Economics of Agricultural Commodities

SERIES

Plantation Crops

Tea, Coffee, Rubber and Cocoa

Economics of
Agricultural Commodities

Economics of
Agricultural Commodities

SERIES

Plantation
Crops

Tea, Coffee, Rubber and Cocoa

PC Bansil PhD

Director
Techno Economic Research Institute
New Delhi

CBS

CBS Publishers & Distributors Pvt Ltd

New Delhi • Bengaluru • Chennai • Kochi • Mumbai • Pune
Hyderabad • Kolkata • Nagpur • Patna • Vijayawada

Economics of Agricultural Commodities SERIES

Plantation Crops

Tea, Coffee, Rubber and Cocoa

ISBN: 978-81-239-2623-0

Copyright © Author and Publisher

First Edition: 2015

Published by Satish Kumar Jain and produced by Varun Jain for

CBS Publishers & Distributors Pvt Ltd

4819/XI Prahlad Street, 24 Ansari Road, Daryaganj, New Delhi 110 002, India.

Ph: 23289259, 23266861, 23266867   Website: www.cbspd.com

Fax: 011-23243014   e-mail: delhi@cbspd.com; cbspubs@airtelmall.in.

Corporate Office: 204 FIE, Industrial Area, Patparganj, Delhi 110 092

Ph: 4934 4934   Fax: 4934 4935   e-mail: publishing@cbspd.com; publicity@cbspd.com

Branches

- **Bengaluru:** Seema House 2975, 17th Cross, K.R. Road, Banasankari 2nd Stage, Bengaluru 560 070, Karnataka

    Ph: +91-80-26771678/79   Fax: +91-80-26771680   e-mail: bangalore@cbspd.com

- **Chennai:** 7, Subbaraya Street, Shenoy Nagar, Chennai 600 030, Tamil Nadu

    Ph: +91-44-26260666, 26208620   Fax: +91-44-42032115   e-mail: chennai@cbspd.com

- **Kochi:** Ashana House, No. 39/1904, A.M. Thomas Road, Valanjambalam, Ernakulam 682016, Kochi, Kerala

    Ph: +91-484-4059061-65, 67   Fax: +91-484-4059065   e-mail: kochi@cbspd.com

- **Mumbai:** 83-C, Dr E Moses Road, Worli, Mumbai-400018, Maharashtra

    Ph: +91-22-24902340/41   Fax: +91-22-24902342   e-mail: mumbai@cbspd.com

- **Pune:** Bhuruk Prestige, Sr. No. 52/12/2+1+3/2 Narhe, Haveli (Near Katraj-Dehu Road Bypass), Pune 411 041, Maharashtra

    Ph: +91-20-64704058, 64704059, 32392277 Fax: +91-20-24300160   e-mail: pune@cbspd.com

Representatives

- **Hyderabad** 0-9885175004   • **Kolkata** 0-9831437309, 0-9051152362
- **Nagpur**   0-9021734563   • **Patna** 0-9334159340
- **Vijayawada** 0-9000660880

Printed at: India Binding House, Noida, UP

to
Aadi – Jaiditya

My great grandson is a naughty boy—master of his own will.
He is quite respectful to the elders and unlike many children of
his age goes to school happily. He is fond of cars and there is
possibly no car or truck the prototype of which he does not
have. I wish that he grows up as a responsible citizen of India
and being the youngest male member of the family upholds the
name of the Bansil family. May God bless him with a happy,
healthy and prosperous long life.

Preface

This book *Plantation Crops* is one of the volumes in the series, **Economics of Agricultural Commodities**. The contents of this book comprises 5 chapters. Besides giving an overview of plantation crops (Chapter 1), it deals comprehensively with Tea, Coffee, Rubber and Cocoa in separate chapters. Each chapter covers national and international aspects of the commodity in a comprehensive way.

We have made extensive use of the data from Tea, Rubber and Coffee Boards. The study is the result of innumerable sources—published or unpublished, quite a large number of daily newspapers, journals, magazines and books. The final presentation, however, is in a specific order so as to give the reader the required information at one place. The entire work depends on secondary sources including the net. Although every possible source has been studied to provide data, there are a number of difficulties one faces.

Our special thanks are due to Mr Ravi Shankar, Dr ML Srivastav and Dr PN Radhakrishnan—Institute faculties who took upon themselves the arduous task of not only going through the first draft but also giving their most valuable time to search through the net. The whole of the net data search is their contribution. Total responsibility of providing office support fell on our two diligent staff—Mrs Ajitha Gangatharan and Mrs Vasantha R Pillai—who cheerfully helped in printing/reprinting of various drafts from time to time.

I most gratefully acknowledge the contribution of the editorial staff of CBS Publishers and Distributors, who read the first draft word to word, which led to a lot of improvement in the quality of the final version.

I must, however, say that none of them is responsible for any errors/omissions from which this work may suffer as at present. I am personally responsible for all this.

PC Bansil

Contents

3 Coffee   261

1

Plantation Crops

DEFINITION

A plantation is a term generally used to describe a large very labor intensive farm. Meaning the crop produced usually requires many workers to harvest. Before the time of machine processing people required huge numbers of laborers to harvest crops like cotton and tobacco. This was the key driving force of the slave trade in the colonial era. However not necessarily related to rule by an imperial power. It is more related to the type of technology available at the time. Plus the fact that colonies had large areas or open land to place plantations on where as in Great Britain every tiny plot of land had been divided or built on. The imperial power distinction is more or less coincidence rather than an intended trademark.

PLANTATION

1. An estate where cash crops are grown on a large scale (especially in tropical areas)
2. Acres, demesne, landed estate, estate, land: Extensive landed property (especially in the country) retained by the owner for his own use; "the family owned a large estate on long Island".
3. Orangery: A place where oranges are grown; a plantation of orange trees in warm climes or a greenhouse in cooler areas
4. Garden consisting of a small cultivated wood without undergrowth orchard, woodlet, grove:

    - *Apple orchard*: A grove of apple trees
    - *Garden*: A plot of ground where plants are cultivated
    - *Lemon grove*: A grove of lemon trees
    - *Orange grove*: A grove of orange trees
    - *Peach orchard*: A grove of peach trees.

A *plantation* is a long, artificially-established forest, farm or estate, where crops are grown for sale, often in distant markets rather than for local on-site consumption. The term *plantation* is informal and not precisely defined. Plantations are grown on a large scale as the crops are grown for commercial purposes, not for local consumption. Crops grown on plantations include fast-growing trees (often conifers), cotton, coffee, tobacco, sugarcane, sisal, some oil seeds (notably oil palms) and rubber trees. Farms that produce alfalfa, lespedeza, clover, and other forage crops are usually not called plantations. The term "plantation" has usually not included large

1

orchards (except for banana plantation). A plantation is always a monoculture over a large area and does not include extensive naturally occurring stands of plants that have economic value. Because of its large size, a plantation takes advantage of economies of scale protectionist policies and natural comparative advantage has contributed to determining where plantations have been located.

Plantation crops constitute a large group of crops. The major plantation crops include coconut, arecanut, oil palm, cashew, tea, coffee and rubber; and the minor plantation crops include cocoa. India is the largest producer and consumer of cashew nuts. The total production of cashew is around 0.57 million tons from an area of 0.24 million hectares. India also occupies number one position in arecanut production.

Tea and coffee are the main and oldest industries in the country which provide ample employment opportunities to the people at large and hold immense potential for export. India is one of the largest tea producers in the world. Coffee is the second largest traded commodity in the world and is an extremely important foreign exchange earner. The coffee industry of India is one of the largest producers of coffee in the world.

India is the third largest producer of coconut and leads 90 coconut-producing countries of the world. The area for coconut plantation in India has been distributed over 18 states and 3 union territories (UTs), under different agroclimatic conditions. India is a premier coir manufacturing country in the world. Wide ranges of coconut products, edible and nonedible are available for both domestic and export market. Tender coconut water concentrate is another product apart from soft drinks which is manufactured and marketed successfully.

But, in India, plantation crops have been continuously facing the problem of lack of investment and depressed yields, and are in great need of modernization. Their total coverage is comparatively less and they are mostly confined to small holdings. Thus, the Government of India has identified some prominent crops as high-value crops of great economic importance. It is taking all possible steps and initiatives to commercialize the sector. Tea, coffee, rubber and coconut industries are providing greater business opportunities to the investors worldwide.

Industrial Plantations

Industrial plantations are established to produce a high volume of wood in a short period of time. Plantations are grown by state forestry authorities (for example, the Forestry Commission in Britain) and/or the paper and wood industries and other private landowners (such as Weyerhaeuser, Rayonier and Plum Creek Timber in the United States, Asia Pulp and Paper in Indonesia). Christmas trees are often grown on plantations as well. In southern and southeastern Asia, teak plantations have recently replaced the natural forest.

Industrial plantations are actively managed for the commercial production of forest products. Industrial plantations are usually large-scale. Individual blocks are usually even-aged and often consist of just one or two species. These species can be exotic or indigenous. The plants used for the plantation are often genetically altered for desired traits such as growth and resistance to pests and diseases in general and specific traits, for example in the case of timber species, volumic wood production and stem straightness. Forest genetic resources are the basis for genetic alteration. Selected individuals grown in seed orchards are a good source for seeds to develop adequate planting material.

Wood production on a tree plantation is generally higher than that of natural forests. While forests managed for wood production commonly yield between 1 and 3 cubic meters per hectare per year, plantations of fast-growing species commonly yield between 20 and 30 cubic meters or more per hectare annually; a Grand Fir plantation at Craigvinean in Scotland has a growth rate of 34 cubic meters per hectare per year (Aldhous and Low, 1974), and Monterey Pine plantations in southern Australia can yield up to 40 cubic meters per hectare per year (Everard and Fourt, 1974). In 2000, while plantations accounted for 5% of global forest, it is estimated that they supplied about 35% of the world's roundwood.

Growth Cycle

- In the first year, the ground is prepared usually by the combination of burning, herbicide spraying, and/or cultivation and then saplings are planted by human crew or by machine.

  The saplings are usually obtained in bulk from industrial nurseries, which may specialize in selective breeding in order to produce fast growing disease and pest-resistant strains.

- In the first few years until the canopy closes, the saplings are looked after, and may be dusted or sprayed with fertilizers or pesticides until established.

- After the canopy closes, with the tree crowns touching each other, the plantation is becoming dense and crowded, and tree growth is slowing due to competition. This stage is termed "pole stage". When competition becomes too intense (for pine trees, when the live crown is less than a third of the tree's total height), it is time to thin out the section. There are several methods for thinning, but where topography permits, the most popular is "row-thinning", where every third or fourth or fifth row of trees is removed, usually with a harvester. Many trees are removed, leaving regular clear lanes through the section so that the remaining trees have room to expand again. The removed trees are delimbed, forwarded to the forest road, loaded onto trucks, and sent to a mill. A typical pole stage plantation tree is 7–30 cm in diameter at breast height (DBH). Such trees are sometimes not suitable for timber, but are used as pulp for paper and particleboard, and as chips for oriented strand board.

- As the trees grow and become dense and crowded again, the thinning process is repeated. Depending on growth rate and species, trees at this age may be large enough for timber milling; if not, they are again used as pulp and chips.

- Around year 10–60 the plantation is now mature and (in economic terms) is falling off the back side of its growth curve. That is to say, it is passing the point of maximum wood growth per hectare per year, and so is ready for the final harvest. All remaining trees are felled, delimbed, and taken to be processed.

- The ground is cleared, and the cycle is repeated.

Some plantation trees, such as pines and eucalyptus, can be at high risk of fire damage because their leaf oils and resins are flammable to the point of a tree being explosive under some conditions. Conversely, an afflicted plantation can in some cases be cleared of pest species cheaply through the use of a prescribed burn, which kills all lesser plants but does not significantly harm the mature trees.

Criticism of Industrial Plantations

In contrast to a naturally regenerated forest, plantations are typically grown as even-aged monocultures, primarily for timber production.

- Plantations are usually near or total monocultures. That is, the same species of tree is planted across a given area, whereas a natural forest would contain a far more diverse range of tree species.
- Plantations may include tree species that would not naturally occur in the area. They may include unconventional types such as hybrids, and genetically modified trees may be used sometime in the future. Since the primary interest in plantations is to produce wood or pulp, the types of trees found in plantations are those that are best-suited to industrial applications. For example, pine, spruce and eucalyptus are widely planted far beyond their natural range because of their fast growth rate, tolerance of rich or degraded agricultural land and potential to produce large volumes of raw material for industrial use.
- Plantations are always young forests in ecological terms. Typically, trees grown in plantations are harvested after 10–60 years, rarely up to 120 years. This means that the forests produced by plantations do not contain the type of growth, soil or wildlife typical of old-growth natural forest ecosystems. Most conspicuous is the absence of decaying dead wood, a crucial component of natural forest ecosystems.

In the 1970s, Brazil began to establish high-yield, intensively managed, short rotation plantations. These types of plantations are sometimes called fast-wood plantations or fiber farms and often managed on a short-rotation basis, as little as 5–15 years. They are becoming more widespread in South America, Asia and other areas. The environmental and social impacts of this type of plantation have caused them to become controversial. In Indonesia, for example, large multinational pulp companies have harvested large areas of natural forest without regard for regeneration. From 1980 to 2000, about 50% of the 1.4 million hectares of pulpwood plantations in Indonesia have been established on what was formerly natural forest land.

The replacement of natural forest with tree plantations has also caused social problems. In some countries, again, notably Indonesia, conversions of natural forest are made with little regard for rights of the local people. Plantations established purely for the production of fiber provide a much narrower range of services than the original natural forest for the local people. India has sought to limit this damage by limiting the amount of land owned by one entity and, as a result, smaller plantations are owned by local farmers who then sell the wood to larger companies. Some large environmental organizations are critical of these high-yield plantations and are running an antiplantation campaign, notably the Rainforest Action Network and Greenpeace.

Farm or Home Plantations

Farm or home plantations are typically established for the production of timber and fire wood for home use and sometimes for sale. Management may be less intensive than with industrial plantations. In time, this type of plantation can become difficult to distinguish from naturally regenerated forest.

Teak and bamboo plantations in India have given good results and an alternative crop solution to farmers of central India, where conventional farming was popular. But due to rising input costs of farming many farmers have done teak and bamboo plantations which require very little water (only during first two years). Teak and bamboo have legal protection from theft. Bamboo, once planted, gives output for 50 years till flowering occurs. Teak requires 20 years to grow to full maturity and fetch returns.

Environmental Plantations

These may be established for watershed or soil protection. They are established for erosion control, landslide stabilization and windbreaks. Such plantations are established to foster native species and promote forest regeneration on degraded lands as a tool of environmental restoration.

Ecological Impact

Probably the single most important factor a plantation has on the local environment is the site where the plantation is established. If natural forest is cleared for a planted forest, then, a reduction in biodiversity and loss of habitat will likely result. In some cases, their establishment may involve draining wetlands to replace mixed hardwoods that formerly predominated with pine species. If a plantation is established on abandoned agricultural land, or highly degraded land, it can result in an increase in both habitat and biodiversity. A planted forest can be profitably established on lands that will not support agriculture or suffer from lack of natural regeneration.

The tree species used in a plantation is also an important factor. Where non-native varieties or species are grown, few of the native fauna are adapted to exploit these and further biodiversity loss occurs. However, even non-native tree species may serve as corridors for wildlife and act as a buffer for native forest, reducing edge effect.

Once a plantation is established, how it is managed becomes the important environmental factor. The single most important factor of management is the rotation period. Plantations harvested on longer rotation periods (30 years or more) can provide similar benefits to a naturally regenerated forest managed for wood production, on a similar rotation. This is especially true if native species are used. In the case of exotic species, the habitat can be improved significantly if the impact is mitigated by measures such as leaving blocks of native species in the plantation, or retaining corridors of natural forest. In Brazil, similar measures are required by government regulations.

Plantations and Natural Forest Loss

Many forestry experts claim that the establishment of plantations will reduce or eliminate the need to exploit natural forest for wood production. In principle this is true because due to the high productivity of plantations less land is needed. Many point to the example of New Zealand, where 19% of the forest area provides 99% of the supply of industrial round wood. It has been estimated that the world's demand for fiber could be met by just 5% of the world forest (Sedjo and Botkin, 1997). However in practice, plantations are replacing natural forest, for example in Indonesia. According to the Food and Agriculture Organization (FAO), about 7%

of the natural closed forest being lost in the tropics is land being converted to plantations. The remaining 93% of the loss is land being converted to agriculture and other uses. Worldwide, an estimated 15% of plantations in tropical countries are established on closed canopy natural forest.

In the Kyoto Protocol, there are proposals encouraging the use of plantations to reduce carbon dioxide (CO_2) levels (although this idea is being challenged by some groups on the grounds that the sequestered CO_2 is eventually released after harvest).

OTHER TYPE OF PLANTATION

Crops may be called plantation crops because of their association with a specific type of farming economy. Most of these involve a large landowner, raising crops with economic value rather than for subsistence, with a number of employees carrying out the work. Often it referred to crops newly introduced to a region. In past times, it has been associated with slavery, indentured labor, and other economic models of high inequity. However, arable and dairy farming are both usually (but not always) excluded from such definitions. A comparable economic structure in antiquity was the latifundia that produced commercial quantities of olive oil or wine, for export. One plantation crop is bananas and there are others as well. Some of the arable crops included are: tobacco, sugarcane, pineapple and cotton, especially in historical usage.

High Value Food Crops

Plantings of a number of trees or shrubs grown for food or beverage, including tea, coffee and cacao are generally called plantations. Some spice and high value crops grown from permanent perennial stock, such as black pepper, may also be so called. When the holding belongs to a single individual, that person may be called a *planter*.

Sugar

Sugar plantations were highly valued in the Caribbean by the British and French colonists in the 19th and 20th centuries and the use of sugar in Europe rose during this period. Sugarcane is still an important crop in Cuba. Sugar plantations also arose in countries such as Barbados and Cuba because of the natural endowments that they had. These natural endowments included soil that was conducive to growing sugar and a high marginal product of labor realized through the increasing number of slaves.

Oil Palm

Oil palm agriculture is rapidly expanding across wet tropical regions, and is usually developed at plantation scale.

Orchards

Fruit orchards are sometimes considered to be plantations.

Arable Crops

These include tobacco, sugarcane, pineapple and cotton, especially in historical usage. Before the rise of cotton in the Southern American, indigo and rice were also sometimes called plantation crops.

Fishing Plantations in Newfoundland and Labrador

When Newfoundland was colonized by England in 1610, the original colonists were called "lanters" and their fishing rooms were known as "fishing plantations". These terms were used well into the 20th century.

The following three plantations are maintained by the Government of Newfoundland and Labrador as provincial heritage sites:

- Sea-Forest Plantation was a 17th-century fishing plantation established at Cuper's Cove (present-day cupids) under a royal charter issued by King James I.
- Mockbeggar Plantation is an 18th-century fishing plantation at Bonavista.
- Pool plantation a 17th-century fishing plantation maintained by Sir David Krike and his heirs at Ferryland. The plantation was destroyed by French invaders in 1696.

Other Fishing Plantations

- Bristol's Hope Plantation, a 17th-century fishing plantation established at Harbor Grace, created by the Bristol Society of Merchant-Adventurers.
- Benger Plantation, an 18th-century fishing plantation maintained by James Benger and his heirs at Ferryland. It was built on the site of Georgia plantation.
- Piggeon's Plantation, an 18th-century fishing plantation maintained by Ellias Piggeon at Ferryland.

Slavery, Para-slavery and Plantations

Slave labor extracted from forcibly transported Africans was used extensively to work on early plantations (such as cotton and sugar plantations) in the American colonies and the United States, throughout the Caribbean, the Americas and in European-occupied areas of Africa. Several notable historians and economists such as Eric Williams, Water Rodney and Karl Marx contend that the global capitalist economy was largely founded on the creation and produce of thousands of slave labor campus based in colonial plantations exploiting 10 millions of abducted Africans.

In modern times, the low wages typically paid to plantation workers are the basis of plantation profitability in some areas. Sugarcane plantations in the Caribbean and Brazil, worked by slave labor, were also examples of the plantation system.

In more recent times, overt slavery has been replaced by "para-slavery" or slavery-in-kind, including the sharecropping system. At its most extreme, workers are in "debt bondage": they must work to pay off a debt at such punitive interest rates that it may never be paid off. Others work unreasonably long hours and are paid subsistence wages that (in practice) may only be spent in the company store.

In Brazil, a sugarcane plantation was termed an *engenho* ("engine"), and the 17th-century English usage for organized colonial production was "factory". Such colonial social and economic structures are discussed at plantation economy. Sugar workers on plantations in Cuba and elsewhere in the Caribbean lived in company towns known as Bateys.

Plantations in the Antebellum Southern American

In the southern American, antebellum plantations were centered on a "plantation house", the residence of the owner, where important business was conducted.

Slavery and plantations had different characteristics in different regions of the South. As the Upper South of the Chesapeake Bay Colony developed first, historians of the antebellum South defined planters as those who held 20 or more slaves. Major planters held many more, especially in the Deep South as it developed. The majority of slaveholders held 10 or fewer slaves, often just a few to labor domestically. By the late 18th century, most planters in the Upper South had switched from exclusive tobacco cultivation to mixed crop production, both because tobacco had exhausted the soil and because of changing markets. The shift away from tobacco meant they had slaves in excess of the number needed for labor, and they began to sell them in the internal slave trade.

There was a variety of domestic architecture on plantations. The largest and wealthiest planter families, for instance, those with estates fronting on the James River in Virginia, constructed mansions in brick and Georgian style, e.g. Shirley Plantation. Common or smaller planters in the late 18th and 19th century had more modest wood frame buildings, such as South all Plantation in Charles City Country.

In the Low Country of South Carolina, by contrast, even before the American Revolution, planters holding large rice and cotton plantations in South Carolina typically owned hundreds of slaves. In Charleston and Savannah, the elite also held numerous slaves to work as household servants. The 19th-century development of the Deep South for cotton cultivation depended on large plantations with much more acreage than was typical of the Chesapeake Bay area, and for labor, planters held hundreds of slaves.

Until December 1865 slavery was legal in parts of the United States. Most slaves were employed in agriculture, and "planter" was a term commonly used to describe a farmer with many slaves. The term "planter" has no universally accepted definition but academic historians have defined it to identify the elite class, "a landowning farmer of substantial means". In the "Black Belt" counties of Albama and Mississippi, the terms "planter" and "farmer" were often synonymous. Robert Fogel and Stanley Engerman define large planters as owning over 50 slaves, and medium planters as owning between 16 and 50 slaves. In his study of Black Belt counties in Alabama, Jonathan Wiener defines planters by ownership of real property, rather than of slaves. A planter, for Wiener, owned at least $10,000 worth of real estate in 1850 and $32,000 worth in 1860, equivalent to about the top 8% of landowners. In his study of southwest Georgia, Lee Formwalt also defines planters in size of land holdings rather than slaves. Formwalt's planters are in the top 4.5% of landowners, translating into real estate worth $6,000 or more in 1850, $24,000 or more in 1860, and $11,000 or more in 1870. In his study of Harrison County, Texas, Randolph B. Campbell classifies large planters as owners of 20 slaves, and small planters as owners of between 10 slaves and 19 slaves. In Chicot and Phillips Counties, Arkansas, Carl H Moneyhon defines large planters as owners of 20 or more slaves, and 600 or more acres.

Among the earliest examples of plantations were the latifundia of the Roman Empire, which produced large quantities of wine and olive oil for export. Plantation agriculture grew rapidly with the increase in international trade and the development of a worldwide economy that followed the expansion of European colonial empires. Like every economic activity, it has changed over time. Earlier forms of plantation agriculture were associated with large disparities of wealth and income, foreign ownership and political influence, and exploitative social systems such as indentured labor and slavery. The history of the environmental, social and economic issues relating to plantation agriculture is covered in articles that focus on those subjects.

Importance of Plantation Crops

The term plantation crops refer to those crops which are cultivated on an extensive scale in a large contiguous area, owned and managed by an individual or a company. The crops include tea, coffee, rubber, cocoa, coconut, arecanut, oil palm, palmyrah, cashew, cinchona, etc. These plantation crops are high value commercial crops of greater economic importance and play a vital role in Indian economy. The main draw back with this sector: of crops in India is that major portion of the area is of small holdings (except tea) which hinders the adoption of intensive cultivation. In the case of coffee, 97.13% of the growers have holdings below 10 hectares and in rubber, 82% of the total area is of small holdings having an average size of 0.5 hectares.

The economic importances of these crops are:

1. They contribute to national economy by way of export earnings. These crops occupy less than 2% of the total cultivated area (i.e. 3.82% of total crop land) but they generate an income of around Rs 16,000 million or about 12.72% of the total export earnings of ail commodities or 75% of total earnings from the export of agricultural produces.

2. India is the leading country in the total production of certain plantation crops in the world. For instance, Indian production meets the share of 47% in tea and 66% in each of cashew and arecanut.

3. Plantation industry provides direct as well as indirect employment lo many millions of people. For instance, tea industry offers direct employment to 10 lakhs and indirect employment to 10 lakhs people; while-cashew processing factories alone provide employment to 3 lakhs people besides 2 lakhs farmers are employed in cashew cultivation.

4. Plantation industry supports many by-product industries and also many rural industries. For example, coconut husk is used to produce coir fiber annually to a tune of 2,19,600 tons in India.

5. These crops help to conserve the soil and ecosystem. Tea planted in hill slopes and cashew in barrel and waste lands protect the land from soil erosion during the rainy season or due to heavy winds.

Area of Plantation Crops in India

The area and production is more in Kerala (1,073,000.7 hectares and 4359000.9 metric tons) followed by Karnataka (679,000.2 hectares and 1,401,000.0 metric tons), Tamil Nadu (503,000.0 hectares and 3,810.6 metric tons), Andhra Pradesh (289,000.0 hectares and 1,021,000.2 metric tons) (Tables 1.1 to 1.6; Charts 1.1 and 1.2). Estimated budgetary requirements during 12th plan for the growth of tea, coffee, natural rubber and spices sector are as in Table 1.7.

Table 1.1: Statewise area and production of plantation crops in 2005–2006

States/UT's	Cashewnut		Arecanut		Cocoa		Coconut		Total	
	A	P	A	P	A	P	A	P	A	P
Andaman & Nicobar	–	–	4.4	4.8	–	–	25.5	59.92432	29.9	64.72432
Andhra Pradesh	170	92	0.3	0.2	11.83	0.715	104	613.6911	286.13	706.6061
Assam	14	10	71.2	66.8	–	–	19.1	140.9701	104.3	217.7701
Goa	55.00	27.00	1.6	2.6	–	–	25.3	86.20571	81.9	115.8057
Gujarat	4.00	4.00	–	–	–	–	16.4	95.14964	20.4	99.14964
Karnataka	100	45	161.6	215.7	6	2.75	385.4	832.3357	653	1095.786
Kerala	80	67	108.6	119.3	10.22	6.49	897.8	4352.253	1096.62	4545.043
Lakshadweep	–	–	–	–	–	–	2.7	36.46371	2.7	36.46371
Maharashtra	160	183	2	5	–	–	18	188.0977	180	376.0977
Meghalaya	6.38	6.36	11.5	15.5	–	–	–	–	17.88	21.86
Mizoram	–	–	2.00	5.3	–	–	–	–	2.00	5.3
Nagaland	–	–	0.2	1.3	–	–	0.9	0.825593	1.1	2.125593
Orissa	120	78	–	–	–	–	50.8	188.9233	170.8	266.9233
Pondicherry	3.00	1.00	0.1	0.1	–	–	2.1	19.19505	5.2	20.29505
Tamil Nadu	121	56	4.8	10.3	1.421	0.22	370.6	3348.538	497.821	3415.058
Tripura	–	–	3.4	6.9	–	–	3.3	4.815961	6.7	11.71596
West Bengal	10.00	10.00	9.4	29.3	–	–	24.9	222.5662	44.3	261.8662
Total	843.38	579.36	381.1	483.1	29.471	10.175	1946.8	10189.96	3200.751	11262.59

Table 1.2: Statewise area and production of plantation crops in 2006–2007

States/UT's	Cashewnut		Arecanut		Cocoa		Coconut		Total	
	A	P	A	P	A	P	A	P	A	P
Andaman & Nicobar			4.1	5.8			21.4	61.24247	25.5	67.042
Andhra Pradesh	171	99	0.3	0.2	11.9	1.52	105	912.4439	288.2	1013.2
Assam	15	11	71	65			19	105.282	105	181.3
Goa	55	29	1.7	2.6			25.5	87.1845	82.2	118.8
Gujarat	4	4					16.4	95.16666	20.4	99.2
Karnataka	102	52	168	224	6.8	2.65	401	1118.191	677.8	1396.8
Kerala	80	72	102.1	110	10.22	5.8	870.9	4165.864	1063.2	4353.7
Lakshadweep							2.7	36.47023	2.7	36.470
Maharashtra	164	197	2.3	3.6			21	120.4894	187.3	321.0894
Meghalaya			12	16.6					12	16.600
Mizoram			2	5.3					2	5.300
Nagaland			0.2	1.3			0.9	0.137624	1.1	1.438
Orissa	125	84					51	189.7828	176	273.8
Pondicherry	5	2	0.1	0.1			2.1	13.21081	7.2	15.311
Tamil Nadu	123	60	5.5	11.9	1.421	0.21	374.6	3736.41	504.5	3808.5
Tripura			3.4	6.9			3.3	4.816823	6.7	11.717
West Bengal	10	10	10	30			25.1	247.103	45.1	287.1
Total	**854.0**	**620.0**	**382.7**	**483.3**	**30.3**	**10.2**	**1939.9**	**10893.8**	**3206.9**	**12007.3**

Table 1.3: Statewise area and production of plantation crops in 2007–2008

States/UT's	Cashewnut		Arecanut		Cocoa		Coconut		Total	
	A	P	A	P	A	P	A	P	A	P
Andaman & Nicobar			4.1	5.7			21.6	55.47144	25.7	61.171
Andhra Pradesh	171	107	0.3	0.2	12.7	1.6	101.32	770.2684	285.32	879.1
Assam	15	12	70.3	68.8			19	93.59945	104.3	174.4
Goa	55	31	1.7	2.6			25.5	87.81831	82.2	121.4
Gujarat	4	4					16.4	95.18238	20.4	99.2
Karnataka	103	56	168	224	7.2	2.8	405	1125.946	683.2	1408.7
Kerala	84	78	108.3	110	10.5	6	818.8	3882.312	1021.6	4076.3
Lakshadweep							2.7	36.47626	2.7	36.476
Maharashtra	167	210	2.2	3.6			21	120.5093	190.2	334.1
Meghalaya			12.1	16.5					12.1	16.500
Mizoram			2	5.3					2	5.300
Nagaland			0.2	1.3			0.9	0.137646	1.1	1.438
Orissa	131	90					51	189.8142	182	279.8
Pondicherry	5	2	0.1	0.1			2.2	18.30695	7.3	20.407
Tamil Nadu	123	65	4.9	9	1.4	0.2	383.37	3419.27	512.67	3493.5
Tripura			3.4	6.9			5.8	7.845836	9.2	14.74584
West Bengal	10	10	9	22			28.6	245.3544	47.6	277.4
Total	**868**	**665**	**386.6**	**476**	**31.8**	**10.6**	**1903.19**	**10148.31**	**3189.59**	**11299.9**

Table 1.4: Statewise area and production of plantation crops in 2008–2009

States/UT's	Cashewnut		Arecanut		Cocoa		Coconut		Total	
	A	P	A	P	A	P	A	P	A	P
Andaman & Nicobar			4.100	6.000			21.600	55.471	25.700	61.471
Andhra Pradesh	182.0	112.0	0.3	0.2	14.1	2.6	101.3	770.3	297.6	885.1
Assam	18.0	13.0	70.0	62.7			19.0	93.6	107.0	169.3
Goa	55.0	30.0	1.9	2.8			25.5	87.8	82.4	120.6
Gujarat	6.0	4.0					16.4	95.2	22.4	99.2
Karnataka	107.0	60.0	168.0	224.0	7.2	2.9	405.0	1125.9	687.2	1412.8
Kerala	70.0	75.0	101.7	116.9	10.7	6.1	818.8	3882.3	1001.2	4080.3
Lakshadweep							2.700	36.476	2.700	36.476
Maharashtra	170.0	225.0	2.2	3.6			21.0	120.5	193.2	349.1
Meghalaya			12.360	17.100					12.360	17.100
Mizoram			6.580	8.210					6.580	8.210
Nagaland			0.200	1.300			0.900	0.138	1.100	1.438
Orissa	137.0	95.0					51.0	189.8	188.0	284.8
Pondicherry	6.000	2.000	0.060	0.080			2.200	18.307	8.260	20.387
Tamil Nadu	131.0	68.0	5.0	10.4	2.1	0.2	383.4	3419.3	521.5	3497.9
Tripura			3.400	6.900			5.800	7.846	9.200	14.746
West Bengal	11.0	11.0	11.4	21.2			28.6	245.4	51.0	277.5
Total	**893.0**	**695.0**	**387.1**	**481.3**	**34.0**	**11.8**	**1903.2**	**10148.3**	**3217.3**	**11336.4**

Table 1.5: Statewise area and production of plantation crops in 2011–2012

States/UT's	Cashewnut		Arecanut		Cocoa		Coconut		Total	
	A	P	A	P	A	P	A	P	A	P
Andaman & Nicobar	4.22	5.95	1.2	0.35			21.8	72.25	27.22	78.55
Andhra Pradesh	5.319	8.51	183.95	113.6	18.71	4	142.025	1270	350.004	1396.11
Assam	73.14	72.85	0.6	0.5			20.78	194.81	94.52	268.16
Bihar							15.24	97.536	15.24	97.536
Chandigarh			13.5	15			0.79	6.32	14.29	21.32
Delhi	1.728	2.867	57.47	28.8			25.73	88.95	84.928	120.617
Goa			7.63	22.86			20.93	217.89	28.56	240.75
Jammu & Kashmir			10.5	4.00					10.5	4.00
Jharkhand	236.8	380.8	121.28	66	10.6	2.00	511	3784.6	879.68	4233.4
Karnataka	97.122	117.3	82.88	74	12.283	5.9	766	3973.87	958.285	4171.07
Kerala							2.568	48.74	2.568	48.74
Madhya Pradesh	2.2	3.58	183	216			21	120	206.2	339.58
Manipur	14.62	19.83	8	9					22.62	28.83
Meghalaya	5.01	12.39	0	2			0.02	0.06	5.03	14.45
Mizoram	0.2	1.3					0.9	0.3	1.1	1.6
Nagaland			157.5	96			53.94	258.04	211.44	354.04
Orissa	0.06	0.08					2.1	20	2.16	20.08
Sikkim	6.43	15.72	136.42	60	21.389	1	430.656	4515.56	594.895	4592.28
Tamil Nadu	5.6	17.73	3.9	5.5			6.21	18.06	15.71	41.29
Uttranchal	11.445	21.8	11	11.6			29.133	252.88	51.578	286.28
Total	**463.894**	**680.71**	**978.83**	**725.21**	**62.982**	**12.9**	**2070.822**	**14939.9**	**3576.53**	**16358.7**

Table 1.6: Statewise area and production of plantation crops in 2012–2013

States/UT's	Cashewnut		Arecanut		Cocoa		Coconut		Total	
	A	P	A	P	A	P	A	P	A	P
Andaman Nicobar	4.23	5.88	1.2	0.38			21.88	89.45	27.31	95.71
Andhra Pradesh	0.58	0.27	183.95	118.14	20.71	4.16	128.897	1,330.40	334.137	1,452.97
Assam	75.06	72.58	0.9	0.52			22.154	110.259	98.114	183.359
Bihar							15.246	97.135	15.246	97.135
Chhattisgarh			13.5	9.6			1.41	7.87	14.91	17.47
Goa	1.73	2.87	57.47	29.95			25.712	84.445	84.912	117.265
Gujarat			7.97	24.52			21.12	221.88	29.09	246.4
Jharkhand			11.5	4.64					11.5	4.64
Karnataka	221.37	358.61	122.11	74.64	10.883	2.08	513.1	4,169.90	867.463	4,605.23
Kerala	96.6	96.3	84.88	76.96	12.483	6.136	798.162	3,990.39	992.125	4,169.79
Lakshadweep							2.57	48.8	2.57	48.8
Maharashtra	2.2	3.58	184.2	224.64			28.082	129.02	214.482	357.24
Meghalaya	14.62	19.83	8.5	9.36					23.12	29.19
Mizoram	7.57	4.32					0.02	0.06	7.59	4.38
Nagaland	0.22	0.12					1.3	10.4	1.52	10.52
Orissa			163.91	100.84			54.29	262.17	218.2	363.01
Puducherry	0.06	0.08					1.952	23.18	2.012	23.26
Tamil Nadu*	6.06	13.2	136.42	62.4	22.389	1.04	465.108	4,760.67	629.977	4,837.31
Tripura	4.7	9.92	4.1	4.72			6.47	18.89	15.27	33.53
West Bengal	11.39	21.16	11	12.06			29.2	254.17	51.59	287.39
Total	**446.39**	**608.72**	**991.61**	**753.37**	**66.465**	**13.416**	**2,136.67**	**15,609.09**	**3,641.14**	**16,984.60**

Sources:

Arecanut: Directorate of Arecanut and Spices Development (DASD).

Cashewnut: Directorate of Cashewnut and Cocoa Development (DCCD) for all States except A&N, Gujrat and Mizoram.

Cocoa: Directorate of Cashewnut and Cocoa Development (DCCD).

Coconut: State Directorate of Horticulture.

*Tamil Nadu has not provided figures for coconut. Therefore, figures recieved during 2012-13 (2nd est.) repeated.

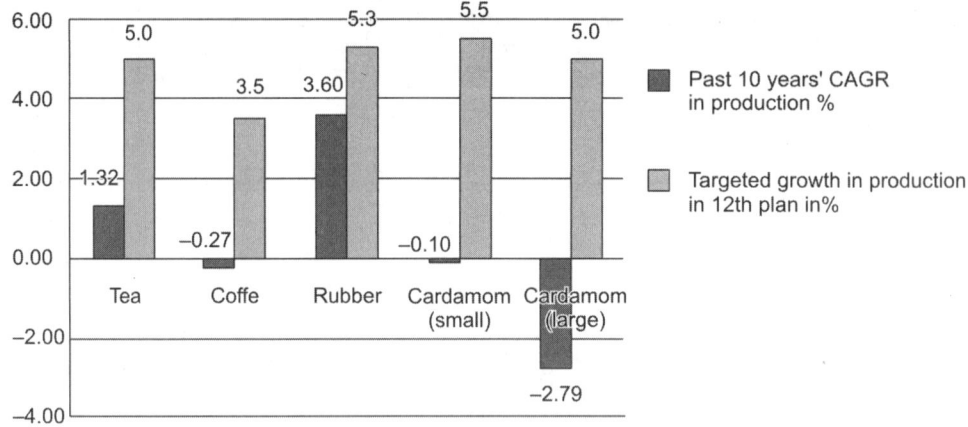

Chart 1.1: Growth rate in production

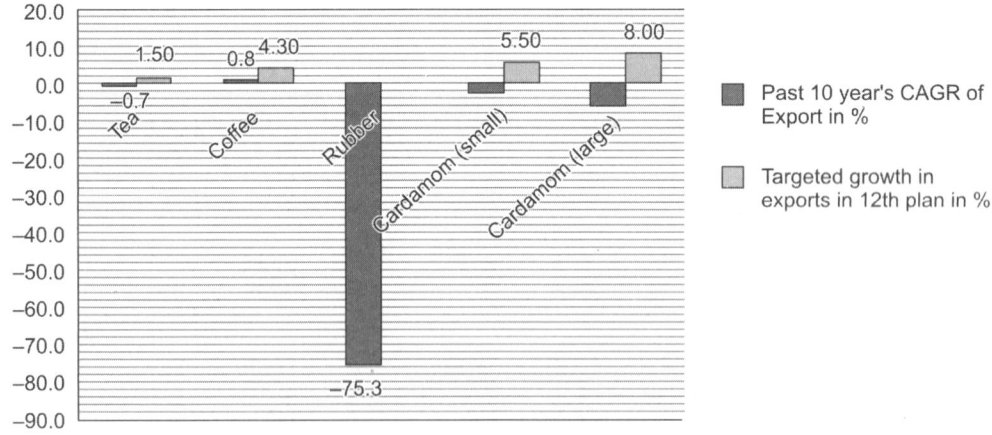

Chart 1.2: Growth rate for export

Table 1.7: Budgetary requirements during 12th plan for the growth of tea, coffee, natural rubber and spices sector

S. No.	Crop	Estimated budgetary requirement during 12th plan in Rs crore
1	Schemes of Tea Board	1,600
2	Schemes of Coffee Board	1,200
3	Schemes of Rubber Board	1,180
4	Schemes of Spice Board	900
	Total	**4,880**

PRODUCTION TECHNOLOGY OF PLANTATION CROPS

Production Technology of Coconut

Origin and Distribution

The home of coconut might have been somewhere in South East Asia, most probably in Malaysia or Indonesia. It moved eastwards to the Pacific region, and further to America. Toward the west, it moved to India and Madagascar over the calm tropical waters; man also played important role, in the spread of this indispensable palm. The crop is grown on an area bf about 9 million hectares with the production of 33,700 million nuts. In India, the area under this crop is 1,513 thousand hectares and production is 9,700 million nuts and in Maharashtra, the crop is grown on the west coast on an area of about 9,300 hectares and production is 50 million nuts.

Soil and Climate

Coconut palm thrives in almost all types of wall drained soils such as coastal sand, red loam, laterals alluvial and reclaimed soils of marshy low lands. Coconut is a crop bumid tropic. Although it is mainly grown in the coastal plains it *is* possible to grown even at elevation of 600–900 m above mean sea-level (MSL) in areas near the equator where the temperature remains favorable. Among the climatic factors affecting the palm, rainfall is the most important. A rainfall of 1,000–2,250 mm per annum evenly distributed throughout the year appears to be most congenial. Regions with long and pronounced dry spells are not suited to its growth.

Coconut palm requires equable climate neither very hot not very cold. The maximum mean annual temperature for good growth is about 27°C with a diurnal venation of about 6–7°. Persistant high humidity is harmful and incidence of budrot is more under such a conditions. The palm requires bright, sunshine of about 2,000 hours a year.

Planting Material (Propagation)

Since, it is a cross-pollinated crop which is propagated only by seeds, the selection of planting material is of vital, importance selection has to be made at the mother palm level and at the seedling stage. The mother palm should be between age group of 25 years and 60 years, should be healthy, high yielding and regular in bearing. Immature arid under-developed seed nuts should not be used. The selection of seedlings at nursery stage is also important. Generally, nuts harvested from January to April are used for raising seedlings.

The seedlings should be:

1. Healthy
2. Should have minimum of 5–6 leaves when they are 1 year old
3. The leaves should have been splitted
4. The girth of seedling at collar region should be more
5. Should have 5–6 roots.

Preparation of Land and Transplanting

The depth of pit depends on soil type in sand loam soil pits of 1 × 1 × m is generally recommended. In laterite soils, the pits of 1.2% 1.2 × 1.2 m are necessary. The pits are taken at the distance of 7.5–9 m apart thus accommodating 177–124 palm/ hectares. The planting is done by square system, deep planting method is adopted. It is good practice to spread two layers of coconut husk at the bottom of the pits in areas where drought conditions prevail. The seedling is placed at the center of the pit in such a way that the top of the husk is just visible from outside. The earth is well-pressed down in order to keep the seedling firmly in position.

In well-drained soil where water stagnation is not a problem transplanting is done at the beginning of the monsoon. In low lying areas, planting is done after monsoon. The transplanted, seedlings should be shaded and irrigated properly during summer. Irrigation with 45 liters of water once in 4 days has been found to be the optimum especially in sandy soils.

Manure Fertilization and Intercultivation

Application of fertilizers in general reduces the pre-hearing age of palms. The palm generally starts bearing at the age of 5 or 7 years after planting and the stabilized yield is obtained from 10th year onward till the age of 60 years. Regular intercultivation and manuring is essential for stepping up and maintaining the productivity of palm. Till age including digging, ploughing the interspaces, making shallow basins with a radius of 2 m and applying fertilizer.

The Columbia Flexible Capital Income Fund (CFCIF) Kasargod has recommended an annual application of following nutrients/palm/year,

Sr. No.	Type of plantation	N	P205	K20
1	Ordinary tall varieties	0.5 kg	0.32 kg	1.2 kg
2	For hybrid and high yielding varieties	1.0 kg	0.50 kg	2.0 kg

Application of the annual dose of fertilizers in two or more splits had been found highly beneficial in increasing the yield and quality of nut. To obtain higher efficiency in the uptake of nutrients of fertilizers are to be applied in circular basis 20–25 cm deep and 1.5–1.8 m radius round the base of the palm.

Intercropping and Multiple Cropping

In pure coconut garden when palms are spaced at 7.5 × 7.5 m as much as 78% of the available area is not effectively utilized. It is also seen that a pure coconut grove utilizes only-half, of the available light. Introduction of cocoa, pineapple and pepper has been found to help to increase the dry matter production from 12.67% to 193% under Kerala conditions. In a crop combination involving coconut, dioscorea, cocoa and pineapple 17,500 coconut, 100 kg of diascofes tubers, 300 kg of dried coco beans, and 2,000 kg of pineapple, fruits were harvested from 1 hectare. The increased income through multiple cropping is about 420% more than that obtained from a pure crop of coconut.

Production of Barren Nuts

The phenomenon of the occurrence of barren nuts (without or with imperfectly developed Kernel) is very old. Only certain trees in the coconut plantation produce large number of barren nuts. The nuts are generally oblong in shape and quantity of husk produce is very much less as compared to normal, nut. The embryo in the barren nut is mostly absent or when present. It is in varying stage of decay. Fungal infection is also sometime noticed in the embryo resulting in the decay of the kernel and loss of water inside. In the barren, nut cracking of shell is relatively more common.

1. Several causes for the phenomenon have been reported
2. Due to defective fertilization resulting in malformation of embryo
3. Nutritional deficiency in the palm
4. Excessive bearing.

Harvesting

Coconut usually ripens in about 12–13 months after opening of the inflorescence. In order to get the maximum yield of copra and oil, only full matured nuts should be harvested [the loss of copra is in 11 months (6%), 10 months (16%) and 9 months (33%) old nuts, respectively]. Similarly, the reduction in the oil percentage in 11, 10 and 9 months old, nut being 5, 15 and 33%, respectively. Generally, harvesting is done once in 45–60 days. Tender nuts which are in great demand as a delicious soft drink particularly in West Bengal and Maharashtra are the best harvested at the age of 6–7 months. A fully matured fruit will have a composition by weight of about husk (35%), shell (12%), meat or kernel (28%) and water (25%).

Yield

The average yield per hectare varies from 10,000 to 14,000 nuts/annum. From a well-maintained garden an annual yield of 25,000 nuts/hectare/5 years can be obtained.

Coconut Global Status

Coconut is grown globally over an area of 12.19 million hectare producing 13.68 million tons (copra equivalent) in 93 countries of the world. Asia and pacific region accounts for a major share of area and production occupying 10.7 million hectare (88%) and 9.6 million tons of copra equivalent (70.18%). Indonesia, Philippines and India are the major producers of coconut in the world. The area, production and productivity of coconut have increased at the global level (0.89, 4.36 and 3.79% per year) during the past 15 years (1990–2004). Compared to this, there has been increased area, production and productivity in the Asian-Pacific Children's Convention (APCC) region to the tune of (1.06, 2.09 and 1.07% per year).

PRODUCTION TECHNOLOGY OF ARECANUT

Botanical name: *Areca eatechu*

Family: *Palmae*

Arecanut (betel nut) is an extensively cultivated tropical palm the nuts of which form a popular masticatory in India, the Middle East and the far East. It belongs to the family Palmae and originated in India and South Eastern Countries.

It is a tall stemmed erect palm reaching a height of 30 m. It is one of the important cash crop of India after coconut. Nearly 4 million peoples in India are engaged in production and processing of arecanut.

Origin

India and South Eastern countries.

Soil

The arecanut palm is grown in a variety of soils such as laterite soils of the West Coast, the *red* loamy soils of the Mettupalayam (Tamil Nadu), the alluvial soils of Assam and West Bengal and the loam of Orissa. The largest area is lateritic soils. The soil also should be deep and well drained. Water logged, soils should be avoided. The depth of soil should be at least 1 m with 4.5–7.6 pH. An adequate irrigation facility is required for its satisfactory production.

Climate

Arecanut is a tropical crop. It *is* capable of growing under variety of climatic conditions. It grows well from sea level upto an altitude of 1,000 m in areas, of abundant and well-distributed rainfall. It is grown in high rainfall area about 200–400 cm. the cultivation is mostly confined to 20° North and South of the equator. It is unable to withstand extremes of temperature and wide diurnal variations. The optimum range of temperature is 15–38°C for its good growth. High humidity and areas free from cyclonic wind and sun scorching are congenial.

Propagation

It is propagated by seeds. The selection of proper planting material is of almost importance as it is perennial crop.

Selection of Mother Palms

Select mother palms showing earliness in bearing and high percentage of fruit set. The age 20–40 years of the palm should have a regular bearing habit. Less than 10 leaves and 4 bunches per year and poor yielding mother trees should be rejected.

Selection of Seed Nuts

Select fully tree ripe nuts for use as seeds. Discard nuts which are undersized, malformed and low in weight.

Raising of Seedlings

Sow selected seednuts soon after harvest in nursery bed with stalk end up and with a spacing of 5–6 cm. Cover the seedniits with sand and irrigate daily. Germination starts about 40 days after sowing and the sprouts are ready for transplanting when they are about 3 months old having 2–3 leases.

Prepare secondary nursery beds of 150 cm. width and a convenient length. Apply FYM5 (farmyard manure 5) tons/kaas basal dose. Transplant sprouts at a spacing of 30 × 30 cm with the onset of the monsoon. Partial shade to the seedlings can also be provided by banana, *Coccinia indica* or by means of artificial pandal. Provide irrigation during hot and dry periods and drainage during monsoon periodical weeding and mulching are necessary.

Selection of Seedlings

Select good seedlings for transplanting in the main field when they are 12–18 months old. Selection of seedlings can be based on selection index, which is calculated by multiplying leaf number by 40 and substracting the seedling height.

Example: Seedling height 90 cm. Leaf numbers 5 selection index $(5 \times 40)-90 = 110$

Select seedlings with higher selection index values, i.e. if index values range between 50 and 150, select seedlings with higher values.

Remove seedlings with ball of earth attached to them for transplanting.

Planting

Plant tall, quick growing shade trees on the Southern and Western sides of the seedlings to provide protection from sun scorching. This helps for better stand of crop in the initial stage.

Dig pits of $90 \times 90 \times 90$ cm at 2.7×2.7 m and fill-up with rich top soil to a , level of 15 cm from the bottom. Plant seedlings in the center of pit, cover with soil upto collar teel and press around.

The planting is to be done during May–June in well-drained soils while in ill-drained soils (clayer) planting is done in August–September to avoid the plantation in water logging.

Banana is raised between rows to provide shade to the seedlings in the initial stages upto 4–5 years.

Manuring

A steady and high yield will depend much on the adequate availability of plant nutrients in the soil. Since almost all the arecanut growing areas are in heavy rainfall tracts, the soils are liable to leaching and erosion thus making them poor in major plant nutrients and organic matter.

The application of NPK (nitrogen-phosphorus-potassium) fertilizers for adult palms 100:40:146 gm/palm/year and 12 kg of each of green manure and compost is recommended and for variety Mangala NPK may be applied 150:60:210 gm/palm/year.

Apply one-third dose of fertilizer and full dose of green manure and compost during first year, two-thirds dose of fertilizer and full dose of green manure and compost during second year and full dose-from third year onward during September–October.

Under irrigated conditions, apply fertilizers in two split doses, the first during September–October and the second during February. Under rainfed conditions apply the second dose during March–April after receipt of summer rains.

Apply manure and fertilizers in circular basins of 15–20 cm depth and with a radius of 0.75–1 m from the palm. Apply second dose of fertilizer around the base of palm after weeding and mix into soil by light forking.

In acidic soils, broadcast lime 0.5 kg per palm once in 2 or 3 years and incorporate into soil during April–May.

Irrigation and Drainage

Palm responds well to irrigation. Irrigate the palms during hot and dry periods at regular intervals of 3–5 days.

In West-Coast where major area of arecanut gardens are irrigated, watering the garden once in 7–8 days during November–December, once in 6 days during January–February and once in 3–5 days during March–April is recommended. In each irrigations give about 175 liters of water per palm, application of organic mulch to the garden help conservation of soil moisture.

Construct drainage channels (25–30 cm deep) between the rows and the drain out water during periods of heavy rainfall to prevent water logging.

Cultural Operation

Keep the garden free of weeds and breakup surface crust by light forking or digging after ceaseastion of monsoon during October–November. Where the land is sloppy, terracing has to be done to prevent soil erosion. The raising of green manure-cum-cover crops in April–May with the onset of pre-monsoon rains and cutting burying the same in September–October was found to be advantageous.

Intercropping

Owing to the long pre-bearing age of the palm practically no income obtained during the first 3–4 years. Intercropping with elephant foot yarn, pineapple, pepper, betel vine, banana, cocoa, ginger and cardamom can be grown. In all cases, the intercrops should be manured adequately and separately. While planting cocoa, a spacing of 5.4 × 2.7 m is recommended.

The cutting out of uneconomic trees and replacing them with good seedlings is important in maintaining a high level of productivity of the garden.

Harvesting

The prehearing age of the palm ranges from 4 years to 5 years. The plant is *monoecious*, producing both male and female flowers on the same tree. The spadix of a grown up palm produces on an average 294 female flowers. The color of the fruit during its growth changes from green to different shades of yellow and red during ripening. Nut matures after 8–9 months after fertilization, 4–5 spadix are produced by the palm per year.

The stage of which nuts are to be harvested depends upon the type of nuts required for the market. Where tender processed nuts are required as finished product, the tender nuts are harvested from July to December. In places where "Chali" or "Gota" (sub-dried whole nut) is required fully ripe nuts are to be harvested from December to March or from May to July. There are found plucking that are done during the whole season.

Production Technology of Coffee

Botanical name: *Coffee arabica, coffee robusta*

Family: *Rubiaceae*

Coffee of commerce consists of seeds of coffee when roasted, ground and soaked in hot water yields a fragrant stimulating infusion used for preparing the beverage called coffee.

It is native of America and introduced in India in 1936 near Chimanglur in Karnataka. Mainly grown in the countries like Brazil, Central Venezuela, Colombia, Central America, West Kenya, East Africa, Jawa, Sumatra and India, etc.

Soil and Climate

Coffee arbica comes up well in high altitude from 800 m to 1,650 m but *C. robust* adapt well to lower elevations. At high altitude the crop is often late and susceptible to frost and high winds.

Evenly distributed rainfall of 2,250 mm is essential. Heavy rainfall is not conducive as it encourages rotting of leaves and plants are easily susceptible to fungal diseases.

The temperature range is 50–80°F. It can also be grown at higher provided shade is there. In India, coffee is grown in hilly areas. There is a distinct dry period of about 90–100 days or from the December. March–April which is the best for harvesting and processing and also for maturity of flower buds.

The shallow soils with little organic matter to virgin soils on steep mountain slopes or almost flat lands are suitable for coffee. In Karnataka where *Coffee arabica* is grown on commercial scale, the soils are red loamy and deep. Soils of coffee estates are generally rich in aluminum and iron content. The nitrogen percentage is also fairly high and low in lime percent. The soils are acidic with pH of 6.0.

Propagation

Propagated both by seeds and cuttings seeds are collected during December. Seed should be heavy broad and boat-shaped. Pulp of the seed is removed by hand: The fruits are rubbed with ash to prevent sticking of seeds and dried in shade and sown at 2.5 cm apart 4,000 seeds are required 5 for 1 hectare seeds germinate within 4–5 weeks. Then, the seedlings are uprooted and transplanted in bags or in nursery bed at 25 cm apart.

Vegetative Propagation

Cuttings have to be selected from bushes of outstanding performance and made to root in the propagation chambers or in specially laid out nursery beds. The cuttings root within 4–5 months. Rooting can be hastened by employing growth regulators like indole-3-butyric acid (IBA) or by dipping the cuttings in cow urine.

Planting

Pits of 45–60 cm cube are dug during January-February at a spacing of 2.5 × 2.5 m or 3 × 3 m depending on species to be planted. For *C. arabica* spacing of 2.5 × 2.5 m is recommended and for *C. robusta* spacing of 3 × 3 m is adopted. Planting is done during June–July. In the initial stage, staking is done for giving support to the seedlings.

Provision of Shade

Coffee: Prefers a subdued light, i.e. partial shade where sunlight is intense. The general practice in East Africa is to provide shade to the plantations grown below 1,600 in and to grow coffee without shade above this altitude. Shade is necessary to protect the soil moisture and soil temperature. In Brazil, coffee is grown without any shade. In India, the environmental conditions are entirely different. The severe heat-often scorches the leaves and dries up the soil resulting in the loss of soil moisture and increase/in soil temperatures which adversely affect the coffee bush.

Advantages of Shade Trees

1. They protect the bushes from torrential rains.
2. Provide a heavy mulch for the bushes.
3. Prevent soil erosion.
4. Add organic matter to enrich fertility status of the soil.
5. Increase nitrogen content of the soil.

The followings are some of the shade trees commonly used in coffee plantations, species of *Ficus, Terminale sp. Artocarpus heterophyllus, Grevillea robusta (silver oak), Albizia, Lebbeck, Erythrina lithosperma; Gliricidia maculata and Deucaene glauea.* Although the shade trees shed leaves and add humus to the soil, they compete for the nutrients with coffee bushes.

Manuring

The recommendations are based on the results of experiments, the nutrient removal and the productivity of coffee bushes under the different conditions of soil, climate and culture. The following fertilizer recommendations are given as the minimum requirements.

Fertilizer requirement of young plants from 1st year to IIIrd year has been described in the below.

Fertilizers	Kg/hectare
Stermeal	336
Urea	17
Muriate of potash	19
Single super phosphate	22

These fertilizers are applied in four split doses each of 106 kg in February/March, May/June, August/September and November/December. The fertilizer doses (NPK, 45:34:45 kg/hectare) are recommended for mature bused of over 3 years age.

Foliar sprays of nutrients mixtures containing nitrogen, phosphoric acid, potash, magnesium and zinc may be applied along with regular spray program.

Foliar sprays of nutrients during the break in monsoon in July–August have also been found to arrest fruit drop in coffee considerably. In problem areas where roots are unable to absorb sufficient nutrients from soil due to very low soil temperature, lack of moisture of a restricted injured or diseased root system, foliar feeding is very effective.

Training and Priming

Arabica coffee is grown in India on single stem. The vertical growth of the plant is checked at two stages with the object of having good lateral spread and to secure a semispherical bearing surface. This object is achieved by topping and countering. The young tree is allowed to grow until it develops of crown wood on the main stem and on the primary branches. When stem is mature, it is topped at a height of 1 m. Timely topping of the young plant helps to develop a good framework on the bush. Centering is done in the 2nd or 3rd year to strengthen the stem and the primaries. Centering provides sufficient aeration to the lower region of the plant.

Crisscross and overriding shoots and unproductive wood are periodically removed, unproductive wood between all primaries and secondaries are also to be removed and only healthy vigorous growth is alone encouraged. These operations are generally carried in June–July and September–October.

Rejuvenation Pruning

This consists of part of pole pruning generally done once in 4 or 5 years to bring back old coffee to shape again and control unwanted shoots. This is needed for the production of healthy vigorous cropping wood after heavy bearing or heavy defoliation due to disease or debility. This type of pruning includes removal of dead, exhausted, dried and worn out branches. This operation is taken up immediately after harvest so that the plants will have the benefit of summer showers after pruning for the production of new flush.

After Culture

Digging and forking open are usually done during September–November and again in February–March. This may be done annually but it is a costly item and also detrimental to feeding roots of the bush. Therefore, some plantar do digging once in 4–5 years weed control is done in initial years. Chemical weedicides like dalapon (controlling grasses and amino salt of 2, 4-D) for controlling broad leaved weed are used.

Mulching and cultivation of green-manuring plants are done with the object of adding D.M. to soil mulching also controls and check the weed growth.

Cropping and Harvesting

1. Bearing commences from 3rd year onward, good yield sectors from the 5th year onward and continue to yield upto 50 years.
2. Fly picking: Small scale of picking of ripe berries is made during October and continued till February.
3. Main picking: Well formed and dripened barriers are harvested during December. Bulks of the yields are obtained during this period.
4. Stripping: Picking of left berries irrespective of ripening.
5. Collection of fruit dropped during harvesting.

Average Yield

1. *Arabica*: 400–650 kg/hectare
2. *Robusta*: 350–725 kg/hectare.

Production Technology of Tea

Botanical name: *Cornelia thea*

Family: *Camelliaceae*

Origin: Tea is believed to be indigenous to Assam in India only.

Area and Production

The crop is mainly grown in Assam (50%) and West Bengal (25%), Karnataka (30%) and Tamil Nadu (10%), respectively. Other minor tea growing/producing areas are located in Tripura, Punjab, U.P, Himachal Pradesh and Bihar.

Varieties

The most important types in cultivation are: (1) Assam and (2) China.

1. Assam: It is a taller plant with soft leaves and can grow at elevations under 1,500 meters.
2. China: It is dwarf bush with leathery leaves and can be grown upto 2,400 meters above sea level. Many hybrids of these two are in cultivation.

Ecology

1. Warm moist climate with plenty sun light
2. Rainfall: 1,500–2,500 mm well distributed
3. Temperature: Mean ranging from 10°C to 38°C
4. High elevations are good for economic life of plants and quality of leaves but total yield at high altitudes is best
5. Frost affects the adversely.

Soil

Deep liable loam and forest land rich in organic matter is very ideal. Generally, tea soils of India are generally with organic matters, N, Potash, low K, lime and magnesia content hence soil reaction is medium to strongly acidic.

Practice of liming is not followed in ease of tea because tea-does not thrive well on a soil which contains more than a trace of active lime subsoil should not be hard and stiff and growth of tea on clay soil is more uniform and tea is of better quality than tea grown on coarse sandy soils.

Land Preparation: Cultural Method

Tea is taken on hilly areas; the land is prepared by cutting of low growing vegetation arid unwanted forest trees are cut and removed. Except few selected ones left for shade stoop slopes are terraced and provided with contour drains and silt traps. A thick-wind-break of silver oak *(Grevillea robusta)* is planted on the periphery. Also shade trees, viz. silver oak, jack are planted at adjoined 12–15 m apart a year in advance of the main plantation to provide protection: to provide protection against, i.e. to provide shade, heat and torrential rains. They are lopped every year to provide adequate light and air.

After field/land preparation pits measuring of 30–45 m deep, 22 cm diameter are dug at distance of 1.2–1.5 m from one another. Filled with mixture of surface soil + FYM leaf mould.

Raising of Seedlings

Generally propagated by seeds; but vegetatively propagated plants give high yield, high quality, budding, grafting and layering have also been found successful.

Seeds sown first in germinating beds, then seedlings transferred to other nurseries or baskets containing, loose friable soil. Here, seedlings are allowed to grow for 6–8 months and subsequently 1.5 year (17 months) old seedlings are planted in April–May or September–October. In pits (previously prepared) dug in the permanent stags, gap filing as well as replacing, in to 30 years old bushes are also done at this time.

Manuring

Fertilizers mixtures supplying 60 kg N, 30 kg P_2O_5, 30 kg/K20 are applied in one or two doses after pruning. Nitrogenous manuring is very essential for promotion for leaf growth. Besides this application of compost and benefit derived from leaf fall of leguminous shade trees are grown for incorporation in the soil as green manures.

Intercultivation

The tea-gardens are hood and weeded three to five times during the rainy season. Shade trees are lopped to promote lateral development which will shade large area.

Topping and Pruning

1. Tea bush is pruned regularly to maintain proper shade, i.e. 1, 2–1.5 m diameter at 1–2 m height.
2. When the plants are 1 year old and have attained a height of 45 cm at this stage entering is done. Main stem is cut a few centimeters above ground. The new materials developed by the plant are again cut a little higher up.
3. This process is repeated every year. In 4 or 5 years, plant becomes a mature bush of 45–60 cm height and is ready to yield a crop. To encourage lateral spread, all shoots growing through center of the bush should be removed.
4. After a cycle of pruning, the bush is cut back to 2–3 cm below the first cut. This encourages fresh laterals and maintains yield at a high level.
5. In Assam, pruning is done in December–March after allowing the bush to grow 25 cm or more.

Plucking and Processing

Tea bush is ready for yielding after 4–5 years of planting and having a height of 45–60 cm. Usually, plucking is restricted to two leaves and a bud. This is called a fine and light plucking. Coarse plucking includes extra one or two leaves. In North, tea is plucked at interval of 7–10 days from April–December in South plucking continues throughout the years at weekly interval during March–May and at 10–14 days during other 3 months, i.e. during June–February (9 months).

Processing

For manufacturing of black tea, the plucked leaves are dried for 18–24 hours in ventilated indoor racks rolled for half an hour mechanically to breakup cells, then fermented or oxidized again for 8 hours at 27–105°C and passed through sieves of different meshes, thus sorting out grades and again graded into:

1. *Leaf*: Orange pekoe, flowery pekoe
2. *Broken*: Broken orange pekoe, broken pekoe, fanning
3. Dust tea.

Yield

The average yield is 1,200–1,500 kg/hectare of made tea. Vegetatively propagated clones often give as much as 2,000 kg/taken during cultivation and processing but on natural factors such as soil, climate, altitude and topography. Leaves are rich in caffeine and tannin.

Economic Use

Tea is an important foreign exchange earning crop, India exported tea worth of Rs 340 crores during 1998–1999. The commercial tea is either green (unfermented) or black (fermented). The leaves are rich in caffeine and tannin. On infefon in boiled water, it gives a well-known beverage known as tea.

Production of Technology Cashew Nut

Botanical name: *Anacardium occidentale*

Family: *Anacardiaceae*

Cashew is an important dollar earning crop of India, remarking second (29%) in the international trade of the nuts. It is a crop of marginal lands and can be grown under rainfed conditions.

Origin and Distribution

Cashew belongs to the family *Anacardiaceae*. It is a native of South Eastern Brazil. Li most tropical areas it is found growing in the coastal areas. The commercial production is mainly confined to India, Mozambique, Tanzania, Kenya; Brazil, Philippines, Malaysia and Sri Lanka.

Area and Production

In India, total area under cashew nut is 5.75 lakh hectares and the annual production of raw nut is only 245,576 tons which works out to only 427 kg of units per hectare. In Maharashtra, it is grown on an area of 22,692 hectare and the annual production is 19,120 tons. India earns about 200 crores of rupees annually through expert of cashew kernels.

Composition and Uses

It is one of the most delicious and nutritious nuts of the world, cashew contains moisture (5.9%), protein (21.2%), fat (46.9%), carbohydrates (22.3%), phosphorus (0.45%), calcium (0.05%), iron (5.0 mg/100 g), minerals and amino acids (2.4%).

Cashew is the most popular nut used by the confectionery industry. Cashew nut shell liquid (CMSD) is in important by-product of cashew nut industry. Cashew which contains a good amount of vitamin C, upto five times that of citrus fruits, used for different preparations like pickle, jam, candy, chutney, etc.

Climate

Cashew is mainly a crop of the tropics. It does not establish well in areas subject to frost. Coastal areas having humid and warm climate are best suited for cashew cultivation. Cashew requires a minimum rainfall of 600 mm and above. However, it does not establish well areas subject to frost. It is a sun loving tree and therefore, does not tolerate excessive shade. It does not thrive below 20°C temperature for long period and very high temperature 39–42°C during the movable stage of fruit development cause fruit drop. Heavy rains and cloudy weather adversely affect the yield in cashew.

Soil

It is generally grown on a wasteland of low fertility also. Being hardy plant, cashew can grow in varkas land on top slope of the hills, red sandy loams arid light coastal sandy soils as well. It requires a well-drained soil. It can be grown on almost all types of soil from sandy sea coast to laterite hill slopes upto an elevation of 700 m above sea level.

Varieties

1. Vengurla-1: Selection from Ansur-1
2. Vengurla-2: Selection from West Bengal Deepal Semuha
3. Vengurla-3: Vengurla-1 × Vectore-56
4. Vengurla-4: Midnapur Red × Vectore-56
5. Vengurla-5: Ansur Barly × Mysore Rotekar 1/61.

Planting

For raising a new plantation, pits of 13 m are dig in summer at 7 × 7 or 8 × 8 distance. The pits are refilled to a depth of 30 cm with a mixture of top soil, 50 mg FYM, 2.5 kg SSP (single super phosphate) just before the onset of monsoon. After first shower of rains, the remaining top of the pit is refilled with a 10 cm layer of dry leaves over which a layer of 8 cm soil is made. Sowing of seeds or planting of grafts is done after receiving of 3–4 rains.

Manuring and Fertilization

Cashew responds, very well to manuring. To ensure early and higher yield, regular fertilizer application is needed. The fertilizer recommendation for cashew is 500 kg N, 125 kg P_2O_5 and 125 kg K20 per tree from 4th year onward and to be applied in split doses before and after the South West monsoon.

The fertilizers should be applied within the radius of 2 m of tree. The application of fertilizer may be done after complete weeding and cleaning of basins of each tree to avoid the competition for nutrients from weeds.

Stage of growth	Per tree per year in gram					
	May–June			September–October		
	N	P_2O_5	K20	N	P_2O_5	K20
1st year	50	40	–	50	40	–
2nd year	100	40	30	100	40	30
3rd year	200	60	60	200	60	60
4th year onward	250	65	65	250	60	60

Irrigation

Cashew is a hardy and rainfed crop. Its extensive root system is capable of absorbing moisture from sub soil. The irrigations are therefore not required by this crop. However, it is advised to irrigate newly planted grafts/seedlings for the initial period of 2 years till their root system is established well. The irrigation during flowering and fruiting period helps to reduce the fruit drop.

Interculture

Keeping orchard free from weeds is important aspect of management. The first weeding may be done before heavy rains and before application of first dose of fertilizers. The second weeding may carried out after monsoon.

Use of Mulch

Mulching in cashew plantation is helpful in regulating soil temperature and conserve soil moisture. It also prevents soil erosion and improves soil fertility. Mulching to bearing cashew trees with black polythene mulch during pest-monsoon has given higher yields than the trees without mulching.

Intercropping

Intercropping in cashew plantation would enable higher returns during the initial years. There should be no scope for intercropping once the cashew canopy comers the area and shades the interspace.

Harvesting

Cashew planted by grails gives yield after 3–4 years and that from seedlings 5–6 years after planting. Flowering commences in the month of December–January on new shoots and fruits will be ready for harvest, after 50–55 days. Harvesting and collection of nuts are done over a period of 10–12 weeks. Harvesting commences from February and continues upto May. The crop is gathered from the ground after the apple is allowed, to drop down naturally with the attached nut. The fruits are collected every day and the nuts are separated allowing the fruits by itself ensures the fully matured nut. The nuts gathered are Sun dried for 2–3 days before storing.

Yield

The yield per tree is estimated at 8–15 kg. However, the maximum yield produced by Vengurla-3 (20.78 kg), Vengurla-4 (27.34 kg) and Vengurla-5 (31.26 kg), respectively.

Production Technology of Cocoa

Botanical name: *Theobroma cacao*

Family: *Sterauliaceae*

2n = 20

The word cacao is often used for the tree and its parts whereas the word "cocoa" for the product of manufacture. In this account, the word "cocoa" is used throughout for both tree and its products.

It is most nutritious of all beverages has been cultivated since ancient time in Central America from Mexico to the Southern Costa Rican border for over 2000 years. It was first introduced into India in 1796.

Area and Production

West Africa is leading country in cocoa trade. For last 40 years, China, Ivory coast, French Cameroon and Nigeria contribute 84% of the world production.

Ghana (36%), America (33%), rest of Africa (30%) and other (1%), respectively.

In India, cocoa is grown in a small area of about 17,600 hectares in arecanut and coconut gardens in scattered holdings of Southern States of Tamil Nadu and Kerala. 7,000 tons of cocoa beans are produced. The Hindu Survey of Indian Agriculture, Statewise area and production is as shown below:

Sr. No.	State	Area (hectare)	Production (tons)
1	Kerala	15,000	6,036
2	Karnataka	1,530	700
3	Tamil Nadu	470	264
	Total	**17,000**	**7,000**

Climate and Soil

It is strictly tropical crop and cultivation restricted in 20°N and South of latitude, grows at low elevation, i.e. below 1,000 feet. However, it can be cultivated upto 4,000 feet in Venezuela and upto 3,000 feet in Colombia.

The optimum temperature range is 15–25°C and rainfall requirement is 1,000–2,500 mm and should be well distributed, grows under dense shade.

Cocoa requires well-drained sols with good crumb structure and adequate, supply of water and nutrients. The best soils are clays or loams of sandy loams. The optimum pH is around 6.5.

Propagation

Progagated both by-seeds and by vegetative means seed propagation cheapest. The pulp adhering to the seed is removed by treating the seed with earth, ash or lime. Seeds are sown individually in polythene bags or can be grown in nursery beds with natural or artificial shade. Seeds sown soon after extraction. Seedlings are ready for transplanting when they attain height of 60.

Vegetative Propagation

Cocoa can be propagated vegetatively by cutting, budding and grafting. Cutting of 15 cm length bearing four terminal leaves were treated with naphthalene acetic acid (NNA) + *indole butyric acid* (IBA) dip and planted in polybags, rooting of 60–70% reported after 1 month. Cutting 2–4 cm long with one or two leaves treated with IBA and planted in medium of rotten palm fiber and coarse river sand in equal part gave 90–100% rooting.

Inarchaing in cocoa was highly successful (70–100%) at Kalian and Burliar Fruit Research Station. Saddle and wedge grafting of leaf bearing shoot is also possible.

Planting

Usually planted at 3.5 × 3.5 m. The spacing will depend upon the environmental conditions and cultivar grown. Closer spacing gives higher yield in early years and also provides a quicker closed canopy. Closer spacing of 2.7 × 2.7 m gives higher yield than 3.5 × 3.5 m as seen by the spacing trials in Trinidad. In Sri Lanka and New guinea, usually spacing of 5 × 5 m is kept. In India, cocoa is generally planted in the coconut and arecanut gardens. In arecanut garden, a spacing of 2.7 × 5.4 m and in coconut gardens at 7.5 × 7.5 m, thus accommodating about 550–650 cocoa trees either in coconut or arecanut garden.

Manuring

Ten kilogram organic manure, 100 kg N, 40 kg P_2O_5 and 140 kg K20 per plant per year is the recommended dose of fertilizers, fertilizers are applied in two equal split doses, one in April–May alongwith organic manures and other in August–September full dose of organic manure is applied from first year itself. However, the fertilizers are applied in graded doses, i.e. one-third dose in first year, two-thirds and full dose from 3rd year.

Irrigations

Young cocoa plantation is irrigated regularly at an interval of 3–4 days; during summer months.

Harvesting

Bearing starts from 2nd year onward. Pods mature in about 5–6 months. Two crops are there, first from October–January and 2nd from April–June. The ripen pods are harvested without causing injury to cushions from which they are developed. This is necessary as flowers are produced again from these "Cushions". The pods are opened by heating on a hard surface or using a mallet. Knife is not used as it may cut the beans inside. The beans are scooped out from the pod. To get 1 kg of dry cocoa beans about 15–30 pods are required.

Yield

The average yield of cocoa in Trinidad is 200 kg/hectare from seedling progenies. From selected cuttings, yield of 600–1,000 kg/hectare dried bean may be obtained. Hybrid seedlings of Trinitario may yield over 2,000 kg/hectare. Well care plantation has yielded above 3,000 kg of beam/hectare.

Production Technology of Oil Palm

There is an ever increasing demand for vegetable oils all over the world today. Oil palm is one of the important crops which can meet the demand for vegetable oils. It provides both palm oil and kernel oil. The yield of palm oil is not only very high but this can also be grown in wider range of soils.

Climate

Hot humid equatorial climate with a mean annual temperature of 20–27°C is preferred. The optimum rainfall for oil palm lies between 2,000 nm and 3,000 mm (80–120"). In relatively low rainfall areas, the oil palm flourishes only when rain and sunshine frequently alternate with one another and the soil moisture is sufficient high. It can be planted throughout the year.

Soil

High yields are obtained in deep, permeable soils which are rich in humus and have a crumby structure. Optimum soil reaction is from pH 6.5 to 7.5.

Varieties

1. Tanera
2. Dura.

Propagation

Collect fresh, ripe fruits and remove the mesocarp. The basic requirement for germination of seeds is temperature about 40°C, adequate aeration and moisture content of about 22%. The seedlings will be ready for transplanting in 12–14 months.

Planning

1. Dig pits of 60 cm³ in 10 m rows at 10 m apart.
2. Fill the pits with top soil, FYM and 125 g superphosphate.
3. Plant good healthy seedling with a ball of earth in the center of pit.

Manure and Fertilizers

Apply 50 kg FYM/plant before and after planting. The phosphorous should also be given before planting 125 g/plant. After 7 years of planting apply NPK every year 450 g N, 450 g P and 900 g K alongwith 350 g Mg/plant.

Intercultivation

Remove the woods around the plants regularly. Carry out initial pruning just before assisted pollination begins maintaining two fronds below the lowest developing bunch. Maintain a minimum of 37 trends per palm.

Assisted Pollination

It is necessary in order to ensure fertilization of all females flowers in the bunch especially during rainy season. Collect pollen from male inflorescence and dry in Sun for about 5 hours and store in a moisture free containers. It remains viable for over 30 days. Mix this pollen with chalk powder (1:4) and use for pollination. The stigma remains receptive for 3 days, after they have opened.

Harvesting

Ripe fruits become loose on the bunch and this stage can be considered as stage for harvesting. A chisel or harvesting knife attached to a bamboo pole is used for harvesting fruit bunches.

Processing

The fruit bunches are sterilized in steam or boiling water for 30–60 minutes. The object of this process is to inactivate the fat splitting enzymes which are present in fruit which may raise the free, fatty acid content of the oil and also to soften the fruits for easy pounding strip. Sterilize fruits from the bunch and then pound, reheat. The pounded fruit mass should be squazed on or the hydraulic press. Then boil in a clarification drum. When the sludge will deposit in the bottom and pure oil float over the water, drain out the oil.

Plant Production

1. *Insects*: *Rhioceros beetles* and *Slug caterpillar.*
2. *Diseases*: Stem rot, bud rot, crown disease, morasmius disease.

Schedule

1. To control *Rhicocerous beetle* remove the adult beetles from the infected frantls and fill the hole with a mixture of *benzenehexachloride* (BHC) (10%) or dichlorodiphenyltrichloroethane (DDT) (10%) and fine sand (1:1)
2. Treat the breeding ground with BHC (50%) or carbaryl (50%) at 350°.
3. To control the stem rot, prune the diseased frontals and burn them.
4. To control morasmius disease, remove the unpollinated branches when they show signs of decay and burn them.
5. Gramodenues can be controlled by removing severely affected palms along with roots from the garden. Apply 1 kg mancoreb or capton or thiram in deep trenches, 1 m away from base of the palms.
6. To control the damages of *Slug caterpillar,* remove and burn affected leaflets and spray the plants with 40 g carbaryl in 10 liters of water.

2

Tea

DEFINITION

Tea is an aromatic beverage commonly prepared by pouring hot or boiling water over cured leaves of the tea plant, *Camellia sinensis*. After water, tea is the most widely consumed beverage in the world.

- An eastern Asian evergreen shrub or small tree *(Camellia sinensis)* having fragrant, nodding, cup-shaped white flowers and glossy leaves.
- The young, dried leaves of this plant prepared by various processes and used to make a hot beverage.
- An aromatic, slightly bitter beverage made by steeping tea leaves in boiling water.
- An afternoon refreshment consisting usually of sandwiches and cakes served with tea.
- An afternoon reception or social gathering at which tea is served.

Tea can refer to any of several different meals or mealtimes, depending on a country's customs and its history of drinking tea. However, in those countries where the term's use is common, the influences are generally those of the former British Empire (now the Commonwealth or Nations). Tea as a meal can be small or large.

Derived from the Chinese, the word tea occurs in almost all languages of the world. This is the name by which the beverage came to be known in the countries. It initially arrived via sea (in French, *tee* in Germany, *te* in Italian). Mean while, the countries it reached by land adopted a derivative of the more common Chinese pronunciation *cha*. Thus, at home (India), the Arab nations and the Slavonic world, *chai* is the identity for tea. Interestingly, infusions made from other plants are often also referred to as "tea;" the correct term for a fruit or herbal tea is *tisane*.

Varied *avatars of tea* demanded a deeper query into its antecedents. Hence, the endeavor. After all, tea is much more than just a hot or cold infusion, particularly if one were to ponder over mythical Chinese emperor and scholar Shen Nung's wise words: "tea arouses the intellect and arouses wise thoughts. It refreshes the body and calms the soul".

> Tea has stirred conflicts and created chaos. The destinies of several individuals and even the world have been decided, rulers overthrown, peace treaties signed and declarations of war made over cups of tea, writes Suparna-Saraswati Puri.

HISTORY OF TEA

The history of tea is long and complex, spreading across multiple cultures over the span of thousands of years. Tea likely originated in Yunnan, China during the Shang Dynasty (1500–1046 BC) as a medicinal drink. The earliest credible record of tea drinking dates to the 3rd century AD, in a medical text written by Hua T'o. Tea was first introduced to Portuguese priests and merchants in China during the 16th century. Drinking tea became popular in Britain during the 17th century. The British introduced tea production, as well as consumption to India, in order to compete with the Chinese monopoly on tea.

Geographic Origin

According to Mondal (2007): "*Camellia sinensis* originated in Southeast Asia, specifically around the intersection of latitude 29°N and longitude 98°E, the point of confluence of the lands of Northeast India, North Burma, Southwest China and Tibet. The plant was introduced to more than 52 countries, from this 'center of origin', rather than as a medicinal concoction".

The story of tea began in ancient China over 5,000 years ago. According to legend, Shen Nung, 2737–269 BC an early emperor was a skilled ruler, creative scientist and patron of the arts and inventor of agriculture and Chinese medicine. His far-sighted edicts required, among other things, that all drinking water be boiled as a hygienic precaution. One summer day while visiting a distant region of his realm, he and the court stopped to rest. In accordance with his ruling, the servants began to boil water for the court to drink. Dried leaves from the nearby bush fell into the boiling water, and a brown liquid was infused into the water. As a scientist, the Emperor was interested in the new liquid, drank some, and found it very refreshing. And so, according to legend, tea was created (this myth maintains such a practical narrative, that many mythologists believe it may relate closely to the actual events, now lost in ancient history). The first mention of tea, however, is found in the Erh Ya—an ancient Chinese dictionary published around 350 BC. Lu Yu, a renowned author in the time of the Tang Dynasty (618–907 AD), wrote a treatize on tea called Ch'a Ching. His book says that sometimes onions, ginger, jujuke, orange peel and peppermint were boiled along with tea. The book also mentions the medicinal properties of tea. Buddhist monks brought tea from China to Japan. Teas stimulating properties helped the monks to stay awake during meditation, which helped its spread in Japanese culture. Commercial cultivation did not start in Japan until the 12th century. Japan, unlike China, drank its tea ceremoniously. In China, small farmers traditionally grew tea, and large traders bought the tea and transported it to distant countries. Laborers carrying 300 lb. of tea on their backs walked mountain passes at 6 miles per day and used opium packs on the back of their ears to deaden the pain from the heavy loads.

Tea resonates of culture and enjoys a long eventful occasionally turbulent journey in the annals of history. Strange as it may sound but tea has stirred conflicts and created chaos. The destinies of innumerable individuals and even the world itself have been decided, rulers overthrown, peace treaties signed and declarations of war made over cups of tea. Probably, mankind's oldest cultivated plant, the origins of tea, can be traced to China where it is known to have been grown for 2,500 years. Even today, visitors and guests alike are greeted with a bowl of tea as a symbol of friendship, a tradition that we Indians carry as well rather proudly. The oldest reliable records mention dates from 221 BC when scrolls document the introduction of a tea tax.

Tea *(Camellia spp.)* is an important beverage and the world drinks more of it than any other beverage. It is made from the tender or young leaves and unopened buds of the evergreen tea-plant, popular as a "healthful herb". The tea plant is in the polymorphic species *Camellia sinensis* Kuntz, but recent findings show that this plant of commerce is derived more than one species. Two distinct varieties of tea-plant are generally recognized, the small-leaved China *(sinensis)* and the large-leaved Assam *(assamica)* which have been raised to a specific rank by a well-known tea botanist. Careful field observations, however, reveal that more than one or two species are involved in the evolution of the present-day tea-plant of commerce. Considerable interspecific hybridization has taken place in nature. Thus, the taxonomy of the tea-complex is confounded.

The Chinese Influence

Tea consumption spread throughout the Chinese culture reaching into every aspect of the society. In 800 AD, Lu Yu wrote the first definitive book on tea, the Ch'a Ching. This amazing man was orphaned as a child and raised by scholarly Buddhist monks in one of China's finest monasteries. However, as a young man, he rebelled against the discipline of priestly training which had made him a skilled observer. His fame as a performer increased with each year, but he felt his life lacked meaning. Finally, in mid-life, he retired for 5 years into seclusion. Drawing from his vast memory of observed events and places, he codified the various methods of tea cultivation and preparation in ancient China. The vast definitive nature of his work projected him into near sainthood within his own lifetime. Patronized by the Emperor himself, his work clearly showed the Zen Buddhist philosophy to which he was exposed as a child. It was this form of tea service that Zen Buddhist missionaries would later introduce to imperial Japan.

China's monopoly over tea was broken by Buddhist monks who, under their robes, smuggled, tea out to Japan between 520 AD and 800 AD. This precious commodity was initially reserved for the Japanese imperial family and upper echelons of society and only became more widely available during the 12th century.

In the 16th century, Christian missionaries and sailors carried the knowledge of the cultivation and advantages of tea to the land of the colonizers, Europe. It began in 1610, with the Dutch seafarers shipping tea to Amsterdam. Perhaps, this would then explain the use of the word, "orange" in orange pekoe tea (orange being the color associated with the royalty of the Netherlands). The trade in tea soon meandered from Holland to Italy, France, Germany and Portugal. Initially, the trade was focused on import of green tea. In Russia tea was called *cha* and was transported by Caravan of traders along the silk route, travelling from Peking through the Gobi desert and Siberia to Volga. It was in the middle of the 17th century that 200 packets of tea were sent to Czar Michael I as a birthday present. Interestingly, along with tea, precious Chinese porcelain was imported into European markets. The original teacups had no handles, as is still used in Japan and China even today.

The Japanese Influence

The first tea seeds were brought to Japan by the returning Buddhist priest Yeisei, who had seen the value of tea in China in enhancing religious mediation. As a result, he is known as the "Father of Tea" in Japan. Because of this early association, tea in Japan has always been associated with Zen Buddhism. Tea received almost instant imperial sponsorship and spread rapidly from the royal court and monasteries to the other sections of Japanese society.

Tea was elevated to an art form resulting in the creation of the Japanese Tea Ceremony ("Cha-no-yu" or "the hot water for tea"). The best description of this complex art form was probably written by the Irish-Greek journalist-historian Lafcadio Hearn, one of the few foreigners ever to be granted Japanese citizenship during this era. He wrote from personal observation, "The tea ceremony requires years of training and practice to graduate in art...yet the whole of this art, as to its detail, signifies no more than the making and serving of a cup of tea. The supremely important matter is that the act be performed in the most perfect, most polite, most graceful, most charming mr possible".

Such a purity of form, of expression prompted the creation of supportive arts and services. A special form of architecture (chaseki) developed for "tea houses", based on the duplication of the simplicity of a forest cottage. The cultural/artistic hostesses of Japan, the Geishi, began to specialize in the presentation of the tea ceremony. As more and more people became involved in the excitement surrounding tea, the purity of the original Zen concept was lost. The tea ceremony became corrupted, boisterous and highly embellished. "Tea Tournaments" were held among the wealthy where nobles competed among each other for rich prizes in naming various tea blends. Rewarding winners with gifts of silk, armor, and jewelry was totally alien to the original Zen attitude of the ceremony.

Three great Zen priests restored tea to its original place in Japanese society:

1. *Ikkyu (1394–1481)*: A prince who became a priest and was successful in guiding the nobles away from their corruption of the tea ceremony.
2. *Murata Shuko (1422–1502)*: The student of Ikkyu and very influential in re-introducing the tea ceremony into Japanese society.
3. *Sen-no Rikkyu (1521–1591)*: Priest who set the rigid standards for the ceremony largely used intact today. Rikyo was successful in influencing the Shogun Toyotomi Hideyoshi, who became Japan's greatest patron of the "art of tea". A brilliant general, strategist, poet, and artist this unique leader facilitated the final and complete integration of tea into the pattern of Japanese life. So, complete was this acceptance that tea was viewed as the ultimate gift, and warlords paused for tea before battles.

Europe Learns of Tea

While tea was at this high level of development in both Japan and China, information concerning this then unknown beverage began to filter back to Europe. Earlier Caravan leaders had mentioned it, but were unclear as to its service format or appearance. (One reference suggests the leaves be boiled, salted, buttered, and eaten!). The first European to personally encounter tea and write about it was the Portuguese Jesuit Father Jasper de Cruz in 1560. Portugal with her technologically advanced navy had been successful in gaining the first right of trade with China. It was as a missionary on that first commercial mission that Father de Cruz had tasted tea 4 years before.

The Portuguese developed a trade route by which they shipped their tea to Lisbon, and then Dutch ships transported it to France, Holland, and the Baltic countries (at that time Holland was politically affiliated with Portugal. When this alliance was altered in 1602, Holland with her excellent navy entered into full Pacific trade in her own right).

Tea Comes to Europe

When tea finally arrived in Europe, Elizabeth I had more years to live, and Rembrandt was only 6 years old. Because of the success of the Dutch navy in the Pacific, tea became very fashionable in the Dutch capital, the Hague. This was due in part to the high cost of the tea (over $100 per pound) which immediately made it the domain of the wealthy. Slowly, as the amount of tea imported increased, the price fell as the volume of sale expanded. Initially, available to the public in apothecaries along with such rare and new spices as ginger and sugar, by 1675, it was available in common food shops throughout Holland.

As the consumption of tea increased dramatically in Dutch society, doctors and university authorities argued back and forth as to the negative and/or positive benefits of tea. Known as "tea heretics", the public largely ignored the scholarly debate and continued to enjoy their new beverage though the controversy lasted from 1635 to roughly 1657. Throughout this period France and Holland led Europe in the use of tea.

In 1610 in Europe, tea was initially introduced as a medicinal brew. By the 1700s, the Duke's wife began the tradition of afternoon tea to ward off hunger pangs between lunch and dinner. Asians used it for years together as a warm welcoming beverage for guests. Before long, it became the most popular beverage, both for pleasure and medicinal purposes.

In Europe, tea was sold as a medicinal drink in the 1650s. Tea drinking really took hold when Catherine of Bragaza, a Portuguese princess, married Charles II in 1662. She brought tea and served it to friends at court. The tea started being served at what was called tea gardens all over London. Many of the tea gardens closed as people migrated to the suburbs in the 19th century. About the same time Anna, the Dutchess of Bedford, started serving tea and snacks to her afternoon guests. This started the fashion of afternoon teatime in Britain. Tea was associated with social functions and was served with great ceremony including the best porcelain tea wares. In the 1950s, tea bags appeared and changed the way Britain brewed tea. The tea gardens and tea functions disappeared and were changed to fast food restaurants where tea was also being served. Tea remained popular in homes. In the 1980s, a new trend developed where specialty shops started selling a variety of fine teas. The media took hold of the event and tea once again came into fashion and has kept up the momentum.

As the craze for things oriental swept Europe, tea became part of the way of life. The social critic Marie de Rabutin-Chantal, the Marquise de Seven makes the first mention in 1680 of adding milk to tea. During the same period, Dutch inns provided the first restaurant service of tea. Tavern owners would furnish guests with a portable tea set complete with a heating unit. The independent Dutchman would then prepare tea for himself and his friends outside in the tavern's garden. Tea remained popular in France for only about 50 years, being replaced by a stronger preference for wine, chocolate, and exotic coffees.

Tea Arrives in England

Great Britain was the last of the three great sea-faring nations to break into the Chinese and East Indian trade routes. This was due in part to the unsteady ascension to the throne of the Stuarts and the Cromwellian Civil War. The first samples of tea reached England between 1652 and 1654. Tea quickly proved popular enough to replace ale as the national drink of England.

As in Holland, it was the nobility that provided the necessary stamp of approval and so insured its acceptance. King Charles II had married, while in exile, the Portuguese Infanta Catherine de Braganza (1662). Charles himself had grown up in the Dutch capital. As a result, both he and his Portuguese bride were confirmed tea drinkers. When the monarchy was re-established, the two rulers brought this foreign tea tradition to England with them. As early as 1600 Elizabeth I had founded the John Company for the purpose of promoting Asian trade. When Catherine de Braganza married Charles, she brought as part of her dowry the territories of Tangier and Bombay. Suddenly, the John Company had a base of operations.

The John Company

The John Company was granted the unbelievably wide monopoly of all trade east of the Cape of Good Hope and west of Cape Horn. Its powers were almost without limit and included among others the right to:

- Legally acquire territory and govern it
- Coin money
- Raise arms and build forts
- Form foreign alliances
- Declare war
- Conclude peace
- Pass laws
- Try and punish law breakers.

It was the single largest, most powerful monopoly to ever exist in the world. And its power was based on the importation of tea.

At the same time, the newer East India Company floundered against such competition. Appealing to Parliament for relief, the decision was made to merge the John Company and the East India Company (1773). Their redrafted charts gave the new East India Company a complete and total trade monopoly on all commerce in China and India. As a result, the price of tea was kept artificially high, leading to later global difficulties for the British crown.

Afternoon Tea in England

Tea mania swept across England as it had earlier spread throughout France and Holland. Tea importation rose from 40,000 pounds in 1699 to an annual average of 240,000 pounds by 1708. Tea was drunk by all levels of society.

Prior to the introduction of tea into Britain, the English had two main meals- breakfast and dinner. Breakfast was ale, bread and beef. Dinner was a long, massive meal at the end of the day. It was no wonder that Anna, the Duchess of Bedford (1788–1861) experienced a "sinking feeling" in the late afternoon. Adopting the European tea service format, she invited friends to join her for an additional afternoon meal at 5 o'clock in her rooms at Belvoir Castle. The menu centered around small cakes, bread and butter sandwiches, assorted sweets, and, of course, tea. This summer practice proved so popular, the Duchess continued it when she returned to London, sending cards to her friends asking them to join her for "tea and a walking the fields" (London at that time still contained large open meadows within the city). The practice of inviting friends to come for tea in the afternoon was quickly picked up by other social hostesses. A common pattern of service soon merged. The first pot of tea was made in the kitchen and carried to the lady of the house who waited with her invited guests, surrounded by fine porcelain from China. The first pot was warmed by the hostess from a second pot (usually silver) that was kept heated over a small flame. Food and tea was then passed among the guests, the main purpose of the visiting being conversation.

Tea Cuisine

Tea cuisine quickly expanded in range to quickly include wafer thin crustless sandwiches, shrimp or fish pates, toasted breads with jams, and regional British pastries such as scones (Scottish) and crumpets (English).

At this time, two distinct forms of tea services evolved: "High" and "Low". "Low" tea (served in the low part of the afternoon) was served in aristocratic homes of the wealthy and featured gourmet tidbits rather than solid meals. The emphasis was on presentation and conversation. "High" tea or "Meat tea" was the main or "High" meal of the day. It was the major meal of the middle and lower classes and consisted of mostly full dinner items such as roast beef, mashed potatoes, peas, and of course, tea.

Coffee Houses

Tea was the major beverage served in the coffee houses, but they were so named because coffee arrived in England some years before tea. Exclusively for men, they were called "Penny Universities" because for a penny any man could obtain a pot of tea, a copy of the newspaper, and engage in conversation with the sharpest wits of the day. The various houses specialized in selected areas of interest, some serving attorneys, some authors and others military. They were the forerunner of the English gentlemen's private club. One such beverage house was owned by Edward Lloyd and was favored by shipowners, merchants and marine insurers. That simple shop was the origin of Lloyd's, the worldwide insurance firm. Attempts to close the coffee houses were made throughout the eighteenth century because of the free speech they encouraged, but such measures proved so unpopular they were always quickly revoked.

Tea Gardens

Experiencing the Dutch "tavern garden teas", the English developed the idea of Tea Gardens. Here ladies and gentlemen took their tea out of doors surrounded by entertainment such as orchestras, hidden arbors, flowered walks, bowling greens, concerts, gambling, or fireworks at night. It was at just such a Tea Garden that Lord Nelson, who defeated Napoleon by sea, met the great love of his life, Emma, later Lady Hamilton. Women were permitted to enter a mixed, public gathering for the first time without social criticism. As the gardens were public, British society mixed here freely for the first time, cutting across lines of class and birth.

Tipping as a response to proper service developed in the Tea Gardens of England. Small, locked wooden boxes were placed on the tables throughout the Garden. Inscribed on each were the letters "TIPS" which stood for the sentence "To Insure Prompt Service". If a guest wished the waiter to hurry (and so insure the tea arrived hot from the often distant kitchen), he dropped a coin into the box on being seated "to insure prompt service". Hence, the custom of tipping servers was created.

Russian Tea Tradition

Imperial Russia was attempting to engage China and Japan in trade at the same time as the East Indian Company. The Russian interest in tea began as early as 1618 when the Chinese embassy in Moscow presented several chests of tea to Czar Alexis. By 1689, the Trade Treaty of Newchinsk established common border between Russia and China, allowing caravans to then cross back and forth freely. Still, the journey was not easy. The trip was 11,000 miles long and took over 16 months to complete. The average caravan consisted of 200–300 camels. As a result of such factors, the cost of tea was initially prohibitive and available only to the wealthy. By the time Catherine, the Great died (1796), the price had dropped some, and tea was spreading throughout Russian society. Tea was ideally suited to Russian life: hearty, warm and sustaining.

The samovar, adopted from the Tibetan "hot pot", is a combination bubbling hot water heater and tea pot. Placed in the center of the Russian home, it could run all day and serve up to forty cups of tea at a time. Again showing the Asian influence in the Russian culture, guests sipped their tea from glasses in silver holders, very similar to Turkish coffee cups. The Russians have always favored strong tea highly sweetened with sugar, honey or jam.

With the completion of the Trans-Siberian Railroad in 1900, the overland caravans were abandoned. Although the Revolution intervened in the flow of the Russian society, tea remained a staple throughout. Tea (along with vodka) is the national drink of the Russians today.

Tea Comes to America

By 1650, the Dutch were actively involved in trade throughout the Western world. Peter Stuyvesant brought the first tea to America to the colonists in the Dutch settlement of New Amsterdam (later renamed New York by the English). Settlers here were confirmed tea drinkers. And indeed, on acquiring the colony, the English found that the small settlement consumed more tea at that time then all of England put together.

It was not until 1670 that English colonists in Boston became aware of tea, and it was not publicly available for sale until 20 years later. Tea Gardens were first opened in New York City, already aware of tea as a former Dutch colony. The new Gardens were centered around the natural springs, which the city fathers now equipped with pumps to facilitate the "tea craze". The most famous of these "tea springs" was at Roosevelt and Chatham (later Park Row Street).

By 1720, tea was a generally accepted staple of trade between the Colony and the Mother country. It was especially a favorite of colonial women, a factor England was to base a major political decision on later. Tea trade was centered in Boston, New York, and Philadelphia, future centers of American rebellion. As tea was heavily taxed, even at this early date, contraband tea was smuggled into the colonies by the independent minded American merchants from ports far away and adopted herbal teas from the Indians. The directors of the then John Company (to merge later with the East India Company) fumed as they saw their profits diminish and they pressured Parliament to take action. It was not long in coming.

Tea and the American Revolution

England had recently completed the French and Indian War fought from England's point of view, to free the colony from French influence and stabilize trade. It was the feeling of Parliament that as a result, it was not unreasonable that the colonists shoulder the majority of the cost. After all, the war had been fought for their benefit. Charles Townshend presented the first tax measures which today are known by his name. They imposed a higher tax on newspapers (which they considered far too outspoken in America), tavern licenses (too much free speech there), legal documents, marriage licenses, and docking papers. The colonists rebelled against taxes imposed upon them without their consent and which were so repressive. New, heavier taxes were leveled by Parliament for such rebellion. Among these was, in June 1767, the tea tax that was to become the watershed of America's desire for freedom (Townshend died 3 months later of a fever never to know his tax measures helped to create a free nation).

The colonists rebelled and openly purchased imported tea, largely Dutch in origin. The John Company already in deep financial trouble saw its profits fall even further. By 1773, the John Company merged with the East India Company for structural stability and pleaded with the Crown for assistance. The new Lord of the Treasury, Lord North, as a response to this pressure, granted to the new company permission to sell directly to the colonists, by-passing the colonial merchants and pocketing the difference. In plotting this strategy, England was counting on the well-known passion among American women for tea to force consumption. It was a major miscalculation. Throughout the colonies, women pledged publicly at meetings and in newspapers not to drink English sold tea until their free rights (and those of their merchant husbands) were restored.

The Boston Tea Party

By December 16 events had deteriorated enough that the men of Boston, dressed as Indians (remember the original justification for taxation had been the expense of the French and Indian War) threw hundreds of pounds of tea into the harbor: the Boston Tea Party. Such leading citizens as Samuel Adams and John Hancock took part. England had enough. In retaliation, the port of Boston was closed and the city occupied by royal troops. The colonial leaders met and revolution was declared.

The Company of merchants of London trading into the East Indies is granted a royal charter by Queen Elizabeth I, established with 125 shareholders and £72,000 of capital. Sir Thomas Smythe is The Company's first Governor. Elizabeth also limited the liability of the Equity Investment Corporations (EICs) investors as well as her liabilities in granting a Royal Charter. This made The Company the world's first limited liability corporation.

Sir Thomas Roe was instructed by James I to arrange a commercial treaty with Emperor Nurudin Salim Jahangir. This gave the company exclusive rights to reside and build factories around Surat in exchange for rare commodities from Europe.

This provided a secure base for operations to wage trade wars with Portuguese and Dutch governments and merchants.

The company receives Chinese permission to trade from Guangzhou (Canton) importing silk, tea and porcelain. Trade was made with the Chinese Hongs (trading companies) who controlled trade within China. In England, the demand for tea booms in 1664. The Company placed an order for tea for 100 lbs by 1750 annual imports had reached 4,727,992 lbs. Having initially traded tea for silver, the English are concerned that too much silver is leaving their shores. They begin to trade the highly addictive drug opium for tea, this leads directly to the opium wars between Britain and China, as the Chinese government tries to stop this trade.

The Boston Tea party was driven by resistance throughout British America against the Tea Act, passed by the British Parliament in 1773. Colonists objected to the Tea Act because it violated their right to be taxed only by their own elected representatives. Men thinly disguised as Mohawk Indians dumped 342 chests overboard three ships: (1) the "Dartmouth", (2) the "Eleanor" and (3) the "Beaver", loaded with tea from the East India Company.

The Trade Continued in the Orient

Though concerned over developments in America, English tea interests still centered on the product's source-the Orient. There the trading of tea had become a way of life, developing its own language known as "Pidgin English". Created solely to facilitate commerce, the language was composed of English, Portuguese, and Indian words all pronounced in Chinese. Indeed, the word "Pidgin" is a corrupted form of the Chinese word for "do business".

So, dominant was the tea culture within the English speaking cultures that many of these words came to hold a permanent place in our language.

- "Mandarin" (from the Portuguese "mandar" meaning to order): The court official empowered by the emperor to trade tea.
- "Cash" (from the Portuguese "caixa" meaning case or money box): The currency of tea transactions.
- "Caddy" (from the Chinese word for one pound weight): The standard tea trade container.
- "Chow" (from the Indian word for food cargo): Slang for food.

The Opium Wars

Not only was language a problem, but so was the currency. Vast sums of money were spent on tea. To take such large amounts of money physically out of England would have financially collapsed the country and been impossible to transport safely half way around the world. With plantations in newly occupied India, the John Company saw a solution. In India, they could grow the inexpensive crop of opium and use it as a means of exchange. Because of its addictive nature, the demand for the drug would be lifelong insuring an unending market.

Chinese emperors tried to maintain the forced distance between the Chinese people and the "devils". But, disorder in the Chinese culture and foreign military might prevented it. The Opium Wars broke out with the English ready to go to war for free trade (their right to sell opium). By 1842, England had gained enough military advantages to enable her to sell opium in China undisturbed until 1908.

America Enters the Tea Trade

The first three American millionaires, TH Perkins of Boston, Stephen Girard of Philadelphia, and John Jacob Astor of New York, all made their fortunes in the China trade. America began direct trade with China soon after the Revolution was over in 1789. America's newer, faster clipper ships outsailed the slower, heavier English "tea wagons" that had until then dominated the trade. This forced the English navy to update their fleet, a fact America would have to address in the War of 1812.

The new American ships established sailing records that still stand for speed and distance. John Jacob Astor began his tea trading in 1800. He required a minimum profit on each venture of 50% and often made 100%. Stephen Girard of Philadelphia was known as the "gentle tea merchant". His critical loans to the young (and still weak) American government enabled the nation to rearm for the War of 1812. The orphanage founded by him still perpetuates his good name. Thomas Perkins was from one of Boston's oldest sailing families. The Chinese trust in him as a gentleman of his word enabled him to conduct enormous transactions half way around the world without a single written contract. His word and his handshake was enough so great was his honor in the eyes of the Chinese.

It is to their everlasting credit that none of these men ever paid for tea with opium. America was able to break the English tea monopoly because its ships were faster and America paid in gold.

The Clipper Days

By the mid-1800s, the world was involved in a global clipper race as nations competed with each other to claim the fastest ships. England and America were the leading rivals. Each year the tall ships would race from China to the Tea Exchange in London to bring in the first tea for auction. Although beginning half way around the world, the mastery of the crews was such that the great ships often raced up the Thames separated by only by minutes. But by 1871, the newer steamships began to replace these great ships.

Global Tea Plantations Develop

The Scottish botanist/adventurer Robert Fortune, who spoke fluent Chinese, was able to sneak into mainland China the first year after the Opium War. He obtained some of the closely guarded tea seeds and made notes on tea cultivation. With support from the Crown, various experiments in growing tea in India were attempted. Many of these failed due to bad soil selection and incorrect planting techniques, ruining many a younger son of a noble family. Through each failure, however, the technology was perfected. Finally, after years of trial and error, fortunes made and lost; the English tea plantations in India and other parts of Asia flourished. The great English tea marketing companies were founded and production mechanized as the world industrialized in the late 1880s.

Tea Rooms, Tea Courts and Tea Dances

Beginning in the late 1880s in both America and England, fine hotels began to offer tea service in tea rooms and tea courts. Served in the late afternoon, Victorian ladies (and their gentlemen friends) could meet for tea and conversation. Many of these tea services became the hallmark of the elegance of the hotel, such as the tea services at the Ritz (Boston) and the Plaza (New York).

By 1910, hotels began to host afternoon tea dances as dance craze after dance craze swept the United States and England. Often considered wasteful by older people they provided a place for the new "working girl" to meet men in a city, far from home and family. (Indeed, the editor of Vogue once fired a large number of female secretarial workers for "wasting their time at tea dances").

Afternoon Tea Today in the USA

Tea is more popular than ever in America today. Currently, there is a reawakening of interest in tea as many Americans seek a more positive, healthy lifestyle. Fine hotels throughout the United States are reestablishing or planning for the first time afternoon tea services.

Tea Inventions in America: Iced Tea and Teabags

America stabilized her government, strengthened her economy, and expanded her borders and interests. By 1904, the United States was ready for the world to see her development at the St Louis World's Fair. Trade exhibitors from around the world brought their products to America's first World's Fair. One such merchant was Richard Blechynden, a tea plantation owner. Originally, he had pld to give away free samples of hot tea to fair visitors. But when a heat wave hit, no one was interested. To save his investment of time and travel, he dumped a load of ice into the brewed tea and served the first "iced tea". It was (along with the Egyptian fan dancer) the hit of the fair.

Four years later, Thomas Sullivan of New York developed the concept of "bagged tea". As a tea merchant, he carefully wrapped each sample delivered to restaurants for their consideration. He recognized a natural marketing opportunity when he realized the restaurants were brewing the samples "in the bags" to avoid the mess of tea leaves in the kitchens.

Types of Tea

Commonly believed even today is that green tea and black tea originate from different plants. But the fact is that black, oolong, and green tea comes from the same plant. The real difference, however, is that black tea is fermented and green tea is not. Although there are different varieties of tea (as discussed below), basically it is classified into five main types: (1) green tea, (2) black tea, (3) white tea, (4) oolong tea and (5) pu-erh tea. For instance, gunpowder tea made in China and Taiwan is a variety of the Green tea. Curiously, it takes its name from the appearance of the leaves that are rolled into tight pellets and unfold like tiny flowers when infused. The tea emits a yellow-green infusion with a fresh, tart taste.

Different Types of Tea

All the tea that we drink comes from the Camellia Sinensis or tea plant. Although there are different varieties of tea grown across the world, the three main varieties are: (1) Assam tea, (2) China tea and (3) the hybrid tea. It is from these that the different types like green tea, black tea, white tea, herbal tea and oolong tea are prepared.

Green Tea

When green tea is manufactured, it is not allowed to oxidize. The leaves are dried very quickly, either in a pan or an oven, to dehydrate them and then stored. This process retains the polyphenols, catechins and flavanoids, which makes drinking green tea a healthy option. Some of the benefits of green tea are its antioxidant, inflammatory, anticarcinogenic, antiarteriosclerotic properties which aid in preventing cancer, raising the metabolic rate to cut fat and even reducing the probability of heart diseases. Due to its short brewing time, green tea is stimulating.

Black Tea

This is stronger than any other type of tea. The caffeine content is higher in black tea than in the less oxidized varieties. It retains its flavor for many years. Black tea enjoys the maximum sales in the world. Plain black tea without sugar contains antioxidants and helps in preventing cardiovascular (CV) diseases.

White Tea

This is the rarest variety of tea. The leaves are picked and harvested before they are fully open and the buds still have a covering of white "hair" on them. White tea undergoes the least processing and is also not fermented. It has a light, sweet flavor and contains less caffeine and more antioxidants than any other type of tea. The ideal temperature to brew white tea is 76–85°C. The leaves should be steeped in water for at least 7–8 minutes.

Herbal Tea

Tisane is a herbal infusion. It is made with any part of a herb—either the dried or fresh flowers, roots, seeds and leaves—over which boiling water is poured. Flavored teas are prepared by adding this to regular tea like the jasmine tea of China. Herbal teas contain no caffeine but often have substances with soothing, stimulating or euphoric effects. Long-term use of ginseng may produce hypertension, nervousness, sleeplessness and edema. There are different types of herbal tea that can be consumed for medicinal purposes.

Oolong Tea

The uniqueness of this tea is attributed to the different mr in which its leaves are treated and, owing to this reason, its taste is distinct from other types of tea. The traditional oolong tea is brewed in a special type of pot known as a *gaiwan*.

Even though it all comes from the same plant, there are more types of tea out there than one can think you can shake a stick at.

- *Bubble tea shopping for tea herbal tea*
  - *Sweet leaf iced tea*: A review of bottled iced tea from sweet leaf
  - *Yerba mate*: Yerba Mate is a popular herbal tea drink found in many South American countries.
  - *Pu-erh tea*: Pu-erh tea is a very old and unusual form of Chinese tea
  - *Mighty leaf tea*: Review of several varieties of mighty leaf tea
  - *Types of tea*: An illustrated look at the different varieties of tea
  - *Tetley chai tea*: Review of tetley chai tea, a spiced chai tea in a teabag.

- o *Lipton's tea to go*: A review of lipton's tea to go, instant iced tea you can take with you
- o *Top varieties of earl gray tea*: Top brands of earl gray tea that add a little something extra to the taste.
- o *Anteadote bottled iced tea*: A review of anteadote, a bottled iced tea from adagio teas.
- *Salute to Chai*: More on spiced chai tea, including several great recipes.
- *Top green teas*: There are many kinds of green tea, and these are the best choices.
- *Top black teas*: Some of the most well-known black teas.
- *Introduction to green tea*: Don't be afraid to try green tea. Here are some basics you need to know, like how to brew it, where it comes from and what it tastes like.
- *Black teas*: Black teas from various regions are described in this online catalog. For centuries it was thought that black and green teas came from different plants. In fact, they come from the same species, but black tea is fermented.
- *Grades of tea*: Orange pekoe is a grade of tea, not a flavor. There are several other grade levels that are even better.
- *Kombucha tea*: A fermented tea drink that just might cure all your ills. You'll need a starter culture to make your own.
- *Olive leaf tea*: Olive leaf tea from olivus makes an interesting and healthy herbal tea.
- *Reali tea teabags*: Review of adagio tea's reali tea teabags. Whole-leaf tea in a bag.
- *Rooibos tea*: Rooibos is a red herbal tea from South Africa, with a sweet and nutty taste. Best of all, there is no caffeine.
- *White tea*: White tea is a unique and rare form of tea that is high in antioxidants and low in caffeine.
- *Top bottled tea are you?* If you enjoy bottled teas, you don't have to settle for over sweetened drinks with no tea taste.
  - o *What kind of tea are you?* Another personality quiz, to match you up with the kind of tea that suits you the best.
  - o *Yerba mate*: An herbal tea that is popular in South America and that you drink with a straw.

Health Benefits of Tea

In the year 1823, a Singpho (a region falling across parts of present day Arunachal Pradesh and Assam) king is said to have offered an English army officer tea as a medicinal drink.

1. Tea can boost endurance. Scientists have found that the catechins (antioxidants) in green tea increase the body's ability to burn fat as fuel, which accounts for improved muscle endurance.
2. Tea is believed to protect against cancers of the breast, colon, colorectal region, skin, lung, esophagus, stomach, small intestine, pancreas, liver, ovaries, prostate gland and mouth. But, it does not rely solely on tea to stay healthy and it is not a miracle cure, after all. While several studies suggest that tea has cancer fighting benefits, overall, the current research does not present a very clear verdict on the matter.

3. Tea helps fight free radicals. It has a high oxygen radical absorbance capacity (ORAC)—a fancy way of saying that it helps destroy free radicals (which can damage DNA) in the body. While our bodies are designed to fight free radicals on their own, they are not 100% effective—and since damage from free radicals has been linked to cancer, heart disease and neurological degeneration, let's take all the help we can get.
4. Tea is hydrating to the body (despite the caffeine!).
5. When considered with other factors like smoking, physical activity, age and body mass index, regular tea drinking was associated with a lowered risk of Parkinson's disease in both men and women.
6. Green tea is believed to offer protection from ultraviolet rays.
7. Tea could keep out waist circumference in check. In one study, participants who regularly consumed hot tea had a lower waist circumference and lower body mass index (BMI) than non-consuming participants. Scientists speculate that regular tea drinking lowers the risk of metabolic syndrome (which increases the risk of diabetes, artery disease and strokes).

Herbal Infusions

Chado tea, which introduced the joys of drinking tea to the people of Los Angeles, has now come to India with an immense assortment of flavored, organic and decaf teas along with chai blends, rooibos blends, herb infusions and fruit tisanes. It also has an impressive list of tea accessories like infusers, cups, saucers, mugs, sugar and creamer pots and teabag holders.

> From Darjeeling silver needle white tea that costs Rs 10,000 for 1 kg to the Ceylon silver tips tea at an eye-popping price of Rs 60,000 for 1 kg, costly teas are the new status symbol.

Newby tea, a subsidiary of Newby Teas (UK) has setup a preservation and packing facility in Kolkata and claims to offer discerning Indian consumer the "finest teas money can buy". Its traditional black tea has a fuller body and goes particularly well with milk. However, its green, white and oolong teas and more fragrant, delicate black teas and herbal infusions are not suited to being taken with milk.

There's a word of caution though. These new-age teas come with fancy price tags. For example, Darjeeling silver needle white tea costs Rs 10,000 for 1 kg at the Chado Tea outlet in Delhi's Ambience Mall. The Gopaldhara Estate-II flush wonder tea costs Rs 14,000 for 1 kg and the Ceylon silver tips tea is an eye-popping Rs 60,000 for 1 kg.

But despite the steep prices, it is tea time for discerning aficionados, who keep thronging the bars, lounges and tea rooms for their hot (or cold) cuppa makaibari chais, earl grays, sencha kyotos, chamomiles, fruit tisanes and even the teapuccinos!

Benefits of Green Tea

Green tea is less processed, thereby retaining a lot of its nutrients. The polyphenols and catechins retained in this tea are good antioxidants. They help in eradicating free radical sin the body and are thus good detoxifiers—an aspect that aids in weight loss. Studies have shown that green tea helps to prevent and fight cancer, among other things. These studies are meant to encourage tea drinking, but not promote it as a cure for cancer. Similarly, green tea helps to reduce the bad cholesterol in the body while increasing good cholesterol—thus indirectly reducing the risk of a heart attack and stroke. Green tea nutrients help in arthritis and other joint-related problems. Green tea should be part of a lifestyle that includes regular healthy food and exercise to get the best out of it.

A Brewing Scandal

Herbal brews and some tea brands contain ingredients unlisted on the packet. The unlisted contents include weeds that could result in allergic reactions. Teas are made from leaves of the plant Camellia sinensis, native to India and South Western China. Herbal infusions, commonly referred to as teas, use roots, leaves, stems, seeds or flowers of several plants. Molecular biologists at the Rockefeller University and botanists from Tufts University in New York used a technique known as DNA barcoding to analyze 146 herbal teas and 70 regular tea samples from 14 countries. DNA barcoding quickly and accurately identifies and distinguishes plant, animal and fungal species based on a snippet of genetic code.

The researchers developed DNA barcodes (short genetic sequence) of the plants present in the samples and compared them to the reference database. They found unlisted ingredients in 21 out of 60 herbal teas and three out of 70 regular teas. The unlisted ingredients included 16 plants. For instance, an herbal tea which mentioned St John's wart as one of its ingredients also contained fern, *Terpsichore sp.*, which was not listed. Another herbal product which showed ginger root and lemongrass as its ingredients was found to additionally contain annual bluegrass, a common weed. Other unlisted ingredients included parsley, white goosefoot (a relative of spinach), traces of ornamental tree Taiwanese cheesewood, alfalfa and papaya. The most common non-labeled ingredient was chamomile, says the study published in the July issue of Scientific Reports.

The extra ingredients could have been accidentally added during harvesting. "Or perhaps, inclusion of chamomile and parsley could have been intentional to enhance flavor or color. They could also be used as fillers to make tea bags look fuller". "After tea ingredients are dried and processed it is difficult to determine which species the ingredients came from". DNA barcoding solves this problem. The study could help regulators tighten labeling rules for teabags and make manufacturers improve what they put in the brews, says Stoeckle.

HISTORY OF TEA IN INDIA

The cultivation and brewing of tea in India has a long history of applications in traditional systems of medicine and for consumption. The consumption of tea in India was first clearly documented in the (750–500 BC). Research shows that tea is indigenous to Eastern and Northern India, and was cultivated and consumed there for thousands of years. However, commercial production of tea in India did not begin until the arrival of the British East India Company.

The Indian tea industry has a long history. It has undergone a sea change from manufacturing orthodox teas to moving on to cut, turned and curled (CTC) teas, and now green teas. Darjeeling tea, Assam tea and Nilgiri tea are very popular in India. The tea available in South India is mainly dust, whereas the North Indians prefer leaf tea. India, Sri Lanka and Kenya account for 70% of the global black tea output. In the past, most of the tea produced in the southern part of India was exported to the erstwhile Soviet Union.

Today, India is one of the largest tea producers in the world, and over 70% of the tea is consumed within India itself. A number of renown teas, such as Darjeeling, also grow exclusively in India. The Indian tea industry has grown to own many global tea brands, and has evolved to one of the most technologically equipped tea industries in the world. Tea production, certification, exportation, and all other facets of the tea trade in India are controlled by the Tea Board of India.

Ancient India and the Ramayana

Tea cultivation in India has somewhat ambiguous origins. Although the extent of the popularity of tea in Ancient India is unknown, it is known that the tea plant was a wild plant in India that was indeed brewed by local inhabitants of different regions. The first recorded reference to tea in India was in the ancient epic of the Ramayana, when Hanuman was sent to the Himalayas to bring the Sanjeevani tea plant for medicinal use. The Singpho tribe and the Khamti tribe also validate that they have been consuming tea since the 12th century.

In India, the tale on tea revolves around a missionary named Dharma. He had vowed to meditate rather than sleep at night during his 7-year *yatra* to China in order to achieve heavenly support for his missionary work. When after 5 years exhaustion overcame him, he got up and went for a walk among the tea bushes. While chewing the leaves, he realized that fatigue departed from his body and he was able to pass the final 2 years of his pilgrimage without sleeping. Whether one believes these legends or not, the fact remains China is tea's place of birth.

The East Asian Legends of Bodhidharma and Gan Lu

Japanese legends ascribe the origin of tea in China to the Indian monk Bodhidharma (460–534 CA), a monk born near Madras, India, and the founder of the Ch'an (or Zen) sect of Buddhism.

Chinese legends credit a monk called Gan Lu, whose family name was Wu-Li-chien, with traveling to India during the Later Han dynasty, 25–221 AD, to pursue Buddhist studies. Gan Lee is said to have taken seven tea plants home to China from India, which he planted on Meng Mountain in Szechwan.

East India Company

Until then all the tea for Europe came from China. The commercial production of tea was slow in developing because the use of Chinese plants, which were good for a colder climate, did not do as well in the low lands. The British were slow to recognize the indigenous plants and their commercial importance. However, when it looked like the Chinese might not renew their treaty with Britain in 1833, the British really became committed to growing tea in India. They then recognized the indigenous plants and commercial tea production took off in the Assam area. Private investors from Britain came to India to start tea plantations. Many forests were cut down and tea was planted. Tea cultivation came at great expense to the entrepreneurs, the environment and the labor they brought in from nearby Nepal. The weather and diseases like Malaria took their toll. A large number of Chinese laborers were brought in and later deported because they were "turbulent", "obstinate" and "rapacious". People from nearby districts in India were brought in and paid very low wages. Working conditions were harsh and inhumane. They worked long hours and their ranks were disseminated by disease. Any laborer that left the garden could be sent to prison. Absenteeism was punished by flogging. The laborers were underfed and lived in swampy, mosquito infested grounds and worked in the monsoon rains. About one-third of the employees died on site. Women and children were subject to the same treatment. In 1869 when the Suez Canal opened and the advancement of railways came about, tea export increased tremendously. This encouraged tea production in many areas of India. Darjeeling in the foothills of the Himalayas produced one of the best and prized teas from Chinese varieties. Other places in the Northeast of India as well as the hills of Nilgiri in South India produced tea, again at great expense to the environment and the people. India in a short time became the largest exporter of tea. The consumption of tea by local people also increased tremendously. The best teas are grown at elevations of 5,000–6,000 feet in Darjeeling in the North and in the Nilgiri Hills in Southern India.

The Origins of Indian Tea

Long before the commercial production of tea started in India in the late 1830s, the tea plant was growing wild in the jungles of Northeast (Assam). In 1598, a Dutch traveler, Jan Huyghen van Linschoten, noted in a book about his adventures that the Indians ate the leaves as a vegetable with garlic and oil and boiled the leaves to make a brew.

In 1788, the British botanist, Joseph Banks, reported to the British East India Company that the climate in certain British-controlled parts of Northeast India was ideal for tea growing. However, he seems to have missed the fact that the plant was a native to Bengal and suggested transplanting tea bushes from China. But, his idea was ignored.

In the early 1820s, the British East India Company began large-scale production of tea in Assam, India, of a tea variety traditionally brewed by the Singpho tribe. In 1826, the British East India Company took over the region from the Ahom kings through the Yandaboo Treaty. In 1837, the first English tea garden was established at Chabua in Upper Assam; in 1840.

In 1823 and 1831, Robert Bruce and his brother Charles, an employee of the East India Company, confirmed that the tea plant was indeed a native of the Assam area and sent seeds and specimen plants to officials at the newly established Botanical Gardens in Kolkata. But again, nothing was done—perhaps because the East India Company had a monopoly on the trading of tea from China and, as they were doing very nicely, probably saw no reason to spend time and money elsewhere.

But in 1833, everything changed. The company lost its monopoly and suddenly woke up to the fact that India might prove a profitable alternative. A committee was set up, Charles Bruce was given the task of establishing the first nurseries, and the secretary of the committee was sent off to China to collect 80,000 tea seeds. Because they were still not sure that the tea plant really was indigenous to India, committee members insisted on importing the Chinese variety.

The seeds were planted in the Botanical Gardens in Kolkata and nurtured until they were sturdy enough to travel 1000 miles to the newly prepared tea gardens. Meanwhile, up in Assam, Charles Bruce and the other pioneers were clearing suitable areas of land on which to develop plantations, pruning existing tea trees to encourage new growth, and experimenting with the freshly plucked leaves from the native bushes to manufacture black tea. Bruce had recruited two tea makers from China and with their help, he steadily learnt the secrets of successful tea production.

The conditions were incredibly harsh. The area was remote and hostile, cold in winter and steamy hot in summer. Tigers, leopards and wolves constantly threatened the lives of the workers, and the primitive settlements of the tea workers were subject to regular raids by local hill tribes. But they persevered and gradually the jungle was opened up, the best tea tracts cultivated under the light shade of surrounding trees, and new seedlings planted to fill gaps and create true tea gardens.

Ironically, the native plants flourished, while the Chinese seedlings struggled to survive in the intense Assam heat and it was eventually decided to make subsequent plantings with seedlings from the native tea bush. The first twelve chests of manufactured tea to be made from indigenous Assam leaf were shipped to London in 1838 and were sold at the London auctions. The East India Company wrote to Assam to say that the teas had been well received by some "houses of character", and there was a similar response to the next shipment, some buyers declaring it "excellent".

Having established a successful industry in Assam's Brahmaputra valley, with factories and housing settlements, the Assam Tea Company began to expand into other districts of north east India. Cultivation started around the town of Darjeeling in the foothills of the Himalayas in the mid-1850s. By 1857, between 60 acres and 70 acres were under tea and, whereas the China variety of the tea plant had not liked the conditions in Assam, here at elevations of 2,500–6,000 feet, it grew well. The company pushed on into Terai and Dooars and even into the remote Kangra valley, 800 miles West of Darjeeling.

In the south western tip of the country, experimental plantings had been made in 1835, while the first nurseries were being established in Assam, and by the mid 1850s tea was growing successfully alongside coffee. The climate of the Nilgiri Hills, or Blue Mountains, seemed to suit the plant, and the area under tea steadily expanded.

In 1853, India exported 183.4 tons of tea. By 1870, that figure had increased to 6,700 tons; and by 1885, 35,274 tons exported. Today, India is one of the world's largest producers of tea with 13,000 gardens and a workforce of more than 2 million people.

There is another story goes like this in 1849 British horticulturist, Dr A Campbell, brought tea seeds from China and planted them in the backyard of his Darjeeling house. The results were astounding. The tea leaves that sprouted had an exquisite aroma which Dr Campbell thought was far superior to that of the Chinese varieties. Soon enough, cultivation of tea spread rapidly to Assam, Darjeeling, Cachar, Sylhet and the Dooars. By 1874, there were 113 gardens in Darjeeling district alone. For the next century and a half, the tea industry was set to boom like none other. By 1951, the total area under tea cultivation was 317 hectares. Today, more than six decades later, it stands at a mindboggling 6,00,000 hectares spread mainly across Assam, West Bengal, Sikkim, Uttarakhand, Himachal Pradesh, Karnataka, Tamil Nadu and Kerala. With the annual production breaching the 1 billion kg mark and the total output expected to touch Rs 33,000 crore, India is the world's largest consumer and the second largest producer of tea (after China). Even as the industry grows at a breakneck pace, high-end tea gardens across the country are busy promoting tea as a health drink.

The story of "discoveries" is the story of chance. And so it was with tea in India. In 1833, the East India Company sour at the end of monopoly over Chinese trade was looking for alternate sources. The plant was found growing in the wild in Assam.

"Chubwa" in Dibrugarh was India's first tea garden. Our leaf was found to be longer than the Chinese variety. The first lot of Indian tea was auctioned in London in 1838. Goradia joined the Kolkata office of J Thomas and Company, the single largest tea auctioneer in the world in his twenties.

Goradia's book is both a photographic account—there is plenty of text as well—of his time in tea and of a certain professional class of 19th century Englishmen who as planters, botanists, managers and agents were making a living in the east and south of pre-independence India. Despite the climate change, for their memsahibs, it was a plush life. Picnics, elephant rides, birdshoots and all this while trussed up in crinoline, bonnet and lace.

Writing in *The Cambridge World History of Food, Weisburger and Comer write:* "The tea cultivation begun there (India) in the 19th century by the British, however, has accelerated to the point that today India is listed as the world's leading producer, its 715,000 tons well ahead of China's 540,000 tons, and of course, the teas of Assam, Ceylon (from the island nation known as Sri Lanka), and Darjeeling are world famous. However, because Indians average half a cup daily on per capita basis, fully 70% of India's immense crop is consumed locally".

MODERN TEA PRODUCTION IN INDIA

Tea, one of the widely consumed beverages in the world, shares an inextricable history with India. The country is one of the largest producers as well as the largest consumer of tea. Indian tea stands as the epitome of flavor, quality and uniqueness. Whether it is the world famous muscatel flavored Darjeeling, the action-packed Assam, or the mellow blue mountain Nilgiri, each tea-producing region lends a special and distinctive taste to the tea that emerges from its soil. Indian tea companies have acquired a number of iconic foreign tea enterprises including British brands Tetley and Typhoo. India is also the world's largest tea-drinking nation. However, the per capita consumption of tea in India remains a modest 750 g per person every year due to the large population base and high poverty levels.

The present Tea Board, setup under Section 4 of the Tea Act 1953, was constituted on April 1, 1954 functioning as a Statutory Body of the Central Government under the Union Ministry of Commerce and Industry. While the Tea Act mainly focuses on controls, the scope of the Tea Board's activities over the years has considerably changed. Currently the Tea Board is functioning as an apex body concerned with overall development of the tea industry in India by providing necessary assistance for R and D activities.

These activities are aimed at increasing production, productivity and quality; facilitation of trade and promotion of exports so as to ensure maximum returns to the producers, including small growers, as also safeguarding the interests of the workers and the consumers. They are also aimed at gathering statistical and other relevant data and disseminating information to various segments of the industry and acting as the recognized spokesperson on behalf of the industry to government, media, trade and general public.

Growth of Tea

Orange carrots, delicate brown baby potatoes, snow-white cabbages, once they accounted for a sizable patch of the Nilgiris' rolling blue mountain. But, the tea gardens are cutting a swathe through the vegetables. Farmers increasingly prefer to farm tea because it is the cup that cheers and brings good returns. From just 20,000 hectares in the 1980s, the tea gardens are three times larger today. And the 65,000 small tea growers, who were pushed to the brink by falling prices over the last few years, now say they will expand cultivation. Tea has everything going for it in the Nilgiris: incentives are flowing in from the Tamil Nadu government and unpredictable rain has been washing away the vegetable crops. Small wonder the local Badaga community is shifting to tea. "Kenya and Sri Lanka, the major tea producers are facing severe drought conditions. As tea is a rain-fed crop, production has come down globally. So, Nilgiri tea is in great demand now. Today, tea-growers can expect to earn Rs 14/kg of leaves—up by Rs 10 since last year. Much of the produce [92 million kg (mkg)] heads for Russia, Europe and the US. But, agricultural scientists caution that the Nilgiris' teascape needs value addition to remain green. "Right now, Nilgiri tea is enjoying the benefits of drought in other tea-growing countries. But for long-term growth, quality is the key.

In Southern India, the pruning cycle extends over a period of 4, 5 or 6 years depending on the elevation and growth. In some cases, a "skiff" is given at a convenient height and the pruning cycle extended for 2 or 3 years. Pruning and skiffing are done periodically to keep the height of the bush at a convenient level for the pluckers to operate and to encourage vegetative growth. Annual pruning is a practice in Northeastern India (Assam), but even there the present trend is toward an extended pruning cycle. After a series of pruning cycle, the bushes are rejuvenated by hard pruning, removing all cankered and diseased portions of the stem.

In Northern India, the economic life of the tea bush is generally 40–50 years and therefore 2–2 and a ½% of the area is uprooted and replanted every year. In Southern, such regular uprooting and replanting is not practiced, because economic yields are obtained from sections which are 80 years or more old. Usually, plucking is restricted to the terminal bud and two expanded leaves, or to the bud and three succulent leaves, known as fine or medium plucking. Coarse plucking includes extra leaves. In Northern India, the tea bush is plucked at weekly intervals from April to December and there is a dormant season during winter. In Southern India the crop is harvested during the cold and dry months (December to March).

Value Addition

In India, about 5.21 lakh hectares of land is under cultivation of tea. The industry provides direct employment to more than million workers. Backed by a strong domestic consumption, it has been growing at 3–3.3% per year. In 2007, the industry saw lower production and lower exports than 2006—a year which had witnessed a record and exports.

India produces around 980 mkg of tea, of which around 180 mkg is exported. Of the remaining, around 350 mkg is sold as packaged tea, while the rest is sold in loose form. Currently, India also imports 15 mkg of tea from South Asian Association for Regional Cooperation (SAARC) countries. Indian consumption rose to 797 mkg in 2008 (85% of the total production) from 780 mkg in 2007. Indian tea is becoming more and more popular in the international market. For instance, Egypt finds Indian tea tasty. Tea exports to Egypt grew more than threefold from 4.5 mkg in 2007–2008 to nearly 16 mkg in 2008–2009.

Tea firms are progressively leaning toward tea bags as a means of value addition. This sector is witnessing a growth of 15% and the potential market for the tea bags industry is estimated to touch Rs 4,410 million by 2012–2013. According to some estimates, about 6,900 tons were sold in tea bags in 2007–2008. This, however, is a very small quantity as total consumption was of the order of 800 mkg.

There are attempts to boost organic tea. At present, about 37% of the total crop grown on the slopes of the Eastern Himalayas is organic. India would be offering around 5 mkg of the brew as an organically grown product. It takes about 3 years to convert a garden from conventional plantation into an organic one. This involves not only a total ban on chemical fertilizers and pesticides but also restrictions on the use of some natural items. For instance the use of tobacco extract for pest control is being used. Drinking organic tea was initially fashionable in the US and Europe, but now it has emerged as a necessity in many other global markets. Germany is expected to become a major market for Darjeeling organic tea. Project werkstatt GmbH, Berlin, a leading Darjeeling tea buyer, has decided to go for 100% organic Darjeeling tea from 2010. Organic is a state of mind. The demand for organic is high and supply is rather limited as of now, because truly certified organic teas are rare. With big growth in demand, natural calamities remain the biggest worry for growers in these Himalayan hills. Despite a recession, there's huge demand for organic tea and Indian tea producers are not being able to meet the growing demand.*

The tea industry is looking at alternative cropping as a means to derricking its business. This would also ensure tea garden workers a sustainable livelihood. The Indian Tea Association (ITA) feels that efforts should be made to identify surplus/ marginal yields are not economical on these patches. The advantages of utilizing surplus tea land for multicropping are many. Jatropha cultivation is one of the top choices.

There is a proposal to accord agri-export zone (AEZ) status to Darjeeling tea industry. There are about 87 tea estates in Darjeeling. With AEZ status they will have access to a number of central and state government schemes to improve productivity and earn better revenue through value addition. It may be noted that unlike special. It may be noted that unlike special economic zones, an AEZ does not comprise a physically defined area, but is an amalgamation of various schemes for a particular commodity.

Global tea shortage has risen to unprecedented levels. The deficit would be in the range of 80–100 mkg for the three major producing countries: (1) India, (2) Sri Lanka and (2) Kenya. These three countries account for 80% of the total black tea production. By the end of September 2008, the world production was marginally down by 6.3 mkg. Kenya suffered a fall of 35 mkg, while India and Sri Lanka together were up by 46 mkg. However, all African countries showed downward trend in output. Countries such as Germany which imports about 50% of the total Darjeeling tea output (both organic and inorganic) often re-export this to European countries like the Netherlands and Switzerland. The **Food and** *Agriculture* **Organization** (FAO) is planning to setup a body of tea producing nations. India, Sri Lanka, Kenya, China and Vietnam have

---

* The Economic Times December 10, 2009.

decided to setup body to coordinate their activities relating to tea production and trade. India feels that the competitiveness of its tea needs to be enhanced.

The year 2009 has been a significant period for the tea industry. After almost a gap of 10 years. Three things have largely contributed to this turnaround. Firstly, a crop shortage in India as well as in other tea producing nations pushed up the prices at the auctions by Rs 20–25 per kg. Secondly, the quality of Indian tea has improved over the years, which has enabled the Indian tea to fetch better prices in both domestic and global markets. "The rising domestic consumption has also increased the demand of tea within the country. The domestic consumption is increasing at the rate of 3–3.5%, which the tea industry has to meet". The industry is now all set to catch up with China's annual tea production of 1,160 mkg. So much so in 2010, the tea industry hopes to race past the 1,000 kg production mark if weather remains favorable throughout the year.

Tea for Health

Tea for health is dedicated to bringing you the facts about how tea, the world's favorite drink, can help you maintain your health as part of a balanced diet and healthy, active lifestyle. If you need questions answering about tea and looking after your health or if you want to know why drinking at least four cups of tea a day is a good way for you to help to maintain your health, then look no further—this site provides a wealth of information that can help you.

For the science behind the facts, health professionals can access peer-reviewed evidence in a bespoke section of the site. The latest research from around the world is presented and you can also register for the "updates" service so you will see the most recent research first. The site provides a number of Monographs to help you with the background that can be downloaded in PDF format, including an information leaflet that also gives an overview on why tea can be an important part of a healthy lifestyle.

The cuppa has long been the nation's number one pick-me-up of choice—you just have to think how many cups you or your friends and colleagues drink each day. We often reach for a cuppa when our spirits need reviving; but is there any truth in the fact that people say tea is good for you?

Long stressful days at work, lack of exercise, too much convenience food that is high in fat and sugar but low in fiber, can all take its toll. A well-earned tea break is often the way to catch your breath, but it can also help to maintain heart health as part of your healthy diet and lifestyle that includes plenty of exercise. Studies from around the world are finding that the some of the ingredients in tea may help toward maintaining a healthy heart. A national study of 1,764 women in Saudi Arabia showed that tea drinkers were 19% less likely to suffer from CV disease than non-tea drinkers. In Holland, 806 men who consumed the greatest amount of catechins (a type of flavonoid) were 51% less likely to die of heart disease during the 10-year study period, compared with men who consumed the lowest amount.

Further studies are looking into how tea could help your heart. The results from trials so far show that flavonoids may prevent the oxidation of the so-called bad cholesterol in the blood that leads to the buildup of plaque in artery walls, as well as helping to maintain a healthy CV system. Still more research is becoming available every day which continues to point to tea being a good option for consumers who want tea as part of their healthy lifestyle. When you are puckering up for that kiss it is nice to know you have got a perfect set of pearlies and drinking tea can help to contribute toward your teeth and a clean bill of health.

Tea is a great natural source of fluoride, which is added to water and toothpaste because it can actually strengthen tooth enamel. Tea can also help to cut down the buildup of plaque on your pearly whites and apart from the fluoride in water, the tea plant is in itself a rich source of fluoride since it actually absorbs the compound from the soil via its roots. Both black and green teas contain fluoride and they appear to help control bacterial growth that can result in dental plaque.

The Cup that Cheers

Although many may call the new-found love for tea a fad or a passing fancy, there's some cheering news from the medical fraternity. Research is finding increasing evidence which

> Tea drinkers have a lower risk of heart attack and stroke.

suggests that green, black, white and oolong teas contain an overabundance of disease-fighting qualities.

Doctors point out that the antioxidant compounds called flavonoids in these four basic types of teas may help to keep at bay a host of physical problems ranging from obesity to heart attacks and from seizures to diabetes and even cancer.

Flavonoids are said to kill cell-damaging free radicals, which are linked to cancer, atherosclerosis and heart attack. These can decrease risk of cataract and slow the progression of Parkinson's disease.

A research by the American Heart Association says that drinking green, white, black or oolong tea promotes healthy arteries and tea drinkers have a lower risk of heart attack and stroke. It adds that that drinking tea relaxes and dilates arteries, increasing blood flow to the heart.

Although most scientists point to the need for further studies to establish a definitive link between tea drinking and health, the current research is unearthing a treasure of the many benefits about this age-old beverage that was discovered more than 5,000 years ago when a few leaves fell into the water cup of Chinese Emperor Shennong, who is also considered the father of the traditional Chinese medicine. Several studies have suggested drinking either green or black tea may lower blood cholesterol concentration, blood pressure and inhibit clothing of blood.

Tea can Help Fight Terror Attack

A cup of tea could be a secret weapon to fight poison used in terror attacks according UK scientists. Academics at Cardiff University's School of Pharmacy and Pharmaceutical Sciences discovered a chemical, polyphenol found in tea can deactivate ricin—a highly toxic ingredient used in fatal terrorist attacks, the "Daily Mail" reported.

Professor Les Baillie was quoted by the paper as saying: "We already knew that tea had the ability to inhibit anthrax as long as it is black tea with no milk. Our new findings suggest that if the security services want to counter the threat of ricin, they may find the answer in their morning cup of tea".

Since the First World War ricin has had a gruesome reputation as a bioweapon. A tiny amount of ricin after getting into the bloodstream can kill a person within 2–3 days. And it comes from the humble castor oil bean, a powerful laxative, used medicinally for centuries that are available in many health food shops and online.

Ricin is used in an arsenal of terrorist weapons, and has already been at the center of a number of attempted terrorist attacks in the US, the report said.

The new discovery follows on from research done by Cardiff scientists which showed chemicals in English breakfast tea known as polyphenols were able to kill bacillus anthracis, the organism which causes anthrax and was used in the 2001 US anthrax mail attacks. The new discovery follows on from research done by Cardiff scientists which showed tea has an unexpected array of talents outside the morning cuppa. "These toxins, such as ricin have been shown to have been used by nasty people, and nasty countries, to do nasty things".

Tea Board Summons Help to Strain Polluted Yield

With tea containing nicotine and heavy metals like arsenic making its entry into the market, the Tea Board of India has engaged the Tea Research Association (TRA) and the United Planters' Association of Southern India (UPASI) to study the source from where these substances come. Tea planters feel that there is nothing to worry about this and only quality tea will make it to export markets.

Nicotine content was reported from one of the tea consignments from Germany. There are instances of heavy metal like arsenic being detected in tea. Even the base line survey done by the Assam government and Tea Board in 14 tea-producing districts has pointed that some growers use dangerous insecticides such as phenol and dichlorodiphenyl-trichloroethane (DDT) in the tea bushes to fight insecticides. However, this claim has not gone down well with the industry.

"Those countries which are importing teas from us follow the European Union (EU) standards of maximum residue limit or have evolved their own stringent measures of laboratory test. Any tea that is not up to the standard will not find place in exporting countries". "There might be some instance of inferior quality tea getting circulated. But, the Tea Board has made it clear that quality parameters have to be complied with and only good tea reaches the market".

"The basic problem is that till now no one knows from where these substances get in. The study, expected to be completed shortly, will tell us precisely whether these nonpermissible substances make their entry in the farm, or during the processing or in the handling". The board has even decided to go for random sampling, like the way it did in the Siliguri Tea Auction Center.

"There must be a system of multiple checks as tea changes several hands and places before it finally reaches the market. Small growers comply with *maximum residue levels* (MRL)".

Tea20 Varieties

The Tea Board of India has tossed the coin in favor of Tea20, a futures trading concept involving 20 qualities of tea considered among the best at the time of e-auctioning. The Information Technology wing of the National Stock Exchange (NSE-IT), has been asked to design the online auctioning program. The program is at a nascent stage, but we hope it will work wonders for futures trading of the best of Assam, Darjeeling and other qualities of Indian teas, According to NSE-IT. India pioneered the e-auction concept that other tea producing countries are keen on adopting. Tea20 will add a new dimension to e-auctioning that makes bidding very simple and transparent besides ensuring fair price discovery mechanism with the ever-increasing volume of trade. Tea20, although, is not expected to be click-ready before Assam CTC tea gets its exclusive logo. The logo would help ensure a stringent quality control mechanism for the export market where Assam tea is facing stiff competition from cheaper teas offered by Kenya and Sri Lanka.

Organic by Compulsion

Tea cultivation in Darjeeling began in the 1840s after a colonial official experimented with tea seeds in his garden in what was then a sparsely populated hill resort for the affluent. Commercial plantations mushroomed in the next two decades. Plantations required workers to plant, tend, pluck and finally manufacture the tea— a labor-intensive process which continues till today. The steady supply of cheap labor came from across the border in Nepal. The turning point came in 1971 when Russia became the bulk importer of Indian tea. An assured market made the planters sacrifice quality for quantity. Chemical fertilizers and pesticides were used for the first time in tea estates to boost productivity. Post-1991, with the breakup of Soviet Union—and new producers like Kenya and Sri Lanka entering the market—the demand for the tea suddenly dwindled. "It was during this time that Europe became quality conscious, with standards for chemical and pesticide residues introduced for food items. The famed Darjeeling tea could not be marketed there. The entire tea industry shared the fate".

Unable to deal with the stress some gardens discontinued use of chemical fertilizers—simply to cut cost—while others were closed and finally abandoned. Within a decade several gardens became "organic by default". The next big change came around 2000 when a handful of entrepreneurs bought a host of the "sick and abandoned gardens" and converted Darjeeling into a niche brand. Ashok Lohia of the Chamong group, for instance, bought 11 gardens between 2001 and 2004. "For the industry, the real challenge was to prevent misuse of the brand. The tea estates were certainly not benefiting", he says. While Darjeeling produced barely 10 mkg in a year, world over an estimated 40 mkg was sold in its name. A painstaking campaign later, Darjeeling got the geographical indication status in 2004. Simultaneously, to cater to the discerning international consumer, gardens started an organic transition. Today 38 gardens, accounting for more than half of the tea grown in the region are chemical-free (see "Organic Certification and Technology").

Longjing Tea

From the mountain lakes of Hangzhou in China, this is one of the most purest and popular green tea variants. These pan fired leaves yield a pale yellow liqueur and a slightly sweet cherry blossom aroma. Shah says, "It aids in a healthy detox process. If had after meals it helps in weight loss, however, only if alongside a healthy diet and lifestyle".

Darjeeling Black Tea

This is a good mid-morning tea, that comes from a late spring first flush, it is also known as India's Champagne of teas as it yields a bold orange liqueur and bouquet of straw, wood berries and honeysuckle. As for its health benefits, "It is a soothing pick me up tea that does not have any side effects of caffeine and at the same time gives one the needed stimulant to go through a hectic day".

Zoraat Flower Tea

This is a Middle Eastern flower blend that is bedecked with colorful flecks of dried flower petals of rose, chrysanthemum, marigold and jasmine. It gives out a floral aroma and is a graceful addition to a romantic and exquisite after luncheon tea. This is an excellent digestive post a heavy meal. Zoraat also has the calming properties of de-stressing and relieving from the chaos of a hectic life.

Oolong Shanghai Tea

Oolong Shanghai tea is regarded as the ultimate accompaniment to meals due to its oven-fried toasty aroma that exudes a light toasty sweetness.

Elaborating on its health benefits, "oolong has known to help heal heart related issues, cholesterol, blood pressure and diabetes. A smooth semi fermented tea gives the benefits of taste and health".

Fruity Lover's Tea

This is an exquisite blend of fresh fruits and dry fruits. Shah says, "this delectable concoction of fruits and herbs aids in a healthy sleep pattern and is great for the sleep deprived".

A Tea Pill

The tiny tea tablet developed by scientists in Tocklai Experimental Station (TES) of the TRA, in Jorhat in Upper Assam, may soon become an alternative for the age-old tea bag, a favorite with tea drinkers all over the world, if a refined version of the pill hits the market. Tea tablets can be chewed or added to a cup of hot water for a cup of tea. Chewing a tablet will freshen and cheer up a person with nearly the same effect as having a hot cup of brewed tea.

The tea pill is one of the innovations of the TES in Jorhat, the oldest and the largest research station of its kind in the world. Since its inception in 1911, TES has become synonymous with the research on tea. Its scientists have developed many technologies for boosting the tea production especially in the Northeast India.

Eight research departments in the TES: (1) botany, (2) soil, (3) agronomy, (4) plant protection, (5) biochemistry, (6) engineering and manufacturing technology, (7) statistics and agricultural economics and (8) tea tasting—have carried many research projects, besides providing services like soil analysis, testing of agrochemical, identification of pests and disease samples, supply of elite planting materials. Some of major contributions of the TES to the tea industry include technique for vegetative propagation of tea by internodal cuttings, development of 30 high-yielding and better quality clones and 14 hybrid seeds, selecting 154 region specific clones.TES also takes up collaborative projects with some leading research institutes of the country, which include making tea manufacture a continuous process by an integrated monitoring system, studies on the pharmacological, physiological and medicinal values of tea, tissue culture.

Tea from Mulberry Leaves

Scientists at Jammu and Kashmir's Sher-e-Kashmir University of Agriculture Science and Technology (SKUAST) have extracted various tea varieties from mulberry leaves and say they could be marketed in Kashmir and outside within next 2 years. They egan trials for mulberry tea in 2007 at the university; the results were very encouraging. "Mulberry is grown for silk production in Kashmir. Its surplus leaves can now be used to extract tea. This can be marketed once the department is ready with its findings. We have to conduct trials on a few more varieties over the next year".

During the trials it was found that mulberry tea could be best developed from indigenous varieties. Around 70 varieties of mulberry are grown in Kashmir. This tea was also found to have medicinal values. It tastes much like Kashmir's famous sweet tea kehwa. It also has medicinal values and could be useful for patients suffering from type II diabetes and blood pressure. Trials in this respect are also underway. Jammu and Kashmir is the country's fourth largest silk producing state and the mulberry trees are also grown in forest areas here.

Tea Exports and Imports

Indian tea exports are gaining momentum. This is attributed to decline in production in Kenya. Of course, the Russian offtake is strong. There has been an increase enquiry from Pakistan, Egypt and, of late, Iraq. The upturn in demand has been aided by reports of decline in tea production in Kenya. Egypt imported 4.88 mkg of tea in 2007, up from 2.75 mkg in 2006. Pakistan purchased 14.73 mkg of Indian tea in 2006, but the offtake slumped to 5.15 mkg in 2007. Tea exports to Pakistan may pickup soon. Global economic slowdown had affected the tea industry. Tea export volumes rose in 2008 and reached a level of 156 mkg by October. But, since then demand for tea in Western nations and Russian has declined.

Imports of tea into India increased during 2008 to a level of 20.3 mkg against 15.4 mkg in 2007. The ITA has expressed its concern over the imports substandard teas. Their average value in 2008 was Rs 79.9 for 1 kg. In recent years, the average cost, insurance and freight (CIF) value of imported teas, especially from countries like Vietnam, was significantly lower than prices prevailing in India. The industry feels that the prevailing rate of import duty which is 100% should be maintained. However, a phased rate reduction is inevitable under the India-ASEAN (Association of South East Asian Nations) Free Trade Agreement.

There are Toxic Pesticides in Your Tea

A Greenpeace India study, released on Monday, says it has identified the presence of pesticides in leading brands of tea sold in India, both national and international. These include pesticides that the World Health Organization has classified as both highly and moderately hazardous, says the report and adds that tea cultivation in India is on a "pesticide treadmill".

The non-government organization (NGO) studied a sample of 49 branded packages of tea from eight of the 11 companies that dominate the Indian market and which also export tea. The samples were taken from Mumbai, Delhi, Kolkata and Bangalore, and sent to a certified laboratory in Europe for testing.

"The pesticides result in both acute and chronic toxicity. Acute toxicity is a result of direct contact with the pesticides, and is seen in farmers and tea cultivators who experience body ache, respiratory and skin problems. Chronic impacts are seen with low doses over a long period of time. Pesticides consumed in this mr can be potentially carcinogenic, affect hormones as well as the reproductive system", says Neha Saigal, senior campaigner, Greenpeace India.

Some of the Toxins the Study Found in Tea

- *Monocrotophos*: Highly toxic orally killed 23 children in Bihar who consumed it in a meal in 2013.
- *Imidacloprid*: Potential liver, kidney, thyroid, heart and spleen toxicant.
- *Thiaclopride*: Possible liver and thyroid toxin.
- *Bifenthrin*: Skin sensitizer, may cause tremors and staggered galt.
- *Fipronil*: Thyroid, liver, kidney toxicant.

The study says, "A large number of the samples tested positive for a cocktail of toxic pesticides. DDT was present in almost 67% of the tea samples, even though it is no longer registered for use in agriculture".

Worse, the report says several samples tested positive for monocrotophos—a pesticide responsible for killing 23 students in a Bihar school; it was present in their meal. The Food and Agriculture Organization urged developing countries to phase it out after the incident.

"The study results indicate that the tea sector is caught in a pesticide treadmill", says the NGO, which has shared its results with tea companies, and asked them for a time-bound roadmap to replace pesticides with ecological agriculture methods.

To spotlight the issue, Greenpeace India has placed several billboards at the Bandra-Worli Sea Link urging tea companies to "Clean Chai Now". Volunteers have climbed up on these and won't come down till tea companies give a commitment to phase pesticides.

The Tea Board of India on Monday released a statement saying, "Indian teas are well regarded the world over and are totally safe following stringent standards". It added the industry, led by the Board, has been taking steps to make tea cultivation more sustainable and reduce reliance on synthetic plant protection products. It said the Board is open to collaborating with all stakeholders.

Statement by Tea Board of India

The Tea Board of India having reviewed the findings of the Greenpeace study can confirm that all the samples tested comply with the Indian laws and regulations, designed to protect consumers. Indian teas are well regarded the world over and are totally safe following stringent standards.

The Tea Board of India would like to dispel any misconceptions about Indian tea in the eyes of consumers at large. The Indian tea industry led by the Tea Board of India has been constantly taking steps to make tea cultivation even more sustainable and reduce reliance on synthetic plant protection products to ensure that Indian tea continues to meet the high standards consumers expect. These steps include:

- The launch of trustea, an initiative which will have certified at least 50 mkg of tea by December 2014.
- The development of the Plant Protection Code to aid best practice in tea cultivation. Identifying, and advocating for, even higher standards by partnering with the industry on a scientific pilot that will ascertain the feasibility of nonsynthetic plant protection products for tea cultivation.

Tea Board of India is open to collaborating with all stakeholders to help make tea production in India more sustainable in the long run. It was in this vein that Tea Board organized a seminar for Greenpeace to interact with the small growers in the tea sector recently.

Organic Certification and Technology

Happy Valley tea estate at an altitude of about 1,980 meters was once "sick and abandoned". It now supplies organic tea to Harrods in London. For Anjan Medhi, manager of the estate, green manuring is no less of an art compared to tasting the brew. Cow pat pit, a fermented concoction of broken egg shells and basalt salt mixed with cow dung is a biodynamic preparation that acts as a rich source of nutrients besides strengthening tea bushes against pest attacks.

Vermicompost is used while a brew produced from locally grown herbs serves as natural pesticides. During winter months, as the tea bushes enter a dormant phase and plucking stops, meticulous bush sanitation is practiced. This involves removing the field of weeds that would otherwise compete with tea bushes for precious nutrients. Organic fertilizers and pesticides are often a guarded secret for the tea estates, but many swear by Vrishkayurveda—an ancient treatize by Surapala.

Indranil Ghosh, principal officer for the Chamong Tea group explained the certification process. Once a garden decides to go organic, it will approach a certifier who undertakes a thorough check for any use of chemical ingredients during cultivation and manufacturing. After laying down the standard guidelines, the certifier keeps a tab on the garden activities for three consecutive years—checks soil and tea samples—after which the certification is granted. The gardens are inspected every year. Institut Fur Marktokologie (IMO), Switzerland is the principal certifying agency for Darjeeling tea. The agency has been accredited by the National Program for Organic Production for carrying out inspection and certification of organic agriculture in India. IMO certification is used for further certification from the US Department of Agriculture (USDA). For a medium-sized garden (200 hectares) the cost of certification is Rs 1.5 lakh per year (Down to Earth, May, 1–15).

Tea as National Drink

Government will support the industry's move to declare tea as the national drink of India.

Ahluwalia, who was in Jorhat to attend the celebration marking 75 years of Assam Tea Planters' Association (ATPA), told ET, "I am going to write to Union Commerce Minister Anand Sharma if tea can declared a national drink. This also has historical connection as the first indigenous tea planter Maniram Dewan was hanged by the Britishers in 1857. So, tea has its roots in the freedom struggle". He added the tag will definitely help in brand-building. Tea is now grown and consumed across the country and its consumption is much larger than that of coffee. "However, we need to thoroughly look into it".

Cup that Cheers

Nation	Consumption
Australia	700
Canada	720
India	730
Pakistan	840
Egypt	970
Russia	1,640
UK	2,100

(per capita consumption in grams)

Nation	National drink
Britain	Tea
China	Tea
Pakistan	Sugar
Scotland	Whisky

Tea Cuts Risk of Deaths not Related to Cardiac Woes

Drinking tea reduces the risk of dying from causes unrelated to the heart, a new study has claimed. Researchers investigated the effects of coffee and tea on CV mortality and non-CV mortality in a large French population at low risk of CV diseases. They found that drinking tea reduces non-CV mortality by 24%.

The study, presented at European Society of Cardiology (ESC) Congress in Barcelona, included 131,401 people aged 18–95 years who had a health checkup at the Paris IPC Preventive Medicine Center between January 2001 and December 2008. During a mean 3.5 years follow-up there were 95 deaths from CV and 632 deaths from non-CV causes. Coffee or tea consumption was assessed by a self-administered questionnaire as one of three classes: none, 1–4, or more than 4 cups per day.

The researchers found that coffee drinkers had a higher CV risk profile than non-drinkers, particularly for smoking. The percentage of current smokers was 17% for nondrinkers compared with 31% in those who drank 1–4 cups per day and 57% in those who drank more than 4 cups per day. Noncoffee drinkers were more physically active, with 45% having a good level of physical activity compared to 41% of the heavy coffee drinkers.

AREA AND PRODUCTION UNDER TEA

Beginning of tea in India: The discovery of indigenous tea in Assam in 1823 led to the origins of the tea industry in India. However, the Kolkata Agricultural Society differs from the above opinion. It has consistently held that in the early 1700's, the ships of the East India Company frequently brought the tea plants in the country by way of curiosity. Col. Kyd, a resident of Kolkata and a famous botanist, saw tea plants growing in his garden in 1780. This information was sent to Sir Joseph Bank and in 1782 his garden was handed over to Botanical Garden of Kolkata. In 1788, Sir Joseph Bank recorded the existence of indigenous tea growing wild in Coochbehar and Rangpur districts of Bengal and suggested the cultivation of this plant. The wild teas of Coochbehar confirmed the first discovery of indigenous tea in India.

Birth of Indian tea industry: The birth of Indian tea industry was marked by the discovery of indigenous teas plant in Assam in 1823 by Robert Bush. This received momentum when the East India Company in 1833 lost the tea trading monopoly in China. In 1835, a scientific deputation was sent to Assam to report on prospects of the tea industry and the team saw tea plants in many parts in the hills between Assam and Burma. In 1836 CA, Bruce was made the Superintendent of Tea Forests. Among others, he formed the Bengal Tea Company at Kolkata with the objective of purchasing the produce from the East India Company's tea plantations in India. A similar Company was also established in the same year in London with the same objectives.

In 1839, the first consignment of tea from India (eight chests) was shipped to London and it was auctioned at a price ranging from 6 to 34 shillings per pound. In 1840, two-thirds of experimental teas were handed over to new company. In 1852, the first tea company in India paid its final dividends. The second limited company in 1859 was formed in Assam called Jorhat Company. During 1862–1867, tea cultivation started in Chittagong and Chotta Nagpur. Ultimately, tea cultivation was commissioned in many districts in India wherever there was some hope of a success. Within a few months, India along with Sri Lanka dominated the world tea trade/market.

Tea trade: In 1874, the land located in the East of Teesta river was explored with the foreign liability of growing tea plants. By 1876, as many as 13 gardens had started cultivating tea. In 1878, the first two Indian tea gardens by name Megalkat Tea Estate and Indian Tea Company Ltd. were established although the Company actually received a grant of 741 acres on 19 March 1981. The first tea auction started on May 26, 1841 in London under the pioneering leadership of Lyal & Co., Mincing Lane, London was the center of World Tea activities prior to World War II. The first tea auction in Kolkata in December 27, 1861 and the second in Cochin in 1947 for South Indian teas were held. Subsequently, many tea auction centers were opened in Coonoor, Guwahati, Amritsar, Siliguri etc.

Formation of tea association: The Tea planters formed an association named ITA in 18 May 1881, with its headquarters at Kolkata for promoting their common interest and objectives. Subsequently many associations were formed in various tea regions of North and South India.

Tea growing regions in India are located in the monsoon belt comprising Assam, West Bengal and the foot hills of the Himalayas in the North and moist slopes and the plateaus of the Western Ghats in the South. The climate and the soil of these widely separated locations exhibit wide variations, the impact of which is naturally noticed in wide difference in productivity and cultural practices.

Zonewise classification of tea, etc: Tea units and tea growing regions are classified into revenue units and zones. At present there are two zones. Zone I includes Dibrugarh, Lakhimpur, Shibsagar, and Darrang (excluding Barsola circle in North India) while Zone II includes all other North Indian districts excluding Barsola circle of Darrang and also South Indian districts.

Areawise distribution: Tea estates are distributed according to the various size groups. Ninety six per cent of the total tea estates belong to the size group of upto 9 hectares and the remaining 4% falls in the size group of above 9 hectares. Total No. between 9–100 hectares was 469, 100–400 hectares and above 400 hectares as 390. Moreover, a little less than 400 tea estates have size holding above 400 hectares. Sizewise and statewise categorization of tea estimates show that the No. of Estates upto 8.09 hectares is maximum in Tamil Nadu followed by Kerala and Himachal Pradesh (Table 2.1).

Age-wise classification of states: Bushes are the assets of the tea estate-owners as they provide green leaves which are the basic raw material for made/green tea. The composition of assets, i.e. bushes are classified into three age groups: (1) tender (below 5 years), (2) economic (5–50 years) and (3) old (above 50 years). On an average, 30% of the total areas under tea contain bushes which have attained the economic

Table 2.1: Sizewise categorization of tea estates in India for 1997

Statewise	Up to 8.09 hectares			Above 8.09 and up to 100 hectares			Above 100 and up to 400 hectares			Above 400 hectares		
	No. of estates	Area in hectares	Pdn. in thousand kg	No. of estates	Area in hectares	Pdn. in thousand kg	No. of estates	Area in hectares	Pdn. in thousand kg	No. of estates	Area in hectares	Pdn. in thousand kg
Assam	1,697	1,936	5,714	114	10,520	16,677	322	72,385	128,426	239	145,002	274,298
West Bengal	157	1,305	3,313	31	1,669	2,877	152	35,316	46,796	113	64,718	11,772
Tripura	6	39	5	27	1,381	1,564	26	4,325	4,155	1	490	711
Bihar	16	51	20	1	25	115	–	–	–	–	–	–
Uttar Pradesh	2	13	–	5	136	45	4	919	305	–	–	–
Himachal Pradesh	3,679	3,225	1,442	–	–	–	–	–	–	–	–	–
Manipur	1	5	–	3	133	–	1	209	27	–	–	–
Sikkim	–	–	–	–	–	–	1	172	105	–	–	–
Arunachal Pradesh	4	14	3	27	790	434	6	1,014	438	–	–	–
Nagaland	2	9	–	6	194	17	2	319	14	–	–	–
Orissa	1	5	–	–	–	–	1	213	24	–	–	–
Tamil Nadu	25,526	17,067	49,667	177	4,393	5,753	77	19,639	53,082	16	8,572	20,506
Kerala	5,965	4,740	2,161	64	2,195	1,747	76	18,415	36,831	21	11,466	29,037
Karnataka	14	61	–	14	317	549	8	1,726	4,800	–	–	–
Total All India	37,070	28,470	62,325	469	21,753	29,778	676	154,652	275,003	390	230,248	336,324

age group while 65% are old age bushes and only 5% are tender bushes. As about two-thirds of the total area is covered by overage bushes, there is a need for rehabilitation programs in the form of new planting (extension/replanting), etc.

Tea growing areas in India can be divided into North East, North and South West (Table 2.1A). Statewise details of number of tea estates in North and South India (Tables 2.1B and C) show that in North India Assam shows over 71% of the number of estates in North India, West Bengal (14%) and others are small players. North India, however, account for about 47% of total India. As regards South India, Tamil Nadu is at the top followed by Kerala details about extension replacement and replanting area separately for North and South is as Table 2.1D. Production of tea in India has different methods of manufacturing (Table 2.1E). This shows that CTC accounts for nearly 90% of total production, followed by orthodox just 7–8%.

The widespread closing down of estates and the neglect of the existing plantations were the major reasons for the decline in tea production in the 1999–2001 period. No plucking was done in many of the small/medium gardens due to low profit. The unequal cost-profit ratio also leads the producers to neglect production. However, the tea industry in India overcame sluggishness in production and has been increasing production since 2002. Many tea gardens have also reopened and the move has also started to reopen more closed gardens in India. Total production of tea in India shows an increasing trend from 2002, and although the trend fluctuates from year to year, the production has moved positively upward. Tea production increased from 423 mkg in 1970–1971 to 874 mkg, whereas it sharply declined to 825.9 mkg in 1999. It has again gone up to 1095 mkg in 2011–2012 and 1,035.1 mkg in 2012–2013. Figure 2.1 shows the trend of tea production in India since 1996.

Table 2.1A: Tea growing areas in India

Region	Site	State	Distribution
N-E India	Darjeeling	West Bengal	Darjeeling District
	Dooars	West Bengal	Jalpaiguri, Coochbehar
	Surma Valley	Assam	Cachhar
	Tripura	Tripura	Agartala, Dharmapur, Badamura, Maheshpur
	Brahamaputra Valley	Assam	Lakhimpur, Kamrut Darrang, Shivsagar, Nagaon, Tejpur, Goalpara
North India	Chhoto Nagpur	Bihar	Ranchi, Hazaribag,
	Tarai	Uttar Pradesh and Himachal Pradesh	Purnea Narendra Nagar, Garwal, Almora, Dehradun, Nahar Solan, Mandi
South West India	Nilgiri, Annamalai and adjacent highland	Kerala, Karnataka, Tamil Nadu	Nilgiri, Cochin, Coimbatore, Madurai, Tirunelveli, Nagar coil, etc.

Table 2.1B: Area under tea in North India

(hectares)

District/States	1951+	1961	1971	1981	1991	1993	1998	1999	2000	2001	2001	2003
1	2	3	4	5	6	7	8	9	10	11	12	13
Darrang	25,320	26,509	30,897	35,198	40,126	39,878	40,950	40,499	41,037	41,367	41,693	41,158
Goalpara	1,467	1,603	2,098	2,576	3,188	3,300	3,338	3,295	3,460	3,471	3,523	3,635
Kamrup	1,881	2,074	2,713	3,159	3,660	3,461	3,307	3,269	3,442	3,436	3,454	3,466
Lakhimpur	46,926	50,243	57,297	3,680	4,287	4,258	4,809	4,744	4,815	4,763	4,793	4,839
Dibrugarh	—	—	—	60,273	68,385	69,049	83,380	88,442	93,076	93,484	93,698	95,118
Nowgong	5,064	5,577	6,372	6,822	7,829	7,630	7,746	7,975	7,994	8,004	8,041	8,114
Sibsagar	44,571	46,433	51,930	58,962	64,895	64,111	71,362	72,377	74,807	76,113	76,762	77,135
Cachar	30,445	29,928	31,018	32,368	35,314	34,385	30,565	31,721	32,008	32,703	32,775	32,137
North Cachar	—	—	—	—	4,233	4,326	4,516	4,532	4,004	4,065	4,071	4,064
Karbi Anglong	—	—	—	—	1,367	1,544	1,652	1,601	1,869	1,748	n03	1,923
Total Assam	155,674	162,367	182,325	203,038	233,284	231,942	251,625	258,455	266,512	269,154	270,683	271,589
Darjeeling	16,569	18,605	18,245	19,239	20,085	19,324	17,830	17,604	17,228	17,453	17,463	17,580
Dooars	54,609	54,756	59,485	63,418	13,783	67,510	70,479	69,708	69,703	72,109	72,792	72,800
Terai	8,402	9,344	10,769	11,314	68,054	13,655	17,315	20,118	20,548	21,258	22,858	22,971
Total West Bengal	79,580	82,705	88,499	93,971	101,922	100,489	105,624	107,430	107,479	110,820	113,113	113,351
Tripura	4,773	5,055	5,444	5,333	5,898	5,991	6,355	6,482	6,623	7,200	7,591	8,268
Bihar	1,644	534	460	460	22	25	762	1,348	1,350	1,445	1,877	2,000
Uttaranchal	2,605	2,084	1,818	1,804	903	848	1,068	1,068	1,068	1,068	1,068	1,471
Himachal Pradesh	4,317	4,183	4,183	4,183	2,063	2,063	2,325	2,325	2,325	2,312	2,312	2,348

(Contd.)

Table 2.1B: Area under tea in North India

(hectares)

District/States	1951+	1961	1971	1981	1991	1993	1998	1999	2000	2001	2001	2003
1	2	3	4	5	6	7	8	9	10	11	12	13
Manipur	—	—	—	80	144	180	536	746	907	450	450	1,319
Sikkim	—	—	—	192	171	163	202	296	296	300	300	195
Arunachal Pradesh	—	—	—	5	526	687	1,953	2,179	2,176	1,067	1,067	1,229
Nagaland	—	—	—	—	35	187	472	1,012	1,214	580	1,878	1,898
Orissa	—	—	—	—	214	214	214	214	214	214	214	214
Meghalaya	—	—	—	—	—	—	145	215	351	103	117	252
Mizoram	—	—	—	—	—	—	350	360	391	400	448	750
North India Total	248,593	256,928	282,729	309,066	345,182	342,789	371,631	382,130	390,906	395,113	401,118	404,884

Table 2.1C: Area under tea in South India

(hectares)

District/States	1951+	1961	1971	1981	1991	1993	1998	1999	2000	2001	2001	2003
1	2	3	4	5	6	7	8	9	10	11	12	13
Nilgiris		20,840	22,651	24,849	26,260	26,451	49,759	55,319	60,427	61,634	61,679	61,679
Total Tamil Nadu	33,375	32,723	34,646	37,073	38,634	38,831	63,543	69,103	74,398	75,625	75,619	75,619
Cannanore		1,448	1,505	–	–	–	–	–	–	–	–	–
Palghat		574	635	665	688	744	841	R40	850	850	852	85'2
Kozhikode		4,014	3,874	–	–	–	–	–	–	–	–	–
Malapuram		–	174	174	174	174	174	174	174	174	174	174
Trichur		401	459	447	466	481	523	530	530	530	529	529
Trivandrum		1,082	1,057	1,071	1,023	1,023	965	965	965	965	965	965
Quilon		3,006	2,673	1,653	1,362	1,362	1,348	1,348	1,348	1,348	1,348	1,348
Ernakulam		161	147	30	2	2	2	2	2	2	2	2
Kottayam		29,098	26,747	2,232	2,026	2,039	840	840	840	840	840	840
Idukki		–	–	23,930	23,571	23,440	26,608	26,678	26,748	26,748	26,753	26,753
Wayanaad		–	–	5,387	5,366	5,418	5,447	5,468	5,483	5,483	5,504	5,504
Total Kerala	33,203	39,784	37,271	35,589	34,678	34,683	36,748	36,845	36,940	36,940	36,967	36,967
Chikamagalur		1,168	1,222	1,317	1,320	1,390	1,420	1,428	1,428	1,434	1,434	1,434
Coorg		178	205	188	261	275	290	299	299	299	299	299
Hassan		448	443	396	395	395	395	395	395	395	395	395
Total Karnataka	1,669	1,794	1,870	1,901	1,976	2,060	2,105	2,122	2,122	2,128	2,128	2,128
Total South India	68,247	74,301	73,787	74,563	75,288	75,574	102,396	108,070	113,460	114,693	114,714	114,714
Total All India	**316,840**	**331,229**	**356,516**	**383,629**	**420,470**	**418,363**	**474,027**	**490,200**	**504,366**	**509,806**	**515,832**	**519,598**

Table 2.1D: Extensions, replacement and replanting area in India

(hectares)

Year	North India			South India			All India		
	Extensions	Replacements	Replantings	Extensions	Replacements	Replantings	Extensions	Replacements	Replantings
1955–1956	251.98	239.03	1,980.87	403.03	25.00	23.85	655.01	264.03	2,004.72
1956–1957	679.57	473.31	2,385.69	274.72	7.49	14.77	954.29	480.80	2,400.46
1957–1958	1,621.05	749.19	2,372.72	331.23	6.10	27.25	1,952.28	755.29	2,399.97
1958–1959	1,835.09	580.08	2,374.64	274.23	–	59.69	2,109.32	580.08	2,434.33
1959–1960	2,009.25	488.34	1,878.36	307.31	37.66	8.50	2,316.56	526.00	1,886.86
1960–1961	1,626.73	345.99	1,769.40	86.74	6.78	1247	1,713.47	352.77	1,781.87
1961–1962	1,638.96	389.09	1,601.04	113.24	4.09	6.34	1,752.20	393.18	1,607.38
1962–1963	2,009.45	399.31	1,548.19	215.43	1.82	22.97	2,224.88	401.13	1,571.16
1963–1964	2,915.96	377.22	1,738.04	219.42	34.40	20.80	3,135.38	411.62	1,758.84
1964–1965	3,612.57	540.50	1,957.48	247.58	10.64	66.42	3,860.15	551.14	2,023.90
1965–1966	3,245.13	509.35	1,866.01	249.60	1.10	71.35	3,494.73	510.45	1,937.36
1966–1967	2,965.07	436.76	1,606.77	363.81	23.07	21.30	3,328.88	459.83	1,628.07
1967–1968	2,637.97	460.78	1,290.49	322.84	13.85	16.62	2,960.81	474.63	1307.11
1968–1969	2,,453.95	364.87	150.93	181.24	8.33	37.75	2,635.19	373.20	188.68
1969–1970	1985.82	277.20	955.12	188.66	0.78	32.30	2,174.48	277.98	987.42
1970–1971	2,151.04	195.57	1,076.51	204.31	5.55	42.55	2,355.35	201.12	1,119.06
1971–1972	1,557.86	176.61	1,258.73	273.77	18.05	63.48	1,831.63	194.66	1,322.21
1972–1973	1,390.52	173.20	1,046.42	242.39	7.16	62.80	1,632.91	180.36	1,109.22
1973–1974	1,516.66	307.61	1,015.98	284.95	14.87	74.37	1,801.61	322.48	1,090.35

Table 2.1D: Extensions, replacement and replanting area in India *(Contd.)*

(hectares)

Year	North India			South India			All India		
	Extensions	Replacements	Replantings	Extensions	Replacements	Replantings	Extensions	Replacements	Replantings
1975–1976	1,421.60	354.50	1,117.40	237.29	7.72	60.43	1,658.89	362.22	1,177.83
1976–1977	1,421.62	360.68	1,166.67	248.07	5.58	36.09	1,669.69	366.26	1,202.76
1977–1978	2,145.68	265.14	1,183.11	188.43	2.00	42.25	2,334.11	267.14	1,225.36
1978–1979	3117.46	383.49	1,221.33	347.09	5.73	24.89	3,464.55	399.22	1,246.22
1981	1,921.43	470.06	1,251.32	65.07	5.69	37.66	1,986.50	475.75	1,288.98
1991	2,286.74	383.42	1,334.50	136.31	51.48	160.98	2,423.05	434.90	1,495.48
1992	2,179.74	462.08	1199.95	212.97	56.54	82.20	2,392.71	518.62	1,282.15
1993	2,124.77	397.23	1300.74	337.76	53.24	37.91	2,462.53	450.47	1,338.65
1994	2,160.56	400.74	1,314.35	1,342.77	63.81	10.05	3,503.33	464.55	1,324.40
1995	1,465.52	235.46	1,243.98	176.74	–	36.49	1,642.26	235.46	1,280.47
1996	4,799.30	1,362.36	1,762.57	80.33	47.30	13.39	4,879.63	1,409.66	1,775.96
1997	1,920.00	945.00	1,419.00	719.45	61.57	2.17	2,639.45	1,006.57	1,421.17
1998	3,893.57	1,096.96	1,490.53	125.80	12.25	5.36	4,019.37	1,109.21	1,495.89
1999	2,974.23	826.32	1,315.16	55.10	87.24	5.05	3,029.33	913.56	1,320.21
2000	2,750.00	785.00	1,180.00	94.94	11.00	17.35	2,844.94	796.00	1,197.35
2001	2,470.00	632.00	945.00	136.02	–	14.68	2,606.02	632.00	959.68
2002	2,794.13	760.00	1,141.00	75.87	–	19.00	2,870.00	760.00	1,160.00
2003	3,012.10	824.00	1,277.00	21.24	3.00	15.21	3,033.34	827.00	1,292.21

Note: Figures up to 1978–1979 are as on 31st March and onward as on 31st December.

Table 2.1E: The trends in production of various types of teas in India

Year	North India					South India				All India				
	CTC	Orthdx.	Darjlng.	Green	Total	CTC	Orthdx.	Green	Total	CTC	Orthdx.	Darjlng.	Green	Total
1961	118.8	115.1	10.1	29.3	273.3	3.3	76.2	1.6	81.1	122.1	191.3	10.1	30.9	354.4
1971	210.2	93.2	10.3	18.6	332.3	29.8	71.4	2	103.2	240	164.6	10.3	20.6	435.5
1981	299.3	119.3	12.2	7	437.8	58.2	63.8	0.6	122.6	357.5	183.1	12.2	7.6	560.4
1991	461.9	79.5	13.9	7.6	562.9	141.7	47.4	2.2	191.3	603.6	126.9	13.9	9.8	754.2
1992	485.1	65.9	12.4	7	570.4	125.6	33.9	2.4	161.9	610.7	99.8	12.4	9.4	732.3
1993	507	55.7	13	5.8	581.5	139.3	38.5	1.5	179.3	646.3	94.2	13	7.3	760.8
1994	498.8	50.8	11.1	7.3	568	137	47.4	0.5	184.9	635.8	98.2	11.1	7.8	752.9
1995	520.7	29.2	11.3	7.4	568.6	141.7	45.2	0.5	187.4	662.4	74.4	11.3	7.9	756
1996	542.8	36.9	10.6	7.8	598.1	138.1	43.4	0.5	182	680.9	80.3	10.6	8.3	780.1
1997	549.5	37.1	10.1	8	604.7	150.6	54.2	0.5	205.3	700.1	91.3	10.1	8.5	810
1998	594.1	59.5	10.3	6.8	670.7	144.1	58.8	0.5	203.4	738.2	118.3	10.3	7.3	874.1
1999	576	32.5	8.7	6	623.2	172.1	30.2	0.4	202.7	748.1	62.7	8.7	6.4	825.9
2000	590.1	35.7	9.3	5.6	640.7	170.3	35.3	0.6	206.2	760.4	71	9.3	6.2	846.9
2001	592.1	44.4	9.8	4.5	650.8	167.4	34.8	0.9	203.1	759.5	79.2	9.8	5.4	853.9
2002	570.4	48.4	9.2	3.8	631.8	174.7	31.1	0.9	206.7	745.1	79.5	9.2	5.4	838.5
2003	608	26.9	9.6	3.8	648.3	191.6	37.2	1	229.8	799.6	64.1	9.6	4.7	878.1
2004	618	28.8	10.1	5.3	662.2	196.8	32.5	1.5	230.8	814.8	61.3	10.1	6.8	893
2005	649.8	32.3	11.3	7.6	701	181.8	43.3	1.9	227	831.6	75.6	11.3	9.5	928
2006	678.5	30.6	11.7	8.8	729.6	189.6	34.9	1.8	226.3	868.1	65.5	11.7	10.6	955.9

Source: Tea Statistics (2005–2006), Tea Board of India.

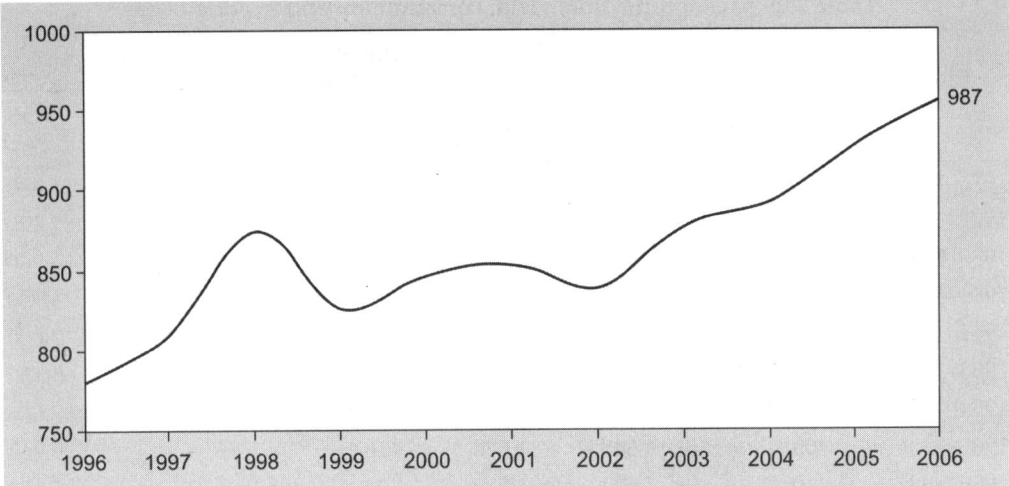

Fig. 2.1: Trend of tea production in India

The increase is primarily due to the area going up from 316 thousand hectares in 1950–1951 to 579 thousand hectares in 2011–2012. India's tea production in 2012 was 1126 mkg. Area during 2012 remaining the same as in 2011, increased production was due to increase in productivity (Table 2.2). Productivity increased steady from 881 kg/hectares. In 1950 to 1,174 kg/hectares in 1970–1971 to 1,481 kg/hectares by 1980–1981; 1,608 kg/hectares in 1984–1985 and 1,794 kg/hectares in 1990–1991. Thereafter, it has been fluctuating around 1,800 kg/hectares. Between 2000 and 2009, global tea production increased by 1,000 mkg and consumption by 879 mkg. Thus supply continued to surpass consumption in the last decade. The global production mix over the last decade has undergone significant change, with the share of green tea going up from 23% in 2000 to 33% in 2009, mainly because of the huge expansion in cultivation areas in China. Black tea production has remained static at around 2,400 mkg with the entire increase in global production over the last decade being accounted for by green tea. In India, lower output and increasing domestic consumption over the past four years resulted in a cumulative deficit of 130 mkg by June 2012.

Tea producers may look at increasing orthodox or hand-rolled varieties of production in the new season beginning March 2013, as the payment crisis with Iran—one of the largest buyers of Indian orthodox tea—has been sorted out. Orthodox tea production is likely to go up by 10 mkg in the new season. Prices too may rise by 10–12%, and orthodox tea is expected to command a price of Rs 190–200 per kg. In the first half of 2012, prices of orthodox tea had crashed as there was very little buying from Iran. Generally, Iran lifts 25–30 mkg of orthodox tea. Erratic weather throughout 2012 has cut tea production in India to 970–973 mkg compared to 980 mkg in 2011.

Top Three Tea Manufacturing Companies

1. Godrej Tea Limited
2. Tata Tea Limited
3. Hindustan Unilever Limited.

Table 2.2: Area, production, yield, consumption and exports of tea

Year	Area (Th. hectares)	Production (mkg)	Yield (kg/ha)	Per capita availability (gm)	Exports Quantity (mkg)	Exports Value (Rs million)
1970–1971	357	423	1,174	387	199	1,480
1975–1976	363	483	1,347	455	212	2,370
1980–1981	382	569	1,492	487	231	4,260
1981–1982	378	560	1,481	464	224	3,950
1982–1983	395	561	1,420	367	194	3,600
1983–1984	396	582	1,467	399	202	5,150
1984–1985	398	640	1,608	422	214	7,666
1985–1986	400	648	1,620	426	206	6,263
1986–1987	410	624	1,522	420	196	5,800
1987–1988	414	665	1,606	592	197	5,920
1988–1989	415	701	1,689	612	222	6,740
1989–1990	415	685	1,651	571	209	9,045
1990–1991	421	754	1,794	612	199	10,701
1991–1992	420	754	1,794	655	216	12,116
1992–1993	420	732	1,742	649	168	9,777
1993–1994	418	761	1,819	664	155	10,620
1994–1995	426	753	1,768	667	151	9,750
1995–1996	428	754	1,761	646	159	11,710
1996–1997	434	780	1,797	657	140	10,370
1997–1998	400	838	1,865	636	212	19,539
1998–1999	470	850	1,995	684	210	22,650
1999–2000	490	816	1,702	641	179	17,850
2000–2001	500	800	1,663	638	202	19,760
2001–2002	510	854	1,800	657	180	17,190
2002–2003	520	846	1,640	600	184	16,520
2003–2004	520	879	1,691	651	183	16,370
2004–2005	520	907	1,739	646	206	18,403
2005–2006	569	949	1,785	665	197	17,936
2006–2007	570	973	1,732	854	218	20,457
2007–2008	570	987	1,633	859	185	18,887
2008–2009	570	973	1,727	884	190	23,818
2009–2010	570	991	1,739	847	213	30,387
2010–2011	570	967	1,696	815	180	24,505
2011–2012	579	1095	1,891	641	214	33,048
2012–2013	579	1059	1829	727	156*	30,627*

* Apr-Dec.

Statewise Production of Tea

Tea gardens and tea industries are largely scattered covering a major part of India. The crop is grown in the certain districts located in Assam, West Bengal, Kerala, Karnataka and Tamil Nadu and to some extent in Tripura, Uttar Pradesh and Himachal Pradesh. Major states producing tea are Assam, West Bengal, Tamil Nadu and Kerala. Other small players are Himachal Pradesh, Tripura and Bihar (Tables 2.3 and 2.3A). Assam is the major producer of tea accounting for more than percentage of area. Production increased from 293.8 thousand tons in 1977–1976 to 425 thousand tons in 1996–1997, 451.2 thousand tons in 2000, 589.1 thousand tons in 2011 and 542.1 in 2012. This is followed by West Bengal sharing over 20% the total production. Tamil Nadu producing around 16% of the total production on an area of around 11% follows.

Balance of production is shared between Kerala and quite a number of States like Mizoram and Nagaland, etc. which are taken producers (Table 2.3B). What is however, most interesting is Karnataka, a very small player (5.5 million tons in 2000) has the highest yield nearly 2,600 kg/hectares against all India 1,669 kg/hectares.

Production of tea in India during last three financial years

(in Mkg)

Year	North India	South India	All India
2010-11	728.52	238.21	966.73
2011-12	865.59	229.87	1095.46
2012-13	893.38	241.69	1136.07

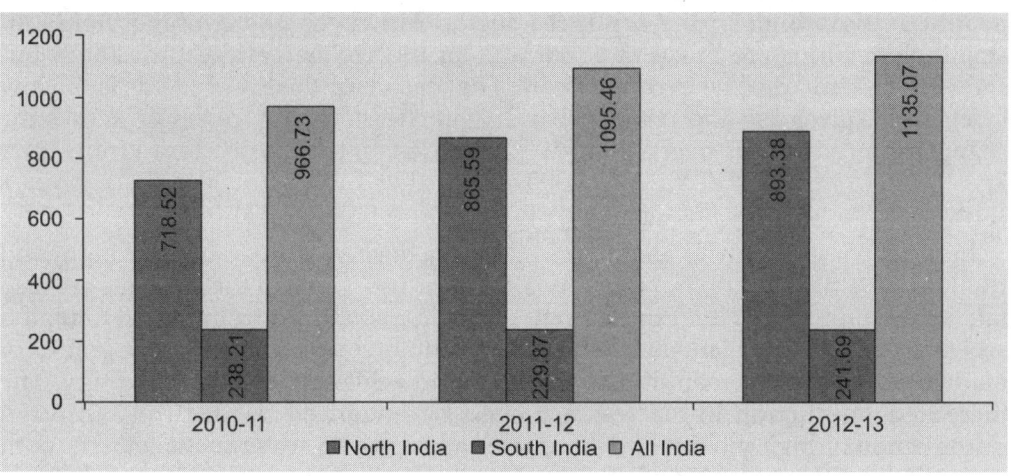

Production of tea in India (Mkg)

Category wise production of tea in India during 2012-13

(in Mkg)

Category	North India	South India	All India
CTC	827.61	195.07	1022.68
Orthodx (Darjeeling + Green)	65.77	46.62	112.39
Total	**893.38**	**241.69**	**1135.07**

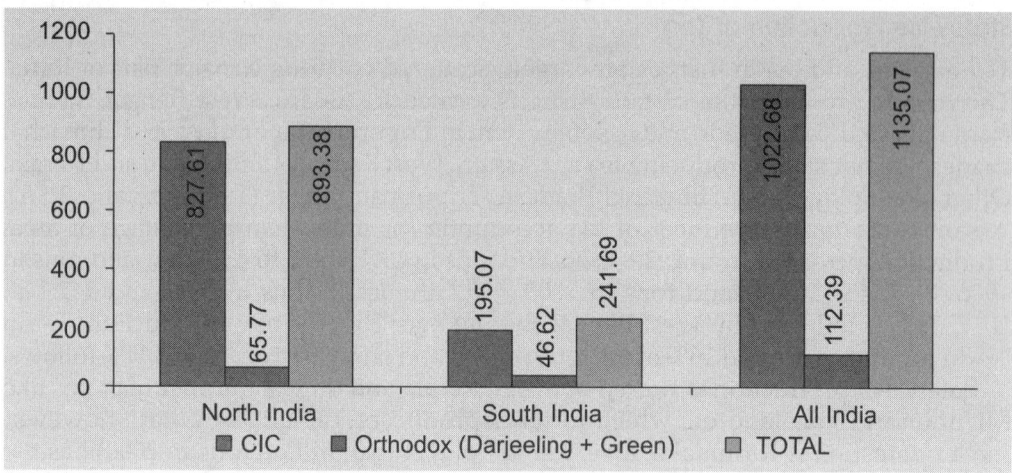

Category breakup production 2012-13

Productivity of Tea Cultivation in India

India's performance in terms of productivity (1,944 kg/hectares) is lower than Kenya's (2,235 kg) but better than Sri Lanka's (1,611 kg). India has shown steady growth since 1960–1961 (971 kg/hectares), 1,182 kg in 1970–1971 and 1,491 kg/hectares in 1980–1981 as against Kenya's growth, which has been very rapid productivity patterns in the small tea gardens and large-estate sectors vary and productivity is high in the small tea sector. However, the average yields on smallholder farms are lower at about 60% of the yields realized on estates, but showing a steady decline in recent years. The reason for the lower yields is the low levels of fertilizer use and poor husbandry practices. The figure below shows the changes in productivity over a period. Productivity of tea has decreased from 1,809 kg in 1996 to 1,669 kg/hectares in 2000 and further 1,774 kg in 2005. Recent years show that productivity is decreasing over a period (Table 2.3B).

Productivity is highly related to the age of tea bushes, temperature, drought and changes in rainfall. South or North-facing tea bushes, slope of the land, etc are also important in productivity. Productivity varies in plantations from region to region and even within one plantation. The same plantation provides different grades of made tea. The management is also influential in achieving high productivity. The increased production in tea was achieved by enhanced productivity through introduction of high-yielding quality material improved water management (both irrigation and drainage) (Fig. 2.2).

Recent data from Tata Tea estates, KDHB (Kannan Devan Hills Plantations Company Private Limited) in Munnar shows that the productivity has increased drastically after the new management. The productivity has increased from 687 kg/hectare to 3,743/hectare in the phase of new management. This management is known as participatory tea management where all workers and employees are shareholders in plantation sector. It is reported that they feel it belongs to them and this has been influential in achieving high production and productivity. The yield per hectare in Southern India (2,004 kg) is higher than that of the Northern India (1,601 kg). It has to be noted however, that in Northern tea gardens unlike in the

Table 2.3: Area production and average yield statewise tea

Area: in thousand hectares; Production: in thousand tons; Yield: per hectare in kg.

Year	Assam			Kerala			Tamil Nadu			West Bengal			Others			All India		
	Area	Prod.	Yield	Area	Produ.	Yield	Area	Produ.	Yield	Area	Prod.	Yield	Area	Produ.	Yield	Area	Prod.	Yield
1970-71	—	—	—	—	—	—	—	—	—	—	—	—	—	—	—	354.0	419.0	1184
1971-72	—	—	—	—	—	—	—	—	—	—	—	—	—	—	—	357.0	435.0	1218
1972-73	—	—	—	—	—	—	—	—	—	—	—	—	—	—	—	359.0	456.0	1270
1973-74	—	—	—	—	—	—	—	—	—	—	—	—	—	—	—	360.0	472.0	1311
1974-75	—	—	—	—	—	—	—	—	—	—	—	—	—	—	—	362.0	489.0	1351
1975-76	—	—	—	—	—	—	—	—	—	—	—	—	—	—	—	363.0	487.0	1342
1976-77	—	—	—	—	—	—	—	—	—	—	—	—	—	—	—	364.0	512.0	1407
1977-78	190.6	293.8	1541	36.2	51.7	1428	36.3	73.3	2019	89.3	128.7	1441	13.9	8.8	633	366.3	556.3	1519
1978-79	192.4	297.0	1544	36.2	51.3	1417	36.6	75.8	2071	90.0	131.9	1466	14.0	7.8	557	369.2	563.8	1527
1979-80	195.4	276.2	1414	36.1	58.3	1615	36.8	77.6	2109	91.0	124.0	1363	14.4	7.7	535	373.7	543.8	1455
1980-81	200.6	300.7	1499	36.1	53.6	1485	37.0	74.0	2000	93.5	133.2	1425	14.7	8.1	551	381.9	569.6	1491
1981-82	203.0	305.1	1503	35.6	47.6	1337	37.1	71.6	1930	94.0	128.3	1365	13.9	7.8	561	383.6	560.4	1461
1982-83	211.3	302.9	1434	35.3	48.5	1374	36.9	71.4	1935	96.6	133.3	1380	14.1	4.5	319	394.2	560.6	1422
1983-84	213.0	321.7	1510	35.0	44.6	1274	37.0	67.4	1822	97.2	139.7	1437	13.9	8.1	583	396.1	581.5	1468
1984-85	214.8	338.6	1576	35.1	58.2	1658	36.9	86.1	2333	97.8	148.3	1516	13.9	8.7	626	398.5	639.9	1606
1985-86	216.1	352.5	1631	34.8	53.1	1526	37.0	84.9	2295	98.0	157.4	1606	14.0	8.3	593	399.9	656.2	1641
1986-87	224.7	335.5	1493	34.7	48.6	1401	38.0	86.7	2282	100.1	141.3	1412	14.2	8.7	613	411.7	620.8	1508
1987-88	226.9	363.8	1603	34.7	56.3	1622	38.2	86.3	2259	100.5	149.6	1489	14.1	9.3	660	414.4	665.3	1605
1988-89	229.4	379.9	1656	34.7	53.9	1553	38.2	100.7	2636	101.0	143.2	1418	11.7	10.4	889	415.0	688.1	1658
1989-90	230.4	388.2	1685	34.7	60.6	1746	38.6	110.6	2865	101.2	149.7	1479	11.4	11.2	982	416.3	720.3	1730
1990-91	233.3	396.6	1700	34.7	66.8	1925	38.6	119.9	3106	101.9	159.2	1562	12.0	11.7	975	420.5	754.2	1794
1991-92	233.7	412.0	1763	34.5	54.6	1583	38.7	103.1	2664	102.0	150.7	1477	21.4	11.9	556	430.3	732.3	1702

(Contd.)

Table 2.3: Area production and average yield statewise tea

Area: in thousand hectares   Production: in thousand tons   Yield: per hectare in kg.

Year	Assam			Kerala			Tamil Nadu			West Bengal			Others			All India		
	Area	Prod.	Yield	Area	Produ.	Yield	Area	Produ.	Yield	Area	Prod.	Yield	Area	Produ.	Yield	Area	Prod.	Yield
1992-93	231.9	410.4	1770	34.7	62.0	1787	38.8	112.8	2907	100.5	162.7	1619	12.4	12.9	1040	418.3	760.8	1819
1993-94	227.1	400.8	1765	36.8	63.1	1715	48.9	117.5	2403	100.0	158.8	1588	13.2	12.7	962	426.0	752.9	1767
1994-95	226.3	402.6	1779	36.8	64.8	1761	49.0	117.9	2406	101.2	157.5	1556	13.8	13.2	957	427.1	756.0	1770
1995-96	227.2	424.9	1870	36.8	64.8	1762	49.0	117.9	2408	102.5	165.4	1614	14.2	14.0	986	429.7	780.0	1815
1996-97	227.2	424.9	1870	36.8	62.0	1684	49.0	113.8	2319	102.5	165.4	1613	14.2	15.1	1063	429.7	780.0	1815
1997-98	229.6	425.4	1853	36.8	69.6	1893	49.0	130.6	2663	103.5	169.9	1641	–	–	–	433.8	810.6	1869
1998-99	231.0	462.8	2004	36.8	70.6	1918	49.1	125.1	2548	104.2	195.7	1878	–	–	–	436.1	870.4	1996
1999-00	231.0	414.1	1793	36.8	67.8	1842	49.1	128.1	2610	104.2	180.2	1729	–	–	–	436.1	805.6	1848
2000-01	231.0	414.1	1793	36.8	67.8	1842	49.1	128.1	2610	104.2	180.2	1729	16.9	10.0	592	504.4	846.9	1679
2001-02	269.2	453.6	1685	36.9	65.2	1764	75.6	132.4	1751	110.8	186.8	1686	15.1	10.4	689	509.8	853.9	1675
2002-03	270.7	433.3	1601	37.0	57.8	1563	75.6	143.1	1893	113.1	188.0	1662	17.3	10.4	601	515.8	838.5	1625
2003-04	271.6	434.8	1601	37.0	58.0	1569	75.6	166.6	2203	113.4	200.6	1770	19.9	13.2	663	519.6	878.1	1690
2004-05	271.8	435.6	1603	37.1	62.1	1675	76.0	163.0	2146	114.0	214.5	1882	20.4	12.0	588	521.4	893.0	1713
2005-06	300.5	487.5	1622	36.8	63.3	1723	80.9	158.8	1962	114.5	217.5	1900	20.8	13.4	644	555.6	946.0	1703
2006-07	311.8	502.0	1610	36.2	59.5	1641	81.3	163.7	2014	114.8	237.1	2066	20.8	14.1	678	567.0	981.8	1732
2007-08	312.8	479.9	1534	36.2	61.8	1706	81.3	153.1	1884	114.8	231.4	2016	20.8	13.3	639	568.0	944.7	1663
2008	322.2	487.5	1513	37.1	70.3	1895	80.4	170.5	2121	115.0	233.1	2027	–	–	–	579.4	980.8	1693
2009	322.2	500.0	1552	37.1	69.0	1860	80.4	169.4	2107	115.0	221.6	1927	–	–	–	579.4	979.0	1690
2010	322.2	480.3	1491	37.1	66.8	1801	80.4	170.7	2123	115.0	229.8	1998	–	–	–	579.4	966.4	1668
2011	322.2	589.1	1828	37.1	68.9	1857	80.4	165.9	2063	115.0	271.6	2362	–	–	–	579.4	1115.7	1926
2012	322.2	590.1	1831	37.1	63.1	1701	80.4	170.6	2122	115.0	279.3	2429	–	–	–	579.4	1126.3	1944

Source: Area and Production of Principal Crops in India (Various Issues), Directorate of Economics and Statistics, Department of Agriculture and Co-operation Ministry of Agriculture.

Table 2.3A: Statewise production of tea (in thousand kg) in India

States	1986	1992	1993	1994	1995	1996	1997	1998	1999	2000	2003	2005	2006	2007	2008*	2009*	2010*	2011*	2012*
Assam	335,492	412,010	410,430	400,732	402,617	423,965	425,115	467,046	432,925	451,236	55434,759	487,487	502,041	511,885	487,497	499,997	480,286	589,110	590,120
West Bengal	141,270	150,690	162,669	158,825	157,522	164,768	170,158	193,789	180,212	180,724	200,635	217,546	237,106	236,344	233,133	221,573	229,784	271,600	279,300
Tripura	3,427	5,484	5,927	5,827	5,679	5,474	6,435	6,199	6,385	6,431	8,577	7,515	7,272	7,856					
Bihar	17	100	116	136	130	127	135	138	473	538	1,130	1,122	1,122	1,098					
Uttar Pradesh	407	471	379	338	341	345	350	359	309	264	141	427	427	231					
Himachal Pradesh	636	1,192	1,303	1,314	1,359	1,423	1,442	1,701	1,222	1,247	605	971	789	769					
Manipur	50	32	42	60	74	21	27	76	97	96	119	108	110	110					
Sikkim	50	97	84	96	102	67	105	112	102	105	107	157	87	82					
Arunachal Pradesh	–	308	522	569	704	853	875	965	1063	993	1745	2624	3884	5842					
Nagaland	–	7	7	12	17	69	31	29	39	43	195	190	191	191					
Meghalaya	–	–	–	–	–	–	–	127	135	140	81	99	139	259					
Mizoram	–	–	–	–	–	–	–	23	35	39	78	73	75	75					
Orissa	–	33	55	46	83	116	24	94	100	105	105	101			13,290	13,298	12,959	14,860	17,530
Tamil Nadu	86,742	103,066	112,832	117,520	117,915	115,840	130,761	132,046	128,088	129,699	166,572	163,676	163,656	160,531	170,532	169,356	170,723	165,890	170,560
Kerala	48,616	54,627	62,003	63,127	64,778	61,581	69,776	65,943	67,796	69,355	58,012	58,502	59,462	55,966	70,287	68,964	66,754	68,830	63,100
Karnataka	4,146	4,205	4,457	4,293	4,692	4,578	5,379	5,461	5,427	5,468	5,268	5,376	5,444	5,188	6,079	5,811	5,897	5,430	5,720
Total All India	620,853	732,322	760,826	752,895	756,013	779,227	810,613	874,108	824,408	846,483	878,129	945,974	981,805	986,427	980,818	978,999	966,403	1,115,720	1,126,330

* Breakup not available.

Table 2.3B: Average yield of tea (in kg/hectares) in India

States	Year																	
	1986	1992	1993	1994	1995	1996	1998	1999	2000	2003	2005	2006	2007	2008	2009	2010	2011	2012
Assam	1,507	1,763	1,770	1,764	1,779	1,858	1,856	1,680	1,693	204,113	1,622	1,610	1,593	1,513	1,552	1,491	1,828	1,831
West Bengal	1,426	1,492	1,619	1,589	1,557	1,605	1,835	1,657	1,681	1,770	1,900	207	2,053	2,026	1,925	1,996	2,360	2,427
Tripura	531	905	989	981	954	1,068	975	985	971	1,037	863	835	877					
Bihar	38	4,545	4,620	1,790	1,711	1,671	181	351	399	565	561	561	549					
Uttar Pradesh	225	528	447	370	319	323	327	289	247	96	293	293	146					
Himachal Pradesh	308	578	632	637	588	612	736	526	536	258	414	336	328					
Manipur	–	208	233	175	213	193	142	130	106	90	82	83	83					
Sikkim	281	571	515	558	593	674	554	345	355	549	805	446	423					
Arunachal Pradesh	–	448	760	494	519	469	494	488	456	1,420	1526	2,259	2,273					
Nagaland	–	37	37	51	66	46	61	39	35	103	100	101	101					
Meghalaya	–	–	–	–	–	–	876	628	654	321	393	552	459					
Mizoram	–	–	–	–	–	–	66	97	111	104	112	115	115					
Orissa	–	154	257	210	379	315	439	467	269	491	472	–	–	596	596	581	666	786
Tamil Nadu	2,282	2,665	2,906	2,406	2,408	2,365	2,078	1,852	1,743	2,203	2,022	2,014	1,995	2,119	2,105	2,122	2,062	2,120
Kerala	1,399	1,582	1,788	1,715	1,761	1,675	1,794	1,845	1,878	1,569	1,591	1,641	1,507	1,893	1,857	1,798	1,853	1,699
Karnataka	2,172	2,087	2,164	2,049	2,235	2,181	2,594	2,577	2,577	2,476	2,545	2,547	2,423	2,839	2,714	2,754	2,537	2,673
Total All India	**1,523**	**1,742**	**1,819**	**1,768**	**1,770**	**1,809**	**1,844**	**1,680**	**1,678**	**1,690**	**1,703**	**1,732**	**1,705**	**1,693**	**1,690**	**1,668**	**1,926**	**1,944**

* Breakup not released.

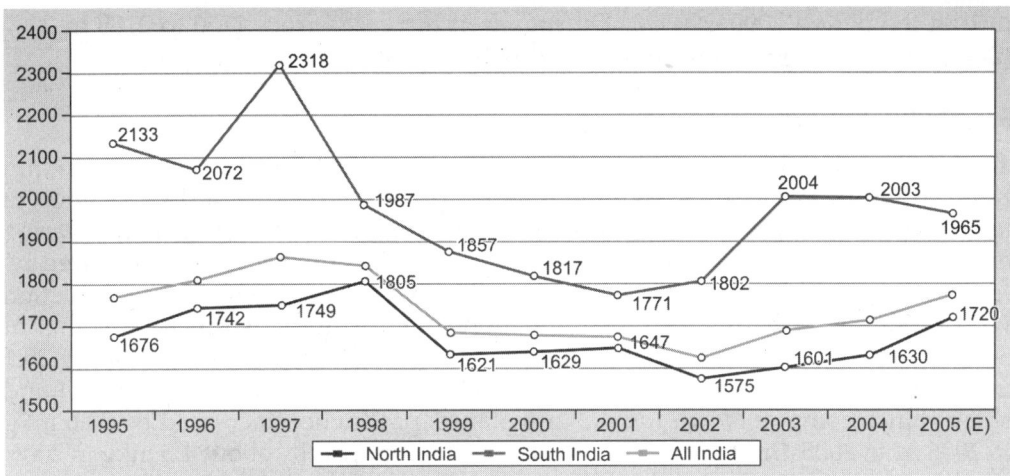

Fig. 2.2: Productivity of Indian tea industry

southern gardens, plucking does not take place throughout the year and hence the volume is low (Fig. 2.3).

In South India, tea yields are high in Madurai, Trichur and Coimbatore. By comparison, tea yields are low in North India in general, and Darjeeling in particular. Yields in Darjeeling are low, because they collect only the finest two leaves and the bud to enhance the unique flavor which has been described as "muscatel". The low productivity in Darjeeling tea is also due to its old age bushes. The productivity of Darjeeling is very low (545 kg), and it has pushed down the total productivity of West Bengal (1770 kg) which is given in the following table (figures in kg/hectares). Except Darrang and Dibrugarh, in all other districts, productivity has declined

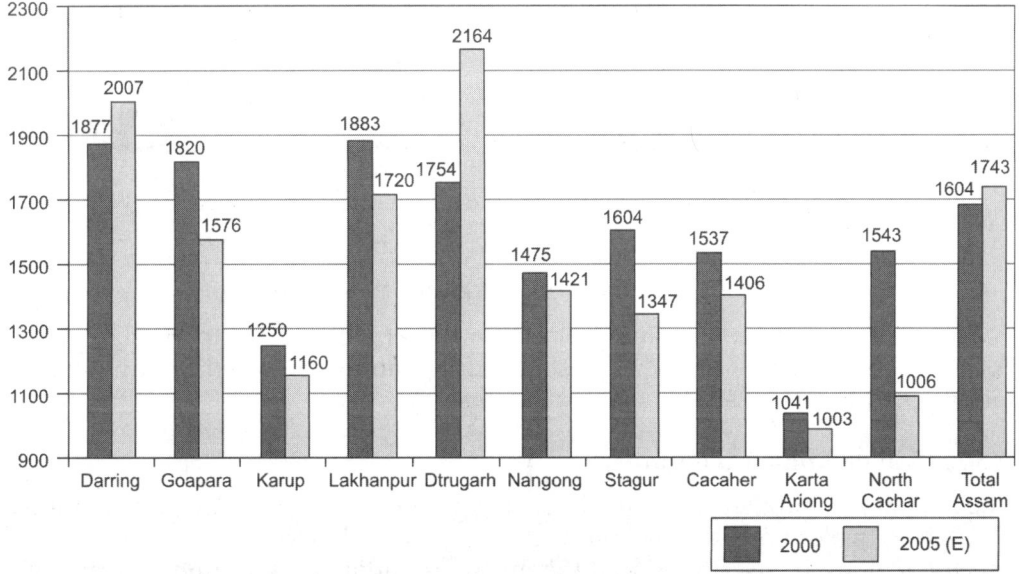

Fig. 2.3: Productivity in districts of Assam

during the period 2000–2005. In Dibrugarh, it increased from 1750 to 2105 in 2005 (Fig. 2.3). The figure below shows productivity in West Bengal (Fig. 2.4).

Production in North and South India

Tea is grown in 16 Indian States, of which Assam, West Bengal, Tamil Nadu and Kerala account for about 96% of the total tea production. Area and production of tea region wise is as in Tables 2.4 and 2.4A to D. District Nilgiri (Tamil Nadu) sharing over 11% in area and production is the topper in the country. This is followed by Iduki in Kerala. This shows that Northern India holds a major share in tea production with 76.3% share. Both area and production of North India is three times that of South (Table 2.4E). However, there was a fall in North Indian production by 29.1 mkg, i.e. 634.5 mkg against 663.6 mkg in 2003. But since 2003, the production and share is increasing in North India. For instance, production increased by 28.6 mkg in 2006 from 2005. But in South India, the output dropped by about 4.5 mkg in 2006. District-wise area and production data for each region has been described.

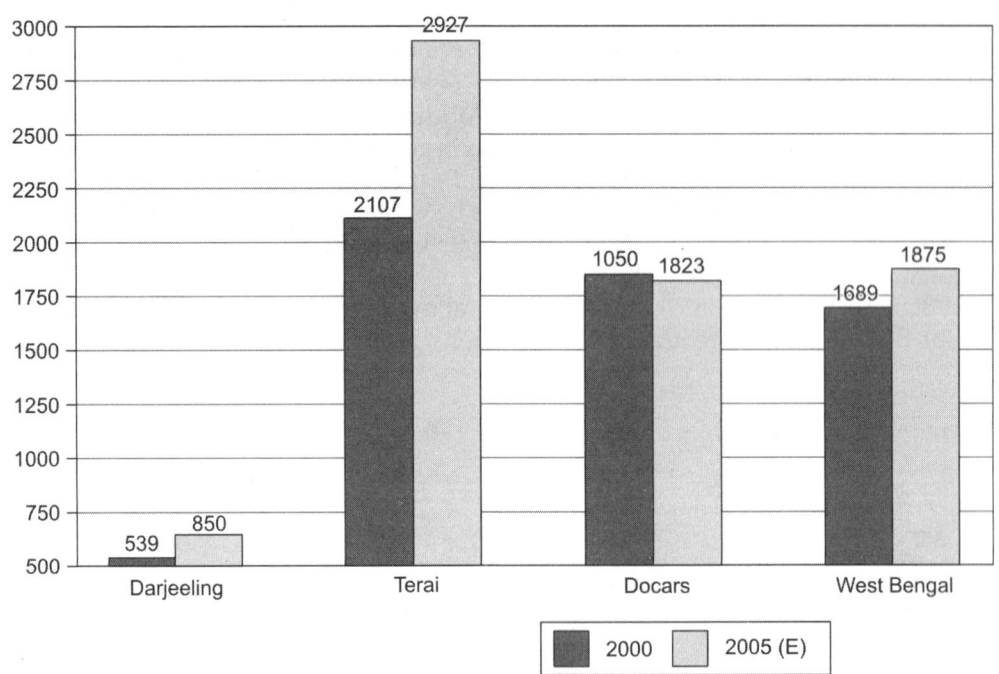

Fig. 2.4: Productivity of tea industry in West Bengal

Months and district-wise tea production data (Tables 2.4 F to H) shows that September and October are the highest producing months followed by July, August, January and February are the earnest months.

Production of Small Tea Growers

The industry in India includes small and big growers and government plantations. Though the major portion of tea production in India is highly concentrated in some specific regions, it is scattered in different states. India holds around 19% (521,403 hectares) of the total area of tea cultivation in the world (2,774,797 hectares). On the

Table 2.4: Tea Area as on 31-12-2011 and production in 2011-12 to 31-12-2013 and production in 2013-14

State/Districts	Area under tea (in the hectares) 2011	Production (million kgs.) 2011-12	Area under tea (in the hectares) 2011	Production (million kgs.) 2011-12
Assam Valley	285.83	531.26	270.92	581.03
Cachar	36.38	50.00	33.48	48.02
Total Assam	322.21	581.26	304.40	629.05
Darjeeling	17.82	9.02	17.82	8.91
Dooars	72.92	147.59	72.92	177.85
Terai	24.36	112.82	49.70	125.34
Total West Bengal	**115.10**	**269.43**	**140.44**	**312.10**
Other North Indian States (includes Tripura, Uttarakhand, Bihar, Manipur, Sikkim, Arunachal Pradesh, Himachal Pradesh,Nagaland, Meghalaya, Mizoram and Orissa	22.30	14.90	12.29	23.92
Total North India	459.61	865.59	457.13	965.07
Tamil Nadu	80.46	162.79	69.62	174.71
Kerala	37.14	61.62	35.01	63.48
Karnataka	2.14	5.46	2.22	5.52
Total South India	119.74	229.87	106.85	243.71
All total	**579.35**	**1095.46**	**563.98**	**1208.78**

basis of the ownership pattern, tea estates can be broadly classified under the following heads:

- Small holdings, which may be anything from 1 acre to 25 acres (10.12 hectares) in extent, owned by the proprietors
- Small gardens, having a tea area below 200 hectares, owned by a single proprietor or partnership firms. this may be further subdivided into:
  o Where tea is cultivated and the green leaf is taken to a nearby factory for processing
  o Where both the cultivation and the processing of tea is undertaken.
- Estates owned by limited liability companies. It may again be further subdivided into Public Limited and Private Limited Companies
- Estates owned by big companies
- Estates owned by government undertakings and cooperatives.

Small growers have been a part of the Indian Tea Industry only since early 1960s. They were initially confined to Nilgiris district in Tamil Nadu, and to a small extent in Kerala and Himachal Pradesh. Reliable secondary data on Small Tea Growers (STGs) is limited. Therefore, only primary survey and field studies may provide an understanding of the problems and issues. Some macro-level information is available in Tea Statistics published by Tea Board of India since 1998. But, this cannot be treated as comprehensive because many of the growers are not registered with Tea Board and out of the ambit all kinds of data sources (Table 2.4I).

Table 2.4A: Area under tea: North India

(Area in hectare)

Districts/States	1938	1948	1950	1960	1971	1980	1990	1995	1996	1997	1998	2000	2003	2005	2006	2007	2008	2009	2010	2011	2012
Darrang	119,882	122,264	124,265	26,529	30,897	34,798	39,989	40,284	41,575	41,669	40,950	41,037	41,158	41,388	41,677	41,710					
Goalpara				1,604	2,098	3,486	3,141	3,176	3,112	3,143	3,338	3,460	3,635	4,215	4,451	4,451					
Kamrup				2,075	2,713	3,122	3,557	3,013	3,252	3,265	3,307	3,442	3,466	3,787	3,782	3,953					
Lakhimpur				50,282	57,297	3,593	4,212	4,494	4,362	4,497	4,809	4,815	4,839	6,301	6,724	6,756					
Dibrugarh						59,572	68,207	68,998	70,022	70,806	8,3380	93,076	95,118	114,435	120,489	122,514	Breakup not released	Breakup not released	Breakup not released	Breakup not released	Breakup not released
Nowgong				5,581	6,372	7,004	7,780	7,723	7524	7,715	7,746	7,994	8,114	8,605	8,709	8,758					
Sibsagar				46,469	51,930	57,823	63,348	62,810	62,751	63,196	71,362	74,807	77,135	83,971	88,008	94,611					
Cachar	21,674	30,379	30,525	29,951	31,018	3,2171	35,075	29,969	29,534	29,503	30,565	3,2008	32,137	31,894	31,805	32,312					
Karbi Anlong							1,358	1,550	1,559	1,563	1,652	4,004	1,923	1,885	2,201	2,185					
North Cachar							3,696	4,263	4,514	4,486	4,516	1,869	4,064	4,021	3,976	4,069					
Total Assam	**141,556**	**152,643**	**154,790**	**162,491**	**182,325**	**201,569**	**230,363**	**226,280**	**228,205**	**229,843**	**251,625**	**266,512**	**271,589**	**300,502**	**311,822**	**321,319**	**322,214**	**322,214**	**322,214**	**322,210**	**322,210**
Darjeeling	25,329	25,386	26,005	27,971	18,245	19,241	20,065	18,932	17,551	17,760	17,830	17,228	17,580	17,539	17,542	17,818	17,818	17,818	17,818	17,820	17,820
Terai (a)					10,769	11,474	1,3345	13,083	15,351	15,618	17,315	69,703	22,971	24,313	24,340	24,359	24,359	24,359	24,359	24,360	24,360
Dooars (b)	53,331	53,289	54,061	54,798	59,485	62,782	67,760	69,175	69,748	69,630	70,479	20,548	72,800	72,673	72,906	72,918	72918	72,918	72,918	72,920	72,920
Total West Bengal	**78,660**	**78,675**	**80,066**	**82,769**	**88,499**	**93,497**	**101,170**	**101,190**	**102,650**	**103,008**	**105,624**	**107,479**	**113,351**	**114,525**	**114,788**	**115,095**	**115,095**	**115,095**	**115,095**	**115,100**	**115,100**
Tripura				5059	5,444	6,062	5,778	5,952	6,064	6,235	6,355	6,623	8,268	8,710	8,710	8,962	22,304				
Bihar					460	459	22	76	76	76	762	1,350	2,000	2,000	2,000	2,000					
Uttaranchal				1,818	1,818	1,804	876	1,068	1,068	1,068	1,068	1,068	1,471	1,456	1,456	1,585					
Himachal Pradesh				4,183	4,183	4,183	2,063	2,312	2,325	2,325	2,325	2,325	2,348	2,348	2,348	2,348					

Table 2.4A: Area under tea: North India (Contd.)

(Area in hectare)

Districts/States	1938	1948	1950	1960	1971	1980	1990	1995	1996	1997	1998	2000	2003	2005	2006	2007	2008	2009	2010	2011	2012
Manipur						80	140	347	347	347	536	907	1,319	1,319	1,319	1,319	22,304	22,304	22,304	22,304	22,304
Sikkim	12,589	12,423	12,286	6,806		185	171	172	172	172	202	296	195	195	195	194	(Breakup not released)	(Breakup not released)	(Breakup not released)	(Breakup not released)	(Breakup not released)
Arunachal Pradesh						5	195	1,361	1,818	1,818	1953	2,176	1,229	1,719	1,719	2,570	released)	released)	released)	released)	released)
Nagaland							13	256	415	472	472	1,214	1,898	1898	1,898	1,898					
Meghalaya										120	145	214	252	252	252	564					
Mizoram											350	351	750	650	650	650					
Odissa							213	219	219	218	214	391	214	214	214	214					
Total North India	232,805	243,741	247,142	257,125	282,729	307,844	341,004	339,233	343,359	345,702	371,631	390,906	404,884	435,788	447,371	458,718	437,309	459,613	459,613	459,610	459,610
Total All India	298,441	310,931	314,883	331,479	73,787	381,891	416,269	42,7065	431,204	434,294	474,027	504,366	519,598	555,611	567,020	578,458	579,353	579,353	579,353	579,350	579,350

(a) Including West Dinajpur (b) Including Cooch Behar (E) - Subject to revision
Source: Tea Board of India.

Table 2.4B: Area under tea: South India

(Area in hectare)

Districts/States	1938	1948	1950	1960	1971	1980	1990	1995	1996	1997	1998	2000	2003	2005	2006	2007	2008	2009	2010	2011	2012
Kanyakumari					484	443	434	434	434	434	434	434	433	410	410	310	310	Breakup not released	Breakup not released	Breakup not released	Breakup not released
Tirunelveli					509	772	800	800	800	800	800	800	800	800	800	818	818				
Madurai					944	964	945	946	941	941	941	973	973	991	991	550	550				
Coimbatore					10058	10008	10187	11241	11224	11457	11609	11764	11734	12623	12623	12628	12628				
Nilgiris					22651	24843	26237	35537	35585	36039	49759	60427	61679	66115	66452	66156	66156				
Total Tamil Nadu				32748	34646	37030	38603	48958	48984	49671	63543	74398	75619	80939	81276	80462	80462	80462	80462	80460	80460
Cannanore					1505																
Palghat					635	664	681	829	829	829	841	850	852	815	860	860	860				
Kozhikode					3874																
Malapuram	Breakup not abailable	Breakup not abailable	Breakup not abailable		174	174	174	174	174	174	174	174	174	174	174	174	174				
Trichur					459	442	466	496	515	533	523	530	529	530	530	530	530				
Trivandrum					2673	1071	1023	965	965	965	965	965	965	769	433	433	433				
Quilon					26747	1999	1362	1348	1348	1348	1348	1348	1348	1348	1149	1149	1149	Breakup not released	Breakup not released	Breakup not released	Breakup not released
Kottayam					147	2266	2019	776	776	776	840	840	840	840	827	827	827				
Ernakulam						30	2	2	2	2	2	2	2	2	2	2	2				
Idukki						24130	23584	26710	26729	26764	26608	26748	26753	27100	27122	27692	27692				
Wynaad						5354	5375	5475	5424	5426	5447	5483	5504	5194	5139	5470	5470				
Total Kerala					36214	36130	34686	36775	36762	36817	36748	36940	36967	36772	36236	37137	37137	37137	37137	37140	37140
Chikmagalur					1222	1311	1320	1414	1414	1418	1420	1428	1434	1430	1455	1459	1459	Breakup not released	Breakup not released	Breakup not released	Breakup not released
Coorg					205	189	261	290	290	291	290	299	299	296	296	296	296				
Hassan					443	387	395	395	395	395	395	395	395	386	386	386	386				
Total Karnataka				1791	1870	1887	1976	2099	2099	2104	2105	2122	2128	2112	2137	2141	2141	2141	2141	2140	2140
Total South India	**65636**	**67190**	**67741**	**74354**	**72230**	**75047**	**75265**	**87832**	**87845**	**88592**	**102396**	**113460**	**114714**	**119823**	**119649**	**119740**	**119740**	**119740**	**119740**	**119740**	**119740**
Total All India	**298441**	**310931**	**314883**	**331479**	**373787**	**381891**	**416269**	**427065**	**431204**	**434294**	**474027**	**504366**	**519598**	**555611**	**567020**	**578458**	**579353**	**579353**	**579353**	**579350**	**579350**

E - Subject to revision.
No figure available after 2008.
Source: Tea Board of India.

Table 2.4C: District wise tea production: South India

(Figures in thousand kg)

Districts/States	1938	1948	1951	1960	1971	1980	1990	1995	1996	1997	1998	2000	2003	2005	2006	2007	2008	2009	2010	2011	2012
Kanyakumari					247	192	182	120	101	99	119	120	101	108	82	70					
Tirunelveli					858	2073	2262	2447	2174	1992	1883	2100	1658	1660	1226	1360					
Madurai					1738	2988	3397	2906	2871	3682	3075	3650	2036	3098	2084	2129					
Coimbatore					18434	23745	28210	28168	28097	32234	32997	32100	29208	33127	35291	32189					
Nilgiris					36254	45008	76525	84274	82597	92172	93972	91729	133569	125683	124973	124783					
Total Tamil Nadu	17181	24875	25225	37429	57531	74006	110576	117915	115840	130179	132046	129699	166572	163676	163656	160531	170532	169356	170723	165890	170560
Cannanore																					
Palghat					975	1336	1697	1999	1980	2466	2398	1950	2444	1887	2117	2012					
Kozhikode					6140																
Malapuram					138	91	97														
Trichur					674	1099	1503	1553	1614	1922	1951	1650	1002	1863	1921	1594					
Trivandrum					940	836	744	433	561	641	582	475	298	209	213	220					
Quilon					1648	960	423	438	343	417	366	375	322	232	227	166					
Kottayam					30706	198	324	140	169	139	244	320	645	208	165	177					
Ernakulam					67																
Idukki						39699	46697	49473	46434	52394	48254	52000	41848	41932	43639	38484					
Wynaad						9395	9180	10742	10480	11797	12148	12585	11453	12171	11180	13313					
Total Kerala	16152	21712	25775	30056	41288	53614	60665	64778	61581	69776	65943	69355	58012	58502	59462	55966	70287	68964	66754	68830	63100
Chikmagalur					2022	2445	2701	2993	2974	3239	3484	3288	3563	3619	3543	3541					
Coorg					273	376	497	606	591	746	768	760	756	776	752	652					
Hassan					582	654	793	1093	1013	1394	1209	1420	949	981	1149	995					
Total Karnataka	470	1745	874	1673	2877	3475	3991	4692	4578	5379	5461	5468	5268	5376	5444	5188	6079	5811	5897	5430	5720
Total South India	33803	48332	51874	77158	101696	131095	175232	187385	181999	205334	203450	204522	229852	227554	228562	221685	246898	244131	243374	240150	239380
Total All India	203335	260009	285399	318534	435468	569550	720338	756016	780140	810031	874108	846683	878129	945974	981805	986427	980818	978999	966403	1115720	1126330

Source: Tea Board of India.

Table 2.4D: District wise tea production: North India

(Figures in thousand kgs)

Districts/States	1938	1948	1951	1960	1971	1980	1990	1995	1996	1997	1998	2000	2003	2005	2006	2007	2008	2009	2010	2011	2012
Darrang	18168	26770	26909	26648	41283	62701	79632	80538	83240	81112	86942	80227	80291	82281	83404	84976					
Goalpara	1022	1610	1616	1434	2428	3885	5027	5779	5226	5844	6099	5855	6137	5271	6327	6847					
Kamrup	879	1211	1157	1400	2557	4498	4702	4766	4044	4498	5146	5003	4333	4021	3720	3982					
Lakhimpur	36393	49354	55996	68324	91949	6193	8257	8678	8494	8590	9995	9701	8502	8387	8993	9165	432246	445126	428736	538820	537250
Dibrugarh						110276	140447	143931	146435	146074	164463	155932	175339	211376	223876	225321					
Nowgong	2933	3724	3691	3786	7423	9274	11690	13846	12888	12788	14684	14073	11587	11821	10742	12429					
Sibsagar	26750	39200	41174	39315	55289	72422	92331	98186	110278	109933	119749	118324	100693	113392	117231	118622					
Cachar	31321	18119	19827	15344	22736	31451	40174	40180	45768	48453	51850	53722	41411	44858	41832	44131	55151	54871	51550	50290	52870
Karbi Anlong							1048	1598	1427	1487	1375	1878	2028	1663	1682	1677					
North Cachar							4873	5115	5765	6336	6743	6521	4438	4417	4234	4735					
Total Assam	117466	139988	150370	156251	223665	300700	388181	402617	423565	425115	467046	451236	434759	487487	502041	511885	487497	499997	480286	589110	590120
Darjeeling	10270	12879	7838	10043	10293	12689	14499	11298	10614	10054	10253	9814	9582	11312	10854	10007	11586	8909	8626	9140	8930
Terai (a)			6376	8053	12954	15872	21130	24804	28901	30344	36403	34947	59786	77078	87064	87502	79517	74041	76355	114040	113660
Dooars (b)	36661	54727	63944	62781	80840	104624	114124	121420	125253	129760	147133	135963	131267	129156	139188	138835	142030	138623	144803	148420	156710
Total	46931	67606	78158	80877	104087	133185	149753	157522	164768	170158	193789	180724	200635	217546	237106	236344	233133	221573	229784	271600	279300
West Bengal																					
Tripura	1504	1688	1873	2138	2960	3688	5205	5679	6474	6435	6199	6431	8577	7515	7272	7856					
Bihar	3631	2395	3124	2108	41	20	76	130	127	135	138	538	1130	1122	1122	1098					
Uttaranchal					690	285	534	341	345	1442	349	264	141	427	427	231					

Table 2.4D: District wise tea production: North India (*Contd.*)

(Figures in thousand kgs)

Districts/States	1938	1948	1951	1960	1971	1980	1990	1995	1996	1997	1998	2000	2003	2005	2006	2007	2008	2009	2010	2011	2012
Himachal Pradesh					888	551	1180	1359	1423	105	1711	1247	605	971	789	769					
Manipur							18	102	21	24	76	96	119	108	110	110					
Sikkim						26	90	83	67	875	112	105	107	157	87	82	13290	13298	12959	14860	17530
Arunachal Pradesh							38	707	853	27	965	993	1745	2624	3884	5842					
Nagaland								74	29		29	43	195	190	191	191					
Meghalaya											127	140	81	99	139	259					
Mizoram											23	39	78	73	75	75					
Odissa							31	17	69	31	94	105	105	101							
Total North India	169532	211677	233525	241374	332331	439455	545106	568631	597741	604347	670658	641961	648277	718420	753243	764742	733920	734868	723029	875570	886950
Total All India	203335	260009	285399	318534	435468	569550	720338	756016	780140	810031	874108	846483	878129	945974	981805	986427	980818	978999	966403	1115720	1126330

Source: Tea Board of India.

Table 2.4E: Tea production and share between North India and South India

Year	Total production (Qnty. mkg)			Share of the total production (as %)	
	N. India	S. India	All India	N. India	S. India
1995	568.63	187.4	756.01	75.2	24.8
1996	598.22	182	780.2	76.7	23.3
1997	604.9	205.3	810	74.7	25.3
1998	670.7	203.4	874.1	76.7	23.3
1999	623.2	202.7	825.9	75.5	24.5
2000	640.7	206.2	846.9	75.7	24.3
2001	650.8	203.1	853.9	76.2	23.8
2002	631.8	206.7	838.5	75.3	24.7
2003	648.3	229.8	878.1	73.8	26.2
2004	662.2	230.8	893	74.2	25.8
2005	701	227	928	75.5	24.5
2006	729.6	226.3	955.9	76.3	23.7

Source: Tea Statistics, J. Thomas & Co. Pvt. Ltd. and www.indiateaporatal.com

Available data indicates that at the national level, there is an absolute increase in the number of STGs across India from 110,396 in 2000 to 157,504 in 2007 (Table 2.5). At the same time, the area under tea cultivation has gone up from 109.2 thousand hectares in 2003 to 162.4 thousand hectares in 2007. During the same period, the area under estate gardens/big growers seem to be almost constant. Interestingly, the percentage share of area under cultivation for tea shows that the small growers constituted 21.02% in 2003 and have further increased to 28.08% in 2007. Similar trends for the estate gardens/big growers have rather shown a declining trend from 78.98% to 71.92% during the same period. The share of tea production of the small-holders has also increased substantially from 20.57% to 26.10% during the period between 2003 and 2007.

The absolute increase from small holdings is 76.80 mkg during the corresponding period, against 21.50 mkg from the estate sector. The average farm size of small-holders is 1.03 hectares as compared to 246.75 hectares in case of estates. Productivity has been decreasing from 1,654 kg/hectares in 2003 to 1,585 kg/hectares in 2007. It may be due to varying nature of age structure of bushes in smallholder gardens and growing nature of new areas into tea cultivation. It is also to be noted that since the small growers sell the green leaves to the Bought Leaf Factories (BLF), co-operative factories and estate garden factories, there is a possibility that the data on tea production by the smallholders gets recorded in estate gardens account. Hence, there may be an extent of under-reporting of production by STGs which ultimately overestimate the productivity and efficiency of estate gardens. It is also contradictory as Hayami (2004) mentions: "the advantage of smallholders lies in their predominant reliance on the labor of family members which provides a strong incentive to elicit conscientious work efforts for the sake of family well-being, in contrast to hired wage workers which require close supervision for attaining comparative performance levels. This advantage applies to both "farm" and "non-farm" family

Table 2.4F: Statewise and month wise production data for the year 2011

(Quantity in mkg)

State/Month	Jan	Feb	Mar	Apr	May	Jun	Jul	Aug	Sep	Oct	Nov	Dec	Jan-Dec 2011
Assam Valley	0.32	0.12	17.94	35.54	46.45	66.19	77.35	78.93	84.28	73.95	41.85	15.90	538.82
Cachar	0.46	0.06	1.24	3.53	3.92	5.68	6.76	7.17	6.79	7.68	4.77	2.23	50.29
Total Assam	**0.78**	**0.18**	**19.18**	**39.07**	**50.37**	**71.87**	**84.11**	**86.10**	**91.07**	**81.63**	**46.62**	**18.13**	**589.11**
Dooars	0.83	0.19	7.91	7.35	15.10	16.30	18.39	19.80	20.35	20.17	14.56	7.47	148.42
Terai	2.27	0.58	7.30	4.08	11.42	12.45	13.42	14.94	14.60	14.39	11.70	6.89	114.04
Darj	0.00	0.00	0.33	1.17	0.64	1.18	1.26	1.30	1.53	1.03	0.57	0.13	9.14
Total West Bengal	**3.10**	**0.77**	**15.54**	**12.60**	**27.16**	**29.93**	**33.07**	**36.04**	**36.48**	**35.59**	**26.83**	**14.49**	**271.60**
Others	0.08	0.00	0.35	0.75	1.34	1.66	2.17	2.19	2.07	1.99	1.41	0.85	14.86
Total North India	**3.96**	**0.95**	**35.07**	**52.42**	**78.87**	**103.46**	**119.35**	**124.33**	**129.62**	**119.21**	**74.86**	**33.47**	**875.57**
Tamil Nadu	11.72	9.88	13.41	15.21	18.07	16.32	13.89	11.13	12.52	16.48	15.28	11.98	165.89
Kerala	6.63	5.45	6.42	5.48	8.25	6.73	4.61	3.49	4.06	6.24	6.19	5.28	68.83
Karnataka	0.41	0.30	0.38	0.50	0.64	0.44	0.50	0.29	0.33	0.61	0.62	0.41	5.43
Total South India	**18.76**	**15.63**	**20.21**	**21.19**	**26.96**	**23.49**	**19.00**	**14.91**	**16.91**	**23.33**	**22.09**	**17.67**	**240.15**
Total All India	**22.72**	**16.58**	**55.28**	**73.61**	**105.83**	**126.95**	**138.35**	**139.24**	**146.53**	**142.54**	**96.95**	**51.14**	**1115.72**

Source: Tea Board Govt. of India.

Table 2.4G: Statewise and month wise production data for the year 2012

(Quantity in mkg)

State/Month	Jan	Feb	Mar	Apr	May	Jun	Jul	Aug	Sep	Oct	Nov	Dec	Jan-Dec 2012
Assam Valley	0.20	0.10	10.52	32.26	49.50	67.04	70.45	84.93	80.81	68.50	53.45	19.49	537.25
Cachar	0.22	0.03	1.22	3.79	4.14	5.70	6.84	7.51	7.69	7.12	5.59	3.02	52.87
Total Assam	**0.42**	**0.13**	**11.74**	**36.05**	**53.64**	**72.74**	**77.29**	**92.44**	**88.50**	**75.62**	**59.04**	**22.51**	**590.12**
Dooars	0.65	0.41	7.04	7.25	12.71	17.97	18.98	22.08	21.54	23.39	16.94	7.75	156.71
Terai	1.56	0.38	6.99	3.80	10.00	10.79	12.55	14.91	14.88	17.03	12.96	7.81	113.66
Darj	0.00	0.00	0.21	1.18	0.85	0.83	1.34	1.59	1.28	0.87	0.57	0.21	8.93
Total West Bengal	**2.21**	**0.79**	**14.24**	**12.23**	**23.56**	**29.59**	**32.87**	**38.58**	**37.70**	**41.29**	**30.47**	**15.77**	**279.30**
Others	0.06	0.00	0.41	0.81	1.65	2.23	2.37	2.60	2.56	2.20	1.74	0.90	17.53
Total North India	**2.69**	**0.92**	**26.39**	**49.09**	**78.85**	**104.56**	**112.53**	**133.62**	**128.76**	**119.11**	**91.25**	**39.18**	**886.95**
Tamil Nadu	11.24	9.57	11.10	17.82	15.86	19.56	15.02	12.15	10.99	16.84	15.40	15.01	170.56
Kerala	4.58	3.33	3.38	3.67	7.93	6.55	5.00	4.83	4.00	7.87	6.41	5.55	63.10
Karnataka	0.38	0.32	0.42	0.41	0.78	0.53	0.47	0.30	0.36	0.67	0.53	0.55	5.72
Total South India	**16.20**	**13.22**	**14.90**	**21.90**	**24.57**	**26.64**	**20.49**	**17.28**	**15.35**	**25.38**	**22.34**	**21.11**	**239.38**
Total All India	**18.89**	**14.14**	**41.29**	**70.99**	**103.42**	**131.20**	**133.02**	**150.90**	**144.11**	**144.49**	**113.59**	**60.29**	**1126.33**

Source: Tea Board Govt. of India.

Table 2.4H: Statewise and month wise estimated production data for the year 2013 (Jan to October)

(Quantity in mkg)

State/Month	Jan	Feb	Mar	Apr	May	Jun	Jul	Aug	Sep	October	Jan–Oct, 2013
Assam Valley	0.41	0.11	8.62	39.69	42.66	69.71	86.03	85.23	81.45	87.31	501.22
Cachar	0.39	0.02	0.76	2.18	3.99	4.58	6.87	8.04	6.39	7.66	40.88
Total Assam	**0.80**	**0.13**	**9.38**	**41.87**	**46.65**	**74.29**	**92.90**	**93.27**	**87.84**	**94.97**	**542.10**
Dooars	0.69	0.40	10.46	6.97	16.48	18.24	24.91	25.12	24.94	25.40	153.61
Terai	1.26	0.23	10.85	3.80	10.78	14.86	15.65	16.24	15.62	17.29	106.58
Darjeeling	0.00	0.77	0.60	0.90	0.91	1.57	1.15	1.67	1.16	0.95	9.68
Total West Bengal	**1.95**	**1.40**	**21.91**	**11.67**	**28.17**	**34.67**	**41.71**	**43.03**	**41.72**	**43.64**	**269.87**
Others	0.05	0.01	0.80	1.44	2.18	2.75	3.62	3.41	3.26	3.42	20.94
Total North India	**2.80**	**1.54**	**32.09**	**54.98**	**77.00**	**111.71**	**138.23**	**139.71**	**132.82**	**142.03**	**832.91**
Tamil Nadu	13.53	8.82	10.93	14.55	16.08	18.95	13.35	10.73	16.30	18.72	141.96
Kerala	5.12	3.10	3.73	5.15	7.65	5.06	3.16	3.58	7.00	5.89	49.44
Karnataka	0.47	0.40	0.53	0.45	0.45	0.46	0.32	0.24	0.58	0.47	4.37
Total South India	**19.12**	**12.32**	**15.19**	**20.15**	**24.18**	**24.47**	**16.83**	**14.55**	**23.88**	**25.08**	**195.77**
Total All India	**21.92**	**13.86**	**47.28**	**75.13**	**101.18**	**136.18**	**155.06**	**154.26**	**156.70**	**167.11**	**1028.68**

Source: Tea Board Govt. of India.

Table 2.4I: Area (in hectares) under tea cultivation in India

States	1986	1992	1993	1994	1995	1996	1997	1998	1999	2000	2003	2005	2006	2007	2008	2009	2010	2011	2012
Assam	222,618	233,648	231,942	227,120	226,280	228,205	229,843	251,625	257735	266,512	271,589	300,502	311,822	321,319	322,214	322,214	322,214	322,210	322,210
West Bengal	99,129	100,971	100,489	99,967	101,190	102,650	103008	105,624	108,,754	107,479	113,351	114,525	1147,788	115,095	115,095	115,095	115,095	115,100	115,100
Tripura	6,453	6,058	5,991	5,938	5,952	6,064	6,235	6,355	6,482	6,623	8,268	8,710	8,710	8,962					
Bihar	444	22	25	76	76	76	76	762	1,348	1,350	2,000	2,000	2,000	2,000					
Uttar Pradesh	1,804	892	848	914	1,068	1,068	1,068	1,068	1,068	1,068	1,471	1,456	1,456	1,585					
Himachal Pradesh	2,063	2,063	2,063	2,063	2,312	2,325	2,325	2,325	2,325	2,325	2,348	2,348	2,348	2,348					
Manipur	104	154	180	343	347	347	347	536	746	907	1,319	1,319	1,319	1,319					
Sikkim	233	170	163	172	172	172	172	202	296	296	195	195	195	194					
Arunachal Pradesh	5	687	687	1,151	1,361	1,818	1,818	1,953	2,179	2,176	1,229	1,719	1,719	2,570					
Nagaland	8	187	187	237	256	415	472	472	1,012	1,,214	1,898	1,898	1,898	1,898					
Meghalaya	–	–	–	–	–	–	–	145	215	214	252	252	252	564					
Mizoram	–	–	–	–	–	–	–	350	360	351	750	650	650	650					
Orissa	100	14	214	219	219	219	218	214	214	391	214	214	214	214	22,304*	22,304*	22,304*	22,304*	22,304*
Tamil Nadu	38,041	38,673	38,831	48,854	48,958	48,984	49,671	63,543	69,155	74,398	75,619	80,939	81,276	80,462	80,462	80,462	80,462	80,460	80,460
Kerala	34,736	34,525	34,683	36,817	36,775	36,762	36,817	36,748	36,752	36,940	36,967	36,772	36,236	37,137	37,137	37,137	37,137	37,140	37,140
Karnataka	1,909	2,015	2,060	2,095	2,099	2,099	2,104	2,105	2,106	2,122	2,128	2,112	2,137	2,141	2,141	2,141	2,141	2,140	2,140
Total All India	407,647	420,289	418,363	425,966	427,065	431,245	434,294	474,027	490,747	504,366	519,598	555,,611	567020	578,458	579,353	579,353	579,353	579,350	579,350

* Breakup not released.

Table 2.5: Number, area, farm size, production level and productivity in smallholders and estate gardens

India: national level/years	2000	2003	2005	2007
A. Smallholders				
a. Number of STGs	110,396	127,366	13,9041	157,504
(Upto 10.12 hectares)				
b. Area under tea in hectare	NA	109,198	142,985	162,431
(% of total area)		(21.02)	(25.73)	(28.08)
c. Production in mkg	NA	180.66	231.29	257.46
(% of total tea)		(20.57)	(24.45)	(26.10)
d. Average farm size (hectare)	NA	0.86	1.03	1.03
e. Productivity (kg/hectare)	NA	1,654	1,617	1,585
B. Big growers/estates				
a. Number of big growers/estates	1,614	1,661	1,672	1,686
b. Area under tea in hectare	NA	410,400	412,626	416,027
(% of total area)		(78.98)	(74.27)	(71.92)
c. Production in mkg	NA	697.47	714.68	728.97
(% of total tea)		(79.43)	(75.55)	(73.90)
d. Average farm size (hectare)	NA	247.08	246.81	246.75
e. Productivity (kg/hectare)	NA	1,699	1,732	1,752

Note: NA - Not Available as data provided in Tea Statistics are not segregated between Smallholders and Estate Gardens.

enterprises but it is specially pronounced for agricultural production". Since most of the estate gardens suffer from old age bush, the Tea Board of India has already announced Special Purpose Tea Fund (SPTF) for replantation and rejuvenation of the sector.

As per the membership of various small growers' associations in different states, the number of small holdings is high. It was only during the late 1980s or early 1990s when started spreading to North-Eastern States such as Assam and West Bengal. The smallholders are unorganized and operate in fragmented landholdings. They face challenges of landownership regulations and related procedural problems. Technical know-how on tea husbandry and cultivation is very low and the integration of this unorganized sector with the plantation industry seems to be a challenging task. At present various agencies such as Smallholders Associations, Primary Producing Societies [Self-Help Groups (SHGs)], Bought-Leaf Factories (BLFs), and Co-operative Factories (CPFs) exist in the 15 small tea growing states. However, most of these agencies are found to be ineffective due to the lack of proper coordination and collective action in an integrated mr. By analyzing organizational innovations like BLFs, CPFs, SHGs, Federations-Associations-Confederations against the back drop of the emergence of STGs and their national and regional growth pattern, the present study try to identify the gaps in the existing policies and suggests new areas of research (Table 2.5A).

Despite the number of small growers having increased over the period, especially in the post 90s, large estates still account for major production of tea (78.8%) in

Table 2.5A: Registered small tea gardens in India

Region	Registered with tea board	Reported by associations	Percentage of registered growers
South India	61,773	68,000	90.8
North East	5,595	45,132	12.4
North India	9,903	58,256	17.0
Total India	**71,676**	**126,256**	**56.8**

Source: Compiled Report on Small Tea Growers (2006), Tea Board of India.

India. In Sri Lanka however, small growers produce 61% of the country's tea and in Kenya, small holdings accounted for 61.6% of production in 2000. In India, the majority of small tea growers are from Southern India, mainly the Nilgiris region.

It is a matter of serious concern that in spite of the significant differences between the large tea and the small tea plantations, very little attention has been given to identify the problems specific to small farms. Most often they are treated on par with the large tea estates. Farmer-based tea cultivation in India has started in 1930s in Nilgiris mainly by Bagada community (Hayami and Damodaran, 2004). A comprehensive study of Smallholders and Cooperative tea factories on the emergence of small tea growers in India was made by Bhowmik (1989). However, some information on small tea growers is available based on various official reports and studies conducted by different committees appointed by the government from time to time. Most of the reports suggest that the small tea plantations emerged in early 1960s in India and these were mainly concentrated in south Indian states of Tamil Nadu, Kerala and Karnataka. It is only during the late 1980s or in early 1990s that they spread in North-Eastern States including Assam and West Bengal.

Although the origin of small tea plantation in India is only a recent phenomena, during this short span of time it has acquired two distinct types of operations for the unorganized and organized sectors completely in tune with the international trends: The organized sector has a history of pld development extending over one and a half century since the third phase of colonial rule in India, and it was mainly developed to meet the needs of the colonial rulers.

Today, the situation is diametrically opposite of what it was under the colonial rule and the unorganized sector of tea industry is an outcome of the survival and sustainability of the thousands of unemployed youths in the backward pockets of the country. Most of the farms are small and owned mostly by individual owners using labor-intensive production techniques. The size of workforce in these individual farms is too small as compared to traditional estate gardens. Some studies have been made to trace the changing nature of organizational structure of tea plantations and suggest some survival strategy for small shareholders (Tables 2.5B and C).

The number of small tea gardens has registered a high increase in Southern India, particularly in Tamil Nadu. Around 53.9% of small growers are concentrated in Southern India whereas the share of small tea growers in Northern India is 46.1%.

Out of the tea produced by small tea growers in India, Northern India's share is 54.5%. Of this, small tea growers in Assam constitute the major share, both in the number of estates as well as in the production. In Southern India, the major share of

Table 2.5B: Share of small and estate tea gardens in India

Region	Small growers			Big growers		
	No. of estates	Area in hectare	Production	No. of estates	Area in hectare	Production
Assam	98.2	15.2	14.5	1.8	84.8	85.5
W. Bengal	96.5	8.4	17.1	3.5	91.6	82.9
Others	98.0	42.5	20.3	2.0	57.5	79.7
Northern India	**97.9**	**14.5**	**15.4**	**2.1**	**85.5**	**84.6**
Tamil Nadu	99.6	57.1	55.0	0.4	42.9	45.0
Kerala	97.5	13.0	3.4	2.5	87.0	96.6
Karnataka	50.0	3.9	4.0	50.0	96.1	96.0
Southern India	**99.4**	**41.9**	**39.2**	**0.6**	**58.1**	**60.8**
All India	**98.7**	**20.6**	**21.2**	**1.3**	**79.4**	**78.8**

Source: Tea Statistics (2003), Tea Board of India.

Table 2.5C: Share of small growers in various states
(Figures in brackets show the percentage share against All India levels)

Region	Small growers			Big growers			Total		
	Nos	Area	Pdn.	Nos	Area	Pdn.	Nos.	Area	Pdn.
Assam	42,492 (33.7)	41,249 (38.9)	62,770 (35.2)	780 (47.7)	229,434 (56.0)	370,557 (56.1)	43,272 (33.9)	270,683 (52.5)	433,327 (51.7)
W. Bengal	8,398 (6.7)	9,500 (8.9)	32,245 (18.1)	308 (18.8)	103,613 (25.3)	155,776 (23.6)	8,706 (6.8)	113,113 (21.9)	188,021 (22.4)
Others	7,277 (5.8)	7,355 (6.9)	2,108 (1.2)	148 (9.1)	9,967 (2.4)	8,292 (1.3)	7,425 (5.8)	17,322 (3.4)	10,400 (1.2)
North India	**58,167 (46.1)**	**58,104 (54.7)**	**9,712 (54.5)**	**1,236 (75.6)**	**343,014 (83.7)**	**534,625 (81.0)**	**59,403 (46.5)**	**401,118 (77.8)**	**631,748 (75.3)**
TN	61,985 (49.1)	43,157 (40.7)	78,764 (44.2)	228 (14.0)	32,462 (7.9)	64,357 (9.7)	62,213 (48.7)	75,619 (14.7)	143,121 (17.1)
Kerala	5,999 (4.8)	4,810 (4.5)	1,969 (1.1)	154 (9.4)	32,157 (7.8)	55,803 (8.5)	6,153 (4.8)	36,967 (7.2)	57,772 (6.9)
Karnataka	16 (0.0)	83 (0.1)	232 (0.1)	16 (1.0)	2,045 (0.5)	5,601 (0.8)	32 (0.0)	2,128 (0.4)	5,833 (0.7)
South India	**68,000 (53.9)**	**48,050 (45.3)**	**80,965 (45.5)**	**398 (24.4)**	**66,664 (16.3)**	**125,761 (19.0)**	**68,398 (53.5)**	**114,714 (22.2)**	**206,726 (24.7)**
Total India	**100.0**	**100.0**	**100.0**	**100.0**	**100.0**	**100.0**	**100.0**	**100.0**	**100.0**

Source: Tea Statistics (2003), Tea Board of India.

production as well as the number and area of production of small tea gardens belongs to Tamil Nadu.

Types of Tea Production in India

The pattern and types of production tea of directly linked to the market demand and different sale practices of each region. The market demands sometimes force producers to change the nature of production and mode of manufacturing of tea. The nature of production mainly includes chemical to organic forms; and the type of tea shifts from orthodox tea to CTC. The consistent demand for organic tea from Germany, for instance, forced some producers in Coonoor to stay with organic cultivation. The high demand from the EU countries for Darjeeling tea forced them to stick to orthodox production in some of the Darjeeling plantations. Tea is traditionally classified based on the degree or period of fermentation (oxidation) the leaves have undergone.

White tea: Made from young leaves (new growth buds) that have undergone no oxidation. White tea is produced in lesser quantities than most of the other types, and can be correspondingly more expensive than tea from the same plant processed by other methods. It is also less well-known in countries outside China.

Green tea: In the manufacture of green tea, the oxidation process is stopped after a minimal amount of oxidation by application of heat. The tea is processed within 1–2 days of harvesting.

Oolong: Oolong is semi-fermented tea, where the oxidation process takes 2–3 days.

Black tea: In black tea production, the tea leaves are allowed to completely oxidize. Black tea is the most common form of tea in South Asia (India, Sri Lanka, Bangladesh, etc) and also in Kenya. Black tea is further classified as either orthodox or CTC. Orthodox and CTC teas are further graded according to the post-production leaf quality by the Orange Pekoe (OP) system. Black tea contributes 97.7% of production, and Darjeeling tea 1.2% of production (or around 5 mkg annum) (Fig. 2.5).

Till the 1960s, orthodox tea dominated India's tea production. The share of orthodox tea was significant (32%) till the 1980s as given in the Table 2.6. However,

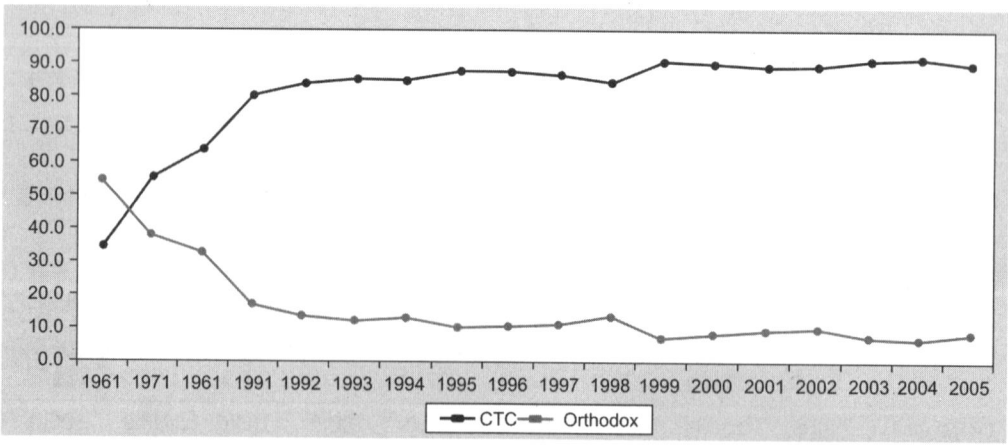

Fig. 2.5: Production of orthodox and CTC tea in India

Table 2.6: The trends in production of various types of teas in India

	North India					South India				Total				
	CTC	Orthd	Darjlng	Green	Total	CTC	Orthd	Darjlng	Green	CTC	Orthd	Darjlng	Green	Total
1961	118.8	115.1	10.1	29.3	273.3	3.3	76.2	1.6	81.1	122.1	191.3	10.1	30.9	354.4
1971	210.2	93.2	10.3	18.6	332.3	29.8	71.4	2	103.2	240	164.6	10.3	20.6	435.5
1981	299.3	119.3	12.2	7	437.8	58.2	63.8	0.6	122.6	357.5	183.1	12.2	7.6	560.4
1991	461.9	79.5	13.9	7.6	562.9	141.7	47.4	2.2	191.3	603.6	126.9	13.9	9.8	754.2
1992	485.1	65.9	12.4	7	570.4	125.6	33.9	2.4	161.9	610.7	99.8	12.4	9.4	732.3
1993	507	55.7	13	5.8	581.5	139.3	38.5	1.5	179.3	646.3	94.2	13	7.3	760.8
1994	498.8	50.8	11.1	7.3	568	137	47.4	0.5	184.9	635.8	98.2	11.1	7.8	752.9
1995	520.7	29.2	11.3	7.4	568.6	141.7	45.2	0.5	187.4	662.4	74.4	11.3	7.9	756
1996	542.8	36.9	10.6	7.8	598.1	138.1	43.4	0.5	182	680.9	80.3	10.6	8.3	780.1
1997	549.5	37.1	10.1	8	604.7	150.6	54.2	0.5	205.3	700.1	91.3	10.1	8.5	810
1998	594.1	59.5	10.3	6.8	670.7	144.1	58.8	0.5	203.4	738.2	118.3	10.3	7.3	874.1
1999	576	32.5	8.7	6	623.2	172.1	30.2	0.4	202.7	748.1	62.7	8.7	6.4	825.9
2000	590.1	35.7	9.3	5.6	640.7	170.3	35.3	0.6	206.2	760.4	71	9.3	6.2	846.9
2001	592.1	44.4	9.8	4.5	650.8	167.4	34.8	0.9	203.1	759.5	79.2	9.8	5.4	853.9
2002	570.4	48.4	9.2	3.8	631.8	174.7	31.1	0.9	206.7	745.1	79.5	9.2	4.7	838.5
2003	608	26.9	9.6	3.8	648.3	191.6	37.2	1	229.8	799.6	64.1	9.6	4.8	878.1
2004	618	28.8	10.1	5.3	662.2	196.8	32.5	1.5	230.8	814.8	61.3	10.1	6.8	893
2005	649.8	32.3	11.3	7.6	701	181.8	43.3	1.9	227	831.6	75.6	11.3	9.5	928
2006	678.5	30.6	11.7	8.8	729.6	189.6	34.9	1.8	226.3	868.1	65.5	11.7	10.6	955.9

Source: Tea Statistics (2005–2006), Tea Board of India.

since the 1990s, the constitutes of CTC tea have recorded a sharp rise and now shares 90.8% of tea production in India. The shares of orthodox tea (6.9%), Darjeeling tea (1.2%), Green tea (1.1%) are very marginal (Table 2.6A).

Made tea or tea manufactured from green tea leaves is generally classified into two types: (1) black tea and (2) green tea. Green tea is different from black tea since fermentation of green leaves is arrested in manufacturing green tea. Black tea includes two types, such as Orthodox tea and CTC tea. Both of these teas vary due to their manufacturing differences. Orthodox teas are manufactured with the help of orthodox roller in the process of rolling while CTC machine/Rotervan is used in rolling process in manufacturing CTC teas. India and Kenya produce more CTC whereas Sri Lanka produces more orthodox tea. The tea processing in any factory in the traditional way includes five phases, such as Withering, Rolling, Fermentation, Drying, Sorting and Grading (Table 2.6A).

The production method of orthodox tea consists of five stages: (1) withering, (2) rolling, (3) fermentation, (4) drying and (5) sorting.

- The freshly-picked green leaves are spread out to dry on ventilated trays. During this process, approximately 30% moisture is extracted from the leaves, making them soft and pliable for further processing. The leaves are then rolled by applying mechanical pressure to break up the cells and extract the cell sap. After 30 minutes, the leaves still damp from the sap are sieved to separate the finer leaves. These are spread out immediately for fermentation, while the remaining coarse leaves are rolled for a further 30 minutes under higher pressure. If necessary, this process is repeated several times. A short rolling time produces larger leaf grades, while longer rolling breaks the leaves up more resulting in smaller grades. During the rolling process, the cell sap runs out and reacts with oxygen, thus triggering the fermentation process. At the same time, the essential oils responsible for the aroma are released.

- After rolling, the tea is spread out in layers approximately 10 cm high for one to three hours in a cool, damp atmosphere to finish off the fermentation process. During this process, the substances contained in the cell sap oxidize. In this production phase, the green leaf gradually turns a copper color. The color and typical odor tell the person supervising the process how far the fermentation has progressed. Various chemical reactions cause the leaf to heat up during fermentation. It is critical for the quality of the tea that the fermentation process be interrupted at its peak, when the temperature is at its highest.

- Next, the tea is dried with hot air at a temperature of approximately 85–88°C in order to interrupt the oxidation process. The residual moisture is thereby extracted from the leaves, the extracted sap dries on the leaf and the copper-colored leaf turns dark brown to black. Finally, the dried tea is sieved to separate the different leaf grades. The orthodox production method provides teas of all leaf grades: leaf, broken, fanning and dust. Leaf grades only refer to the leaf size, however: they are not necessarily an indication of the quality of the tea.

Apart from orthodox, CTC and green tea, powder tea which is known as "Instant tea" is also being manufactured in India and in a few other tea-producing countries of the world like Kenya and Sri Lanka. The Instant tea is manufacture in separate factories known as Instant tea factories. The procedure for manufacturing Instant tea is different from that of black tea or green tea. The raw materials used for

Table 2.6A: Description and characteristics of CTC tea

Category	Size	Grade name	Appearance	Liquor
CTC leaf grade	Over mesh 10	Flower pekoe (FP)	Biggest granular size tea with embedded fiber or clean appearance	Thin and plain, 150–200 cups/kg.
	Over mesh 12	Pekoe (PEK)	Bolder grade with granulation and black and clean appearance	Color with medium strength 170–200 cups/kg.
	Over mesh 16	Broken orange pekoe (BOP)	Medium sized and granular clean teas	Very colory and strong with brightness and briskness, 250–300 cups/kg.
	Over mesh 16	Broken pekoe (BP)	Medium granulation with a little flaky particles	Very colory and strong with brightness and briskness, 300–350 cups/kg.
	Over mesh 24	Pekoe fannings (PF)	Small sized andgranular shape with a little flackiness	Very strong and colorywith some brightness and briskness, 300–350 cups/kg.
	Over mesh 24	Pekoe fannings one	–	–
	Through mesh 24	Pekoe dust one (PD1)	Granular finer particles with clean appearances	Very colory and strong, 300–350 cups/kg.
CTC dust grade	Over mesh 30	Pekoe dust (PD)	–	–
	Over mesh 40	Red dust (RD)	Finer particles of dust with clan appearance smaller than PD	Colory and strong withsome brightness and briskness, 300–350 cups/kg.
	Over mesh 50	Super red dust (SRD)	Black and cleanpowdery appearance smaller than RD	Good color with morestrength and brightness, 350–400 cups/kg.
	Through mesh 50	Super fine dust (SFD)	Black clean very fine particles with heavy density	Colory and more strength and some brightness, 450–500 cups/kg.
	Through mesh 50	Fine dust (FD)	Finer powdery dust clean fiber	Colory with some strength, brightness and briskness, 450–500 cups/kg.

manufacturing instant tea are green tea leaves and/or tea waste. The manufacture of Instant tea in India started in 1960. The Fig. 2.6 shows the share of export of value added tea.

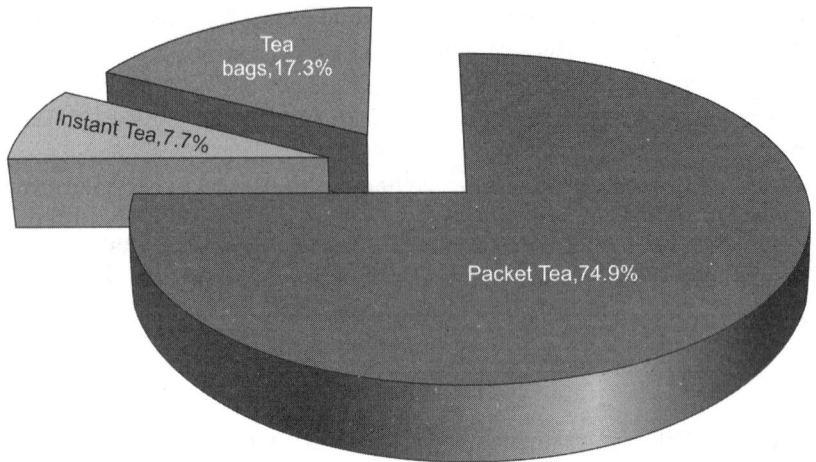

Fig. 2.6: Total value added tea (figures in 2005)

Instant tea and tea bags are generally known as "convenience tea" since these are convenient for consumers and less hazardous. Moreover, in order to preserve the quality of tea during its different stages of trading activities particularly in retail trading and also to maintain the uniformity of the quality to the extent possible, black tea or green tea are packed either in original form or in blended form in small consumer packs. These are known as "Packet tea". Depending on the system of tea processing, tea is classified into black tea and green tea. Black tea is obtained by so called fermentation process whereas for making green tea, fermentation is prevented. The type of the tea and its production such as orthodox, CTC or even organic tea mainly depends on the demand from the domestic and international market. The changes in international demands greatly influence the production of various types of tea.

Bought Leaf Factories

The BLFs have a major role in controlling the mechanism of price determination and quality of tea. BLFs do not have their own tea plantations and depend on small farmers for green leaves to produce made tea. BLFs have direct linkage to the wholesalers, up country buyers and foreign market. Several BLFs have mushroomed in West Bengal and in South India in recent years. Several BLFs do not have efficient technicians. This has led to the flooding of inferior quality tea in the domestic market. Smaller players offer this tea at cheaper rates. Market analysts say that the poor quality tea produced by these players not only affects domestic price levels, but also damages the quality perception of the Indian tea in export markets (Table 2.6B).

There has been a steady growth in the numbers of private tea manufacturing factories in India in the post 90s. During 2004, there were more than 162 tea factories in Assam producing 77 mkg of tea, 79 factories in West Bengal producing 50 mkg of tea and 185 factories in Tamil Nadu producing 81 mkg of tea. In Kerala, 18 factories produced 3 mkg of tea.

Table 2.6B: Growth of BLFs in India

Region	2001		2002		2003		2004	
	No.	Production (in Mn .kg)	No.	Production (in Mn. kg)	No.	Production (in Mn. kg)	No.	Production (in Mn. kg)
Assam	119	43.0	139	53.29	151	65.32	162	77.6
WB	44	24.6	56	33.44	69	37.74	79	49.59
Others	4	0.5	4	1.67	8	2.78	9	3.04
North India	163	67.5	199	88.4	228	105.8	250	130.23
TN	155	65.6	159	67.43	182	75.9	185	80.72
Kerala	13	2.1	13	1.49	17	3.03	18	2.95
South India	168	67.6	172	68.6	200	78.19	205	83.79
India	331	135.2	371	157	428	183.99	455	214.02

Source: Tea Statistics (2003), Tea Board of India and Tea Statistics (2005), J Thomas Pvt. Ltd.

The average price at state level shows that estate factories fetch a higher price compared to co-operative and BLFs except in Tripura. In Tripura, BLFs get better price than estate factories. The adoption of advanced technology in BLFs also facilitates many of them to achieve the production of high quality tea and a high price from auction. The newly-opened BLFs are technically better off with upgraded technologies than many of the estate factories. Hence, the made tea is also better in terms of quality at the level of manufacturing. In many of the BLFs, performance is mainly influenced by the basic raw materials, i.e. green leaves from the small growers. Since the competition from BLFs has been high in recent period the BLFs owners never strictly monitor the leaf standards. At the same time, it is also noted that some of the BLF owners are in constant contact with small growers and maintain the standards and so they can maintain good quality and get higher price in auctions. Even if new BLFs also sell tea outside, it can be seen that BLFs produced tea fetches lesser price in the tea auctions compared to the estate factories. However, in individual cases, some of the BLFs get high price for their tea in auctions. In the Niligiris itself, there are 55 BL factories and some of them obtain an average price that is higher than estate factories. On the other hand, some of the BLFs could auction only at a lower price which is far below the average auction price. However, the average auction price of the BLF is far below the average price of the estate factories.

Quality Constraints of Green Leaves

The term "quality" in its broadest sense is used as a description of all the characters of tea by which it is judged on its market value. So, quality means the summation of the desirable attributes comprising internal and external characters like aroma/ flavor, strength, color, briskness and character of infused leaf. In scientific terminology, a maximum platform of quality in terms of chemical characterization of tea has been set by the Bureau of Indian Standard (BIS), followed by setting up of "safety" requirement of teas under the Prevention of Food Adulteration Act, 1954 and Rules, 1955 (PFA). It should be made clear that terminologies like super fine, pekoe, tipsy, broken, silvery and so on, associated with tea culture, are different from the specifications on the minimum chemical limits of tea. Most of the chemical parameters are influenced by standard of plucking, climate and seasonal variations. The quality of tea is a highly variable attribute. There is a saying that teas of today may not match with those of tomorrow even in the same garden and factory.

The "quality" of the tea conforming to the specification laid down in the PFA Act may vary. The quality of tea also varies between garden to garden and also between the teas manufactured at different times in a particular garden. The green tea leaves of the plant belonging to the species of Camellia Sinensis have a natural "aroma". The efforts of the tea manufacturer are generally aimed at to maintain the natural aroma in the made tea as far as possible.

The quality of "tea" depends primarily on the nature and chemical composition of the plucked leaf which is again dependent on the type of bush, the growing conditions and the kind of plucked leaf like coarseness, fineness, etc. Only careful and proper processing will bring out the full potential of the green leaf. Each of the characteristics on which tea is assessed by trade is affected by one or more the factors involved both in the field and in the factory. Since a variety of factors play a role and the production of a particular character is usually obtained at the expense of another, pre-processing and processing conditions are generally adjusted so as to bring about the most desirable characters in a tea made from a given material.

So, the factors affecting tea quality apart from those involved in processing can be distinguished into three groups: (1) genetic, (2) environmental and (3) cultural:

1. Tea quality is primarily determined by the genetic properties of the tea planted and those of the tea bush in particular.
2. Both soil and climate is influence the quality of tea. Climatic condition including temperature, humidity, sunshine duration, rainfall, North-South facing gardens are important in determining quality.
3. Field operation like pruning, fertilizing, shading, plucking round and plucking standard are also playing the important role in determining the quality of tea.

South and north facing of tea gardens/bushes and other climatic conditions, shade/rain fall also affect quality of leaf. Generally, the producer and the Tea Board control the quality of the product, but at different levels. At the same time, brokers also play an influential role in maintaining the quality of the product. On the one hand, they maintain continuous interaction with the producers and on the other hand, they get an indication of the market from the buyers.

The intervention of the Tea Board and other agencies to create awareness to increase quality and technical upgradation among BLFs has however increased productivity and quality of mad e tea. Table 2.6C shows the impact of quality upgradation programs for BLFs in Coonoor.

Tea Processing

Tea processing is an agro based non-conventional industrial sector with activities concentrated mostly in hilly areas. The environmental status of the sector has not been compiled so far even though it is already recognized as an industrial activity by the Government. The Central Pollution Control Board has therefore undertaken a project for preparation of "Comprehensive Industry Document on Tea Processing Industry". The report covers the national and international scenario of tea processing

Table 2.6C: Impact of quality upgradation programs for BLFs

Parameters	Existing practices	QUP technologies	Achievement in QUP
		Recommended	Exp. conducted factories (in per cent)
Raw material	Three to four leaf and bud	Three to four leaf and bud	38.5
Withering	5 hours	12 hours	92.8
Rolling (temp.) 38.5%	> 350°C	> 350°C	38.5
Fermentation	30 minutes	90 minutes	85.7
Drying	290°F	250°F	42.8
Theaflavin (TF)% for brightening and briskness	< 0.5	> 1.0	10
Total liquor color (TLC)	< 2	> 3	32.8
No. of cups per kg of tea	< 300	> 450	–
Tea grade	Moderate	Premium	38.5
Price realization	Rs 35/-	Rs 45/-	25

Source: Tea Board & UPASI–KVK (2004).

industry, and its categorization, process details, environment aspects related to wastewater, air pollution and solid waste management along with the proposed environmental standards.

One of the important agro-industrial crop which supports Indian economy largely, is tea. Tea is indigenous to India and is an area where the country can obviously take a lot of pride. Not only because tea is a major player in the earning of foreign exchange but also contributes substantially to the country's gross domestic product (GNP). The technology of tea cultivation and processing has been developed within the industry aided by applied research which was largely funded by the tea companies themselves. This has helped to grow tea industry as a technically competent entity and also allowed the generation of more academic and fundamental investigations which might bring future rewards. Now, when global market has opened, all commodities are facing stiff competitions tea is not an exception. In fact, one of the major reasons for the refusal of Indian tea by the consumer worldwide is the cost of production and marketing.

Packing

Sorted and graded black tea is normally packed in a plywood tea chest. The chests are assembled using various components, like the plywood shooks, battens, metal fittings, iron nails and aluminum foil with tissue paper lining. Recently, attention has been drawn to the use of non-conventional materials like paper, multiwall paper sacks and polythene lined jute bags.

Fuel and Power Requirements

Factories require a power source for driving machinery and a fuel source for heat generation. The nature and combination of fuel and power sources varies considerably depending on the natural resources of the tea growing area concerned, and on the economics applying to possible alternatives. The efficiency of the drying system and local meteorological conditions will also effect the fuel consumption. An indicative energy consumption pattern of different sources of energy is presented in Table 2.6D.

Table 2.6D: Thermal energy consumption of different energy sources

Fuel	Average calorific value	Amount of fuel consumption per kg. of made tea	Average energy consumed (KW hr/kg. made tea)
Coal	5,830 kcal/kg	1.125 kg	7.62
Leco wood natural gas	6,900 kcal/kg	0.625 kg	5.01
TD oil direct	3,500 kcal/kg	2.000 kg	8.13
TD oil indirect	9,000 kcal/Nm³	0.62500 Nm³	6.53
	10,500 kcal/kg	0.300 kg	3.65
	–	0.500 kg	6.10

Black Tea Processing

Overall Steps

Black tea manufacturing technology involves disruption of the cellular integrity of tea shoots; in doing so, the mixing of substrates, polyphenols and the enzymes, polyphenols oxidase is facilitated. This results in the initiation of a series of biochemical and chemical reactions with the uptake of atmospheric oxygen and formation of pigmented hot water soluble polyphenolic compounds, characteristic of black tea.

Black tea processing consists of the following unit operations:

- Withering (partial removal of moisture)
- Rolling/disruption (size reduction)
- Oxidation/fermentation (biochemical reactions in the presence of oxygen)
- Drying (completion of moisture removal)
- Sorting (fiber removal; grading based on size)

Of these, chemical changes occur primarily during withering, fermentation and drying.

Withering

Withering is carried out to prepare the green tea shoots biochemically and physically for subsequent manufacturing operations. Withering essentially consists of storage of green shoots for about 12–20 hours with the partial removal of moisture (known as physical wither) from the leaf. Withering is accompanied by certain chemical changes (known as chemical wither) which may affect fermentation and thereby, the quality of the final product. Chemical wither is essentially a time-temperature dependent process. Some of these changes are dependent on moisture loss while others are independent.

The major physical change during withering is the increase in cell membrane permeability and consequently, the leaf becomes flaccid. The increased permeability of the membrane has a great effect on the mixing of substrates and enzymes during fermentation.

Withering is also accompanied by the activation of oxidative, hydrolytic and proteolytic enzymes, causing significant changes in the chemical composition of tea shoot, as a result the levels of soluble protein, free amino acids and simple sugars increase in the withered leaf. Amino acids increase due to the breakdown of proteins by the enzyme pepsidase. Amino acids are primarily the precursors of the aromatic compounds.

Caffeine content increases with withering. The increase in caffeine content is greater if the withering is accompanied by loss of moisture. Caffeine forms a complex with theaflavins (TF) thearubigins and "Creams" down from the liquor; this creaming down is a desirable cup character for black tea.

The chemical wither also increases the level of organic acids and improves polyphenol oxidase (PPO) activity. The increase in organic acids will have an obvious effect of reducing pH and TF formation is increased as pH tends toward 5.0. The effect of increased PPO activity is beneficial for more TF formation provided oxygen availability is not limited during catechin oxidation. Volatile compounds essentially impart aroma to the finished product. Volatile compounds present in the tea are classified into two groups: (1) Group-I compounds, which are deleterious to the tea quality and (2) Group-II compounds, which impart sweet flowery aroma to tea and its presence is highly desirable. The ratio of Group-II compounds to Group-I compounds is known as the flavor index and it is a semiquantitative method of describing the aroma quality of tea. Tea with higher values of flavor index normally has better aroma quality. Withering improves flavor index and thereby, sweet aroma.

Leaf Disruption

This stage in processing is described in a number of ways, e.g. rolling, cutting, crushing, tearing, but the basic requirements are size reduction with a degree of cell disruption to allow the exposure of the new surfaces to air in the subsequent fermentation stage.

The LTP machine consists of a central rotor with a number of knives and beaters, where the leaf is bruised and cut by the rotating knives and beaters. The leaf next enters into the rolling section. The rolling is done either by orthodox rollers or by a combination of orthodox rolling and the CTC machines. The surface of each roller is made up of a number of segments made of stainless steel. The withered leaf passes through a battery of three to five such CTC machines which cause the leaf to get CTC.

Fermentation

Tea fermentation is essentially the oxidation of simple substrates into complex characteristic substances by endogenous enzymes present in the tea leaf. This distinguishes tea manufacture from other food processes in which exogenous fermentation inducing agents are added to the raw material.

Fermentation is not confined only to the period during which the leaf lies in the fermenting drums, racks or floors. It commences from the time the cells are bruised and extends until the enzymes are deactivated in the drier. As a first step during fermentation, the catechins are oxidized to highly reactive transient orthoquinones by PPO. The quinones in turn dimerize to produce TF, which are orange red substances that contribute significantly to astringency, briskness, brightness and the color of tea beverage. TF comprise 0.3–2.0% of the dry weight of black tea.

Further transformations of dicatechins and TF yield compounds which are known as the arubigins, comprising about 9–19% of black tea, are red brown in color and contribute to color, strength and mouth feel of liquor.

While TF content of tea increases during fermentation and starts declining after reaching a peak the arubigin content continually increases throughout the fermentation. In actual practices, the completion of fermentation is judged by the change in color (green to coppery) and the pleasant aroma that develops. However, chemically optimum fermentation may be assessed by monitoring the profile of TF content and taking the time required for the production of maximum. TF Proper balance between TF and the arubigins is also essential for a good cup of tea.

Like any other enzymic reaction, the rate of fermentation primarily depends upon the concentration and relative proportion of individual substrates, availability of oxygen, the activity of enzyme, pH and the temperature. Since it is not a homogeneous system, the degree of contact between the enzyme and the substrate will be important. In addition, mass transfer of air to the reaction side is crucial in controlling the rate and product profile of fermentation.

During fermentation, the PPO activity is known to decrease due to the formation of insoluble complexes of polyphenol oxidation products with the enzyme protein by feedback action. This precipitation process increases as fermentation continues and the temperature of the fermentation leaf increases.

Both reaction rate and the ultimate concentration of products are affected by the concentration of oxygen. TF production will be inhibited if the concentration of the oxygen in the air falls below normal, which can occur in dead spots' in a forced-air fermentation system. By increasing the oxygen concentration of the air in a fermentation unit, it is possible to achieve higher TF levels.

Temperature is one of the most important factors influencing the complex series of enzymic and chemical reactions during fermentation. Temperature not only affects the rate of fermentation but also the ultimate level of TF in tea. As a rule of thumb for altering the fermentation times to suit ambient temperature conditions, the rate of fermentation at any temperature will be taken as 1.7 to 1.8 times as fast as that a 10°C cooler. Although, increase in temperature accelerates the fermentation rate, maximum TF occurs, when fermented at low temperature for a long time. This happens because as the temperature increases, the breakdowns reactions become more rapid than the TF formation reaction, and ultimately less TF is produced. Another advantage of low temperature fermentation is that the peak of TF production is maintained for a longer period. Even a delay in firing results in a detectable difference in quality.

Drying

The drying of fermented tea has three major objectives; to terminate the biochemical functions by heat denaturation of the enzyme; to reduce the moisture to increase the shelf-stability of black tea and finally, to enhance chemical reactions responsible for black tea character and flavor.

The PPO enzymes which convert catechins into TF are not inactivated as soon as the leaf enters the drier. In fact, the fermentation process is actually accelerated and continues at a faster rate till the temperature of leaf reaches 55°C at which the enzyme is completely inactivated. Hence, any unoxidized catechin will continue to be converted into TF until oxidase enzyme has been inactivated. It has been reported that 10–15% of TF content in black tea is formed during the first 10 minutes of drying.

A noticeable effect of drying is the change in color of dried leaf brought about by the transformation of chlorophyll into pheophytin, which imparts the desired black color. During drying, the reduction in stringency of fermented tea occurs due to the combination of polyphenols with tea leaf proteins at the elevated drying temperature. Drying causes an overall reduction in the quantity of volatile compounds, although certain aromatic compounds continue to be formed. Relative distribution of chemical compounds in the tea bush is presented in Table 2.6E.

The fermented tea leaf is dried by exposing to a draft of hot air; the process takes about 30 minutes. Some of the flavor characteristics of the final product are developed as the leaf heats up during the drying process, and eventually the leaf temperature and moisture levels bring about the enzyme destruction or inactivation necessary for preservation of the product. The conventional tea dryer is basically a rectangular chamber. The tea to be dried is spread on perforated trays. These dryers are driven by trays-carrying chains and sprockets running on angle iron runners. The movement of the trays with the leaf is counter-current to the draft of hot air.

Table 2.6E: Relative distribution of chemical compounds in the tea bush

Compound	Flush	Mature leaf	Green stem	Mature stem	Root	Seed
Polyphenols	++	+	+	+	+	+
Amino acids	++	+	+	+	++	+
Nucleotides	+	+	+	+	+	+
Phosphate ester	+	+	ND	ND	ND	ND
Caffeine,	++	+	+	+	+	+
Theobromine	+	+	+	+	+	+
Carbodase	+	+	+	ND	ND	+
Lipids	+	+	+	+	+	+
Organic acids	+	+	+	+	+	+
Chlorophyll	+	++	+	+	+	ND
Carotenoids	+	+	+	+	+	+
Unsaponifiables	+	+	+	+	+++	+++
Saponin	+	+	+	+	+	++
Minerals	+	+	+	+	+	+
Volatile compound	+	+	+	+	+	+

Note: ND denotes not determined and signs denote relative distribution of each compound.

Recently, the technology of fluid-bed drying at 125°C for 20 minutes is being followed in many cases. Normally, the leaf enters the dryer with 60–72% moisture, depending on the cutting process used, and is dried down to 2.5–3.5% moisture.

Cooling, Sorting and Grading

The hot dried tea is cooled on the factory floor before it is sent for sorting and grading. Sorting is the operation in which tea particles of the bulk are separated into various grades of different sizes and forms confirming to trade requirements. In other words, it basically converts the bulk into finished products. The process of sorting has two objectives: (1) to enhance the value (2) to impart quality.

Sorting enhances the appearance and quality of liquor; at the same time it can also deteriorate the quality. The presence of fiber or flakes of coarse leaf in a primary grade causes harshness and their removal makes the liquor mellow. The cleaning of fiber also improves the black appearance of tea which is desirable. Bloom is indicative of liquor character; over sorting and over cleaning can result in loss of bloom. Usually, a tea which has not been well fired, loses bloom more quickly. If tea absorbs moisture during the cleaning process, liquors can deteriorate and its keeping quality reduces. Sorting of bulk has to be done in three stages: (1) cleaning of fiber (2) grading and (3) winnowing.

The initial separation of leaf and dust can be carried out on a Middleton fitted with a sieve on No. 24 mesh on the top and No. 10 mesh on the bottom. Tea particles which pass through mesh No. 24 are collected separately and graded further in the dust grade sorter. Similarly, particles which are retained on No. 24 mesh and pass through mesh No. 10 are graded separately in the leaf grade sorter. Particles retained over 10 are generally taken for reconditioning.

Both leaf and dust grades are further fractionated either in Trinic sorters or vibro sorters. The recommended standard mesh sizes are opening for different CTC grades. After sifting, each grade is finally cleaned by winnowing during which fibers and flaky teas are removed. Generally, super fine dust (SFD) and fine dust (FD) grades are cleaned separately in the fibrex after winnowing.

Labor Problems

The Indian tea industry which is on a revival path is now faced with a new challenge an acute labor shortage. While the labor crisis has taken an acute shape in the Southern Indian tea estates, the gardens in Assam and West Bengal have just started to feel the pinch of labor shortage.

Neither the tea industry nor the labor unions attribute the crisis to the wage structure. Both agree that the change in the aspirational level of the estate workers is prompting them to look around for jobs that do not put them in the "worker" category.

"In recent times, we are witnessing much absenteeism in the estates. There are three reasons. One, the workers are aspiring for a job, which will free them from the brand name of a "tea estate worker". Second, the continuous agitation for a separate Gorkhaland is forcing some to leave the hills of Darjeeling and look elsewhere for a job. And thirdly, the central government's scheme for 100-day work is also attracting quite a number of temporary workers, who are generally employed for a 9-month period. If this trend continues then Darjeeling tea estates will face an acute labor shortage in the coming years". There are nearly 55,000 permanent workers at the Darjeeling tea estates. An additional 35,000 people work as temporary workers during the tea season. "Productivity has emerged as a crucial issue for us. The Darjeeling tea industry is now planning to tie-up with Indian Institute of Plantation Management (IIPM) to find out ways to increase the productivity of our existing workforce".

Labor unions feel that workers at the tea estates are aspiring for an urban life. "The wage structure at the gardens can meet the requirement of the workers. They now aspire to enjoy an urban lifestyle". To tide over the crisis of labor shortage, South Indian tea estates have gone for mechanization of certain operations in the estates. Some of the estates have started sourcing people from Bihar and Orissa. "In some of the gardens in South India, machines carry out 50–55% of the estate jobs. However, we always see that quality does not suffer due to the usage of machines".

However, estates in Assam do not think mechanization is the answer to a drop in supply of workers. "In Assam, there is some shortage of temporary workers during the peak season in certain pockets. This is happening as these workers are availing the central government's 100-day (NREGA) scheme as now the labor shortage has not acquired any acute shape".

Workers in Tea Industry

Tea plantation industry not only occupies a very important role in the national economy as an earner of foreign exchange but it also provides gainful employment to a large number of people. This industry which is largely labor intensive provides employment to a large number of female workers. The industry accounted for 20% and 10% of the total labor force employed in the private sector in 1961 and in 2002, respectively. The ratio of tea labor to total labor employed in the private sector has registered a declining trend in recent years (Table 2.7).

Table 2.7: Ratio of tea labor to total labor employed

(Number in lakhs)

Year	Total number of labor employed in private sector	Number of labor employed in tea**	Share
1961	50	10	19.8
1971	67	8	11.3
1981	73	8	11.0
1991	76	8	10.5
1997	79	8	10.1
1998	80	8	10.0
1999	79	8	10.1
2000	80	8	10.0
2001	81	8	10.0
2002	82	8	10.0

* Tea Statistics, Tea Board, Kolkata.

Tea plantation in the country provides employment opportunities to the rural poor living in the remotest areas. It is a highly labor intensive industry and engages maximum employment per household. Laborers are employed in the tea industry both in fields and factory operations. They are mainly resident and also outside workers. Resident workers are the permanent laborers of the estate whereas outside workers are temporary and casual laborers. Both resident and outside workers are again divided into male, female, children and adolescent depending upon the nature of the work involved. Productivity and labor per hectare is given below Table 2.7A.

The tea industry is labor intensive and women are major workers among them. Although there is only a marginal increase of women workers from 2001 to 2005 (Table 2.7B), women workers still constitute the majority of workers of tea industry in India. In the context of closure of tea gardens and crisis in tea industry, a number of studies have pointed out the issues and challenges of workers in tea industry. Over the years, adolescent workers have declined and now they account for only 2.8% at the all India level (Table 2.7C).

Table 2.7A: Productivity and labor per hectare during 2000 in North India

State	District	No. of estates	Area in hect.	Prod. in Th, kg	Est. avg. daily labor	Lab. per haect.	Prod. per hect.	Prod. per lab.
Assam	Darrang	829	41,037	77,030	11,4629	2.79	1,877	672
	Goalpara	249	3,460	6,297	9,508	2.75	1,820	662
	Kamrup	54	3,442	4,302	8,918	2.59	1,250	482
	Dibrugarh	21,388	93,076	163,426	19,7145	2.12	1,756	829
	Lakhimpur	326	4,815	9,068	14,056	2.92	1,883	645
	Nowgong	213	7,994	11788	18,910	2.37	1,475	623
	Sibsagar	15,735	74,807	119,978	15,6825	2.1	1,604	765
	Karbi Anglong	143	1,869	1,945	4,512	2.41	1,041	431
	N. Cachar	8	4,004	6,179	10,320	2.58	1,543	599
	Cachar	206	32,008	49,206	67,708	2.12	1,537	727
	Total Assam	39,151	26,652	44,9219	60,2531	2.26	1,686	746
West Bengal	Darjeeling	85	17,228	9,281	51,515	2.99	539	180
	Terai	910	20,548	43,291	38,420	1.87	2,107	1,127
	Dooars	545	69,703	128,964	16,3524	2.35	1,850	789
	Total W. Bengal	1,540	10,7479	18,1536	25,3459	2.36	1,689	716
Others	Tripura	292	6,623	6,431	12,105	1.83	971	531
	Bihar	244	1,350	538	50	0.04	399	10,760
	Uttar Pradesh	11	1,068	264	387	0.36	247	682
	Manipur	39	907	96	504	0.56	106	190
	Sikkim	74	296	105	392	1.32	355	268
	Arunachal Pradesh	50	2,176	993	2,086	0.96	456	476
	Nagaland	94	1214	43	228	0.19	35	189

Table 2.7B: Estimated number of labor employed in tea industry

Category	2001	2002	2003	2004	2005
Women workers	606,009 (49.2)	618,134 (49.2)	618,630 (49.2)	620,750 (49.4)	623,727 (49.5)
Male workers	579,471 (47.0)	589,607 (47.0)	589,854 (47.0)	597,835 (47.5)	600,035 (47.7)
Adolescent	46,670 (3.8)	47,359 (3.8)	47,726 (3.8)	39,025 (3.1)	35,038 (2.8)
Total	**1,232,150**	**1,255,100**	**1,256,210**	**1,257,610**	**1,258,800**

Table 2.7C: Workforce in Indian tea industry-state wise

Category	2001	2002	2003	2004	2005
All India	1,232,150	1,256,210	1,256,210	1,257,610	1,258,800
Assam	611,063	619,663	619,322	617,518	618,139
Karnataka	3,837	3,953	4,403	4,508	4,769
Kerala	77,198	79,524	87,184	90,358	90,148
Other States	16,818	17,055	16,614	16,527	16,659
Tamil Nadu	267,665	275,723	268,351	266,027	266,383
Total North India	8834,50	895,900	896,272	896,717	8975,00
Total South India	348,700	359,200	359,938	360,893	361,300
West Bengal	255,569	259,182	260,336	262,672	262,702

Source: Tea Statistics (2003), Tea Board of India, www.teaboardofindia.com

Indian Tea Industry—Supply Side Constraints

The Indian tea industry is facing various supply side constraints. The rate of growth of land under tea cultivation dropped from the level of 15%+ during the 1970s and the 1980s to about 6–7% during the 1990s. Growth in land under tea cultivation was much higher in Kenya and Indonesia during the 1990s. India already has the second highest area under tea cultivation after China and further scope for expansion is limited.

India's cost of production is higher than that of Kenya and Sri Lanka essentially due to the higher production overheads, besides labor costs. Thus Indian CTC tea is less competitive than Kenyan produced tea on the issue of pricing alone. With the opening up of the Indian market post-*World Trade Organization* (post-WTO); a possible scenario is that cheaper imports may cater to the domestic demand while finer quality tea could be diverted to export markets.

The inward-looking nature of the tea industry has resulted in a lack of innovation and genuine value creation efforts and the result is a rather diluted export focus due to lack of competitiveness in international markets. Consumer satisfaction more than production efficiency is the key to long-term survival and growth. The Indian tea industry thus has to move toward "productizing" Indian tea into a "consumer product". It needs to shift away from the commodities, nature of exports in order to move up the value-curve.

The industry needs to address the issue of value creation through a concerted effort that addresses the product form and the delivery system (with the accent on convenience and innovation in packaging). Focused brand building and a marketing campaign that positions tea as a "healthy alternative to other beverages" and reinforces the superior value of Indian tea, are critical. The industry also needs to establish strategic alliances in its major markets.

Small Tea Growers—Assam

The days of large plantations seem to be finally over. Assam now has a record number of STGs. A recent survey (New Emerging Sector) by the state government has put the number at around 68,465 in 14 districts. Assam produces nearly 55% of India's total tea production of 980 mkg. Major concentration of the small growers is in five upper Assam districts, which accounts for 94% of small growers in 14 districts of the Brahmaputra valley. The small growers now produce nearly 100 mkg of tea annually, which is largely of CTC variety.

The peak growth of small growers, according to the Assam government, came in 1995–2005. The most insurgency-infested districts of Tinsukia and Dibrugarh have witnessed the highest number of small growers. Presently, around 117,000 acres of land are under unorganized sector of small growers in the Brahmaputra Valley, the traditional tea growing area. The survey has revealed that around 5 lakh families are involved in this sector where 87% of the holdings are less than 3 acres and only 0.4% holdings are above 15 acres. Around 67% of the bushes are over 10 years of age and only 8% of tea bushes are over 15 years of age. While average productivity of the state is 2,379 kg per acre, Dibrugarh small growers produce 4,609 kg per acre and Tinsukias 3,947 kg per acre. Only 1,297 small growers are registered with Tea Board and only 1,055 small growers availed incentives from the board. A senior Tea Board official said that efforts are on to register all the small growers and implement schemes to facilitate them.

New Rules for Assam Tea Units

India's largest tea producer, Assam, will adopt Kenyan model of regulating tea processing units to ensure quality. The state government will regulate the opening of BLFs in the state. The government has put on hold issue of fresh registration of BLFs for the last 3 years in view of the mushrooming of BLFs. The state government in consultation with Tea Board and tea planters' bodies has come up with a new set of guidelines for opening BLFs and stand alone factories. Hundreds of applications are pending for BLFs.

According to guidelines, the availability of green leaf per BLFs should be around 25 lakh kg annually. The government is now armed with production database of green leaf in each tea producing districts. Under the regulation, area under 20-km radius from the proposed BLFs will be considered as catchments area. Instead of present practice of plucking in the day time and drooping in the factory in the evening, the green leaf must reach BLFs within 1 hour from the plucking. The expected quantity of leaf available in the area both in the lean and peak season will be submitted along with application seeking permission for setting up processing unit. The factories are barred from procuring leaf from agents and will have to get the same from small tea growers. Agreement with growers has to be furnished along with the application. A techno-economic viability report is required to be submitted from reputed firm/planter/TRA/Assam Agriculture University about the viability of the project. Tea Board will prepare a panel of such accredited bodies.

The stipulation also enumerated that the BLF will invariably obtain the license under the Tea Marketing Control Order (TMCO) from Tea Board prior to all other clearances and permissions required for setting up the processing unit. However, priority will be given to BLFs that produce certified organic, orthodox manufacturing units, green and white manufacturing units and other specialty tea manufacturing. However, violation of these parameters will attract cancellation of license. These stipulations will be proposed to be endorsed by Tea Board for incorporating in the MCO guidelines for registration. There are around 177 BLFs with a total capacity of 261 mkg.

Secretary of Tea Association of India, Guwahati, Dipanjal Deka told ET: "These guidelines will help to produce quality tea. Only genuine people related to the trade will stay and others will move out. Till recently, anybody can come and set up a BLFs producing whatever tea they wanted without any quality check." He added with the implementation of new guidelines there will quality check in every stage right from the sourcing of green leaf. This will also check theft of green leaf. Bidyananda Barkakoty, chairman, North Eastern Tea Association (NETA) told ET those planters who have plantation of over 100 acres has must be allowed to set BLFs without undergoing all this stipulations. Small factories in the vicinity of the tea estate will help in getting quality tea.

Revival of Kangra Tea

Once renowned as among the best in the world, the one and a half century old Kangra tea might be on its way to a comeback if the government's efforts bear fruit. There is new hope for the dying tea sector after the Centre evinced an interest in the revival of the industry. A high-powered committee of the National Tea Board which recently traveled to the tea belt at the instance of Union Minister for Commerce and Industry has already held discussion with state government officials in the matter.

"The Kangra tea industry has gone through a troubled phase. But, things will change drastically once the government starts implementation of the package. We are targeting bringing an additional 10,000 hectares of area under tea cultivation. The government will take the help of the scientists at Chaudhary Sarwan Kumar Karishi Vishvavidyalaya Palampur to draw-up detailed expansion and rehabilitation plans for Kangra tea".

More than 1,200 hectares of tea plantations lie abandoned, reducing the total plantation to barely 1,000 hectares. With the quality of the produce unable to withstand the competition in the tea market, the production has also hit a low of eight lakh kg per annum. Known for its floral aroma and distinct flavor—which had led the British to promote Kangra as the tea destination of India—the tea is grown on the picturesque slopes of Palampur, Baijnath, Bir and Dharamshala in Kangra district. Some area of Chamba and Mandi are also seen as suitable from tea cultivation in view of climatic conditions.

An approach paper prepared by the Tea Board of India says that Kangra tea has an international demand and Palampur University had recently produced "Dhauladhar Tea"—a new brand of Kangra tea and has been trying to impart production and marketing skills. The Kangra Valley has been home to tea cultivation since the middle of the last century. Rated the finest in the world for its flavor and quality until 1905, it was the Kangra earthquake that year that proved catastrophic for the industry. It destroyed a large number of tea gardens, several tea factories and killed a number of tea planters. However, things are beginning to look up for the beleagured industry with the tea even receiving recognition for a "geographic indicator" in 2006. The renewed interest on the part of the Center may yet restore the sector its lost glory.

The first survey (new emerging Sector, 2011) of tea grown in the unorganized sector has revealed a link between the success story of small tea growers and the mushrooming growth of "BLFs" leading to output leakage. BLFs are standalone units distinguished from factories owned by major tea estates. The quality loss of Assam tea linked with uncontrollable rise of small tea growers and BLFs was the primary driver of this survey. So this was gap between production of tea leaves and processed tea, both CTC and orthodox. Assam produces the most CTC tea in the world.

"It took 500 people 6 months from November 2009 to complete the survey. This report has given the tea industry in India a benchmark for better management", The report, though, has thrown up figures that don't match up. For instance, 68,465 STGs in Assam annually produce 400 mkg of tea leaves and offload the bulk to BLFs. But, 450 estate factories source 377 mkg of tea leaves from STGs besides producing 1,623 mkg themselves. Officials underscored the need to rein in the BLFs—177 at the last count—make them register, demarcate sourcing areas for each and make them accountable. They also sought the Tea Board's help in drawing up a mechanism to provide expertise to STGs.

Gurgur Cha

People in the Himalayan region, the highest mountain range in the world know how to beat this cold with a cup of warm gurgur cha. The beverage, also called butter tea, is a must in Ladakh and the upper reaches of Himachal Pradesh, including Kinnaur and Lahaul-Spiti. But, it does not get misled by the name; the beverage is not made form tea leaves. Instead, it is a heady concoction of milk, yak butter, salt and an infusion prepared from plants available in the Himalayan region. Chunks of yak butter in the cha provide energy that keeps the body warm at such a high altitude. Yak butter also helps to prevent chapped lips and flaky skin from cold dry winds.

Till a few years ago, people had cultural reluctance to have a toilet within the house, and the cold winds would make it difficult to go out for urination. Salt, instead of sugar, in the drink helps to absorb excess water from the body and reduces thirst, thereby preventing frequent urination. Infusion is prepared from chathang leaves or yamdal bark. The plant used differs from region to region depending on the altitude. People in Ladakh, for instance, prepare the concentrate from fresh leaves of chathang, usually found in the upper reaches of the Himalaya.

The leaves impart a subtle flavor to the beverage. They also protect against cold and fever, and help to reduce flatulence. The leaves are boiled and then allowed to simmer for 7–8 hours. People in Kinnaur prefer using the yamdal bark. They roast the bark and grind before boiling it in water. One can drink as many cups of gurgur cha in a day as one wants. It has no ill effects; in fact it protects from heart diseases.

Tea in Bihar

Following a modest beginning in the early 90s, tea plantation has made a quantum jump in Kishanganj, the only district in the state where tea is grown and has thus put Bihar on the tea map of the country. Within a short span of nearly two decades, the tea plantation has risen from 0 acre to some 25,000 acres which was once barren and uncultivated. It has not just generated huge employment opportunities, but could indeed reverse the migration of farm workers from Bihar. Kishanganj produces 150 mkg of green leaves annually and net 33 mkg of tea annually.

An entrepreneur indeed foresaw the huge potential of tea plantation in this district situated as it is on the foothills of the Himalayas and in the vicinity of Darjeeling district. Its tea as already carved a niche among tea lovers, globally. When he started planting tea on a small patch of barren and undulating land in Pothia and Thakurganj blocks the district, he was simply mocked and derided. But once, it captured people's imagination, more and more small and marginal farmers turned toward it. Entrepreneurs from outside the state, too, jumped on the tea bandwagon. The green tea leaves grown in the district are now in high demand and has thrown a big challenge to the traditional tea-growing states of West Bengal and Assam.

Bihar State Tea Planters Association sources claimed that the tea plantation was likely to generate 80.30 lakh man-days annually if things work according to plan. The Tea Board of India, foreseeing the tremendous potential, has declared five blocks of Pothia, Thakurganj, Kishanganj, Bahadurganj and Dighalbank nontraditional areas for growing Tea under its new area development scheme. And, as a mandatory incentive, the board has offered a subsidy of Rs 40,000 per acre of plantation.

Changing Contours of Indian Tea Industry

The Indian tea industry is facing threats on account of its high cost of production. The threat is particularly acute in the international arena where India is now a distant fourth with a global share of 12% in 2009 and after Kenya, China and Sri Lanka. That is nothing new, but over the last few years, the organized industry has been exposed to threat from within the country too—from the STG who now account for 28% of total Indian tea output. The phenomenon is more pronounced in the South where 44% of the produce is from this segment while in North India 24% comes from STG. The industry construct is changing with a new paradigm evolving.

High cost: During the Eighth and the Ninth Plan periods, a large number of agriculturalists in North Bengal and Assam switched over to tea cultivation lured by good tea prices. Small growers holding upto 10–12 hectares thus started co-existing with corporates/proprietary gardens in North and South India and now perhaps no policy is formulated by the Government without keeping in mind this sector's interest. However, the organized sector faces competition from this sector as STG is outside the ambit of the Plantation Labor Act under which the organized industry has to fulfill certain social obligations which results in shouldering the highest cost of production (COP) in the world. The organized industry has addressed this challenge in two ways—while some corporates like the Tatas have de-risked their operations by evolving as a beverage company rather than remaining as a plantation outfit only, others have chosen to take benefit of this development (of emergence of STG) by increasing their purchases from BLF to which the STG sell their green leaves. There has been a mushrooming of BLF units in Assam and North

Bengal. Currently, the share of BLF in total tea production is about 23% against 10% in 2001. However, their teas are sold privately and inadequate quality control or expertise makes this sector produce a low quality product mostly.

Status paper: A recent status paper by the Indian Tea Association says that "Due to various reasons, the sector has much lower cost of production and thus can offload tea at lower prices. This adversely affects the general tea market because of uneven competition". During 1998 and 2007 while the organized sector has lost 57 mkg of crop, the BLF sector registered a 169 mkg jump, just as the area cropped by the corporate sector increased by a mere 0.3% while that of the STG by 14.3%.

Now, steps have been initiated to achieve the requisite quality standards as the organized sector is increasingly sourcing their teas from this sector, as part of its strategy to tackle competition as well as to meet the increasing demand. These facets on the Indian tea industry has been highlighted in a recent status paper published by the Indian Tea Association which says that over the years, India has slipped to the fourth position in world tea exports as its competitors like Kenya and Sri Lanka, serviced by well-organized low-cost high quality small-holder sector is outdoing India. Boosting exports and higher overall price-realization will be the main thrust of the industry, the report said.

Tea prices: Because of poor rains in June and July 2009, tea prices rose sharply by Rs 35 per kilogram. Good quality Assam tea was selling at Rs 160 per kilogram and South India tea at Rs 90–110 was up Rs 20–30 per kg. Tea prices are expected to remain firm in 2011 with global tea deficit expected to reach as much as 130 mkg. The shortage in tea production in India alone was likely to reach 80–100 mkg in the new season beginning April 2011. In March 2011, good Assam tea fetched Rs 200 to 300 per kilogram compared to Rs 200 per kg the previous year. Dooars and Cachar tea where sold at Rs 300 to 400 per kg against Rs 300 per kilogram the previous year.

Guwahati to Get Northeast's First Integrated Tea Park

The first integrated tea park of the Northeast will come up at Chaygaon on the outskirts of Guwahati. Around Rs 23 crore will be invested in the project. The pre-feasibility report of the park is already prepared. Sources in Assam Industrial Development Corporation (AIDC) told ET: "We have identified 200 bighas of land for the tea park. We have already purchased and acquired 60 bighas. Process is on for procuring the remaining." Assam chief minister Tarun Gogoi, during his meeting with deputy chairman of the Planning Commission Montek Singh Ahluwalia, said that though tea is the biggest industry in Assam there was not a single integrated tea park in the state, which could cater to the needs of the industry. "The AIDC has taken steps to setup the tea park, which will create world class infrastructure for processing, warehousing, blending and packaging on the industry cluster concept. Tea export from the state will increase substantially with the operation of the park", the sources added. Based on the techno-economic feasibility report, AIDC has recasted the project cost from Rs 39.67 crore to Rs 23.40 crore. The fund is expected to be generated from the leased out space and assistance to the state for developing export infrastructure and allied activities. Currently, Guwahati has around 14 lakh square feet of warehousing facilities scattered in different locations.

Assam's tea production was estimated at 480.2 mkg last year, which was down by 19.7 mkg compared to the previous year's production of 499.9 mkg. Tea plantation is expanding fast in nontraditional areas and the park is expected to assist the growers in the nontraditional areas. While Assam and Tripura are traditional tea-growing states, Meghalaya, Nagaland, Arunachal Pradesh, Manipur, Mizoram and Sikkim constitute the nontraditional areas. The Northeastern region accounts for 55% of the area under tea and 53% of the production. Tripura produces 7.5 mkg annually. The nontraditional areas together produce 2.98 mkg annually.

Tea Cooperative in Bengal

Generally, 6,000 tea bushes can be planted in an acre of plot. These 6,000 bushes can produce 10,000 kg of green leaf. The cost of production varies between Rs 8.50 and Rs 10.50 per kg. The producer gets Rs 13.50 per kg. So, his net earning is Rs 3 per kg.

These growers are now forming self help groups and later cooperative societies to set up their own bought-leaf factories to ensure higher price for their produce. The state government is delaying the issue of no objection certificates to thousands of small tea plantations in north Bengal. As a result, we are not getting government funds and assistance from the Tea Board. So, we have decided to form self-help groups so that we can access different schemes, said Chakroborty, who is also associated with one such cooperative society, Panbari Small Tea Growers Association.

Green leaf production is finding new converts in rural North Bengal as a few first time entrepreneurs are looking at it as an alternative source of income.

The Panbari Small Tea Growers Association has 340 small tea growers in its fold. The growers have contributed Rs 78 lakh from their profit. With some financial assistance from the Tea Board and bank loans, we are planning to setup a factory which will become operational from next fiscal, says Chakroborty. Added Dilip Das: Our association of small growers, Nabajagarn Self-Help Growers Association, is also planning to setup factories. This will help us to process tea leaves and command better price for our made teas.

The big tea companies which buy leaves from these small tea producers are ready to lend a helping hand to them. AN Singh, managing director and CEO of Goodricke Group, said his company has appointed a dedicated manager to help these small growers to adopt better agricultural practices to produce quality tea leaves. Quality is an issue that needs to be addressed immediately. If that is taken care of, small tea growers will be able to garner better prices for their produce, said Mr DP Maheswari, managing director of Jay Shree Tea and Industries.

Goodricke Group which buys 3.5–4 mkg of green leaf has setup a soil testing laboratory at Danguajhar, a place closer to Jalpaiguri town where small tea growers can test their soil at a discounted price. We are offering Rs 14 per kg to the green leaf producers and if they provide good quality leaves we reward them with an annual bonus. We have also convinced Axis Bank to provide financial assistance to small tea growers, said Mr Singh. The small tea growers are there to stay and flourish as domestic consumption of tea is increasing at the rate of 3.5%. It has also given a boost to the local economy. What is needed is monitoring of the quality of tea. Most of them now have motorcycles. They are also buying TVs, refrigerators, music systems and desktop computers. Eating out is fast catching up among the youths.

And they are ready to spend more on their children education. Suddenly, a lot is happening over tea.

Cup Brimmeth Over

People in the age group of 35–50 years are entering the business; 80% are from rural areas. Ninety-five percent are literate.

Tea guarantees a steady flow:

- Of income through the year which is why they are venturing in to this business.
- Rs 8.50–10.50
- What is costs to produce a kg of green leaf?
- Rs 3–4 per kg. Is the profit?
- Small tea growers are jointly setting up factories to process green leaves, produce black tea.
- Some have started: dealing with processing units to avoid brokers or middlemen.

Major Moves

As a result of a conference held in New Delhi in September 2004 by the stakeholders, a Special Purpose Tea Fund (SPTF) came into being. It envisages accelerating the pace of replanting and rejuvenation by ensuring availability of funds to the extent of 75% of the unit cost by way of long-term loan (50%) and subsidy (25%) so that the growers can take up the program in right earnest. The program is targeted at the organized sector comprising about 160 tea estates spread over 4 lakh hectares. The Rs 47,610 million program spread over 15 years is expected to increase yields from 1,662 kg per hectares now to 2,120 kg for north India, and to 2,420 kg for South India. This is expected to reduce the cost of production of Indian tea. In March 2008, the union cabinet has approved a fund of Rs 2,300 million under the Eleventh Five-Year Plan for quality upgradation and product diversification of tea. Of this, Rs 1,000 million will be spent as subsidy on orthodox tea. Nearly, Rs 870 million will be utilized for modernization of tea processing factories and Rs 370 million on creating infrastructure for value-added exports of high-quality tea. The total outlay for tea under the Eleventh Five-Year Plan has been fixed at Rs 8,000 million against Rs 3,500 million in the Tenth Five-Year Plan. As a result of labor shortage, and declining productivity, tea plantations may take to mechanization in a big way. The measure needs support from trade unions and governments. Some say that the manual skill in plucking cannot be matched by machines. Japan has mechanized plucking of tea leaves because the terrain is mostly even.

Major Problems

The tea industry is not free from problems. In early 2005, the industry witnessed major companies withdrawing from production and concentrating on packaging/retailing sector. They intended to focus on brand-building business and exploring the market substantially, rather than on the plantation business, which is a low-margin segment. The problem of tea-shortage is likely to worsen as pest's damage this crop. In 2010, excess rains hurt tea crop in North eastern States which accounted for more than 70% of production. Also, the increasing use of tea bags and soluble instant tea effectively reduces the quality of tea needed per cup and raise the demand of plain cheaper tea. Tea bags account for 10% of the volume of world consumption, and it still increasing. A major problem is the poor yield because of poor condition of the gardens.

The biggest challenge facing the Indian tea industry is its ageing tea bushes. In Darjeeling for instance, 75% of tea bushes are between 50 years old to 100 years old. Data reveals that 38% of the bushes in South and North India are between 50 years to 100 years of age and thus the yield is very low compared to Kenya and Sri Lanka where the bushes are relatively younger.

More than 30% of the tea-growing areas are above the economic threshold age limit. The auction mechanism is defective and factory set-ups are old. Poor and frequent changes of garden management are another problem. Some owners are inexperienced. Added to these, the managements depend heavily on bank debts with negligible fresh equity infusion. Indian tea industry suffers from a defective auction system. Nearly, 55% of the output is sold through auction houses, and the rest sold through private sales. Of course, the compulsory auction was abolished in 2001. The fact is that big tea companies are benefiting from fall in auction prices and rise in retail prices of tea. Longer transaction time and high transaction cost (like warehousing charges, transportation cost, brokerage charges, etc.) are some other problems. It takes about 35 days for the entire transaction processes to complete. The wide fluctuation in prices is causing hardships to the growers. The price of tea has been on a long-term decline while production costs are rising, putting pressure on tea growers. The laborers too suffer because losses due to the low prices of tea are generally passed on to the workers in the form of low wages and withdrawal of basic facilities.

Present Status on Research and Development in Tea

R and D Contributions on Tea

TRA and *United Planters' Association of Southern India* (UPASI) Tea Research Foundation (TRF) have released 30 high-yielding vegetative clones each. This has enhanced productivity from 1,416 kg per hectare in 1981 to 1,850 kg per hectare in 2000 in North India and 1,645 kg per hectare to 2,300 kg per hectare in 2000 in South India. UPASI-TRF-I recently released in South India has yield potential upto 11,000 kg per hectare.

Biotechnological approach in tea breeding has progressed toward protoplast fusion, haploid line and market developments in pruning, DNA, finger printing and patenting of elite clones. Nutrition in Tea is now based on computerized model and green leaf yield potential. Sulfur and zinc nutrients have been accommodated along with NPK requirements.

Cultivation aspects like pruning, shade management, organic nutrition in soil, soil amendment and application of weedicides and balanced application of fertilizers have been refined over the years to harvest increasing yield. Further, Irrigation Drainage Technologies in tea have been improved and their requirement in improving yields has been established.

Protection of crops is linked to minimum application of pesticides and its linkage to follow Integrated Pest Management (IPM) practice. Maintaining biodiversity and minimum or no pesticide residue is the call of the day. Biocides and biocontrols have been developed. Chemistry of tea manufacture and flavor chemistry of tea have helped in refining manufacture of tea on scientific basis and understanding the role of enzymes involved in it.

Quality improvement in tea has been achieved through training, modernization of factory, upgrading of plucking standard and improving sanitation and hygienic situations. ISO-9000 and *hazard analysis and critical control points* (HACCP) as a package for quality improvement have been introduced.

Research on health benefit aspects has yielded positive results. Tea drinking is beneficial in the cure of hypertensions, diabetes, cancer, kidney, malfunction, dental caries, etc. Tea contains antioxidants which help human beings to avoid many health complications. Packaging of tea is now being done with recently developed packaging materials like jute, laminated bags, multi-wallpaper sacks and use of flexible packaging substances.

Approach to 10th Plan Period

Specific areas of research can be identified to launch new areas of fundamental research in different fields, like advance programs in biotechnology, characterization of clones, etc. Nutrition of Tea Plants is a gray area. Computer simulation models for balanced nutrition for Tea will be a step to apply non-contents of fertilizer to the tea plant based on variable criteria like soil conditions, bush frame and age, environmental factors, etc. This will help in scientific management of tea estates in accordance with the production need.

Computer aided database, if stored for future utilization and guidance to the management and sectional information of tea gardens will help both the research institutes and tea estates to save time and initiate prompt action in taking corrective actions. Quality of Tea can be enhanced from the information on biochemical pathways if these are identified and packages are developed.

Electronics can play a big role once the biochemical pathways are identified and these are linked to computer sensors by-products of tea can be gainfully utilized for other industrial use. Similarly, value added items like real time database (RTD), flavored tea are the areas on which new research could be thought of.

Sustainability is a major problem in tea. It is observed that tea productivity is not increasing in the replanted areas. This has been linked to soil sickness, reasons for which are not well established. Bioagriculture is a new research area, which can give answers to the problems as indicated, in organic tea estates with stable yields.

Quality control is a major issue in Tea. The Quality Control Laboratory Chain in South India as well as in North India needs to be strengthened soon. Well developed field laboratories for quality testing of tea and monitoring of adversities with Tea Estate is essential. The conducive environment for trade has prompted such steps to ensure quality tea production. If needed, a phased program can be developed and computer net work monitoring may be essential.

Tea infrastructure has been created to setup future programs on DNA markers and hybridization. Tissue culture techniques and technology for production of haploid lines were standardized. Production technology of tea has been redefined to harvest, increasing yield.

Nutrition in tea is adopted based on the computer model and green leaf yield potential. Role of sulfur, zinc and other micro nutrients like Ma, Mn, Bo has been proved necessary in high yielding areas. Biocides and bio control measures in plant protection have been developed to minimize pesticide residues. Improved packaging of tea has been developed by using jute, laminated bags, multiwalled paper sacks and flexible packaging substances. ISO 9000 and HACCP as the package for quality improvement have been introduced.

The Indian tea industry will have to evolve strategies in terms of quality improvement, market intelligence and market promotion to counter the competing forces unleashed by globalization.

With the world supply position steadily increasing, our target should no longer be production oriented, but on improving productivity, value addition and marketability. Special emphasis has to given for enhancing productivity in the small holder sector.

In the post-liberalization period, the main thrust should be on quality improvement so as to make Indian tea competitive. Apart from this, there should be a continued effort towards further increasing the profitability of tea gardens through replanting/rejuvenation and mechanization of operations. Special emphasis needs to be given on irrigation and drainage in tea gardens.

Special efforts have to be made for improving the market promotion and marketing capabilities, improving the packaging and reducing package cost and for value addition to Indian tea and tapping overseas market.

Conversion to organic system of tea growing will have to be encouraged. Information technology needs to be used effectively for making available ready information to the tea industry and for promotion of our produce in other markets. Vigorous support will be needed to the promotion of Indian value added teas in overseas markets.

Tea-processing facilities need to be augmented by construction of new tea factories to meet the processing needs of additional products. Product diversification, creation of facilities for dual manufacture of tea (orthodox and CTC) need to be encouraged. The existing factories require modernization in order to ensure production of clean tea without any trace of foreign material in the end product. The competitive advantage of tea industry depends primarily on the quality of human resource. Therefore, human resource development (HRD) inputs need to be augmented for the future developments of the tea industry.

MAJOR TAXES ON TEA

Tea is a major source of revenue to the National Exchequer. The major imposts are excise duty, cess on tea as well as various Central and State taxes like sales tax, entry tax, agriculture income tax, etc. Present taxes and duties (Central Levy and State Levy) on tea in India are given below.

Central Levy

1. **Tea cess:**
    i. Thirty paisa/kg on tea produced except in Darjeeling Plantation District.
    ii. Twelve paisa/kg on tea produced in Darjeeling Plantation District.
2. **Excise duty:**
    i. Rs 1/kg on tea imposed on 01.03.2002 has been abolished w.e.f. 01.03.2003. However, an additional excise duty of Rs 1/kg has been introduced w.e.f. 01.03.2003 for development purposes.
    ii. Sixteen percent ad valorem on instant tea falling under heading 2101.20.

3. **Export duty:** Nil
4. **Import duty:**
    i. Hundred percent ad valorem on teas falling under heading 09.02
    ii. Thirty-five percent on instant tea falling under heading 2101.20F
    iii. 7.5% on teas imported under Indo-Sri Lanka Free Trade Agreement (FTA)
    iv. Nil when imported for re-export under duty exemption scheme and/or by export oriented unit (EOU)/export processing zones (EPZ)/special economic zone (SEZ) units.
5. **Corporation tax 35% plus 2% surcharge**
6. **Central sales tax**
    i. Two percent on teas sold at Kolkata/Siliguri/Coonoor and Coimbatore Auctions.
    ii. Nil on teas sold at Guwahati Auction.
    iii. Four percent on ex-garden sale against Form C
    iv. Eight percent on teas sold to unregistered dealers.

State Levy

A. Assam

1. **Assam Sales Tax**
    i. Two percent on all teas sold through Guwahati auction, orthodox teas are exempted.
    ii. Eight percent on sales outside auction but within Assam.
2. **Assam Taxation on Specified Land (Amendment) Act, 1994**
    i. Twenty paisa/kg on green leaf produced by producers having tea area of 40 hectares.
    ii. Thirty-two paisa/kg on green leaf produced by producers having tea area above 40 hectares in upper Assam.
    iii. Twenty-nine paisa/kg on green leaf produced by producers having tea area above 40 hectares in Cachar/Barak valley.
    v. Producers having tea area up to 4 hectares exempted.
3. **Agricultural income tax:** Up to Rs 1 lakh is 40% and above Rs 1 lakh is 45%.

B. West Bengal

1. **Sales tax (w.e.f. 01.01.2000)**
    a. Tea sold in Kolkata or Siliguri auction
      i. Tea sold to registered dealer for exports : Nil
      ii. Tea sold to registered dealer for re-sale in original form : 1%
      iii. Tea sold to an unregistered dealer : 8%
    b. Tea sold other than in Kolkata or Siliguri auction
      i. Tea sold to registered dealer for exports : Nil
      ii. Tea sold to registered dealer for re-sale in original form : 1%
      iii. Tea sold to an unregistered dealer : 8%
2. **Inter-State Sale**
    a. Tea Purchased in Kolkata or Siliguri auctions in course of Inter-State Trade : 2% CST
    b. Tea sold ex-garden in the course of Inter-State Trade : 4% CST
3. **Purchase Tax:** Tea purchased for blending/packing but disposed of otherwise than by way of sale in West Bengal : 1%

4. West Bengal Rural Employment and Production Cess (w.e.f. 01.04.1981). Twelve paisa/kg of green leaf produced for estates producing over 2.5 lakh kg of green leaf.
5. West Bengal Primary Education (w.e.f. 01.04.1981). Four paisa/kg of green leaf produced for estates producing over 2.5 lakh kg of green leaf.
6. Agriculture Income Tax. Forty-five percent brought down to 30% (w.e.f. 01.04.2003).

C. Tamil Nadu

1. Sales Tax
   a. Four percent on sale through Auction
   b. Eight percent on sale through other than Auction Infrastructure Surcharge 5% on Sales Tax
2. Inter-State Sale: Two percent on teas sold in Auction for Inter-State Sale
3. Agricultural Income Tax:
   a. Up to Rs 25,000 thousands : 45%
   b. Above Rs 25,000–1 lakh   : 50%
   c. Above Rs 1–3 lakhs   : 55%
   d. Above Rs 3–10 lakhs   : 60%
   e. Above Rs 10 lakhs   : 65%

(D) Kerala

1. Sales Tax
   i. Unbranded   : 8%
   ii. Branded   : 8%
   iii. Additional Sales Tax   : 15%
2. Inter-State Sale: Two percent on teas sold in Auction for Inter-State Sale
3. Agricultural Income Tax:
   a. Up to Rs 25,000 thousands : 45%
   b. Above Rs 25,000–1 lakh   : 50%
   c. Above Rs 1–3 lakhs   : 55%
   d. Above Rs 3–10 lakhs   : 60%
   e. Above Rs 10 lakhs   : 65%
4. Plantation Tax (w.e.f. 01.04.2000)
   a. First 5 hectares   : Nil
   b. Next 3 hectares   : Rs 350 per hectare
   c. Next 3 hectares   : Rs 500 per hectare
   d. Next 3 hectares   : Rs 900 per hectare
   e. Up to 500 hectares   : Rs 1,500 per hectare

E. Karnataka

1. Sales Tax
   a. Unbranded   : 8–12%
   b. Branded   : 15%
2. Turn Over Tax:
   a. Above Rs 5 lakh but less than Rs 5 crores   : 1%
   b. Above Rs 5 crore but less than Rs 10 crores : 2%
   c. Above Rs 10 crores   : 3%
3. Infrastructure Development Tax   : 5% on tax payable

4. Agricultural Income Tax:

a. Up to Rs 1 lakh : 30%

b. Above Rs 1–5 lakh : Rs 30,000 plus 40% of the amount by which total income exceeds Rs 1 lakh

c. Where the total income exceeds Rs 5 lakh: Rs 190,00 plus 40% of the amount by which total income exceeds Rs 5 lakh.

Table 2.7D shows the taxes levied in other producing and non-tea producing states.

Table 2.7D: Taxes levied in other producing states, non-tea producing states/union territories

State	Central sales tax	State sales tax	Other taxes
Andhra Pradesh	4%	10%	CST without Form "C" (10%)
Bihar	NA	10%	Additional tax (1%). CST without Form "C" (10%)
Delhi	2%	5.5%	–
Goa, Daman, Diu	NA	4% (w.e.f. 30.5.95)	–
Gujarat	4%	8%	Packages below 20 kg (12%), for packages above 20 kg (80%) + surcharge (10%), octroi (1%)
Haryana	4%	8%	CST without form "C" (10%)
Himachal Pradesh	4%	7%	–
Madhya Pradesh	NA	8%	On loose tea and on tea in packets (10%)
Maharashtra	4%	8%	Surcharge (10%)
Meghalaya	4%	7%	Surcharge (1%)
Mizoram	NIL	NIL	–
Nagaland	4%	6%	–
Orissa	4%	12%	Entry tax (1%), CST without form "C" (12%)
Pondichery	3%	3%	–
Punjab	2%	4%	–
Rajasthan	4%	4%	–
Tripura	4%	8%	–
Uttar Pradesh	4%	6%	Single point and additional tax (2%)
Sikkim	4%	8%	

Source: Various issues of tea Statistics, Tea Board, Kolkata.

CONSUMPTION

In fact, there are two parallel tea worlds that are being established in India. The old world being where tea is consumed in the traditional style sweetened and enriched with sugar and milk and sometimes infused with tulsi, adhrak, cardamom, black pepper, dalchini, mulethi (liquorice), etc. This delicious concoction is consumed in most Indian homes and brewed fresh at tea stalls in virtually every street corner and at all railway stations.

There is emerging a new world of tea connoisseurs who are not found at these tea stalls but at the chai bars, tearooms and tea lounges dotting big cities where they sample teas made from herbs, fruits, seeds and roots steeped in hot water. From the basic four varieties: (1) green, (2) black, (3) white and (4) oolong—other exotica on offer includes blooming or flowering tea, chamomile tea, hibiscus tea, jasmine tea, orange pekoe, rooibos, pu-erh and an array of other flavors.

> Blooming teas, chamomile, hibiscus, orange pekoes, rooibos and an array of other flavors tease the palate as chai bars, tearooms and tea lounges provide a modern setting for an old tradition.

Tea has almost acquired the status of a national drink, and as this article shows, it is also packed with health benefits.

Tea is a very popular beverage in India. Indians have to have their cup of hot steaming tea, first thing in the morning, in order to stimulate their senses and refresh themselves. In fact, tea as a beverage is much preferred to coffee in India. Tea is like a comfort drink for many Indians, especially on rainy days, when it is savored along with pakoras. Tea is popular all over India, both as a breakfast drink as well as evening refreshment. Nothing complements a family get-together or a college reunion more than an endless supply of tea throughout the day. In fact, it is the cultural norm to offer tea to guests and visitors instead of alcoholic drinks. Although in recent years many people have shifted to drinking black tea, traditionally, tea is blended with a little bit of milk, and sugar is added in accordance to one's tastes. India is the world's largest tea producer, where tea is mostly cultivated in West Bengal and Assam, with a small percentage coming from the Nilgiri Hills in Tamil Nadu.

The History of Tea Drinking in India

This is documented evidence that tea drinking in India dates back to 750 BC. Buddhist monks in India have used tea for its medicinal value for thousands of years. According to a very interesting legend, tea drinking in India began with a saintly Buddhist monk about 2000 years ago. It so happened that this monk, who later became the founder of Zen Buddhism, decided to spend 7 sleepless years contemplating the life and teachings of Buddha. While he was in the fifth year of his contemplation and prayer, he almost fell asleep. He took some leaves from a nearby bush and began chewing them. These leaves revived him and enabled him to stay awake as he chewed on them whenever he felt drowsy. Thus, he was able to complete his penance of 7 years. These were the leaves of the wild tea plant.

According to local traditions, people used to brew and drink tea using the leaves of the wild native tea plants. In the 16th century, Indians prepared a vegetable dish using tea leaves along with garlic and oil, and the boiled tea leaves were used to prepare a drink as well. Since that time, different varieties of tea have emerged; the most famous among them is Darjeeling tea. The commercial production of tea in India was started by the British East India Company and vast tracts of land were exclusively developed into tea estates for producing various types of tea. The first tea garden was established by the Company by the end of the 19th century in Assam. One popular anecdote related to the history of tea drinking in India dates back to the 19th century when an Englishman noticed that the people of Assam drank a dark liquid which was a type of tea brewed from a local wild plant. In the year 1823, a Singpho (a region falling across parts of present day Arunachal Pradesh and Assam) king is said to have offered an English army officer tea as a medicinal drink.

Domestic Consumption

Internal

Tea consumption in India has increased from 98.5 mkg in 1947 to 221 mkg in 1971 to 500 mkg in 1990 and 890 mkg in 1212 (Table 2.8). Internal consumption of tea grew appreciably. It was 38.7% of total production in 1947 which went up to 78% of the total production in 2004. The position today is that international consumption

Table 2.8: Estimates of domestic consumption of tea in India

Year	Domestic consumption (mkg)	Year	Domestic consumption (mkg)
1971	221	1992	540
1972	233	1993	560
1973	244	1994	580
1974	258	1995	595
1975	272	1996	618
1976	287	1997	633
1977	302	1998	615
1978	320	1999	633
1979	332	2000	653
1980	346	2001	673
1981	360	2002	693
1982	372	2003	714
1983	386	2004	735
1984	400	2005	757
1985	415	2006	771
1986	431	2007	786
1987	446	2008	802
1988	462	2009	838
1989	480	2010	856
1990	500	2011	873
1991	520	2012	890

increased to over 81% of production in 2012 (Table 2.8A). Thus, the task before the government is to fix up trade priorities. If the priority is to make available tea in the domestic market, the export front is neglected. On the other hand, if the priority is to ensure maximization of export earnings, the tea may not be available in the internal market at reasonable prices (Table 2.8A).

There are various demographic, economic, social and psychological factors that determine demand for a commodity like tea in a developing economy like India. Income, prices of tea and its substitutes and complements, change in consumer taste, preferences, population, social satisfaction, and health aspects are some of the important factors in this regard. Another factor is urbanization, the pace of which in the developing countries is very rapid. The details of internal consumption are given below.

Indian domestic market continues to grow at around 2% per annum. The 1999 domestic consumption was about 670 mkg. By 2004, this figure reached 725 mkg. If export of 205 mkg is added, production in 2004 was about 940 mkg. The CTC element of Indian consumption is over 94% (Table 2.8B).

A look at the state-wise consumption (Table 2.8B) shows that since early days Maharashtra has been the biggest consumer.

Table 2.8A: Indian tea consumption—as percentage of production

Particulars/year	1947	1957	1967	1977	1987	1991	1997	1999	2004
Consumption in mkg	98.5	112.9	180.7	302.0	446.0	520.0	635.0	670.0	740.0
Production in mkg	254.8	310.8	384.8	556.3	674.3	741.7	810.6	880.2	950.0
Percent of production	38.7	36.3	47.0	54.3	66.0	70.1	78.3	76.1	77.9

Table 2.8B: Indian consumption of tea during 1947–2004

(In mkg)

Particulars/year	1947	1957	1967	1977	1987	1991	1997	1999	2004
Consumption	98.5	112.9	180.7	302.0	446.0	520.0	635	670	740
Growth (%)	–	14.6	60.1	67.1	47.6	16.6	22.1	5.5	10.5
Average annual rate of growth (%)	–	1.46	6.01	6.7	4.76	4.1	3.6	2.3	2.1

India is still the largest consumer of Black Tea in the world with domestic consumption accounting for almost 80% of the total tea production in the country. The pattern of domestic consumption has shown a steady and positive growth since 2000. From a mere 73 mkg in 1951, domestic consumption has increased to 653 mkg in 2000. In addition, compared to the previous years, there is a marginal increase in 2004, 2005 and 2006 at 735, 757 and 771 mkg, respectively. The following Fig. 2.7 shows the pattern of domestic consumption in India.

The major tea-consuming states in India include Maharashtra (99 mkg), Uttar Pradesh (67 mkg), Gujarat (67 mkg), Rajasthan (56 mkg) and Madhya Pradesh (43 mkg). The average annual per capita consumption of tea in India varies considerably from region to region. It fluctuates from a maximum of 1.2 kg in Punjab to a minimum of 0.36 kg in Orissa.

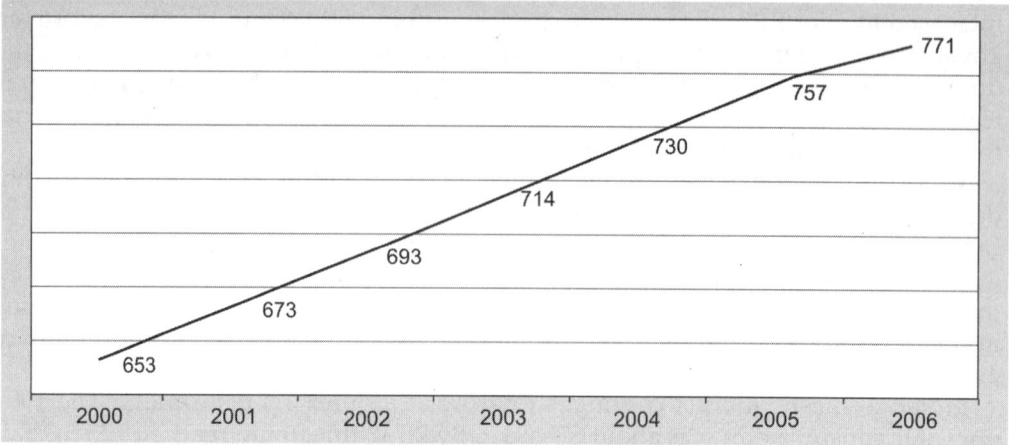

Fig. 2.7: Domestic consumption (mkg)

The Indian domestic tea market is predominantly a loose tea market, constituting around 60% of the total tea consumption, while the rest is served by packet tea. Over the past couple of years however, there has been a shift in the domestic market from loose tea to branded packet tea. The growth of packet tea has increased in the overall domestic consumption in India. The share of packet tea has increased from a meager 15% in the early 1980s to over 40% currently. Big companies sell tea in branded loose and packet tea. Since 1985, the branded tea segment has registered good growth and its share in the total tea market is currently around 40%. Fig. 2.8 shows the trend of loose and packet tea consumption in the domestic market in India.

Small local players in the unorganized sector are major stakeholders in loose tea markets at various levels. Later on, large players such as Hindustan Unilever Limited and Tata Tea took over the tea market as branded packed tea producers. They created and nurtured the perception that non-branded packet tea is inferior. Consumers were offered branded teas in a variety of aromas and flavors, packed in compact, attractive packets. Most of the big players such as Tata Tea and Hindustan Lever

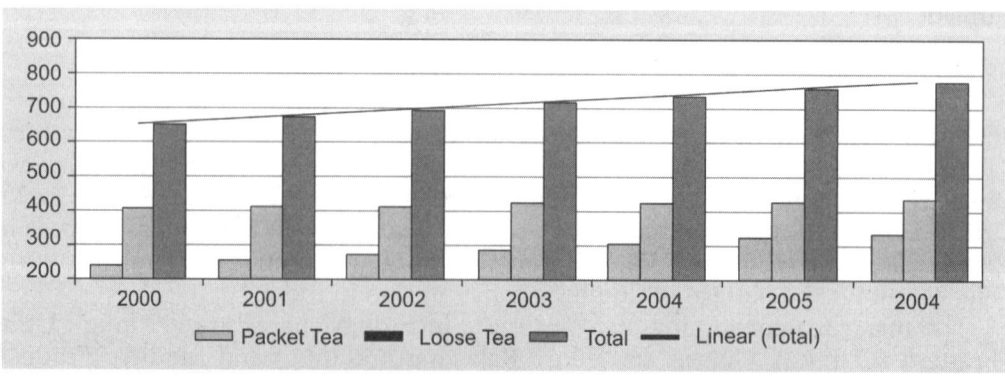

Fig. 2.8: Domestic consumption of packet and loose tea (mkg)

Source: Tea Statistics (2005) J Thomas and Company Pvt. Ltd., and www.indiateaportal .com

Limited claim through their marketing strategies that they provide good quality tea at economical prices in order to capture the market from all strata of society.

Per Capita Domestic Consumption of Tea

Domestic consumption constitutes around 80% of total tea production in India. However, the per capita consumption of tea in India is very low compared to other countries. Figure 2.2.9 shows that per capita consumption of tea in India is very low and it is stagnant during the period 1999–01 to 2001–03, compared to other major countries. Despite a steady growth rate in domestic consumption, the per capita consumption in India is still one of the lowest in the world at 0.65 gm per head. The average annual per capita consumption of tea in India is relatively low vis-à-vis other countries like UK (2.24 kg), Ireland (2.96 kg), Turkey (2.6 kg) and Sri Lanka (over 1.38 kg).

It is noted that there is a need for joint venture promotion of domestic consumption in India. It shows that there is high potential to explore in domestic market. The per capita consumption of tea is very low among the young population in India. Therefore, the regulatory body of the tea industry along with the other stakeholders have to come together to sustain the domestic market and explore fresh market potential in the future.

The break-up of the Soviet Union had a strong impact on the Indian tea market. However, it gained momentum over the years. Russia and other **Commonwealth of Independent States** (CIS) members did not cross 45 mkg. Total Indian exports thus touched 205 mkg. Indian domestic market continues to grow at around 2% per annum. The 1999 domestic consumption was about 670 mkg. By 2004, this figure was 725 mkg. If export of 205 mkg is added, production in 2004 was about 940 mkg. The CTC element of Indian consumption is over 94%. It is estimated that in 2010 the Indian requirement for CTC teas has been estimated at 1,034 mkg which would go up to 1,050 mkg in 2012. State-wise split of estimated consumption of tea is furnished below (Table 2.9):

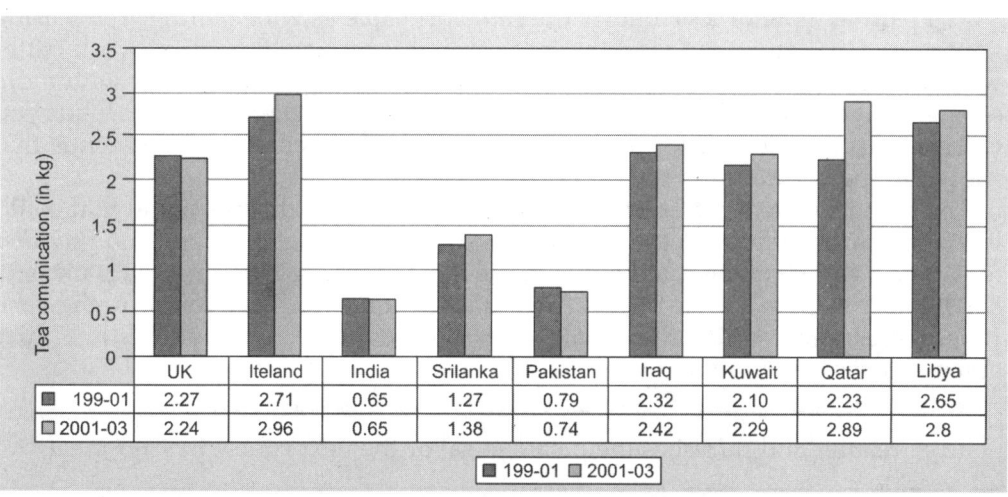

	UK	Iteland	India	Srilanka	Pakistan	Iraq	Kuwait	Qatar	Libya
199-01	2.27	2.71	0.65	1.27	0.79	2.32	2.10	2.23	2.65
2001-03	2.24	2.96	0.65	1.38	0.74	2.42	2.29	2.89	2.8

■ 199-01 □ 2001-03

Fig. 2.9: Per capita consumption of tea in various countries
Source: Tea Statistics (2003), Tea Board of India.

Table 2.9: A statewise split of estimated consumption during 1991–2004

(mkg)

Particulars/year	1991	1995	1999	2004
Uttar Pradesh	44	50	57	67
Bihar	18	23	25	25
Maharashtra	67	76	86	99
West Bengal	38	43	48	52
Andhra Pradesh	25	30	32	33
Madhya Pradesh	32	38	40	43
Tamil Nadu	21	23	26	28
Rajasthan	45	48	52	56
Gujarat	45	50	57	67
Orissa	10	12	18	20
Kerala	33	37	40	44
Assam	18	20	23	25
Punjab	40	45	50	55
Haryana	18	20	22	24
Jammu and Kashmir	10	15	20	22
Karnataka	26	30	34	36
Others	30	35	40	44
Total	**520**	**595**	**670**	**740**

New strategies will have to be evolved for the Russian Federation, CIS and Pakistan. Above all, exports will have to be given a clear priority over domestic need. While future supply and demand, on the overall, appears 'hand to-mouth' the future of specialty varieties, such as Darjeeling and Assam orthodox, would depend upon aggressive marketing.

Tea pairing more or less follows the same principle as wine pairing. Tea pairing lighter teas like green tea work better with lighter foods like salads work better with lighter foods likes salads. While the stronger black tea pairs best with more strongly flavored and spicy foods. Many tea brands now suggest specific foods you can eat with their leas. They are also roping in chefs to create special menus that showcase the versatility of the beverage.

Tea brand Typhoo got Chief Vicky Ratnani to create a distinct menu that could be offered with different teas. Not everyone drinks alcohol or wine. And flavored tea offers a variety of taste and enriches the accompanying food too. Tea is like any small mid-course palate cleanser, a great flavor bridge from one course to the next. It refreshes and readies the palate to savor the next course and is healthier accompaniment to food that wine.

> Tea readies and refreshes the palate to savor the next course in your meal.

A Sweet Match

Light teas like jasmine and chamomile go with most chocolate flavors.

Pairing Tricks

Ratnani pairs Moroccan spiced cottage cheese or chicken with mint tea. Moroccans use a lot of mint in their food, so I thought mint tea would go well with this cuisine. Similarly, something like oolong tea would go nicely with grilled oriental food, and jasmine tea with, say, grilled chicken.

Cha bar, the tea cage chain also pairs their wide in-house variety of teas with different kinds of food. Whenever we have a cup of tea, we like to have something with it whether it s a cookie, a toast or our favorite pakoras sas Priti Paul, owner of cha bar and a passionate tea aficionado herself. So after talking to various tea drinkers, we decided to work out the combinations so that the next time you want to have chai with something, you know exactly what to ask for. So, while our masala chai or the chai Hindustani works with pakoras, the breakfast teas work best with patties or tea cakes, the Arabic tea goes well with kebab wraps and hummus and organic tea with basil pesto and vegetable Panini. Similarly, Typhoo, which also has a wide range of falvors, offers interesting suggestions about what to pair your favorite tea with. Says the brand's spokesperson, Renu Kakkar, Typhoo Darjeeling goes excellently with creamy desserts , while typhoo Classic Assam is perfect with rich re meats, pastas and samosas. Yu can sip the English breakfast with your egg bhurger and aloo paratha while the Earl Gray is good with mild English cheeses, lemon-flavored cakes and desserts, like rabdi, falooda and kulfi.

Interestingly, the brew that most of India has with biscuits is also a good match with a variety of chocolate. According to Rajesh Variyath, Corporate Chief, Radisson Blu MRD, Nodia, most heavy, rich chocolates go well with light teas. You can pair an orange truffle chocolate with honey ginger tea. In case, you are trying a dark chocolate then go for strong back tea like onlong, or Earl Gray with more fruity fillings. Light teas like jasmine and Chamomile also go with most chocolate flavors.

However, do not go by the book. In the end, you should just go by what suits your own palate. Total tea consumption in the world has risen from 3.76 million tons in 2002 to 4.66 million tons in 2007 (Table 2.10). Per capita consumption, however, does not show much change. It has remained around 0.6–0.7 kg (Table 2.11). But, various types of tea available today provide a wide range to choose from (masala chai, green tea, Arabic tea and even white). Domestic tea consumption has increased from 221 kg in 1971 to 615 kg in 1998 to 837 kg.

TEA IMPORTS

Production vis-à-vis-Consumption

Whilst it was unlikely that the government would impose any restriction on exports in the foreseeable future, the pressure from the domestic market would limit the quantum of Indian tea exports in the years to come. AS stated earlier that with the country's population touched to 100 crore, ever if an Indian was to drink one extra cup a year, the additional requirement of tea would be 2.55 mkg; again, if 10 cups extra were to be taken every day by every Indian, the additional requirement would be 931 mkg per annum. But, how much the industry with its present capacity can produce at the maximum? It may be mentioned, however, that highest tea production was achieved in 2004 at 950 mkg. And it was high in 1999 with the crop amounting to 880 mkg, indicated by Mr AK Bothra, Chairman, North Bengal branch of the India

Table 2.10: Tea consumption (total)

Countries	Unit	2002	2003	2004	2005	2006	2007
Albania	kt	0.308978	0.31067	0.312486	0.31418	0.315661	0.316967
Algeria	kt	6.28837	9.574039	9.718814	9.866535	10.01759	10.17198
Argentina	kt	256.0699	250.8083	230.0447	243.6914	249.7526	255.8924
Armenia	kt	0.306107	0.306055	0.306261	0.306595	0.306984	0.307418
Australia	kt	15.72112	13.92678	14.08918	14.27636	14.48853	14.71113
Austria	kt	1.616391	0.812142	1.634393	14.81009	12.40296	9.130867
Azerbaijan	kt	4.085975	3.29364	3.3226	3.35674	0.848455	10.29756
Belarus	kt	0.9865	4.8985	1.946	2.8989	4.802	6.692
Belgium	kt	1.033279	3.11284	3.126341	2.095723	3.164387	3.18771
Bosnia and Herzegovina	kt						
Brazil	kt	484.0809	454.0827	349.3594	371.9739	394.7122	398.5759
Bulgaria	kt		0.782356				
Canada	kt	18.8172	19.0056	15.9975	16.156	13.03043	16.46376
Chile	kt	20.51919	20.74773	25.81153	22.82242	24.70302	24.94988
China	kt	512.16	515.36	518.43	651.86	786.612	922.5195
Colombia	kt			4.238571			
Croatia	kt						
Czech Republic	kt	3.061456	3.062209	3.064805	3.070748	2.053827	8.267328
Denmark	kt	1.612779	2.15623	2.702262	3.251659	2.718636	1.638431
Egypt	kt	70.17463	64.34859		7.420322	7.556845	23.08247
Estonia	kt	0.679322	0.541423	0.674645	0.673049	0.671774	0.670836
European Union	kt	243.0346	292.8969	294.2471	344.8355	346.295	347.8733
Finland	kt	1.04012	2.085206	2.091269	2.623048	2.106507	1.586616
France	kt	18.54091	18.67268	18.81056	18.95278	25.44703	32.00603
Georgia	kt	14.8138	15.58404	12.9549	17.00868	3.5184	6.14376
Germany	kt	24.74655	49.52051	74.26463	65.97554	90.6141	82.26637
Ghana	kt	4.022872	4.122179	10.55996	8.655922	8.868222	6.813721
Greece	kt	1.098754	1.102351	1.10617	2.220793	1.114846	1.119276
Hungary	kt	3.047582	3.038866	3.032144	2.017413	3.021411	2.011156
Iceland	kt	0.115009	0.115808	0.11683	0.148367	0.151891	0.18694
India	kt	653.2164	663.5314	673.7947	798.03	809.927	821.7801
Indonesia	kt	65.70791	88.73569	67.38196	68.19095	45.98371	69.73852
Iran	kt	53.77028	54.44936	41.33599	83.67841	28.23283	71.4355
Ireland	kt	11.79584	14.38748	9.768629	9.983794	9.798784	9.149555
Israel	kt	1.314	2.00691	1.3618	1.38602	1.41074	0.71801
Italy	kt	5.715741	5.760466	5.817531	5.860704	5.89415	5.937529
Japan	kt	140.1895	140.4898	166.0893	153.3276	140.5316	140.5478
Kazakhstan	kt	19.31663	22.36353	30.02597	24.23525	27.55455	27.87155
Kenya	kt	6.585573	6.76106	10.41065		3.654095	3.748525
Kyrgyzstan	kt	1.99628	3.02598	3.06282	3.61382	3.65288	3.68788
Latvia	kt	1.169312	1.162671	1.15641	0.920205	0.915179	1.13805

Table 2.10: Tea consumption (total) *(Contd.)*

Countries	Unit	2002	2003	2004	2005	2006	2007
Lithuania	kt				1.365722	1.357633	1.350247
Luxembourg	kt	0.089235	0.361304	0.183238	0.139547	0.094527	0.143998
Macedonia	kt	1.011128	0.811128	0.609912	0.611433	0.612927	
Malaysia	kt	14.70919	15.03611	17.91332	15.66014	18.6104	18.9358
Malta	kt	0.593954	0.518157	0.561775	0.484604	0.48769	0.531765
Mexico	kt						
Moldova	kt	0.362306	0.722574	0.720787	0.719036	0.717104	0.715381
Mongolia	kt	2.212968	2.236659	2.263016	1.528403	2.325729	2.624509
Montenegro	kt						
Morocco	kt	44.1809	44.65547	45.12323	48.62796	49.12333	55.82016
Netherlands	kt	19.37871	19.47036	17.90996	24.4798	21.24993	16.3817
New Zealand	kt	2.3691	2.0136	1.635	2.06695	2.51076	2.11415
Nigeria	kt	12.98324	13.30671				14.69515
Norway	kt	1.361448	1.825942	1.377573	1.386987	1.398203	1.412746
Pakistan	kt	90.24435	107.1979	109.102	126.9164	129.2107	115.1119
Peru	kt	5.31585	5.383268	2.724203	5.511754	5.573277	2.816608
Philippines	kt						
Poland	kt	26.76125	26.7432	26.72756	26.71581	22.88476	22.87234
Portugal	kt	1.03684		1.050197	1.054942	1.058434	1.060834
Romania	kt						2.154687
Russia	kt	159.8297	173.5193	172.6195	171.78	171	170.52
Serbia	kt						
Singapore	kt						
Slovakia	kt	0.537906	0.537961	1.076488	1.6161	1.617423	5.397318
Slovenia	kt	0.199453	0.199573	0.199701	0.200047	0.200687	0.403624
South Africa	kt	18.21332	23.05825	13.99943	37.75878	23.86547	19.30291
South Korea	kt			4.8039	4.8138	4.8372	4.8598
Spain	kt	4.131397	4.200452	4.269169	4.339814	8.823288	13.46368
Sweden	kt	2.677487	3.583292	4.496766	3.611829	2.724152	3.659237
Switzerland	kt	2.185426	2.2017	2.95585	2.231135	2.993574	1.510223
Tajikistan	kt	4.400066	5.069379	5.752008	5.807916	5.219707	3.962656
Thailand	kt	32.32147	45.75919	52.84831	53.35879	53.82111	54.23716
Turkey	kt	130.8923	152.5807	201.7078	218.0582	200.2843	209.9783
Turkmenistan	kt	5.060102	2.323956	1.878708	8.071326	3.841478	2.915306
Ukraine	kt	19.281	19.12518	4.74516	23.55258	23.39388	23.25468
United Kingdom	kt	136.4494	119.1325	131.7093	126.471	139.37	140.2693
USA	kt	143.8126	145.054	175.6832	147.7583	179.0279	150.6156
Uzbekistan	kt	22.74462	2.55677	20.69152	26.167	21.19056	21.4944
Venezuela	kt						2.7483
Vietnam	kt	15.90774	48.28104	16.28754	41.19675	41.6565	50.53266
World	kt	3763.35	3809.353	3855.47	4551.973	4606.085	4660.551

Table 2.11: Tea consumption per capita

Countries	Unit	2002	2003	2004	2005	2006	2007
Albania	kg	0.1	0.1	0.1	0.1	0.1	0.1
Algeria	kg	0.2	0.3	0.3	0.3	0.3	0.3
Argentina	kg	6.8	6.6	6	6.3	6.4	6.5
Armenia	kg	0.1	0.1	0.1	0.1	0.1	0.1
Australia	kg	0.8	0.7	0.7	0.7	0.7	0.7
Austria	kg	0.2	0.1	0.2	1.8	1.5	1.1
Azerbaijan	kg	0.5	0.4	0.4	0.4	0.1	1.2
Belarus	kg	0.1	0.5	0.2	0.3	0.5	0.7
Belgium	kg	0.1	0.3	0.3	0.2	0.3	0.3
Bosnia and Herzegovina	kg						
Brazil	kg	2.7	2.5	1.9	2	2.1	2.1
Bulgaria	kg		0.1				
Canada	kg	0.6	0.6	0.5	0.5	0.4	0.5
Chile	kg	1.3	1.3	1.6	1.4	1.5	1.5
China	kg	0.4	0.4	0.4	0.5	0.6	0.7
Colombia	kg			0.1			
Croatia	kg						
Czech Republic	kg	0.3	0.3	0.3	0.3	0.2	0.8
Denmark	kg	0.3	0.4	0.5	0.6	0.5	0.3
Egypt	kg	1	0.9		0.1	0.1	0.3
Estonia	kg	0.5	0.4	0.5	0.5	0.5	0.5
European Union	kg	0.5	0.6	0.6	0.7	0.7	0.7
Finland	kg	0.2	0.4	0.4	0.5	0.4	0.3
France	kg	0.3	0.3	0.3	0.3	0.4	0.5
Georgia	kg	3.4	3.6	3	3.9	0.8	1.4
Germany	kg	0.3	0.6	0.9	0.8	1.1	1
Ghana	kg	0.2	0.2	0.5	0.4	0.4	0.3
Greece	kg	0.1	0.1	0.1	0.2	0.1	0.1
Hungary	kg	0.3	0.3	0.3	0.2	0.3	0.2
Iceland	kg	0.4	0.4	0.4	0.5	0.5	0.6
India	kg	0.6	0.6	0.6	0.7	0.7	0.7
Indonesia	kg	0.3	0.4	0.3	0.3	0.2	0.3
Iran	kg	0.8	0.8	0.6	1.2	0.4	1
Ireland	kg	3	3.6	2.4	2.4	2.3	2.1
Israel	kg	0.2	0.3	0.2	0.2	0.2	0.1
Italy	kg	0.1	0.1	0.1	0.1	0.1	0.1
Japan	kg	1.1	1.1	1.3	1.2	1.1	1.1
Kazakhstan	kg	1.3	1.5	2	1.6	1.8	1.8
Kenya	kg	0.2	0.2	0.3		0.1	0.1
Kyrgyzstan	kg	0.4	0.6	0.6	0.7	0.7	0.7
Latvia	kg	0.5	0.5	0.5	0.4	0.4	0.5

Table 2.11: Tea consumption per capita *(Contd.)*

Countries	Unit	2002	2003	2004	2005	2006	2007
Lithuania	kg				0.4	0.4	0.4
Luxembourg	kg	0.2	0.8	0.4	0.3	0.2	0.3
Macedonia	kg	0.5	0.4	0.3	0.3	0.3	
Malaysia	kg	0.6	0.6	0.7	0.6	0.7	0.7
Malta	kg	1.5	1.3	1.4	1.2	1.2	1.3
Mexico	kg						
Moldova	kg	0.1	0.2	0.2	0.2	0.2	0.2
Mongolia	kg	0.9	0.9	0.9	0.6	0.9	1
Montenegro	kg						
Morocco	kg	1.5	1.5	1.5	1.6	1.6	1.8
Netherlands	kg	1.2	1.2	1.1	1.5	1.3	1
New Zealand	kg	0.6	0.5	0.4	0.5	0.6	0.5
Nigeria	kg	0.1	0.1				0.1
Norway	kg	0.3	0.4	0.3	0.3	0.3	0.3
Pakistan	kg	0.6	0.7	0.7	0.8	0.8	0.7
Peru	kg	0.2	0.2	0.1	0.2	0.2	0.1
Philippines	kg						
Poland	kg	0.7	0.7	0.7	0.7	0.6	0.6
Portugal	kg	0.1		0.1	0.1	0.1	0.1
Romania	kg						0.1
Russia	kg	1.1	1.2	1.2	1.2	1.2	1.2
Serbia	kg						
Singapore	kg						
Slovakia	kg	0.1	0.1	0.2	0.3	0.3	1
Slovenia	kg	0.1	0.1	0.1	0.1	0.1	0.2
South Africa	kg	0.4	0.5	0.3	0.8	0.5	0.4
South Korea	kg			0.1	0.1	0.1	0.1
Spain	kg	0.1	0.1	0.1	0.1	0.2	0.3
Sweden	kg	0.3	0.4	0.5	0.4	0.3	0.4
Switzerland	kg	0.3	0.3	0.4	0.3	0.4	0.2
Tajikistan	kg	0.7	0.8	0.9	0.9	0.8	0.6
Thailand	kg	0.5	0.7	0.8	0.8	0.8	0.8
Turkey	kg	2	2.3	3	3.2	2.9	3
Turkmenistan	kg	1.1	0.5	0.4	1.7	0.8	0.6
Ukraine	kg	0.4	0.4	0.1	0.5	0.5	0.5
United Kingdom	kg	2.3	2	2.2	2.1	2.3	2.3
USA	kg	0.5	0.5	0.6	0.5	0.6	0.5
Uzbekistan	kg	0.9	0.1	0.8	1	0.8	0.8
Venezuela	kg						0.1
Vietnam	kg	0.2	0.6	0.2	0.5	0.5	0.6
World	kg	0.6	0.6	0.6	0.7	0.7	0.7

Tea Association at the 27th annual general meeting of the association. And this achievement is, of course, due to maximum favor of all inputs, practically the climatic condition. But, he reiterated that the tea industry immediately requires more additional plantation area to meet the target of 1,000 mkg by the end of the 21st century. Otherwise, tea production will grow at a small rate of around 3% per annum. Nevertheless, it is necessary to renovate tea areas, which are more than 60 years of age. A replanting program of 2% per annum will ensure a rotation over 50 years. Obviously, the argument in favor of "exportable surplus" needs be reconsidered. It is a plain truth that if not today, tomorrow India will have to import sizeable quantity of tea either, or to curtail its export for the sake of domestic consumer. Otherwise, where is the guarantee that, in the near future, domestic consumers will not be strangulated with severe pressure of demand-pull inflation? Where is the guarantee that the industry will be able to maintain exportable surplus, as expected? These matters are indeed, related with the industry's social obligation to two segments-first, obligations to domestic consumers in terms of right price for the right product at the right time; second, obligation to the nation in terms of helping earn foreign exchange.

Imports for Re-export

There are countries like UK, USA, importing huge quantity of teas, of course, high grade, to re-export them in the value added from. It should not go unnoticed that international buyers are fast leaning towards packet tea, instant tea and tea bags. So, it is high time to catch them young. Indian tea barons should realize this fact. They should further appreciate that endeavor to re-export value added teas will help to find new markets and to contribute more foreign exchange in the national exchequer through nontraditional way. This is likely to attract new investment also. This besides, two other significant matter should not go unescaped from our view. First, India's overwhelming dependence on traditional buyers-Russia and CIS who were the principal buyers of Indian tea? Although, at the moment, India enjoys comfortable position the possibility of creating discomfort by the infiltrated sellers in these markets should not be over-looked. The "seller's market" at that time was turned to "buyer's market". Second, China is preparing vigorously to exert its pressure in the international market. Tea is listed as one of the key export commodities. Due to over-whelming importance of hard currency earnings it was very likely that the China government provided all sorts of incentive to the tea industry. It is worth noting that between 1950 and 2004 total tea area in that country increased by more than 7 times, 155,000 hectares to 1,115,300 hectares. Output increased by more than three times over the same period from 255 mkg to 950 mkg. Export-increase accounted for 10 times from 18 mkg in 1950 to 205 mkg in 2004. Nevertheless, China has the greatest range of tea in different grades and varieties. China intends to be at the top of the list of tea traders in the world market. And no denying the fact, China may, at the earliest opportunity, penetrate in the Russian and CIS market. Keeping in view this possibility, the industry should right now find new market, which may easily be possible with selling value-added teas.

Standard of Quality

Of course, the standard of quality matters much at any export trade. It may be recollected that only a few years back the quality of tea sold to Russia was so bad that mkg of tea were destroyed. Serious complaints were lodged to the tea board. Russian television cautioned the domestic consumers with the words: "Don't sip Indian tea". No doubt, industry's goodwill has been severely damaged by this act of the exporters. The questions are obviously, who has to be blamed for this event; what measures have been taken so far to prevent recurrences. The Tea Board, being the appropriate authority, should devise full-proof measures to ensure quality. Tea Board should (1) scrutinize every export order received; (2) ensure the creditworthiness of the exporter; (3) arrange intensive checking at the time of shipment; (4) arrange random checking after un-loading; (5) introduce mandatory use of the Tea Board's logo, subject to the fulfillment of stipulated conditions, for every export.

It is unlikely that with further liberalization of imports, the domestic market will be flooded with low-grade imported tea. For the Gresham's Law does not hold good in an open market, the law reacts in the opposite mr-good product drives away bad product. As far as India's domestic tea market is concerned, consumers here drink the best of CTCs. Not only that, they are prepared to pay a premium for quality. Because of the strong domestic demand Indian tea prices are generally higher than the world prices. And it is to be noted further that in volume terms India is the largest consumer. Evidently, in the perspective of the country's consumer behavior it is doubtful that to what extent importers will be able to sell the low-grade imported stuff to increase their profits and be able to exert dominant voice in the domestic market.

It was unwise to view that once India started buying of low priced tea, the price of its produce in the international market would have fallen. Some Asian sellers would have been benefited out of this transaction. From the viewpoint of open market economy, however, it was felt that the aforesaid promise was not correct. In an open market mechanism only the appropriate substitute and its price played a dominant role in determining the demand of the principal product the vice-versa. Since Indian importers intended to import only cheap variety of teas, the price of Indian tea was likely too remain unaffected until now suppliers entered the market. And in this matter, the only threat was likely to come from China-the Asian Dragon-having a large variety and quantity of tea at its disposal.

In the light of the above study, it was viewed that there was no point of becoming shaky even though the Ministry of Commerce allowed free import of teas for re-exports in bulk as well. The only necessity is to remain alert against the unscrupulous traders who may take the advantage of import liberalization policy of the Government of India just to further their own interest.

Unrestricted Import of Tea: To Allow or Not

Proposal of ministry of commerce, Government of India, modified the export-import policy (1992–1997) with a view to facilitating the export oriented unit (EOU)/export processing zones (EPZ) to freely import teas for bulk-re-exports generated unfathomable dissatisfaction among many Barons of the India's tea industry. Tea imports were allowed with the rider that they should be used only for re-export with a 20% value addition. But, the imports were insignificant because the facility was limited to re-export of packaged teas, tea bags and instant tea. The Commerce Ministry sought the industry's view on allowing bulk re-export of tea blended with the imported product. Barons of the Indian tea association asserted: (1) having an exportable surplus, India does not need to import teas; (2) if the imported low grade teas are blended with better stuff of the country to export as tea bags, packets, instant tea, its image would be damaged at the international market and exports suffer in the long run; (3) under the Exim policy (1997–2002) for tea, exporters were not allowed to sell any portion of the manufactured items in the domestic market. But, the leaders of the Indian tea industry feared that once bulk teas, allowed to be imported, there would also be an option for unloading these teas in the domestic market. And a few larger business houses, facing stiff competition in the domestic market, would practically use the cheap imported product to reduce their prices in a bid to earn and maintain substantial profit and hold the domestic share; (4) import of teas by India would raise international prices of teas while depressing domestic markets, a situation, which would adversely effect the growth of tea industry that may eventually lead to recession. The aforesaid premises, as a corollary, led many barons of the industry to raise strong objection against the government's intention of further liberalizing the Exim policy, which may open the floodgates for import of teas. They felt that the policy, if implemented, would not, in anyway, help the growth of the country's tea industry. But, however, one should not be touchy and emotional while considering the policy of import. Rather, it was imperative to visualize the necessity of imports in the perspective of reality. And no denying the fact, that only such a study can help comment judiciously either in favor or against the proposed policy.

Recent Position

Indian tea exports are gaining momentum. This is attributed to decline in production in Kenya. Of course, the Russian offtake is strong. There has been an increase enquiry from Pakistan, Egypt and, of late, Iraq. The upturn in demand has been aided by reports of decline in tea production in Kenya. Egypt imported 4.88 mkg of tea in 2007, up from 2.75 mkg in 2006. Pakistan purchased 14.73 mkg of Indian tea in 2006, but the offtake slumped to 5.15 mkg in 2007. Tea exports to Pakistan may pick up soon. Global economic slowdown had affected the tea industry. Tea export volumes rese in 2008 and reached a level of 156 mkg by October. But, since then demand for tea in Western nations and Russian has declined. Tea balance sheet is as in Table 2.12.

Imports touched around 14 mkg in 2004 against average levels of 1 to 2 mkg in the past. The unit CIF value of tea imported from a few countries was lower than the prices faced at Indian auctions. This has affected market sentiments. With the emerging trends in the globalized economy, markets can no longer be protected. Indian Tea Industry will have to compete in the domestic market. Protecting the home market is going to be a challenging task and the Tea Industry has to evolve some strategy to counter the new competing forces unleashed by globalization.

Table 2.12: Tea balance sheet

(mkg)

Year	Import	Estimated supply	Export	Dom. demand
2008–2009	22.03	995.03	190.64	804.39
2009–2010	25.84	1,016.84	213.43	803.41
2010–2011	19.26	985.99	213.79	772.2
2011–2012	19.21	1,114.67	214.35	900.32

Continued supplies of tea at reasonable prices to the domestic market and to maintain and improve the export share in the global tea trade were the twin objectives of the previous plan period. These twin objectives hold good for the X-plan period and they could be fulfilled, only if the industry continues to grow with profit and remains healthy.

Imports of tea into India have further increased during 2009–1010 to a level of 25.8 mkg against 16 mkg in 2007. Imports have been moving around 20 mkg in the subsequent years (Tables 2.13 and 2.13A). The ITA has expressed its concern over the imports of substandard teas. Their average value in 2010 was Rs 64.5 a kg. This is estimated at Rs 128.2 per kg during 2012–2013 (Table 2.13). In recent years, the average CIF value of imported teas, especially from countries like Vietnam, was significantly lower than prices prevailing in India. The industry feels that the prevailing rate of import duty which is 100% should be maintained. However, a phased rate of reduction is inevitable under the India-ASEAN Free Trade Agreement.

Table 2.13: Import of tea into India

Year	Quantity (mkg)	Value (Rs crores)	Unit CIF price(Rs/Kg)
1992–1993	1.37	5.14	37.52
1993–1994	0.87	3.99	45.86
1994–1995	0.20	1.10	55.00
1995–1996	0.45	2.41	53.56
1996–1997	1.25	6.21	49.68
1997–1998	2.61	17.79	68.16
1998–1999	8.93	64.73	72.49
1999–2000	10.36	61.97	59.80
2000–2001	15.35	96.67	63.00
2001–2002	16.79	86.59	51.56
2002–2003	22.49	105.32	46.82
2007–2008	16.75	108.07	64.51
2008–2009	22.03	181.45	82.36
2009–2010	25.84	214.44	82.97
2010–2011	19.26	186.82	97.02
2011–2012	19.21	186.04	96.85
2012–2013	21.90	282.56	129.02
2011–2012 (Apr-Dec)	16.94	166.04	98.02

Calendar Year

Year	Quantity (mkg)	CIF value (crores)	Unit price (kg)	CIF value (Mill US$)	Unit price (US$/kg)
2007	15.99	104.60	65.43	25.27	1.58
2008	20.28	161.97	79.90	37.31	1.84
2009	25.67	216.03	84.16	44.64	1.74
2010	20.04	184.94	92.26	40.46	2.02
2011	21.17	206.54	97.57	44.30	2.09
2012	20.50	253.60	123.71	47.45	2.31

With regard to the future two questions arise in this context: (1) despite the export price advantage enjoyed by some of the ASEAN countries vis-à-vis India's tea import price, why is only 22% of India's import demand met by ASEAN (and a mere 5% from Vietnam)? (2) why is India importing around 78% of its tea imports from other countries at higher prices? Of India's total tea imports, black tea constitutes around 90%. According to the UN Comtrade data, during 2008, India imported around 46% of black tea from Nepal, 17% from Kenya, 13% from Indonesia and 6% from Vietnam. Thus, India imported around 63% of black tea from Nepal and Kenya even though importing from these countries was more expensive than doing so from Indonesia and Vietnam. This is because India has given preferential market access to Nepal under the Generalized System of Preference (GSP), and India imposes zero tariffs on tea imports, which are used for re-export. In the case of Indonesia and Vietnam, India imposes *most favored nation* (MFN) applied tariffs of 100%, making tea imports from these countries relatively expensive. Under the ASEAN- India free trade agreement (FTA), India kept most of the black tea under the special products category. Applied MFN tariff rates on special products will be brought down in a phased mr. In case of most of the black tea, it will be brought down from 100% to 50% by 2019. This will make tea from Indonesia and even more so from Vietnam (since the latter has a larger negative price difference) relatively cheap.

Safeguard Duty

Imports have been a cause for concern to the Indian growers especially in view of the two FTA in force now—the India-Sri Lanka and the India-ASEAN one—under which duties will come down progressively to 40% in 10 years from 100% now. The industry wants this to continue as a safeguard duty. At its recently held annual general meeting, the ITA Chairman highlighted this issue before the Union Finance Minister also.

Country-wise imports of tea in India (Table 2.13A) show that Nepal has its share of nearly 30% followed by Indonesia 8–9% of Kenya 8–9%. Strange enough major tea producers China and Sri Lanka are small players. Tables 2.13A and 2.14 provide the data regarding, quantity, value and unit price of tea imported during the recent years. After 2008, unit price has increased both because of increase in unit value and depreciation of the rupee.

TEA EXPORTS

India is one of the major producer and exporter of tea. Starting from 191.7 mkg in 1947, it went upto 229.6 million tons in 1977—the highest ever till now. Exports have been moving below this level all these years. Britain is known for tea drinking. It is a major consumer of Indian tea, and hence a great source of revenue for the Indian tea industry. In fact, Britons are the biggest consumers of tea per capita. However, this is changing. According to the FAO, Britain will be consuming 15% less tea than 15 years earlier. This is worrying India's tea exporters. In fact, during the last 5 years, tea exports to the UK have come down to 16 mkg from 22 mkg. Britain consumes 100 mkg of tea annually, of which nearly 60 mkg is imported from Africa. The country is gradually leaning toward variants with less tea content, like chamomile tea and lemon tea.

Table 2.13A: Country-wise import of tea into India

Country	Jan–May, 2010			Jan–Dec, 2009 (P)			Jan–Dec, 2008		
	Qty. (mkg)	CIF Value (Crores Rs)	unit (mkg)	Qty. (mkg)	CIF value (Cr. Rs)	Unit (Rs/kg)	Qty. (mkg)	CIF value (Cr. Rs)	Unit (Rs/kg)
Argentina	0.08	0.45	55.73	0.65	3.8	58.22	0.63	2.88	45.43
Bangladesh	–	–	–	0.02	0.27	113.77	–	–	–
Canada	0.20	0.74	36.76	0.23	0.84	37.12	–	–	–
China	0.38	3.67	96.97	0.49	5.22	105.99	1.38	8.84	64.34
Germany	0.01	0.09	277.99	–	–	–	0.01	0.31	308.48
Hong Kong	–	–	–	0.02	0.11	71.56	–	–	–
Indonesia	0.40	4.10	101.36	2.76	24.9	90.25	3.39	22.30	65.86
Iran	1.04	5.59	53.87	1.42	8.6	60.42	0.24	1.00	42.2
Japan	0.05	0.79	152.97	0.01	0.03	186.48	–	–	–
Kenya	0.75	9.30	124.01	2.64	35.79	135.68	3.32	36.03	108.55
Malawi	0.35	3.60	102.39	0.51	4.82	94.16	0.52	3.85	74.09
Nepal	1.63	12.82	78.75	7.86	65.48	83.21	7.87	59.03	75.13
Papua New Guinea	0.13	1.00	78.34	0.6	4.9	81.88	0.41	2.68	65.25
South Africa	0.00	0.01	112.16	0	0.05	131.14	–	–	–
Sri Lanka	0.14	2.16	151.83	0.94	12.85	136.83	0.51	9.97	194.22
Tanzania	0.01	0.15	117.56	–	–	–	0.02	0.1	51.39
UAE	0.47	3.59	76.89	0.61	2.53	41.67	0	0.01	66.89
United Kingdom	0.05	1.38	258.41	0.29	5.27	179.63	0.2	4.58	227.78
USA	–	–	–	0.01	0.23	414.79	–	–	–
Vietnam	1.80	11.92	66.09	6.4	38.73	60.55	1.77	10.29	58.16
Zimbabwe	–	–	–	–	–	–	0.01	0.1	51.39
Total	**7.49**	**61.36**	**81.89**	**25.46**	**214.42**	**84.23**	**20.28**	**161.97**	**79.90**

"0" is less than 500.
(P) Provisional

Table 2.14: Origin wise import of tea into India during April to December

Country	April–March, 2010			2009 (P)			2008		
	Qty. (mkg)	CIF value (Crores Rs)	Unit price	Qty. ((Th kg)	CIF value (Th. Rs)	Unit price (Rs/kg)	Qty. (Th. kg)	CIF value (Th. Rs)	Unit price (Rs/kg)
Argentina	0.38	2.39	62.33	0.30	1.94	64.10	0.43	1.91	44.89
Bangladesh	0.02	0.27	113.77	0.02	0.27	113.77	–	–	–
Canada	0.30	1.10	37.07	0.17	0.64	36.72	–	–	–
China	0.51	5.34	105.72	0.23	2.69	118.58	1.20	7.65	63.78
Germany	0.00	0.00	0.00	–	–	–	0.01	0.31	308.48
Hong Kong	0.02	0.11	71.56	0.02	0.11	71.56	–	–	–
Indonesia	2.22	21.94	98.71	1.96	19.29	97.97	2.56	17.68	68.99
Iran	2.20	12.36	56.10	1.42	8.60	60.42	0.24	1.00	42.20
Japan	0.01	0.03	27.56	0.01	0.03	186.48	–	–	–
Kenya	2.27	31.49	138.76	1.85	26.08	141.14	2.64	30.20	114.15
Malawi	0.61	6.07	99.08	0.42	4.08	96.62	0.46	3.49	75.23
Nepal	7.29	61.90	84.90	6.76	58.05	85.86	7.26	55.73	76.68
Papua New Guinea	0.44	3.38	76.22	0.34	2.59	75.95	0.22	1.55	70.94
South Africa	0.01	0.04	32.14	0.01	0.02	124.68	–	–	–
Sri Lanka	0.93	11.55	124.69	0.84	10.46	124.85	0.43	8.95	208.15
Tanzania	0.01	0.15	117.56	–	–	–	0.02	0.10	51.39
UAE	1.03	5.92	57.77	0.56	2.33	41.24	0.01	0.01	66.89
United Kingdom	0.20	4.08	205.73	0.17	3.25	194.77	0.15	3.57	239.48
USA	0.01	0.23	414.79	0.01	0.23	414.79	–	–	–
Vietnam	7.21	44.75	62.05	5.56	33.85	60.89	1.60	9.39	58.87
Total	**25.67**	**213.10**	**83.01**	**20.65**	**174.51**	**84.52**	**17.23**	**141.54**	**82.17**

"0" is less than 500.
(P) Provisional

The share of United Kingdom 66.3% in 1947 increased slightly to 68% in 1957, went down from year to year and is around 9% currently. USSR which had a minor share of 2.1% in the total Indian exports increased to 51.5%, in 1991, has continued to be the major importer with a little fall to around 44%. It has fallen further to 21% recently. Pakistan (around 10%) along with UAI (11%) are other important importer of tea from India and the USA had a share of 9% in 1947, but cane down to less than 2% by mid eighties, has again improved its share to 5–6%.

Global warming including a shortfall in rain and prolonged dry periods has created problems for tea growers. Added to this, there are pests and outbreaks of disease that adversely affect tea productivity. Also, the tea companies that export have to obtain quality management certification and food safety management certification such as ISO 9001, HACCP and ISO 22000.

Recent Developments

The Indian tea industry is keen on upgrading quality and hiking production to meet growing demand in the domestic as well as the global market. For starters, the Tea Board has just lined up a Rs 1,500 million corpus for R and D, of which Rs 200 million will be spent to develop weather-resistant tea clones.

Another Rs 3,500 million has been earmarked for replanting ageing bushes that are affecting the overall production of Indian tea, which has stagnated at around 980 mkg for a couple of years. Also, the allocation for improving the living conditions of tea estate workers in the 12th Plan has been hiked to Rs 2,000 million, up from Rs 480 million in the 11th Plan.

It has been observed that the younger plants are more resistant to insects and pests. Hence, the TRA and United Planters' Association of South India have been entrusted with the task of working on developing climate resistant clones.

India is the first country in the world to successfully start an electronic auction for tea. By 2011, more than 400 mkg of tea had been sold through the electronic route. Introduction of the web-based electronic auction will help broaden the base of buyers, increasing the involvement of all stakeholders. Electronic auction makes the bidding process transparent, faster and helps in arriving at a fair price. In future, it may be possible to have a single all-India tea auction and full electronic settlements.

The Tea Board has announced that it will clamp down heavily on import of low quality teas that are meant for re export. According to the Tea Board, imported teas should comply with the Food Safety Standards Act and will have to obtain certificates from the Tea Board empanelled testing laboratories. The Board has also formed two tea councils—one for South India and the other for North India. These will keep a strict vigil on the quality of imported teas.

The Tea Board has dropped the loan component from the purview of the Special Purpose Tea Fund Scheme (SPTFS) as part of restructuring the scheme. The SPTFS was launched in April 2007, but the demand for loans under SPTFS was very poor—far below the target. In a five-year period ending May 2012, the loan demand amounted to Rs 480 million, covering 117 gardens belonging to 70 companies, against the target of Rs 7,500 million. The turnaround of the tea industry from 2008 onwards may be responsible for low loan demand. Also, many garden owners are not happy with the structure of the loan scheme. A technical committee has been constituted to re-evaluate the estimated cost of replanting old bushes.

Shift in the composition of demand for tea in the importing countries has produced adverse effects on export earnings from tea in India. Wide fluctuations in tea prices are a serious problem. There is a fierce competition abroad. Indian tea has lost its competitive advantage to other countries on account of high cost and poor quality. The major competitive countries are Sri Lanka, Kenya, China and Indonesia. China is the major producer of green tea. Sri Lanka and Indonesia mainly produce orthodox varieties of tea. Kenya is basically a CTC tea-producing country. India is facing competition from Sri Lanka and Indonesia with respect to orthodox tea, from China with respect to green tea, and from Kenya and other African countries with respect to CTC tea. Because of their low domestic base, Sri Lanka and Kenya have an edge over India in the international market. Range and types of tea offered by India is as detailed below:

Range of tea offered in India

- Darjeeling tea
- Nilgiri tea
- Assam tea

Speciality teas:

- Black tea
- Instant tea
- Green tea
- Oolong tea
- Biodynamic tea
- White tea
- Flavored tea.

Share of India in the world tea is as in Table 2.15. India's share in the international trade of tea was 42% between 1951 and 1960. It fell to 21.91% during 1981–1990, and further to 12.32% in 2008–2009. In the first half of the financial year, 2012–2013, tea exports fell by 20%. Exports declined to 81.85 mkg as compared to 102.6 mkg in the corresponding period of 2011–2012. This is attributed to higher prices and lower availability. However, because of higher unit value realization, the export value, during this period, fell just marginally from Rs 15,600 million to Rs 15,080 million (Table 2.15; Tables 2.15A and B).

India's tea industry is aiming to increase its exports to ASEAN countries. In the ASEAN region, there has been a declining trend in tea production and an increase in tea imports.

Demand Supply

Following erratic weather conditions where either there were drought conditions or incessant rains triggering a pest attack that will leave Indian crop down by 22 mkg in 2010. The industry now expects a crop level of 957 mkg, with imports of 20 mkg and a consumption of 870 mkg.

There appears to be equilibrium in demand and supply. Exports are being seen at around the level of 190 mkg which is lower than in 2009 but realizations are expected to be better on improved prices. Commenting on the rising consumption of tea, the study is of the view that the demand which is now growing at an annual

Table 2.15: India's share in world tea production and exports (percentage)

Country	Production (based on 5-year global average quantum of 3,727 mkg) (2005–2009)	Exports (based on 5-year global average quantum of 1,594 mkg) (2005–2009)
China	30	18
India	27	13
Kenya	9	22
Sri Lanka	8	19
Indonesia	4	6
Turkey	4	–
Vietnam	4	6
Others	14	16

Source: The Hindu Survey of Indian Industry 2011, p. 295.

Table 2.15A: Country-wise exports from India during 1947–2004

(In mkg)

Country/year	1947	1957	1967	1977	1987	1991	1997	1999	2004
United Kingdom	127.20	135.40	117.20	74.30	22.40	22.50	25.40	25.00	25.10
Percent of export	66.30	68.00	53.80	32.40	11.09	11.09	12.70	12.10	12.11
Ireland	9.00	8.30	6.20	6.40	2.10	2.50	2.60	2.50	2.50
Percent of export	4.70	4.20	2.80	2.80	1.04	1.23	1.28	1.20	1.19
Netherlands	1.50	0.90	3.70	3.40	1.60	1.90	2.70	2.60	2.60
Percent of export	0.80	0.50	1.70	1.50	0.79	0.90	1.33	1.27	1.26
West Germany	NII	1.90	2.20	5.80	4.70	4.70	6.90	6.60	6.65
Percent of export	Nil	0.90	1.00	2.50	2.33	2.30	3.40	3.20	3.21
Rest of West Europe	0.60	0.10	0.50	0.90	0.50	0.60	0.80	0.80	0.80
Percent of export	0.30	0.05	0.20	0.40	0.20	0.30	0.40	0.40	0.40
Poland	NIL	NIL	1.80	5.30	10.70	11.90	14.00	14.70	14.75
Percent of export	NIL	NIL	0.80	2.80	5.30	5.90	6.90	7.10	7.11
Yugoslavia	NIL	NII	0.50	4.70	1.40	0.20	0.30	0.40	0.40
Percent of export	NIL	NIL	0.20	2.00	0.70	0.10	0.15	0.17	0.16
Country/year	1947	1957	1967	1977	1987	1991	1997	1999	2004
Rest of East Europe	NIL	0.10	1.70	1.40	3.30	1.00	1.60	1.40	1.40
Percent of export	NIL	0.05	0.80	0.60	1.60	0.50	0.80	0.70	0.70
USSR	4.00	7.30	20.70	47.70	96.60	104.50	90.70	92.80	94.10
Percent of export	2.10	3.60	9.50	20.80	47.80	51.50	44.70	44.90	44.95

(Contd.)

Table 2.15A: Country-wise exports from India during 1947–2004

(In mkg)

Country/year	1947	1957	1967	1977	1987	1991	1997	1999	2004
Afghanistan	NIL	NIL	5.70	8.60	3.60	1.60	0.80	1.20	1.20
Percent of export	NIL	NIL	2.60	3.70	1.80	0.80	0.40	0.60	0.60
Iran	3.90	5.60	1.80	6.60	18.90	14.80	11.70	12.80	12.80
Percent of export	2.00	2.80	1.10	2.90	9.40	7.30	5.80	6.20	6.15
Iraq	1.40	0.02	2.50	4.60	8.80	–	0.10	0.04	0.40
Percent of export	0.70	0.00	1.10	2.00	4.30	–	0.01	0.02	0.02
Persian Gulf Ports	4.40	2.60	3.00	6.20	7.00	5.20	6.80	7.02	7.02
Percent of export	2.30	1.30	1.40	2.70	3.50	2.60	3.35	3.40	3.40
Jordan	NIL	NIL	1.40	0.60	–	0.50	0.10	0.60	0.60
Percent of export	–	–	0.60	0.30	0.05	0.20	0.20	0.30	0.36
Rest of Middle East	0.60	0.30	0.05	0.07	0.30	–	0.20	0.20	0.20
Percent of export	0.30	0.10	0.02	0.03	0.10	–	0.10	0.10	0.10
Pakistan	NIL	NIL	NIL	4.60	0.60	0.30	0.40	O.4	0.40
Percent of export	–	–	–	2.00	0.30	0.15	0.20	0.20	0.26
Japan	NIL	NIL	0.30	0.80	1.40	2.00	1.90	2.30	2.30
Percent of export	–	–	0.10	0.30	0.30	1.00	0.90	1.10	1.10
Arab Rep. of Egypt	1.80	7.30	16.60	14.10	7.80	7.90	7.20	7.60	7.60
Percent of export	0.90	3.70	7.60	6.10	3.90	3.90	3.50	3.70	3.76
Sudan	0.70	2.00	10.00	13.60	0.10	–	0.10	0.10	0.10
Percent of export	0.40	1.00	4.60	5.70	0.05	–	0.05	0.06	0.06
Tunisia	NIL	NIL	3.80	1.20	1.00	1.70	1.50	1.90	1.90
Percent of export	–	–	1.70	0.50	0.50	0.80	0.70	0.90	0.90
Rest of Africa	NIL	NIL	–	0.40	3.70	7.00	9.80	9.50	9.50
Percent of export	–	–	–	0.20	1.80	3.40	4.80	4.60	4.60
Canada	8.20	7.70	3.90	2.50	0.80	0.60	0.10	0.15	0.15
Percent of export	4.30	3.90	1.80	1.10	0.40	0.30	0.05	0.07	0.07
USA	17.30	10.60	8.40	10.00	1.80	2.50	2.90	3.30	3.30
Percent of export	9.00	5.30	3.90	4.40	0.90	1.20	1.40	1.60	1.60
Australia	7.00	3.40	5.40	4.60	0.70	0.80	0.50	0.60	0.60
Percent of export	3.70	1.70	2.50	2.00	0.30	0.40	0.25	0.30	0.30
New Zealand	0.50	0.70	0.40	1.30	–	–	–	–	–
Percent of export	0.30	0.40	0.20	0.60	–	–	–	–	–
All other countries	3.60	5.00	0.10	0.50	4.30	8.10	13.40	11.95	11.95
Percent of export	1.90	2.50	0.05	0.20	2.10	4.00	6.63	5.81	5.81
Total	**191.70**	**199.20**	**217.80**	**229.60**	**201.90**	**202.90**	**203.00**	**206.50**	**205.00**

Table 2.15B: Quantity and value of tea exports from India

Year	Quantity thousand kg	Value thousand Rs	Year	Quantity thousand kg	Value thousand Rs
1954–1955	208,462	1,482,316	1983–1984	202312	5,575,549
1955–1956	183,769	1,096,448	1984–1985	217,401	7,713,889
1956–1957	233,088	1,451,344	1985–1986	214,234	6,479,796
1957–1958	191,755	1,436,435	1986–1987	196,232	5,794,783
1958–1959	217,322	1296953	1987–1988	201,830	6,277,688
1959–1960	215,459	1,290,846	1988–1989	204,075	6,352,799
1960–1961	196,473	122,349	1989–1990	210,615	9,047,231
1961–1962	205,329	1,221,680	1990–1991	198,240	1,062,0939
1962–1963	220,800	1,296,000	1991–1992	215,166	1,196,4625
1963–1964	209,328	1,231,885	1992–1993	178,950	1,031,6125
1964–1965	212,325	1,246,657	1993–1994	153,427	1,039,8935
1965–1966	197,385	1,148,374	1994–1995	130,836	9,635,458
1966–1967	190,383	1,362,189	1995–1996	166,239	1,218,4298
1967–1968	203,333	1,801,974	1996–1997	167,172	1,256,8167
1968–1969	200,824	1,365,092	1997–1998	208,773	1,945,3207
1969–1970	174,112	1,245,029	1998–1999	203,431	2,128,8720
1970–1971	199,139	1,842,470	1999–2000	189,837	1,867,2822
1971–1972	214,317	1,609,204	2000–2001	200,770	1,806,6853
1972–1973	193,228	1,472,935	2001–2002	190.0	16,957.8
1973–1974	190,268	1,448,490	2002–2003	184.4	16,650.4
1974–1975	225,057	2,235,355	2003–2004	183.07	16,369.9
1975–1976	211,409	2,382,948	2004–2005	205.81	19,247.1
1976–1977	242,418	2,954,777	2005–2006	196.67	17,935.8
1977–1978	221,522	3,637,117	2006–2007	218.15	20,457.2
1978–1979	177,327	3,591,193	2007–2008	185.32	18,886.7
1979–1980	208,448	3,768,961	2008–2009	190.63	23,817.9
1980–1981	231,736	4,352,730	2009–2010	196.35	24,532.4
1981–1982	224,200	4,068,232	2010	193.3	25,952
1982–1983	194,090	3,694,482			

(Excluding instant tea)
Source: Tea Statistics 2000–2001 issued by Tea Board of India, Kolkata.

rate of 3% is still low and the industry has to devise ways of tackling competition especially from the aerated beverage segment. Experts say that this can only be done through innovation as well as promoting the drink as one with health-giving properties. Some broad areas have already been identified in this respect between the ITA and the Tea Board. A domestic consumption level of 870 mkg has been projected for this year.

Exports of tea from India have shown an irregular trend. The country exported 208.5 mkg in 1,954.55. Exports during 1960–1961 were 196.5 mkg 199.1 mkg in 1970–

1971 and 231.7 mkg in 1980–1981. Came down to 198.2 mikg in 1990–1991 and are again quoted as 196.4 mkg in 2009–1910 (Table 2.15C).

Table 2.15C: Exports of tea from India

(Quantity in mkg, value in Rs crores, unit price in Rs/kg)

Year	North India			South India			All India		
	Qty.	*Value*	*UP*	*Qty.*	*Value*	*UP*	*Qty.*	*Value*	*UP*
2006	98.81	1191.70	120.60	119.92	814.83	67.95	218.73	2006.53	91.73
2007	102.72	1215.84	118.37	76.03	594.27	78.16	178.75	1810.11	101.26
2008	116.22	1592.41	137.02	86.90	800.50	92.12	203.12	2392.91	117.81
2009	110.53	1788.00	161.77	87.37	997.85	114.21	197.90	2785.85	140.77
2010-11	115.02	2045.21	177.81	98.77	950.58	96.24	21.3.79	2995.79	140.13
2011 -12	118.74	2337.39	196.85	95.61	967.43	101.19	214.35	3304.82	154.18
2012-13	131.45	2907.34	221.17	84.78	1098.59	129.58	216.23	4005.93	185.26

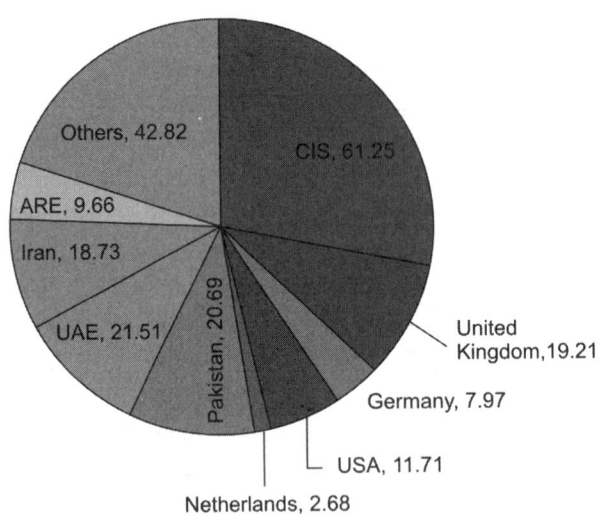

Exports to major countries during 2012–13

Recent Tea Scenario

Exports in 2012 are less although average price realization has been higher: Internationally, black tea prices will go as China, a green tea drinking nation, has developed a taste for black tea.

Significant Changes in 2013

- China will increase sourcing of black tea from India and Africa
- India will introduce all-India e-auction of tea which will allow buyers registered with an auction center to participate in auction at any other center.
- Better price recovery is expected due to this move.

Global shortfall of tea in 2012 with bad weather affecting African production, prices have firmed up by 15–20%. Sri Lankan production (241 mkg) till September has declined from 245 mkg.

According to latest estimates for 2013, exports are estimated at 150–160 mkg.

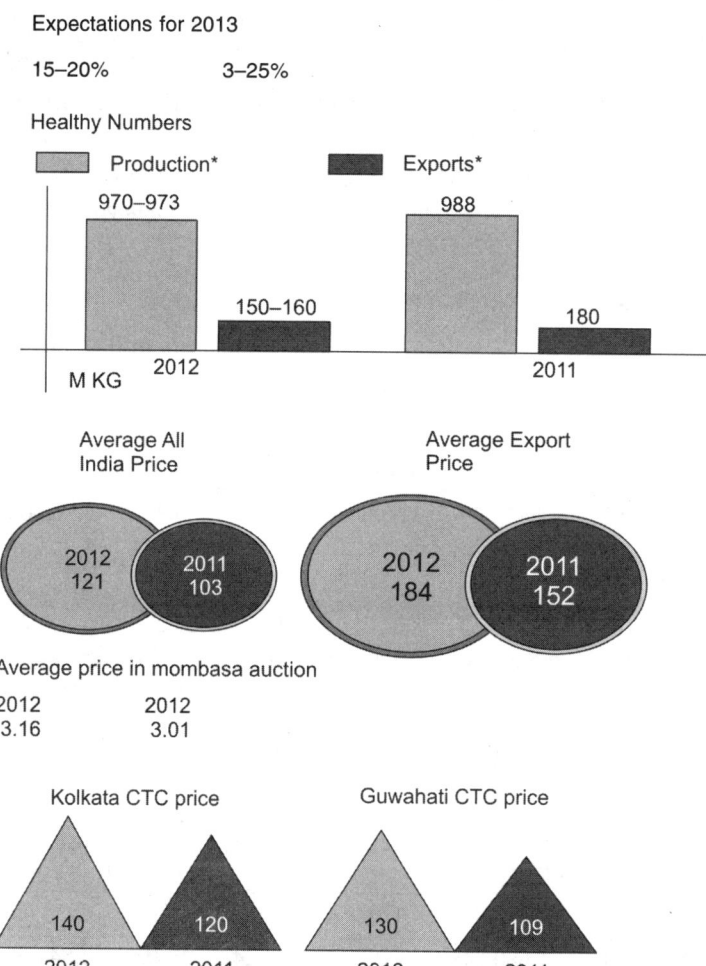

Expectations for 2013

15–20%   3–25%

Healthy Numbers

□ Production*   ■ Exports*

970–973   988

150–160   180

M KG   2012   2011

Average All India Price

2012 121   2011 103

Average Export Price

2012 184   2011 152

Average price in mombasa auction

2012 3.16   2012 3.01

Kolkata CTC price   Guwahati CTC price

140   120   130   109

2012   2011   2012   2011

A look at the country-wise exports data for 2010 (Table 2.15B) shows that Russia is February with 43.2 mkg is at the top, UK comes with 18 mkg and USA comes with 11.6 mkg. UAE imported 22.2 mkg, Iran 15.2 mkg and Pakistan 20.4 mkg. It is interesting that the major world produces Sri Lanka imported 4.7 mkg and Kenya 5.1 mkg.

In total exports of tea separately from North and South India (Tables 2.15C to F), North India has a larger share. With volumes dropping, the emphasis now should be on value-added exports as these teas realize better price. Emphasis should also be placed on enhanced production of orthodox. Exports were 218.7 mkg in 2007, 198 mkg in 2009 against 222 mkg in 2008. Tea is exported from India as packet tea, tea bag and instant tea. Packet tea is highest quantity at 17.1 mkg instant tea being only 3.1 mkg.

Table 2.15D: Financial year

(Quantity in mkg, value in Rs crores, unit price in Rs/kg)

Year	North India			South India			All India		
	Qty.	Value	UP	Qty.	Value	UP	Qty.	Value	UP
2006–07	100.87	1223.20	121.26	117.28	822.52	70.13	218.15	2,045.72	93.77
2007–08	110.15	1291.18	117.22	75.17	597.50	79.48	185.32	1,888.68	101.91
2008–09	106.30	1560.96	146.84	84.34	820.83	97.33	190.64	2,381.79	124.94
2009–10	122.59	2001.36	163.26	90.84	1037.33	114.19	213.43	3,038.69	142.37
2010–11	115.02	2045.21	177.81	98.77	950.58	96.24	213.79	2,995.79	140.13

Table 2.15E: Export of value-added tea from India—calendar year

(Quantity in thousand kg, value in thousand kg)

Year	Packet tea		Tea bags		Instant tea		Total value-added tea	
	Qty.	Value	Qty.	Value	Qty.	Value	Qty.	Value
2006	20,902	2,185,764	6,952	1,543,179	3,062	1,034,092	30,916	4,763,035
2007	9,315	1,197,836	8,303	1,901,099	2,913	914,687	20,531	4,013,622
2008	11,798	1,714,483	8,787	2,302,280	3,047	965,158	23,632	4,981,921
2009	16,267	2,670,284	9,168	2,925,465	2,841	1,107,489	28,276	6,703,238
2010	17,714	3,143,990	10,476	3,261,409	3,359	1,348,411	31,549	7,753,810

Table 2.15F: Export of value-added tea from India—financial year

(Quantity in thousand kg, value in thousand Rs)

Year	Packet tea		Tea bags		Instant tea		Total value-added tea	
	Qty.	Value	Qty.	Value	Qty.	Value	Qty.	Value
2006–07	14,767	1,799,079	7,337	1,680,048	3,095	1,062,424	25,199	4,541,551
2007–08	10,143	1,319,078	8,660	1,952,443	3,036	944,494	21,839	4,216,015
2008–09	10,257	1,621,853	8,636	2,484,356	2,810	951,385	21,703	5,057,594
2009–10	17,722	2,971,091	9,504	2,951,036	2,943	1,177,460	30,169	7,099,587
2010–11	17,141	3,070,304	10,794	3,410,574	3,056	1,271,618	30,991	7,752,496

Export Trade

India is one of the major exporters of black tea. Productions of black tea during 1995 and 1996 in the major tea growing countries are presented in Table 2.15G in xure at the end of the chapter. The table also indicates the quantum of tea exported by the countries during this period. The quantum of tea exported by India during 1991 to 1997 and the value of such exports are presented in Table 2.15H.

Exports over last 3 years in different forms [Tables 15H(a) to 15(d)].

Table 2.15G: Country-wise exports of total tea from India

Name of country	2010 Qty (Th./kg)	2009 Value (Th.)	2008 UP (Th/kg)	Qty (Th./kgs)	Value (Th.)	UP (kg)	Qty (Th./kg)	Value (Th.)	UP (Th/kg)
I. West Europe:									
(a) EEC									
United Kingdom	18126	2588914	142.83	16720	2264167	135.42	19298	2150808	111.45
Ireland	1775	605852	341.33	1441	406052	281.78	1482	345952	233.44
Netherlands	3201	674338	210.66	2572	619963	241.04	2578	554130	214.95
Germany	5608	1226559	218.72	4001	928476	232.06	4329	903921	208.81
Italy	631	99157	157.14	1241	128304	103.39	123	34615	281.42
Sub-Total (a)	**29627**	**5287473**	**178.47**	**26148**	**4408216**	**168.59**	**28018**	**4056004**	**144.76**
(b) Other West									
Finland	124	40101	323.40	27	5678	210.30	4	1676	419.00
Sub-Total (b)	**315**	**110521**	**350.86**	**200**	**75295**	**376.48**	**153**	**50845**	**332.32**
Sub-Total (I)	**29942**	**5397994**	**180.28**	**26348**	**4483511**	**170.17**	**28171**	**4106849**	**145.78**
II. East Europe:									
Russian Fed.	43166	5222321	120.98	46341	5648182	121.88	40439	4077344	100.83
Ukraine	1855	229884	123.93	1626	182697	112.36	1564	146153	93.45
Kazakhstan	11105	1719521	154.84	9435	1425796	151.12	11329	1396194	123.24
Uzbekistan				22	2384	108.36	77	9593	124.58
Kyrgyzstan	229	29077	126.97	262	38796	148.08	350	40551	115.86
Tajikistan	161	19198	119.24	99	13152	132.85	176	19818	112.60
Total CIS	**56674**	**7255908**	**128.03**	**57844**	**7333336**	**126.78**	**54024**	**5719693**	**105.87**

(Contd.)

Table 2.15G: Country-wise exports of total tea from India

Name of country	2010			2009			2008		
	Qty (Th/kg)	Value (Th)	UP (Th/kg)	Qty (Th/kgs)	Value (Th)	UP (kg)	Qty (Th/kg)	Value (Th)	UP (Th/kg)
Poland	4342	546589	125.88	3265	488270	149.55	3449	401780	116.49
Sub-Total II	**61018**	**7804240**	**127.90**	**61119**	**7823515**	**128.00**	**57569**	**6130269**	**106.49**
III. America									
(a) North America and West Indies									
USA	11582	2230012	192.54	9210	1736883	188.59	9547	1536172	160.91
Canada	2358	438714	186.05	2440	430992	176.64	1517	247317	163.03
Sub-Total (a)	**13940**	**2668726**	**191.44**	**11650**	**2167875**	**186.08**	**11064**	**1783489**	**161.20**
(b) Latin America									
Suriname	26	2977	114.50	28	4567	163.11	140	20849	148.92
Brazil	0	172	638.25	2	1471	735.50	2	944	472.00
Sub-Total (b)	**124**	**53484**	**431.32**	**41**	**10723**	**261.54**	**155**	**23021**	**148.52**
Sub-Total (III)	**14064**	**2722210**	**193.56**	**11691**	**2178598**	**186.35**	**11219**	**1806510**	**161.02**
IV. West Asia and North Africa									
(a) North Africa									
AR	5811	518918	89.30	5581	512515	91.83	15040	1117533	74.30
Tunisia	6718	517345	77.01	3750	388914	103.71	2999	223119	74.40
Sudan							18	2684	149.11
Sub-Total (a)	**12576**	**1042547**	**82.90**	**9331**	**901429**	**96.61**	**18234**	**1361334**	**74.66**

Table 2.15G: Country-wise exports of total tea from India (*Contd.*)

Name of country	2010			2009			2008		
	Qty (Th/kg)	Value (Th)	UP (Th/kg)	Qty (Th/kgs)	Value (Th)	UP (kg)	Qty (Th/kg)	Value (Th)	UP (Th/kg)
(b) West Asia									
Iran	15241	2607484	171.08	11525	1781108	154.54	15898	2100032	132.09
UAE	22151	3377040	152.46	19421	2851344	146.82	24804	2825260	113.90
Qatar	444	81767	184.16	390	69837	179.07	436	62015	142.24
Kuwait	462	92124	199.40	205	33572	163.77	361	42901	118.84
Iraq	5961	649118	108.89	16591	2118308	127.68	5109	670009	131.14
Saudi Arabia	2870	419056	146.01	2846	376211	132.19	3398	374468	110.20
Jordan	413	49903	120.83	114	14782	129.67	92	6513	70.79
Yemen	900	70295	78.11	400	32302	80.76	414	30276	73.13
Israel	567	201948	356.17	352	126714	359.98	628	161260	256.78
Sub-Total (b)	**49695**	**7669292**	**154.33**	**52572**	**7522891**	**143.10**	**51942**	**6370881**	**122.65**
Sub-Total IV	**62271**	**8711839**	**139.90**	**61903**	**8424320**	**136.09**	**70176**	**7732215**	**110.18**
V. Asia other than West									
Afghanistan	8808	588783	66.85	13398	1017076	75.91	10739	758302	70.61
Japan	3445	930557	270.12	3008	815131	270.99	2712	668103	246.35
Malaysia	659	66725	101.25	342	40350	117.98	138	19065	138.15
Pakistan	20351	1269576	62.38	7510	672023	89.48	7670	574220	74.87
Sri Lanka	4727	681548	144.18	4028	535903	133.04	5569	555354	99.72
China	717	99513	138.79	213	31246	146.69	75	9795	130.60
Bangladesh	3643	253066	69.47	18	10619	589.94			
Sub-Total (V)	**44260**	**4299612**	**97.14**	**30021**	**3460432**	**115.27**	**28805**	**2960014**	**102.76**

(*Contd.*)

Table 2.15G: Country-wise exports of total tea from India

Name of country	2010			2009			2008		
	Qty (Th/kg)	Value (Th)	UP (Th/kg)	Qty (Th/kgs)	Value (Th)	UP (kg)	Qty (Th/kg)	Value (Th)	UP (Th/kg)
VI. Africa other than North									
Ghana	5	2143	428.60	12	2846	237.17			
Kenya	5137	327576	63.77	1840	118446	64.37	2056	124956	60.78
Sub-Total VI.	**5739**	**420014**	**73.19**	**2176**	**197507**	**90.77**	**2236**	**150747**	**67.42**
VII. Australia and Oceania									
Australia	4692	1218558	259.71	4601	1280987	278.41	4912	1036282	210.97
Sub-Total VII.	**4725**	**1227172**	**259.72**	**4645**	**1290582**	**277.84**	**4941**	**1042532**	**211.00**
GRAND TOTAL	**222019**	**30583081**	**137.75**	**197903**	**27858465**	**140.77**	**203117**	**23929136**	**117.81**
U.P (Rs/kg)					140.77			117.81	

"0" is less than 500.

Table 2.15H: Major country-wise exports of tea from India

(Qty. in: mkg, value in million US$ unit price in $/kg)

Name of the countries	2011-12			2010-11			2009-10			2009			2008		
	Qty.	Value	UP	Qty.	Value	UP	Qty.	Value	UP	Qty.	Value	UP	Qty.	Value	UP
Russian Federation	42.61	115.7	2.72	42.55	111.75	2.63	48.35	129.45	2.68	46.34	116.72	2.52	40.44	93.91	2.32
Kazakhstan	12.00	40.95	3.41	10.49	35.84	3.42	11.10	35.73	3.22	9.43	29.46	3.12	11.33	32.16	2.84
Ukraine	1.82	4.57	2.50	1.82	4.82	2.65	1.78	4.46	2.51	1.63	3.78	2.32	1.56	3.37	2.16
Uzbekistan	–	–	–	–	–	–	–	–	–	0.02	0.05	2.24	0.08	0.22	2.76
Other CIS	2.06	8.32	4.04	0.57	2.16	3.74	0.50	1.70	3.35	0.42	1.53	3.65	0.61	2.08	3.41
Total CIS	58.49	169.71	2.90	55.43	154.57	2.79	61.73	171.34	2.78	57.84	151.54	2.62	54.02	131.74	2.44
United Kingdom	21.02	68.68	3.27	16.85	54.28	3.22	17.79	50.86	2.86	16.72	46.79	2.80	19.30	49.54	2.57
Netherlands	4.03	17.73	4.40	3.25	14.94	4.60	2.73	13.83	5.06	2.57	12.81	4.98	2.58	12.76	4.95
Germany	7.18	35.51	4.95	5.98	28.39	4.75	3.89	19.40	4.99	4.00	19.19	4.80	4.33	20.82	4.81
Ireland	1.75	11.29	6.46	1.84	13.87	7.52	1.51	10.16	6.71	1.44	8.39	5.82	1.48	7.97	5.38
Poland	3.88	11.04	2.85	4.40	11.78	2.68	3.42	10.81	3.16	3.27	10.09	3.09	3.45	9.25	2.68
USA	12.77	69.57	5.45	11.63	48.63	4.18	9.81	39.35	4.01	9.21	35.89	3.90	9.55	35.38	3.71
Canada	1.60	6.86	4.28	2.37	9.79	4.13	2.35	8.40	3.57	2.44	8.91	3.65	1.52	5.70	3.75
UAE	18.05	67.97	3.77	19.76	69.01	3.49	21.97	67.83	3.09	19.42	58.92	3.03	24.80	65.08	2.62
Iran	11.05	45.28	4.10	15.89	62.58	3.94	13.28	44.00	3.31	11.53	36.80	3.19	15.90	48.37	3.04
Iraq	–	–	–	3.86	8.70	2.26	17.36	47.27	2.72	16.59	43.77	2.64	5.11	15.43	3.02
Saudi Arabia	3.57	10.98	3.08	2.88	9.04	3.14	2.82	8.28	2.93	2.85	7.77	2.73	3.40	8.63	2.54

(Contd.)

Table 2.15H: Major country-wise exports of tea from India

(Qty. in: mkg, value in million US$ unit price in $/kg)

Name of the countries	2011-12			2010-11			2009-10			2009			2008		
	Qty.	Value	UP	Qty.	Value	UP	Qty.	Value	UP	Qty.	Value	UP	Qty.	Value	UP
ARE	6.57	12.40	1.89	5.23	9.25	1.77	5.76	11.71	2.03	5.58	10.59	1.90	15.04	25.74	1.71
Turkey	0.10	0.27	2.80	0.14	0.54	3.83	0.01	0.09	8.29	0.01	0.12	8.43	0.11	0.27	2.43
Afghanistan	0.69	1.49	2.16	5.19	7.93	1.53	13.33	20.60	1.55	13.40	21.02	1.57	10.74	17.47	1.63
Singapore	0.34	1.44	4.22	0.35	1.40	3.99	0.36	1.58	4.39	0.37	1.70	4.58	0.32	1.65	5.16
Sri Lanka	3.86	11.01	2.85	4.74	15.52	3.27	5.05	14.19	2.81	4.03	11.07	2.75	5.57	12.79	2.30
Kenya	3.26	5.11	1.57	4.07	5.45	1.34	3.09	4.42	1.43	1.84	2.45	1.33	2.06	2.88	.40
Japan	2.91	21.49	7.38	3.58	21.47	6.01	2.95	16.84	5.71	3.01	16.84	5.60	2.71	15.39	5.68
Pakistan	26.27	37.28	1.42	22.08	29.12	1.32	8.31	16.56	1.99	7.51	13.89	1.85	7.67	13.23	1.72
Australia	3.52	22.53	6.40	4.81	28.86	6.00	4.56	25.49	5.59	4.60	26.47	5.75	4.91	23.87	4.86
Other Countries	23.44	62.50	2.67	19.46	52.69	2.71	11.35	34.79	3.06	9.67	30.65	3.17	8.55	27.21	3.18
Total	**214.35**	**690.14**	**3.22**	**213.79**	**657.81**	**3.08**	**213.43**	**637.80**	**2.99**	**197.90**	**575.67**	**2.91**	**203.12**	**551.17**	**2.71**

Source: Various Annual reports Tea Board.

Table 2.15H: Major country-wise exports of tea from India *(Contd.)*

(Qty. in: mkg, value in million US$ unit price in $/kg)

Name of the countries	2013-14			2012-13		
	Qty.	Value	UP	Qty.	Value	UP
Russian Federation	38.62	639.91	2.74	45.91	139.53	3.04
Kazakhstan	10.26	34.38	3.35	11.73	42.09	3.59
Ukraine	2.21	5.90	2.67	2.42	6.62	2.74
Uzbekistan	–	–	–	–	–	–
Other CIS	1.70	6.25	3.68	1.19	3.92	3.29
Total CIS	52.79	152.46	2.89	61.25	192.16	3.14
United Kingdom	17.64	55.98	3.17	19.21	63.91	3.33
Netherlands	3.26	16.26	4.99	2.68	13.28	4.95
Germany	7.77	42.92	5.52	7.97	39.08	4.90
Ireland	2.21	15.63	7.07	2.17	14.40	6.64
Poland	4.72	11.90	2.52	3.48	9.56	2.75
USA	14.09	65.65	4.66	11.71	58.35	4.98
Canada	1.24	5.19	4.18	1.04	5.00	4.81
UAE	23.33	78.31	3.36	21.51	72.55	3.37
Iran	22.90	99.97	4.37	18.73	71.60	3.82
Iraq	–	–	–	0.09	0.20	2.22
Saudi Arabia	2.63	9.60	3.65	2.57	11.58	4.50
(Egypt) ARE	7.45	14.82	1.99	9.66	19.75	2.04
Turkey	–	–	–	0.38	1.22	3.21
Afghanistan	2.46	4.11	1.67	0.74	1.59	2.14
Singapore	0.34	1.78	5.22	0.35	1.90	5.43
Sri Lanka	1.55	3.83	2.47	1.91	4.99	2.61
Kenya	2.69	4.17	1.55	2.66	5.53	2.08
Japan	3.61	35.70	7.12	3.46	25.85	7.47
Pakistan	19.92	32.45	1.63	20.69	37.46	1.81
Australia	3.16	19.32	6.11	3.66	23.73	6.48
Other Countries	13.92	50.01	3.59	13.33	44.67	3.35
Total	**22.5**	**746.6**	**3.31**	**216.23**	**735.90**	**3.40**

Table 2.15H(a): Bulk tea export

Year	Quantity (Mkg)	Value (Rs Crs)	Unit price (Rs/kg)
2010-11	182.80	2220.54	121.47
2011-12	190.25	2576.48	135.43
2012-13	190.63	3126.29	164.00

Table 2.15H(b): Packet tea export

Year	Quantity (Mkg)	Value (Rs Crs)	Unit price (Rs/kg)
2010-11	17.14	307.03	179.13
2011-12	12.07	307.82	255.03
2012-13	11.09	309.18	278.79

Table 2.15H(c): Tea bags export

Year	Quantity (Mkg)	Value (Rs Crs)	Unit price (Rs/kg)
2010-11	17.79	341.06	316.09
2011-12	9.69	328.02	338.51
2012-13	12.12	455.94	376.19

Table 2.15H(d): Instant tea export

Year	Quantity (Mkg)	Value (Rs Crs)	Unit price (Rs/kg)
2010-11	3.06	127.16	415.56
2011-12	2.34	92.50	395.30
2012-13	2.39	114.52	479.16

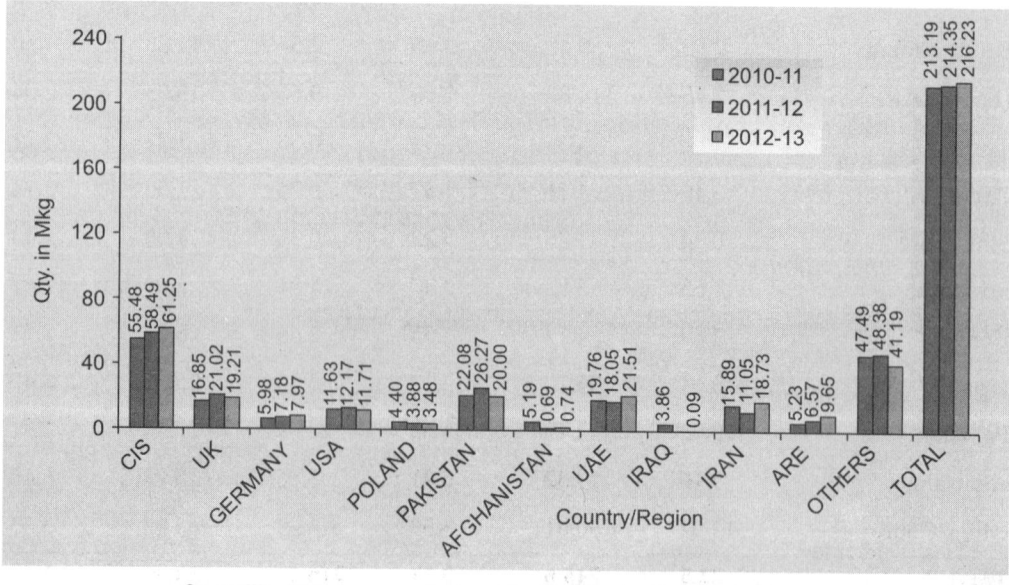

Quantity of tea exports from India (including instant tea)

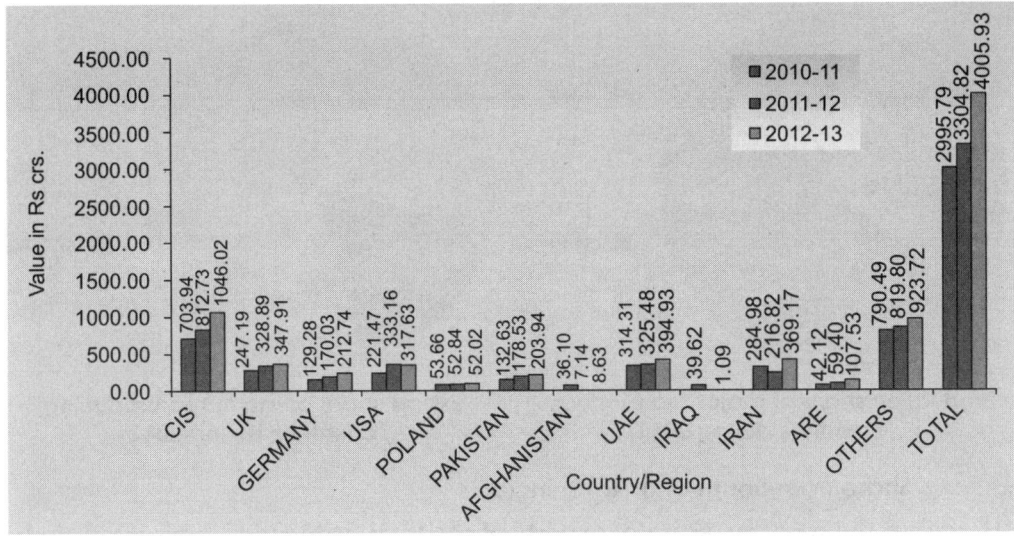

Value of tea exports from India (including instant tea)

Primary Marketing

During the year under report 46% of total tea produced in the country was sold through public auctions, 8% was directly exported through forward contract and the remaining 46% was sold through ex-garden private sale. The different modes of disposal of tea over the last three years and the average price fetched in public auctions are shown in Table 2.15K (a) and 2.15K(b).

Table 2.15K(a): Mode of disposal of tea produced in India

Year	Quantity of tea sold through auction	Ex-garden export under toward contract	Ex-garden private sale
2010	530 (54.87)	41 (4.24)	395 (40.89)
2011	542 (48.57)	90 (8.06)	484 (43.37)
2012	515 (45.74)	87 (7.73)	524 (46.53)

(Volume in million kgs. Figures in brackets denote % to the total production)

Table 2.15K(b): Average price Rs per kg of tea sold through auctions

Year	North India	South India	All India	Financial year	North India	South India	All India
2010	119.51	67.69	104.66	2010-11	120.18	68.37	105.40
2011	117.19	70.17	104.06	2011-12	117.01	70.26	103.94
2012	135.59	87.39	121.81	2012-13	142.09	93.75	127.91

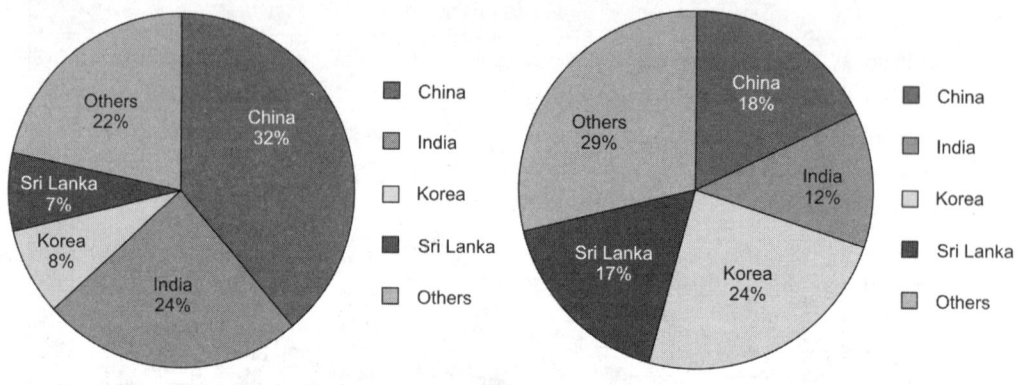

Production share of major tea producing countries during 2012

Export share of major tea producing countries during 2012

Exports Share from South and North India

As against the past, the share of exports of the total production from South India was significantly higher than North India in 2006. It was 119.92 mkg or 5.5% of the total share exported, while exports from North India were a mere 98.81 mkg or 45%. From the year 2007, it is North India which has taken the lead (Table 2.16).

Table 2.16: Exports of tea from India and South India

(Qty in million kg, value in Rs crores, unit price in Rs/kg)

Year	North India			South India			All India		
	Qty.	Value	U.P	Qty.	Value	UP	Qty.	Value	UP
2006	98.81	1,191.70	120.60	119.92	814.83	67.95	218.73	2,006.53	91.73
2007	102.72	1,215.84	118.37	76.03	594.27	78.16	178.75	1,810.11	101.26
2008	116.22	1,592.41	137.02	86.90	800.50	92.12	203.12	2,392.91	117.81
2009	110.53	1,788.00	161.77	87.37	997.85	114.21	197.90	2,785.85	140.77
2010	119.11	2,055.01	172.53	102.91	1,003.30	97.50	222.02	3,058.31	137.75
2011	107.64	2,009.44	186.68	85.23	832.63	97.69	192.87	2,842.07	147.36

Exports of Green Tea

India produces only a small quantity of green tea. Its share in green tea production has been declining from 4.72% in 1978 to 1.23% in 1999. During 1993–1994 India exported 3.36 mkg (nearly 84% of green tea production) to Afghanistan. Thereafter exports to Afghanistan declined rapidly but exports to Russia picked up. Like black tea, Russia has been having a large share in Indian green tea exports. In 1999, India exported around 3 mkg having a 2.07% share in world exports. Although India is not a large consumer of green tea, in the hilly regions of Kangra and Kashmir valleys, green tea goes well with low temperatures. In some Indian markets, green tea is also sold as herbal tea usually mixed with aromatic condiments. Share of green tea export from India was 2.07% in 1999. The procedure in India regarding green tea is as under:

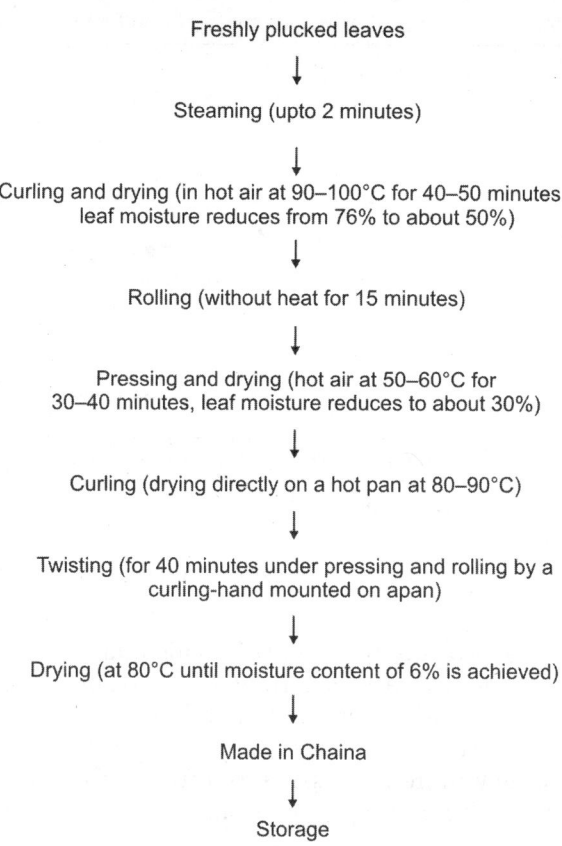

Freshly plucked leaves

↓

Steaming (upto 2 minutes)

↓

Curling and drying (in hot air at 90–100°C for 40–50 minutes the leaf moisture reduces from 76% to about 50%)

↓

Rolling (without heat for 15 minutes)

↓

Pressing and drying (hot air at 50–60°C for 30–40 minutes, leaf moisture reduces to about 30%)

↓

Curling (drying directly on a hot pan at 80–90°C)

↓

Twisting (for 40 minutes under pressing and rolling by a curling-hand mounted on apan)

↓

Drying (at 80°C until moisture content of 6% is achieved)

↓

Made in Chaina

↓

Storage

Process Chart of Indian Green Tea

Temperature below 100°C, moisture content below 6% concentration of oxygen lower than 2% and humidity controlled inert gas packaging.

Trend of Export to Various Destinations

Figure 2.10 shows Russia, the UAE, and Germany were among the countries that imported a slightly higher volume of tea from India between January and June in 2007 compared to 2006. The other major markets include Pakistan, USA and Egypt. India holds a high market share in countries like the UAE, Germany, Poland and Kazakhstan. However, exports to Iraq have declined drastically from 23.42 mkg in 2006 to 3.35 mkg in 2007.

In these countries, India is the top sourcing partner for tea. Exports to the UK, UAE and Germany showed steady gains, but shipments to the CIS and Poland declined substantially. There has been a changing preference toward orthodox tea in India's major markets. Considering India's strengths and global consumption trends, thrust markets identified for export of tea include UAE, Iraq, Kazakhstan, UK, USA, Pakistan, Hong Kong, Netherlands, Canada, Germany, Japan, Russia, Poland and Saudi Arabia.

The exports share of India's tea also goes to the EU market apart from the Russian federation. UK markets share the majority of Indian tea from the EU members. The

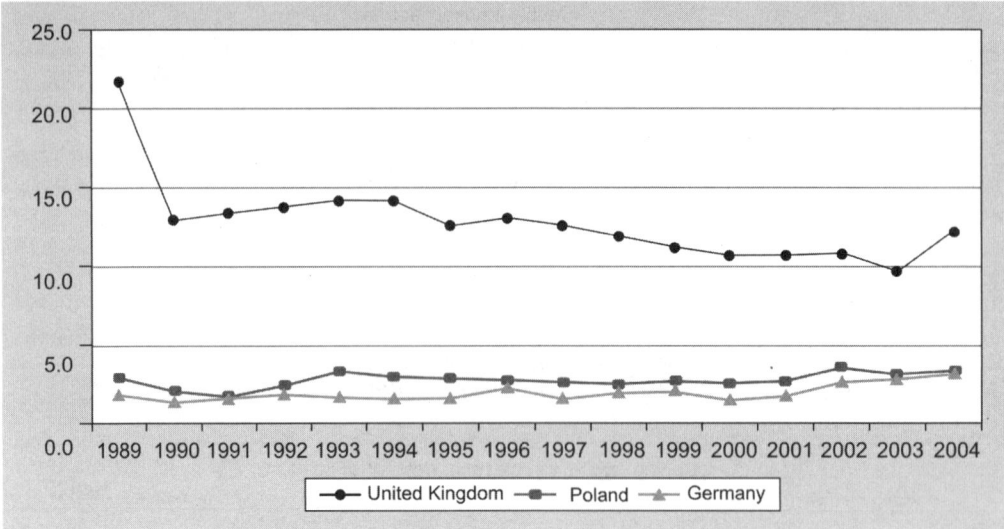

Fig. 2.10: India's tea export to major countries

norms and standards and the drinking habits also vary among the EU countries. The Indian tea industry also faces a serious threat from the export markets to EU countries as the industry and government failed to strengthen existing markets and penetrate newer ones. The emerging trend of supply from other countries forces India to make its policy more aggressive to improve the volume of exports to EU countries. Sri Lanka, China and Kenya dominate EU markets with their higher volume of exports.

There is an emerging market in Pakistan and Iraq, despite the overall decline in exports, which explains the trade prospects in the Indian tea industry. The new trend in exports is Iraq, which is now the second largest importer of India's tea after the Russian Federation and CIS countries. Though Iraq is undergoing political and economic instability, it is a favorable market for Indian tea. Iraq consumes an estimated 110 mkg of tea every year. Exports to Iraq from India were 44 mkg in 2002. However, exports dipped to 12.7 mkg in 2003 due to the war in Iraq. Exports to Iraq in the first three months of 2004 have risen by 0.9 mkg from 0.7 mkg in 2003 to 1.6 mkg in 2004. Going by actual Iraqi imports so far, estimates of a 50 mkg order from Iraq appear too ambitious. It is expected that the export would rise to 9 mkg of tea in the current year and estimates that Iraq could import a total of 17 mkg from India.

VALUE ADDED EXPORTS

Background

Even 50 years ago, tea drinkers abroad used to buy "pure" tea from the producing country of his choice from among the neighboring grocers. The teas of different origins were being sold under well advertised brand names by trading companies located in the importing countries. These companies got their merchandize from a number of tea producing countries. In other words, there was a so-called international division of labor under which tea was grown by poor developing countries especially for the purpose of exports in bulk as raw materials to various developed countries. The imported tea was then sold by the developed countries through a network of large sized companies with substantial capital investment who were marketing the tea in attractive consumer packs under different brand names built up by intensive campaigns. This division of labor was not based on any natural advantage as understood in the theory of international trade. It was based on historical factors and on advantages artificially created for different companies by virtue of dominant position of their countries over the erstwhile colonies. The companies not only controlled over 40% or 50% of the markets of developed countries but also controlled trade chls for marketing and distribution of tea. Moreover, there were some bigger companies which owned plantations and controlled a large part of retail marketing of packaged tea. Thus, it is of vital importance that an attitudinal change must precede our attempts toward boosting of tea exports by the developing countries. This would work as catalyst to mark a departure from the traditional position of tea producing countries being content with export of tea as a primary product to value added items. This change covers the diversification into blending of tea and its packaging would enable the tea producing countries to free themselves from the vagaries of the wholesale market of tea and enter the consumer markets directly where prices are more stable compared to wholesale markets. Packet tea can help the producing countries to earn added value on account of blending and packaging and thereby earn more foreign exchange. Similar is the case of instant tea and tea bags.

It may, therefore, be the strategy of all the developing countries that they should bring in certain structural changes in the product they export. This will help them in improving their share in world trade and in earning more foreign exchange. Besides, this would enable the developing countries to be known not only as exporters of "primary" products but also as exporters of "convenient" products or manufactured goods which can directly find place in the display counters of the consumer stores in the developed countries. In other words, a switch over from "primary" to "processed" goods might open up new vistas of economic growth for the developing countries through increased exports. India, which is one of the developing countries, has progressively ushered in diversification in many of its agricultural commodities in recent years. India started by exporting groundnut seeds and then moved to export of oilseeds and thereafter to products like meal. In case of leather products, India has moved from raw hides to td, semi-processed to processed and finished leather, and for over a decade, India has been developing markets for shoe uppers, shoes and leather as well as leather garments and goods. The same could happen in the case of tea. The question is what type of structural changes in tea exports, i.e. product diversification has been achieved in India so far. Recent data on the export of value added tea of all types are presented in Tables 2.17 and 2.17A.

Export of Packet Tea

India is the largest producer and exporter of tea in the world and is expected to produce 850 mkg in 2004 assuming an average annual growth rate in tea production to the extent of a little over 3%, other things remaining constant. On an average, India produced about 820 mkg annually during the last 5 years. India produced 826 mkg of tea in 2002 and her share in world production was 27%. The volume of

Table 2.17: Export of value-added tea from India—calendar year

(Quantity in thousand. kg, value in thousand kg)

Year	Packet tea		Tea bags		Instant tea		Total value-added tea	
	Qty.	Value	Qty.	Value	Qty.	Value	Qty.	Value
2006	20,902	2,185,764	6,952	1,543,179	3,062	1,034,092	30,916	4,763,035
2007	9,315	1,197,836	8,303	1,901,099	2,913	914,687	20,531	4,013,622
2008	11,798	1,714,483	8,787	2,302,280	3,047	965,158	23,632	4,981,921
2009	16,267	2,670,284	9,168	2,925,465	2,841	1,107,489	28,276	6,703,238
2010	17,714	3,143,990	10,476	3,261,409	3,359	1,348,411	31,549	7,753,810

Table 2.17A: Export of value-added tea from India—financial year

(Quantity in thousand kg, value in thousand Rs)

Year	Packet tea		Tea bags		Instant tea		Total value-added tea	
	Qty.	Value	Qty.	Value	Qty.	Value	Qty.	Value
2006–07	14,767	1799079	7337	1680048	3095	1062424	25199	4541551
2007–08	10,143	1,319,078	8,660	1,952,443	3,036	944,494	21,839	4,216,015
2008–09	10,257	1,621,853	8,636	2,484,356	2,810	951,385	21,703	5,057,594
2009–10	17,722	2,971,091	9,504	2,951,036	2,943	1,177,460	30,169	7,099,587
2010–11	17,141	3,070,304	10,794	3,410,574	3,056	1,271,618	30,991	7,752,496

her tea exports was 201 mkg in 2002 which accounted for 14% of world exports and these are mostly in bulk form. India has been trying to maximize exports particularly in the form of processed tea such as packets, tea bags, and instant tea.

In India, tea packets containing loose tea are still the normal form of packaging. India for the first time started the export of packet tea (in consumer pack upto a size of 1 kg) in 1965. Six years later, India ventured into export of tea bags, instant tea, etc. Since then India has been making steady and consistent progress in the export of packet tea. In 1965, with only two firms in the field, India had exported 2 mkg of packet tea and at the end of 5 years, with entry of few more firms, India tea exports doubled to 4 mkg 1971–1972 and in another 4 years, exports reached the level of about 11 mkg (1975–1976). The progress, since then, noteworthy with the entry of more than 200 firms in the field.

The year-wise growth of exports of packet tea in India for the last two and a half decades since 1973–1974 is in Table 2.18.

India's export of packet tea increased from 5 mkg in 1973–1974 to 43 mkg in 2001–2002. Year-wise data further revealed that on many occasions India could not retain the volume of her preceding year's exports. Export of packet tea showed a record increase of 84 mkg in 1995–1996 followed by 82 mkg in 1998–1999 and 81 mkg in 1996–1997. On an average India exported about 68 mkg fetching Rs 712 crores with average unit price of Rs 105 per kg. India acquired an important position as the world's

Table 2.18: Export of packet tea from India during 1973–1974 to 2001–2002

Year	Quantity (thousand kg)	Value (Rs)	Unit value (Rs/kg)
1973–1974	4,744	50,216.00	10.58
1974–1975	6,095	83,051.00	13.56
1975–1976	10,787	172,457.00	15.99
1976–1977	12,612	193,635.00	15.37
1977–1978	25,187	519,834.00	20.64
1978–1979	38,599	787,384.00	20.40
1979–1980	30,024	580,703.00	19.34
1980–1981	32,322	699,834.00	21.65
1981–1982	20,493	468,216.00	22.85
1982–1983	10,101	263,232.00	26.06
1983–1984	17,368	521,288.00	30.01
1984–1985	21,841	930,552.00	42.61
1985–1986	25,690	994,063.00	38.69
1986–1987	16,847	595,727.00	35.36
1987–1988	21,142	785,994.00	37.18
1988–1989	25,541	879,841.00	34.45
1989–1990	75,817	3,548,148.00	46.80
1990–1991	71,514	3,908,642.00	54.64
1991–1992	78,321	4,520,917.00	57.72
1992–1993	65,245	4,040,263.00	61.92
1993–1994	64,917	4,685,722.00	72.18
1994–1995	52,042	3,577,669.00	68.75
1995–1996	83,965	6,162,394.00	73.39
1996–1997	81,016	5,714,458.00	70.53
1997–1998	78,115	7,490,434.00	97.89
1998–1999	82,013	8,904,328.00	108.57
1999–2000	63,518	674,390.00	106.16
2000–2001	69,315	7,195,601.00	103.89
2001–1002	42,719	5,211,372.00	121.99

Source: Various issues of Tea Statistics, Tea Board, Kolkata.

largest direct exporter of packet tea surpassing the UK. India is the leading exporter of packet tea and accounts for 60% of world trade in packet tea. It is interesting to note that packet tea imports constituted nearly 20% of total world imports and India constitutes for nearly half of it by way of direct export of this item during the year.

Direction—Region-wise Packet Tea Export

During the last four decades major changes have already taken place in the tea market in the world. Countries like USA, UK, Canada and others have preference for packet tea, tea bags, instant tea in recent years. The countries in the region of West Asia and North Africa place their order mostly for these items. The exports of packet tea in the countries of West Europe (UK, Irish, Netherland, Germany, Austria, Finland, etc.) are also gradually falling. On an average, about 4 mkg is exported to West Europe, 21 mkg to East Europe, 1.5 mkg to America (North and Latin America).

Export of Tea Bags

In order to cope up with changing consumer preferences, India started production and export of tea bags from 1971 onward with three firms. Progress made since then has been considerable and at present there are many firms manufacturing tea bags. The progress relating to export of tea bags in India is as in Table 2.18A.

Exports of tea bag in 1973–1974 was 144 thousand kg which went up to 2,524 thousand kg in 2001–2002 showing an increase of 17.6 times. There was an appreciable increase of this item from 1994 to 1995 onward. Except 1995–1996, exports of packet tea boosted up from 1,716 thousand kg in 1996–1997 to 2,169 thousand kg in 1997–1998. It further improved from 2,415 thousand kg in 1998–1999 to 2,542 thousand kg in 2001–2002. Average export of packet tea during last 5 years was to the level of 2,270 thousand kg. fetching Rs 219 per kg. It is also observed that average unit price stands at Rs 201 per kg.

Direction of Tea Bag Exports—Region-wise

Tea bags are exported to mainly countries like United Kingdom, Irish Republic, Germany, France, Belgium and Luxembourg of West Europe. A substantial quantity is also exported to east Europe, i.e. CIS countries (Russian Federation, Ukraine, Latvia, Kazakhstan, etc.) and Poland. Meagre quantities are exported to USA, Canada and Brazil of America as well as Iran, UAE, Kuwait, Bahrain, Muscat, Yemen of West Asia and North Africa. Further less quantity in the level of 20 thousand is exported to Asia other than West (Japan), Africa other than North (Angola, South Africa) and Australia and Oceania (Australia). It is interesting to note that over the last 3 years quantities exported to East Europe has increased from 1,816 thousand kg in 1999–2000 to 2,115 in 2001–2002, while it was 16 thousand kg 84 thousand kg during the period in America. There was fall in exports from 207 thousand kg to 106 thousand kg in West Asia and north Africa (Tables 2.18B to H).

Value Added Concept

By introducing structural changes in tea exports, India has been sharing the value added market. Before making any attempt to define "value added" concept it would be worthwhile to mention that despite over a century of India's entry in world tea export market Indian tea has been hardly known by name or origin except in the country like UK and Germany. In these countries, there was good demand for fine Darjeeling Tea while Chinese and Sri Lankan Tea are well known in export markets abroad. Even the small amount of value that may be added on account of the consumer preference for a particular origin of tea has not reached us. The first value added exercise could, therefore, start with Indian tea known for superior quality and flavor to create among consumers a purchasing preference for Indian tea. The next stage would be to create awareness among the consumers about the regional varieties such as Darjeeling tea, the Nilgiris tea, the Assam tea, Kangra tea, etc.

Forms of Value Addition

There are three methods by which values are added to tea. These are (1) breaking bulk and blending involving no technology but require skills that we possess; (2) consumer packing in attractive packets, cans or bags using modern packing materials, if sold in other brand names (to devote attention toward marketing and

Table 2.18A: Export of tea bags during 1973–1974 to 2001–2002

Year	Quantity (thousand kg)	Value (Rs)	Unit value (Rs/kg)
1973–1974	4,744	50,216.00	10.58
1973–1974	144	3,571.00	24.80
1974–1975	108	2,752.00	25.48
1975–1976	157	5,914.00	37.67
1976–1977	285	10,560.00	37.05
1977–1978	390	18,522.00	47.49
1978–1979	238	10,570.00	44.41
1979–1980	493	20,275.00	41.13
1980–1981	754	32,591.00	43.22
1981–1982	777	33,531.00	43.15
1982–1983	618	23,172.00	37.50
1983–1984	514	24,259.00	47.20
1984–1985	631	36,551.00	57.93
1985–1986	590	37,839.00	64.13
1986–1987	467	31,845.00	68.19
1987–1988	498	32,424.00	65.11
1988–1989	626	44,409.00	70.94
1989–1990	546	46,875.00	85.85
1990–1991	496	43,715.00	89.20
1991–1992	483	71,408.00	147.84
1992–1993	520	72,536.00	139.49
1993–1994	1,007	101,456.00	100.75
1994–1995	1,008	144,180.00	143.04
1995–1996	861	125,811.00	146.15
1996–1997	1,716	252,479.00	147.16
1997–1998	2,169	449,957.00	207.45
1998–1999	2,415	498,180.00	206.29
1999–2000	2,305	557,207.00	241.74
2000–2001	1,917	385,332.00	200.96
2001–2002	2,542	597,103.00	234.89
2002–2003			

promotional skills) and cost, if sold under own brand name and (3) Product processing and qualitative improvement extracting tea soluble, i.e. solids and flavor. The country which exports tea in bulk quantities without recourse to value added system is, therefore, not only deprived of legitimate share or value added but also fails to reach the consumer directly. The value added items of tea which are sold in the retail market, are in the forms of tea in consumer package and tea bags.

The Global Production in 2012 was increased 171.16.

Sharing of Value Added Tea

The sharing of value added which could be seen from the price differentials in respect of packet teas and tea bags as compared to bulk teas is as in Table 2.19.

Table 2.18B: World tea: production

(Unit: 1,000 metric tons)

Country	1992	1999	2000	2001	2002	Annual growth rate (%) 1992–2002
Developing Countries						
Southeast Asia						
1. Indonesia	153.7	161.0	162.1	163.4	163.4	0.7
2. Lao PDR	1.0	.4	.2	.2	.2	–20.5
3. Malaysia	5.9	5.9	5.6	5.4	5.4	–0.9
4. Myanmar	14.4	18.4	19.0	19.4	19.4	3.4
5. Thailand	5.0	5.5	5.5	5.6	5.6	1.3
6. Vietnam	36.2	70.3	69.9	75.7	89.6	9.7
South Asia						
7. Bangladesh	45.6	56.0	46.0	52.0	52.0	0.8
8. India	754.2	855.0	835.0	848.0	826.2	1.7
9. Nepal	1.6	4.5	5.1	6.6	7.5	15.7
10. Sri Lanka	178.9	283.8	305.8	295.1	310.0	4.4
Other Asia						
11. China	580.0	697.0	703.7	721.5	759.8	2.5
12. Iran (Islamic Rep. of)	55.0	61.7	49.9	51.2	51.2	–0.8
13. Rep. of Korea	.7	1.1	1.4	1.6	1.6	10.5
14. Papua New Guinea	8.50	9.00	9.00	9.00	9.00	2.1
Subtotal	1,840.7	2,229.5	2,218.3	2,254.7	2,300.9	2.4
Developed Countries						
15. Japan	92.1	88.5	85.0	85.0	85.0	–0.7
Subtotal	92.1	88.5	85.0	85.0	85.0	–0.7
Asia and Pacific	1,932.8	2,318.0	2,303.3	2,339.7	2,385.9	2.2
Rest of World	561.7	744.1	643.8	640.1	713.9	2.0
World	2,494.5	3,062.1	2,947.1	2,979.8	3,099.8	2.2

Table 2.18C: Top rank countries of tea, 2000

Rank	Country	Production (Int $1000)	Flag	Production (MT)	Flag
1	India	878,432	*	826,000	
2	China, mainland	726,699	*	683,324	
3	Sri Lanka	325,253	*	305,840	
4	Kenya	251,284	*	236,286	
5	Indonesia	172,906	*	162,586	
6	Turkey	147,578	*	138,770	
7	Japan	90,395	*	85,000	
8	Argentina	78,969	*	74,256	
9	Vietnam	74,337	*	69,900	
10	Iran (Islamic Republic of)	53,039	*	49,874	
11	Bangladesh	48,919	*	46,000	
12	Malawi	45,091	*	42,400	
13	Thailand	34,379	*	32,327	
14	Uganda	31,091	*	29,236	
15	Georgia	25,523	*	24,000	
16	United Republic of Tanzania	25,098	*	23,600	
17	Zimbabwe	23,396	*	22,000	*
18	China, Taiwan Province of	21,640	*	20,349	
19	Myanmar	20,206	*	19,000	*
20	Rwanda	15,400	*	14,481	

* : Unofficial figure

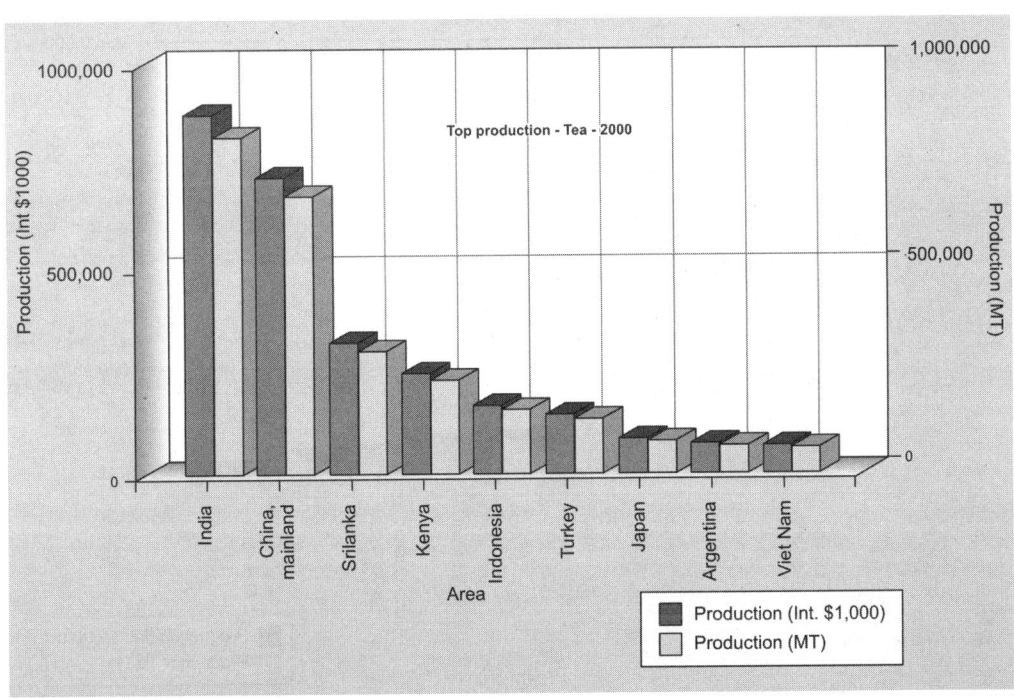

Table 2.18D: Top rank countries of tea, 2011

Rank	Country	Production (Int $1000)	Flag	Production (MT)	Flag
1	China, mainland	1,726,023	*	1,623,000	
2	India	1,028,098	*	966,733	
3	Kenya	401,900	*	377,912	
4	Sri Lanka	348,288	*	327,500	
5	Turkey	235,666	*	221,600	
6	Vietnam	219,714	*	206,600	
7	Iran (Islamic Republic of)	172,833	*	162,517	Im
8	Indonesia	151,439	*	142,400	
9	Argentina	102,702	*	96,572	
10	Japan	87,311	*	82,100	
11	Thailand	77,974	*	73,320	
12	Bangladesh	64,340	*	60,500	
13	Malawi	55,300	*	52,000	F
14	Uganda	37,428	*	35,194	
15	United Republic of Tanzania	34,031	*	32,000	
16	Myanmar	32,967	*	31,000	*
17	Mozambique	28,713	*	27,000	
18	Rwanda	25,593	*	24,066	
19	Malaysia	21,935	*	20,626	
20	Zimbabwe	19,379	*	18,223	Im

* :   Unofficial figure
F :   FAO estimate
Im: FAO data based on imputation methodology.

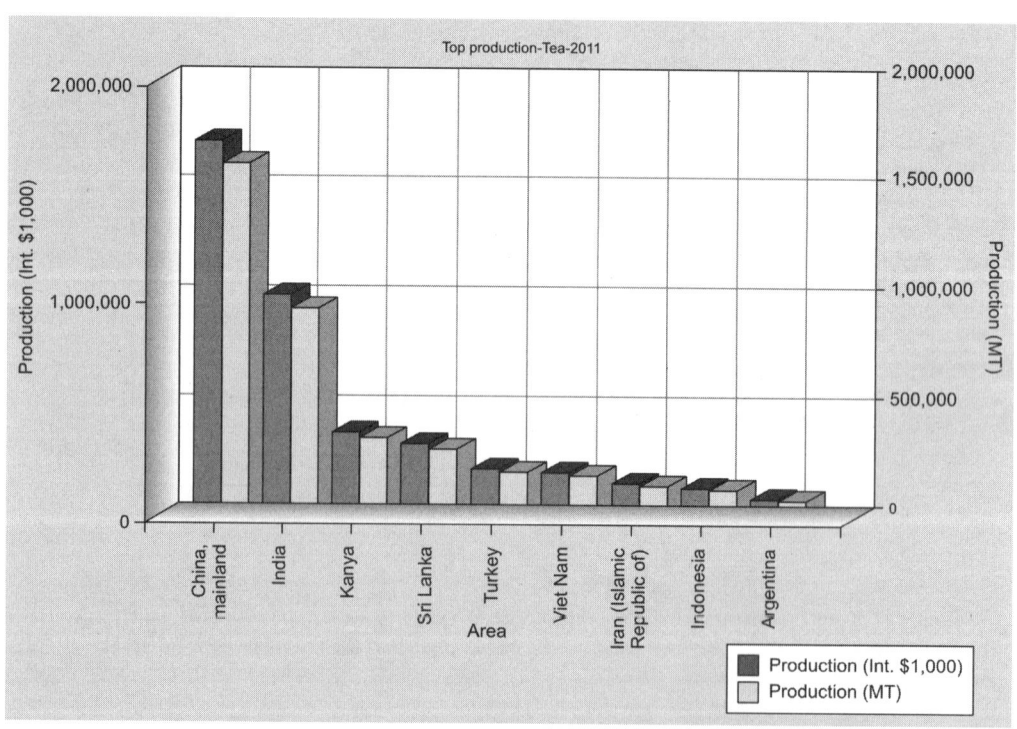

Table 2.18E: World production

(Figures in mkg)

Country	2012 (P)	2011	2010	2009	2008
China	1,761.00	1,623.21	1,475.06	1,358.64	1,257.60
India	1,111.76	1,115.72	966.40	979.00	980.82
Kenya	369.56	377.91	399.01	314.20	345.82
Sri Lanka	326.28	328.63	331.43	289.78	318.70
Vietnam	158.00	178.00	170.00	175.00	166.38
Turkey	147.00	145.00	148.00	153.00	155.00
Indonesia	130.50	142.34	151.01	152.59	153.28
Bangladesh	62.16	59.32	59.27	60.00	58.66
Malawi	42.49	47.06	51.59	52.56	41.64
Uganda	55.08	54.18	59.14	50.98	42.75
Tanzania	32.28	32.78	31.65	32.09	31.61
Others	330.87	345.16	349.45	342.65	327.01
Total	**4,526.98**	**4,449.31**	**4,192.01**	**3,960.49**	**3,879.27**

(P) – Provisional.
Source: ITC Annual Bulletin Supplement, 2012 and MSS - March, 2013.

Table 2.18F: Average yield of tea per hectare in principal producing countries

(yield in kg per hectare)

Country	1986	1990	1992	1994	1995	1996	1997
India	1523	1,780	1,742	1,768	1,770	1,809	NA
Bangladesh	805	963	1,024	1,079	992	1115	NA
Sri Lanka	954	1,056	806	NA	NA	NA	NA
Indonesia	1,043	1,076	1,050	1,010	NA	1,078	NA
Japan	1,597	1,537	1,624	1,584	1,579	1,683	NA
Turkey	1,723	1,448	1749	1,745	1,366	1,493	NA
Kenya	1,846	2,031	1847	1,900	2,172	2,189	NA
Argentina	966	NA	NA	NA	800	1,103	NA
USSR/CLS	1,801	NA	NA	NA	NA	NA	NA

The data presented in the above table showed that packet tea and tea bags added more value approximately 27% and 173%, respectively than the bulk tea during 1971–1972. Value addition in respect of packet tea and tea bags stood at 37% and 164%, respectively in 2001–2002. Value addition for packet tea ranged from 3% to 39% during the period from 1966–1967 to 2001–2002, while it ranged from 55% to 235% during the same period in respect of tea bags. Value addition was reduced to minimum during 1990–1991 and 1992–1993 in respect of packet tea and tea bags as compared to bulk tea because of increase in the price per kg of bulk tea.

Table 2.18G: World's total product mix

(In million kgs)

	2011	2012	Increase over 2011
Green tea	1370.92	1495.77	124.85
Black tea	3082.55	3128.86	46.31
Total	**4453.47**	**4624.63**	**171.16**

Table 2.18H: Tea production in major black tea producing countries

(In million kgs)

Country	2011	2012	Increase decrease over 2011
India	1115.72	1126.33	10.61
Sri Lanka	328.63	328.40	−0.23
Kenya	377.91	369.56	−8.35

Packet tea can offer a dependable and standardized product to a consumer while tea bags standardization simplifies the process of brewing. In the second stage, by marketing tea under a brand name, although being a costly process in terms of high costs of distribution and consumer promotion, the exporter gets an easy access to preferences and some command over the market, together with increase in profitability comparatively higher than the returns available from the export of loose tea.

Instant Tea—Its Development

As regards instant tea, India is still on the threshold of product development. With the gradual acceptance of instant tea by the consumer, its demand is bound to rise gradually in the near future. Instant tea is processed in two forms, the cold water soluble (CWS) and hot water soluble (HWS). These are manufactured both from the green leaf and from the black tea or from a combination of both types. HWS has limited market in the UK, Australia, etc. While CWS has markets in USA, tata Finlay is specializing in CWS and food specialities in HWS. Both the products are manufactured in South India. The data relating to export of instant tea from India is in Table 2.19A.

It will be seen from the above table that the export of instant tea increased from 295,000 kg in 1973–1974 to 2,594,000 kg in 2001–2002 showing an improvement of less than 10 times. Similarly, in value terms it was Rs 92.17 lakh in 1973–1974 and 7,419.79 lakh in 2001–2002.

Problems of Value Added Instant Tea

For expansion of exports of value added items of tea, India is facing various problems. These are: (1) dearth of indigenous know how in international market; (2) inadequate production capacity of tea bags; (3) lack of investment for establishment of firm's brand name and entry into the super markets in foreign countries and (4) imposition of various tariff as well as nontariff barriers created by developed countries against the entry of Indian tea in consumer packs.

Table 2.19: Price differentials during 1966–1967 to 2001–2002

(Rs/kg)

Year	Packet tea	Tea bag	Bulk tea	Percentage of value addition in packet/bag to bulk tea	
1966–1967	9.88	–	8.18	20.80	–
1971–1972	9.48	20.39	7.47	26.90	173
1973–1974	10.58	24.80	7.63	27.90	225
1974–1975	13.76	25.48	9.16	50.20	178
1975–1976	15.99	37.67	11.22	42.50	178
1976–1977	15.36	37.05	12.01	27.90	235
1977–1978	20.64	47.49	23.29	–14.00	208
1978–1979	20.40	44.41	20.61	–1.90	113
1979–1980	19.34	41.13	18.12	6.70	127
1980–1981	21.65	43.22	19.15	12.80	122
1981–1982	22.85	43.15	18.15	25.90	138
1982–1983	26.06	37.50	18.72	39.20	101
1983–1984	30.01	47.20	24.79	21.00	91
1984–1985	42.61	57.93	34.12	24.80	70
1985–1986	38.69	64.23	30.25	27.70	112
1986–1987	37.42	63.84	29.53	26.50	116
1987–1988	37.18	65.11	31.10	19.50	109
1988–1989	34.45	70.94	31.13	10.60	128
1989–1990	46.80	85.88	42.97	8.90	100
1990–1091	54.64	89.20	53.58	3.50	69
1991–1992	57.72	147.84	55.61	3.80	62
1992–1993	61.92	139.49	56.05	10.50	148
1993–1994	72.18	100.75	65.19	10.70	55
1994–1995	68.75	143.05	64.64	6.40	0
1995–1996	73.39	146.15	71.25	3.10	105
1996–1997	70.53	147.13	75.44	–6.50	95
1997–1998	97.89	207.45	85.79	14.10	142
1998–1999	108.57	207.45	107.81	–0.70	91
1999–2000	106.16	241.74	100.61	5.60	143
2000–2001	103.81	200.96	89.41	16.10	125
2001–2002	121.99	234.89	89.98	36.90	164

Source: Various issues of Tea Statistics, Tea Board, Kolkata.

Table 2.19A: Export of instant tea from India: 1974–1975 to 2001–2002

Year	Quantity (Th/kg)	Value (Rs)	Unit value (Rs/Kg)
1973–1974	295	9,217.00	31.24
1974–1975	255	563.00	33.58
1975–1976	478	19,162.00	40.09
1976–1977	584	25,064.00	42.92
1977–1978	598	31,533.00	52.73
1978–1979	686	35,500.00	51.75
1979–1980	656	30,509.00	46.51
1980–1981	761	36,608.00	48.11
1981–1982	832	41,712.00	50.13
1982–1983	799	43,185.00	54.05
1983–1984	1,049	66,874.00	63.75
1984–1985	1,138	95,538.00	83.95
1985–1986	938	80,428.00	85.74
1986–1987	1,134	94,896.00	83.68
1987–1988	8,661	66,611.00	7.36
1988–1989	1,147	100,986.00	88.04
1989–1990	925	90,068.00	97.39
1990–1991	1,283	158,039.00	123.18
1991–1992	1,740	270,592.00	155.51
1992–1993	1,122	221,463.00	197.56
1993–1994	1,320	228,667.00	173.23
1994–1995	1,230	260,940.00	212.15
1995–1996	1,868	446,403.00	238.97
1996–1997	2,483	578,336.00	232.92
1997–1998	2,428	629,703.00	259.35
1998–1999	2,602	653,770.00	252.26
1999–2000	2,783	831,013.00	298.60
2000–2001	2,574	741,979.00	286.04
2001–2002			

Source: Various issues of Tea Statistics, Tea Board, Kolkata.

Long-term Strategy for Marketing of Value Added Items

For evolving a long-term strategy for marketing of value added items, the "Committee on Tea Marketing" setup by the Government of India (GoI) recommended in its report a three-phased approach which is quoted below:

1. In the first phase, packet tea export should be confined to our neighboring countries through local collaboration particularly in those cases where there are no packeting facilities and tea is imported in packages especially in premium range. This would mean less investment, no clash of interest among own customers and a price advantage on account of lower freight. On both sides of

India upto Africa and South East Asia, there is great demand for imported packet teas where India exported tea could successfully compete with others.

2. The second phase would be collaborating with existing packers in Europe and supplying the blends in bulk and sharing part of their profits.

3. The third phase could be independent marketing efforts in value added, medium priced tea in major markets of UK and Ireland. Over riding all these phases, there are at least two considerations to ponder over.

First, research into new tea products and tea blending continues. Second, to support export of value added tea abroad in the form of packets, bags and instant tea, we should first encourage and organize markets at home. It was noted by the Committee that exact strategy would depend on three factors like creating favorable market conditions, increasing investment on export promotion and building of organizational marketing strengths.

As regards tea bags, the Committee has recommended that the facilities for manufacturing units in India with tea bagging facilities should be carefully examined and maximum encouragements may be given. It has also been observed that to acquire market facilities and skills abroad, the cost will be high and will have to be standardized. The public sector agencies like Tea Trading Corporation and State Trading Corporation will be able to work on the problem of external marketing of value added items of tea. As regards instant tea, the Committee recommended that the existing companies in the field as well as new entrants should be encouraged. The company should invest capital in promoting technical and marketing skills by encouraging only or part acquisition of R and D equipments and sharing international promotion expenditure on time bounds which must be result oriented and monitored against expected returns.

Potential and Scope for Instant Teas

Tea is probably one of the most widely consumed beverages in the world and is accepted and acclaimed everywhere. The worldwide acceptance of tea is because of its zero alcohol content, stimulating effect and aroma, etc. Many types like black, green, orange, flavored, golden, pekoe, etc. grades of tea are available in the market. These types are mainly classified according to their manufacturing process, compiled with spices and other flavor rendering substances. Brewing of instant tea is a common and old practice. Black and green teas are only products obtained on a large scale from the tea bush and at present none of the other products mentioned above are being exploited on a commercial scale. Efforts will be made for developing and standardizing suitable and effective technologies for tea industry to keep pace with other tea producing countries like China, Sri Lanka and Kenya who has already made their mark in the world export market for tea.

Tea Powder

Although commercial production of instant tea began in the 1940s, little information is available as to what sort of process is suitable, as these techniques have been kept a secret by patent rights over the manufactured products. Generally, tea powder, the basic material is derived from the fermented leaf. The usual steps adopted in the preparation of powder are extraction of tea solids followed by concentration of extracts and finally drying of these concentrates, to convert them into powder.

Extraction is generally carried out by recovering the solids in water. Concentration of extracts is effected by evaporation of the water at low temperature and under reduced pressure. The final step of drying the concentrated leaf is achieved by subjecting the concentrate to either low temperature, spray, fridge or foam drying. The solid thus obtained is brown in color and amorphous in nature but on breeding it turns into brown powder.

One such study was conducted in the tea research laboratory in Himachal Pradesh Krishi Vishwa Vidhyalaya, Palampur. The yield of powder from the fermented tea was generally better than that of made tea. At present a number of laboratories are setup which have invented the technologies for preparation of tea powder.

Major Determinant Factors of Export from India

The international demand and export is also determined by the various standards and norms at the international and national level. The standards and norms vary from country to country. These norms may not be the same for other countries. The consumer's consciousness and initiative regarding the issues have a major role in influencing sale practices. For instance, in New Zealand, the consumer has the option of choosing the packet by reading the label, which gives details of quality and environmental justice. In a similar way, organic tea producers in Tamil Nadu are selling their tea to the market through direct marketing. The tea packet describes the quality and procedures of tea production and their environmental consciousness.

The high demand for organic tea from the EU countries and specifically for Darjeeling tea from the UK market can be considered specific choices of export. The price and quality are also important to the export of Indian Tea. The low price product from Kenya and other countries badly affected India's export. Also, the new economic policies affect the export–import trend. The hike in the exports is attributed to the opening up of markets in Iraq, Pakistan and other Gulf countries. The emerging demand from the Middle Eastern countries is one of the factors for high exports growth from Southern India.

Along with international demands, the increase in production of Kenya also affects monthly exports of India in 2006–2007. For instance, in the first eight months of 2007, exports fell 19.3% to 86.03 mkg while the production remained steady, exports in July fell 46% to 10.3 mkg. The high competition from other producing and exporting countries has affected competition in international market. Some other factors challenging the export potential of Indian tea include various tariff and non-tariff measures imposed by some tea importing countries, lower off take by Russia due to change in consumer preferences, lower production of orthodox teas which have a larger demand worldwide, quality problems and the higher cost of production and prices of Indian tea.

New policies and opening up of route through the border areas of Pakistan also led to high increase in export in 2006–2007. Exports from south India are expected to go up, following the opening up of non-traditional markets like Libya. International relations and political stability are also important to promote exports. The political and economic instability of Russia in the 90s, for instance, affected the demand for orthodox tea that was mainly produced in the Coonoor area of Tamil Nadu.

The political conflict and economic strategy of the ruling government also have a direct impact on trade-offs between the countries. The tea export market in Pakistan is one of the examples of this regime. However, the export prospect to Pakistan is highly persuasive in the future. Industry sources said tea export prospects to Pakistan have brightened to some extent, after the country recently announced a 5% reduction in duties from 30% to 25%. The reopening of the Iraqi market coupled with loosening import restrictions in Iran indicates that exports should grow in the near future.

There is a lack of pld strategy for marketing of Indian tea in the international market. It is widely shared by all stakeholders that as a regulatory body of the tea industry, the India Tea Board has to take more initiatives to promote tea in both the Indian and the international market. An extensive campaign and aggressive intervention is the only the first step to improve the international market, especially in the context of competitive participation from other countries. The trend in the world market shows that Sri Lanka, China and Kenya have edged out India, where they already have a higher volume of exports than India. India is also facing a high volume of imports and this increasing trend has many implications on the tea industry. It is directly linked to the price of Indian tea and to the domestic market. The following section looks into the domestic consumption of India and its implications on the Indian tea industry (Tables 2.19B and C).

Geographical Indication (GI) Tag to Boost Darjeeling Tea Exports

Darjeeling tea exports are set to increase by volume and value, following its registration as a protected geographical indication (PGI) product from India. The industry closed 2011 by registering a 10% increase in total Darjeeling tea exports. "In value terms, the rise has been 20%. This will rise further following the GI registration". Exports of Darjeeling tea stood at around 6.9 mkg in 2011, when production was around 9.2 mkg. Darjeeling tea is the first Indian product to be

Table 2.19B: World export

(Figures in mkg)

Country	2012 (P)	2011	2010	2009	2008
Kenya	430.21	421.27	441.02	342.48	383.44
China	321.79	322.58	302.53	302.95	296.94
Sri Lanka	304.49	301.27	296.38	279.84	298.82
India	201.08	215.42	222.02	197.90	203.12
Vietnam	135.00	143.00	127.97	120.00	104.00
Indonesia	71.00	75.45	87.10	92.30	96.21
Argentina	78.00	86.20	85.35	69.19	77.23
Malawi	41.83	44.89	48.58	46.55	40.07
Uganda	48.22	46.15	53.18	47.92	42.39
Tanzania	26.30	27.11	26.13	21.51	24.77
Zimbabwe	7.00	8.57	8.50	7.54	5.65
Bangladesh	1.51	1.45	0.91	3.15	8.39
Others	59.24	26.78	77.98	73.77	72.03
Total	**1,725.7**	**1,720.4**	**1,777.7**	**1,605.1**	**1,653.1**

Source: ITC Annual Bulletin Supplement, 2012 and MSS- March, 2013.
P - Provisional.

Table 2.19C: World production and export

(Figures in mkg)

Countries	Production		Export	
	1996	1995	1996	1995
India	780	756	162	164
Sri Lanka	258	246	234	235
Indonesia	166	145	102	79
Bangladesh	53	48	26	25
China	593	588	170	167
Kenya	257	245	244	237
Tanzania	20	24	18	21
Malawi	38	35	37	33
Argentina	43	32	41	41
Others	496	449	21	83
Total	**2,704**	**2,566**	**1,115**	**1,084**

recognized by the EU as a protected GI. "This has been a historical achievement for all the stakeholders and consumers of this globally famous product". Only around 10 mkg of this premium agricultural produce is grown on the slopes of the Eastern Himalayas in some 87 gardens spread over 17,500 acres with some gardens being located at an altitude of 5,000 meters above sea-level.

Cup Brimmeth Over

People in the age group of 35–50 years are entering the business, 80% are form rural areas, 95% are literate.

Tea guarantees a steady flow of income through the year which is why they are venturing in to this business.

Rs 8.50–10.50

What it costs to produce a kg of green leaf.

Rs 3–4 per kg is the profit.

Small tea growers are jointly setting factories to process green leaves, produce black tea.

Some have started dealing with processing units to avoid brokers or middlemen.

Indian Tea Stages a Comeback in Russia

Indian tea has bounced back in popularity stakes in Russia. Thanks to a slew of innovative steps taken by the Tea Board of India and the India embassy in Moscow, tea exports to Russia from India surged in 2013, both in terms of quality and value. Today, Russia is the largest buyer of Indian tea, with its imports around 41 mkg tea per annum, mainly as bulk tea, which constitutes 25% of Indian tea exports.

Backed by innovative promotional drive and quality upgrade, Indian tea which once dominated the Russian market, is regaining its popularity.

The Tea Board of India, under the launched a series of programs aimed at restoring the "image of Indian Tea" in Russia, including public tea tasting, competitions and visits to tea growing areas, charity auction, publicity through social media and print media. The board has also been conducting frequent and mass tea tasting and sampling programs during various festivals and events Moscow and other regions of Russia. Indian tea videos, photographs and tea related interesting stories were publicized through social media and You Tube. For example, at a charity auction held in Moscow, India's Darjeeling Tea fetched the highest-ever record price of Rs 89,000 per kg of tea.

With per capita consumption of 1.2 kg tea annually, Russia consumes 192 mkg per annum. Although the annual demand for tea remained more or less the same in Russia over the years, consumer preferences have shifted to specific teas and premium quality segments. Before the collapse of the Soviet Union, India tea was the sole tea available in the Russian market. However, after the break-up to the Soviet Union, teas from countries such as Sri Lanka, Kenya and Vietnam started coming to Russian market. Sri Lanka, with its aggressive marketing, became the number one supplier of tea to Russia, Pushing down India to the second place.

It is expected that with Russia's accession to WTO the custom duty will be reduced from 20% to 12.5% by 2017.

There were many reasons for India ceding its leading position to Sri Lanka in tea exports to Russia, which included collapse of barter system (rupee rouble trade), strong growth in domestic consumption in India, dismantling of central purchase system, deterioration of quality of exported tea from India, demand for cheap Indian teas in Russian market, payment problems and diversion of export business to European and Middle East markets.

An identity crisis gripped the Indian tea in Russia as traders started selling low-quality tea blended with other origin tea as Indian tea, which severely dented the image of the Indian tea in the Russian market. Even today people in Russia fondly remember the good old Elephant brand Assam Tea from India during the Soviet era.

This bad phase of Indian tea in Russia is over. Driven by consistent efforts made by the Tea Board of India and the Union Ministry of Commerce and Industry, the popularity of Indian tea is on an upward curve. Russians have again started liking the taste of Indian tea and are buying more and more of the Indian brands. Exclusive brands of the Assam, Darjeeling and Nilgiri tea have started reappearing in many retail chains and boutiques in Russia. Recently ORIMI Trade, the highest stakeholder in tea industry in Russia, launched and exclusive Premium Assam brand in the market, which was followed by other players like Mayski and Ahmed Tea.

Within India also, the Tea Board has taken many steps to ensure the quality of tea being exported to Russia like registering the logos of Assam, Darjeeling and Nilgiri teas in Russia known as GI of Assam, Darjeeling and Nilgiri teas though mixing of these teas with other varieties in Russia.

Recently, besides the GI brands of Assam, Darjeeling and Nilgiri teas, the demand for Indian Masala Tea in the Russian market is also increasing. According to experts, there is a lot of scope for developing the Indian Masala Tea as a health drink under a specialty tea category in Russia. It has already become a hot selling item in Indian restaurant chains across Russia.

It is expected that with Russia's recent accession to the WTO, the customs duty will be reduced from 20% to 12.5% by 2017, which will be an additional advantage for Indian tea exports to Russia.

US Emerging as a Major Market for Black Tea

The US has emerged as a major market for black tea and is now the third largest importer of tea. The present market size of US is about 126 mkg of which 84.4% is black tea.

The Commerce and Industry Ministry has chosen five countries—the US, Russia, Kazakhstan, Iran and Egypt—for extensive and intensive promotional intervention through five specific activities over 5 years. These five countries account for 42% of the total tea exported from India. Indian tea exports average 200 mkg with the unit realization averaging at about Rs 175.3 a kg, said Minister of State for Commerce and Industry D Purandeswari in the Lok Sabha. India is the world's second largest producer after China and second largest consumer of tea, accounting for nearly 25–27% of world tea production. India accounts for around 10–12% of world tea exports. Further, certain varieties of tea (for example, Darjeeling) are grown only in India and are in great demand across the world. However, India has been losing its share of the global tea exports in the face of the threat coming from newer competitors such as China, Sri Lanka and Kenya.

A new online system had been introduced from June this year to enforce strict quality check of tea exported as well as tea imported for re-export. For this purpose, two advisory tea councils have been setup, one each for the South and North India to monitor and take appropriate corrective action against the exporters concerned whose tea have failed the quality checks. The Tea Board has also launched special promotional campaign in rural areas aimed at increasing tea consumption.

Loss of London Market

With the loss of London market, former USSR and East European countries appeared on the scene, strengthened by a long-term friendship treaty involving rupee trade agreement. Tea became an important item in this pact. Within a short time, the share of former USSR and East European countries surpassed 50% of Indian export quantum. So, the need for exporting more than what India could conveniently do was not strong. However, an ambitious projection of 370 mkg export by the turn of century, kept the tea industry busy all the while. The slogan of need for exporting more value added products like packet tea; tea bag and instant tea was heard from all corners. It was all for increasing the foreign exchange earnings. Some meek attempts were made to popularize Indian tea in foreign markets by way of subsiding advertising expenditure on India exporters for their packs with the mention of Indian tea on it. Foreign packers would also receive subsidy if they used a certain percentage of Indian tea in their blends and advertised that point. Funds for such activity were small and mechanism of payment was complicated. As a result, real big tea marketers hardly cared for such schemes. But year after year some money, which appeared large in Indian context, but chicken feed in the context of global operations, used to be dissipated. After the loss of USSR market when exports fell sharply, there was hardly any scope for toying with such experiments. Collaboration with global operators, attempts to establish brand image, realizing need for consumer research, production of Bio-tea and specialties etc. gave Indian tea industry a smart appearance convertibility of rupee as a part of liberalization plan provided necessary support for taking right steps. Devalued rupees had positively encouraged larger interest from general currency areas. Indian tea was found more competitive in the world markets. Breakdown of the buying system in CIS countries created such an impact in the international trade that the normal rules of demand and supply did not work. Export projection called for substantial efforts in the field of marketing.

This part deals with marketing system of tea, modes of disposal of tea, seven marketing modes, primary marketing, development of auction centers, tea auction facilities, tea auction systems, advantage of auction sale, Tandon Committee on Tea Marketing, ex-garden sales, mini-auction, auction for blended and packet teas. Besides, efforts have been made to devote critical analysis on new auction rules—Ahuja committee 1981, marketing of Indian tea—domestic vs. exports, unrestricted import of tea to allow or not etc. Tea is the most popular of all the beverages in the world. As the largest organized sector, tea is one of the oldest industries in India and holds a considerable potential for the economic development of the country. India has the largest area under tea and is also the largest producer, consumer and exporter of tea in the world. In 2000, India's production was estimated at 950 mkg accounting for 29% of world production. Tea export from India was about 210 mkg, which represents 18% of world exports. In addition to contributing substantially to national and state ex-checkers directly and indirectly, it is the largest single export commodity earning foreign exchange.

Recent Trends

Tea industry has experienced many structural changes in recent years. These include emergence of small tea growers in place of large plantations and introduction of BLF. India's large tea plantations are mostly concentrated in Assam, and North Bengal. Assam alone produces 51% of the national production. As an agro-based industry, the development of plantation industry has contributed greatly towards rural development and urbanization of remote hilly regions by optimum use of land, creation of roads and other communication networks in such areas. In India, there are about 1,700 processing units engaged in tea production, while around 1,671 big (more than 100 hectares) planters produce an output of 700–725 mkg. At least 16 plantations in West Bengal were shut down in last few years after production fell and profits plummeted due to low yields from ageing tea bushes. According to the Tea Board, production during the first ten months of 2010 stood at 813 mkg as against 830 mkg during the same period last year. Looking at the cumulative figures, tea production in the first 2 months of 2011 was down by nearly 16.4–37.66 mkg compared with 45.06 mkg of the commodity produced in the same period of 2010. Production in February was down in West Bengal as well as in most parts of North India.

In case of Assam, production rose significantly to 94,000 kg as against 44,000 kg in February 2010. Consumption of black tea in the world market is expected to increase. In India alone, black tea consumption is expected to grow by 3.5%. The pressure on supply is expected to push up prices. In India, prices of quality tea fetched Rs 15–20 higher per kg in 2010 compared to the previous year. Darjeeling Tea, which is known world over as the champagne of teas, may get exclusive status in the EU. India has sent a proposal, seeking patent protection for Darjeeling Tea in the EU. The European Commission has sought some clarifications from the Tea Board on Darjeeling Tea before granting PGI. Over Rs 6 million is spent every year on the legal requirements to protect "Darjeeling" word and logo globally. A welcome development is that quality tea is finding takers even in smaller cities. Tier 2 and Tier 3 cities are emerging as major growth drivers for domestic consumption of tea. One reason for this is increase in purchasing power of the people.

Measures Needed

The Indian tea has to become globally competitive. No doubt, there are large estates, but not sufficient attention is paid toward processing and improving the quality of tea. India has to promote a powerful brand to win back the confidence of lost foreign markets. Attention should be paid to reducing unit cost of production through productivity gains, capacity building of small growers and streamlining marketing chls to suit foreign markets' demand. There is also a need to propagate the health benefits of tea. Promotion of organic tea is also important as its international demand is growing (Facts For You, August 2011).

Issues Impacting India's Export Performance

There are various issues which have some impacts on the performance of Indian exports. If these issues are addressed squarely, there are hopes of increasing India's exports. These are as follows:

- Inadequate efforts made in respect of marketing and brand building of Indian tea in overseas market.
- Exposing India's tea exports to concentration of risk arising out of over-dependence on CIS, UK and UAE.
- For CIS and UK markets, growth rates have been slower as compared to other import destinations.
- Indian teas are getting edged out of emerging higher growth markets by competing produce from Sri Lanka, Kenya and China.
- A large market like Pakistan which accounts for 9% of world imports remains closed to India. Black CTC tea from Kenya dominates consumption in Pakistan. Although Indian Tea would work out cheaper on landed cost basis in Pakistan, trade in tea remains marginal because of political sensitivities.
- Stagnant export realization.
- Limited presence in emerging markets.
- Market share depleting in matured markets.
- Tea exports constitute less than 2% of India's export revenues and hence it has not been covered under the priority list.
- Given policies and regulations are oriented towards protection of domestic market; availability of tea in domestic market and price stability are the over-riding concerns dictating policy formulation.

India's Competitive Position in World Tea Trade

India's competitive position has weakened in the world tea trade due to various reasons which are discussed in various interaction meets/workshops/seminars, etc of national and international nature. The following factors are held responsible for such weakness:

- India's tea exports are facing a double crunch with a production slow down and loss of share in major markets served and inability to make significant headway in potential/emerging markets.
- World export growth 5.3% Compound Annual Growth Rate (CAGR) was higher than India's export growth 3.4% CAGR during the period 1995–1999.
- Export realizations in dollar terms have been stagnant during the 1990s.
- Region-wise trends indicate that other than the CIS countries, India's share has been declining (in North America, India continues to be a marginal player).
- In UK, the second largest importer after the CIS group, Indian tea has lost significant market share to Kenyan produce.

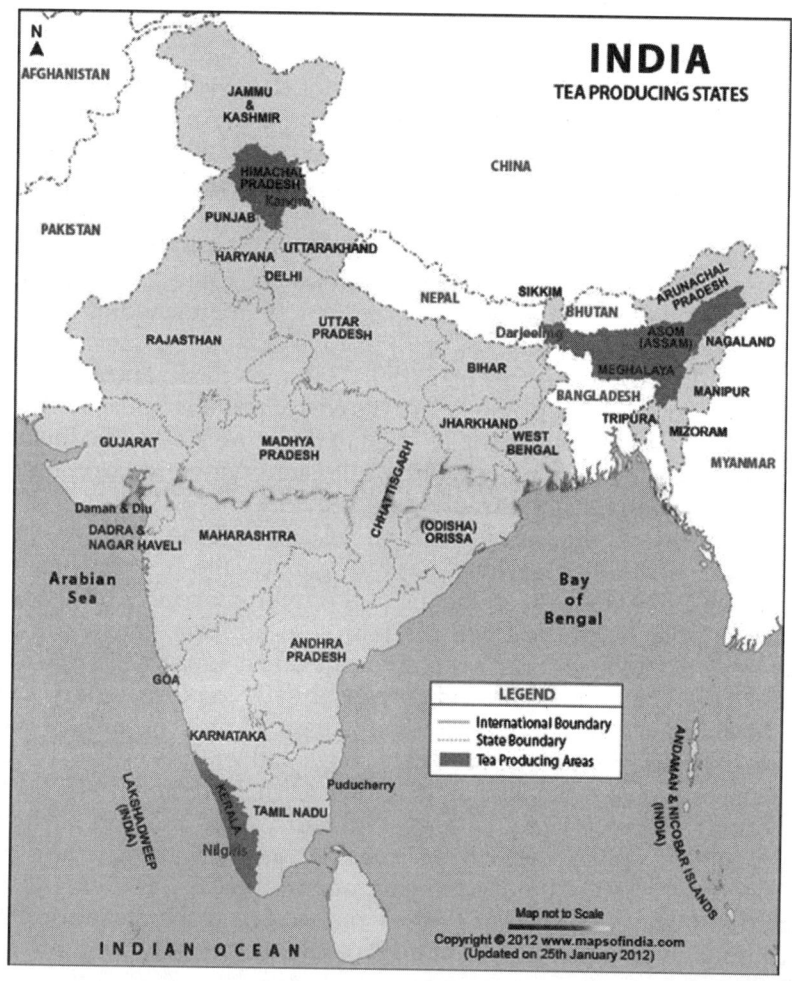

- In green tea, China has registered a much higher growth rate (15.3% CAGR, than Indian tea exports (3.4% CAGR) during 1995–1999.
- Even in India's traditional strongholds, CIS, Sri Lanka has made significant inroads since 1993 following the disbanding of the centralized marketing system. The main reasons attributed to Sri Lanka's success are better and more organized marketing efforts.

THE HISTORY OF THE TEA BAG

Tea Infusers and Origin of the Tea Bag

The arrival of tea in Britain in the seventeenth century altered the drinking habits of this nation forever. The late eighteenth century saw black tea overtake green tea in popularity for the first time, which also accelerated the addition of milk. In the 19th century widespread cultivation of tea in India began, leading to the imports of Indian tea into Britain overtaking the imports of Chinese tea. And in the 19th century, there was a further development that would radically change our tea-drinking habits—the invention of the tea bag.

Popular Infusers Included Tea Eggs and Tea Balls

The purpose of the tea bag is rooted in the belief that for tea to taste its best, the leaves ought to remove from the hot water at the end of a specific brewing period. Then there is the added benefit of convenience—a removable device means that tea can be made as easily in a mug as in a pot, without the need for a tea strainer, and that tea pots can be kept clean more easily. But, the earliest examples of removable infusing devices for holding tea were not bags. Popular infusers included tea eggs and tea balls—perforated metal containers which were filled with loose leaves and immersed in boiling water, and then removed using an attached chain.

Needless to say, it was in America, with its love of labor-saving devices, that tea bags were first developed. In around 1908, Thomas Sullivan, a New York tea merchant, started to send samples of tea to his customers in small silken bags. Some assumed that these were supposed to be used in the same way as the metal infusers, by putting the entire bag into the pot, rather than emptying out the contents. It was thus by accident that the tea bag was born!

Responding to the comments from his customers that the mesh on the silk was too fine, Sullivan developed sachets made of gauze—the first purpose-made tea bags. During the 1920s, these were developed for commercial production, and the bags grew in popularity in the USA. Made first of all from gauze and later from paper, they came in two sizes, a larger bag for the pot, and a smaller one for the cup. The features that we still recognize today were already in place—a string that hung over the side so the bag could be removed easily, with a decorated tag on the end.

While the American population took to tea bags with enthusiasm, the British were naturally wary of such a radical change in their tea-making methods. This was not helped by horror stories told by Britons who had visited the USA, who reported being served cups of tepid water with a tea bag on the side waiting to be dunked into it (an experience which is still not as uncommon in the USA as it should be!).

The material shortages of World War Two also stalled the mass adoption of tea bags in Britain, and it was not until the 1950s that they really took off. The 1950s were a time when all mr of household gadgets were being promoted as eliminating tedious household chores, and in keeping with this tea bags gained popularity on the grounds that they removed the need to empty out the used tea leaves from the tea pot. The convenience factor was more important to the British tea-drinker than the desire to control the length of infusion time, hence the appearance of tea bags that did not have strings attached.

It was Tetley in 1953 that drove the introduction of tea bags in Britain, but other companies soon caught up. In the early 1960s, tea bags made up less than 3% of the British market, but this has been growing steadily ever since. By 2007 tea bags made up a phenomenal 96% of the British market, and there can hardly be a home or workplace in Britain that does not have a stash of the humble, but vital, tea bag.

Tea consumption is growing by 3% every year. "It is more of a common man's drink and used in 90% of the households in the country", said Sujit Patra, Joint Secretary of Indian Tea Association.

TEA BOARD OF INDIA

About Tea Board

Tea is one of the industries, which by an Act of Parliament comes under the control of the Union Government. The genesis of the Tea Board India dates back to 1903 when the Indian Tea Cess Bill was passed. The Bill provided for levying a Cess on tea exports—the proceeds of which were to be used for the promotion of Indian tea both within and outside India. The present Tea Board setup under section 4 of the Tea Act 1953 was constituted on 1st April 1954. It has succeeded the Central Tea Board and the Indian Tea Licensing Committee which functioned respectively under the Central Tea Board Act, 1949 and the Indian Tea Control Act, 1938 which were repealed. The activities of the two previous bodies had been confined largely to regulation of tea cultivation and export of tea as required by the International Tea Agreement then in force, and promotion of tea consumption.

Tea Board Organization and Functions

Organization of the Board: The present Tea Board is functioning as a statutory body of the Central Government under the Ministry of Commerce. The Board is constituted of 31 members (including Chairman) drawn from Members of Parliament, tea producers, tea traders, tea brokers, consumers, and representatives of Governments from the principal tea producing states, and trade unions. The Board is reconstituted every 3 years.

The following are the standing committees of the Board:

1. Executive Committee
2. Tea Promotion Committee
3. Labor Welfare Committee
4. Development Committee
5. Licensing Committee for North India
6. Licensing Committee for South India.

The Executive Committee deals with the administrative matters of the Board.

The Export Promotion Committee deals with the work in relation to the export promotion of tea.

Labor Welfare Committee guides the Board in implementation of various welfare schemes for the benefit of the plantation workers and their wards.

The Development Committee is responsible for overseeing the various developmental schemes run by the Board.

Licensing Committee for North and South India will act as per direction of the Board or the Executive Committee pertaining to Chapter III and IV of the Tea Act relating to Tea Estate of North India and South India, respectively.

1. Administrative Setup: The functional activities of the Board's Head Office located in Kolkata, West Bengal are as under:

   a. The Secretariat headed by Secretary looks after Establishment/ administrative works and coordinates with the various departments of the Board's office.

   b. The Establishment branch headed by Assistant Secretary looks after administrative/policy matter and deal with the staff matter of the Board's office.

   c. The Finance wing headed by Financial Advisor and Chief Accounts Officer is responsible for the maintenance of accounts, release of financial assistance to tea gardens and internal audit.

   d. The Development Directorate headed by the Director of Tea Development is responsible for formulation and implementation of various developmental schemes and rendering assistance to the industry in the procurement, distribution and movement of essential inputs.

   e. The Promotion Directorate headed by the Director of Tea Promotion looks after the works relating to Marketing and Promotion of tea in India and abroad.

   f. The Research Directorate headed by the Director of Research is responsible for co-ordination of tea research carried out by the different tea research institutions in the country and monitoring the functions the Tea Board's own Research Station.

   g. The Licensing Department headed by the Controller of licensing is responsible for issue of business licenses for tea exporters and distributors, recording the ownership of all tea gardens in India and implementation of the Tea Waste (control) Order and Tea Warehousing (control) Order.

   h. The Labor Welfare Department headed by Welfare Liaison Officer (North) looks after the work relating to implementation of welfare schemes of the Board.

   i. The Statistics Department headed by the Statistician is responsible for the collection of Statistics relating to tea area production, tea prices, export, import, labor and all other related data and carrying out techno-economic surveys of various tea growing areas in the country including cost studies.

   j. The Law Cell headed by Law Officer looks after all legal matters arising in various functional departments mentioned above.

   k. Hindi Cell headed by the Deputy Director (Hindi) is responsible for the implementation of the provisions of Official Languages Act and various related measures.

   l. Vigilance Cell: Tea Board's Vigilance Cell is headed by the Deputy Chairman of the Board who has been appointed as the Chief Vigilance Officer of the

Board by the Central Vigilance Commission. The Cell engages itself with surveillance and preventive vigilance, in addition to taking appropriate action in matters arising out of information/complaints. The Cell attends to queries of the Government of India and the Central Vigilance Commission as and when such queries are received. Monthly and Quarterly Reports are prepared and sent to the Ministry of Commerce and the Central Vigilance Commission. The overall vigilance activities are looked after by the Chief Vigilance Officer who is assisted by the Vigilance officer.

2. Functions: The Tea Board has wide functions and responsibilities under the direction of the Central Government. Briefly the primary functions of the Tea Board are as under:

   a. Rendering financial and technical assistance for cultivation, manufacture and marketing of tea.

   b. Export Promotion

   c. Aiding Research and Development activities for augmentation of tea production and improvement of tea quality.

   d. Extend financial assistance in a limited way to the plantation workers and their wards through labor welfare schemes.

   e. To encourage and assist both financially and technically the unorganized small growers sector.

   f. Collection and maintenance of Statistical data and publication.

   g. Such other activities as are assigned from time to time by the Central Government.

3. Funds for the aforesaid functions are made available to the Board by the Government through Plan and Non-Plan Budgetary allocations.

   The Plan funds are being used exclusively for the activities mentioned at (a) above. Funds for all other activities mentioned above (F and g) are met from Non-Plan Budget allocation for which Cess levied on tea is the major source.

   Tea Cess is levied on all teas produced in India under Section 25(1) of the Tea Act, 1953. The said Act provides for levying Cess upto 50 paise per kilogram of tea produced in India. Currently, however, the Cess is collected at the rate of 30 paise per kg excepting Darjeeling teas for which only 12 paise is levied. The Cess at present is collected by the Central Excise Department and credited to the Consolidated Fund of India after deducting the expenses of collection. Funds are released by the Central Government in favor of Tea Board from time to time on the basis of the sanctioned budget after due appropriation by the Parliament. Such funds received by the Board are being utilized for meeting the non-plan expenditure.

   Plan Funds: Funds are provided under the plan budget with the prior approval of Planning Commission and EFC for implementing various developments, promotional and R and D schemes.

4. Offices of Tea Board:

   a. Offices in India: With Head Office located in Kolkata, West Bengal it has 21 offices which include Zonal, Regional and Sub-Regional Offices located at the following cities/towns:

Coonoor	Jorhat	New Delhi
Siliguri	Mumbai	Kochi
Coimbatore	Silchar	Kottayam
Agartala	Guwahati	Tezpur
Kurseong	Palampur	Jalpaiguri
Dibrugarh	SGDD-Dibrugarh	Gudalur
Kumily	Itanagar	Chennai
Tirumala	Bongaigaon	

It also maintains four Tea Bar/Buffets.

b. Foreign Offices: Currently, Tea Board has three overseas offices located at London, Dubai and Moscow. All these foreign offices of the Board are designed to undertake the various promotional measures to boost up export of Indian tea. These offices also act as a liaison office for interaction between importers of Indian tea of the respective regions as well as Indian Exporters.

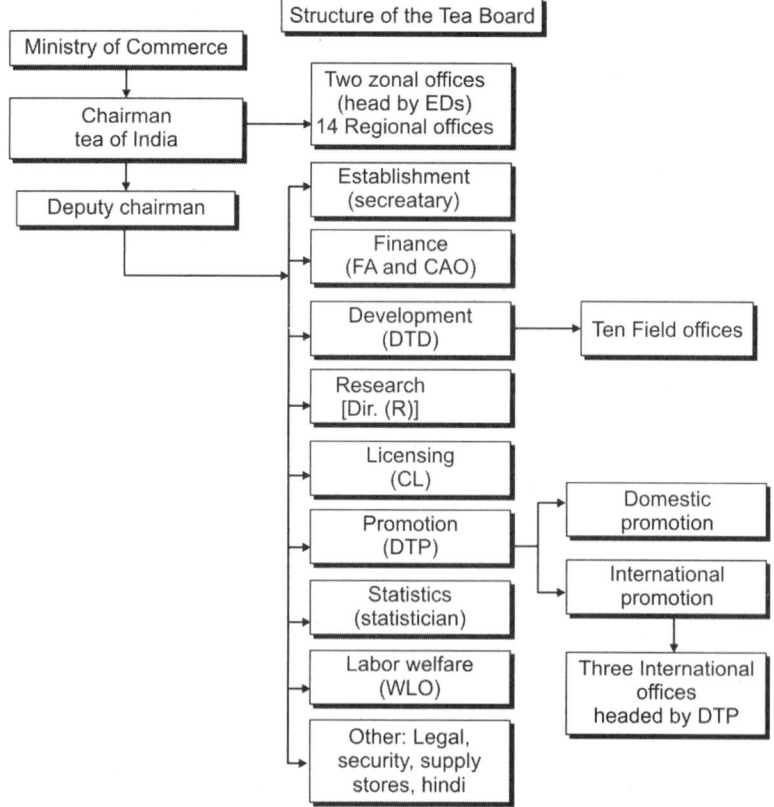

Books published

1. Role of Enzyme in Tea Processing - April 1998.
2. Package of practices for production of Organic Tea in India jointly with Tea Board - 2001.

3. Guidelines for Research Funding - National Tea *Research* Foundation (NTRF) (2000).
4. Road Map on Product Diversification in Tea (2002).
5. Medicinal Properties of Tea - (2006).
6. Natural Enemies of some tea pests with special reference to Darjeeling, Terai and Dooars.
7. Insects Attacking Shade Trees of Tea Plantation in the Dooars and Darjeeling.
8. A notes on Internalization of various NTRF Projects.

Internalization of the research findings is effected using specific recommendations emerging out of NTRF funded studies. At the field level, the recommendations are being implemented by Tea Research Institutes at North and South through their extension services operating in different tea producing districts of North and South India.

Collateral activities

1. In specific cases, on the recommendations of the Governing Body, NTRF gives one-time grant to eminent scientists to attend or address conventions or conversions pertaining to marketing of tea.
2. NTRF publishes its Quarterly News Bulletin, Annul Scientific Reports and specialized publications.
3. The data generated by NTRF projects on pesticide residues and their metabolites form the basis of the national protocol on pesticide residues on tea.

TEA IN THE WORLD—WORLD AREA AND PRODUCTION

About 80 countries produce tea in the world now. Asia alone produces about 83% of world's tea. Five countries contribute 78% of world's total tea production: China (38%), India (23%), Kenya (9%), Sri Lanka (8%) and Vietnam (4%).

India is the world's second-largest producer and the biggest consumer of tea. According to the latest data of the Tea Board, the country's production in November 2012 was 114.03 mkg. This was 13% higher as compared to the previous year's production. Assam and West Bengal together account for more than 50% of total tea produced in the country. Tea production in Assam rose by 25% to 60.41 mkg in November 2012 from 48.30 million kg from the same month in 2011. The production in West Bengal was up by 8% to 30.02 million kg from 27.77 million kg during the same period.

World area under tea increased from 1366 thousand hectares in 1961 to 2.8 million hectares in 2007. Major countries which shared 75% of the total area in 1961 were India, China, Sri Lanka and Indonesia—of these China topped the list, followed by India, Sri Lanka and Indonesia. During the following 46 years (by 2007), world area increased by over 48% and while China, India and Sri Lanka continue to have the top three positions, Kenya has gone ahead of Indonesia and Vietnam which was having just 17.8 thousand hectares in 1961 jumped to 149.2 thousand hectares just close to Indonesia's 110.5 thousand hectares (Tables 2.20 and 2.20A).

Country-wise data of tea production in the major produces for the period 1961–2012 is given in Table 2.20B. What is most interesting is that India was the leader upto 2004 when China was following closely. This is despite the fact that area under

Table 2.20: Area of tea in selected countries in world

Area (hectare)

Year	Bangladesh area		China area		India area		Indonesia area		Kenya area	Malawi area		Sri Lanka area	Vietnam area		World area	
2007	57,580	F	1,165,732	F	558,000	F	110,524	F	149,190	19,000	F	212,720	106,500		2,805,502	A
2006	52,609	F	1,116,740	F	523,000		111,055		147,080	19,000	F	212,720	102,100		2,708,366	A
2005	53,239		1,058,564		521,000		142,847		141,300	18,000	F	212,720	122,500		2,716,075	A
2004	53,215		989,262		520,000		116,200		136,700	18,694		212,720	120,800		2,601,131	A
2003	50,977		943,400		516,000		116,200		131,450	18,694		210,620	86,100		2,508,339	A
2002	50,990		913,100		510,000		115,803		131,450	18,800		210,620	98,000	F	2,480,092	A
2001	48,600		905,662		504,000		115,416		124,290	18,800		188,970	80,000		2,415,365	A
2000	48,600		898,012		490,000		121,200	F	120,390	18,162		188,970	70,300		2,384,046	A
1999	48,562		928,542		474,000		110,000	F	118,540	21,565		195,460	69,500		2,383,831	A
1998	48,598		878,989		434,000		109,745		118,650	18,800		188,970	66,879		2,285,378	A
1997	48,308		888,572		431,000		114,287		113,892	18,800		190,473	63,900		2,287,504	A
1996	48,015		891,435		427,000		114,592		113,680	18,800		187,563	71,000	F	2,303,506	A
1995	47,780		888,132		428,000		113,426		112,556	18,800		188,970	70,800		2,298,290	A
1994	47,786		903,701		426,000		109,939		110,221	18,800	F	187,309	70,500		2,310,856	A
1993	47,782		900,740		448,000		102,542		104,860	18,500	F	197,230	63,395		2,319,631	A
1992	47,657		861,106		444,000		94,666		101,845	18,300	F	221,836	62,862		2,308,157	A
1991	47,629		851,370		421,000		94,647		100,626	18,500	F	221,691	59,981		2,285,963	A
1990	47,418	F	842,695		415,000		94,510		96,981	18,500	F	221,758	59,997		2,260,328	A
1989	46,470	F	847,253		414,300		89,935		87,473	18,400	F	222,110	58,307		2,245,429	A
1988	46,424	F	843,426		414,200		87,064		86,800	18,600	F	221,683	43,400		2,214,688	A
1987	45,785	F	832,663		411,700		98,463		85,400	18,400	F	221,498	43,540		2,204,518	A
1986	45,700	F	819,180		411,673		97,773		84,400	18,000	F	222,905	42,600		2,193,147	A
1985	44,610	F	834,313		399,929		61,854		83,719	18,000	F	231,650	41,600		2,152,785	A
1984	44,553		1,103,931		398,453		60,108		83,350	17,800	F	227,874	49,300		2,417,035	A
1983	44,575		1,131,074		396,066		89,000		82,142	17,000	F	242,130	49,000		2,483,658	A

Table 2.20: Area of tea in selected countries in world (*Contd.*)

Area (hectare)

Year	Bangladesh area	China area		India area	Indonesia area		Kenya area	Malawi area		Sri Lanka area	Vietnam area		World area	
1982	44,543	1,122,995		394,999	86,000		81,082	17,500	F	242,141	38,920		2,449,667	A
1981	45,165	1,087,516		384,242	85,023		78,896	17,500	F	244,918	36,000		2,384,664	A
1980	44,091	1,068,134		381,891	86,178		76,541	17,500	F	244,710	34,690		2,369,480	A
1979	43,183	1,077,859		378,447	84,400		74,300	17,500	F	244,099	34,380		2,363,163	A
1978	43,183	1,075,425		373,747	81,334		72,048	17,700		242,899	48,886		2,379,015	A
1977	42,998	1,041,832		369,184	79,079		68,392	17,300		242,012	43,042		2,317,781	A
1976	43,099	992,800		366,276	82,000		65,957	17,200		240,581	38,618		2,245,608	A
1975	43,161	931,449	F	364,275	84,000	F	61,542	16,000		241,880	38,800		2,167,122	A
1974	43,162	831,825	F	363,303	84,000	F	58,419	16,500	F	242,193	36,000	F	2,053,260	A
1973	45,604	732,068	F	361,663	80,000	F	54,818	15,200	F	242,298	35,000	F	1,933,553	A
1972	45,604	632,529	F	360,108	76,000	F	49,763	14,800	F	241,855	33,000	F	1,801,084	A
1971	45,604	582,957	F	358,675	79,000	F	43,400	14,500		241,667	31,300		1,737,148	A
1970	45,604	519,253		356,516	89,000	F	40,278	14,300		241,799	29,200		1,668,290	A
1969	43,302	473,704	F	354,133	86,000	F	36,524	15,000	F	241,401	27,000	F	1,598,201	A
1968	42,443	444,278	F	353,359	87,000	F	33,562	14,000	F	241,796	25,000	F	1,553,831	A
1967	40,975	414,495	F	351,065	91,000	F	30,078	13,500	F	242,331	23,000	F	1,503,397	A
1966	39,765	374,516	F	347,653	94,000	F	27,340	13,000	F	241,373	22,400		1,454,455	A
1965	38,000	369,607	F	345,256	101,000	F	24,756	13,643		240,508	26,300		1,442,275	A
1964	37,000	365,236	F	341,762	102,000	F	23,062	13,230		239,569	22,000	F	1,415,496	A
1963	36,000	356,308	F	334,036	105,000	F	21,448	12,804		237,702	21,000		1,397,016	A
1962	33,000	351,043	F	332,524	107,000	F	19,893	12,507		239,217	21,000		1,379,866	A
1961	32,000	354,979	F	331,229	107,000	F	17,756	11,000		237,713	19,100		1,366,126	A

A, May include official.
F, Semi-official or estimated data.

Table 2.20A: Percentage share of tea in production

Year	Bangladesh	China	India	Indonesia	Kenya	Malawi	Sri Lanka	Vietnam	World
2012	1.4	38.9	24.6	2.9	8.2	0.9	7.2	3.5	100
2011	1.3	36.5	25.1	3.2	8.5	1.1	7.4	4.0	100
2010	1.4	35.2	23.1	3.6	9.5	1.2	7.9	4.1	100
2009	1.5	34.3	24.7	3.9	7.9	1.3	7.3	4.4	100
2008	1.5	32.4	25.3	4.0	8.9	1.1	8.2	4.3	100
2007	1.5	30.4	24.4	3.9	9.5	1.2	7.9	4.2	100
2006	1.6	28.7	25.4	4.0	8.5	1.2	8.5	4.1	100
2005	1.6	26.5	24.8	4.9	9.1	1.1	8.8	3.7	100
2004	1.7	25.1	25.8	5.0	9.5	1.5	9.0	3.5	100
2003	1.8	24.6	26.1	5.3	9.1	1.3	9.4	3.2	100
2002	1.8	24.2	27.0	5.1	9.1	1.2	9.8	3.0	100
2001	1.7	23.5	27.6	5.3	9.6	1.2	9.6	2.5	100
2000	1.6	23.7	27.9	5.5	8.0	1.4	10.3	2.4	100
1999	1.8	22.6	28.4	5.2	8.1	1.3	9.2	2.3	100
1998	1.7	23.0	27.1	5.6	9.8	1.4	9.4	1.9	100
1997	1.9	23.1	28.3	5.6	8.0	1.1	10.0	1.9	100
1996	1.8	22.9	28.1	6.2	9.5	1.3	9.6	1.7	100
1995	2.0	23.2	28.8	5.9	9.3	1.3	9.4	1.5	100
1994	1.9	23.2	28.6	5.3	7.9	1.3	9.2	1.6	100
1993	1.9	23.7	26.9	6.3	8.1	1.5	8.9	1.4	100
1992	1.8	23.3	30.3	6.2	7.5	1.1	7.2	1.5	100
1991	1.8	22.0	28.1	5.4	7.9	1.6	9.4	1.3	100
1990	1.5	22.3	27.3	6.2	7.8	1.5	9.2	1.3	100
1989	1.8	22.5	28.4	5.7	7.3	1.6	8.4	1.2	100
1988	1.7	23.2	27.5	5.5	6.7	1.6	9.3	1.2	100
1987	1.6	22.7	26.3	5.3	6.6	1.4	9.0	1.2	100
1986	1.7	21.1	27.1	5.6	6.2	1.7	9.2	1.3	100
1985	1.9	19.8	28.5	5.5	6.4	1.7	9.3	1.2	100
1984	1.7	19.9	29.1	5.7	5.3	1.7	9.5	1.2	100
1983	2.0	20.6	28.2	5.3	5.8	1.6	8.7	1.2	100
1982	2.1	21.5	28.6	4.7	4.9	2.0	9.6	1.3	100
1981	2.1	19.5	29.7	5.8	4.8	1.7	11.1	1.1	100
1980	2.1	17.3	30.1	5.6	4.7	1.6	10.1	1.1	100
1979	2.0	16.6	29.6	5.3	5.4	1.8	11.4	1.1	100

Table 2.20A: Percentage share of tea in production *(Contd.)*

Year	Bangladesh	China	India	Indonesia	Kenya	Malawi	Sri Lanka	Vietnam	World
1978	2.1	16.3	31.2	5.1	5.2	1.8	11.0	1.1	100
1977	2.1	15.7	31.4	4.7	4.9	1.8	11.8	1.0	100
1976	2.1	16.2	32.2	4.6	3.9	1.8	12.4	1.1	100
1975	1.9	15.3	31.4	4.5	3.7	1.7	13.8	1.2	100
1974	2.2	14.9	32.8	4.4	3.6	1.6	13.7	1.1	100
1973	1.9	14.4	32.2	4.6	3.9	1.6	14.4	1.0	100
1972	1.7	14.0	32.4	4.3	3.8	1.5	14.9	1.1	100
1971	0.9	13.8	33.3	4.7	2.8	1.4	16.6	1.2	100
1970	2.4	12.7	32.5	5.0	3.2	1.5	16.5	1.1	100
1969	2.4	12.0	31.8	5.8	2.9	1.4	17.7	1.1	100
1968	2.3	11.7	33.1	6.2	2.4	1.3	18.5	1.1	100
1967	2.5	11.8	33.1	6.5	2.0	1.4	19.0	0.8	100
1966	2.5	11.1	32.9	6.3	2.2	1.3	19.4	1.0	100
1965	2.4	11.1	33.5	7.3	1.8	1.2	20.9	1.0	100
1964	2.7	10.4	35.0	7.0	1.9	1.2	20.6	0.8	100
1963	2.4	10.3	33.9	7.4	1.8	1.2	21.5	0.8	100
1962	2.4	9.5	35.1	8.1	1.7	1.4	21.5	0.8	100
1961	2.7	9.9	36.0	7.8	1.3	1.5	21.0	0.8	100

tea in China during 1996 was 891.4 thousand hectares against India 428 thousand hectares only (Table 2.20A). During 2004, when India shared 25.8% of world production, China was having 25.1% (Table 2.20C), Kenya and Sri Lanka followed with 9.5 and 9.0%, respectively. From 2005 onward. China took the lead with 26.5% against India 24.8%. By 2008, China improved to over 30% and India went down to 24%. Data for 2012 gives the share of India as 24.6% and that of China as nearly 39% (Tables 2.20B to D), and production often in different producing countries. Area of tea in India and World, and production of tea are given in Table 2.20D.

Sri Lanka produced 211.3 thousand tons in 1986 increased to 310 thousand tons by 2002, 318.7 thousand tons in 2008 and over 326 thousand tons by 2012. Kenya produced 143.3 thousand tons in 1986, lower than Vietnam. It produced 324.6 thousand (little higher than Sri Lanka) in 2004 and 399 in 2010 which fell-down lightly in the subsequent years. An interesting feature of tea scenario today is that Kenya has come to the third position (Fig. 2.11), surpassing Sri Lanka (Table 2.20B). Besides the eight major producers, there are a few other smaller mes. Area and production of tea producers including these major ones is as in Tables 2.21 to 2.21B.

A look at productivity of tea levels (Table 2.22) shows that of all the countries Netherland a minor producer has the highest productivity at over 7,000 kg per hectares. From among the major producers Kenya is at the top with over 2,200 kg hectares followed by India and Sri Lanka. China with a little over 600 kg per hectares is one of the poorest in so far as productivity levels are concerned.

Table 2.20B: Production of tea

(Tons)

Countries	1994–1996	1999–2001	2003–2005	2006	2007	2008	2009
Argentina	49,846	67,058	69,375	72,129	76,000	76,000	76,000
Azerbaijan	3,595	1,745	910	655	484	323	447
Bangladesh	50,063	51,333	57,553	58,000	58,500	59,000	
Bolivia	692	830	854	872	889	889	889
Brazil	8,198	7,919	5,126	4,052	1,083	4,752	
Burundi	6,499	7,681	7,531		7,700	7,700	
Cameroon	3,674	4,267	3,800	4,000	4,000	4,000	4,000
China	612,954	707,400	865,966	1,047,345	1,183,002	1,275,384	1,317,384
Colombia		97	120	118	120	120	134
Congo, Democratic Rep. of the	3,418	1,892	1,563	1,760	1,760	2,220	
Ecuador	3,090	1,368	1,369	1,870	1,925	1,925	
Ethiopia	1,867	3,786	4,520	4,800	4,800	4,800	
Georgia	44,733	35,777	22,404	6,600	7,500	5,400	
Guatemala	447	450	440	450	480	480	
India	754,300	849,000	869,667	928,000	949,220	805,180	
Indonesia	153,164	162,218	172,906	146,858	150,224	150,851	160,000
Iran, Islamic Republic of	57,352	54,240	54,360	59,180	49,680	42,348	
Japan	86,567	86,167	97,533	91,800	94,100	96,500	86,000
Kenya	237,037	259,869	315,590	310,580	369,600	345,800	314,100
Korea, Republic of	782	1,298	1,500	1,500	1,550	1,550	
Lao People's Democratic Republic	936	272	282	300	260	560	470
Madagascar	300	444	495	560	580	580	
Malawi	34,708	39,233	43,261	45,009	48,140	48,140	
Malaysia	5,800	5,652	3,625	2,850	5,540	5,570	9,120

(Tons)

Table 2.20B: Production of tea (*Contd.*)

Countries	1994–1996	1999–2001	2003–2005	2006	2007	2008	2009
Mali	156	57	112	135	135	135	
Mauritius	3,790	1,434	1,435	1,567	1,563	1,668	1,481
Mozambique	1,549	7,032	14,606	16,256	16,256	16,866	
Myanmar	15,733	19,575	24,160	26,500	26,500	26,500	
Nepal	2,510	5,405	10,783	13,043	15,168	16,160	16,208
Panama	155	110	172	141	145	151	
Papua New Guinea	6,104	9,500	8,133	9,000	9,000	9,000	
Peru	7,356	6,567	3,806	4,820	3,597	4,009	3,169
Portugal	62	120	118	115	115	115	
Russian Federation	6,804	1,587	1,123	1,150	630	820	630
Rwanda	6,202	15,085	15,478	16,000	20,474	19,965	20,000
Seychelles	232	238	231	189	222	137	
South Africa	10,784	12,421	12,734	3,328	4,200	4,200	
Sri Lanka	248,867	294,897	309,507	310,800	305,220	318,700	290,000
Tanzania, United Republic of	24,367	24,700	29,467	30,300	31,300	34,800	
Thailand	5,100	5,533	24,167	6,000	57,362	61,557	63,707
Turkey	117,201	160,275	191,001	201,866	206,160	198,046	198,601
Uganda	14,524	28,944	36,778	34,334	44,923	42,808	48,663
Vietnam	43,000	71,967	118,775	151,000	164,000	174,900	
Zambia	483	800	783	750	750	750	
World	**2,650,455**	**3,037,586**	**3,426,690**	**3,646,452**	**3,947,527**	**3,894,029**	**3,885,302**

Table 2.20C: Production of tea in different producing countries

(Figure in thousand kg)

Name of the countries	1986	1990	1991	1992	1993	1994	1995	1996	1997	2000	2001	2002	2003	2008	2009	2010	2011	2012
India	620,853	720,338	754,192	732,322	760,826	752,895	756,013	779,227	810,613	846,922	853,923	838,474	878,129	980,820	979,000	966,400	1,115,720	1,111,760
Bangladesh	37,593	45,894	45,030	48,935	50,507	51,655	145,422	53,406	53,495	52,639	56,820	53,624	58,298	58,660	60,000	59,270	59,320	62,160
Sri Lanka	212,705	234,074	241,552	178,870	233,276	243,563	246,424	258,969	277,428	306,794	296,301	310,604	303,254	318,700	289,780	331,430	328,630	326,280
Indonesia	–	–	152,898	144,834	136,587	–	–	166,256	153,619	162,586	166,868	162,194	169,819	153,280	152,590	151,010	142,340	130,500
China	460,468	540,100	541,600	559,827	599,941	588,468	588,423	593,386	613,366	683,324	701,699	745,374	768,140	1,257,600	1,358,640	1,475,060	1,623,210	1,761,000
Japan	93,601	89,903	87,903	92,103	92,103	86,303	84,804	88,709	91,211	89,309	90,371	83,677	91,930	–	–	–	–	–
Turkey	143,849	126,768	136,887	156,269	127,715	134,350	104,680	114,540	139,523	130,671	142,900	142,000	155,000	155,000	153,000	148,000	145,000	147,000
Vietnam	301,000	32,200	33,000	36,200	37,700	36,000	40,000	40,000	42,000	70,000	80,000	88,000	93,000	166,380	175,000	170,000	178,000	158,000
Kenya	143,317	197,008	203,589	188,072	211,168	209,422	244,552	257,162	220,722	236,286	294,631	287,102	293,670	345,820	314,200	399,010	377,910	369,560
Malawi	38,976	39,059	40,530	28,136	39,497	35,140	34,526	38,312	43,930	42,114	36,770	39,185	41,693	41,640	52,560	51,590	47,060	42,490
Tanzania	15,079	18,414	19,321	18,365	23,249	23,764	23,705	19,768	22,475	23,897	24,745	2,751	29,482	31,610	32,090	31,650	32,780	32,280
Uganda	3,335	6,704	8,950	9,129	12,289	3,000	12,692	17,418	21,075	29,282	33,255	33,831	36,475	42,750	50,980	59,140	54,180	55,080
Argentina	40,920	43,000	43,700	44,000	46,000	42,000	32,000	43,000	55,000	63,000	59,000	58,000	60,000	–	–	–	–	–
USSR/CIS	146,600	131,000	116,000	55,000	30,000	18,000	10,000	8,000	16,000	14,900	15,000	14,300	14,500	–	–	–	–	–
Others	–	689,000							738,000	673,000	692,000	701,000		327,010	342,650	349,450	345,160	330,870
Total	–	2,584,000							2,883,000	2,992,000	3,091,000	3,099,000		3,879,270	3,960,490	4,192,010	4,449,310	4,526,980

Source: Tea Board.

Table 2.20D: Area and production of tea in India and world

Area (hectares); Production (tons)

Year	India Area		India Produ.	World Area		World Produ.	
2007	558,000	F	949,220	2,805,502	A	3,887,308	A
2006	523,000		928,000	2,708,366	A	3,646,452	A
2005	521,000		893,000	2,716,075	A	3,603,197	A
2004	520,000		878,000	2,601,131	A	3,409,055	A
2003	516,000		838,000	2,508,339	A	3,212,516	A
2002	510,000		854,000	2,480,092	A	3,165,432	A
2001	504,000		847,000	2,415,365	A	3,071,601	A
2000	490,000		826,000	2,384,046	A	2,963,588	A
1999	474,000		874,000	2,383,831	A	3,077,588	A
1998	434,000		810,000	2,285,378	A	2,989,032	A
1997	431,000		780,000	2,287,504	A	2,758,006	A
1996	427,000		756,000	2,303,506	A	2,692,866	A
1995	428,000		753,900	2,298,290	A	2,621,082	A
1994	426,000		753,000	2,310,856	A	2,637,418	A
1993	448,000		703,900	2,319,631	A	2,612,797	A
1992	444,000		754,200	2,308,157	A	2,492,432	A
1991	421,000		720,300	2,285,963	A	2,561,050	A
1990	415,000		688,100	2,260,328	A	2,524,165	A
1989	414,300		701,100	2,245,429	A	2,472,861	A
1988	414,200		674,300	2,214,688	A	2,448,034	A
1987	411,700		620,800	2,204,518	A	2,358,977	A
1986	411,673		620,803	2,193,147	A	2,293,102	A
1985	399,929		656,162	2,152,785	A	2,304,834	A
1984	398,453		639,864	2,417,035	A	2,200,532	A
1983	396,066		581,484	2,483,658	A	2,062,325	A
1982	394,999		560,732	2,449,667	A	1,961,781	A
1981	384,242		559,583	2,384,664	A	1,885,907	A
1980	381,891		569,550	2,369,480	A	1,893,527	A
1979	378,447		543,776	2,363,163	A	1,834,132	A
1978	373,747		563,846	2,379,015	A	1,805,757	A
1977	369,184		556,267	2,317,781	A	1,771,000	A
1976	366,276		511,817	2,245,608	A	1,591,872	A

(Contd.)

Table 2.20D: Area and production of tea in India and world *(Contd.)*

Area (hectares); Production (tons)

	India		World	
Year	Area	Produ.	Area	Produ.
1975	364,275	487,137	2,167,122 A	1,549,347 A
1974	363,303	489,475	2,053,260 A	1,492,601 A
1973	361,663	471,952	1,933,553 A	1,465,134 A
1972	360,108	455,996	1,801,084 A	1,405,269 A
1971	358,675	435,468	1,737,148 A	1,308,424 A
1970	356,516	418,517	1,668,290 A	1,286,757 A
1969	354,133	393,588	1,598,201 A	1,238,984 A
1968	353,359	402,489	1,553,831 A	1,216,441 A
1967	351,065	384,759	1,503,397 A	1,161,581 A
1966	347,653	375,983	1,454,455 A	1,144,061 A
1965	345,256	366,374	1,442,275 A	1,092,631 A
1964	341,762	372,486	1,415,496 A	1,063,199 A
1963	334,036	346,413	1,397,016 A	1,021,949 A
1962	332,524	346,736	1,379,866 A	987,350 A
1961	331,229	354,397	1,366,126 A	983,785 A

A, May include official.
Semi-official or estimated data.

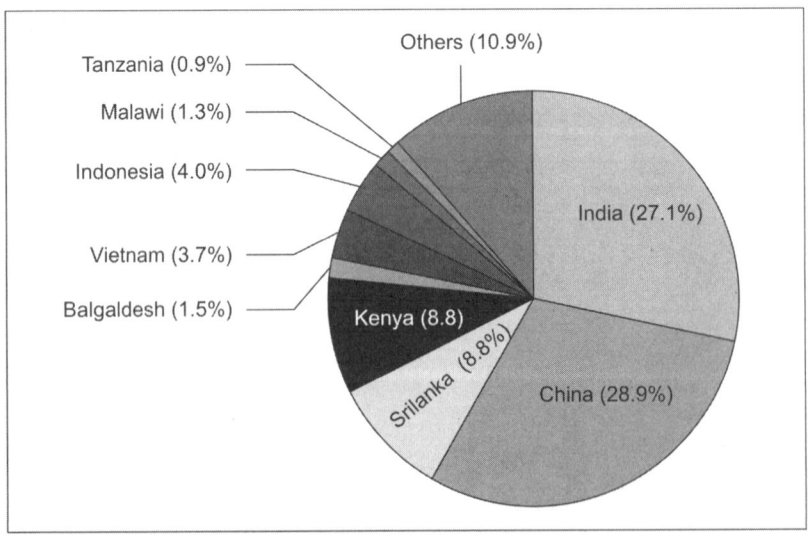

Fig. 2.11: Share of tea production

Table 2.21: Area under tea in different producing countries

(Area in hectares)

Name of the countries	1986	1990	1991	1992	1993	1994	1995	1996	2000	2000	2001	2002	2003
India	407,647	416,269	420,470	420,289	418,363	425,966	427,065	431,245	504,366	504,366	509,806	515,832	519,598
Bangladesh	46,703	47,650	47,677	47,781	47,888	47,847	48,036	47,889	49,195	49,195	49,313	49,500	50,000
Sri Lanka	222,905	221,758	221,691	221,836	221,836	NA	NA	NA	188,971	188,971	188,971	187,971	188,199
Indonesia	124,093	134,934	137,055	138,736	129,231	128,503	NA	514,185	153,667	153,667	150,938	150,723	143,620
China	1,023,933	1,061,864	1,060,530	1,084,200	1,170,800	1,134,600	1,115,300	1,10,3000	1,089,000	1,089,000	1140,700	1,134,200	1,207,300
Japan	60,200	58,500	57,600	56,700	55,700	54,500	53,700	52,700	50,400	50,400	50,100	49,700	50,000
Turkey	83,470	90,575	88,639	89,345.	89,330	76,971	76,609	76,743	76,749	76,749	76,653	76,600	76,639
Vietnam	58,100	59,900	65,000	68,000	70,000	64,000	71,000	64,000	80,000	80,000	82,000	85,000	87,000
Kenya	84,400	97,020	100629	101,845	104,864	110,222	112,556	117,457	126,203	126,203	131,581	139,976	131,419
Malawi	18,790	18,204	18,300	18,587	18,705	18,801	18,963	18,986	18,782	18,782	18,761	18,800	18,694
Tanzania	18,875	18,875	19,415	19,415	19,415	19,881	20,153	20,564	21,212	21,212	21,371	21,316	21,984
Uganda	20,905	20,905	20,500	20,500	20,500	20,500	20,500	20,500	20,570	20,570	20,870	21,170	21,570
Argentina	42,350	41,276	41,406	41,406	41,406	NA	40,000	39,000	39,000	39,000	36,000	36,000	36,000
USSR/CIS	81,400	NA	81,400	1,600	1,600	NA	NA	NA	40,500	40,500	40,600	40,500	41,300

NA, non-available.

Table 2.21A: Percentage share of major countries in global production of tea

Name of the countries	1991	1992	1993	2000	2001	2002	2003*	2004	2005	2006	2011
India	28.67	30.04	29.50	29.06	28.13	27.45	27.67	27.0	27.14	27.1	22.00
China	20.58	22.96	23.50	23.45	23.12	24.40	24.20	25.5	27.34	28.9	37.76
Sri Lanka	9.1S	7.34	9.14	10.53	9.76	10.17	9.55	9.3	9.28	8.8	7.64
Kenya	7.74	7.71	5.27	–	9.71	9.40	9.25	9.8	9.59	8.8	8.79
Bangladesh	1.71	2.01	1.98	1.81	1.87	1.76	1.S4	1.7	1.71	1.5	
Vietnam	1.25	1.48	1.48	2.40	2.64	2.88	2.93	2.9	3.19	3.7	
Indonesia	5.81	5.94	5.35	5.58	550	5.31	5.35	5	4.85	4.0	
Malawi	1.54	1.15	1.55	1.45	1.21	1.28	1.31	1.5	1.11	1.3	
Tanzania	0.73	0.75	0.91	0.82	0.S2	0.90	0.93	0.9	0.89	0.9	
USSR/CIS	4.41	2.26	1.17	0.51	0.49	0.47	0.46				
Iran	1.71	1.97	1.96	1.52	1.94	1.62	1.83				
Turkey	5.20	6.41	5.00	4.48	4.71	4.65	4.88				
Uganda	0.34	0.37	0.48	1.00	1.10	1.11	1.15				
Mozambique	0.08	0.06	0.08	0.09	0.10	0.10	0.10				
Zaire	0.11	0.12	0.12	0.09	0.09	0.09	0.09				
Mauritius	0.22	0.24	0.23	0.04	0.02	0.05	0.05				
Rwanda	0.51	0.56	0.37	0.49	0.59	0.49	0.49				
Burundi	0.20	0.24	0.22	0.24	0.30	0.22	0.23				
Cameroon	0.13	0.14	0.15	0.14	0.14	0.14	0.14				
Argentina	1.66	LSO	1.80	2.16	1.94	1.90	1.89				

Table 2.21A: Percentage share of major countries in global production of tea *(Contd.)*

Name of the countries	1991	1992	1993	2000	2001	2002	2003*	2004	2005	2006	2011
Brazil	0.36	0.37	0.39	0.12	0.15	0.15	0.15				
Peru	0.13	0.12	0.12	0.09	0.09	0.09	0.09				
Ecuador	0.08	0.06	0.06	0.06	0.05	0.06	0.06				
Zimbabwe	0.59	0.32	0.55	0.77	0.74	0.74	0.69				
Myanmar	1.80	0.00	0.00	0.00	0.00	0.00	0.00				
Malaysia	0.27	0.27	0.23	0.19	0.18	0.17	0.13				
South Africa	0.46	0.40	0.42	0.36	0.35	0.38	0.34				
Australia	0.03	0.02	0.03	0.04	0.04	0.05	0.05				
Ethiopia	0.06	–	–	0.15	0.15	0.15	0.15				
Nepal	0.06	–	–	0.26	0.25	0.26	0.25				
World total	**100.00**	**100.00**	**100.00**	**100.00**	**100.00**	**100.00**	**100.00**				**100.00**

* Provisional.
Source: TEA statistics.

Table 2.21B: Percentage share of tea in production

Year	Bangladesh	China	India	Indonesia	Kenya	Malawi	Sri Lanka	Vietnam	World
2012	1.4	38.9	24.6	2.9	8.2	0.9	7.2	3.5	100
2011	1.3	36.5	25.1	3.2	8.5	1.1	7.4	4.0	100
2010	1.4	35.2	23.1	3.6	9.5	1.2	7.9	4.1	100
2009	1.5	34.3	24.7	3.9	7.9	1.3	7.3	4.4	100
2008	1.5	32.4	25.3	4.0	8.9	1.1	8.2	4.3	100
2007	1.5	30.4	24.4	3.9	9.5	1.2	7.9	4.2	100
2006	1.6	28.7	25.4	4.0	8.5	1.2	8.5	4.1	100
2005	1.6	26.5	24.8	4.9	9.1	1.1	8.8	3.7	100
2004	1.7	25.1	25.8	5.0	9.5	1.5	9.0	3.5	100
2003	1.8	24.6	26.1	5.3	9.1	1.3	9.4	3.2	100
2002	1.8	24.2	27.0	5.1	9.1	1.2	9.8	3.0	100
2001	1.7	23.5	27.6	5.3	9.6	1.2	9.6	2.5	100
2000	1.6	23.7	27.9	5.5	8.0	1.4	10.3	2.4	100
1999	1.8	22.6	28.4	5.2	8.1	1.3	9.2	2.3	100
1998	1.7	23.0	27.1	5.6	9.8	1.4	9.4	1.9	100
1997	1.9	23.1	28.3	5.6	8.0	1.1	10.0	1.9	100
1996	1.8	22.9	28.1	6.2	9.5	1.3	9.6	1.7	100
1995	2.0	23.2	28.8	5.9	9.3	1.3	9.4	1.5	100
1994	1.9	23.2	28.6	5.3	7.9	1.3	9.2	1.6	100
1993	1.9	23.7	26.9	6.3	8.1	1.5	8.9	1.4	100
1992	1.8	23.3	30.3	6.2	7.5	1.1	7.2	1.5	100
1991	1.8	22.0	28.1	5.4	7.9	1.6	9.4	1.3	100
1990	1.5	22.3	27.3	6.2	7.8	1.5	9.2	1.3	100
1989	1.8	22.5	28.4	5.7	7.3	1.6	8.4	1.2	100
1988	1.7	23.2	27.5	5.5	6.7	1.6	9.3	1.2	100
1987	1.6	22.7	26.3	5.3	6.6	1.4	9.0	1.2	100
1986	1.7	21.1	27.1	5.6	6.2	1.7	9.2	1.3	100
1985	1.9	19.8	28.5	5.5	6.4	1.7	9.3	1.2	100
1984	1.7	19.9	29.1	5.7	5.3	1.7	9.5	1.2	100
1983	2.0	20.6	28.2	5.3	5.8	1.6	8.7	1.2	100
1982	2.1	21.5	28.6	4.7	4.9	2.0	9.6	1.3	100
1981	2.1	19.5	29.7	5.8	4.8	1.7	11.1	1.1	100
1980	2.1	17.3	30.1	5.6	4.7	1.6	10.1	1.1	100
1979	2.0	16.6	29.6	5.3	5.4	1.8	11.4	1.1	100
1978	2.1	16.3	31.2	5.1	5.2	1.8	11.0	1.1	100
1977	2.1	15.7	31.4	4.7	4.9	1.8	11.8	1.0	100
1976	2.1	16.2	32.2	4.6	3.9	1.8	12.4	1.1	100
1975	1.9	15.3	31.4	4.5	3.7	1.7	13.8	1.2	100

Table 2.21B: Percentage share of tea in production *(Contd.)*

Year	Bangladesh	China	India	Indonesia	Kenya	Malawi	Sri Lanka	Vietnam	World
1974	2.2	14.9	32.8	4.4	3.6	1.6	13.7	1.1	100
1973	1.9	14.4	32.2	4.6	3.9	1.6	14.4	1.0	100
1972	1.7	14.0	32.4	4.3	3.8	1.5	14.9	1.1	100
1971	0.9	13.8	33.3	4.7	2.8	1.4	16.6	1.2	100
1970	2.4	12.7	32.5	5.0	3.2	1.5	16.5	1.1	100
1969	2.4	12.0	31.8	5.8	2.9	1.4	17.7	1.1	100
1968	2.3	11.7	33.1	6.2	2.4	1.3	18.5	1.1	100
1967	2.5	11.8	33.1	6.5	2.0	1.4	19.0	0.8	100
1966	2.5	11.1	32.9	6.3	2.2	1.3	19.4	1.0	100
1965	2.4	11.1	33.5	7.3	1.8	1.2	20.9	1.0	100
1964	2.7	10.4	35.0	7.0	1.9	1.2	20.6	0.8	100
1963	2.4	10.3	33.9	7.4	1.8	1.2	21.5	0.8	100
1962	2.4	9.5	35.1	8.1	1.7	1.4	21.5	0.8	100
1961	2.7	9.9	36.0	7.8	1.3	1.5	21.0	0.8	100

World Tea Exports

World exports of tea have been rising fast—359.5 mkg in 1947, 1,125 mkg in 1989 and 1,725.7 mkg in 2012 (Table 2.23). The growth has been steady with minor fluctuation all these years. But, what is most interesting is that while India was the top exporter (over 53% share), followed by Sri Lanka (36.3%), Kenya and Indonesia shared only 4.4 and 3.9%, respectively during 1947. The most interesting feature is that China one of the major exporter today, did not figure anywhere. Of the total world exports of 359.5 mkg in 1947, the total share of India Sri Lanka, Kenya and Indonesia was over 92%.

By 1977, the share of India was reduced to 28% and Sri Lanka (22.7%). Kenya which shared only 1.2% in world exports in 1947, jumped to 8.6% in 1977 and further to 22.7% by 2004. Kenya today is the top exporter with 430.2 mkg, followed by China, Sri Lanka and India. The whole scenario in the world tea market has changed. Indonesia is now in the fifth position, closely followed by Vietnam (Table 2.23).

In a global context, developing countries in South Asia and East Africa account for more than 85% of world tea production and exports. India and Sri Lanka are dominant in both these respects. Developed countries account for about 62% of world tea imports. Kenya has dominated the world market for several years and its rate of growth is much faster as compared to other competitive countries including India. India has 12.9% of the market share and is ranked fourth among tea-exporting countries in the international market. While Kenya still dominates the international market with 19.9, China and Sri Lanka have declined their market share in 2006 as compared to the previous year. India's exports on the other hand, have increased from 12.3% in 2005 to 12.9% in 2006. Table 2.23A shows the recent trend of world export and the country's position in a global scenario.

Table 2.22: Average yield rate of tea in major producing countries

(Yield in kg/hectare)

Name of the countries*	1986	1990	1991	1992	1993	1994	1995	1996	2000	2001	2002	2003
India	1,523	1,780	1,794	1,742	1,819	1,768	1,770	1,809	1,679	1,675	1,625	1,690
Sri Lanka	954	1,056	1,090	806	1,052	806	NA	NA	1,623	1,568	1652	1,611
Indonesia	1,043	1,076	1,116	1044	1,057	1,010	NA	1,078	1,058	1,106	1,076	1,182
Bangladesh	805	963	944	1,024	1,055	1,979	992	1,115	1,070	1,152	1,083	1,166
China			511	516	512				627	615	657	636
Taiwan			896	933	884				1,033	1,047	1,110	1,135
Japan	1,597	1,537	1,526	1,624	1,654	1,584	1,579	1,683	1,772	1,804	1,684	1,839
Vietnam			508	532	539				875	976	1,035	1,069
Papua and New Guinea			1375	1,488	1500				1,550	L,605	1,676	1,730
USSR/CIS	1,801	NA	1,425	34,375	18750	NA	NA	NA	368	369	353	351
Iran			1406	1506	1443				1,276	1,702	1,435	1,683
Turkey	1,723	1,448	1,544	1,749	1,430	1,745	1,366	1,493	1,703	1,864	1,854	2,022
Kenya	1,846	2,031	2,023	1,847	2,014	1900	2172	2189	1,872	2,239	2,051	2,235
Uganda			437	445	599				1,424	1,593	1,598	1,691
Tanzania			995	946	1,197				1,127	1,158	1,291	1,341
Malawi			2,215	1,514	2,112				2,242	1,960	2,084	2,230
Mozambique			1,000	750	1,000				893	938	938	1,000
Zaire			333	333	333				417	433	435	452

Table 2.22: Average yield rate of tea in major producing countries *(Contd.)*

(Yield in kg/hectare)

Name of the countries*	1986	1990	1991	1992	1993	1994	1995	1996	2000	2001	2002	2003
Mauritius			2063	1865	1882				1,954	929	2,032	2,109
Rwanda			L,093	1,086	756				1,170	1,389	1,162	1,204
Burundi			676	708	631				868	1,035	766	839
Cameroon			2,255	2,260	2,549				2,590	2,800	2,800	2,774
Argentina	966		1,055	1,063	1,111	NA	800	1103	1,615	1,639	1,611	1,667
Brazil			1,727	1,500	1,667				644	885	912	960
Peru			1,167	1,500	1,500				962	963	1,000	964
Ecuador			2,395	1,769	1,601				1,809	1,684	1,789	1,895
Zimbabwe			2,458	1,214	2,183				3,296	3,291	32,91	32,08
Myanmar			820	847	915				853	867	875	882
Malaysia			2,285	2,139	1,959				1,820	1,746	1,632	1,224
South Africa			1,808	1,580	1,753				1,556	1,463	1,766	1,699
Australia			929	670	1,118				1,625	1,625	1,750	1,765
Ethiopia		NA	926	–	–				1,957	1,957	1,958	2,000
Netherlands			660	–	–				7,500	7,000	7,182	6,957

* Provisional

NA, non-available.

Table 2.23: India's share in world exports during 1947–2004

(In mkg)

Country/year	1947	1957	1967	1977	1987	1991	1997	1999	2004
India	191.70	199.20	217.80	229.60	201.90	202.90	203.00	204.20	205.60
Share (%)	53.30	39.90	35.60	28.20	20.70	17.90	13.20	18.50	18.25
Sri Lanka	130.30	166.80	216.50	185.50	201.20	212.40	234.85	238.05	242.50
Share (%)	36.30	33.40	35.40	22.70	20.60	18.80	21.24	21.52	21.60
Indonesia	3.90	38.80	26.60	51.30	90.40	109.60	103.90	102.50	104.20
Share (%)	1.10	7.80	4.30	6.30	9.20	9.70	9.40	9.60	9.70
Bangladesh	NA	4.50	N	26.00	21.60	25.30	24.30	25.40	25.45
Share (%)	N	0.90	N	3.20	2.20	2.20	2.40	2.30	2.32
Country/Year	1947	1957	1967	1977	1987	1991	1997	1999	2004
Kenya	4.40	8.20	19.70	70.20	135.00	191.60	245.50	251.10	255.20
Share (%)	1.20	1.60	3.20	8.60	13.80	16.90	22.20	22.70	22.73
Uganda	1.10	2.80	9.60	14.70	2.10	4.70	15.20	15.10	16.10
Share (%)	0.30	0.60	1.60	1.80	0.20	0.40	1.40	1.40	1.42
Tanzania	0.50	2.40	6.20	12.00	11.40	15.00	18.80	19.90	20.95
Share (%)	0.10	0.50	1.00	1.50	1.20	1.30	1.70	1.80	1.82
Malawi	5.90	8.80	16.80	29.90	33.40	41.20	36.50	35.40	36.20
Share (%)	1.70	1.80	2.70	3.70	3.40	3.60	3.30	3.20	3.21
Mozambique	1.50	5.90	14.40	15.60	2.10	1.00	0.42	0.95	0.97
Share (%)	0.40	1.20	2.40	1.90	0.20	0.09	0.04	0.05	0.08
Others	20.20	61.70	84.40	180.60	277.50	338.40	223.23	213.60	216.15
Share (%)	5.60	12.30	13.80	22.10	28.40	29.90	25.12	18.93	19.25
Total	359.50	499.10	612.00	815.40	976.60	1132.10	1105.70	1106.20	1122.72

N: Negligible.
Source: Same as Table 2.1.

Indian exports at 203.86 mkg (including 21.9 mkg of imports from other countries for re-export) showed a welcome increase over the previous year. In 2003, India exported 183.63 mkg of tea with an export value of Rs 1,636.9 crores. Having touched 222.02 mkg in 2010, three is a small decline in the previous 2 years (Fig. 2.12).

At the world level, a study of world demand and supply of tea shows that there is a surplus, although quite small (Table 2.23B). A study of international prices for the last 5 years shows that Sri Lanka has been having the highest unit price, followed by Kenya and then India.

Tea in India and World

Of the 80 or so countries producing tea in the world, India occupies a place of pride in the production and export of the commodity. A comparative study of India in the world tea shows that the share of India in the world area under tea was 24.2% in 1961 showing an unsteady movement. It was 20% in 1972, touched the ever lowest 15.7% in 1978 and is hovering around 20% since then. With 36% share in world tea

Table 2.23A: Tea world export

(Quantity in mkg)

Name of the countries	1989	1990	1991	1992	1993	1997	1998	1999	2000	2001	2002	2003	2008	2009	2010	2011	2012 (P)
Kenya	163.0	170.0	175.5	166.5	188.4	220.0	230.0	242.0	217.0	258.0	272.5	269.3	383.44	342.48	441.02	421.27	430.21
China	204.0	195.0	184.9	175.5	201.4	194.0	195.0	194.0	227.7	249.7	252.3	260.0	296.94	302.95	302.53	322.58	321.79
Sri Lanka	204.0	215.0	210.8	177.8	209.9	256.0	260.0	262.0	280.1	287.5	285.9	290.6	298.82	279.84	296.38	301.27	304.49
India	213.0	210.0	202.9	174.5	175.3	188.0	189.0	191.0	206.8	182.6	201.0	173.7	203.12	197.90	222.02	215.42	201.08
Vietnam	–	–	100.0	129.7	180.0	–	–	–	556.6	682.1	748.1	599.0	104.00	120.00	127.97	143.00	135.00
Indonesia	115.0	111.0	110.2	121.2	123.9	105.0	102.0	99.0	105.6	99.7	100.1	88.2	96.21	92.30	87.10	75.45	71.00
Argentina	–	–	36.0	36.5	43.5	–	–	–	49.8	56.6	57.1	58.2	77.23	69.19	85.35	86.20	78.00
Malawi	–	–	37.1	35.4	35.3	–	–	–	38.4	38.3	39.4	42.0	40.07	46.55	48.58	44.89	41.83
Uganda	3.0	5.0	7.0	7.8	10.3	18.0	20.0	22.0	26.4	30.4	31.1	34.1	42.39	47.92	53.18	46.15	48.22
Tanzania	–	–	17.5	17.8	19.4	–	–	–	22.5	22.1	22.6	20.4	24.77	21.51	26.13	27.11	26.30
Zimbabwe	–	–	11.3	6.1	8.1	–	–	–	16.9	17.2	17.6	17.1	5.65	7.54	8.50	8.57	7.00
Bangladesh	–	–	25.4	27.2	31.9	–	–	–	18.1	12.9	13.7	12.2	8.39	3.15	0.91	1.45	1.51
Others	218.0	224.0	–	–	–	244.0	234.0	225.0	–	–	–	–	72.03	73.77	77.98	26.78	· 59.24
Total	1,125.0	1,135.0	1,078.0	1,017.0	1,156.0	1,250.0	1,255.0	1,265.0	1,331.4	1,391.7	1,440.8	1,400.8	1,653.06	1,605.10	1,777.65	1,750.14	1,725.67

P: Provisional.
Sources: Tea Statistics + ITC Annual bulletin supplement, 2012, MSS-March 2013.

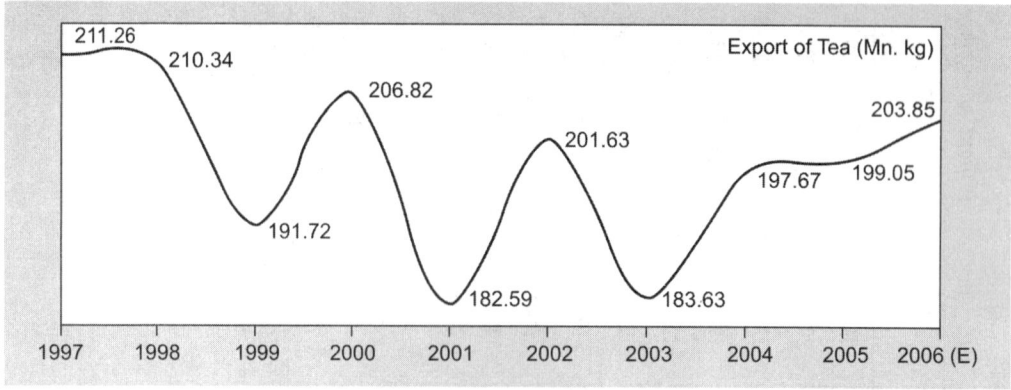

Fig. 2.12: Tea exports from India

Source: Tea Statistics (2005) J Thomas and Company Pvt. Ltd and www.teaboardofindia.com

Table 2.23B: World exports of

	2004		2005		2006	
	(mkg)	*Share*	*(mkg)*	*Share*	*(mkg)*	*Share*
India	197.67	12.8	191.85	12.3	203.86	12.9
China	280.19	18.2	286.56	18.4	286.46	18.1
Sri Lanka	290.6	18.9	298.77	19.1	298.77	18.9
Kenya	333.8	21.7	339.13	21.7	313.72	19.9
Vietnam	70	4.5	88	5.6	106	6.7
Tanzania	24.17	1.6	22.5	1.4	24.13	1.5
Indonesia	98.57	6.4	102.29	6.6	96	6.1
Malawi	46.6	3.0	42.98	2.8	42.5	2.7
Zimbabwe	14.91	1.0	8.45	0.5	11.38	0.7
Others	183.39	11.9	179.8	11.5	108.96	6.9
Total	**1,539.9**	**100.0**	**1,560.33**	**100.0**	**1,578.56**	**100.0**

Sources: Tea Statistics (2005) J Thomas and Company Pvt. Ltd and www.teaboardofindia.com

production, India was the top producer in 1961, it touched 30% in 1992 and is moving around 25% since then.

A historical study of world tea exports shows interesting results. During 1947, India was the leader with 53.3% as its share. Sri Lanka came second with 36.3%. China was included among others with a total of only 5.6% as their share (Table 2.23C). By 1987, there was a drastic change to 28% and Sri Lanka as 20%. Kenya which had only 1.2% shared in 1947 increased to 22% in 1997. We have the data for world production of tea from the same source (the Tea Board of India, Kolkata) (Tables 2.23A and C). This shows that although India was the leader till 1989 with an export of 213 mkg, both China and Sri Lanka at 204 mkg were at

Table 2.23C: Percentage share of major countries in global exports of tea

Name of the countries	1991	1992	1993	2000	2001	2002	2003*	2004	2005	2006	2011
India	18.82	17.20	15.17	15.53	13.12	13.95	12.40	12.8	12.3	12.9	12.11
China	17.15	17.26	17.43	17.10	17.94	17.51	18.56	18.2	18.4	18.1	18.44
Sri Lanka	19.55	17.48	18.16	21.04	20.66	19.85	20.74	18.9	19.1	18.9	17.22
Kenya	16.28	16.37	16.30	16.30	18.55	18.91	19.22	21.7	21.7	19.9	24.08
Vietnam	0.93	1.27	1.56	4.18	4.90	5.19	4.28	4.5	5.6	6.7	
Tanzania	1.62	1.75	1.68	1.69	1.59	1.57	1.46	1.6	1.4	1.5	
Indonesia	10.22	11.92	10.72	7.93	7.17	6.95	6.29	6.4	6.6	6.1	
Malawi	3.44	3.48	3.05	2.89	2.75	2.73	3.00	3.0	2.8	2.7	
Zimbabwe	1.05	0.60	0.70	1.27	1.23	1.22	1.22	1.0	0.5	0.7	
Bangladesh	235	2.67	2.76	1.36	0.93	0.95	0.87				
Taiwan	0.49	0.52	0.44	0.23	0.18	0.18	0.19				
Japan	0.03	0.03	0.03	0.05	0.05	0.06	0.06				
Malaysia	0.03	0.03	0.02	0.03	0.03	0.03	0.03				
Nepal	0.00	0.00	0.00	0.01	0.01	0.15	0.20				
Iran	0.14	0.10	0.15	0.26	0.29	0.59	0.50				
Turkey	0.21	0.50	3.43	0.48	0.35	0.36	0.50				
Uganda	0.65	0.77	0.89	1.98	2.19	2.16	2.43				
Mozambique	0.12	0.08	0.03	0.05	0.05	0.05	0.06				
Zaire	0.19	0.15	0.20	0.15	0.14	0.15	0.16				
Ethiopia	–	–	–	0.07	0.07	0.08	0.09				

(Contd.)

Table 2.23C: Percentage share of major countries in global exports of tea

Name of the countries	1991	1992	1993	2000	2001	2002	2003	2004	2005	2006	2011
Mauritius	0.42	0.54	0.38	0.00	0.00	0.00	0.00				
Rwanda	1.02	1.28	0.62	0.77	0.79	0.78	0.82				
Burundi	0.45	0.56	0.50	0.48	0.63	0.45	0.49				
South Africa	–	–	–	0.45	0.48	0.51	0.51				
Georgia/CIS	–	–	–	0.60	0.57	0.49	0.50				
Argentina	3.34	3.59	3.77	3.74	4.07	3.96	4.15				
Brazil	0.68	0.81	0.72	0.28	0.29	0.28	0.30				
Peru	0.02	0.02	0.03	0.01	0.01	0.01	0.01				
Ecuador	0.13	0.14	0.13	0.09	0.09	0.08	0.08				
Cameroon	0.25	0.24	0.50	0.32	0.30	0.30	0.31				
Papua and New Guinea	0.35	0.56	0.56	0.51	0.44	0.38	0.40				
Other countries	0.06	0.08	0.09	0.15	0.14	0.14	0.16	11.9	11.5	6.9	28.15
Grand total	**100.00**	**100.00**	**100.00**	**100.00**	**100.00**	**100.00**	**100.00**	**100.00**	**100.00**	**100.00**	**100.00**

Source: TEA statistics.

Table 2.23D: Value of exports of tea to total value of exports of all commodities

(Rs in crores)

Year	Value of exports of all commodities	Absolute change	Value of exports of tea	Absolute change	Share of tea to value of exports of all commodities
1961–1962	661	–	122	–	18.46
1971–1972	1,608	(+) 947	184	(+) 62	11.44
1981–1982	7,808	(+) 6,200	406	(+) 222	5.20
1991–1992	33,452	(+) 25,644	1,194	(+) 788	3.57
1997–1998	38,752	(+) 5,300	1,945	(+) 751	5.01
1998–1999	39,892	(+) 1,140	2,129	(+) 184	5.33
1999–2000	41,285	(+) 1,393	1,867	(+) 262	4.52
2000–2001	41,875	(+) 590	1,967	(+) 100	4.70
2001–2002	42,453	(+) 578	2,157	(+) 190	5.08

Table 2.23E: World demand and supply of tea

(Figures in mkg)

Year	World production	Apparent global consumption	(+) or (–)
2008	3,879	3,724	155
2009	3,960	3,839	121
2010	4,192	4,038	154
2011	4,449	4,275	174
2012 (P)	4,527	4,440	87

P: Provisional.
Source: ITC Annual supplement 2012.

Table 2.23F: World auction price of tea sold

Year	International price (US $/kg)					
	India	Bangladesh	Sri Lanka	Indonesia	Kenya	Zimbabwe
2008	2.00	1.62	2.83	1.51	2.18	1.37
2009	2.18	1.98	3.15	1.80	2.29	1.58
2010	2.29	2.61	3.28	1.82	2.54	1.58
2011	2.23	2.14	3.25	1.97	2.72	1.61
2012	2.28	2.40	3.07	1.97	2.88	1.70

Source: ITC Bulletin.

number two. Sri Lanka continued its leadership till early 2000 when Kenya took the first position which it is continuing till today. China comes number 2 and Sri Lanka number three followed by India.

Tea industry: Earner of foreign exchange—a considerable volume of tea is being exported from India and this has given the tea industry a place of importance in the national economy of the country as an earner of foreign exchange. Tables 2.23D to F show the value of exports of tea as compared to total value of exports of all commodities.

GREEN TEA

Conservation ratio: On an average 4.2–4.8 kg of green tea leaves are required to manufacture 1 kg of manufactured black tea, whereas 4.6–6.1 kg of leaf are required for making 1 kg of made green tea. Green tea is more vulnerable to spoilage under adverse keeping conditions than black tea and it has to be stored under controlled atmospheric conditions.

World Production

World production of green tea has been growing consistently and increased from 167.06 mkg in 1978 to 667.61 mkg in 1999. The share of green tea in total tea produced has been consistently increasing and Japan dominated with more than 60% share. From September 1980 onward, China started having a much larger share. However, Japanese production of green tea has declined so much so that it has only 12.81% share in comparison with China which produces nearly 75% of the world production of green tea. Vietnam has been also increasing production of green tea and of late it has a stable 5% share.

The share of green tea produced in total tea has been consistently increasing from 9.35% in 1978 to 23.45% in 1999 (Tables 2.24 and 2.25). However, green tea has less than 10% share in world exports of tea and that share has been fluctuating. More and more green tea production is retained in producing countries for domestic consumption.

World imports prior to 1990 Pakistan was a key importer of green tea but thereafter Morocco emerged as the most significant importer with over half of world imports (Table 2.26).

Producers of Green Tea

Indonesia produces about 37 mkg of green tea with 5.54% share in world production. Indonesia has a large demand for scented teas and a significant proportion of Indonesia green tea is scented using jasmine, red gambir and other types of flowers (Table 2.27). Therefore, Indonesia has only 5.06% share in world exports of green tea. Since 1989, Indonesia has exported sizable quantity of green tea to the Middle East and Morocco (Tables 2.27 and 2.28).

Importers of Green Tea

Consumer preference: Major importers of green tea are Japan, USA, Indonesia, North African countries and Afghanistan. The consumers in these markets have different tastes and preferences. However, a common feature generally sought is that the

Table 2.24: Percentage of green tea production

	1978	1979	1980	1981	1982	1983	1984	1985	1986	1987	1988
India	4.72	3.73	2.40	1.96	1.97	1.66	1.86	1.96	1.80	2.13	1.55
Bangladesh	0.31	0.12	0.12	0.11	0.11	0.09	0.06	0.22	0.23	0.19	0.20
Sri Lanka (Med)	0.00	0.00	0.00	0.00	0.19	0.16	0.27	0.28	0.32	0.26	0.24
Indonesia	10.43	11.75	5.82	7.89	5.29	6.78	6.85	7.93	7.34	6.38	5.97
China	0.00	0.00	50.70	52.11	58.26	56.12	57.04	55.18	57.71	61.89	65.76
Japan	62.69	60.38	29.06	26.46	23.22	23.81	21.76	22.10	21.02	19.79	17.45
Vietnam	8.56	9.55	4.52	4.40	4.36	4.64	5.06	5.30	5.01	4.42	4.27
Georgia	0.00	0.00	0.00	0.00	0.00	0.00	0.00	0.00	0.00	0.00	0.00
Russian Fed.	0.00	0.00	0.00	0.00	0.00	0.00	0.00	0.00	0.00	0.00	0.00
USSR/CIS	13.29	14.48	7.39	7.06	6.60	6.75	7.10	7.03	6.58	4.93	4.55
Total green tea production (mkg)	167.06	162.32	352.00	386.65	424.21	431.26	425.15	432.17	445.32	486.50	514.72
Percent share of green tea in total tea produced	9.35	8.93	19.05	20.53	21.79	21.00	19.39	18.88	19.56	20.78	20.79

Table 2.25: Percentage share of green tea exporting countries

	1978	1979	1980	1981	1982	1983	1984	1985	1986	1987	1988
India (e)	3.77	3.27	1.44	4.58	4.32	4.93	1.58	2.23	2.59	5.72	3.21
Sri Lanka	0.00	0.00	0.00	0.00	0.11	1.33	1.10	1.74	1.89	1.23	1.35
Indonesia	0.05	0.16	0.14	0.15	0.31	0.15	0.19	0.16	0.14	0.21	0.14
China (Mainland)	60.75	61.82	67.57	64.82	70.96	69.96	83.40	83.22	85.07	84.41	84.07
Taiwan	20.38	19.10	14.66	12.18	5.25	6.46	3.66	3.37	3.05	1.70	2.11
Japan	4.55	3.99	3.70	4.18	3.90	2.96	3.80	2.42	1.69	1.27	1.32
Vietnam	10.50	11.65	12.48	14.09	15.16	14.22	6.27	6.86	5.57	5.46	7.81
Total green tea exports (mkg)	74.25	76.38	72.10	63.88	62.67	70.33	71.80	72.89	71.77	82.38	93.51
Percent of green tea	9.24	8.98	8.39	7.50	7.64	8.08	7.63	7.65	7.38	8.47	9.03
Percent of green tea Production exported	44.46	47.15	20.48	16.51	14.78	16.32	16.89	16.87	16.13	16.92	18.16
Percent of green tea production retained	55.54	52.85	79.52	83.49	85.22	83.68	83.11	83.13	83.87	83.08	81.84

Table 2.26: Countries importing green tea (% share)

	1993	1994	1995	1996	1997	1998	1999
Austria	0.04	0.06	0.3	0.17	0.28	0.36	0.48
UK	1.77	2.93	2	1.47	1.1	0.71	0.89
Belgium and Lux.	0.88	1.13	0.41	0.38	0.16	1.17	0
Denmark	0.01	0.01	0.02	0.01	0.02	0.06	0.03
Finland	0.01	0.02	0	0.08	0.14	0.04	0
Germany	0.58	0.51	0.88	2	3.27	7.15	9.74
Ireland (Rep.)	1.13	0.11	0.05	0.01	0.18	1.47	0.17
Italy	0.42	0.24	0	0.58	0.5	0.32	0
Netherlands	1.36	1.18	1.52	2.15	2.25	1.83	1.32
Switzerland	0.05	0.04	0.06	0.17	0.23	0.4	0.57
Total (mkg)	52.23	60.29	62.4	62.38	70.19	72.92	76.15
Japan	10.49	7.83	10.36	17.35	16.11	8.66	15.82
Pakistan	8.03	6.02	3.24	2.89	0.8	1.32	1.57
Egypt	0	1.97	0.29	0	0.25	0.03	0.21
Morocco	50.56	54.35	60.18	45.32	49.79	54.85	46.26
Australia	0.41	0.37	0.41	0.51	0.4	0.49	0.57
New Zealand	0.04	0.1	0.02	0.02	0.29	0.2	0.06
Tunisia	2.87	3.32	3.4	3.37	3.56	2.71	1.84
USA	9.39	9.66	8.51	9.26	5.9	8.62	10.1
Canada	1.7	2.04	2.13	2	2.26	2.31	3.39
France	10.25	8.11	6.21	12.26	12.5	7.3	6.97

Source: Various issues of ITC Bulletin, London.

Table 2.27: Percentage share and unit value of exports of green tea from Indonesia 4.86% share of world green tea exports

(1990–1999 averages)

	1990	1991	1992	1993	1994	1995	1996	1997
Green tea (%)	1.56	2.35	3.72	9.06	8.94	4.08	4.26	6.56
Green tea (mkg)	1.73	2.6	4.53	11.23	7.59	3.23	4.33	4.39
All teas (mkg)	110.96	110.33	121.78	123.93	84.92	79.23	101.53	66.84

(Contd.)

	1998	1999	Avg.	CV	G. rate	Min.	Max.
Green tea (%)	5.26	7.56	5.34	49.1	12.62	1.56	9.06
Green tea (mkg)	3.54	7.33	5.05	56.67	7.06	1.73	11.23
All teas (mkg)	67.22	96.99	96.37	21.84	-4.93	66.84	123.93

Source: Various issues of ITC Bulletin London.

Table 2.28: Exports of green tea from Indonesia (1990–1999 averages)

	Avg.	CV	Growth Rate	Min.	Max.
Green tea	5.05	56.67	7.06	1.73	11.23
All teas	96.37	21.84	−4.93	66.84	123.93

Source: Various issues of ITC Bulletin London.

dried green tea leaves should have bright olive green color without any brown or red. The Chinese green tea is preferred in Japan and USA. Chinese green tea leaves are generally polished using French chalks or gypsum and colored with indigo. Afghans prefer the green tea liquor similar to Chinese green tea and unlike the Moroccans, they are much less fussy about the appearance of the dry tea leaves.

Morocco: Morocco has the largest market for green tea having imported as much as 35.23 mkg in 1999 and almost all of that came from mainland China. Imports of green tea in Morocco have been rising and so also its share in the world imports. During 1990–1999, Morocco imported an average of 33.67 mkg having a 51.62% share at a moderate unit import price of US$2.10. Imports from China have been consistently increasing (98.4% share in 1999). Per head consumption of tea in Morocco is in excess of 1 kg.

Japan: Japan has been a significant consumer of green tea but its imports have been less than one-fourth of the imports of Morocco. Of the total tea imported during 1993–1999, black tea had taken an increasing share between 28% tand 42%. In terms of per unit import value in 1993, green tea was only 44% of the black tea and 59% of the other teas. While the volume and unit value of imports of other teas has been somewhat declining, the unit import value of green tea has increased slightly from US$ 2.20 in 1993 to US$ 2.45 per kg in 1999.

France: Nearly 82% of green tea imported in France is from China and 13% is re-exports from Belgium. The French market had paid an average of US$ 3.71 per kg. The quantity imported has fluctuated and the average for 1990–1999 was 5.36 mkg in 1997 as much as 8.78 mkg of green tea was imported.

USA: USA imported an average of 6.20 mkg of green tea during 1990–1999 in which China had nearly 77.68% share. The popularity of green tea in US is largely on account of its health benefits which has been receiving increasingly more and more media attention. Although imports from other countries are small, they receive higher unit import value when compared to China, which on average received just about US$ 1.11 per kg.

Tunisia: Although in 1997 Tunisia imported 2.5 mkg of green tea imports, this was abruptly halved in 1999. A highly fluctuating pattern of imports of green tea in Tunisia from China existed during the years 1990–1999 with the average of 82.46% Further the quantity-wise (mkg) average imports of green tea in Tunisia from China for the period 1990–1997 is 1.38.

Canada: In 1999, Canada imported 2.58 mkg of green tea. Imports have been increasing consistently and exhibiting a good growth rate. China, Hong Kong, Japan and Taiwan are the main sources although US also had nearly 34% share. Green tea from Taiwan fetched the highest price at US$ 4.49 per kg whereas China, Hong Kong and USA teas fetched under US$ 3.5 per kg.

Oolong Tea

China: Oolong tea is produced mainly in Fujian and Guangdong provinces of mainland China and Taiwan. Oolong tea is semifermented. In 1990, 90 million cases of Oolong tea and 70 million cases of black tea were produced in Japan. Oolong tea is more stable than other beverages and is therefore easier to pack in tins, cans or bottles. As black tea is milk or lemon flavored, its storage in vending machines is somewhat difficult. For these reasons, Oolong tea has found favor with the food processors particularly in Japan.

Taiwan: Tea production in Taiwan has been declining and production in 1999 at 3.07 mkg was less than one-third of the production in 1987. Production of green tea has been declining and reached a low of 0.55 mkg in 1999. However, Taiwan is a key producer of Oolong tea and almost all of its production in 1999 was of this type. During 1990–1999, the share of green tea in tea exports has been between 14% and 33%. Information on exports of green and other teas from Taiwan is not available.

World Consumption

Total consumption of tea in the world increased from 3.76 million tons in 2002 to 4.7 million tons in 2007. World per capita consumption is just 0.7 kg per annum. The top consumer is Argentina with 6.5 kg, followed by UK 2.3 kg and Ireland 2.1 kg. Consumption in India is just 0.7 kg. Kenya is major producer and consumer only 0.1 kg tea per annum.

Tea Producing Nations Unite to Create a Forum

Seven major tea producing countries including India have decided to setup a global platform for addressing common concerns of the industry. The main objectives of the International Tea Producers' Forum (ITPF) include protecting interests of the tea-producing countries, sharing knowledge and boosting demand for tea to raise prices. Global tea prices are around $2.5 a kg, down from $2.84 a year earlier. Worldwide tea consumption, meanwhile, is set to rise over one per cent this year.

The decision to form ITPF was taken at a ministerial meeting held in Colombo on January 21. The Indian delegation was led by D Purandeswari, Union Minister of State for Commerce. The meeting saw representatives from India, China, Sri Lanka, Indonesia, Malawi, Kenya and Rwanda. Iran, a major tea consumer, was also present at the meeting. The first attempt to form such a forum was made in 1933. Again, in 1979, the International Tea Producers' Association was formed. But, it became defunct in 1984. In 1994, Colombo proposed a tea forum on the lines of the Organization of Petroleum Exporting Countries (OPEC). But, there was no unity among producing nations at the time.

The recent meeting has adopted the draft constitution of ITPF, subject to ratification by the governments of the respective countries. Any country producing more than 2 mkg of tea in a year can become a member of the forum. Consuming countries can also participate in the meetings but they will not have voting rights. The forum will also make efforts for technical cooperation and sharing expertise by the member countries, undertaking market studies and research on issues concerning the tea sector.

ITPF will be initially headquartered in Colombo. It will initially be an independent body and in future could be got affiliated to the FAO of the United Nations. Apart from India the other countries that have signed the ITPF statement are Kenya, Sri Lanka, Indonesia, Rwanda and Malawi. Iran and China did not sign the statement.

WORLD RECENT DEVELOPMENT

Decline in UK Tea

Britain is known for tea drinking. It is a major consumer of Indian tea, and hence a great source of revenue for the Indian. In fact, Britons are the consumers of tea per capita. However, this is changing. According to the FAO, Britain will be consuming 15% less tea than 15 years earlier. This is worrying India's tea exporters. In fact, during the last 5 years, tea exports to the UK have come down to 16 mkg from 22 mkg. Britain consumes 100 mkg of tea annually, of which nearly 60 mkg is imported from Africa. The country is gradually leaning toward variants with less tea content like chamomile tea and lemon tea.

Global warming, including a shortfall in rain and prolonged dry periods, has created problems for tea growers. Added to this, there are pests and outbreaks of disease that adversely affect tea productivity. Also, the tea companies that export have to obtain quality management certification and food safety management certification such as ISO 9001, HACCP and ISO 22000.

Tea drinking has for centuries been a proud UK tradition, leading to such coinage as tea parties, tea breaks, and also a great source of revenue for India's tea industry as Britons are the biggest consumers of tea per capita. That could change in the next decade.

The United Nations Food Agency, the FAO, has forecast that by 2021, Britons will be consuming 15% less tea than 15 years earlier. This decline has emerged as a concern for the Indian tea industry, whose exports to the UK have dwindled to 16 mkg from 22 mkg over the last 5 years.

The UK tea market has become stagnant. The country consumes 100 mkg of tea annually, of which nearly 60 mkg is imported from Africa. UK is gradually leaning toward tea variants where tea content is less, like camomile tea and lemon tea. In this way, per cup consumption of tea has gone up in the UK. What we are seeing in the UK is that supermarket brands have shown a decline while sales of better packeteers like Taylors of Harrogate are increasing. McLeod is the largest integrated tea company in the world.

Tighter European Union laws on maximum residue limit (MRL) may be one of the reasons for declining Indian tea exports. "We have to cater to the UK market according to their choice. In fact, Britons have developed a taste for instant tea. In calendar 2011, we sold more instant tea to Typhoo. Nearly 30% of our total production of 400 tons was sold to Typhoo". UK first imported tea in 1660. After the first official import in the 1660s of two ounces, tea shipments to the UK soared to 24 million pounds by the start of the 1800s, and at their most recent high in 2006, topped 136,000 tons. However, tea shipments have declined since then to 119,200 tons by 2010. The downtrend will continue, according to the FAO.

A research in the UK market "suggested that as household expenditure of non-alcoholic beverages increased, consumers tended to spend proportionately less on black tea and more on coffee". Per capita consumption of coffee rose from 2.78 kg in 2007 to 3.14 kg in 2009, according to the International Coffee Organization, although even here consumption growth has not been smooth, falling to 3.04 kg in 2010. In fact, the FAO observes that tea producing countries need to look to themselves if they wish to keep tea prices near the 2011 level of $2.85 a kg on average, despite production growth estimated at 1.9% a year over the next decade. "Greater efforts should be directed at expanding demand", the FAO said in comments following a tea summit.

Indian Tea Cost in Africa

Some of the Indian companies that have already entered Africa are McLeod Russel India and Jay Shree Tea and Industries. These two companies have plans to expand their footprints in the continent. Dhunseri Petrochem and Tea and Rossell Tea are also exploring opportunities in Africa. "The entire process has slowed down in Africa. Though we are keen to acquire more gardens there, the present situation does not allow us to do so. A new government has also taken over, which is further delaying privatization". The rules of the game have changed in South Africa. Earlier, private parties were offered 90% stake in a tea company but now this has been reduced to 60%. The government will keep 30% and 10% will be offered to the cooperatives that run the estates. Rwandan government has one garden and five factories, which it will privatize soon Rwanda has privatized 8–9 gardens. "Burundi is another region looking at privatization. It produces 10 mkg tea annually. Burundi is expected to follow the same shareholding matrix for private parties".

The likes of Rossell Tea, which are keen to make a foray into Africa, are keenly watching the developments. "The Rwandan government has planted teas across the region. Now, it plans to invite private parties for handing over these estates. Private parties will get the control of the tea estates but they have to build the infrastructure. However, it will take some time to happen". Acquisitions will be costly as tea prices are going up across the globe.

Drop in World Tea Output

The United Planters' Association of Southern India (UPASI) has outlined the world tea supply situation. In a statement issued at Coonoor, UPASI Tea Committee says that the prospects for tea exports were picking up. Listing out the reasons for his optimism and referring to the trends in the tea sector in the first half of the current year, he said out that there was a shortage in the world supply.

The subdued supply level in the world tea market was a result of lower Kenyan crop by 34.5 mkg. Though this was partially compensated by higher North India crop of 23.9 mkg, world tea production in the first half was lower by 20.6 mkg. In the South, the crop was down by 4.6 mkg due to dry weather in the first quarter of this calendar year. The price realization across auction centers around the world was more in the first half due to the tight supply situation. In South India, the average price realization was higher by Rs 1.92 a kg and accordingly the average realization was Rs 71.17 a kg during January–June 2011. Despite a decline in production, the quantity of tea sold at south Indian auction centers was higher by 2.3 mkg compared to the corresponding period of last year. In the orthodox category, sales have come down by about 17.3%. But increasing export demand for this is expected to have a positive effect on the prices. The increase in the price realization from South India despite lower exports of 9.7 mkg is mainly on account of an increase in the domestic demand for CTC teas.

The lower export (16.2 mkg) from India in general and South India in particular was on account of disturbance in the West Asia North Africa (WANA) region and also due to payment problem with Iran. As the situation is improving in the WANA region, export to the region is bound to pickup in the second half of 2011.

Nursery Construction and Management, Farm Management, Cultivation and Agronomic Practices

Tea nursery management practices should comply with the recommendations in the Tea Growers' Handbook or an approved producer manual. Materials used should be from a sustainable source while complying with the legislation on protection of plant species.

Material chosen when establishing a nursery should be suitable for the particular agroecological zone. The young seedlings are ready for transplanting after 8 months. The seedlings should be hardened off prior to transplanting when they are about 20 cm, by reducing the frequency of watering and fertilizing and gradual exposure of the seedlings by removal of the shade. Complete exposure should be for 2 months before transplanting.

Cultivation techniques (time, methods and technology) applied should be such that they minimize soil erosion and compaction, and safeguard the environment. Field planting should conform to the recommendations in the tea growers' handbook or an approved producer manual.

Agronomic practices should comply with the recommendations in the Tea Growers Handbook or an approved producer manual.

TEA IN SRI LANKA

The Importance of Origin

The tea-growing regions of Sri Lanka are clustered mostly among the mountains of the Island's Central Massif and its Southern Foothills. Once thickly forested and largely inaccessible to humans, the central mountains were known to the ancient Sinhalese as Mayarata, the Country of Illusions. It was said to be haunted by demons and spirits. This fearsome reputation, together with more tangible threats posed by wild beasts, venomous snakes, landslides, rockfalls and the ever-present danger of simply losing one's way in the forest, kept most people away from the high hills. Settlement was almost non-existent except in the valleys and around the city of Kandy. Only foresters, hermits and fugitives had any reason to enter the Mayarata.

Thus, it was that after the xation of the Kandyan kingdom in 1815, the British found themselves in possession of vast tracts of virgin montaine forest. Imperial enterprise soon found a way of putting the acquisition to good use. By 1840, there were already about two hundred coffee-estates dotted about the hills; then came a boom in coffee on the London market, fuelling a land-rush. Down came the high forests, acre after acre, to be replaced by endless, regimented rows of coffee-bushes. At the peak of the coffee enterprise in 1878, no less than 113,000 hectares (278,000 acres) were under cultivation.

Tea is not indigenous to Ceylon. According to records in the country's Archives, tea seed was first imported from China in the year 1824 and from Assam in 1839. James Tayler-father of Ceylon's tea industry planted the first tea clearing of 20 acres on the Loole-Condera Estate, Deltota. Early efforts, however, did not offer any inducement to cultivate it on a large scale and progress was did not offer any inducement to cultivate it on a large scale and progress was slow until experience was brought from India. Thereafter organized knowledge regarding tea started only in 1867, after half a century, when it was first shown at the Royal Botanical Garden, Paradeniya.

Major portion of the hill country area was thus purchased by big landlords or the Britishers themselves, and coffee plantations started. Area under coffee went up from 4 thousand acres in 1836 to 275 thousand acres in 1878. But, the coffee economy had to give way to tea cultivation soon after as a result of the coffee blight which visited the Island somewhere in 1868. Area under coffee dwindled down to 5 thousand acres by 1903 and a much bigger increase took place in tea, under which the area went up from a mere 250 acres in 1873 to 450 thousand acres in 1922.

Before 1840, practically the whole land in the Island belonged to the Crown. During the period, 1840–1931, three main principles dominated Government policy with regard to the administration of such Crown land. The Crown lands Encroachment Ordinance declared all the undeveloped land as Crown property. Secondly, it was laid down that the initiative in the alienation of Crown land had to come from the individual who wanted the land. The third principle was that Crown land must be paid for either by outright purchase or by means of rent in connection with lease-hold tenancy.

Since most of the alienation took place by auction, it was rather impossible for the poor cultivator to bid for these lands and purchase them. He had neither the financial resources nor the technical capability of making use of these lands.

Development of tea during 1836–1920

		(thousand acres)
Year	*Tea*	*Coffee*
1836	–	38.0
1845	–	Depression (low price)
1847	–	60.0
1848	–	121.0
1857	–	168.0
1867	–	Blight
1868	–	–
1873	0.25	275.0
1878	–	–
1880	9.3	–
1883	35.0	–
1890	220.0	–
1893	255.0	–
1896	330.0	–
1900	392.0	–
1903	406.0	5.0
1920	450.0	–

Source: Kandyan Commission Report.

Certainly, it meant considerable hardship to the peasantry who were deprived of their village forests, village pasture and chena lands which became crown property.

Development of the tea industry took place more or less in a pld mr. All the increases in the area under tea were closely connected with the extension of railway lines and the opening up of these new areas with proper means of transportation. Below table would give an idea of the area under tea and the opening of new railway lines in this region.

Area under tea and opening of new railway lines

(Acres)

Area under tea	Year	Railway to
1,083	1873	Gampola
1,750	1874	Nawalapitiya
70,000	1884	Hattan
273,000	1893	Haputale
305,000	1894	Bandarawela
380,000	1894	N'Eliya and Ragalla
400,000	1924	Badulla

Source: SF De Silva, A Regional Geography of Ceylon. page 165.

Establishment of the Sri Lanka Tea Board

Sri Lanka Tea Board has been established as a fully government owned statutory institution on 1st January 1976 by an Act of Parliament of the Democratic Socialist Republic of Sri Lanka and comes under the purview of the Ministry of Plantation Industries. Year 2006 was the year celebrating the 30th anniversary of the Sri Lanka Tea Board. Sri Lanka Tea Board being the apex regulatory body of the tea industry in Sri Lanka is directing responsibilities for the supervision, regulation, monitoring, extension and all maters connected with the promotion of "Ceylon Tea" in and outside of Sri Lanka. Name of the "Quality Ceylon Tea" is because the Sri Lanka Tea Board adopts strict control on tea to ensure all teas marketed and exported conform to ISO 3720 minimum quality standards and free of any contamination. The quality of teas is examined by the experienced tea tasters followed by the Analytical Laboratory of the Sri Lanka Tea Board by its chemical, microbiological and pesticide residue analysis units headed by academically qualified experienced analysts.

The Tea Commissioner's Division as the regulatory arm of the Sri Lanka Tea Board operates its regulatory functions through decentralized seven Regional Offices.

Sri Lanka Tea Board continues promotion of teas in the overseas markets through four tea promotion offices located in Poland (Covering Poland, Hungary, Czech Republic, Romania, Latvia, Estonia, Lithuania, Germany, UK, Yugoslavia, France, Netherlands and Italy), Japan (Covering Japan, China, South Korea, Hong Kong, Taiwan, Singapore, Thailand, Malaysia, Philippines, Vietnam, Indonesia, Australia, New Zealand and Fiji Islands), Russia (Covering Russian Federation, Ukraine, Belarus, Azerbaijan, Kazakhstan, Uzbekistan, Kyrgyzstan, Turkmenistan, Moldova,

Georgia, Armenia and Tajikistan) and Dubai (Covering UAE, Syria, Turkey, Saudi Arabia, Iran, Jordan, Kuwait, Egypt, Tunisia, Lebanon, Iraq, Libya and Yemen).

The "Lion Logo" (Lion emblem with 17 spots) depicted in the "Ceylon Tea" packs a trade mark owned by Sri Lanka Tea Board under the Intellectual Property Law which is registered internationally, is the Sri Lankan government guarantee of the quality of tea and its genuineness. The "Lion Logo" is a symbol, which guarantees a 100% pure "Ceylon Tea" blend of the finest quality tea, pre-packed in Sri Lanka.

Ceylon Tea Museum

It was in the Kandy district that the first successful experiments in tea cultivation were made, and it was from this ancient Sinhalese capital that the dominant modern industry of Sri Lanka spread out to cover the entire hill country. Kandy was thus the appropriate choice for a museum dedicated to the history of Ceylon Tea. The Ceylon Tea Museum is located at the Hantane Tea Factory, about 5 km (3 miles) from Kandy. Hantane was one of the first areas successfully opened up to tea cultivation after the failure of the coffee enterprise, but the factory that now houses the Museum is a relatively modern building, constructed in 1925. It is a typical example of its kind, large, light and airy, with most factory machinery housed on the ground floor and the three upper floors originally used to wither the freshly plucked tea-leaves. Today, the ground floor remains much as it was when the factory was operational, demonstrating the process of manufacture while the upper floors house are used to house other exhibits and a library, a space for audio-visual presentations and a restaurant.

Why "Ceylon" Tea?

Green and lushly fertile, the island republic of Sri Lanka lies in the Bay of Bengal, just below the Southeastern tip of India. Sri Lanka was formerly a British crown colony known as Ceylon, a name it kept for nearly a quarter-century after independence. It was during the British era that tea first began to be cultivated and manufactured here. Tea from Ceylon soon gained the reputation of being the finest in the world, and tea exports became the mainstay of the colonial economy. Housewives and restaurateurs across the globe grew familiar with the name of the country, learning that its appearance on a tin or packet reliably guaranteed the quality of the tea inside. Independence brought new markets, and production continued to increase. In 1965 Ceylon became, for the first time, the world's largest exporter of tea.

When the country changed its name to Sri Lanka in 1972, its premier industry was faced with a knotty problem. Ceylon was not only the former name of the country; it was also one of the world's leading brands, familiar to consumers from Virginia to Vladivostok—a brand the industry had been actively promoting and investing in since the early 1930s. Abandoning it would deliver a setback from which there could be no easy recovery. And the cost of promoting and establishing an unfamiliar new brand "Sri Lanka Tea" would be ruinous.

Although opposed by some who demanded a complete break with the colonial past and a new start for the country, industry leaders managed to persuade the socialist government then in power to permit the continued use of the name Ceylon to refer to the country's most famous product. Tea from Sri Lanka would still be marketed as Ceylon Tea; a priceless world brand had been saved.

HISTORY OF TEA IN KENYA

In Kenya, there are both large plantations and what are called smallholdings. Kenya is the largest producers of tea in Africa, and it has quadrupled its exports over the last decade. Tea is also one of the most important drinks in the country itself. The Tea Board of Kenya (Table 2.29) and the Tea Research Institute work constantly to help the industry, and the returns from the industry, help the country.

Currently, Kenya prides itself as one of the world's leading black tea producers. The tea industry operates under the auspices of the Ministry of Agriculture for technical and policy guidance. The industry is well-structured right from the apex regulatory body, the Tea Board of Kenya (TBK), the Tea Research Foundation of Kenya, through to the producers.

Tea was introduced to Kenya in 1903 by GWL. Canine and in the 1930s commercial planting began. Although planting was cut back in 1933 because of a depressed market, tea is today one of Kenya's most important cash crops. The first tea bushes have grown into large trees, forming an historical feature on what is now Unilever's Mabroukie Tea Estate.

Kenya tea has certain advantages which cannot be replicated elsewhere:

1. Kenya tea is *free* of pests and/or diseases. This means that Kenya tea is produced without use of any *agrochemicals*. The only item used in growing is the fertilizer which is used to replenish the soils. There is no doubt that such pure and healthy tea will be relished by the increasingly health conscious world population.

2. Kenya tea is grown along the equator. This means that the tea receives 12 hours of sunlight throughout the year. Kenya Tea is grown in areas of altitude between 1,500 meters and 2,700 meters above sea level, receiving 1,200–1,400 mm of

Table 2.29: The tea board of Kenya

(Qty. in mkg)

| | | | | | Ten-year monthly tea production | | | | | | |
Month	2003	2004	2005	2006	2007	2008	2009	2010	2011	2012	2013
January	32.8	31.1	34.1	17.9	41.6	29.7	25.5	37.7	35.9	36.2	45.3
February	23.6	28.1	25.8	11.7	34.8	24.1	21.5	34.8	26.7	18.4	38.5
March	15.0	28.9	24.8	19.9	32.2	16.9	18.8	39.2	22.4	17.8	33.3
April	19.3	29.4	29.1	30.4	30.7	27.4	18.3	35.9	31.4	18.1	38.2
May	26.0	28.4	28.8	26.4	32.1	36.4	29.8	35.6	32.8	37.3	39.6
June	19.5	23.9	24.0	27.7	27.3	22.8	25.3	29.8	28.9	30.2	30.5
July	18.9	18.6	20.8	23.8	22.7	24.2	21.5	24.4	26.3	24.3	26.2
August	19.9	18.9	21.8	23.2	22.7	24.5	21.2	23.1	24.4	31.9	26.3
September	26.4	23.0	26.9	28.6	28.9	32.0	27.4	28.8	30.5	33.5	
October	31.6	27.4	32.3	34.8	35.2	35.3	32.8	34.1	39.9	40.2	
November	27.0	32.0	30.0	31.6	32.3	34.4	35.9	37.0	36.8	39.9	
December	32.9	34.6	29.8	34.4	28.8	37.9	36.1	38.3	41.3	41.4	
Total	**292.9**	**324.3**	**328.2**	**310.4**	**369.3**	**345.6**	**314.1**	**398.5**	**377**	**369.2**	**277.9**

rainfall annually which is spread throughout the year. This makes the supply of Kenya tea consistent throughout the year both in quantity and quality.

3. Kenya has about 50 varieties of tea, which are developed to suit the seven tea growing regions. Research continues to be undertaken in this area. With each new variety developed, chemical properties of the produce is enhanced. This implies that the health attributes that tea is associated with can be found in abundance in tea from Kenya.

Over 90% of tea from Kenya is hand-picked. Only the finest top two leaves and the bud are used for tea production. This explains the excellent cuppage and aroma. Over and above this, Kenya has over the years developed skills in tea production which can be attested to by the quality of the tea. Kenya tea factories/producing facilities are certified with the internationally acclaimed standards (ISO 22000; HACCP; Rain forest alliance, fair trade GMP).

Windows for Sales/Exports

Kenya tea can be purchased by international importers in two main ways:

1. *Auction sales:* An importer can purchase tea through the Mombasa Tea Auction or directly or through an agent. This option avails a wide range of teas from the different origins in Kenya. Infrastructure for making special blends is available.
2. *Direct/contract sales:* This option allows for teas straightline/unblended teas straight from the factory.

Requirements for Use of Mark of Origin

1. The use of the mark of origin shall be granted solely by TBK upon satisfying the requirements as per the management system of certification [system operating procedure (SOP) to be developed].
2. The consumer tea packets and containers bearing the mark must contain 100% tea produced in Kenya.
3. The Kenya tea branded with the mark of origin must be manufactured according to the Tea Industry Code of Practice (KS 2128). Exceptions may be made for tea grades necessary for production of tea bags or meeting specific market demand. However in all cases, item 2.2 *must* apply.
4. The Tea Packets and Containers using this mark shall be of the quantity specified in the Tea Regulations 2008 of the Tea Act.
5. The tea packets and containers bearing the mark must conform to the standards for packets and containers for respective markets and where the standard is not specified, Kenya standard for tea packets and containers (KS 1927:2005) shall apply.
6. The packets and containers bearing the mark of origin must be packed in premises registered by the TBK.

Tea Growing and Production

The Tea Industry in Kenya is unique in that it is comprised of two distinct sectors; the plantation or large scale sector and the small holder sector. The plantation sector is owned by large scale tea producers and companies while the small holders sector is by small scale growers. The small holder sector has registered more than half a million growers who are located across tea growing areas in the country. The small holder sector factories are managed by Kenya Tea Development Agency Ltd. (KTDA).

The tea growing regions in Kenya are endowed with the ideal climate for tea. Tropical, volcanic red soils and well distributed rainfall ranging between 1,200 mm and 1,400 mm per annum that alternates with long sunny days; which attribute to these favorable conditions. Production goes on all round the year with two main peak seasons of high crop between March and June and October and December which coincide with the rain seasons. Kenya tea is grown free of agrochemicals because the ideal environment in which the tea is grown acts as a natural deterrent to pests' infestation and diseases attack; This natural conditions guarantees the consumer the safest and most refreshing health drink.

The main tea growing areas in Kenya are situated in and around the highland areas on both sides of the Great Rift Valley; and astride the Equator within altitudes of between 1,500 meters and 2,700 meters above the sea level. These regions include the areas around Mt. Kenya, the Aberdares, and the Nyambene hills in the Central Kenya and the Mau Escarpment, Kericho Highlands, Nandi and Kisii Highlands and the the Cherangani Hills.

Clonal planting materials are developed through scientific innovations by the Tea Research Foundation of Kenya (TRFK) which have made vegetative propagation possible resulting in high yielding well adapted varieties. The selection of planting materials is enhanced by mapping the genetic and environmental conditions; where genotype—environment interaction trials are carried out as useful selection criteria for determining clonal genetic potential and adaptation so as to match the clones to specific areas where productivity can be maximized. The developed clones are subjected to environmental response tests are various representative sites. So far the TRFK has developed about 50 varieties.

Plucking, Manufacturing and Quality

Kenya's distinct and high quality teas are made from the upper two leaves and a bud. The young shoots are plucked in regular cycles ranging from seven to fourteen days. Kenya teas are mainly manufactured using the CTC method to ensure maximum cuppage per unit weight. Kenya prides itself as the producer of the best black tea in the world due to the good agronomical and manufacturing practices and the ideal tea growing conditions. Kenya tea liquors range between good medium to very fine qualities, attributes that make Kenya tea the most sought after beverage in the world. To assure the local and international markets of sustained safety and quality of the Kenya tea, the Board conducts continuous tea factories compliance audits on tea regulations and guidelines as well as on aspects of good agricultural practices (GAPS), good manufacturing practices (GMPS) and best practices. There is a Tea Growers Handbook which provides detailed instructions regarding basic data regarding production, exports and consumption is as Tables 2.30 to 2.31.

TEA IN THE ASEAN COUNTRIES

Area, production and yield are as given in Tables 2.32 to 2.34. Data on tea, export/ imports for the ASEAN countries is given in Tables 2.35 to 2.37. The share of Indian imports from ASEAN increased from 16.86% in 2005 to 21.94% in 2008 (Table 2.35).

Table 2.30: Year Kenya tea export

(Qty. in mkg)

Months	2003	2004	2005	2006	2007	2008	2009	2010	2011	2012	2013
January	24.9	28.8	27.3	29.7	35.0	30.4	34.9	39.2	33.6	37.9	39.8
February	26.4	26.2	30.6	24.7	31.9	27.9	25.1	37.6	32.2	44.7	42.9
March	30.8	35.2	31.6	20.9	33.4	23.9	33.8	40.2	41.5	35.4	36.1
April	23.4	30.4	27.6	17.8	29.8	35.2	24.8	31.8	32.1	29.4	40.1
May	23.4	29.4	26.5	28.1	33.8	28.8	22.4	31.0	34.4	29.9	45.4
June	25.8	22.6	28.3	26.2	32.0	33.0	26.9	36.8	37.7	30.1	42.3
July	26.7	27.2	35.5	29.6	24.7	31.6	32.4	38.3	37.4	33.2	46.1
August	23.6	24.3	35.0	30.4	28.3	40.2	25.6	37.7	37.2	37.2	43.7
September	23.1	28.2	28.6	26.7	21.2	36.6	30.9	43.8	28.8	35.7	
October	25.9	22.7	21.3	22.2	21.4	34.1	27.1	27.8	30.2	38.6	
November	25.3	30.4	25.1	31.9	36.4	32.6	30.3	41.5	39.3	44.0	
December	26.9	28.4	32.5	25.5	17.9	29.1	28.3	34.9	36.2	33.5	
Total	**306**	**334**	**350**	**314**	**345.8**	**383**	**343**	**441**	**421**	**429.6**	**336.3**

Table 2.31: Monthly local tea consumption

(Qty. in mkg)

Month	2008	2009	2010	2011	2012	2013
January	1.1	1.5	1.4	1.4	1.3	2.2
February	1.1	1.5	1.3	1.6	1.6	1.8
March	1.1	1.4	1.3	1.5	1.6	1.7
April	1.5	1.6	1.5	1.8	1.2	2.6
May	2.1	1.6	1.6	2.0	1.5	2.2
June	1.7	1.5	1.6	1.7	1.5	1.9
July	1.1	1.3	1.5	1.5	1.5	1.7
August	1.6	1.4	1.6	1.6	2.2	1.7
September	1.3	1.4	1.8	1.9	2.6	
October	1.4	1.5	1.6	1.7	2.9	
November	1.5	1.5	1.7	1.7	2.8	
December	1.9	1.8	1.8	1.6	2.0	
Total	**17.4**	**18.0**	**18.7**	**20.0**	**22.7**	**15.8**

Source: The tea board of Kenya.

Total ASEAN imports increased from 14.23 thousand tons in 1991 to 39.11 thousand tons in 2007 (Table 2.36). Table 2.37 shows the difference between export unit value if India and import unit value of ASEAN countries. Production, exports and domestic consumption in some of the selected countries is as in Table 2.38. Domestic price of tea and India is unit value of tea from Vietnam is as in Table 2.39. Export unit value and important unit value id India is as Tables 2.40 to 2.44.

Table 2.32: Tea production: ASEAN and India (1991–2008)

(in '000 tons)

Year	Thailand	Malaysia	Indonesia	Vietnam	Total-4	India	World
1991	5.0 (0.20)	7.0 (0.27)	139.5 (5.45)	33.1 (1.29)	184.6 (7.21)	720.3 (28.13)	2,561.1
1994	5.1 (0.19)	5.4 (0.20)	139.2 (5.28)	42.0 (1.59)	191.7 (7.27)	753.0 (28.55)	2,637.4
1997	5.3 (0.19)	6.0 (0.22)	153.6 (5.57)	52.2 (1.89)	217.1 (7.87)	780.0 (28.28)	2,758.0
2000	5.5 (0.19)	5.6 (0.19)	162.6 (5.49)	69.9 (2.36)	243.6 (8.22)	826.0 (27.87)	2,963.6
2003	5.6 (0.17)	4.1 (0.13)	169.8 (5.29)	104.3 (3.25)	283.8 (8.84)	838.0 (26.09)	3,212.5
2006	6.0 (0.16)	6.2 (0.17)	146.9 (4.03)	151.0 (4.14)	310.1 (8.50)	928.0 (25.45)	3,646.5
2007	6.0 (0.15)	5.5 (0.14)	150.2 (3.86)	164.0 (4.22)	325.8 (8.38)	949.2 (24.42)	3,887.3
2008	6.0 (0.13)	5.6 (0.12)	150.9 (3.19)	174.9 (3.69)	337.3 (7.12)	805.2 (17.00)	4,736.0
CAGR (1991–2008)	1.24	−1.87	0.36	10.97	3.60	1.4	3.06

Figures in parenthesis show percentage share in world production.
Source: Estimation based on Food and Agriculture Organization (FAO) statistics.

Table 2.33: Tea yield in major ASEAN exporting countries (kg/hectare)

Year	Thailand	Malaysia	Indonesia	Vietnam	India	World
1991	303	2,117	1,474	552	1,711	1,120
1994	300	2,002	1,266	596	1,768	1,141
1997	294	2,068	1,344	817	1,810	1,206
2000	297	1,879	1,341	994	1,686	1,243
2003	295	1,179	1,461	1,211	1,624	1,281
2006	300	1,871	1,322	1,229	1,774	1,346
2008	300	2,011	1,411	1,353	1,699	1,688
CAGR (1991–2008)	−0.07	−2.45	−0.56	5.71	−0.07	1.74

Source: Same as Table 2.1.

Table 2.34: Tea area harvested in major ASEAN exporting countries and India

(In '000 hectares)

Year	Thailand	Malaysia	Indonesia	Vietnam	Total-4	India	World
1991	17 (0.72)	3 (0.14)	95 (4.14)	60 (2.62)	174.43 (7.63)	421 (18.42)	2,286
1996	17 (0.74)	3 (0.13)	115 (4.97)	71 (3.08)	205.54 (8.92)	427 (18.54)	2,304
2001	19 (0.79)	4 (0.14)	115 (4.78)	80 (3.31)	217.92 (9.02)	504 (20.87)	2,415
2008	20 (0.71)	3 (0.10)	107 (3.81)	129 (4.61)	259.02 (9.23)	474 (16.89)	2,806
CAGR (1991–2008)	1.31	0.60	1.16	4.97	2.78	1.46	1.30

Figures in parenthesis show percentage share in world area.
Source: Same as Table 2.1.

Table 2.35: ASEAN countries' tea exports to India and World

(Quantity in '000 tons)

Year	Malaysia		Thailand		Vietnam		Indonesia		Total AS export		India's total import	India's imports from ASEAN as a % of its total imports from the World
	To India	To World	To India	To World	To India	To World	To India	To World	To India	To World		
2000	NA	0.65	0.01 (2.46)	0.59	2.46 (4.41)	55.66	6.01 (5.69)	105.58	NA	NA	NA	
2005	0.17 (14.95)	1.16	0.01* (0.25)	1.47*	0.80 (2.44)	32.79	2.17 (2.12)	102.29	3.14 (2.28)	137.72	18.65	16.86
2008	0.02 (1.28)	1.61	0.01 (0.28)	2.36	1.26** (1.09)	115.73**	3.80 (3.95)	96.21	5.09 (2.36)	215.91	23.20	21.94
2009									10.35		31.56	

Figures in parenthesis show India's import share in total ASEAN countries' tea exports.
NA, non-available.
* For the year 2006.
** For the year 2007.

Source: Estimation based on UN Comtrade Database, viewed on 28 January 2010 (http://comtrade.un.org/db/)
EPW, Issue No. 44, 2010.

Table 2.36: Tea imports of ASEAN countries

(Quantity in '000 tons)

Year	Indonesia	Malaysia	Cambodia	Singapore	Other Asian countries	Total ASEAN imports	World imports	ASEAN % share in World import	ASEAN % share in India's total tea exports
1991	0.71	5.11	NA	7.49	0.92	14.23	1,137.35	1.25	7.18
1994	0.45	7.36	NA	7.06	1.18	16.06	1,150.51	1.40	10.48
1997	2.82	6.70	0.07	5.56	1.40	16.55	1,241.68	1.33	11.96
2000	2.63	9.42	0.04	6.20	2.01	20.29	1,343.77	1.51	11.43
2003	4.00	12.67	0.04	3.48	3.05	23.23	1,385.70	1.68	12.79
2006	5.29	14.79	7.13	4.58	2.77	34.56	1,470.64	2.35	21.72
2007	8.70	15.66	6.67	4.46	3.62	39.11	1,463.74	2.67	21.57
CAGR	22.07	7.14	48.00	-4.35	10.67	5.84	1.70		

NA, Data not available for Vietnam.
Source: As specified in Table 2.1.

Table 2.37: Difference between export unit value of India and import unit value of ASEAN countries

Year	Indonesia	Malaysia	Thailand	Philippines	Singapore	Brunei	Laos	Cambodia	Myanmar
2000	83.0	104.6	–17.8	–22.1	–23.0	24.6	–46.3	296.7	296.7
2001	67.4	106.1	–15.1	0.3	–32.9	–52.4	–27.6	71.8	71.8
2002	73.6	53.1	–33.6	–28.6	–41.3	–65.3	NA	48.2	48.2
2003	99.5	79.7	–31.4	–36.3	–42.4	–58.7	NA	50.6	50.6
2004	53.4	83.0	75.9	–18.5	–38.7	–55.2	294.0	48.2	48.2
2005	79.0	82.5	48.6	–56.2	–33.8	–55.9	283.5	40.1	40.1
2006	36.7	63.5	–3.1	–59.0	–42.1	–44.7	171.1	62.6	62.6
2007	97.9	56.4	15.3	–60.1	–39.4	–29.0	115.4	68.5	68.5

(i) Price difference = (EUV of India/IUV of respective ASEAN importing country)*100-100.
(ii) Data for Vietnam are not available in the FAO.
EPW, Issue No. 44, 2010.
NA, Non-available.
Source: As specified in Table 2.1.

Table 2.38: Production, export and domestic consumption of tea

(Quantity in '000 tons)

Year	Malaysia			Thailand			Vietnam			Indonesia			India		
	P	E	P-E*	P	E	P-E*	P	E	P-E*	P	E	P-E*	P	E	P-E*
1991	7.0	0.3 (3.7)	6.7 (96)	5.0	0.3 (5.20)	4.7 (95)	33.1	8.0 (24.0)	25.1 (76)	139.5	110.2 (79.0)	29.3 (21)	720.3	215.1 (29.9)	505.2 (70)
1994	5.4	0.4 (7.0)	5.0 (93)	5.1	0.2 (4.6)	4.9 (95)	42.0	23.5 (55.9)	18.5 (44)	139.2	84.9 (61.0)	54.3 (39)	753.0	150.9 (20.1)	602.1 (80)
1997	6.0	0.4 (5.8)	5.7 (9.4)	5.3	0.2 (4.1)	5.1 (96)	52.2	32.9 (63.0)	19.3 (37)	153.6	66.8 (43.5)	86.8 (56)	780.0	191.5 (24.6)	588.5 (75)
2000	5.6	0.6 (11.5)	5.0 (89)	5.5	0.6 (10.7)	4.9 (89)	69.9	55.6 (79.5)	14.3 (20)	162.6	105.6 (64.9)	57.0 (35)	826.0	200.9 (24.3)	625.1 (76)
2003	4.1	1.6 (39.5)	2.5 (60)	5.6	1.1 (19.1)	4.5 (81)	104.3	58.6 (56.2)	45.7 (44)	169.8	88.2 (51.9)	81.6 (48)	838.0	174.2 (20.8)	663.8 (79)
2006	6.2	1.1 (17.6)	5.1 (82)	6.0	1.5 (24.5)	4.5 (75)	151.0	105.0 (69.5)	46.0 (30)	146.9	95.3 (64.9)	51.5 (35)	928.0	181.3 (19.5)	746.7 (80)
2007	5.5	1.1 (20)	4.4 (80)	6.0	2.7 (45)	3.3 (55)	164.0	114.0 (69.5)	50.0 (30.5)	150.2	83.7 (56)	66.6 (44)	949.2	193.5 (20.4)	755.8 (79.6)
2008	5.6	NA	NA	6.0	NA	NA	174.9	NA	NA	150.9	NA	NA	805.2	NA	NA
CAGR (1991–2008)	-1.9	13.2	-5.04	1.24	18.1	-1.18	10.97	16.5	3.70	0.36	-0.65	3.47	1.40	0.43	2.07

NA, not available.
P–Production, E–Exports,
*Domestic consumption from production.
Figures in parenthesis show percentage share in production.

Table 2.39: Domestic price of tea and India's import unit value of tea from Vietnam and Indonesia

(Price in Rs per quintal)

Year	All India domestic tea price	India IUV of tea from Vietnam	Price difference	India IUV of tea from Indonesia	Price difference
2004	6,454	3,490	–46	5,350	–17.1
2006	6,601	3,507	–47	6,850	3.8
2008	8,699	5,908	–32	6,485	–25.4

(i) India IUV – India's import unit value represents the unit price at which India imports from the respective country.

(ii) The dollar import unit value is converted into Indian rupees by multiplying with Indian exchange rates in respective years.

(iii) Price difference – (India's import unit value of tea from the respective country/domestic price of Indian tea) *100-100.

Sources: (i) All India domestic tea price is taken from Tea Board of India Statistics.

(ii) Import Unit Value (IUV) of Tea from Indonesia and Vietnam is estimated from UN Comtrade Database.

Table 2.40: Export unit value of tea and import unit value of India

(US$ per quintal)

Year	China EUV	Price difference	Vietnam EUV	Price difference	Indonesia EUV	Price difference	Thailand EUV	Price difference	Malaysia EUV	Price difference	India IUV
2000	157.9	19.68	125.2	−5.15	106.2	−19.54	151.6	14.89	213.6	61.85	132.0
2001	142.1	−0.83	115.5	−19.41	100.2	−30.09	155.0	8.18	144.8	1.05	143.3
2002	136.5	26.86	106.5	−1.00	103.2	−4.03	143.5	33.36	165.3	53.63	107.6
2003	146.6	15.50	99.6	−21.51	108.7	−14.41	137.0	7.94	188.8	48.74	127.0
2004	160.5	59.15	93.0	−7.82	117.7	16.70	231.8	129.85	234.6	132.58	100.9
2005	173.1	33.30	110.2	−15.15	118.8	−8.51	178.3	37.35	197.7	52.29	129.8
2006	195.1	64.17	105.2	−11.50	141.1	18.72	175.3	47.54	223.7	88.26	118.8
2007	212.3	35.65	114.8	−26.68	151.3	−3.31	148.8	−4.92	258.4	65.05	156.5

EUV-Export Unit Value; IUV-Import Unit Value.
EPW, Issue No. 44, 2010.
Source: Same as Table 2.1.

Table 2.41: Workers on the rolls of the tea estates

State	Permanent workers			Temporary workers			Total (permanent + temporary)		
	Male	*Female*	*Total*	*Male*	*Female*	*Total*	*Male*	*Female*	*Total*
North India	310936	332868	643804	156087	226465	382552	467023	559333	1026356
South India	30819	44795	75614	7444	13005	20449	38263	57800	96063
All India	**341755**	**377663**	**71418**	**163531**	**239470**	**403001**	**505286**	**617133**	**1122419**

Table 2.42: Production share of major producing countries in 2012

(Qty in Mkg)

Country	2012	Share in total production (%)
China	1789.75	38.70
India	1126.33	24.36
Kenya	369.56	7.99
Sri Lanka	328.40	7.10
Vietnam	190.00	4.11
Turkey	147.00	3.18
Indonesia	137.25	2.97
Bangladesh	62.16	1.34
Malawi	42.49	0.92
Uganda	57.94	1.25
Tanzania	32.28	0.70
Others	341.47	7.38
Total	**4624.63**	**100.00**

Source: ITC Annual Bulletin, 2013.

Table 2.43: Exports share by major producing countries in 2012

(Qty in Mkg)

Country	2012	Share in total exports (%)
Kenya	430.21	24.22
China	321.79	18.11
Sri Lanka	306.04	17.23
India	208.26	11.72
Vietnam	150.00	8.44
Argentina	76.84	4.33
Indonesia	70.07	3.94
Uganda	52.27	2.94
Malalai	41.83	2.35
Tanzania	27.78	1.56
Zimbabwe	8.00	0.46
Bangladesh	1.51	0.08
Others	81.91	4.61
Total	**1776.51**	**100.00**

Source: ITC Annual Bulletin, 2013.

Table 2.44: World demand and supply of tea

Year	World production	Apparent global consumption	(+) or (−)
2010-11	4200	4053	147
2011-12	4453	4285	168
2012-13	4625	4440	185

Source: ITC Annual Bulletin, 2013.

Annexures

Annexure 1: Statewise value of output - tea

State/UTs	At current prices							At 2004-05 prices						
	2004-05	2005-06	2006-07	2007-08	2008-09	2009-10	2010-11	2004-05	2005-06	2006-07	2007-08	2008-09	2009-10	2010-11
Arunachal Pradesh	641	715	1060	1594	1594	1594	1594	641	756	1121	1686	1686	1686	1686
Assam	168139	188146	256594	224342	249446	297380	338888	168139	188146	193760	197563	188150	192119	188039
Bihar	0	432	430	424	463	507	549	0	0	0	0	424	424	424
Himachal Pradesh	747	520	777	407	887	929	1083	747	490	739	388	739	739	739
Karnataka	1080	1018	1031	980	1790	1789	2188	1080	1018	1031	980	1148	1148	1148
Kerala	18847	19294	17366	16243	21356	26834	26593	18847	19064	16377	15962	14738	16488	16340
Manipur	45	45	45	49	52	52	52	45	45	45	45	45	45	45
Meghalaya	341	517	587	706	417	457	478	341	253	262	277	164	171	178
Mizoram	5	29	31	31	31	31	31	5	23	25	25	25	25	25
Nagaland	318	328	335	373	10175	8085	10175	318	137	140	156	1486	1043	1486
Orissa	38	40	42	0	0	0	0	38	39	38	0	0	0	0
Sikkim	0	65	0	0	27	27	27	0	65	47	34	27	27	27
Tamil Nadu	47441	36073	57762	49019	85815	100235	65422	47441	45606	47523	44986	48478	52518	49024
Tripura	1010	1039	1079	1292	4431	4948	4286	1010	1010	1010	1208	1208	1208	1169
West Bengal	74658	83460	93373	92782	104110	125061	148410	74658	69150	82025	75815	76629	74221	77541
Uttarakhand	110	210	207	113	108	108	108	110	45	45	24	23	23	23
Total	313419	331933	430720	388354	480703	568037	599884	313419	325847	344187	339150	334970	341884	337894

Annexure 2: The most common teas and their benefits

Green
Types: Sencha, matcha, gyokuro, etc.
Benefits: It activates the body's natural detox system, prevents brain cell deteriorates damaged cells. It aids in weight loss and prevents the progression of type diabetes.

Black
Types: Keemum, Assam, Darjeeling and chai (black tea is its base).
Benefits: With a high concentration of antioxidant compounds like theaflavins and thearubigins, it works as a blood thindder which prevents blood clots and thus, strokes.

White
Types: Silver needle, white peony, etc.
Benefits: Mild in flavor and low in caffeine content, white tea has youth-friendly benefits. It preserves the skin's natural elastin and collagen, and speeds up the fat-burning process.

Oolong
Types: Darjeeling, wu-yi, formosa, etc.
Benefits: It reduces clot formation, lowers cholesterol and aids weight loss by boosting metabolism.

Herbal
Types: Chamomile, echinacea, mint, roolibos, hibiscus, etc.
Benefits: Herbal tea is not technically tea since it's made from herbs, flowers, fruit, seeds, and not the camellia sinensis shrub. Yet, they have a lot of health benefits. While rooibos treats cramps and relaxes muscles, hibiscus tea reduces sugar absorption in the body. Also, chamomile promotes sleep while peppermint soothes the stomach.

Annexure 3: Tea prices

Summary

- Tea prices continued with their buoyant trend over the last 2 years with average auction realizations increasing from Rs 106/kg during CY11 to Rs 131/kg during CY13: Over a longer horizon of 5 years, prices have increased at a compound annual growth rate (CAGR) of 8.4%; prices at both North Indian and South Indian auctions have grown at a largely similar rate. However, the quality tea of North India continued to command a premium over South India tea.

- The buoyancy can primarily be attributed to a steady growth of around 3% in domestic demand. Tea, apart from being acknowledged to be a healthier drink among other beverages, also finds favor in the price sensitive Indian market because of its competitive per cup cost.

- Tea production in India during calendar year 2013 (CY13) witnessed an increase of around 73.7 million kg (Mkg) reflecting an increase of 6.5% over the previous year. While production from North India (NI) was up by around 70.5 Mkg (y-o-y increase of 7.9%), that from South India (SI) witnessed a marginal increase of around 3.2 Mkg (y-o-y increase of 1.3%).

- During CY13, total exports of tea from India, in volume terms, remained almost flat, with a small increase of around 1.7% to reach 211.9 Mkg; however, a sharp depreciation of the INR resulted in the value of exports increasing by 12%.

- In CY13, global tea production was up by around 153 Mkg (around 7.4%); apart from India, which contributed around 50% to the increase, production was also up in Kenya (y-o-y increase of 17.0%) and in Sri Lanka (y-o-y increase of 3.6%), the two other major producers of black tea. Tea prices at Mombasa auction center corrected more sharply (around 20% fall) than at Indian auction. The Colombo auction prices which is primarily an orthodox market, however, increased by around 12% during CY13.

- With domestic demand growing at a steady rate and production unlikely to witness a sharp increase on account of limited availability of incremental land to grow tea bushes, prices are expected to remain at elevated levels compared with historical trends, going forward. However, the global demand-supply position and therefore the international prices would continue to influence domestic prices, since around 20% of the domestic produce is exported currently.

- The buoyancy in tea prices during the last few years has considerably strengthened the financial position of large and established tea producers in India. In the current calendar year (CY14), the drop in tea production till May 2014 due to an unfavorable weather conditions is expected to firm up tea prices; however, the impact of the same on the profits and cash accruals of the black tea producers would be determined by the extent of increase in tea realizations vis-à-vis production loss. Moreover, input costs are also expected to continue with their rising trend, which is likely to keep the profitability of bulk tea producers under check. However, the debt-service capabilities of large bulk tea companies are likely to remain comfortable on account of their strong balance sheet position.

India is the single largest producer of black tea accounting for over 50% of the total black tea produced globally; primarily manufactures *Crush-Tear-Curl* (CTC) variety of tea.

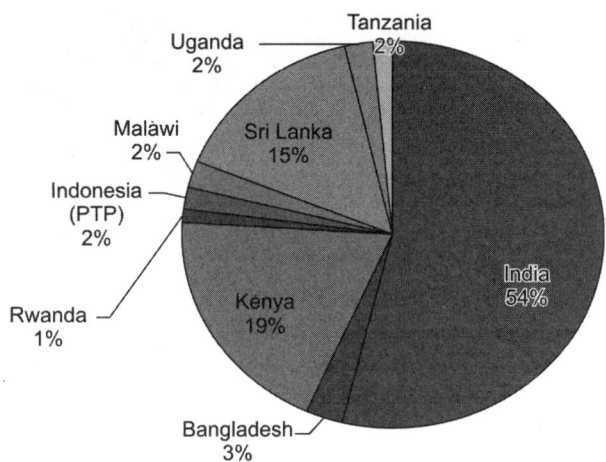

Chart 1: Share of global black tea production (CY13)
Source: ICRA Research.

While Kenya is entirely a CTC producers, orthodox production accounts for almost the entire produce of Sri Lanka. India primarily manufactures the CTC variety of tea which has accounted for around 90% of its production, on an average, with the balance being the orthodox variety of teas. The share of orthodox tea production is higher in SI production compared to that of NI (almost 2.5 times). Although tea is produced in 14 States in India, five of them—Assam and West Bengal in North India (NI), and Tamil Nadu, Kerala and Karnataka in South India (SI), account for over 98% of India's tea production. Within that, the North Indian states alone account for around 80% of India's total tea production.

Globally, black tea production is dominated by India, Sri Lanka and the African continent (with Kenya being the largest). Other large producers (apart from China) are Indonesia, Malawi, Bangladesh, Vietnam, Uganda and Tanzania. As per ITA1 estimates, the world black tea production increased by around 153 Mkg to reach around 2,231 Mkg during CY13, witnessing a y-o-y growth of around 7.4%. All countries mentioned in the chart recorded increased production, except Indonesia and Tanzania where production was marginally down due to adverse weather condition.

In India, production increased significantly during CY13 owing to a favorable weather pattern; however, it remains exposed to agroclimatic risks as seen in the current year so far.

Tea production in India during CY13 witnessed an increase of around 73.7 Mkg (y-o-y increase of 6.5%), primarily driven by an increase in the NI production, by around 70.5 Mkg (y-o-y increase of 7.9%,) while SI production increased by only around 3.2 Mkg (y-o-y increase of 1.3%). The major increase in NI production

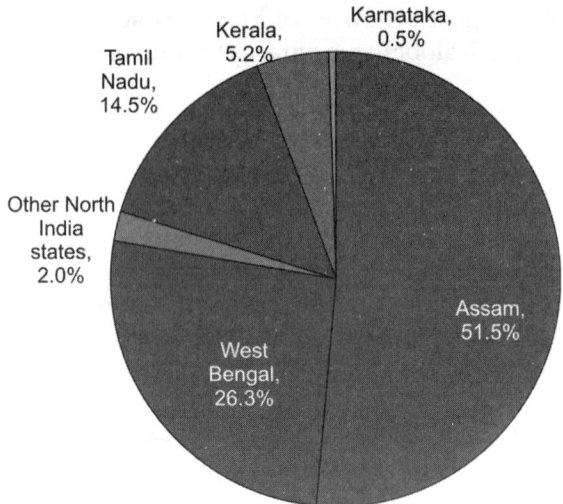

Chart 2: Major tea producing states in India
Source: ICRA Research.

happened during the second half of the year (July–Oct) due to favorable weather condition during the peak tea producing months. In contrast to that, the tea production during CY12 was almost flat due to unfavorable weather pattern during the first half of the year. In the past too, the adverse climatic conditions and associated pest attacks had impacted the domestic production. An adverse weather condition apart, growth in domestic production, has also been constrained by the limited availability of incremental land to increase the acreage under cultivation.

In the first 4 months (January to April) of CY14, production from NI is down by around 11.0 MKg (y-o-y decrease of 12%) on the back of unfavorable weather conditions. However, the production till April typically accounts for around 9–10% of the total NI tea production. So, the weather pattern during the peak tea producing

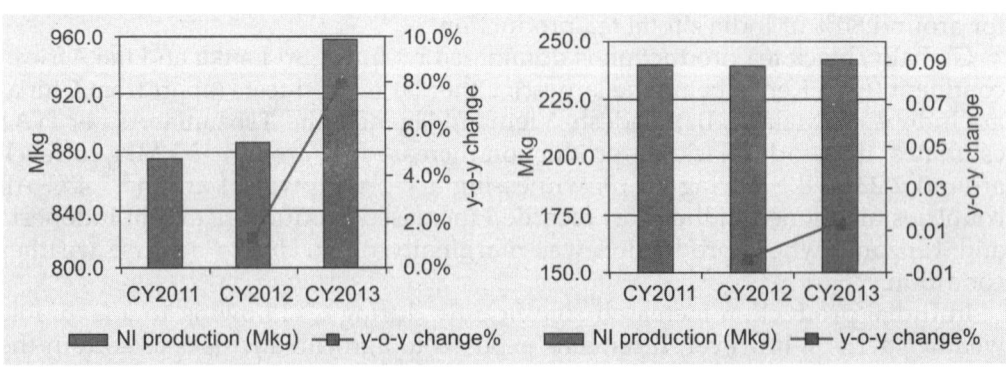

Chart 3: Trend in NI tea production   **Chart 4:** Trend in SI tea production

Since the production data was revised by Tea Board of India from CY11, the y-o-y growth for CY11 has not been plotted in the above charts.
Source: ICRA Research.

months (June–Oct) would be an important determinant of the overall tea production in India in the current calendar year.

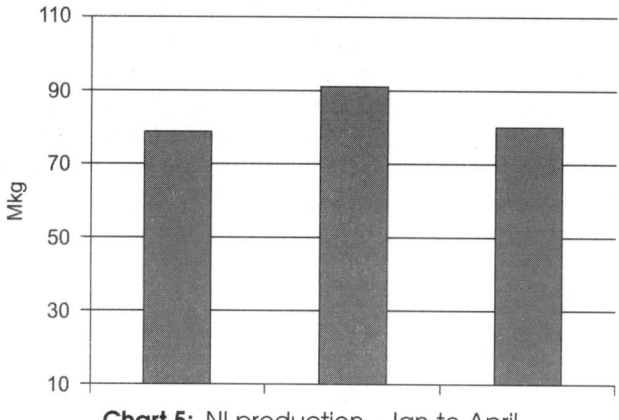

Chart 5: NI production - Jan to April

While domestic consumption absorbs an overwhelming majority of production in India, other key producing countries are more dependent on the exports market.

As depicted in the adjacent chart, exports account for less than 20% of India's tea production, implying that over 80% of the total tea production in India is consumed domestically. However, in case of Kenya and Sri Lanka, the other two major black tea producing countries, export comprise a significant portion of the total production. Notwithstanding the large domestic consumption base that India has, exports play a vital role in maintaining the overall demand-supply balance in the domestic market. Healthy export realization is also crucial for maintaining domestic realizations, as unremunerative prices in the export market may lead to exporters dumping the produce in the domestic market which in turn would exert a downward pressure on domestic prices.

Exports from India remained flat in volume terms during CY13; sharp depreciation of the INR against most of the global currencies resulted in a 12% increase in value

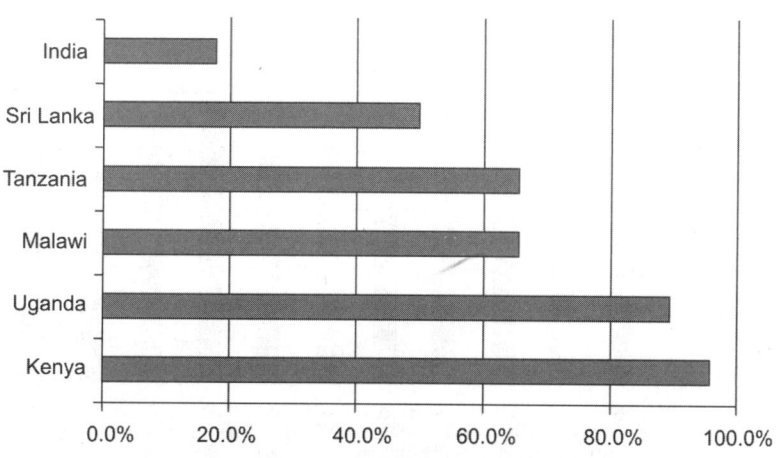

Chart 6: Export percentage of production

of exports During CY13, total exports of tea from India, in volume terms, remained almost flat at 211.8 Mkg as against 208.3 Mkg in CY12; while exports from NI witnessed a marginal decline of around 2.0 Mkg (y-o-y decline of around 1.6%), exports from SI increased by around 5.50 Mkg (y-o-y increase of 6.7%). Although exports volume was flat, in terms of value it witnessed an increase of around 12%, primarily led by sharp depreciation of the Indian Rupee against the US Dollar, which resulted in average realization of exports from NI increasing from Rs 217/kg in CY12 to around Rs 240/kg during CY13 and from SI increasing from Rs 124/kg in CY12 to around Rs 141/kg during CY13. In dollar terms, however, the prices, remained almost flat (both for NI and SI).

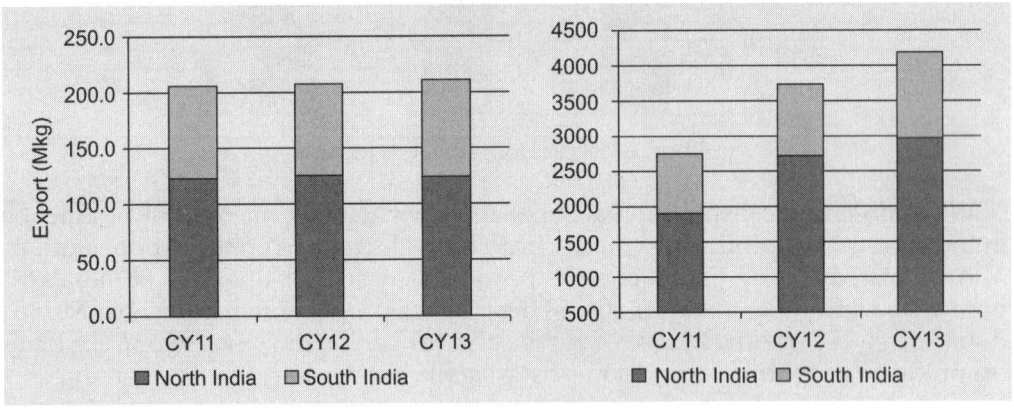

Chart 7: Export volume (CY2011 to CY2013) **Chart 8:** Export value (CY2011 to CY2013)

Source: ICRA Research.

The tea exports have averaged at around 200 Mkg (roughly 20% of overall domestic production) over the last decade (refer Chart 9 for a trend in tea exports during the last 10 years). India exports most of its orthodox production but only a small proportion of its CTC production. Of the total exports, around 58% is accounted for by NI and around 42% by SI. Thus, only around 13% of the total NI production

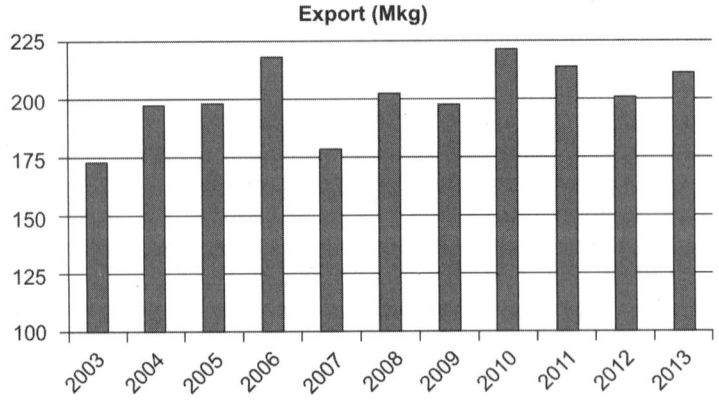

Chart 9: Trend in exports

is exported as against more than a third for SI. While most of the exports from NI are high quality orthodox and CTC teas which fetch a premium in the exports market, SI primarily exports low to medium quality teas, which finds use mainly as "fillers" in tea blending in the international packet tea market. Thus, average export realizations of SI teas are significantly lower than that of NI teas.

Indian teas are primarily exported to CIS countries, European countries, USA, Middle East region and other countries like Pakistan, Sri Lanka, Afghanistan, etc. In CY13, more than one-fourth of the total export was to CIS countries, primarily Russia and Kazakhstan. The teas are also exported to the premium European market viz. UK (7.3%), Germany (3.5%), Netherlands (1.4%). In recent years, the export to Middle East region has picked up, primarily on account of higher exports to Iran posts settlement of payment-related issues and has contributed a significant proportion of the total export volume.

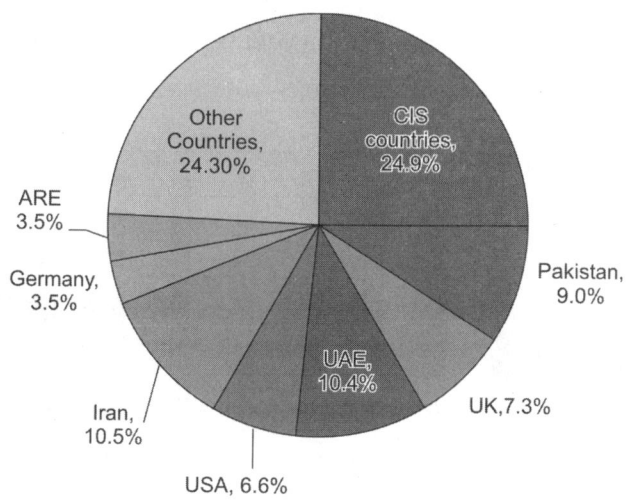

Chart 10: Country-wise export (CY13)

During CY13, domestic tea prices continued to remain firm, notwithstanding higher tea production, primarily driven by a healthy increase in domestic consumption.

Notwithstanding the increase in domestic production (of around 74 Mkg) and almost stagnant exports (increase of only 3.6 Mkg) which resulted in higher availability of tea in the domestic market in CY13, the domestic tea prices continued to remain firm primarily driven by healthy increase in domestic consumption. The NI auction realization increased by Rs 4.0/Kg (y-o-y increase of 2.9%) while SI auction realization increased by Rs 11.9/kg (y-o-y increase of 13.4%) during CY13.

Average prices at NI auction centers remained firm during the first half of CY13 (refer Chart 11 below), as compared to the corresponding previous. Tea production in NI is seasonal with production starting from around march end and ending by around November end with the peak production months being June to September when almost 50% of the total tea is produced. As a result, there are temporary mismatches in the supply-demand scenario for NI teas. Hence auction prices during

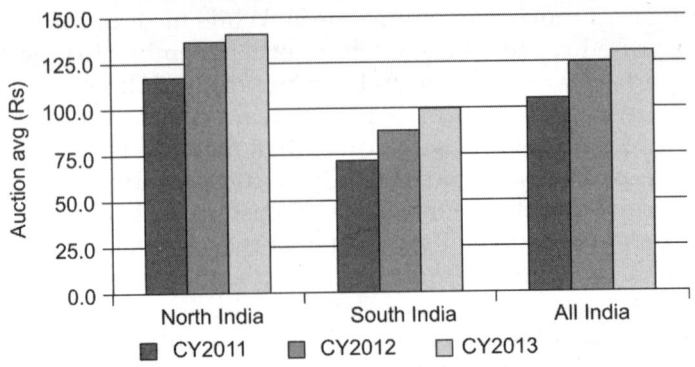

Chart 11: Average Auction Realizations

Source: ICRA Research.

the first half of the year are primarily influenced by carry over stock from the previous year.

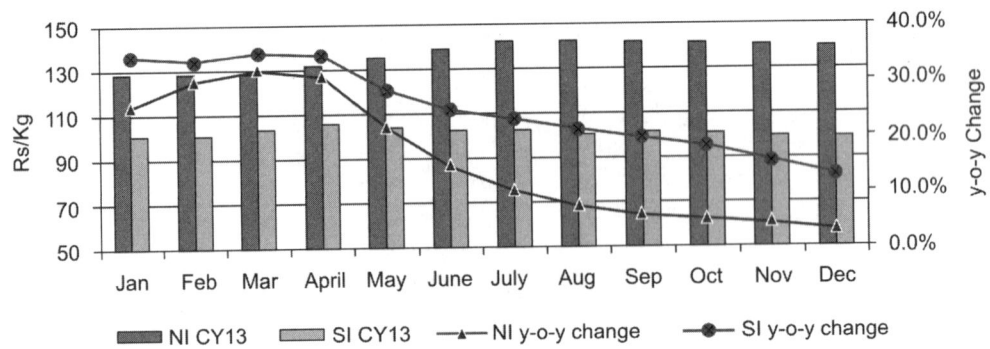

Chart 12: Monthly (cumulative) price movement at NI and SI auction centers

Source: ICRA Research.

With production in NI during CY12 remained almost flat, the low carry over inventory from last year had kept the tea prices firm at NI auction centers till April–May 2013. However with production witnessing, a significant increase during the peak tea producing months, the prices started moderating during the second half of the year and for the full year it witnessed only a marginal increase of around Rs 4.0/Kg (y-o-y increase of 2.9%) compared to the corresponding previous.

At south India, the share of orthodox tea production is significantly higher than NI (almost 2.5 times). So with higher increase in orthodox tea prices over CTC tea prices during CY13, coupled with higher volume of exports of tea from SI primarily led to an increase in SI auction realizations by around Rs 12/kg during CY13.

Sale number 1 represents the auction sale during 1st week of CY14 and henceforth; in NI the auction prices are not available for sale no. 9, 11 and 12 for CY14 and for sale no 11 and 13 for CY13.

In the current calendar year (CY14), the tea realization in NI auction centers was slightly lower till Mar'14 (up to sale number 13), post which it started increasing

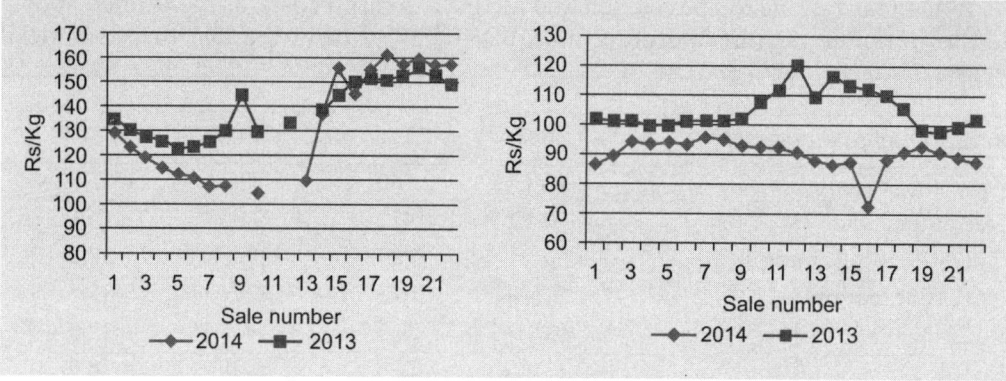

Chart 13: NI weekly auction prices   **Chart 14:** SI weekly auction prices

Source: ICRA Research

during April and May 2014 primarily due to low availability of tea in the auction market with unfavorable weather conditions affecting production during March to May. A low carry over inventory and fall in production also led to cancellation of three auctions in the month of March 2014. In SI auction centers, the realizations are lower over last year till mid-May 2014.

Firm tea prices led to increase in operating income; input cost pressures, however, moderated margins; capital structure and debt coverage indicators continue to remain comfortable.

In bulk tea manufacturing, labor constitutes one of the major cost accounting for around 45–50% of the total cost of production. The wage rate of laborers is decided by bipartite agreement between trade unions and producers' association in Assam and tripartite agreement in West Bengal, wherein the State Government is also involved. The last wage rate increase in West Bengal happened during CY11, which forced the tea companies in Assam too, to negotiate, and increase the wage rates with a retrospective effect before the expiry of the then prevailing agreement. The hike in wage rates coupled with increase in power and fuel expenses led to around 20% increase in operating cost/kg for the sample companies during FY13. The raw material cost/kg also increased during FY13 on account of increase in proportion of bought leaf production for the sample companies.

Cost structure (Rs/kg of sales volume)*	Units	CY10/FY11	CY11/FY12	CY12/FY13
Raw material cost	Rs/kg	17.3	19.8	29.8
Power and fuel cost	Rs/kg	12.7	14.3	17.1
Employee cost	Rs/kg	51.8	55.4	62.3
Other manufacturing cost	Rs/kg	17.3	16.9	18.4
Selling cost	Rs/kg	7.1	8.0	8.9
General and administration cost	Rs/kg	4.1	4.9	5.7
Total operating cost	Rs/kg	110.4	119.4	142.2

* On the basis of aggregate numbers of 11 major NI bulk tea companies rated by ICRA; the cost structure for SI bulk tea companies might be significantly different on account of higher productivity in SI as measured in terms of production (in kg) per hectare of land.

While realizations too have risen, the increase in input costs, as mentioned above, led to a moderation in operating margins (OPM) during the last three financial years.

Key financial parameters[*]	Units	CY10/FY11	CY11/FY12	CY12/FY13
Operating income	Rs Cr	2,560	2,755	3,239
Net profit	Rs Cr	412	344	381
Operating profit margin	%	23.5	19.7	17.1
Net profit margin	%	16.1	12.5	11.8
RoCE	%	25.5	18.3	17.9
RoNW	%	24.8	23.0	18.9
Interest coverage ratio	Times	8.2	6.1	6.1
Debt-equity ratio	Times	0.4	0.3	0.3
Net LT Debt/OPBDITA[**]	Times	0.2	0.1	0.1
NCA/TD	%	59.9	53.5	44.7

[*] On the basis of aggregate numbers of 11 major North India bulk tea companies rated by ICRA.
[**] LT debt is adjusted for cash and bank balances.

The aggregate capital structure has however remained conservative, with healthy accretion to reserves shoring up the net worth of companies from FY08 onward. Healthy cash flows led to accumulation of a healthy cash and bank balance, which stood at almost 87% of the total long-term debt for the sample companies as on 31st March 2013. Working capital bank loans comprise a substantial portion of the net debt (net of cash and bank balance) of these companies. However, it needs to be noted that working capital requirements of bulk tea companies peak during the months of August to October, post which it declines substantially. The debt-coverage indicators although impacted in recent years, remain at comfortable levels.

The quarterly trend of margins for the listed entities is given below:

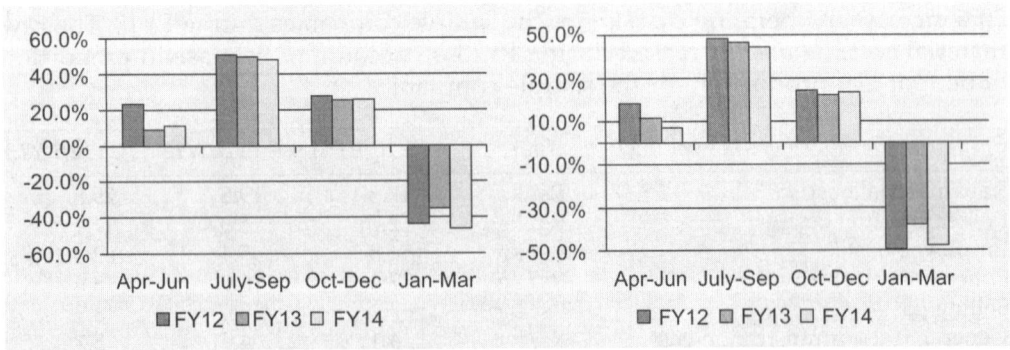

Chart 15: Quarterly trend in operating margin   **Chart 16:** Quarterly trend in PBT margin*

* Margins are calculated based on the aggregate numbers of three listed entities, viz. McLeod Russel India Limited, Goodricke Group Limited and Rossell India Limited.
Source: ICRA Research.

Due to the seasonality involved in the bulk tea industry, the quarterly trend of profits is significantly different from the full year trend. The maximum profits are earned during the period July-September of the calendar year, the peak tea producing months. However, the period January–March is generally loss making for the bulk tea players due to low tea production and high maintenance costs during these months. Nonetheless, as shown in Chart 15 and 16 above, losses in Q4FY14 were higher than those in Q4FY13 because of somewhat lower tea prices in the early months of 2014 compared with 2013.

Outlook

Steady domestic consumption growth, which is estimated at around 3%, and range bound production due to limited availability of incremental land to increase acreage under production, are expected to keep tea prices buoyant at least over the short to medium term. However, input costs, primarily the employee expenses and costs of agrochemicals and power and fuel, are likely to continue to witness an increasing trend. With tea being a fixed cost intensive business, this could be further aggravated in the current financial year (FY) 15 if adverse climatic conditions lead to a significant drop in tea production. Nonetheless, the impact of the same on the profits of bulk tea producers would be determined finally by the trade-off between drop in production and a likely increase in tea prices as a result of that. However, ICRA notes that the debt-service capabilities of large bulk tea companies are likely to remain comfortable on account of their strong balance sheet position at present.

Annexure 4: Priority/focused areas of tea research

1. **Integrated tea agronomy and soil water management program** for the development of package and practices for sustainable tea production.
2. **Integrated tea improvement program** for the development of superior planting materials capable of giving more cuppage than all existing planting materials having yield and quality potential and resistant to biotic and abiotic stress.
3. **Integrated tea protection program** for the development of biopesticides against major pests and diseases of tea and development of package and practices for pest and disease management using physical and cultural methods.
4. **Integrated tea mechanization program** for the development of machines/agricultural appliances required for (i) pruning, (ii) plucking, (iii) fertilizer application and (iv) uprooting, etc. and studies on conservation and efficient use of energy in factory operations.
5. **Integrated tea quality improvement program** for the standardization of factory operations in order to ensure the retention of quality of finished product.
6. **Integrated tea-based product diversification program** for the development of tea based nonedible products (cosmetics, tea oil, medicine, etc. having high-end market value.
7. **Integrated program on climate change and tea** for assessing the impact of climate change on tea and development of strategies to mitigate them.

Annexure 5: How afternoon tea became a trend

While drinking tea as a fashionable event is credited to Catherine of Braganza—known as the tea-drinking queen, the actual idea of having tea in the afternoon was developed into a social event in the late 1830s by Anne, Duchess of Bedford. She enjoyed having light sandwiches and tea in the late afternoon to prevent the sinking feeling she experienced during the long gap between meals. She began inviting others too and it became a trend.

In the 1970s, drinking tea in the house was not encouraged in Bhojpuri villages. Youngsters were forbidden to drink tea; only the older lot who could afford sugar and milk, drank tea. When guests visited, they were offered sherbet. They were offered tea and biscuits only during marriage negotiations. There were only a few tea stalls on high ways. And gossiping over a cup of tea was often looked down upon.

Tea Trail in India

By and large, tea drinkers in India drink doodhwali chai. Depending on the region and locally grown ingredients, there are many popular variations available:

- Since cinnamon and saffron are grown in Kashmir on a large scale, Kashmiri Kahwa is made out of fresh green tea, saffron, sugar, cardamom, cinnamon and almonds.
- Rich, milky and spicy, South Indian tea is known for its distinctive dark color and intense aroma.
- Authentic Darjeeling tea is blackish—green in color.
- The popular brew of Assam is known as Ronga Saah (red tea without milk). It is the main component of English breakfast tea and often had with a slice of lemon.
- A typical North Indian tea is served in a kulhad (earthen pot). Since clay soaks up all the moisture, the tea often has a very strong flavor. The next time you are in Punjab an craving for tea, simply order, Ek kadak chai, malai maar ke.
- The term synonymous with tea in Mumbai is a Cutting Chai, which is based on the concept of addhe se zyada and poore se kam. Afterall, Indians love sharing don't we?

Annexure 6: Promotion scheme for packaged teas of Indian origin (brand support)

The scheme is proposed to be implemented in the 12th 5 year plan period.

I. Scheme Details

To help Indian exporters, in their overseas marketing of teas of Indian origin, on a sustained basis, Tea Board proposes a brand support scheme. Since the scheme is intended to promote teas of Indian origin, it is mandatory for companies wanting to avail of the scheme, to be marketing 100% Indian teas in packets carrying the Indian tea logo or any of the specialty logos after complying with requirements for logo usage. The scheme covers all Indian companies/exporters marketing Indian brand teas in packets less than 1 kg. The brand should be owned by the exporter. Exporters desiring to avail of the scheme would be required to draw up an action plan for 3 years with corresponding projected exports and submit application to Tea Board.

The scheme would be applicable for the following categories:

Tea rooms/boutiques: For display in and retail sale of value added teas from Tea Rooms/Boutiques, exporter may receive reimbursement of the lease/rental charges of floor area or display space on a tapering basis at the following rate subject to submission of valid documents substantiating the claim:

- Year – 1.75%
- Year – 2.50%
- Year – 3.25%

In case of displays from multiple Tea Rooms/Boutiques, maximum reimbursable limit under this head would be Rs 12 lakhs per annum.

Promotional campaign: For intensive publicity campaigns for launching Indian branded products or for promoting branded products, up to 25% of the cost could be considered for reimbursement subject to a ceiling of Rs 50 lakhs per annum per market.

Components eligible under "Promotional Campaign" would be (a) media (covering print, electronic, digital), (b) hoarding, (c) Bus/Tram panels, (d) P-O-P materials and (e) promotional literature. Tea samples or Trade discounts, if given, may not be included in this scheme. PR for the campaign would not be eligible. It is desirable that, wherever possible, Tea Board representative is associated during all stages of the promotion campaign.

Displays in departmental stores plus in-store demonstration/promotion: For promoting value added tea products, tie up with local distributors and major stores is permissible. Level of assistance would be 50% of display and shelf rental cost as well as in-store promotion, subject to a upper ceiling of Rs 25 lakhs per annum per country.

Product literature: For production of literature, to be used for promotion in international markets, assistance to be provided would be 25% of the total cost subject to a ceiling of Rs 50 lakhs per annum per market.

Inspection charges: Inspection charges, incurred prior to shipment of packaged teas carrying Board's logos (adhering to logo usage norms), would be reimbursed. A maximum of 25% costs of such inspection charges would be reimbursable.

II. Eligibility

All Indian registered exporters and exporting value added tea would be eligible if the brand for which support is requested that is owned by them. And all registered exporters and holding permanent exporters license and submitting regular monthly export returns to Tea Board.

III. Conditions

1. All interested exporters are required to apply in advance to Tea Board in the prescribed application form (see page 256 band 257) along with a covering letter on company letterhead.
2. While applying, applicants would be required to provide:
   - Full details of exports (volume and value) of their tea brands in the last year to the particular country for which promotional/financial assistance is sought.
   - Specify the brands to be promoted. Flattened packets may be provided with the application.
   - A 3-year plan.

   For assistance for Promotional Campaign/Brand Promotion, details of the selected media and tariff are to be indicated. After the campaign, copies of invoices along with copy of advertisement released (in the case of publication) prints of digital campaign should be submitted for release of funds. In case of hoardings or Bus/Tram Panel ads, photographs should be submitted duly endorsed by the concerned Director of Tea Promotion or any other authorized official of the Board where such promotion has taken place.

   All claims need to be duly substantiated by proof of payment against invoices. In the event of any false claims being lodged, Tea Board reserves the right to claim refund of the amount granted to the applicant.

   Applications will be processed on "first come first served" basis, subject to availability of funds.
3. There would be an overall ceiling of Rs 50 lakhs per company group per annum. Disbursement would be made subject to the applicant achieving 10% increase in either volume or value of export in the target market at the end of the 2nd year of promotion. While fund disbursement would be made at the end of year – 1, fund disbursement for year – 2 would be subject to 10% increase in either volume or value of exports in the target market. For the purpose of calculating increase in exports, financial year figures would be taken into account.

Application Form for Brand Support

1. Name of the firm with full address	
2. Exporter's Licence issued by Tea Board	No. Date of issue Valid from:
3. Name of the Indian Tea Brand	.............(Brand Name)............ Flattened boxes of the brand to be promoted may be attached for reference
4. Details of exports during the last year to the country where brand promotion is proposed	Financial year ǀ Quantity ǀ Value (Rs Cr.)
5. Particulars of activity and (as per scheme) and country for which support sought with estimated expenditure	(i) Activity: (ii) Country: (iii) Estimated expenditure:
6. Whether assistance/reimbursement availed of in current financial year	Yes/No:
7. If yes, for which activity and country	(i) Activity: (ii) Country:

Signature:

Place:

Name and Designation

Date:

Claim Form for Brand Support

1. Name of the firm with full address	
2. Exporter's Licence issued by Tea Board	No. Date of issue Valid from:
3. Approved Letter No. and Date	

4. Details of exports to the country where brand promotion undertaken	Year 1. 2.	Period From......... To............ From......... To............	Qty.	Value (Rs Cr.)

5. Particulars of activity/country and amount claimed along with supporting documents (i.e. invoice from the media house, receipt of payment made, proof of fund transfer). In case of print advertisement, copy of the publication featuring the advertisements, to be provided.	(i) Activity: (ii) Country: (iii) Expenditure incurred: (iv) Amount claimed:
6. Whether assistance/reimbursement availed of in current financial year	Yes/No.
7. If yes, for which activity and country	(i) Activity: (ii) Country:

Undertaking and Declaration

I/We hereby solemnly undertake/declare that the particulars stated above are true and correct to the best of my/our knowledge and belief.

No other application for claiming assistance for this/these activities and/or cost has been made or will be made in future against purchase or expenditures covered by the application.

Any information if found to be incorrect, wrong or misleading, will render us liable to rejection of our claim without prejudice to any other action that may be taken against us in this behalf.

If as a result of scrutiny any excess payment is found to have been made to me/us, the same may be adjusted against any of the subsequent claims to be made by my/our firm or in the event no claim is preferred, the amount overpaid will be refunded by me/us to the extent of the excess amount paid.

Signature:...

Name in Block Letters:...

Designation:...

Name of the Applicant:...

Firm:...

Company Seal:...

Place:

Date:

Annexure 7: Mirrored tea cups perfectly match these patterned saucers

You have probably heard the story of the painter who was able to perfectly match the color of a room to a priceless vase by simply painting the vase to match. That is the basic idea behind this matching Waltz cup and saucer set, whose mirror-finished tea cup and saucer set, whose mirror finished tea cup will match any surface on which it is placed.

Designed by Japan's D-Bros brand, each cup is made by hand from Hasami porcelain and coated in palladium to ensure the finish is as absolutely perfect as possible. After all even the slightest scratch would ruin the whole effort. The resulting effect is a good reason to get a really wild table cloth for the dining room¯although at $86 (Rs 5,500 approximately) for a single cup and saucer set, your dinner guests might all have to share the same cup.

Annexure 8: Green tea can fight side effects of supplements

Drinking green tea for several weeks or months before you start taking green tea-based dietary supplements for weight loss can protect from potential side effects, a new study has claimed.

As high doses of green tea extract supplements for weight loss become more popular, potential liver toxicity becomes a concern, researchers said. Experts in Penn State's College of Agricultural Sciences gave mice high doses of the green tea polyphenol epigallocatechin-3-gallate (EGCG).

The dosage was equivalent to the amount of the polyphenol that is present in some dietary supplements taken by humans. One group of mice was pretreated with a diet containing a low level of EGCG for 2 weeks prior to receiving high doses of the polyphenol. Another group was fed a diet that did not include EGCG prior to receiving the high, supplement-like doses. After 3 days of high doses, pretreated mice had a 75% reduction in liver toxicity compared to untreated mice.

The research data shows that dietary pretreatment with the green tea polyphenol protects mice from liver toxicity caused by subsequent high oral doses of the same compound, said Josh Lambert, associate professor of food science. "We believe this study indicates that those who are chronic green tea consumers would be less sensitive to potential liver toxicity from green-tea-based dietary supplements. "If you are going to take green tea supplements, drinking green tea for several weeks or months ahead of time may reduce your potential side effects".

Tea is rich in catechins, polyphenols that are natural antioxidants. A number of animal studies have shown the preventive effects of green tea polyphenols against obesity. Lambert pointed out that a recent analysis of 11 human trials with green tea preparations reported a nearly three-pound average body weight loss in intervention groups compared to control groups.

Another recently published research in Food and Chemical Toxicology, has revealed a unique property of the green tea polyphenol EGCG. "It appears that EGCG can modulate its own bioavailability and that dietary treatment may reduce the toxic potential of acute high oral doses of EGCG", said lead researcher Sarah Forester, assistant professor of chemistry, California State University, Bakersfield, a former Penn State postdoctoral fellow.

"These data may partly explain the observed variation in liver toxicity response to dietary supplements containing green tea", Forester said. Lambert suggests that people considering green tea supplements should drink green tea instead. "Drinking green tea rather than taking supplements will allow you to realise the benefits and avoid the risk of liver toxicity.

Annexure 9: Chai Pe Charcha

India's tea production witnessed a slight decline in 2014 when compared to the previous year. In 2014, India produced 1,185 million kg of tea against 1,200 million kg produced in 2013. Tea from the Assam valley constitute about 46% of the total tea produced in the country, the highest among India's three major tea producing regions. The Darjeeling and Nilgiri's regions produced about 28% and 20% respectively of the total.

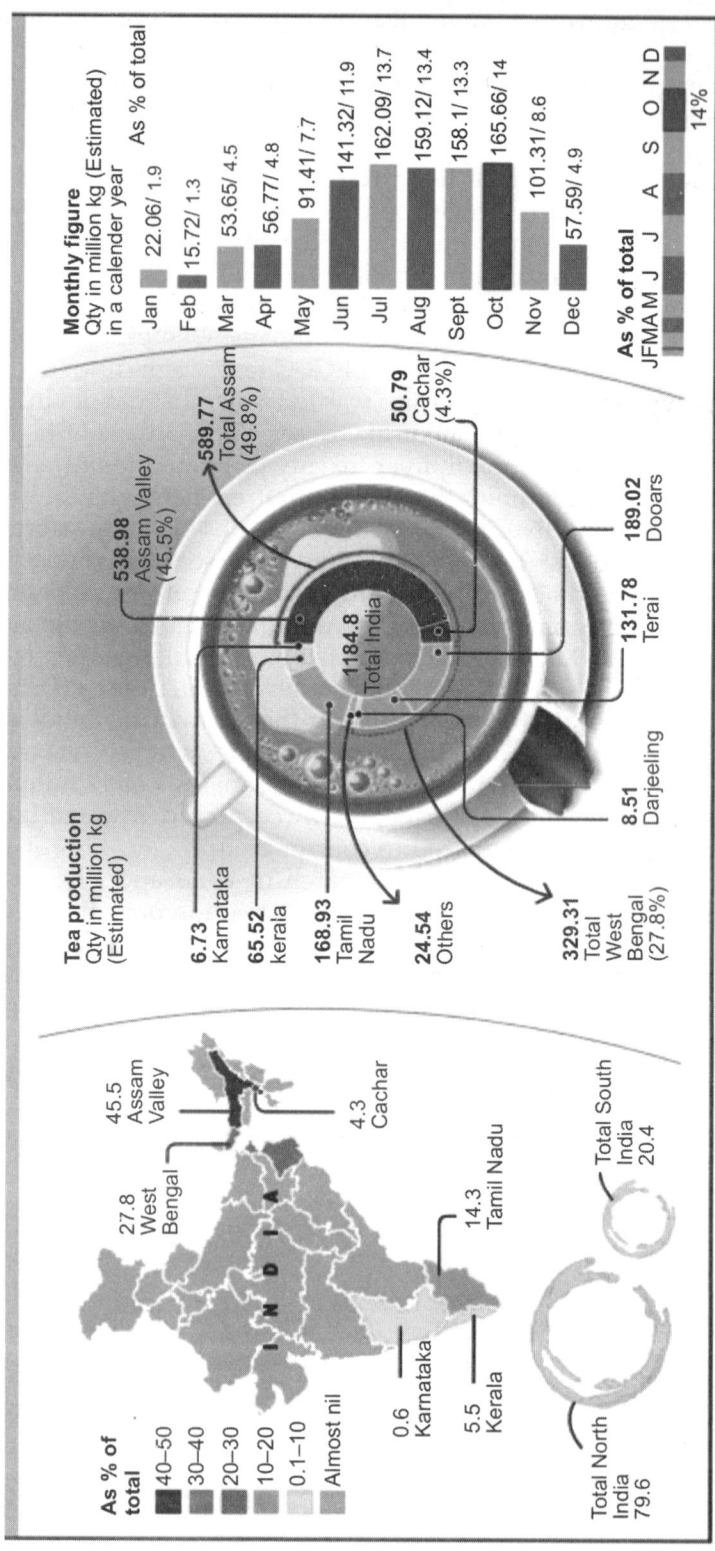

Monthly figure
Qty in million kg (Estimated)
in a calender year   As % of total

Jan	22.06/ 1.9
Feb	15.72/ 1.3
Mar	53.65/ 4.5
Apr	56.77/ 4.8
May	91.41/ 7.7
Jun	141.32/ 11.9
Jul	162.09/ 13.7
Aug	159.12/ 13.4
Sept	158.1/ 13.3
Oct	165.66/ 14
Nov	101.31/ 8.6
Dec	57.59/ 4.9

As % of total
J F M A M J J A S O N D
14%

Tea production
Qty in million kg
(Estimated)

6.73 Karnataka
65.52 kerala
168.93 Tamil Nadu
24.54 Others
329.31 Total West Bengal (27.8%)
1184.8 Total India
538.98 Assam Valley (45.5%)
589.77 Total Assam (49.8%)
50.79 Cachar (4.3%)
189.02 Dooars
131.78 Terai
8.51 Darjeeling

As % of total
- 40–50
- 30–40
- 20–30
- 10–20
- 0.1–10
- Almost nil

45.5 Assam Valley
27.8 West Bengal
4.3 Cachar
14.3 Tamil Nadu
0.6 Karnataka
5.5 Kerala
Total South India 20.4
Total North India 79.6

Source: Tea Board of India

3

Coffee

COFFEE

Coffee growing has a long history that is attributed first to Ethiopia and then to Arabia, mostly to Yemen. However, the earliest history is traced to 875 AD according to the Bibliotheque Nationale in Paris. The original source is also traced to Abyssinia from where it was brought to Arabia in the 15th century.

The history of coffee has been recorded as far back as the 9th century. At first, coffee remained largely confined to Ethiopia, where its native beans were first cultivated by Ethiopian highlanders. It was an Ethiopian shepherd who came lively after eating a shrub with red berries. It was an Ethiopian shepherd who discovered coffee when he watched in wonder as his goats became lively after eating a shrub with red berries. However, the Arab world began expanding its trade horizons, and the beans moved into Yemen, where until 1700 CA the major emporium was Mecha, and thence to North Africa and were mass-cultivated. From there, the beans entered the Indian European markets, and the popularity of the beverage spread.

The word "coffee" entered English in 1598 via Dutch *koffie*. This word was created via Turkish *kahve*, the Turkish pronunciation Arabic *qahwa*, a truncation of *qahhwat al-bun* or *wine of the bean*. One possible origin of the name is the Kingdom of Kaffa in Ethiopia, where the coffee plant originated; its name there is bunn or bunna.

CULTIVARS AND CLASSIFICATION

Coffea Arabica Linne: This species is divided in several varieties, some tall (Bourbon, Typica) and some dwarf (Caturra, Catuai). It is tetraploid species (4n = 44) that yields a clearly superior coffee taste combining low caffeine content with fine aroma. It is generally susceptible to coffee leaf rust and, unfortunately, the more spread varieties like Bourbon tend to be the more susceptible.

Among the more than 200 existing Arabica varieties, the most important tall varieties are:

- Typica: Grown mainly in Brazil; most of the existing varieties originate from it
- Bourbon: Hasa' 25% higher production than Typica
- Mocha: Originates from Ethiopia
- Mundo Novo: This is a natural cross between Bourbon and a variety from Sumatra SL28 and Ruiru ll from Kenya
- Pache Comun and Pache Colis: Both are mutations from Typica

- Maragogype: A mutation from Typica, characterized by broad beans; it originates from Brazil Marella
- Kent, S288 and S288 and S795: All of these originate from India
- Blue Mountain: The famous variety from Jamaica.

The most important dwarf varieties are:

- Caturra: A mutation from Bourbon, known for its productivity and good taste; originates from Brazil
- Catuai: A cross between Caturra and Mundo Novo
- Catimor: A cross between Caturra and Hybrido de Timor.

Coffea canephora Pierre: This is divided in many varieties, but two are mainly grown for commercial purposes: Robusta and Conilon (mainly grown in Brazil). As a whole, it is a diploid species (2n = 22) with an inferior taste but a higher yield. It is more as resistant against coffee leaf rust (*Hemileia vastatrix*), root-knot nematodes (*Meloidogyne exigua, M. incognita, M. paranaensis, Pratylenchus brachyurus, and P. coffeae*) and the coffee berry disease (*Colletotrichum kahawae).* Important varieties are:

- Robusta: The most common variety
- Conilon: Grown mainly in Brazil
- Kouilou or Kwilu: With smaller grains and fruits than Robusta.

There exist also hybrids between *C. arabica and C. canephora*. Some are natural, as for example the Hybrido de Timor, and some are artificial, e.g. arabusta created in Ivory Coast.

Coffea liberuca Hiern: this is a diploid species (2n = 22) which includes several varieties like var. liberica, var. dewevrei and var. excels. It is known for its pungent and earthy tasting coffee. Although it combines good rust resistance, the species is declining and has become less significant as an international commodity.

The genus Coffea, comprising more than 70 species, belongs to the family of *Rubiaceae*. This family forms part of the major group of dicotyledonous sympetales, wherein the petals of the flowers are fused. The flowers are fragrant, with an anise-like scent. Only three coffee species have commercial significance.

Coffee (genus Coffea) is widespread throughout the tropics with more than 70 species. All cultivated species originate from Africa. Economically important today are Coffea Arabica (Arabica, 64% of world production) and Coffea canephora, (var. Robusta, 35%). Coffee is among the most important agricultural commodities on the world market: it is cultivated worldwide on approximately 10.3 million hectares and represents the sole economic income for more than 25 million families. The crop is produced and exported by more than 60 nations and ranks as one of the top cash crops in developing countries.

Coffee is a plantation crop well adapted to different eco-physiological conditions of the tropics. *C. arabica* is adapted to cooler temperatures of the tropical highlands above 1,000 m altitude along the equator; somewhat lower at greater latitude. It needs more than 7 months of rainy weather but a relatively high temperature for an abundant differentiation-of flower buds. The deep root system permits reasonably good drought tolerance. Hence, the crop grows best in tropical highlands. *C. canephora* prefers a hotter climate and is more adapted the lowlands (below 900 m altitude) although quality improves with altitude. It requires a prolonged rainy season because of its shallower root system, tolerates high soil moisture, but needs a short dry season for extensive flowering.

Legendary accounts: There are several legendary accounts of the origin of the drink itself. One account involves the Yemenite Sufi mystic Shaikh ash-Shadhili. When traveling in Ethiopia, the legend goes, he observed goats of unusual vitality, and, upon trying the berries that the goats had been eating, experienced the same vitality. A similar "Legend of Dancing Goats" attributes the discovery of coffee to an Ethiopian goatherder named Kaldi. The story of Kaldi did not appear in writing until 1671, and these stories are considered to be apocryphal.

All commercial coffee species originate from Africa and belong to the genus Coffea. The high quality Coffea Arabica species originates from the rainforests in the southwestern highlands of Ethiopia. One theory suggests that the Ethiopians took it to Yemen when they conquered the country by AD 500. Another hypothesis says that Arab merchants brought it initially to Yemen and the Arabia Peninsula, where it was cultivated and has contributed to the prosperity of the seaport of Mocca. This explains why Arabica coffee is associated with the name Mocca although the prime center of origin and diversity is on the African continent.

It is supposed that the Ethiopians, the ancestors of today's Oromo tribe, were the first to have recognized the energizing effect of the native coffee plant. Studies of genetic diversity have been performed on *Coffea arabica* varieties, found to be of low diversity but which retained some residual heterozygosity from ancestral materials, and closely-related diploid species *Coffea canephora and C. liberica*; however, no direct evidence has ever been found revealing exactly where in Africa coffee grew or who among the natives might have used it as a stimulant or even known about it there earlier than the 17th century. The earliest credible evidence of either coffee drinking or knowledge of the coffee tree appears in the middle of the fifteenth century, in the Sufi monasteries of the Yemen in Southern Arabia. It was in Yemen that coffee beans were first roasted and brewed as they are today. From Mocha, coffee spread to Egypt and North Africa, and by the 15th century, it had reached the rest of the Middle East, Persia and Turkey. From the Muslim World, coffee drinking spread to Italy, then to the rest of Europe, and coffee plants were transported by the Dutch to the East Indies and to the Americas.

The earliest mention of coffee noted by the literary coffee merchant Philippe Sylvestre Dufour is a reference to *bunchum* in the works of the 10th century CE Persian physician Muhammad ibn Zakariya al-Razi, known as Rhazes in the West, but more definite information on the preparation of a beverage from the roasted coffee berries dates from several centuries later.

The most important of the early writers on coffee was Abd al-Qadir al-jaziri, who in 1587 compiled a work tracing the history and legal controversies of coffee entitled *Umdat al safwa fi hill al-qahwa*. He reported that one Sheikh, Jamal-al-Din al-Dhabhani, mufti of Aden, was the first to adopt the use of coffee (circa 1454). Coffee's usefulness in driving away sleep made it popular among Sufis. A translation traces the spread of coffee from Arabia Felix (the present day Yemen) northward to Mecca and Medina and, and then to the larger cities of Cairo, Damascus, Bagdad, and Istanbul.

Though coffee was cultivated as early as the sixth century AD in Yemen, it did not gain popularly until the 15th and 16th centuries when it was cultivated extensively in Yemen, district of Arabia. Coffee beans were first exported from

Ethiopia to Yeman. Yemeni traders brought coffee back to their homeland and began to cultivate the bean. The first coffeehouse opened in Istanbul in 1554. Coffee was at first not well received. In 1511, it was forbidden for its stimulating effect by conservative, orthodox imams at a theological court in Mecca. However, the popularity of the drink led these bans to be overturned in 1524 by an order of the Ottoman Turkish Sulthan Selim, with Grand Mufti Mehmet Ebussuud el-Imadi issuing a celebrated fatwa allowing the consumption of coffee. In Cairo, Egypt, a similar ban was instituted in 1532, and the coffeehouses and warehouses containing coffee beans were sacked.

Similarly, coffee was banned by the Ethiopian Orthodox Church some time before the 17th century. However, in the second half of the 19th century, Ethiopian attitudes softened toward coffee drinking, and its consumption spread rapidly between 1880 and 1886; according to Richard Panhurst, "this was largely due to (Emperor) Menilek, who himself drank it, and to Abuna Matewos who did much to dispel the belief of the clergy that it was a Muslim drink".

Dutchman named Henricus imported seeds to Java from India. This started coffee production in the Dutch Colonies. From here coffee seeds and plants were sent to the botanical conservatory in Amsterdam. These seeds were cultivated at the conservatory and were propagated and sent to many conservatories throughout Europe. Thus, the Dutch took the lead in propagating coffee in their colonies of Java, Sumatra, and Bali.

The French wanted to cultivate coffee in their colonies, but their efforts to transplant plants from Amsterdam were not successful. Finally in 1714, Amsterdam sent a five-foot tree to Louis XIV of France. This tree was successfully planted and propagated in the botanical conservatory of Paris.

In 1723, a French captain, Gabriel Mathieu de Clieu, of French Martinique Island brought a coffee plant from Paris to Martinique. He encountered many difficulties during this historic voyage, but kept the coffee plant alive by sharing his own ration of drinking water and looking after it day and night. In 1727, an earthquake in Martinique destroyed most of the islands cocoa plantations and the island was subsequently replanted with coffee. By 1777, Martinique had about 19 million coffee trees. Coffee was also cultivated in French Guiana and many other nearby islands. Coffee trees from Martinique were introduced to Haiti where they replaced less hardy plants introduced by the French in 1715.

The first coffee in Brazil was planted in 1727 from plants brought from French Guiana. However, significant coffee production in Brazil started after 1760 when Joo Alberto Castello Branco brought plants from Portuguese Goa in India to Rio de Janeiro.

Coffee was introduced to Costa Rica from Cuba by Don Francisco Xavier Navarro in 1779. The English brought coffee to Jamaica in 1730.

Coffee was introduced to Guatemala in the 1750s. However, at that time Guatemala main export was Cochineal (worms used for natural food coloring) and Indigo (a natural dye), so coffee did not take a hold. It was only in the 1850s, when these industries collapsed that farmers started growing coffee in large quantities.

Coffee did not become a major crop in India until the British started emphasizing its production in the 1840s. However, it is said that the coffee seeds that Baba Budan brought from Yemen to India in the 1600s are responsible for the propagation of coffee throughout the world.

Varieties

The four main botanical cultivars of India's coffee include Kent, S.795, Cauvery, and Selection 9. In the 1920s, the earliest variety of Arabica grown in India was named Kent(s) after the Englishman L.P. Kent, a planter of the Doddengudda Estate in Mysore. Probably the most commonly planted Arabica in India and Southeast Asia is S.795, known for its balanced cup and subtle flavor notes of mocca. Released during the 1940s, it is a cross between the Kents and S.288 varieties. Cauvery, commonly known as Catimor, is a derivative of a cross between Caturra with Hybrido-de-Timor while the award-winning Selection 9 is a derivative from the cross between Tafarikela and Hybrido-de-Timor. The dwarf and semi-dwarf hybrids of San Ramon and Caturra were developed to meet the demands for high density plantings. The Devamachy hybrid (*C. arabica* and *C. canephora*) was first discovered around 1930 in India. The Indian Coffee Association's weekly auction includes such varieties as Arabica Cherry, Robusta Cherry, Arabica Plantation, and Robusta Parchment.

Regional logos and brands include: Anamalais, Araku valley, Bababudangiris, Biligiris, Brahmaputra, Chikmagalur, Coorg, Manjarabad, Nilgiris, Pulneys, Sheveroys, Travancore and Wayanad. There are also several specialty brands such as Monsooned Malabar AA, Mysore Nuggets Extra Bold, and Robusta Kaapi Royale.

Organic Coffee

Organic coffee is produced without synthetic agrochemicals and plant protection methods. A certification is essential by the accrediting agency for such coffee to market it (popular forms are of regular, decaffeinated, flavored and instant coffee variety) as such since they are popular in Europe, United States and Japan. The Indian terrain and climatic conditions provide the advantages required for the growth of such coffee in deep and fertile forest soils under the two tier mixed shade using cattle manure, composting and manual weeding coupled with the horticultural operations practiced in its various coffee plantations; small holdings is another advantage for such a variety of coffee. In spite of all these advantages, the certified organic coffee holdings in India, as of 2008, (there are 20 accredited certification agencies in India) was only in an area of 2,600 hectares (6,400 acres) with production estimated at 1,700 tons. In order to promote growth of such coffee, the Coffee Board, based on field experiments, surveys and case studies has evolved many packages for adoption, supplemented with information guidelines and technical documents.

C. canephora varieties, including Robusta coffee, grow at lower altitude and fit well in the equatorial, warm and wet tropics below 1,000 m; they occur naturally in the western Congo basin. Robusta coffee is resistant to coffee leaf rust (*Hemileia vastatrix*) and, therefore, with the expansion of coffee production in the world it replaced Arabica in the area where coffee leave rust was devastating the production. As for Arabica, some early Brazilian coffee was labeled after its major port of export, Santos.

There exist also two additional minor coffee species. *Coffea liberica* originates from West Africa around Liberia. *C. excelsa* comes from the more continental and drier parts of Central Africa, mainly the Central African Republic. Genetically, the latter two species are now considered as a single complex. Nevertheless, practically all present, cultivars are descendants of early coffee introductions from Ethiopia to

Arabia (Yemen) where they were subjected to a relatively dry ecosystem without shade for a thousand years before being introduced to Asia and Latin America.

The early history of coffee growing followed the major colonial routes dominated by France, Great Britain, Spain, Portugal, The Netherlands, Germany and Belgium. The material that followed these routes is of narrow genetic basis, one such cultivar "Bourbon" originates from Bourbon (now Reunion) Island, the then French colony, and formed the basis of a larger part of Arabica plantations worldwide due to its excellent cup taste. Unfortunately, this cultivar is susceptible to coffee leaf rust. Many crossing programs used *Bourbon* to cross with *Hybrido d. e Timor*, a natural. interspecific cross between *C. arabica* and *C. canephora*, but having a lower cup quality.

The expansion of Arabica coffee far beyond its natural ecological requirements resulted not only in overproduction but also into the development of marginal coffee areas which can only make a profit when world market prices are very high. A solution to this problem is to reconvert these threatened regions into other activities. In some cases, horticulture can offer a way-out, though on steep slopes this is less evident due to the difficulty to bring the produce to the markets.

Given below are some specific characteristics and quality parameters of the important commercial grown coffee species discussed above.

Quality parameters of commercially grown coffee species

Coffee species	Berry to dried bean weight rate	Number of green coffee beans per kg.	Caffeine content (%)
C. liberica	10:1	365	1.4–1.6
C. arabica	5–6:1	456	1.0–1.5
C. cancephora	4.5:1	685	2.0–2.5

The proper choice of appropriate coffee varieties, well adapted to the growing region, is very important for the final taste and quality of the coffee in the cup. There is a general tendency to overvalue high yield performances and not enough cup quality as such. Best Agricultural Practices (BAP) combines the principles of sustainable agriculture with coffee quality. Major Arabica coffee varieties in some important producing countries are list below.

Major varieties in arabica coffee growing countries

Origin	Major varieties grown
Colombia	Bourbon, Typica, Caturra and Maragogype
India	Kent and one of its offspring S795; these combine exceptional cup quality with good rust tolerance. S26 and S288 have some Liberica characters in their ancestry. Catimor (Cauvery) and Sin 9 present rust tolerance introgressed from Robusta material.
China	Catimor 7963.
Indonesia	Robusta coffee is widely grown because of the warm and wet climate. In East Java the cv. Kawisari, a cross between Arabica and Liberica, is cultivated. *Cv. Sumatra* is thought to be an interspecific cross between Robusta and Arabica.

(Contd.)

Brazil	Among the better tasting Arabica varieities in Brazil one should cite Bourbon, typical, Maragogype and the shorter Cuturra. The late maturing Mundo Novo and one of its siblings *Cv. catuai* are widely grown.
Ethiopia	There exists a very high genetic diversity of Arabica species in the country. Wild coffee is still found in forests. Famous landraces are Harare, sidamo, Djimmah. Some 20 varieties are now selected for productivity/resistance to the coffee berry disease, and these are currently distributed in farmers.
Kenya	Variety Sl28 is highly appreciated. Ruiru 11 is high yielding, but with some Robusta characteristics.
Tanzania	N197, Typica or French mission varieties are planted.
Jamaica	Besides good tasting Bourbon and Bourbon amarello (Yellow Bourbon) are mostly planted. Jamaica coffee farmers produce the famous Blue mountain variety.
Guatemala	Pache comun, Pache colis.
Panama	Geisha and Geisha grown in Bouquet offer premium quality
Former colonies of Portugal	Catimor (a cross between Timor and Caturra is rust tolerant.

Within the *Coffea canephora* varieties, taste quality differences are not as clear as in *C. arabica*, though this begins to change with the development of washed Robusta vs. Some varieties originating from Angola or Congo-Kinshasa like "Kouilou or Conilon" (Kwilu) are already known for their better cup quality. Vietnam, Indonesia and Uganda have now become leading producers. For simplicity, the terms Arabica (for *C. arabica*) and Robusta (for *C. canephora)* from here onward are used.

Europe

Coffee was noted in Ottoman Aleppo by the German physician botanist Leonhard Rauwolf, the first European to mention it, as *chaube*, in 1573; Rauwolf was closely followed by descriptions from other European travelers.

The vibrant trade between Venice and the Muslims in North Africa, Egypt, and the East brought a large variety of African goods including coffee to this leading European port. Venetian merchants introduced coffee-drinking to the wealthy in Venice, charging them heavily for the beverage. In this way, coffee was introduced to Europe. Coffee became more widely accepted after the controversy over whether it was acceptable for Catholics to consume it, was settled in its favor by Pope Clement VIII in 1600, despite appeals to ban the drink. The first European coffee house (apart from those in the Ottoman Empire, mentioned above) was opened in Venice in 1645.

England

Largely through the efforts of the British East India Company and the Dutch East India Company, coffee became available in England no later than the 16th century according to Leonhard Rauwolf's 1583 account. The first coffeehouse in England was opened in St. Michael's Alley in Cornhill. The proprietor was Pasqua Rosée, the servant of Daniel Edwards, a trader in Turkish goods. Edwards imported the coffee and assisted Rosée in setting up the establishment. Oxford's Queen's Lane Coffee House, established in 1654, is still in existence today. By 1675, there were more than 3,000 coffeehouses throughout England, Popularity of coffeehouses spread rapidly in Europe, and later, America.

But, there were many disruptions in the progressive movement of coffee houses between the 1660s and the 1670s. These coffee houses in England were places used for deep discussion of beliefs during the enlightenment, such as their thoughts on religious and political issues of their time. This practice of religious and political discussion became so common that Charles II made an attempt to crush coffee houses in 1675.

The banning of women from coffeehouses was not universal, but appears to have been commonplace in Europe. In Germany women frequented them, but in England they were banned. Many believed coffee to have several medicinal properties in this period. For example, a 1661 tract entitled "A character of coffee and coffee-houses", written by one "M.P", lists some of these perceived benefits:

- This extolled for drying up the crudities of the stomach, and for expelling fumes out of the head. Excellent Berry! which can cleanse the English-man's stomach of Flegm, and expel Giddiness out of his Head.

    This new commodity proved controversial among some subjects, however. For instance, the anonymous 1674 "Women's Petition Against Coffee" declared:

- The excessive use of that Newfangled, Abominable, Heathenish Liquor called *coffee* has *Eunucht* our Husbands, and Crippled our more kind *Gallants*, that they are become as *Impotent*, as Age.

France

Antoine Galland (1646–1715) in his aforementioned translation described the Muslim association with coffee, tea and chocolate: "We are indebted to these great (Arab) physicians for introducing coffee to the modern world through their writings as well as sugar, tea, and chocolate". Galland reported that he was informed by Mr de la Croix, the interpreter of King Louis XIV of France, that coffee was brought to Paris by a certain Mr Thevenot, who had travelled through the East. On his return to that city in 1657, Thevenot gave some of the beans to his friends, one of whom was de la Croix.

In 1669, Soleiman Agha, Ambassador from Sultan Mehmed IV, arrived in Paris with his entourage bringing with him a large quantity of coffee beans. Not only did they provide their French and European guests with coffee to drink, but they also donated some beans to the royal court. Between July 1669 and May 1670, the Ambassador managed to firmly establish the custom of drinking coffee among Parisians.

Austria

The real first coffeehouse in Austria opened in Vienna in 1683 after the Battle of Vienna, by using supplies from the spoils obtained after defeating the Turks. The officer who received the coffee beans, Polish military officer of Ukrainian origin Jerzy Franciszek Kulczycki, opened the coffee house and helped popularize the custom of adding sugar and milk to the coffee. Melange is the typical Viennese coffee, which comes mixed with hot foamed milk and a glass of water.

Netherlands

The race among Europeans to obtain live coffee trees or beans was eventually won by the Dutch in 1616. Pieter van der Broecke, a Dutch merchant, obtained some of the closely guarded coffee bushes from Mocha, Yemen in 1616. He took them back to Amsterdam and found a home for them in the botanical gardens, where they began to thrive. This apparently minor event received little publicity, but was to have a major impact on the history of coffee.

The beans that van der Broecke stole from Mocha forty years earlier adjusted well to conditions in the greenhouses at the Amsterdam Botanical Garden and produced numerous healthy *Coffea arabica* bushes. In 1658, the Dutch first used them to begin coffee cultivation in Ceylon (now Sri Lanka) and later in southern India. They abandoned these cultivations to focus on their Javanese plantations in order to avoid lowering the price by oversupply. Within a few years the Dutch colonies (Java in Asia, Suriname in the Americas) had become the main suppliers of coffee to Europe.

Americas

Gabriel de Clieu brought coffee seedlings to Martinique in the Caribbean circa 1720. Those sprouts flourished and 50 years later there were 18,680 coffee trees in Martinique enabling the spread of coffee cultivation to Haiti, Mexico and other islands of the Caribbean. The territory of San Domingo (now Hispanola, comprising Haiti and the Dominican Republic) saw coffee cultivated from 1734, and by 1788 it supplied half the world's coffee. Coffee had a major influence on the geography of Latin America. The French colonial plantations relied heavily on African slave laborers. However, the dreadful conditions that the slaves worked in on coffee plantations were a factor in the soon-to-follow Haitian Revolution. The coffee industry never fully recovered there.

Coffee also found its way to the Isle of Bourbon, now known as Réunion, in the Indian Ocean. The plant produced smaller beans and was deemed a different variety of arabica known as *var. Bourbon*. The Santos coffee of Brazil and the Oaxaca coffee of Mexico are the progeny of that Bourbon tree. Circa 1727, the King of Portugal sent Francisco de Mello Palheta to French Guinea to obtain coffee seeds to become a part of the coffee market. Francisco initially had difficulty obtaining these seeds, but he captivated the French Governor's wife and she sent him enough seeds and shoots to commence the coffee industry of Brazil. In 1893, the coffee from Brazil was introduced into Kenya and Tanzania (Tanganyika), not far from its place of origin in Ethiopia, 600 years prior, ending its transcontinental journey.

Meanwhile, coffee had been introduced to Brazil in 1727, although its cultivation did not gather momentum until independence in 1822. After this time, massive tracts of rainforest were cleared first from the vicinity of Rio and later São Paulo for coffee plantations.

Cultivation was taken up by many countries in the latter half of the 19th century, and almost all involved the large-scale displacement and exploitation of the indigenous Indian people. Harsh conditions led to many uprisings, coups and bloody suppression of peasants. The notable exception was Costa Rica where lack of ready labor prevented the formation of large farms. Smaller farms and more egalitarian conditions ameliorated unrest over the 19th and 20th centuries.

In the 1930s, Brazil took off as major producer of coffee, leaving behind their early yerba mate industry, which Argentina then took over.

India

The first record of coffee growing in India is following the introduction of coffee beans from Yemen by Baba Budan to the hills of Chikmagalur in 1670. Since then coffee plantations have become established in the region, extending South to Kodagu.

Japan

Coffee was introduced to Japan by the Dutch in the 17th century, but remained a curiosity until the lifting of trade restrictions in 1858. The first European-style coffeehouse opened in Tokyo in 1888, and closed 4 years later. By the early 1930s, there were over 30,000 coffeehouses across the country; availability in the wartime and immediate postwar period dropped nearly to zero, then rapidly increased as import barriers were removed. The introduction of freeze-dried instant coffee, canned coffee, and franchises such as Starbucks and Doutor Coffee in the late 20th century continued this trend, to the point that Japan is now one of the leading per capita coffee consumers in the world.

South Korea

Coffee's first notable Korean enthusiasts were emperors Sunjong and Gojong, who preferred to consume it after western-style banquets. A disgruntled interpreter at one point attempted to kill both by poisoning their coffee, and nearly succeeded. By the 1980s instant coffee and canned coffee had become fairly popular, with a more minor tradition of independently owned coffeehouses in larger cities; toward the end of the century the growth of franchises such as Caffe Bene and Starbucks brought about a greater demand for European-style coffee.

PRODUCTION

The first step in Europeans' wresting the means of production was effected by Nicolaes Witsen, the enterprising burgomaster of Amsterdam and member of the governing board of the Dutch East India Company who urged Joan van Hoorn, the Dutch governor at Batavia that some coffee plants be obtained at the export port of Mocha in Yemen, the source of Europe's supply, and established in the Dutch East Indies; the project of raising many plants from the seeds of the first shipment met with such success that the Dutch East India Company was able to supply Europe's demand with "Java coffee" by 1719. Encouraged by their success, they soon had coffee plantations in Ceylon Sumatra and other Sunda islands. Coffee trees were soon grown under glass at the Hortus Botanicus of Leiden, whence slips were generously extended to other botanical gardens. Dutch representatives at the negotiations that led to the Treaty of Utrecht presented their French counterparts with a coffee plant, which was grown on at the *Jardin du Roi*, predecessor of the Jardin des Plantes in Paris.

The introduction of coffee to the Americas was effected by Captain Gabriel des Clieux, who obtained cuttings from the reluctant botanist Antoine de Jussieu, who was loath to disfigure the king's coffee tree. Clieux, when water rations dwindled during a difficult voyage, shared his portion with his precious plants and protected them from a Dutchman, perhaps an agent of the Provinces jealous of the Batavian trade. Clieux nurtured the plants on his arrival in the West Indies, and established them in Guadeloupe and Saint-Domingue in addition to Martinique, where a blight had struck the cacao plantations, which were replaced by coffee plantations in a space of 3 years. is attributed to France through its colonization of many parts of the continent starting with the Martinique and the colonies of the West Indies where the first French coffee plantations were founded.

The first coffee plantation in Brazil occurred in 1727 when Lt. Col. Francisco de Melo Palheta smuggled seeds, still essentially from the germ plasm originally taken from Yemen to Batavia, from French Guiana. By the 1800s, Brazil's harvests would turn coffee from an elite indulgence to a drink for the masses. Brazil, which like most other countries cultivates coffee as a commercial commodity, relied heavily on slave labor from Africa for the viability of the plantations until the abolition of slavery in 1888. The success of coffee in 17th century Europe was paralleled with the spread of the habit of tobacco smoking all over the continent during the course of the 30 years war (1618).

For many decades in the 19th and early 20th centuries, Brazil was the biggest producer of coffee and a virtual monopolist in the trade. However, a policy of maintaining high prices soon opened opportunities to other nations, such as Colombia, Guatemala, Nicaragua, Indonesia and Vietnam, now second only to Brazil as the major coffee producer in the world. Large-scale production in Vietnam began following normalization of trade relations with the US in 1995. Nearly all of the coffee grown there is Robusta.

Despite the origins of coffee cultivation in Ethiopia, that country produced only a small amount for export until the 28th century, and much of that not from the South of the country but from the environs of Harar in the northeast. The Kingdom of Kaffa, home of the plant, was estimated to produce between 50,000 kilograms and 60,000 kilograms of coffee beans in the 1880s. Commercial production effectively began in 1907 with the founding of the inland port of Gambela, and greatly increased afterward: 100,000 kilograms of coffee was exported from Gambela in 1908, while in 1927–1928 over 4 million kilograms passed through that port. Coffee plantations were also developed in Arsi Province at the same time, and were eventually exported by means of the Addis Ababa-Djibouti Railway. While only 245,000 kilograms were freighted by the Railway, this amount jumped to 2,240,000 kilograms by 1922, surpassed exports of "Harari" coffee by 1925, and reached 9,260,000 kilograms in 1936.

Australia is a minor coffee producer, with little product for export, but its coffee history goes back to 1880 when the first of 500 acres (2.0 km^2) began to be developed in an area between northern New South Wales and Cooktown. Today, there are several producers of Arabica coffee in Australia that use a mechanical harvesting system invented in 1981.

COFFEE HISTORY

Timeline

c 850

First known discovery of coffee berries. Legend of goat herder Kaldi of Ethiopia who notices goats is friskier after eating red berries of a local shrub. Experiments with the berries himself and begins to feel happier.

c 1100

The coffee first trees are cultivated on the Arabian peninsula. Coffee is first roasted and boiled by Arabs making "qahwa"—a beverage made from plants.

1475

The world first coffee shop opens in Constantinople. It is followed by the establishment of two coffee houses in 1554.

c 1600

Coffee enters Europe through the port of Venice. The first coffeehouse opens in Italy in 1654.

1607

Coffee is introduced to the New World by Captain John Smith, founder of Virginia at Jamestown. Some Canadian historians claim it arrived in previously settled Canada.

1652

The first coffeehouse opens in England. Coffeehouses are called "penny universities" (a penny is charged for admission and a cup of coffee). Edward Lloyd's coffeehouse opens in 1688. It eventually becomes Lloyd's of London, the world's best known insurance company. The word "TIPS" is coined in an English coffee house: A sign reading "To Insure Prompt Service" (TIPS) was place by a cup. Those desiring prompt service and better seating threw a coin into a tin.

1672

The opening of the first Parisian cafe dedicated to serving coffee. In 1713, King Louis XIV is presented with a coffee tree. It is believed that sugar was first used as an additive in his court.

1683

The first coffeehouse opens in Vienna. The Turks, defeated in battle, leave sacks of coffee behind.

1690

The Dutch become the first to transport and cultivate coffee commercially. Coffee is smuggled out of the Arab port of Mocha and transported to Ceylon and East Indies for cultivation.

1721

The first coffeehouse opens in Berlin.

1723

Coffee plants are introduced in the Americas for cultivation. Gabriel de Clieu, a French naval officer, transports a seedling to Martinique. By 1777, 1920 million coffee plants are cultivated on the island.

1727

The Brazilian coffee industry gets its start from seedlings smuggled out of Paris.

1750

One of Europe's first coffeehouses, Cafe Greco, opens in Rome. By 1763, Venice has over 2,000 coffee shops.

1822

The prototype of the first espresso machine is created in France.

1885

A process of using natural gas and hot air becomes the most popular method of roasting coffee.

c 1900

Kaffeeklatsch, afternoon coffee, becomes popular in Germany.

1905

The first commercial espresso machine is manufactured in Italy.

1908

The invention of the worlds, first drip coffeemaker Melitta Bentz makes a filter using blotting paper.

1933

Dr Ernest Illy develops the first automatic espresso machine.

1938

Nescafé instant coffee is invented by the Nestlé company as it assists the Brazilian government in solving its coffee surplus problem.

1945

Achilles Gaggia perfects the espresso machine with a piston that creates a high pressure extraction to produce a thick layer of crema.

1991

Caffè Carissimi Canada, a network of espresso service providers is formed in Canada, modeled after a visit to Franco Carissimi (roaster and equipment manufacturer) in Bergamo Italy. It becomes the fastest growing network of private and independent super automatic machines providers in Canada.

1995

Coffee is the world most popular beverage. More than 400 billion cups are consumed each year. It is a world commodity that is second only to oil.

COFFEE IN INDIA

History

The Indian context started with an Indian Muslim saint, Baba Budan, while on a pilgrimage to Mecca, smuggled seven coffee beans (by tying it around his waist) from Yemen to Mysore in India and planted them on the Chandragiri Hills [1,829 meters (6,001 ft)), now named after the saint as Baba Budan Giri ("Giri" means "hill") in Chikkamagalur district. It was considered an illegal act to take out green coffee seed out of Arabia. As number seven is a sacrosanct number in Islamic religion, the saint's act of carrying seven coffee beans was considered a religious act. This was the beginning of coffee industry in India, and in particular, in the then state of Mysore, now part of the Karnataka State. This was an achievement of considerable bravery of Baba Budan considering the fact that Arabs had exercised strict control over its export to other countries by not permitting coffee beans to be exported in any form other than as in a roasted or boiled form to prevent germination.

Systematic cultivation soon followed Baba Budan's first planting of the seeds, in 1670, mostly by private owners and the first plantation was established in 1840 around Baba Budan Giri and its surrounding hills in Karnataka. It spread to other areas of Wayanad (now part of Kerala), the Shevroys and Nilgiris in Tamil Nadu. With British colonial presence taking strong roots in India in the mid 19th century, coffee plantations flourished for export. The culture of coffee thus spread to South India rapidly.

Initially, Arabica was popular. However, as a result of serious infestation caused to this variety by coffee rust, an alternative robust variety of coffee, appropriately named as robusta and another hybrid between liberica and Arabica, a rust-tolerant hybrid variety of Arabica tree became popular. This is the most common variety of coffee that is grown in the country with Karnataka alone accounting for 70% of production of this variety.

In 1942, the government decided to regulate the export of coffee and protect the small and marginal farmers by passing the Coffee VII Act of 1942, under which the Coffee Board of India got established, operated by the Ministry of Commerce and Industry. The government dramatically increased their control of coffee exports in India and pooled the coffees of its growers. In doing so, they reduced the incentives for farmers to produce high-quality coffee, so quality became stagnant.

Over the last 50 years, coffee production in India has grown by over 15%. From 1991, economic liberalization took place in India, and the industry took full advantage of this and cheaper labor costs of production. In 1993, a monumental Internal Sales Quota (ISQ) made the first step in liberalizing the coffee industry by entitling coffee farmers to sell 30% of their production within India. This was further amended in 1994 when the Free Sale Quota (FSQ) permitted large and small scale growers to sell between 70% and 100% of their coffee either domestically or internationally. A final amendment in September 1996 saw the liberalization of coffee for all growers in the country and a freedom to sell their produce wherever they wished.

Rev. Edward Terry, chaplain to Sir Thomas Roe who was ambassador at the court of Emperor Jehangir, provides a detailed account of its usage (1616):

"Many of the people there (in India), who are strict in their religion, drink no Wine at all; but they use a Liquor more wholesome than pleasant, they call Coffee; made by a black Seed boiled in water, which turns it almost into the same color, but doth very little alter the taste of the water: notwithstanding it is very good to help digestion, to quicken the spirits, and to cleanse the blood".

The British East India Company brought in fresh influences. David Burton, a food historian based in New Zealand writes in his book **The Raj at Table** (1993).

"India's first coffee house opened in Calcutta after the battle of Plassey in 1780. Soon after, John Jackson and Cottrell Barrett opened the original Madras Coffee House, which was followed in 1792 by the Exchange Coffee Tavern at the Muslim, waited at the mouth of the Madras Fort. The enterprising proprietor of the latter announced he was going to run his coffee house on the same lines as Lloyd's in London, by maintaining a register of the arrival and departure of ships, and offering Indian and European newspapers for his customers to read. Other houses also offered free use of billiard tables, recovering their costs with the high price of one rupee for a single dish of coffee".

So, just when and how did coffee, thus far an Arab / Muslim / European experience, percolate into the South Indian, and particularly, the Tamil Brahmin household? Literature and anecdotal evidence provide some clues, as evoked in this extract from the novel **Devadasi** by Kasturi Sreenivasan, under **Chapter I: The Course of True Lovers** (1977):

"Outside the temple, the petty vendors along the dusty street were doing a brisk trade by the light of smokey oil lamps". "Although Palayam was only a small town, one of its eating places started serving a new drink called coffee. It had been introduced by the British rulers and there were many stories about it. Some argued that, since it was of European origin, it must necessarily be unclean; others said it might be alcoholic. In any case, very few tried it, since a tumbler full cost as much as half an anna, while butter-milk was served free in many places and coconut water including the tender coconut meat was only a paisa. Only the most daring or the wealthy could afford the exotic brew. There was animated conversation about this and about various other things among the men who were slowly gathering in the temple courtyard. They talked about a new thing called a railway which had just been extended to the town from Madras recently".

Indian filter coffee was popularized by the India Coffee Houses run by the Coffee Board of India since mid 1940s. It became the drink of millions after the emergence of more popular Indian Coffee House in the mid 1950s. We can read this story in the Malayalam book Coffee Housintekatha by Nadakkal Parameswaran Pillai.

Indian filter coffee even migrated overseas in the early 20th century to Malaysia and Singapore, where *kopi tarik* (pulled coffee) is a close cousin of the Madrasi coffee-by-the-yard/meter, and was introduced at roadside *kopi tiams* run originally by Indian Muslims.

- A term often hard for high-quality coffee. Milk certified as pure with a lactometer was called degree milk owing to a mistaken association with the thermometer. Coffee prepared with degree milk became known as degree coffee.
- Another explanation for degree coffee is that chicory beans were used to make the coffee. The South Indian pronunciation of chickory became chigory then digory and finally degree.
- Yet another explanation is that, when coffee is decocted for the first time, it is called as the first degree or simply as the "Degree Coffee". This has the strongest flavor and the necessary strength to mix with milk without watering down the taste. In less affluent households, in earlier days, coffee was decocted for a second or third time from the same initial load; this became the second degree coffee and naturally, is not as strong. Affluent households drank first degree or the famous "Degree Coffee" only.
- The name derives from the filter used for making the decoction. Interestingly, there is a Kannada name for coffee "Boondh Bisneeru". "Bisneeru" sounds a great deal like " bisi neeru", or "hot water", thus leading to speculation that the terms are connected, although not used currently, this was used by ladies two generations ago. The Tamil name for coffee is "Kottai Vadineer".
- Connoisseurs and respected Coffee tasters world over generally agree that the effectiveness of extracting delicate flavors and aromas from coffee that is prepared using the Indian "degree" filter coffee technique is superior to the extraction techniques, like espresso makers, often used for milk based coffee beverages like lattes.

Indian Scene

South Indian coffee is brewed with a metal device that resembles two cylindrical cups, one of which has a pierced bottom that nests into the top of the "tumbler" cup, leaving ample room underneath to receive the brewed coffee. The upper cup has two removable parts: a pierced pressing disk with a central stem handle, and a covering lid.

The upper cup is loaded with fresh ground coffee mixed with chicory (~ 2 tablespoons of mixture per serving). The grounds are gently compressed with the stemmed disk into a uniform layer across the cup's pierced bottom. With the press disk left in place, the upper cup is nested into the top of the tumbler and boiling water is poured inside. The lid is placed on top, and the device is left to slowly drip the brewed coffee into the bottom. The chicory sort of holds on to the hot water a little longer, letting the water extract more flavor from the coffee powder It is a generally a stronger brew compared to western "drip style" coffee.

Traditional Madras-style Dabarah or Davarah and tumbler placed with the open end facing down as customary. The resulting brew is very potent, and is traditionally consumed by adding 1–2 tablespoons to a cup of boiling milk with the preferred amount of sugar. The coffee is drunk from the tumbler (although a word of English origin, it seems to be the most commonly used name for this vessel), but is often cooled first with a dabarah—"daBbarah" (also pronounced in some regions as "davarah"): a wide metal saucer with lipped walls.

Coffee is typically served after pouring back and forth between the dabarah and the tumbler in huge arc-like motions of the hand. This serves several purposes:

mixing the ingredients (including sugar) thoroughly; cooling the hot coffee down to a sipping temperature; and most importantly, aerating the mix without introducing extra water (such as with a steam wand used for frothing cappucinos).

Benefits

Two cups of coffee a day can help to relieve the movement-related symptoms associated with Parkinson's disease, a new research has claimed. Researchers from McGill University in Montreal found patients given caffeine supplements averaged a five-point improvement in symptoms compared to those given a placebo, the Daily Mail reported.

"This is a modest improvement but may be enough to provide benefit to patients", professor Ronald Postuma from the university, said. "It may not be sufficient to explain the relationship between caffeine non-use and Parkinson's since studies of progression of Parkinson's symptoms early in the disease suggesting a five-point reduction would delay diagnosis by only 6 months", Postuma was quoted by the paper as saying.

Coffee Beans

Special Proteins in Coffee Beans: A team of Brazilian scientists, a compound Legumin, feared in the unroasted coffee beans in coffee seeds, which represents 45% of its total protein content. It protects the plant from pests. Paulo Mazzafera from the University of Campinas in Brazil and his team used the protein from two species: (1) *Coffea arabica* and (2) *C racemosa* against cowpea weevil larvae. This impeded further growth. Experiments showed tiny amounts of the proteins could kill up to 50% of the insects. Weight of the surviving larvae lowered significantly.

"Scientists can insert such genes into important food crops such as wheat and maize so that the crops can produce their own insecticides", The proteins appear harmless to people and can cheaply be produced in large quantities via microbial cultures. According to Dawn Luthe, professor of plant stress biology at Penn State University in USA, if a combination containing a plant protein and a common insecticide is used, it may be more lethal to crop pests than either used alone. It will take longer for the insects to develop resistance to two modes of attack.

The **coffee industry of India** is the sixth largest producer of coffee in the world (Table 3.1), with the bulk of all production taking place in its Southern States. India is most noted for its Monsooned Malabar variety. It is believed that coffee has been cultivated in India longer than anywhere outside of the Arabian peninsula. India is known globally for shade-grown "mild" coffee, and is the only country growing all its coffee in the shade. Grown on an area of 2.92 lakh hectares, Indian, coffee is typically mild and not too acidic, and possesses an exotic full-bodied taste with a fine aroma. Around 75% of India's coffee output is exported.

Coffee production in India is dominated in the hill tracts of South Indian States, with the state of Karnataka accounting 53% followed by Kerala 28% and Tamil Nadu 11% of production of 8,200 tons. Indian coffee is said to be the finest coffee grown in the shade rather than direct sunlight anywhere in the world. There are approximately 250,000 coffee growers in India; 98% of them are small growers. As of 2009, the production of coffee in India was only 4.5% of the total production in the world. Almost 80% of the country's coffee production is exported. Of that which

Table 3.1: Coffee area, production and productivity–India

Season	Bearing area (hectares)			Production (MT)			Productivity (kg/hectares)		
	Arabica	Robusta	Total	Arabica	Robusta	Total	Arabica	Robusta	Overall
1950–51	67613	24910	92523	15511	3382	18893	229	136	204
1960–61	70649	49672	120321	39526	28643	68169	559	577	567
1970–71	80433	55030	135463	58348	51883	110231	725	943	814
1980–81	98005	92071	190076	61262	57384	118646	625	623	624
1985–86	108476	106000	214476	72311	50139	122450	667	473	571
1986–87	108500	107000	215500	88975	103119	192094	820	964	891
1987–88	108500	109500	218000	64556	58157	122713	595	531	563
1988–89	108500	112500	221000	94781	119934	214715	874	1066	972
1989–90	108500	112500	221000	62572	55481	118053	577	493	534
1990–91	108500	115000	223500	78311	91415	169726	722	795	759
1991–92	108500	115000	223500	88320	91680	180000	814	797	805
1992–93	108500	115000	223500	73120	96275	169395	674	837	758
1993–94	108500	118000	226500	98300	113700	212000	906	964	936
1994–95	108500	120000	228500	79000	101100	180100	728	843	788
1995–96	120100	121900	242000	103250	119750	223000	860	982	921
1996–97	125017	126267	251284	90450	114550	205000	724	907	816
1997–98	130664	154988	285652	99300	129000	228300	760	832	799
1998–99	143007	159227	302234	97000	168000	265000	678	1055	877
1999–00	146052	162381	308433	119000	173000	292000	815	1065	947
2000–01	146502	167432	313934	104400	196800	301200	713	1175	959
2001–02	149056	171681	320737	121050	179550	300600	812	1046	937
2002–03	146780	173835	320615	102125	173150	275275	696	996	859
2003–04	148389	176735	325124	101950	168550	270500	687	954	832
2004–05	153280	180058	333338	103400	172100	275500	675	956	826
2005–06	151547	189804	341351	94000	180000	274000	620	948	803
2006–07	151861	191179	343040	99700	188300	288000	657	985	840
2007–08	151013	193495	344508	92500	169500	262000	613	876	761
2008–09	156421	194079	350500	79500	182800	262300	508	942	748
2009–10	159828	195674	355502	94600	195000	289600	592	997	815
2010–11	163737	196748	360485	94140	207860	302000	575	1,056	838
2011–12	169906	198781	368687	101500	212500	314000	597	1,069	852
2012–13*	176131	200174	376305	98600	219600	318200	560	1,097	846

* Provisional (Final Estimate).

is exported, 70% is bound for Germany, Russian federation, Spain, Belgium, Slovenia, United States, Japan, Greece, Netherlands and France, and Italy accounts for 29% of the exports. Most of the export is shipped through the Suez Canal.

Coffee is grown in three regions of India with Karnataka, Kerala and Tamil Nadu forming the traditional coffee growing region of South India, followed by the new areas developed in the nontraditional areas of Andhra Pradesh and Orissa in the eastern coast of the country and with a third region comprising the states of Assam, Manipur, Meghalaya, Mizoram, Tripura, Nagaland and Arunachal Pradesh of Northeastern India, popularly known as "Seven Sister States of India".

Indian coffee, grown mostly in Southern India under monsoon rainfall conditions, is also termed as "Indian monsooned coffee". Its flavor is defined as: "The best Indian coffee reaches the flavor characteristics of Pacific coffees, but at its worst it is simply bland and uninspiring". The two well-known varieties of coffee grown are the Arabica and Robusta. The first variety that was introduced in the Baba Budan Giri hill ranges of Karnataka in the 17th century was marketed over the years under the brand names of Kent and S.795.

Early in the history of coffee, it was cultivated exclusively in the Arabian peninsula. To maintain this monopoly on coffee production, the Arabians forbade the export of coffee beans that had not been roasted or boiled enough to prevent germination. However, in the 17th century, Baba Budan, an Indian pilgrim to Mecca, smuggled seven coffee beans back home to India. There he planted the beans in the Mysore region, establishing the first coffee plantation in India. By 1840, under British rule, India began to grow coffee for export. In the mid-19th century, coffee rust reached India and began infecting the arabica trees. By 1869, the rust had become an epidemic. As a reaction to this, many of the farmers replaced the arabica trees with robusta, liberikca, or a rust-tolerant hybrid variety of arabica tree. These more resistant trees are still commonly grown in India.

There are over 170,000 coffee farms in India, cultivating nearly 900,000 acres of coffee trees. Most coffee production in India is on small farms, with over 90% of all farms consisting of 10 acres or fewer. However, such farms account for just over half of all land used for coffee production and a minority of all coffee produced. Most coffee in India is grown in three states: Karnataka, Kerala and Tamil Nadu. These states accounted for over 92% of India's coffee production in the 2005–2006 growing season.

While India has a tradition as one of the earlier growers of Arabica coffee, it produces currently more substantially more robusta beans. In the 2003–2004 growing season, approximately 52% of all coffee acreage was dedicated to robusta trees. However due to the higher yields of this tree, robusta accounted for 64% of all coffee produced in India. The exotic café wave swept across the country and there are close to 1,900 trendy Western-influenced coffee bars in India has now Bangalore, with more than 150 cafes, boasts of the best among them: Café Coffee Day, Barista lavazza, Costa Coffee, Java City, Mocha, Coffee World, Matteo, Café Pascucci, Gloria Jeans, Java Green and many more, spread across the length and breath of the city.

Production

Coffee is a perennial standing crop in India. It blossoms during February–March and is harvested during November–January, depending on the variety in the coffee-growing regions of India. The coffee-year officially lasts from October to September.

Coffee is mostly grown as a mixed crop in the country. Indian weather conditions—high temperature and long spell of rainfall, followed by a dry season—are not very suitable for coffee production. India produces both the types of coffee: Arabia and Robusta. Every year assessment of crop production is done at the time of blossom period during the month of April–May. Final production estimates are based on post blossom crop forecasts. Final data is thus available upto the year 2012–2013.

Like in Ceylon, coffee production in India declined rapidly from the 1870s and was massively outgrown by the emerging tea industry. The devastating coffee rust affected the output of coffee to the point that the costs of production saw coffee plantations in many parts replaced with tea plantations. However, the coffee industry was not as affected by this disease as in Ceylon, and although overshadowed in scale by the tea industry, India was still one of the strongholds of coffee production in the British Empire along with British Guiana. In the period 1910–1912, the area under coffee plantation was reported to be 203,134 acres (82,205 hectares) in the Southern states, and was mostly exported to England.

In the 1940s, Indian filter coffee, a sweet milky coffee made from dark roasted coffee beans (70–80%) and chicory (20–30%) became a commercial success. It was especially popular in the Southern States of Andhra Pradesh, Karnataka, Kerala and Tamil Nadu. The most commonly used coffee beans are Arabica and Robusta grown in the hills of Karnataka (Kodagu, Chikkamagaluru and Hassan), Kerala (Malabar region)and Tamil Nadu (Nilgiris District, Yercaud and Kodaikanal).

Total area during 1980–1981 was 208–209 thousand hectares which having touched 404.6 thousand hectares in 2010–2011 fell down to 325.3 thousand hectares in 2012–2013.

The share of Robusta area during this period increased from 27% in 1950–1951 to 54% in 1991–1992. Since then it has been hovering around 50% (Table 3.1A). Corresponding production of both the varieties increased from 18.9 thousand tons in 1950–1951 to 1 lakh tons in 1970–1971, to 2 lakh tons in 1980-81, and subsequently to 6 lakh tons in 1999–2000 and 3.47 lakh tones in 2013–2014. With the share of Robusta increasing from 18% in 1950–1951 to 70.0% in 2008–1909 but came down to 67–68% in the recent years (Table 3.1B). According to food and agricultural organization (FAO) production was only 43.2 thousand tons in 1961 and increased to 288 thousand tons in 2007 and has shown a small increase in the subsequent years.

Total coffee production during 2011–2012 and 2012–2013 was 314 and 315.5 thousand tons, respectively. The share of Robusta during 2012–2013 was 69% (Table 3.1C). Of late, coffee planters are shifting to robusta, as pests attack arabica. The robusta variety is slowly replacing arabica due to its lower susceptibility to diseases and higher productivity. Of course, arabica is of superior quality and fetches higher price. Hence any drop in the cultivated area of arabica will have a negative impact on the coffee industry.

Total area under coffee can be distributed into small and large holdings (Table 3.1D). There were approximately 250,000 coffee growers in India; 98% of them are small growers. Over 90% of them are small farms consisting of 10 acres (4.0 hectares) or fewer. According to published statistics for 2001–2002, the total area under coffee in India was 346,995 hectares with small holdings of 175,475 accounting for 71.2%. The area under large holding of more than 100 hectares (250 acres) was 31,571 hectares (78,010 acres) (only 9.1% of all holdings) only under

Table 3.1A: planted area of coffee in India since 1950–1951 to 2012–2013

(In hectares)

Year	Arabica	%	Robusta	%	Total
1950–1951	6,7613	73	24,910	27	92,523
1960–1961	7,0650	59	49,670	41	120,320
1970–1971	8,0433	59	55,030	41	135,463
1980–1981	109,454	53	98,815	47	208,269
1990–1991	127,934	47	142,887	53	270,821
1991–1992	126,889	46	151,742	54	278,631
1992–1993	141,546	49	149,465	51	291,011
1993–1994	143,491	49	148,976	51	292,467
1994–1995	142,644	49	150,465	51	293,109
1995–1996	145,901	48	159,252	52	305,153
1996–1997	143,239	47	160,582	53	303,821
1997–1998	143,928	47	161,974	53	305,902
1998–1999	160,671	49	168,567	51	329,238
1999–2000	168,453	50	171,853	50	340,306
2000–2001	167,679	48	179,037	52	346,716
2001–2002	165,892	48	181,103	52	346,995
2002–2003	171,180	48	182,872	52	354,052
2003–2004	170,294	48	184,546	52	354,840
2004–2005	174,315	48	188,769	52	363,084
2005–2006	177,728	47	201,981	53	379,709
2006–2007	179,096	47	201,989	53	381,085
2007–2008	184,418	48	203,777	52	388,195
2008–2009	189,511	48	204,841	52	394,352
2009–2010	193,995	49	205,688	51	399,683
2010–11	197,930	49	206,715	51	404,645
2011–12	201,070	49	208,620	51	409,690
2012–13*	205,775	50	209,566	50	415,341

* Provisional.

167 holdings. The area under less than 2 hectares (4.9 acres) holdings was 114,546 hectares (283,050 acres) (33% of the total area) among 138,209 holders (Tables 3.1E and F).

Small holdings which covered an area of around 75% produced 70% coffee (Table 3.1D). From among the small holders, those with less than 2 hectares covered more than 37% area and among the large holders, those with more than 25 hectares covered over 17% of the area.

The most important areas of production are in the southern Indian states of Karnataka, Kerala, and Tamil Nadu which accounted for over 92% of India's coffee production in the 2005–2006 growing season. In this same season, India exported

Table 3.1B: Production of coffee in India Since 1950–1951 to 2013–1914

(In tons)

Year	Arabica	%	Robusta	%	Total
1950–1951	15,511	82	3,382	18	18,893
1960–1961	39,526	58	28,643	42	68,169
1970–1971	58,348	53	51,883	47	110,231
1980–1981	61,262	52	57,384	48	118,646
1990–1991	78,311	46	91,415	54	169,726
1991–1992	88,320	49	91,680	51	180,000
1992–1993	73,120	43	96,275	57	169,395
1993–1994	98,300	46	113,700	54	212,000
1994–1995	79,000	44	101,100	56	180,100
1995–1996	103,250	46	119,750	54	223,000
1996–1997	90,450	44	114,550	56	205,000
1997–1998	99,300	43	129,000	57	228,300
1998–1999	97,000	37	168,000	63	265,000
1999–2000	11,9000	41	173,000	59	292,000
2000–2001	104,400	35	196,800	65	301,200
2001–2002	121,050	40	179,550	60	300,600
2002–2003	102,125	37	173,150	63	275,275
2003–2004	101,950	38	168,550	62	270,500
2004–2005	103,400	38	172,100	62	275,500
2005–2006	94,000	34	180,000	66	274,000
2006–2007	99,700	35	188,300	65	288,000
2007–2008	92,500	35	169,500	65	262,000
2008–2009	79,500	30	182,800	70	262,300
2009–2010	94,600	33	195,000	67	289,600
2010–2011	94,140	31	207,860	69	302,000
2011–2012	10,1500	32	212,500	68	314,000
2012–2013*	98,600	31	219,600	69	318,200
2013–2014*	11,1000	32	236,000	68	347,000

* Final Estimate.
** Post Blossom Estimate.

over 440,000 pounds (200,000 kg) of coffee, with over 25% destined for Italy. Traditionally, India has been a noted producer of Arabica coffee but in the last decade robusta beans are growing substantially due to high yields, which now account for over 60% of coffee produced in India. The domestic consumption of coffee increased from 50,000 tons in 1995 to 94,400 tons in 2008. According to the statistics provided by the Coffee Board of India, the estimated production of Robusta and Arabica coffee for the "Post Monsoon Estimation 2009–2010" and "Post Blossom Estimation 2010–2011" in different states accounted for a total of 308,000 tons and 289,600 tons, respectively. As of 2010, between 70% and 80% of Indian grown coffee is exported overseas.

Table 3.1C: Area, production exports and consumption of coffee by types

(Metric tons)

Year	Area (In hectares)	Production Arabica	Production Robusta	Production Total	Exports	Domestic consumption
1979–80	–	71,428	78,407	149,835	61,380	47,683
1980–81	208,269	61,262	57,384	118,646	86,253	50,786
1981–82	–	74,110	75,890	150,000	83,817	53,990
1982–83	–	74,326	55,626	129,952	83,824	56,079
1983–84	–	70,683	34,346	105,029	71,179	53,544
1984–85	–	80,046	115,064	195,110	68,896	54,874
1985–86	–	72,311	50,139	122,450	99,298	54,421
1986–87	–	88,975	103,119	192,094	86,666	58,636
1987–88	–	64,556	58,157	122,713	92,533	55,560
1988–89	–	94,781	119,934	214,715	98,266	63,328
1989–90	–	63,590	56,410	118,053	134,052	54,152
1990–91	270,821	80,535	89,465	170,000	100,110	49,200
1991–92	278,631	88,320	91,680	180,000	111,458	68,554
1992–93	291,011	83,000	86,395	169,395	113,585	55,810
1993–94	292,467	103,900	108,100	212,000	136,690	75,310
1994–95	293,109	87,670	92,430	180,100	137,395	42,705
1995–96	305,153	108,640	114,360	223,000	170,578	52,422
1996–97	303,821	99,790	105,210	205,000	181,237	23,763
1997–98	305,902	123,026	105,262	228,288	179,059	49,229
1998–99	329,238	142,810	122,190	265,000	211,623	53,377
1999–00	340,306	119,000	163,000	282,000	195,000	55,000
2000–01	346,716	104,400	196,800	301,000	247,000	54,000
2001–02	346,995	118,863	206,591	325,454	176,300	149,154
2002–03	354,052	100,436	174,564	275,275	207,333	70,000
2003–04	354,840	100,300	174,500	270,500	232,684	43,000
2004–05	363,084	116,800	175,600	275,500	211,715	75,000
2005–06	379,709	98,550	183,350	274,000	210,555	80,000
2006–07	381,085	104,380	196,000	288,000	249,030	75,000
2007–08	388,195	109,250	169,500	262,000	218,996	85,000
2008–09	394,352	79,500	182,800	262,300	210,000	94,400
2009–10	399,683	94,600	195,000	289,600	197,169	102,000
2010–11	404,645	94,140	207,860	302,000	298,813	108,000
2011–12	409,690	101,500	212,500	314,000	324,253	107,000
2012–13	325,300	100,225	215,275	315,500	332,107	

Source: Coffee Board.

Table 3.1D: Area and share of production of coffee under different coffee holdings in India, 2007–2008

Sr. No.	Size of holdings (in hectares)	No. of holdings		Area under coffee		Share of production (%)
		Number	Total (%)	Area (in hectares)	Total (%)	
1.	**Small holdings**					
	< 2	178585	80.9	144196	37.1	
	2–4	27731	12.6	71905	18.5	
	4–10	11800	5.3	73642	19.0	
	Total	**218116**	**98.8**	**289743**	**74.6**	**70**
2.	**Large holdings**					
	10–25	1789	0.8	29829	7.7	
	> 25	920	0.4	68623	17.7	
	Sub-total	**2709**	**1.2**	**98452**	**25.4**	**30**
3.	**Total (India)**	**220825**	**100.00**	**388195**	**100.00**	**100**

Table 3.1E: Number and area under different size of holding, 2001–2002

Size of holdings	Numbers	Age (%)	Area	Age (%)
Less than 10 and 10 hectares	175,475	71.2	247,087	71.2
Between 10 and 100 hectares and above	2833	28.8	99,908	28.8
Total	178,308	100	346,995	100

Growing Conditions

All coffees grown in India are grown in shade and commonly with two tiers of shade. Often inter-cropped with spices such as cardamom, cinnamon, clove, and nutmeg, the coffees gain aromatics from the inter-cropping, storage, and handling functions. Growing altitudes range between 1,000 m (3,300 feet) and 1,500 m (4,900 feet) above sea level for Arabica(premier coffee), and 500 m (1,600 feet) to 1,000 m (3,300 feet) for Robusta (though of lower quality, it is robust to environment conditions). Ideally, both Arabica and Robusta are planted in well drained soil conditions that favor rich organic matter that is slightly acidic (pH 6.0–6.5). However, India's coffees tend to be moderately acidic which can lead to either a balanced and sweet taste, or a listless and inert one. Slopes of Arabica tend to be gentle to moderate, while Robusta slopes are gentle to fairly level.

Blooming is the time when coffee plants bloom with white flowers which last for about 3–4 days (termed "evanescent" period) before they mature into seeds. When coffee plantations are in full bloom it is a delightful sight to watch. The time period between blooming and maturing of the fruit varies appreciably with the variety and the climate; for the Arabica, it is about 7 months, and for the Robusta, about 9 months. The fruit is gathered by hand when it is fully ripe and red-purple in color.

Coffee productivity is adversely affected by the vagaries of the weather. Other problems include: nonscientific cultivation, unsuitable location, delay in supply of input, improper handling and pruning systems, adverse biological properties of soil, old moribund plants, inadequate irrigation, poor management of pest/diseases, and poor status of the farmers. While during 1950–1951, Arabica yield was 229 kg per hectares, Robusta was only 136 kg/hectares against the overall level 204 kg/hectares. From 1960–1961 onward, Robusta took the lead with fluctuations from year to year. The highest level touched by Arabica has been 906 kg/hectares in 1993–1994 as against 1,175 kg/hectares for Robusta in 2000–2001. Since coffee plants do not give good yield every year, they show regular fluctuations. The Coffee Board has expressed concern over the high use of pesticides such as Lindane (gamma BHC) and chlorphyriphos to combat the white stem borer (WSB). Coffee importing countries have put in place stringent controls to check the residue level in respect of Lindane in coffee.

Statewise area, production and yield (Table 3.2) shows that Karnataka alone has more than half the area and nearly 65% of production. Major states which are producing coffee are Karnataka, Kerala, Tamil Nadu and Andhra Pradesh. Coffee is produced in small quantities in the North East Region. Coffee cultivation in nontraditional areas has expanded by 8% to cross 50,000 hectares in 2008–2009, compared to the previous year. In India, the nontraditional coffee growing areas are in Visakhapatnam and in east Godavari district in Andhra Pradesh, southern districts in Orissa (bordering Andhra Pradesh), and Northeastern states. Coffee cultivation in nontraditional areas has been expanding on an average of 4,000 hectares annually. This is attributed to initiatives of the state governments, and support extended by the Coffee Board. This has provided more employment opportunities to tribal people (Table 3.2A).

District-wise production data (Table 3.3) shows that Kodagu (Karnataka) alone is responsible for over 38% of the production of these two varieties in India of which Robusta alone is more than 80%. Other districts: Chikmagalur (Karnataka) and Wayanad (Kerala) are important. Together they produce over 41%.

Labor Employment

Average daily number of persons employed in recent years has increased from 0.5 million in 2002–2003 to 0.6 million by 2011–2012.

Steps that Need to be Taken

The Board and plantation owners need to give priority to disease-resistance varieties, and good processing methods to ensure quality. Investment must be made in combined use of manual and chemical weed control methods, preservation of soil moisture, better managerial practices and marketing infrastructure. The Indian coffee sector has to be technology and research driven rather than being subsidy driven. Also, while exports are important, the country has to demonstrate the potential in terms of local coffee consumption. According to experts, manufactures should be awarded for retailing and coffee processing systems, as opposed to higher production.

Indian Specialty Coffees

India offers several varieties of specialty coffees that are popular in the West. Continuous research by Indian scientists has helped identify better strains that will

Table 3.2: Area, production and average yield statewise coffee

Area: in thousand hectares;   Production: in thousand tons;   Yield: per hectare in kg.

States	1977 -78	1978 -79	1979 -80	1980 -81	1981 -82	1982 -83	1983 -84	1984 -85	1985 -86	1986 -87	1987 -88	1988 -89	1989 -90	1990 -91	1991 -92	1992 -93	1993 -94	1994 -95	1995 -96	1996 -97
SOUTH																				
Andhra Pradesh																				
Area	2	2.4	2.5	3.1	5.7	5.8	7.4	7.7	7.6	7.8	7.3	7.3	9.1	9.3	9.8	9.3		9.3	9.3	9.3
Prod.	0.3	0.2	0.2	0.3	0.4	0.5	0.5	0.5	0.6	0.4	0.9	0.6	0.5	0.7	0.4	0.7	1.0	2.0	1.5	1.7
Yield	150	83	80	97	70	86	68	0	0	0	0	0	55	75	41	75	0	215	161	183
Karnataka																				
Area	92.3	93.5	100.4	104.5	108.4	110.2	113.1	115.6	117.5	116.7	115.8	113.9	108.8	123.7	134.1			128.4	141.1	143.8
Produ.	88.8	79.3	107.4	82.1	101.9	100	79.3	141.6	84.8	145.0	80.7	161.9	86.7	136.4	139.6	120	144.9	123.1	158.9	141.0
Yield	962	848	1070	786	940	907	701	1225	722	1243	697	1421	797	1103	1041	0	0	959	1126	981
Kerala																				
Area	30.6	36.9	39.1	55.4	55.1	60	61.6	61.7	61.7	62.8	65.4	68.1	63.5	70.4	79.2			67.2	62.6	82.6
Produ.	25.3	19	29.1	21.1	32.7	15.4	9.6	37.3	23.6	33.0	22.6	38.4	14.9	21.9	20.1	25.0	46.8	39	45.0	47.3
Yield	827	515	744	381	593	257	156	605	382	525	346	564	235	311	254	0	0	580	719	573
Tamil Nadu																				
Area	25.1	25.1	28.1	28.5	28.4	28.7	28.4	27.3	30.4	29.5	28.9	29.1	28.8	29.4	27.8			25.4	25.9	28.5
Produ.	10.5	11.7	12.8	15	14.9	14	15.5	15.6	13.8	13.8	18.6	12.8	15.6	10.3	17.8	15.2	15.8	15.9	17.5	15.7
Yield	418	466	456	526	525	488	546	571	454	468	644	440	542	350	640	0	0	626	676	551
Other States																				
Area	1	1	1	1.7	2	2.1	4	4.8	5.0	5.9	7	6.4	7.6	8.6	10.5			1.5	4.2	5.2
Prod.	0.2	0.3	0.2	0.1	0.1	0.1	0.1	0.1	0.2	0.1	0.2	1.0	0.4	0.1	2.1	0.1	0.1	0.1	0.2	0.2
Yield	200	300	200	59	50	48	25	21	40	17	29	156	53	12	200	0	0	67	48	38
All-India																				
Area	149	156.6	168.6	190.1	193.9	201	207.1	209.4	240.6	214.9	217.1	217.5	208.7	232.1	251.6			228.5	242.0	251.8
prod.	125.1	110.5	149.8	118.6	150	130	105	195.1	122.3	192.3	123.0	214.7	118.1	169.7	180.0	161.5	208.0	180.1	223.1	205.9
Yield	840	706	888	624	774	647	507	932	508	895	567	987	566	731	715	0	0	788	922	818

Sources: Area and Production of Principal Crops in India (Various Issues), Directorate of Economics and Statistics, Department of Agriculture and Co-operation, Ministry of Agriculture.

Table 3.2A: State-wise coffee area statistics in NE region

(up to march 2004)

State	Assam	Arunachal Pradesh	Meghalaya	Mizoram	Manipur	Nagaland	Tripura
Planted area (In hectares):							
Arabica	1151.00	209.00	930.00	1003.00	102.00	3018.00	248.00
Robusta	942.50	800	1123.50	3.50	-	400	1019.85
Total	2093.70	1009.00	2053.50	1006.50	102.50	3418.00	1267.85
Non bearing area:							
Arabica	238.60	103.00	140.50	681.50	82.00	458.00	237.45
Robusta	646.90	510.00	48.50	-	-	195.00	933.00
Total	885.50	613.00	189.00	681.50	82.00	653.00	1170.45
Bearing area:							
Arabica	912.60	106.00	789.50	321.50	20.00	2560.00	10.55
Robusta	295.60	290.00	1075.00	3.50	0.00	205.00	86.85
Total	**1208.20**	**396.00**	**1864.50**	**325.00**	**20.00**	**1665.00**	**97.40**

Source: The joint director (Extn.), Coffee Board Guwahati.

make finer coffees with added flavor profiles, in both Arabica and Robusta varieties. *Monsooned coffee.* The "monsooning" of coffee first happened quite by accident. A shipload of coffee bound for Europe acquired a mellow yet unique taste *en route*, with the coffee beans "swelling" due to the moisture in the air and a new kind of coffee was born.

Main grades of monsooned coffee are:

1. Monsooned malabar AA
2. Monsooned basanally
3. Monsooned robusta AA.

Mysore Nuggets Extra Bold

This is a premium-quality coffee. The beans are very large, uniform blush green in colour with a clean polished appearance. In cup, the coffee exhibits full aroma, medium to good body, good acidity and fine flavor with a hint of spice. This coffee is prepared from Arabica plantation coffee (washed coffee) grown in the Mysore, Coorg, Biligiris and Shevaroys regions.

Robusta kaapi royale: This coffee is prepared from robusta parchment AB from the regions of Mysore, Coorg, Wayanad, Shevaroys, Pulneys and Bàbabudans. The beans appear to be bold and round with pointed ends, and gray to bluish gray in color. This cup ensures full body, soft, smooth and mellow flavor.

Cat Coffee

It takes guts to make the most expensive coffee.

Asian palm civet: Natural processor of Kopi Luwak or cat coffee beans.

The shiny, greenish-gray beans look no worse off for having passed through the Asian palm civet's digestive system. One can't tell the difference between this coffee

Table 3.3: Labor employment average daily number of persons employed in coffee plantations of India

Sl. No.	State/District	2002–2003	2003–2004	2004–2005	2005–2006	2006–2007	2007–2008	2008–2009	2009–2010	2010–2011	2011–2012
I.	**Karnataka**										
1	Chikmagalur	128520	131620	131620	132542	132572	132572	133921	134029	134029	134343
2	Coorg	197550	202941	214421	246022	248849	254001	254001	254628	254628	257578
3	Hassan	87300	88146	88663	88663	86663	89115	90537	90796	91856	93149
4	Mysore	729	744	–	–	–	–	–	–	–	–
	Total	**414099**	**423451**	**434704**	**467227**	**468084**	**475688**	**478459**	**479453**	**480513**	**485070**
II.	**Kerala**										
1	Wyanad	31249	31393	31392	31392	31392	31392	31383	31383	31383	31354
2	Travancore	9436	9506	9461	9453	9453	9562	9562	9637	9739	9799
3	Nelliampathies	2502	2515	2515	2515	2515	2515	2515	2515	2515	2515
	Total	**43187**	**43415**	**43368**	**43360**	**43360**	**43469**	**43460**	**43535**	**43637**	**43668**
III.	**Tamil Nadu**										
1	Pulneys	17946	18159	18159	18159	18159	18159	18159	18159	18159	18872
2	Nilgiris	3267	3281	3281	3281	3281	3281	3281	3281	3281	3281
3	Salem (Shevroys)	3447	3471	3471	3471	3941	3941	3941	3941	3941	3526
4	Coimbatore (Anamalais)	2034	2049	2049	2049	2049	2049	2049	2049	2049	2056
	Total	**26694**	**26960**	**26960**	**26960**	**27430**	**27430**	**27430**	**27430**	**27430**	**27735**
IV.	Nontraditional area	12866	33605	37667	40707	40252	40707	44836	44290	47771	50229
	Grand total (India)	**496845**	**527431**	**542699**	**578254**	**579126**	**587294**	**594185**	**594708**	**599351**	**606702**

Note: Estimated based on the average number of permanent and casual labor employed in different zones.

and the normal parchment coffee, but connoisseurs say it has a subtle nuttiness", said septuagenarian coffee planter T S Ganesh, the only producer of this rare coffee in India. He calls it Kari Beck coffee, after the Kannada name for civet. In the 1980s, Ganesh, then a small scale industrialist in Bengaluru, read in the National Geographic about Kopi Luwak or cat coffee. In the 1990s, when he saw lumps of coffee beans lying around in his plantation, he knew instantly he was looking at the world's most expensive coffee.

Passing through the gut of the cat, which eats coffee berries for their juicy pulp, does not change the beans in any visible way. "The scat is clean, containing nothing but beans", assured Ganesh. They just have to be washed, dried and husked. They do not even need to be fermented like parchment coffee-the cat does that job in a single night. The global yield of Kopi Luwak is about 200 kg a year, and its price in the international market is a whopping US$600 a kg. After all, one has to go around looking for the lumps under bushes. Ganesh produces 3–4 kg a year on his 9 hectare plantation in the Biligiri Ranganatha Temple Wildlife Sanctuary in Chamarajanagar district of Karnataka.

The civet that value-adds Ganesh's coffee beans also visits farms of 2,500 Soliga tribal families who cultivate coffee in the sanctuary. Stories of how he sells beans from civet scat at Rs 250 a kg more than twice the price the Soligas receive-have been around for years but no one has tried to process them separately.

Is it not possible to train the tribals how to produce the expensive beans? Ganesh thinks

> **What makes it special**
> - Enzymes in civet's gut remove bitterness and enhance flavour.
> - Less bitter than ordinary coffee.
> - Produced in Indonesia, East Timor, Vietnam, the Philippines
> - Vietnam produces chemically stimulated cat coffee.

not, for several reasons. First, there is no market in India. "I have tried sending samples to several European countries. The response was enthusiastic but I didn't receive any order. Probably they don't trust India because it is not a conventional source of the coffee variety", Ganesh said. He also fears that given the lure of better prices, some could cheat by mixing the excreted seed with ordinary coffee beans, which, in the international market would mean swift and permanent blacklisting of the country.

Farmers Trying Coffee on Lower Hills

The Agriculture Department has started coffee cultivation on a trial basis on 25 bighas each in Mandi, Una, Kangra and Bilaspur districts. Agriculture Director JC Rana said they had started the plantation in collaboration with the Coffee Board, Bangalore. Traditionally, coffee is grown in Karnataka, Kerala and Tamil Nadu and nearly 70% of the crop is exported.

Last year, we wrote a letter to the board to explore the possibilities of coffee cultivation in Himachal". A team from Bangalore visited the state to conduct a survey of the areas in Kangra, Una, Bilaspur, Hamirpur, Mandi and Chamba districts. The team found the potential of coffee in the lower areas of Bilaspur, Mandi, Una and Kangra districts, he said. "Then we sent a team of nine officials for a week-long training to Chikmangalur in Karnataka".

"We also procured seed from Chikmangalur and raised a nursery of 20,000 saplings at Palampur and distributed the plants free of cost among farmers who were willing to experiment with an alternative crop", he said and adding that the saplings were planted in October–November under the supervision of officials and had shown remarkable growth so far. They would also arrange a trip of the farmers to the coffee growing areas in the South and also give them training on fruit processing.

On precautions to be taken, the director said the plants had to be protected from heavy frost during winters and they needed surface irrigation in the months of April and May. On coffee experimentation in the Himalayas, Dr Dharamvir Kanwar, state nodal officer for the coffee plantation and Technical Officer, Tea, Palampur, said some farmers in Bilaspur had already done some experiments with the crop.

He said two main varieties of coffee—Arabica and Robusta—were given to farmers and 200 saplings of Arabica or 150 saplings of Robusta could be planted in a bigha.

Dr Kanwar said the plants would start producing flowers after four years and the fully grown plants, after eight years, could produce 1,600 kg fruits per bigha and a farmer could fetch Rs 250–300 per kg in the market.

Mandi Deputy Director, Agriculture, Dr RK Koundal said the saplings were planted in Dharampur, Chotra, Drang, Sadar and Gopalpur blocks. Sohan Lal, a farmer of Jhmerh village, Chauntra block in Jogindernagar, said he had planted 200 saplings on five bighas of land. Lal said when he was posted in Karnataka, he thought of cultivating coffee in Himachal and when he got an offer from the Agriculture Department, he readily agreed.

Surender Thakur, a specialist, said, "A coffee plant needs natural shade to grow as it has to be protected from direct sunlight and frost. The temperature should not go below 7° in winter and beyond 35 degrees in summer".

A BRAND FOR COFFEE

Criteria were laid down for the Arabicas/Robustas focusing on the bean size, the method of drying and other factors. To qualify as Mysore Nuggets extra bold, for instance, the Arabica bean size needs to be more than 7.5 millimeter. For coffee connoisseurs, Indian coffee was very often called as Mysore coffee. The Robusta Kaapi Royale is made from bold beans with size of 7 millimeters and the beans should be defect-free and bear a neutral taste in the cup. Thanks to the stringent quality norms, the quantum of such specialty coffees is extremely limited.

The output of the Robusta Kaapi Royale is pegged around 4,000 tons while in case of Mysore Nuggets extra bold it is around 8,000–10,000 tons. The Coffee Board has assigned the Nandi (the vehicle of Lord Shiva) logo to Mysore Nuggets extra bold while the Robusta Kaapi Royale logo features an elephant carrying a howdah. In the initial phase, while Mysore Nuggets extra bold was sourced from regions like Bababudangiri and Manzarabad and parts of Chikmagalur (Karnataka), Robusta Kaapi Royale was sourced from parts of Kerala (Waynad and Travancore) and Chikmagalur. The genetic branding of India coffee through Muthamma (the women coffee bean collector depicted in a Madhubani painting) has growing acceptability. Muthamma is India's answer to the person from Colombia's Juan Valdez.

Research and Development

Coffee research and development efforts are well organized in India through its Coffee Research Institute, which is considered the premier research station in South East Asia. It is under the control of the Coffee Board of India, an autonomous body, under the Ministry of Commerce and Industry, Government of India, which was set up under an Act of the Parliament with the objective of promoting "research, development, extension, quality up gradation, market information, and the domestic and external promotion of Indian coffee". It was established near Balehonnur in Chikmagalur district of Karnataka, in the heartland of coffee plantations. Prior to establishing this institute, a temporary research unit was established in 1915 at Koppa primarily to evolve solutions to crop infestation by leaf diseases. This was followed by the field research station established by the then Government of Mysore, titled "Mysore Coffee Experimental Station", in 1925. This was handed over to the Coffee Board which was formed in 1942, and regular research started at this station from 1944. Dr LC Coleman is credited as the founder of coffee research in India. The Coffee Board of India is an autonomous body, functioning under the Ministry of Commerce and Industry, Government of India. The Board serves as a friend, philosopher and guide of the coffee industry in India. Setup under an Act of the Parliament of India in the year 1942, the Board focuses on research, development, extension, quality up gradation, market information, and the domestic and external promotion of Indian coffee.

The research activities covered by the Institute constitute research in seven disciplines such as Agronomy, Soil Science and Agricultural Chemistry, Botany, Entomology/Nematology, Plant Physiology, Biotechnology and Post Harvest Technology with the basic aim of increasing productivity and quality of coffee grown in India. The institute has 60 scientific and technical personnel involved in research activities. The institute has a well-established farm land of 130.94 hectares (323.6 acres) for carrying out crop research, out of which 80.26 hectares (198.3 acres) are dedicated to coffee research 51.32 hectares (126.8 acres) of arabica and 28.94 hectares (71.5 acres) of robusta), 10 hectares (25 acres) are used for growing CXR, 12.38 hectares (30.6 acres) are apportioned for nurseries, roads and buildings, and the balance area of 12.38 hectares (30.6 acres) is a reserve area for future expansion. The research farm has a well established network of check dams that provides a regulated water source to the plantations which offer a wide range of shade tree species under which coffee is grown, and germplasm and exotic material from all the coffee growing countries including Ethiopia which is known as the home land of Arabica. In addition, crop diversification with crops such as pepper and areca are also part of income generating programs of the institute. Part of the institute includes a research laboratory to carry out research in identified disciplines, as well as a stocked library with books and periodicals, not only on coffee but also on other crops. Training of personnel is an important activity of the institute. The training unit of the institute conducts regular training programs for estate managers and supervisory personnel of the coffee plantations and also for the extension officers of the Coffee Board. Recognized by United Nations Development Program (UNDP) and US Department of Agriculture (USDA), the training unit of the institute is providing training to foreign nationals on coffee cultivation in which personnel from Ethiopia, Vietnam, Sri Lanka, Nepal, and Nestle Singapore have been trained. In addition, a Plant Tissue Culture and Biotechnology division, established in

Mysore, is carrying out exclusive research in biotechnology and molecular biology to supplement/complement the conventional breeding programs in developing high yielding, pest and disease resistant varieties. The Coffee Board of India maintains a Quality Control Division in its head office in Bangalore which plays an active role in collaborating with other research disciplines in upgrading the "quality of coffee in the cup".

Regional Research Stations

To cover research specific to each coffee growing region covering different agro-climatic conditions, the following five research stations are fully functional under the overall control of the Central Coffee Research Institute.

- Coffee Research Sub-station (CRSS), Chettalli in Coorg district of Karnataka, was established in 1946. The substation has a well equipped laboratory and covers an area of 131 hectares (320 acres) out of which 80 hectares (200 acres) is exclusive to coffee research activities.
- Regional Coffee Research Station (RCRS), RV Nagar in Visakhapatanam district of Andhra Pradesh also covers the Orissa on the Eastern coast. The research station, established in 1976 to cater to the development of coffee in non-traditional areas has an area of 30 hectares (74 acres) under coffee plantation. The objective of introducing coffee in this area was to wean away the tribal population from growing crops under the "Podu" cultivation (shifting cultivation) in the forest areas, not only to preserve the forest ecology but also to improve the economic condition of the tribal people of the region.
- Regional Coffee Research Station (RCRS), Chundale village in Wayanad district of Kerala was established primarily to develop appropriate technologies to suit the region where robusta is the dominant crop. Kerala is reckoned as the second largest coffee producing state in the country with robusta variety of coffee. The station covers an area of 116 hectares (290 acres) with 30 hectares (74 acres) of farm with an adequate laboratory support for research.
- Regional Coffee Research Station, Thandigudi in Dindigul district of Tamil Nadu. The research station was established with the sole aim of evolving suitable practices for the cultivation of coffee area in Tamil Nadu which receives major rainfall (but scanty) during the Northeast monsoon, unlike the other regions of the country. This station is spread over an area of 12.5 hectares (31 acres) including a research farm of 6.5 hectares (16 acres) with laboratory facilities.
- Regional Coffee Research Station, Diphu in Karbi Anglon district of Assam was established to support coffee plantations which were established in the Northeast region in 1980 to provide an alternate, economically viable agricultural practice to the shifting or jhum cultivation, widely practiced by the tribals in the forested hills, which was a cause of concern to preserve the ecology of the region. This regional station is spread over an area of 25 hectares (62 acres).

Post-Monsoon Coffee Crop Estimate for the Season 2013–2014

The post-monsoon crop forecast for the year 2013–2014 is placed at 311,500 MT, which shown a reduction of 35,500 MT (–10.23%) over the post-blossom estimate of

2013–2014 of 347,000 MT. Of the total estimate, the breakup for Arabica and Robusta is 102,000 MT and 209,500 MT, respectively. Arabica production estimate has shown a decline of 9,000 MT (–8.11%) while robusta declined by 26,500 MT (–11.23%) over the post-blossom estimate of 2013–14. By the states, the decline is mainly seen in Karnataka to the tune of 31,415 MT (–12.61%) while Kerala has shown a marginal decrease of 3,275 MT (–4.64%) compared to the post-blossom estimate.

In Karnataka, Kodagu district experienced a decline of 17,845 MT (–13.28%) both in Arabica (3,025 MT or –12.55%) and robusta (14,820 MT or –13.43%) followed by Chikmangalur (8,060 MT or –10.26%) and Hassan (5,510 MT or –15.25%) over the post-blossom forecast. The reasons for reduction in production estimates is attributed that during the current cropping season, coffee areas have witnessed a long period of drought after receiving blossom showers, followed by an extremely harsh monsoon. The monsoon which started on time continued unabated very heavily with some areas witnessing continuous rainfall for more than 60 days. The continuous showers led to soil saturation and wet feet conditions resulting in defoliation, berry drop and incidences of stalk rot and black rot. Uprooting of shade trees too has been reported. It may be noted that before the onset of monsoon, there was a heavy proliferation of White Stem Borer because of the long period of drought in the months of April/May, but subsequent monsoon rains helped in preventing further spread of this pest. Taking into account of all these factors, the post-monsoon crop estimate for Karnataka is placed at 217,700 MT with a breakup of 78,530 MT of Arabica and 139,170 MT of robusta.

In Kerala, the adverse effect on crop due to premature berry drop, stalk rot and black rot diseases due to continuous rain was less prominent overall, but resulted in marginal decline in Wayana (2800 MT or 4.60%) and Travancore (450 MT or –5.52%) regions over the post blossom estimate. Therefore the post-monsoon forecast is placed at 67.275 MT (Arabica 2000 MT and Robusta 65,275 MT) against the post blossom estimate of 70,550 MT.

In Tamil Nadu post-monsoon forecast is placed at 18,875 MT against 19,125 MT of post-blossom estimate which is a marginal decrease in production of 250 MT mainly observed in Adalur and Bodinayakanur of Pulneys region due to deficit in rainfall.

In nontraditional areas of Andhra Pradesh and Orissa and North Eastern Region, the post-monsoon forecast is placed at 7,650 MT against post-blossom estimate of 8,010 MT.

CONSUMPTION

Coffee consumption is influenced by a number of factors. In the Indian context, the important factors include the promotion of the coffee cafe culture, leading to an increase in the number of coffee bars and cafes; the changing lifestyles of the Indian middle class, and the steady pace of urbanization. Of course, the volume of coffee consumed is very often over estimated because chicory is blended with coffee.

Coffee consumption is concentrated in the Southern States. Around 78% of the total consumption, per capita availability for consumption according to Economic Survey increased from 80 g in 1960–1961 to 95 g in 2011–2012 (Table 3.4). FAO data shows that per capita consumption in India was 100 gm during the period 2002–2007. At the international level, Luxembourg was the highest consumer from 15.2 kg in 2002 to 18.2 kg in 2007.

Steady Rise in India's Coffee Consumption

Despite the fast growth of bottled juices and aerated drinks, consumption of tea and coffee is going up in India. Coffee consumption is up by 6% in the last few years while tea consumption has been showing a 3% annual growth.

Product innovation and better marketing strategy have helped coffee demand to spread to North India. Tea continues to be the common man's drink throughout the country. Widespread popularity of carbonated beverages supported by intense promotional campaigns has not made a dent in the consumption of tea and coffee. Mushrooming coffee bars and cafes have made coffee drinking fashionable in cities. Coffee consumption has been aided by increasing urbanization and greater disposable income. Admittedly, South India as a region has the largest number of coffee drinkers.

A recent survey by Coffee Board shows that of late more than 50% growth has come from non-South regions. Coffee consumption has shown an annual average growth of 6% since 2000. In the previous decades, the growth was just 2%. "Apart from the high-end outlets, the consumption of instant coffee is increasing in North India. Our attempt is to popularize filter coffee in the region by removing the notion that it is difficult to make.

The proportion of occasional coffee drinkers has increased in the last few years in the non-South regions. The board is keen on exploiting this potential of non-South states.

The higher consumption of coffee and tea is taking place at a time when India is fast emerging as a major market for soft drink and fruit juices. "India is a focus market for the Coca-Cola Company. The India business has now been growing for the last 19 quarters".

The India Coffee House chain was first started by the Coffee Board in early 1940s, during British rule. In the mid-1950s, the Board closed down the Coffee Houses, due to a policy change. However, the discharged employees then took over the branches, under the leadership of the then communist leader AK Gopalan and renamed the network as Indian Coffee House. The first Indian Coffee Workers Co-Operative Society was established in Bangalore on 19 August 1957. The first Indian Coffee House was opened in New Delhi on 27 October 1957. Gradually, the Indian Coffee House chain expanded across the country, with branches in Pondicherry, Thrissur, Lucknow, Nagpur, Jabalpur, Mumbai, Kolkata, Tellicherry and Pune by the end of 1958. These coffee houses in the country are run by 13 cooperative societies, which are governed by managing committees elected from the employees. A federation of the cooperative societies is the national umbrella organization to lead these societies. However, now Coffee bars have gained in popularity with other chains such as Barista; Café Coffee Day is the country's largest coffee bar chain. In the Indian home, coffee consumption is greater in south India than elsewhere. Indian coffee has a good reputation in Europe for its less acidic and sweetness of character and thus widely used in Espresso Coffee, though Americans prefer African and South American coffee, which is a more acidic and brighter variety.

Table 3.4: Per capita availability of certain important articles of consumption

Year	Edible oil[a] (kg)	Vanaspati[a] (kg)	Sugar[b] (Nov-Oct) (kg)	Cloth[c] Cotton[e] (meters)	Cloth[c] Man-made (meters)	Cloth[c] Total (meters)	Tea[d] (gram)	Coffee[e] (gram)	Electricity domestic[b] (KWH)
1	2	3	4	5	6	7	8	9	10
1960-61	3.2	0.8	4.8	13.8	1.2	15.0	296.0	80.0	3.4
1970-71	3.5	1.0	7.4	13.6	2.0	15.6	401.0	65.0	7.0
1971-72	3.0	1.1	6.8	12.4	2.2	14.6	426.0	65.0	7.3
1972-73	2.4	1.0	6.2	13.2	2.0	15.2	458.0	69.0	7.3
1973-74	3.4	0.8	6.1	12.0	1.9	13.9	492.0	64.0	8.1
1974-75	3.3	0.6	5.8	12.9	1.7	14.6	471.0	62.0	8.8
1975-76	3.5	0.8	6.1	12.6	2.0	14.6	446.0	62.0	9.7
1976-77	3.2	0.9	6.0	11.4	2.4	13.8	450.0	71.0	10.4
1977-78	3.8	0.9	7.2	9.5	4.0	13.5	516.0	73.0	10.9
1978-79	3.8	1.0	9.6	10.2	4.8	15.0	599.0	77.0	11.9
1979-80	3.7	1.0	7.8	10.1	4.6	14.7	521.0	73.0	12.1
1980-81	3.8	1.2	7.3	12.9	4.4	17.3	511.0	79.0	13.5
1981-82	5.1	1.3	8.2	12.2	4.9	17.1	466.0	79.0	15.1
1982-83	4.5	1.3	9.0	11.8	4.3	16.1	525.0	82.0	17.0
1983-84	5.8	1.2	10.5	12.6	4.7	17.3	519.0	78.0	18.3
1984-85	5.5	1.3	10.7	12.6	4.6	17.2	576.0	72.0	21.0
1985-86	5.0	1.3	11.1	15.4	6.1	21.5	589.0	71.0	22.9
1986-87	5.0	1.2	11.4	15.2	6.6	21.8	545.0	76.0	25.1
1987-88	5.8	1.2	11.7	14.0	7.0	21.0	592.0	72.0	28.2
1988-89	5.3	1.2	12.1	15.0	8.0	23.0	612.0	79.0	30.9
1989-90	5.3	1.1	12.3	14.6	8.1	22.7	571.0	65.0	36.1
1990-91	5.5	1.0	12.7	15.1	9.0	24.1	612.0	59.0	38.2
1991-92	5.4	1.0	13.0	13.7	9.2	22.9	655.0	64.0	41.9
1992-93	5.8	1.0	13.7	15.6	8.9	24.5	649.0	60.0	45.6
1993-94	6.1	1.0	12.5	15.9	10.3	26.2	667.0	56.0	48.8
1994-95	6.3	1.0	13.2	15.2	10.8	26.0	664.0	55.0	53.0
1995-96	7.0	1.0	14.1	16.3	11.7	28.0	646.0	55.0	56.2
1996-97	8.0	1.0	14.6	16.2	13.1	29.3	657.0	58.0	58.6
1997-98	6.2	1.0	14.5	15.9	15.0	30.9	635.0	58.0	62.9
1998-99	8.5	1.3	14.9	13.1	15.1	28.2	684.0	65.0	66.7
1999-00	9.0	1.4	15.6	14.2	16.4	30.6	642.0	55.0	71.2
2000-01	8.2	1.3	15.8	14.2	16.5	30.7	631.0	58.0	75.2
2001-02	8.8	1.4	16.0	14.8	17.2	32.0	650.0	67.0	76.8
2002-03	7.2	1.4	16.3	14.4	17.0	31.4	623.0	67.0	79.0
2003-04	9.9	1.2	16.1	13.4	17.6	31.0	662.0	70.0	83.6
2004-05	10.2	1.1	15.5	14.1	19.4	33.5	663.0	72.0	87.8

(Contd.)

Table 3.4: Per capita availability of certain important articles of consumption *(Contd.)*

Year	Edible oil[a] (kg)	Vanaspati[a] (kg)	Sugar[b] (Nov-Oct) (kg)	Cloth[c] Cotton[e] (meters)	Man-made (meters)	Total (meters)	Tea[d] (gram)	Coffee[e] (gram)	Electricity domestic[b] (KWH)
1	2	3	4	5	6	7	8	9	10
2005-06	10.6	1.1	16.3	16.4	19.7	36.1	687.0	75.0	90.4
2006-07	11.1	1.2	16.8	18.0	21.6	39.6	687.0	77.0	98.8
2007-08	11.4	1.2	17.8	19.0	22.8	41.9	701.0	80.0	106.0
2008-09	12.7	1.3	18.8	17.9	21.1	39.0	704.0	82.0	112.7
2009-10	13.3	1.1	17.9	19.7	23.4	43.1	709.0	86.0	121.2
2010-11	13.6	1.0	17.0	21.4	22.6	44.0	715.0	90.0	130.9
2011-12P	13.8	1.0	18.1	19.8	20.7	40.5	728.0	95.0	NA

Notes: Includes groundnut oil, rapeseed and mustard oil, sesamum oil, nigerseed oil, soyabean oil and sunflower oil but excludes oil for manufacture of vanaspati. Relates to calendar year. Relates to actual releases for domestic consumption.

The data of cloth; prior to 1980-1981 is calender year wise; in meters upto 1984-1985; in square meter from 1985-1986 onward.

NA: Not available. P: Provisional.
[a] Directorate of Vanaspati, Vegetable Oils and Fats.
Ministry of Consumer Affairs, Food and Public Distribution.
[b] Directorate of Sugar, Ministry of Consumer Affairs, Food and Public Distribution; Central Electricity Authority, Ministry of Power.
[c] Ministry of Textiles.
[d] Tea Board.
[e] Coffe Board.

Selection 9 was the winner of the Fine Cup Award for best Arabica at the 2002 Flavor of India—Cupping Competition. In 2004, Indian Coffee with the brand name "Tata Coffee" had the distinction of winning three gold medals at the Grand Cus De Café Competition held in Paris.

COFFEE BOARD

The Coffee Board of India is an organization managed by the Ministry of Commerce and Industry of the government of India to promote coffee production in India. The board was set up by an act of parliament in 1942. Until 1995, the Coffee Board marketed the coffee of many growers from a pooled supply, but after that time coffee marketing became a private-sector activity due to the economic liberalization in India. However, the winds of liberalization swept the Indian coffee industry and since 1995, marketing of coffee is strictly a private sector activity. In fact the Coffee Board went through a massive downsizing and two-thirds of its employees were retired under a voluntary retirement scheme.

The Coffee Board conducts basic and applied research on coffee and can boast of 75 glorious years in coffee research. The Central Coffee Research Institute in the Chikmagalur District, Karnataka State has been in the forefront of coffee research over the years and continues to remain one of the premier institutes of the world as far as coffee research is concerned. The Research Department publishes various journals and periodicals. It also offers various services to growers and exporters.

The Board also has a vast extension network spread over the three main producing states of Karnataka, Kerala and Tamil Nadu, as well as in the non-traditional areas of Andhra Pradesh, Orissa and the seven North-Eastern states. The extension set up provides the day- to- day link with the grower community and this wing facilitates the transfer of technology from **laboratory to land**. The Board also encourages the consumption of coffee in India and abroad. Toward this end, the Board participates in Coffee-centric/Food and Beverages exhibitions in India and abroad. The Board also runs 12 India Coffee Houses/Depots in the country. The *India Coffee* brand of coffee powder is well known in India for its quality and aroma. The Board has for long years worked on the quality of Coffees of India. The Board runs two quality control laboratories in Bangalore and Chikmagalur and one quality testing center in Chettalli, which control and advise the industry on quality issues. The laboratories are equipped with the best roasting and brewing machines. The best cup-tasters and quality evaluators keep a strict vigil on the pre- and post-harvest processes with a view to ensure that the quality of Indian coffee is maintained.

Market Intelligence and Statistical Unit

The Board has a Market Intelligence and Statistical Unit functioning from its head office at Bangalore. The unit undertakes various activities related to market information and intelligence, market research studies, crop forecasting and coffee economics aspects. The unit also undertakes studies on research related to the coffee trade including world trade organization (WTO) issues. Notable publications include the daily market intelligence report and a comprehensive database on coffee (bi-monthly). The periodical reports that are already completed include *Coffee Consumption in India* 2001, 2003, 2005 and 2008 and *Attitude toward coffee drinking* 2007. The unit coordinated studies on (1) logistics and competitiveness of coffee producing countries (India, Vietnam and Brazil) (2) MAI Scheme on promotion of Indian coffee exports to Russia and CIS countries and a manual on coffee retailing. The unit also coordinates the implementation of Price Stabilization Fund Scheme of Government of India and Rainfall Insurance Scheme for Coffee growers.

PUBLICATIONS

Books and bulletins

Sl. No.	Name of the book	Price per copy (Rs)	Registered parcel charges (Rs)
1.	Compendium of Coffee Research in India	500	56
2.	Coffee Guide Book (Revised English Edition)	150	50
3.	Packages of Practices for Coffee-Chikmangalur region	–	–
	Packages of Practices for Coffee-Hassan region.	–	–
	Packages of Practices for Coffee-Coorg region	–	–
	Packages of Practices for Coffee-Kerala region	–	–
	Packages of Practices for Coffee-Tamil Nadu regions	–	–
4.	Coffee Soil Fertility Map of Chikmagalur District	300	50
5.	A Set of English Extension Folders (20 Nos)	–	–
6.	Guidelines for Production of Organic Coffee in India	150	50

7. Platinum Jubilee Souvenior   –   –
8. Compendium on Pests and Diseases of Coffee and
    their management in India   100   50
9. C × R Bulletin
10. Guidelines for Production of Organic Coffee in India   –   –
    (small book)
11. Permitted Inputs for Controlling Pests and Diseases in
    Organic Coffee Estates   –   –
12. Package of Practices for Organic Coffee

In addition to this, extension leaflets on specific topics are also published in regional languages, which are distributed free of cost to growers. Copies of the same could be obtained from the local Liaison offices.

Journals and periodicals

Sl. No.	Journal/Periodical	Subscription rate	Whom to contact
1.	Journal of Coffee Research (Biannual)	Rs 80/year	The Editor, Journal of Coffee Research, CCRI, Coffee Research Station-577117 Chikmagalur Dist., Karnataka

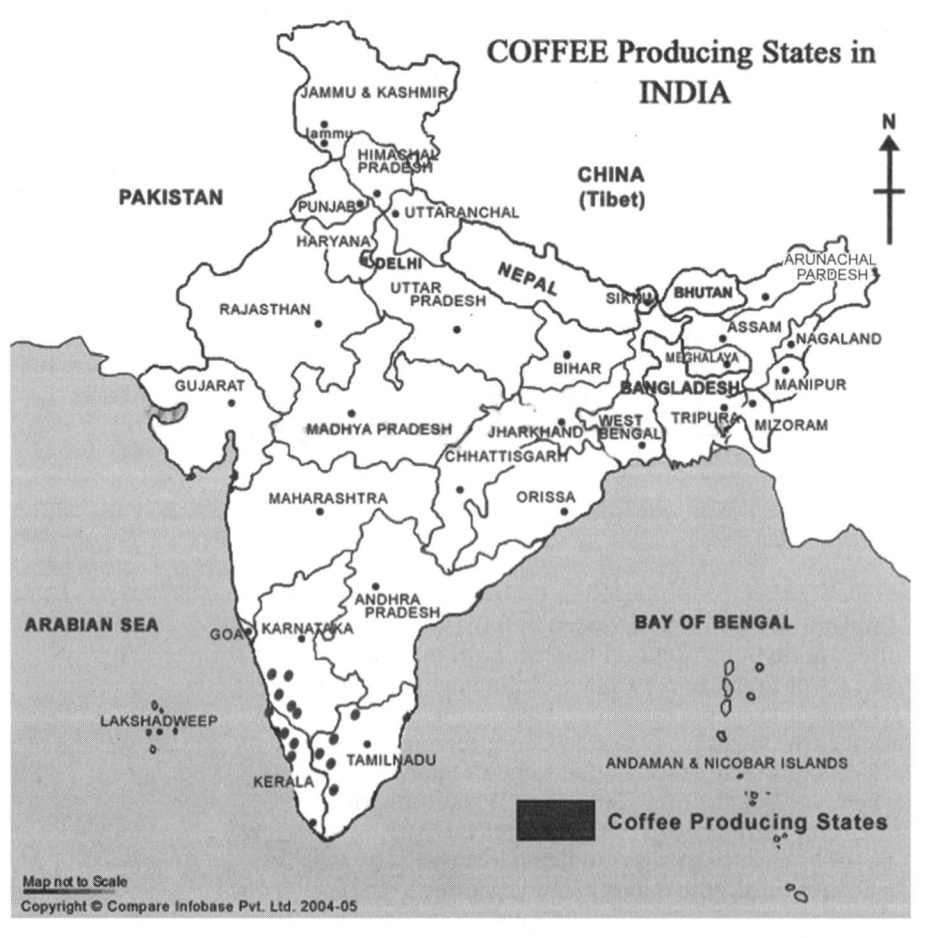

The Coffee Board's traditional duties include the promotion, sale and consumption of coffee in India and abroad; conducting coffee research; financial assistance to establish small coffee growers; safeguarding working conditions for laborers, and managing the surplus pool of unsold coffee. The Exotic café wave has now swept across the country and there are close to 1,900 trendy Western influenced coffee bars in India. Bangalore, with more than 150 cafes, boasts of the best among them— Café Coffee Day, Barista Layazza, Costa Coffee, Jaya City, Mocha, Coffee World, Matteo, Café Pascucci, Gloria Jeans, Java Green and many more spread across the length and breadth of the city.

Attitude toward Coffee Drinking

In order to understand the consumer perceptions and attitudes toward coffee and in the context of other beverages and also to understand the attitude toward coffee with respect to quality, variety, price and additives especially chicory; positive and negative associations related to consumption as well as drivers and barriers to coffee consumption, etc, a consumer attitude survey was commissioned during 2006–2007.

It covers the following:

- Beverage category consumption: Spontaneously recalled beverages, top of mind recalled beverages
- Consumption: Frequency of consumption
- Top beverages consumed by coffee drinkers
- Consideration set of beverages
- Attitudes toward beverages
- Perceived occasions: In-home and out-of-home
- Beverage evaluation criteria
- Barriers and drivers of coffee consumption
- Place of consumption of coffee: In-home and out-of-home
- Usage and attitudes toward R and G (filter) and instant coffee
- Awareness and usage of chicory
- Coffee Additional flavors.

Bands of Coffee Bags

Make Portable Coffee Bags for Better Coffee Anywhere

If you are sick of using generic instant coffee at work or out camping, instructables user claven 20 suggests making your own portable coffee bags using tea bags for delicious coffee no matter where you are.

The core concept of the coffee bag takes its influence from a French press, where the coffee is steeped for a short while and soaked into boiling water. In this case, it works through a tea bag. Grind your favorite brand of coffee on the finest setting, pour the grinds into a tea bag, seal the bag, and take the bags with you wherever you are heading. To drink it, all you need to do is boil some water, pour it over the bag, and let it steep for a few minutes. It is likely not as tasty as French pressed or drip coffee, but it certainly beats out the instant coffee in your desk drawer.

Cafés Excella

- Founded in 1905, Cafés Excella is a French Private Label company
- In 2010, Cafés Excella bought French coffee group Cafés Pivard creating the country's largest private label provider of coffee, as well as one of the biggest suppliers of single portion coffee solutions
- Cafés Excella offers Private Label customers their own brands but it also has its own national brand, "La Tasse", which it sells to French retailers.

Campanini

- Campanini offers own brand, Campanini, to the French out of home market
- It is a strong brand, dedicated to its customers, offers well priced coffee and products of excellence
- It also offers related coffee recipes and products: These include cups, glasses, sugar bowl sticks, stainless steel spoons and nonstick plates.

Cimbali

Cimbali has been producing *espresso and cappuccino machines* since 1912. The extraordinary passion for quality and a renowned talent for innovation led the company to become an ambassador of the espresso coffee culture in the world.

Gala

- Gala is an international coffee brand which was created in 1818 in Hertogenbosch, the Netherlands.
- Gala differentiates itself by producing high-quality products at an affordable price.
- Gala covers all the main coffee segments and is available for retail sale only.

Giger Café

- The brand was created in 1904 in Switzerland and was taken over by Drie Mollen (now United Coffee) in 2003.
- Other brand names as part of the Giger Café range include: GINO Il Tuo Caffè, Heidi Coffee and Indor thea.

Grand Café

- As the leading out-of-home brand in the UK, ethically-sourced Grand Café provides operators with the best flavor together with the option of three different styles of branding, to suit the style and ambience of the operation.
- Branded cups, point-of-sale, signage and full marketing support creates the full café experience, helping the operator to maximize their coffee business.

Grand Chocolate

- Developed by some of the world's finest chocolatiers, the beans for this high cocoa content drink are specially selected for their rich taste and aroma.
- Dried, roasted and finely ground, the beans create an intense flavor resulting in a creamy, luxurious hot chocolate.

Grand Cru

Grand Cru is the "champagne" of the coffee world. Sourced from some of the finest coffee plantations around the globe, this fully traceable "hand-crafted, credible coffee" is a rich, distinctive blend that celebrates what really great coffee is all about.

Lyons

- Originated in 1904. In 1978, Lyons acquired coffee company, Jndor
- Today, the brand focuses on the gastronomy sector of the industry and produces coffee, tea, as well as complementary products and services
- Examples of Lyons products include the Lyons Coffee Bag, which works in a similar way to a tea bag and allows consumers to enjoy real fresh coffee with little more effort than making instant, and the Cafeteria Sachets which contain the exact amount of fresh coffee for a four cup cafeteria
- Sustainability is central to the Lyons coffee brand, and it was the first coffee brand in the UK to be awarded the Rainforest Alliance certification.

Merkur Kaffee

- Merkur was first established in Switzerland in 1905 and changed its name to Merkur Kaffee in 1918. The brand's first central roasting facility was opened 1 year later
- In 2004, the brand was taken over by Drie Mollen, which was then rebranded United Coffee in 2010
- Other brand names as part of the Merkur range include: Merkur Kaffee, Caffè Spettacolo, Café Oncle Tom, Caffè Teatro, La Chiassese, Heidi Coffee and Chocolait.

Rosca Caffè

- One of the leading coffee roasters in Switzerland.
- Rosca has a significant presence in the hotel, restaurant, café and catering sectors. It also supplies selected distributors and a number of private consumers via mail order.
- Other brand name as part of the Rosca caffè range include: Heidi coffee.

Sima Caffè

- Founded in 1969, Sima Caffè is the leading coffee roasting company in Graubünden, Switzerland.
- The brand has a significant presence in the restaurant, hotel and hospital sectors. It also supplies a number of private consumers.

Smit and Dorlas

- Founded in 1822 as a small coffee roaster for hotels and restaurants in Amsterdam.
- Over time the brand has grown into a highly respected full concept coffee supplier with a large market share in the hotel and catering industry and an increasing market share in the business and office segment.

- In addition to selling coffee machines, Smit and Dorlas roasts and delivers coffee beans, as well as, sells, advises on and services the espresso machines.
- Machine brands include Thermoplan and La Cimbali.
- Smit and Dorlas also produce Legends of Tea.

Templo Café

- Templo Cafés was founded during 1996 and services the out-of-home market in Spain under the name "El Templo del café".
- Templo Cafés is the fourth largest brand in the Spanish out-of-home and is backed by the second largest manufacturer in the country.
- Under the concept Espress and Te, Templo Cafés offers several services and products relating to the coffee and tea industry including machinery and customer sales.

Bean Here Bean There

Coffee came to India some 400 years ago and for large sections of the population South of the Vindhyas, filter kaapi is as much a religion as their rice, sambar and curd. Generations of moms have painstakingly brewed decoctions in steel filters every morning and evening and produced steel tumblers full of perfectly steaming hot and frothy servings of the bitter-sweet liquid, without which life would seem incomplete.

But, this drink itself was mostly unidimensional. It is called "filter" coffee as the liquid was brewed in a two-piece steel cylinder where the powder is put in the upper half and hot water poured onto it trickles through tiny holes and collects as coffee decoction in the lower half. The measures could increase or decrease depending on how potent the cup needed to be, with "strong coffee" being the popular keyword to a more bitter and acidic concoction, known for its powers to help defy sleep, to memorize tomes ahead of exams or fight the after-effects of a heavy meal.

That, however, was all the variation there could be, apart from the addition of chicory root powder to milder Arabica coffees to make it "stronger" at a lower cost. Brooke Bond was one major coffee powder brand, which had 70% coffee and 30% chicory. Dozens of regional coffee roasters played on the mix to cater to the taste buds of the more discerning consumers. And then came along Nescafe and Bru, soluble coffee powders, which could be mixed directly with water or milk, doing away with the filtering process. But, they could never compare to the power of filter coffee and no self-respecting south Indian coffee home dared depend on them.

All that changed with the arrival of the modern coffee shop in the mid-1990s. The first of this avatar started off as a giant "cyber café" on two levels on Bangalore's snazzy Brigade Road. Every half hour of browsing came with a complimentary latte, a big mug of milky coffee which connoisseurs-eyed suspiciously. Contrast that with coffee shops offering free Wi-Fi internet and charging a bomb for a cuppa now and you realize the coffee-Internet story has come a full circle. Be that as it may, it is this outlet that spawned the successful Cafe Coffee Day (CCD) chain which is today India's largest, with more than 1,200 coffee shops.

CCD has been followed by Barista, Costa Coffee, Gloria Jean's, Coffee Bean and Tea Leaf and several local chains, all of which specialize in a common range: the popular cappuccino (one part coffee, one part milk, one part milk foam), the latte (one part coffee and two parts milk), the espresso (one part coffee, consumed neat), the americano (one part coffee, two parts hot water) and the macchiato (espresso topped with just a spoon of milk foam). And then there are the cold coffees and ice coffees, which are just coffee-flavored coolers. The cafes have also introduced us to toppings such as cinnamon, nutmeg or chocolate powder that can be sprinkled on cappuccinos or lattes to give them a sweet/spicy twist.

Much of the coffee in these outlets—barring the well-bodied espresso/macchiato crafted from the superior Peaberry—is uniformly unimpressive. A survey conducted by Harish Bijoor, a Bangalore-based independent consultant and former coffee professional, found 67% of coffee sold at cafes in India were cappuccinos and lattes, or "dumbed down coffees" as he rightly calls them. Another 13% were cold coffees and the remaining 20% were espresso/macchiato/americano, or "real coffees". But, the cafes have been successful because they also offer other beverages such as teas, coolers and snacks, and more importantly have become a hip hangout for the young. Although the coffee is a bit incidental, it has gained because new consumers have been introduced to the beverage who have then pursued it at home and elsewhere.

The venerable Starbucks is set to join these worthies. Quite a few books have been written to explain the success of this Seattle-headquartered chain and while there may not be unanimity over the reasons, the rise of Starbucks coincided with the jump in coffee consumption in the US and the company rode that wave by rapidly expanding from coast to coast while maintaining the consistency of its coffees. I have been to less than half-a-dozen Starbucks outlets in different countries and have not found them any different from coffee shops at home. Friends in the US who have more Starbucks experience call their coffees "average", "overpriced" or "over-roasted", among others. Bijoor thinks the price point of Starbucks coffee in India will be a key factor in the chain's success or otherwise. Price has been a critical element behind the success of CCD and the struggles of Barista, and in that sense, India has already woken up and smelt its coffee, even if it is the dumbed-down variety. Starbucks too can ride this wave if it can offer a bang for the buck.

Coffee Consumption In India: Trends and Attitudes

The total pure coffee volume in India is estimated at 102,000 tons in 2009 (Table 3.5).

- Urban consumption dominates with about 73% of total volumes and the remaining 27% accounts for rural consumption (South India).
- In the North, East and West zones, consumption of instant coffee is more predominant than filter coffee. However, in the South zone, consumption of filter coffee is higher than instant coffee.
- South alone consumes nearly 80,538 million tons (78%) of total coffee consumed in India. Among the South Indian States Tamil Nadu accounts for 36% of consumption while Karnataka, Andhra Pradesh and Kerala account for 31%, 18%and 15%, respectively.
- There is more potential in the non-South, where the occasional consumers are high in number. Occasional drinkers contribute to 52% of total, this essentially means that people have started experiencing this beverage, which should be advantageously used to increase in consumption. Converting them to regular coffee drinkers is an opportunity for growth.

Table 3.5: Total releases of coffee from the pool in the internal (domestic) market from 1981–1990 and estimated domestic consumption from 1991 to 2011

(Quantity in million tons)

Calendar Year	Plantation	Arab. cherry	Robusta	Total
1981	21369	7217	22210	50796
1982	22718	7332	23940	53990
1983	23934	7926	24219	56079
1984	31628	8137	13779	53544
1985	28170	5855	20849	54874
1986	25939	6399	22083	54421
1987	26360	6948	25328	58636
1988	25487	6036	24037	55560
1989	26337	6805	30186	63328
1990	22983	8587	22582	54152
1991	26500	11000	17500	55000
1992	26500	11000	17500	55000
1993	22500	10000	17500	50000
1994	22500	10000	17500	50000
1995	22500	10000	17500	50000
1996	22500	10000	17500	50000
1997	22500	10000	17500	50000
1998	22500	10000	17500	50000
1999	25000	10000	20000	55000
2000	29000	8000	23000	60000
2001	28000	6000	30000	64000
2002	30000	10000	28000	68000
2003	32000	10000	28000	70000
2004	–	–	–	75000
2005	–	–	–	80200
2006	–	–	–	85000
2007	–	–	–	90000
2008	–	–	–	94400
2009	–	–	–	102000
2010*	–	–	–	108000
2011*	–	–	–	115000

* Provisional

- Between 2003 and 2009, there is a large reduction of non-drinkers but the proportion of occasional drinkers has increased.

  The potential for growth lies with occasional drinkers and more so in

  o East zone: 80%
  o North zone: 75%
  o Western zone: 63%.

- The attitude surveys bring out the drivers as well as barriers to consumption. The barriers to coffee consumption in the country viz. that the coffee is not good for health, it is too cumbersome to make a cup of coffee and it is hassle to clean the filter/coffee maker every time.

Coffee Makes Its Way Into Fast-Food Restaurants

The good old Indian coffee is steadily making its way into the world of pizzas and burgers in India with quick service restaurant (QSR) chains like Pizza Hut and McDonald's making it an integral part of their offerings. QSR chains, which hitherto focused only on their flagship offerings like pizzas or Big Macs, are diversifying into the cafe concept to lure those customers, who flock to cafes since the concept of coffee and snacks between meals is growing in India. Over the last two quarters, the QSR segment has been posting low same-store sales growth and companies are working their best to increase volume sales by offering value meals and diversifying store formats to increase footfalls. And with a $300 million Indian coffee market, growing at 17% annually, cafes are a clear option for QSRs.

Yum! Brands' Pizza Hut has started a Hut. Cafe in a store-in-store format where a Pizza Hut restaurant houses a cafe that serves coffee, tea, smoothies and coolers; and McDonald's recently brought in its McCafe format to India to sell its range of coffees, pastries, savouries and chilled beverages. Pizza Hut has launched its Hut. Cafe outlet each in Chennai and Kolkata and this mark Pizza Hut's foray into a new category of coffees. "During tough times one of the things we have done is to try and reach out to a whole new segment of customers. The Hut Cafe will help in getting customers who just go out for coffee and snacks between meals", said Sanjiv Razdan, general manager, Pizza Hut India.

The company now has its own range of products and has worked on specialty Indian coffees, but is also open to working with different brands to bring in their signature products to Hut Cafe tables, Razdan said. The company has two such outlets and expects to open 10 more by the end of this year. "McCafe has helped us bring in more customers by building a different day part and increasing footfalls within the McDonald's restaurants", Ranjit Paliath, vice president—business operations, McDonald's India (West and South), said. McDonald's now has three McCafes in India but plans to open 75–150 more in the next 3–5 years.

Coffee is so dear to the Indian consumer that dessert-chains too are looking at putting ice creams parlors and coffee shops together. American icecream brand Mini-Melts, which recently made its foray into India, is planning to setup Mini-Melt Cafes where consumers can step in for coffee or tea, have snacks and finish off the mini-meal with icecreams. "We are working on the design and layout of the cafe and will be launching them in Chennai, Bangalore and Hyderabad in the next three months", said Syed Salim, chairman, Honey Bee Amusements, which has brought the US-based brand to the Indian market. The company will offer a range of Mini Melts-based dishes like "floats", which will have the Mini Melts ice cream on beverages like Coca-Cola, and also serve regular coffees, is looking at typing up with large cafe chains for the coffee.

Processing Coffee

Processing of coffee in India is accomplished using two methods, dry processing and wet processing. Dry processing is the traditional method of drying in the sun which is favored for its flavor producing characteristics. In the wet processing method, coffee beans are fomented and washed, which is the preferred method for improved yields. As to the wet processing, the beans are subject to cleaning to segregate defective seeds. The beans of different varieties and sizes are then blended to derive the best flavor. The next procedure is to roast either through roasters or individual roasters. Then the roasted coffee is ground to appropriate sizes.

The flavor of coffee is determined not only by the variety, but also by the length of time the green beans are roasted. In continuous roasting, hot air (200–260°C/400–500°F) is forced through small quantities of beans for a 5-minute period; in batch roasting, much larger quantities of beans are roasted for a longer time. Dark-roasted coffees (French or espresso roasts) are stronger and mellower than lightly roasted beans. After roasting, the beans are usually ground and vacuum-packed in cans.

Instant coffee is prepared by forcing an atomized spray of very strong coffee extract through a jet of hot air; this evaporates the water in the extract and leaves the dried coffee particles. Another method of producing instant coffee is freeze-drying. To make decaffeinated coffee, the green beans are processed in a steam or chemical bath to remove the caffeine, the substance that produces coffee's stimulating effect.

Between arabica and robusta coffee, demand for the latter is on the rise. Globally, coffee is the second largest traded commodity, after crude oil. The world coffee consumption increased from 109.84 million bags in 2002 to 120.11 million bags in 2006. During this period, coffee consumption in India increase from 68,000 tons to 82,000 tons. Global coffee consumption for 2007 was estimated at around 123 million bags, up 2.5% over the previous year. India's consumption was pegged at 1.33 million bags. Global coffee production in crop year 2006–2007 is increased by 14% to 125 million bags in 2005–2006. The worldwide exports for the year also were up by 9.6% to 96.7 million bags against 88.2 million bags in 2005–2006.

Coffee Crush

Compounded annual rate of growth of India's coffee consumption from 2001–2011 is 5.7%. This is more than the global growth rate, according to the international coffee organization data. India is the sixth largest producer of coffee. Yet, its yearly per capita consumption is 100 gm, tiny as compared to Sweden's 12 kg. No wonder the world best coffee chains are here to tell us how to brew it.

The Convenience of Coffee

Traditionally, coffee in India has been the brew of choice in the South, Mornings have been South-Indian homes waft in the aroma of divinely fresh coffee that has dripped slowly and steadily for years into the receptacles of metallic filters. In fact, a few decades back most households in the south roasted the coffee beans at home before powdering them in a small tabletop hand-operated grinding mill. But that was then. And repeating an oft-repeated cliché, times have changed.

Reinventing Coffee

Over the past few years, coffee has shifted from being the iconic traditional brew of South-India to a beverage with a national presence, reinventing itself smoothly to capture the imagination of a large domestic market. This is a boost to the coffee industry as India is not a traditional coffee market. The regular consumers of coffee with 2-cups-a-day are just about 8% of the middle-class population. In order to understand the present and future of coffee, it is perhaps pragmatic to take a look at a few numbers.

Call it a cup of java, mocha or just plain kaap coffee consumption in India is witnessing a heartening climb upward. The journey of coffee in the past decades, however, has seen a fair bit of convolutions before its remarkable turnaround.

Coffee consumption in India has shown an annual average growth of about 2% from 1951 to 2000, i.e. 18,400 tons in 1951 to 60,000 tons in 2000. In the last 9 years, however, the consumption has grown to almost one lakh tons if this is further analyzed according by region, in 2000. In the last 9 years, however, the consumption has grown to almost 1 lakh tons. If this is further analyzed according by region in 2002 more than 90% consumption was from South-India. But between 2003 and 2008, the consumption growth was reversed, with the rest of India contributing 60% of the growth (i.e. 14,760 metric tons out of 24,100 metric tons consumption growth seen in the five-year period). Also, in the period of 2003–2008, the penetration level (the number of people who have tasted coffee at least once in the last 1 year) increased from 59% to a phenomenal 92%. The reasons could be anything as simple as the fact that people wanted to taste coffee or that there are more coffee outlets all over India or coffee is more easily available and affordable. According to FAO data shows per capita consumption of coffee in India is only 0.1 kg as against 18.2 kg in Luxemburg, 14.5 kg in Montenegro and 10 kg both in Norway and Sweeden. Consumption level in UK is only 2.6 kg against that of USA and 4.2 kg.

Excitement in the Market

The increase in coffee consumption is due to several factors such as higher disposable incomes, especially with the youth, café culture and changing lifestyles. It pointed out that "in recent years, most of the growth has come from instant coffee consumption". This is highlighted by the fact that during the period of 2003–2008, there has been about 48% increase in the consumption of instant coffee. This increase is driven by the desire for speed and convenience. One doesn't really need to put in effort to know how to make coffee using instant coffee. Until instant coffee captured the attention of consumers in rest of India, for most of them, drinking an after-dinner coffee at a restaurant was one thing, but laboring to prepare filter coffee as not so popular.

The rise of the consumption of instant coffee, from 36,000 tons in 2003 to 53,000 tons in 2008, is about 9% per annum which is clearly way ahead of the per annum growth of roasted coffee that hovers at 3.5%. This impressive growth in consumption was, in turn, made possible by the different formats of coffee sold in the market today. The single serve instant coffee packs to 3-in 1 mixtures along with vending machines, seem to drive the instant coffee usage. There are various styles and forms which coffee is consumed in the domestic market which is clearly treading the path of regular coffee drinking markets. With newer options like espresso and espresso-based products like cappuccino, lattee, mocha and so on, the Indian consumers are treated to a whole lot of choices.

A World of Opportunities

Instant coffee manufacturing has always been a source of strength for the Indian coffee industry. Even in the past, a sizeable quantity of coffee exports used to be in the form of instant coffee. The instant coffee presence in the domestic market for long was confined to the MNCs operating in India. The recent upbeat mood has opened up opportunities not only for Indian entrepreneurs to start instant coffee manufacturing units. With two such units coming into production in 2009, but has also paved the way for a large number of small operators to enter the market with their own labels of instant coffee. Even today, there are hardly seven companies manufacturing in the country. The small entrepreneurs are able to source coffee with their own labels from different manufacturers and use their marketing skills. Apart from the powder itself, there are opportunities galore for manufacturers of vending machines for offices, malls and stores and brewing machines or coffees makers for home use.

As instant coffee offers the taste or experience of coffee with convenience to occasional drinkers, there is an expectation that such consumers will move up to roast and ground coffee to experience coffee at its best. All over the world, people drink coffee purely for the pleasure of its aroma and flavor. It is almost like a package deal to savor.

Banishing Barriers

However, the beverage itself is not without its share of skeptics. One barrier is that most respondents (non-drinkers) say that they have "heard" that coffee is not good for health. According to Rau, there are no studies that attribute any ill-effects to coffee. Most studies on which the negative image is built were on the effects of different levels of caffeine intake. The fact is that too much of caffeine is bad to health and that principle holds good for everything we consume. Incidentally, one less-known fact of coffee is that it contains a lot many compounds and the best known are the chlorogenic acids which are the source of antioxidants. Therefore, contrary to popular belief, several studies show a positive correlation between regular moderate consumption of coffee and the reduction in the risk of contracting alzheimers, parkinsons, type-2 diabetes, liver cirrhosis, colon cancer etc. a cup of coffee has about four times more anti-oxidants than tea. Green coffee extract which has higher concentration of chlorogenic acids is, in fact, used in several skin care and cosmetic products.

The next barrier is the perception that coffee making is too cumbersome. The advent of instant coffee has taken away that hurdle to a great extent. But for those who crave for the taste of filter coffee without the hassle of preparation, the answer lies in "A single-serve coffee powder pod in a sachet that will go into a coffee maker is just the answer. With this, anyone can have a cup of freshly brewed coffee at any time. There will be no bother of cleaning the coffee maker as the paper sachet contains the power within. This, in turn, will take away the third barrier of having to clean up after making the coffee. The business opportunities this idea presents are phenomenal both for coffee powder ant the coffee maker, especially when you consider regular consumers of coffee are less than 8% of even the middle-class population".

A Promising Future

The Indian domestic market stands at the crossroads with the coffee industry viewing it with great expectations. For a long time, there was no focus on the domestic market. A robust coffee market is important for the coffee industry. With the Indian middle-class at 350 million and growing, the domestic market becomes crucial for sustaining the coffee industry. All elements are in place for a sustainable and holistic growth of the coffee market. Today, there is a glowing certainty in the industry that the coffee market will get the right stimulus as a wide range of functional and convenient coffee products enter the market, enticing consumers to start their day with an energy kick.

SOME PROBLEMS

The decline in area under Arabica is worrying the Coffee Board. According to the Board, the area under arabica variety fell to 48% of the total planted area in 2010–2011 from around 73% in 1950–1951. Similarly, the area under robusta increased from 27% of the total cultivated area in 1950–1951 to 52% in 2010–2011. In 2010–2011, while the area under arabica stood at 193,155 hectares, constituting 48% of the total area under coffee, it was 206,646 hectares under robusta (52%). India is one of the important arabica producers in Asia. Any drop in production will reduce export revenues for the country. Usually, arabica fetches double the value of robusta in both domestic and international markets.

Any fall in world coffee output is impacting consumption not just in emerging markets like Russia, Algeria and Ukraine but also producing nations such as Indonesia and Brazil. Un-seasonal rains and typhoon attack are adversely affecting coffee output in India and Vietnam. While lower output is a problem, another serious problem is rising cost of production, notably in the form of higher fertilizer and input costs.

Production costs in India are higher than those of Brazil, Vietnam, Indonesia and Peru because of increasing wages; mandatory social costs like providing housing, healthcare and provident fund to the workforce; rising overheads like fuel hikes, and state taxes/levies. The cost of labor has increased enormously. The present wage is Rs 190 per day, up from Rs 27 per day in 1994. Arabica has been hit very badly by the white stem borer pest attacks, which have a long term impact as they destroy the plants. Also, it takes 4 years before a newly grown coffee plant can be productive.

India experienced a 6% growth in output in 2011–2012. Over the same period, Ethiopia suffered a loss in production from 7.5 million bags in 2010–2011 to 6.5 million bags in 2011–2012.

Indian coffee planters achieved a record production of 5.33 million bags of 60 kg each (314,000 tons) in 2011. Yet, the country's ranking in world coffee production fell from the sixth to the seventh position in 2010. Peru now occupies the sixth position with a marginally higher production of 54.4 million bags. While India's share in world output is 4%, Peru's share stands at 4.1%.

Brazil, Vietnam and Indonesia continue to hold the top three positions with 33%, 15.2% and 6.3% of the world's coffee trade, respectively. Though Brazil has suffered a setback, it tops the world in production with 43.4 million bags. Vietnam and Indonesia produced 20 million bags, and 8.2 million bags, respectively in 2010–2011. New players like Peru, and even smaller states like Ethiopia in Africa, are performing well compared to India due to climatic reasons and state patronage.

Coffee production in Vietnam, the world's biggest grower of the Robusta variety, which is used by Nestle in instant coffee, is likely to decline because of dry weather. The yields have come down, and prices have risen. In 2011–2012, the country witnessed a record output of 1.6 million tons. In 2012–2013, this may come down to 1.45 million tons. Vietnam needs to harvest at least 26 million bags in the marketing season starting from October 2012, to ensure supplies of the Robusta variety to meet demand.

In India, growers have sought full exemption from paying tax on the sale of coffee grown and cured by them. As of now, 25% of the income derived from such a sale is taxed as per Rule 7B of the Income Tax Rules, 1962. The growers say that instead of getting a benefit for value-addition, they are being taxed. After the introduction of Rule 7B, no grower is selling coffee through the Indian Coffee Trade Association (ICTA). This scenario has led to deterioration of coffee quality in India.

The coffee growers of Karnataka, who account for 70% of India's coffee output, have sought a subsidy package of Rs.3000 million from the union government for mechanization during the 12th Plan period (2012–2017). Coffee growers in Orissa have demanded that subsidies for the expansion of coffee plantations in non-traditional areas should be at the level granted to traditional areas. They are also demanding that the subsidy for bringing new areas under coffee should cover 50% of the costs of doing so with a cap of Rs 175,000 per hectare. Currently, the subsidy they get is 25% of the cost with a cap of Rs 60,000 per hectare on plantation project cost. During the 11th Plan period, the center allocated Rs 500 million in the fifth year of the Plan, but released only Rs 220 million. Because of labor shortage, the growers feel that there is a strong case for massive mechanization in the coffee plantations.

Measures Needed

The Coffee Board is taking all possible steps to increase the average production of coffee. Andhra Pradesh and Orissa have shown promising possibilities in this regard. Also, there is an urgent need to boost domestic coffee consumption. Industry estimates that there is a scope for another 5,000 outlets in the country.

Coffee producers feel that the industry requires implementation of various measures like improvement in the existing schemes in the plantation sector, along with discovery of new disease-resistant strains, in the 12th plan period (2012–2017) to increase the production and productivity of the commodity. Allocation for these schemes is around Rs 5,000 million during the 11th plan period (2007–2012).

Domestic coffee exporters and planters look for eco-friendly certification from international certifying bodies like UT2, Rainforest Alliance and Fairtrade. This is sought to increase sales in the international market and realize higher price per unit. In 2010, the certifying area in the country was around 202.34 square kilometers (50,000 acres). Now, even individual coffee estates from major growing regions of Coorg and Chikmagalur are seeking such certification.

The certification is issued on the basis of good agricultural and business practices, social criteria and environmental parameters. Certification is sought to obtain long-term gains as organizational rules, sound crop practices and efficient use of natural resources become a part of the coffee production process. Certification will help domestic planters to get right price at the time of crisis. Of course, small planters are certified under "group certification scheme" to reduce the cost of certification.

The Coffee Board has urged the government to increase mechanization subsidy to planters, along with sound plan-allocation for marketing development in this sector. This is necessary in view of labor shortage. The major concern relating to stagnating production should be addressed at the earliest. The government should also try to reduce the operating cost of planters and exporters in an inflationary environment.

Coffee to Boost Memory

A double espresso after revision might be the best way of preparing for an examination, new research suggests. Scientists have found the first clear evidence of caffeine's memory-boosting effect, and shown that it lasts for at least 24 hours. Volunteers took part in a double-blind trial in which they were either given a 200 mg caffeine pill or a placebo 5 minutes after studying a series of images. Tests a day later proved that the memory of those who took caffeine had been enhanced at a deep level. The amount of caffeine used was roughly equivalent to a double shot of strong espresso coffee.

Caffeine's effect on mind lasts for at least 24 hours

We have always known that caffeine has cognitive-enhancing effects, but its particular effects on strengthening memories and making them resistant to forgetting has never been examined in detail in humans. We report for the first time a specific effect of caffeine on reducing forgetting over 24 hours. More than 100 participants took part in the study, none of whom were regular users of caffeinated products. Before being given the caffeine or placebo, they were asked to identify a series of pictured objects as either outdoor or indoor items. The next day, both groups were tested on their ability to recognize the images they had been shown earlier. Some of the images were the same as the ones they had seen, some were new, and some similar but not identical.

Although all the volunteers correctly identified "new" and "old" pictures, those who had taken the caffeine pill were better able to spot "similar" images. Participants not dosed with caffeine were more likely to be fooled into thinking the similar pictures were the ones viewed the previous day. Recognizing the difference between two similar but not identical items reflects a deep level of memory retention, the researchers reported in the Journal Nature Neuroscience.

IMPORT/EXPORTS

An analysis of India's production and export data in the world context shows that the share of coffee production and exports have remained quite near to each other varying from 2% to 4% in the corresponding years (Table 3.6). Although total production of Coffee in India is not consumed during the year, after consumption and exports, there is every year a significant proportion which goes into stocks (Table 3.6A). At the same time, India is also importing small quantities of coffee (Table 3.6B) for re-export. We have, therefore, to examine all the three components—production, consumption and stocks independently.

Annual imports of coffee by type (Table 3.6C), the six types being imported. It is primarily coffee which is neither roasted nor decaffeinated. Various countries from which coffee is being imported (Table 3.6D). Vietnam alone accounts for over 56%.

Table 3.6: Production and exports: India vs world[*]

(In '000 bags of 60 kg each)

Year	Production		India's share (%)	Exports		India's share (%)
	World	India[@]		World[#]	India[@]	
1993–94	90366	3533	3.91	73911	2907	3.93
1994–95	95154	3002	3.15	65718	2070	3.15
1995–96	85250	3717	4.36	74014	3572	4.83
1996–97	101865	3417	3.35	81745	2476	3.03
1997–98	95872	3805	3.97	77806	3685	4.74
1998–99	106163	4417	4.16	82554	3442	4.17
1999–00	115117	4867	4.23	92282	4214	4.57
2000–01	116619	5020	4.30	89248	4229	4.74
2001–02	108451	5010	4.62	90564	3730	4.12
2002–03	123723	4588	3.71	90007	3567	3.96
2003–04	103982	4508	4.34	87527	3826	4.37
2004–05	116062	4592	3.96	91095	2790	3.06
2005–06	111247	4567	4.11	85648	3359	3.92
2006–07	128209	4800	3.74	98143	4150	4.23
2007–08	116455	4367	3.75	96296	3569	3.71
2008/09	128637	4372	3.40	97593	3547	3.63
2009/10	122941	4827	3.93	96205	3005	3.12
2010/11	133357	5033	3.77	96927	4647	4.79
2011/12	134140	5233	3.90	104573	5327	5.09
2012/13[**]	144611	5303	3.67	113157	5130	4.53

 * Production and exports of ICO members.
 ** Provisional, subject to revision.
 # ICO Exports – ICO Coffee Statistics 10/ICA 2007 – July 2013 and Coffee Board.
 @ Boards Estimates.

Table 3.6A: India's Coffee production, consumption, exports and stock (1985–2006)

Year	Production (60 kg bags)	Consumption (60 kg bags)	Exports (60 kg bags)	Opening stocks (60 kg bags)
1985	1571000	538333	1695000	1878658
1986	3618000	1301000	1587000	1216835
1987	1941000	815000	1387000	1946722
1988	3033000	1066667	1918000	1686000
1989	1785000	667000	2025600	1734000
1990	2829000	867000	1510687	826000
1991	3000000	1000000	1727359	1277000
1992	2818000	775000	1816341	1253000
1993	3448000	1000000	2101593	1479000
1994	2984000	1000000	2496085	1020000

Table 3.6A: India's Coffee production, consumption, exports and stock (1985–2006) *(Contd.)*

Year	Production (60 kg bags)	Consumption (60 kg bags)	Exports (60 kg bags)	Opening stocks (60 kg bags)
1995	3727000	1000000	2469337	934000
1996	3469000	1000000	3119736	89000
1997	4729000	916000	2640111	82000
1998	4372000	833000	3487014	210000
1999	5457000	916000	3612690	323000
2000	4526000	917000	4440570	364000
2001	5011000	1134000	3362370	354000
2002	4588000	1134000	3515742	653000
2003	4508000	1134000	3670955	658000
2004	4672000	1250000	2790010	1120000
2005	4617000	1336667	3581307	1752000
2006	5005000	1336667	NA	1451000

Updated on May 16, 2007.

Coffee balance sheet for the latest few years of the total coffee produced in India, a little over 40% was exported during 1979–1980. There was a steady increase in the export share at 67% by 1991–1992 although it represented only 2.54% of total world exports. The share of India in world exports touched 4.8% during 1995–1996. It has since been fluctuating around 3%.

Country-wise export data for coffee is presented in Tables 3.7 and 3.7A. Total exports increased from 213.6 thousand tons in 2001–2002 to 298.1 thousand tons in 2012–2013. With marginal changes from year to year, there is a constant trend toward increased exports. As for value, the increase is four times from Rs 1,050 crore in 2001–02 to Rs 4,662.8 crore in 2011–2012. For the recent 2 years, there is a decline both in quantity and value.

Italy is the major importer of Indian coffee and has been constantly increasing its share from 20% in 2001–2002 to 23% in 2012–2013. Italy is followed by Russian Federation (403 thousand tons in 2001–02 with a continuous decline to 270.8 thousand tons in 2012–2013, Germany (275.9 thousand tons in 2011–2012) and Spain where again imports declined from 122 thousand tons in 2001–2002 to only 6.5 thousand tons in 2012–2013. Slovakia on the other hand increased its share from 8.9 thousand tons to 13.4 thousand tons during this period.

Indian coffee export is on a high. Exports started picking up from 2010 to 2011 when they touched 299.8 thousand tons and have been increasing steadily since then. Exports increased nearly 60% to touch 333 thousand tons in 2011–2012 valued at 4662.78 crores. This is the highest quantity ever exported by the country. The value in dollar terms touched $811.09 million, up 83%, while in terms of rupee the value was Rs 4,680 crore, a 75% rise. According to a senior official of Coffee Board, besides the surge in quantity, the earnings have gone up due to a higher unit value. The unit value stood at Rs 116 per kg compared with Rs 106 per kg in the previous year. If one takes the last 6 months of the year, the unit value is still higher at Rs 131 per kg (Tables 3.7A and B).

The coffee crop was also good during 2009–2010. As a result of the high demand, over 30,000 tons of carryover stock was shipped during 2011–2012. Even the coffee harvested between December 2010 and February 2011 was also exported. Normally, it is included in the next year's crop. India registered a 28% year-on-year export growth by shipping 299.7 million kg in 2010–2011 as against 196.0 million kg in 2009–2010.

Coffee Exports to Scale a New Peak This Fiscal Year

Indian coffee exports are heading for a new peak this fiscal year aided by a good crop and higher imports for re-exporting. As on March 2011, exports touched 287,396 tons, a 47% gain over the previous year. "There was a strong demand for Indian coffee as prices were comparatively lower during the year. The coffee crop was reasonably good and imports for re-export were high. All these factors contributed to the surge in exports", The previous highest export of 249,029 tons was achieved in 2006–2007. Imports of 40,895 tons of coffee beans during 2009–2010 pushed up the export of value-added coffee.

Coffee Exports in 2013–2014 May Slip Below Last Year's Level

India's coffee exports may drop from the last year's record level to 306 thousand tons in the 2013–2014 marketing year due to a dip in production as well as low export prices. The country is estimated to have shipped a record 312 thousand tons of coffee in the 2012–2013 marketing year (October–September). Exports for 2013–2014 marketing year are forecast at 306 thousand tons, according to the US Department of Agriculture (USDA).

Lower export prices, domestic crop reduced by monsoons and better yield in major coffee-producing countries are expected to temper Indian exports, but exporters are optimistic that significant volumes of coffee will be exported. However, foreign demand for Indian beans and processed coffee is expected to remain strong on the back of weaker rupee.

On weak export prices, the USDA said while Indian Arabica remained steady, prices of Robusta, which comprises the bulk of Indian exports, have dropped sharply in anticipation of a larger global supply. This supported the expectation that exports will be competitively priced. The USDA's projection of India coffee production is significantly less than the Coffee Board of India's estimate of 342 thousand tons million bags for 2013–2014. According to the report, heavy rain in major coffee-growing regions, especially in Karnataka that contributes 70% of the total production, appears to have reduced yields.

In addition India is also exporting specialty and value added products. It increased from 54,857.1 tons valued at Rs 35,349 lakhs in 2003–2004 to 107.7 thousand tons valued at Rs 176,421.7 lakhs in 2012–2013 (Table 3.7C and 3.7D) from among the specialty coffee, the major share was that of Robusta Kapi. As for the value added coffee, instant coffee alone accounted for 99%. From among the various type of coffee, it is primarily the instant one which is re-exported (Table 3.8). Russian Federation is the main importer of this variety. Total quantity re-exported in this category increased from 23.2 thousand tons valued at Rs 24.5 lakhs to 30.0 thousand tons in 2007–2008 to 30 thousand tons valued at Rs 72.2 lakhs in 2011–2012, Major ports which ship coffee for export are Cochin and Mangalore accounting for more than 50% (Tables 3.8 and 3.8A) main exporters are M/s NKG Jayanti Coffee Pvt. Ltd. and M/s Allanasons Limited.

Table 3.6B: Import of coffee by type (quantity and value)

Import volume coffee by type (Quantity in MT)

HS_CODE	Type	2003–04	2004–05	2005–06	2006–07	2007–08	2008–09	2009–10	2010–11	2011–12	2012–13*
090111	Coffee neither nor roasted decaffeinated	8756.94	22189.08	38172.16	19507.30	26476.39	28838.99	40681.93	44804.88	45706.48	32701.57
090112	Not roasted but decaffeinated coffee	0.34	0.06	–	–	–	–	–	–		0.10
090121	Roasted not decaffeinated coffee	5.16	6.40	9.54	22.72	43.13	46.85	58.57	75.05	43.19	34.63
090122	Roasted decaffeinated coffee	0.83	2.25	5.55	1.79	6.65	0.34	0.03	–		1.63
090190	Other coffee	6.57	3.49	5.92	10.47	14.00	11.99	10.36	6.75	32.04	0.99
210111	Extracts essences & concentrates of coffee	115.39	203.55	232.23	198.34	257.82	259.99	133.24	193.50	273.80	124.25
210112	Preparation with a basis of extracts essences or concentrates or with a basis of coffee	1.71	9.99	4.91	28.69	18.54	1.99	0.89	0.75	0.28	0.47
	Grand Total	8886.94	22414.82	38430.31	19769.31	26816.53	29160.15	40885.02	45080.93	46055.79	32863.64

Table 3.6B: Import of coffee by type (quantity and value) *(Contd.)*

Import value of coffee by type (lakhs)

HS_CODE	Type	2003–04	2004–05	2005–06	2006–07	2007–08	2008–09	2009–10	2010–11	2011–12*	2012–13*
090111	Coffee neither roasted nor decaffeinated	2133.15	6335.99	16633.9	10686.19	16891.36	25302.80	28834.06	28138.46	45160.38	35463.36
090112	Not roasted but decaffeinated coffee	0.34	0.09	–	–	–	–	–	–	–	0.58
090121	Roasted not decaffeinated coffee	24.53	29.65	25.55	61.41	94.20	217.15	297.75	412.19	277.12	237.91
090122	Roasted deca-feinated coffee	5.27	14.89	14.43	9.16	12.32	5.67	0.29	–		10.39
090190	Other coffee	12.54	4.71	9.77	14.92	34.73	43.98	54.30	32.12	154.86	9.94
210111	Extracts essences & concentrates of coffee	339.68	350.36	568.05	472.50	515.75	985.05	547.75	916.9	1355.14	829.59
210112	Preparation with a basis of extracts essences or concentrates or with a basis of coffee	4.47	19.25	34.16	105.85	104.29	14.74	1.76	4.07	1.97	3.63
	Grand Total	**2519.98**	**6754.94**	**17285.86**	**11350.03**	**17652.65**	**26569.39**	**29735.91**	**29503.74**	**46949.47**	**36555.40**

Source: DGCI and S, Kolkata, MoC and I, GOI (*April to Sep).

Table 3.6C: Imports of coffee imports of coffee by India by countries and types 2011–12

HS_CODE	Type/country	Quantity (MT)	Value (Rs lakhs)	Value (US$ Mln)
090111	**Coffee neither roasted nor decaffeinated**			
	Vietnam Soc Rep	26105.79	26582.18	55.42
	Indonesia	7531.54	7201.04	15.57
	Uganda	5572.73	4789.43	9.86
	China P. Rp.	1339.61	1409.01	3.01
	Kenya	865.07	792.69	1.68
	Germany	825.60	903.18	1.98
	USA	758.00	697.88	1.56
	Taiwan	481.86	480.76	1.00
	Guinea	469.80	445.14	0.99
	Mexico	357.51	512.47	1.00
	Canada	306.80	323.53	0.73
	Ghana	208.97	168.84	0.38
	Cameroon	155.24	127.32	0.27
	Singapore	126.00	119.06	0.27
	Japan	95.80	126.61	0.24
	Korea Republic	95.69	90.34	0.20
	Malaysia	94.92	96.87	0.19
	Portugal	82.50	81.61	0.18
	Papua N Gna	75.00	82.02	0.18
	New Zealand	48.60	34.99	0.08
	Tanzania Rep	36.00	35.29	0.07
	Italy	35.14	30.97	0.07
	Sri Lanka Dsr	18.93	15.47	0.03
	Spain	17.89	9.63	0.02
	Jamaica	1.00	3.60	0.01
	UK	0.49	0.45	0.00
	Total	**45706.48**	**45160.38**	**94.99**
090121	**Roasted not decaffeinated coffee**			
	Italy	36.98	239.31	0.48
	China P Rp	3.21	21.01	0.04
	UK	1.79	9.23	0.02
	USA	0.70	4.62	0.01
	Germany	0.35	1.52	0.00
	Belgium	0.16	1.43	0.00
	Total	**43.19**	**277.12**	**0.55**
090190	**Other coffee**			
	Italy	18.14	83.33	0.18
	Japan	4.02	23.19	0.05
	Australia	2.74	8.80	0.02
	USA	2.12	17.16	0.03
	Germany	1.42	3.39	0.01
	Korea rp	0.66	2.00	0.00
	Guatemala	0.60	4.79	0.01
	Netherland	0.52	2.32	0.00
	France	0.31	1.19	0.00

(Contd.)

Table 3.6C: Imports of coffee imports of coffee by India by countries and types 2011–12

HS_CODE	Type/country	Quantity (MT)	Value (Rs lakhs)	Value (US$ Mln)
	Saudi Arab	0.30	3.53	0.01
	UK	0.26	0.70	0.00
	U. Arab Emts	0.23	1.17	0.00
	China P Rp.	0.20	0.46	0.00
	Belgium	0.18	1.05	0.00
	Philippines	0.17	0.42	0.00
	Switzerland	0.11	0.58	0.00
	Denmark	0.03	0.42	0.00
	Hong Kong	0.02	0.10	0.00
	Spain	0.01	0.26	0.00
	Total	**32.04**	**154.86**	**0.31**
210111	**Extracts essences and concentrates of coffee**			
	Malaysia	116.50	558.91	1.17
	Korea Rp	82.89	328.19	0.66
	Brazil	27.12	157.40	0.35
	UK	11.18	54.28	0.12
	China P. Rp.	8.48	43.42	0.09
	Netherland	7.96	88.55	0.20
	USA	4.45	33.31	0.07
	Germany	4.19	27.45	0.06
	U. Arab Emts	2.19	8.71	0.02
	Thailand	1.77	7.92	0.02
	Portugal	1.69	19.83	0.04
	Indonesia	0.90	2.07	0.00
	Italy	0.72	4.65	0.01
	Saudi Arab	0.72	1.36	0.00
	France	0.71	4.68	0.01
	Turkey	0.57	2.75	0.01
	Austria	0.31	2.48	0.01
	Switzerland	0.30	0.80	0.00
	Hong Kong	0.28	2.24	0.00
	Singapore	0.22	3.31	0.01
	Japan	0.17	0.20	0.00
	Australia	0.16	0.46	0.00
	Spain	0.13	0.99	0.00
	Taiwan	0.10	0.38	0.00
	Canada	0.06	0.37	0.00
	South Africa	0.03	0.43	0.00
	Total	**273.80**	**1355.14**	**2.85**
210112	**Preparation with a basis of extracts essences or concentrates or with a basis of coffee**			
	Belgium	0.28	1.97	0.00
	Subtotal	0.28	1.97	0.00
	Grandtotal	**46055.79**	**46949.47**	**98.70**

Source: DGCI&S, Kolkata, MoC & I, GOI.

Table 3.6D: Imports of coffee by India by countries and types (FY 2012–2013*)

HS_CODE	Type/country	Quntity (MT)	Value (Rs lakhs)	Value (US$ Mln)
090111	**Coffee neither roasted nor decaffeinated**			
	Vietnam Soc Rep	19,535.71	21,294.49	38.74
	Indonesia	7,047.72	7,768.92	14.12
	Uganda	3,263.69	3,232.00	5.88
	Kenya	360.00	375.63	0.68
	China P Rp	345.25	361.22	0.65
	Mexico	321.55	367.24	0.67
	Ghana	309.50	299.54	0.55
	Taiwan	303.20	351.15	0.63
	Korea Rp	243.60	278.02	0.50
	Nigeria	210.70	273.74	0.50
	Egypt A Rp	188.80	243.52	0.44
	Czech Republic	175.00	191.45	0.35
	USA	90.00	86.37	0.16
	Spain	87.00	99.95	0.18
	Ukraine	72.00	69.48	0.13
	UK	57.13	75.82	0.14
	Cameroon	52.69	48.05	0.09
	Myanmar	36.00	37.56	0.07
	Australia	1.59	6.81	0.01
	Italy	0.43	2.39	0.00
	Turkey	0.01	0.03	0.00
	Total	**32,701.57**	**35,463.36**	**64.49**
090112	**Not roasted but decaffeinated coffee**			
	Switzerland	0.10	0.58	0.00
	Subtotal	**0.10**	**0.58**	**0.00**
090121	**Roasted not decaffeinated coffee**			
	Italy	32.68	219.39	0.40
	USA	1.38	12.37	0.02
	Germany	0.36	1.81	0.00
	UK	0.10	0.72	0.00
	Belgium	0.05	1.66	0.00
	Korea Rp	0.05	1.52	0.00
	Turkey	0.01	0.05	0.00
	China P Rp	0.00	0.28	0.00
	Switzerland	0.00	0.09	0.00
	Total	**34.63**	**237.91**	**0.43**
090122	**Roasted decaffeinated coffee**			
	Italy	1.44	6.90	0.01
	UK	0.18	2.94	0.01

(Contd.)

Table 3.6D: Imports of Coffee by India by countries and types (FY 2012–2013*)

HS_CODE	Type/country	Quntity (MT)	Value (Rs lakhs)	Value (US$ Mln)
	Australia	0.01	0.54	0.00
	Total	**1.63**	**10.39**	**0.02**
090190	**Other coffee**			
	Australia	0.58	3.14	0.01
	Netherland	0.20	0.64	0.00
	U. Arab Emts	0.19	4.60	0.01
	Belgium	0.01	0.73	0.00
	USA	0.01	0.12	0.00
	Germany	0.00	0.38	0.00
	Spain	0.00	0.35	0.00
	Total	**0.99**	**9.94**	**0.02**
210111	**Extracts essences and concentrates of coffee**			
	Malaysia	54.47	270.65	0.49
	Brazil	17.40	121.12	0.22
	Germany	13.37	139.50	0.27
	Korea Rp	10.77	151.15	0.28
	USA	7.01	46.91	0.08
	UK	6.70	24.76	0.05
	Singapore	2.73	2.50	0.00
	Switzerland	2.72	37.36	0.07
	U. Arab Emts	2.66	8.15	0.01
	Italy	1.79	10.35	0.02
	Turkey	1.04	2.18	0.00
	France	0.74	4.73	0.01
	Thailand	0.65	1.53	0.00
	Netherland	0.58	2.40	0.00
	Saudi Arab	0.51	1.03	0.00
	Israel	0.36	0.46	0.00
	Baharain Is	0.31	0.60	0.00
	Hong Kong	0.23	2.81	0.01
	Nepal	0.20	0.99	0.00
	China P Rp	0.01	0.40	0.00
	Total	**124.25**	**829.59**	**1.53**
210112	**Preparation with a basis of extracts essences or concentrates or with a basis of coffee**			
	Thailand	0.25	2.11	0.00
	Belgium	0.22	1.51	0.00
	Italy	0.00	0.02	0.00
	Total	**0.47**	**3.63**	**0.01**
	Grand total	**32863.64**	**36555.40**	**66.50**

Source: DGCI & S, Kolkata, MoC & I, GOI (April to Sep).

Table 3.7: Coffee exports-quantity and value

Year	Quantity (tons)	Value (US$ millions)	Value (Rs/crores)	Unit value (Rs/tons)
1991	103638	62.26	324.41	31302
1992	108988	87.27	347.99	31929
1993	126152	138.83	507.32	40214
1994	151532	329.07	1032.58	68142
1995	149290	428.68	1407.56	94283
1996	186841	438.21	1449.12	77558
1997	161590	438.30	1513.68	93674
1998	209687	469.11	1868.28	89098
1999	218230	326.66	1648.51	75540
2000	253524	316.81	1682.59	66368
2001	223782	208.16	1136.93	50805
2002	213008	244.97	1043.87	49006
2003	222425	247.98	1112.35	50010
2004	228246	288.12	1203.52	52729
2005	203768	338.39	1451.65	71240
2006	244989	434.73	1930.95	78817
2007	214155	457.93	1906.52	89025
2008	212806	563.09	2358.37	110822
2009	180298	390.97	1929.67	107026
2010	278837	615.87	2877.94	103212
2011	324818	977.80	4448.02	136938
2012	302260	885.06	4607.57	152437
2013*	254865	692.03	3804.63	149280

Includes re-exports from 2004 onwards.
* Provisional Based on export permits (01.01.2013 to 30.09.2013).

Table 3.7A: Exports of coffee from India by countries

(Rs crores)

Destination	2002–03	2003–04	2004–05	2005–06	2006–07	2007–08	2008–09	2009–10	2010–11	2011–12	2012–13	2013–14*
Algeria	4123	4293	614	1306	4294	727	2448	1318	2490	7395	1664	751
Australia	1743	2469	2393	2615	3389	3195	3140	3325	4035	4819	6003	2775
Austria	677	749	230	69	849	799	870	1008	1618	906	1345	153
Belgium	17430	18777	9204	11190	13989	10615	9653	6680	18236	18900	19907	10840
Canada	1422	2665	1263	1169	1850	1289	1158	1200	1890	1712	1140	620
China	–	–	18	–	959	1173	821	877	427	431	238	66
Czech Republic	144	–		17	53	20	12	38	46	6	70	110
Denmark	515	63	80	160			20	22	2	44	662	227
Dubai	99	253	318	32	34	245	286	85	263	163	48	57
Egypt	1913	1754	966	593	2698	1373	2566	3977	4349	5598	3031	308
Finland	875	4762	3677	4245	6147	7888	5299	5077	4787	5638	5332	2730
France	3676	6214	4283	3811	5837	3856	3803	2512	4424	3232	3121	2658
Germany	23344	25680	16518	16742	21835	14236	14642	13171	33371	38138	24855	16570
Greece	4936	4224	5642	4392	6061	5470	4614	4572	5122	6848	6468	2845
Hungary	1606	2479	2607	2976	2947	3572	2774	2438	609	373	374	171
Israel	1487	1853	1529	1581	3588	2714	2745	2842	4085	3716	3574	2034
Italy	45594	52197	49232	53413	62768	53804	51119	47065	80653	71010	75554	36837
Japan	4899	3538	5918	4147	4650	2158	1612	1079	1315	1812	2751	1552
Jordan	1519	3169	2727	1784	2980	4813	5168	5604	5927	9436	7389	5934
Kuwait	3088	3150	2657	2877	3452	3906	3482	3081	3412	4238	4223	2475
Netherlands	2566	3205	3604	2949	3445	2858	2106	229	1035	2939	1179	661

Table 3.7A: Exports of coffee from India by countries (*contd.*)

(Rs Crores)

Destination	2002–03	2003–04	2004–05	2005–06	2006–07	2007–08	2008–09	2009–10	2010–11	2011–12	2012–13	2013–14*
Norway	1091	1189	934	983	1056	873	794	713	872	830	558	169
Oman	–	923	691	460	676	483	598	569	560	879	774	375
Poland	1846	1018	1302	1021	1119	1518	1336	1426	2747	4492	3485	1021
Portugal	2967	3218	3253	3504	3603	3387	2898	3565	4207	3293	2942	2089
Romania	565	532	450	543	1127	1100	972	992	527	959	587	365
Russian Federation	36578	33592	34459	29432	27447	25183	16143	27482	29978	33112	24770	10158
Saudi Arabia	1714	1041	1181	1012	1346	1398	1738	1791	1119	6816	3132	1887
Singapore	705	713	1767	1961	3091	4207	2566	1823	3857	3587	2109	1493
Slovakia	56			39	45	58	38	58	19	77	77	77
Slovenia	8698	10795	8441	7458	8106	5400	4715	3352	5154	9629	13388	5735
Spain	11142	13898	11499	10292	11091	8781	8556	6169	11043	13451	6650	3679
Switzerland	2872	3301	3244	2440	3200	4758	3873	4069	4808	3455	3499	1322
Syria	275	2337	212	489	1383	397	1150	1828	3302	4974	3699	1189
Tunisia	19	–	440	–		409	721	307	2189	5083	425	145
Ukraine	2908	3190	6131	6920	6962	4943	5445	3620	4300	4784	6188	3674
United Arab Emirates	2840	2120	1781	1529.5	2029	1539	1716	1273	1125	1969	1638	1074
United Kingdom	667	710	1222	1104	1144	1047	1285	1222	2204	2483	1826	1105
USA	3505	3237	5646	2448	4255	4304	1950	3843	6985	6157	6078	2634
Others	7233	9378	15633	13856	19489	24361	21931	25706	36693	39797	47387	28406
Total	**207333**	**232684**	**211765**	**201555**	**248991**	**218852**	**196762**	**196002**	**299778**	**333181**	**298062**	**156966**

*FY - Financial year (April to March). Includes re-exports from 2004–05 onwards (Provisional from 01.04.2013 to 30.09.2013).

Table 3.7B: Export earnings from coffee by countries – FY 2002/03 to 2013/14*

(Rs crores)

Destination	2002–03	2003–04	2004–05	2005–06	2006–07	2007–08	2008–09	2009–10	2010–11	2011–12	2012–13	2013–14*
Algeria	14.44	15.51	2.22	8.38	26.86	5.45	23.10	11.11	19.17	85.47	19.93	9.58
Australia	8.21	12.04	13.52	21.00	27.91	30.28	37.03	39.37	52.13	75.04	111.38	46.27
Austria	3.17	4.16	1.78	0.71	6.07	5.99	8.16	7.96	12.76	11.06	15.80	1.83
Belgium	70.14	86.64	47.34	84.72	109.13	99.99	102.13	77.00	227.73	294.47	335.07	175.18
Canada	5.70	9.41	5.66	8.19	13.20	11.25	12.46	9.72	17.76	20.76	16.11	8.53
China	–	–	0.16	–	6.39	9.25	8.80	8.05	3.93	5.32	3.42	0.94
Czech Republic	0.57	–	–	0.23	–	–	0.21	0.59	0.96	0.17	1.22	1.82
Denmark	2.43	0.14	0.87	1.81	0.47	0.18	0.25	0.23	0.04	0.50	8.06	2.88
Dubai	0.76	1.65	2.41	0.39	0.47	2.98	4.15	1.41	0.95	5.05	1.12	1.08
Egypt	7.16	6.44	4.21	4.18	18.61	11.92	24.11	34.05	38.33	69.32	37.69	4.42
Finland	6.71	36.01	26.76	33.48	51.17	72.85	69.44	59.37	53.13	83.88	83.72	47.11
France	17.16	28.47	22.41	26.75	46.01	35.85	42.54	25.26	52.96	57.21	50.82	41.61
Germany	102.60	123.46	106.16	147.58	190.91	144.77	180.62	148.95	459.55	541.01	387.39	239.31
Greece	18.37	15.33	22.44	26.17	40.83	43.80	44.99	37.70	45.64	76.57	82.01	36.68
Hungary	6.94	11.00	12.22	17.96	21.13	31.02	32.75	24.73	5.67	4.08	4.21	2.43
Israel	7.61	8.66	8.33	13.02	27.15	23.61	28.16	28.28	46.29	52.28	51.18	28.15
Italy	184.64	231.70	254.81	365.86	469.19	476.52	554.29	438.98	805.15	973.10	1091.04	525.49
Japan	25.37	17.72	40.49	37.27	43.96	20.78	22.37	14.21	16.21	26.06	46.76	26.29
Jordan	8.29	14.97	15.85	15.83	26.63	53.17	58.07	71.45	72.79	156.77	132.39	96.37
Kuwait	17.82	20.74	21.71	28.56	36.93	44.94	44.75	42.92	53.88	88.77	81.39	42.74
Netherlands	9.92	15.31	26.10	26.03	30.51	26.25	24.41	2.73	20.54	40.70	21.56	9.66

Table 3.7B: Export earnings from coffee by countries – FY 2002/03 to 2013/14* *(Contd.)*

(Rs crores)

Destination	2002–03	2003–04	2004–05	2005–06	2006–07	2007–08	2008–09	2009–10	2010–11	2011–12	2012–13	2013–14*
Norway	5.59	5.96	5.19	7.23	8.70	8.00	9.06	8.03	9.61	11.56	10.55	3.59
Oman	0.00	3.67	3.62	3.11	4.86	4.22	6.51	5.30	5.28	12.50	11.68	5.47
Poland	9.67	6.06	8.83	6.63	8.46	13.85	14.80	13.22	28.39	51.48	37.52	14.87
Portugal	11.10	12.29	13.50	20.44	27.81	27.59	28.28	28.71	35.66	37.72	37.09	27.11
Romania	1.92	2.12	2.39	3.25	7.70	8.74	9.49	8.28	4.48	12.86	7.73	4.43
Russian Federation	307.74	225.42	235.74	228.25	244.09	253.48	197.50	313.69	332.13	484.76	408.26	155.65
Saudi Arabia	10.19	6.28	8.33	10.93	15.96	16.26	24.06	29.70	16.26	100.49	53.89	30.80
Singapore	5.06	5.37	9.71	14.65	22.92	34.95	30.26	22.03	38.70	40.23	31.91	23.04
Slovakia	0.20	–	–	0.20	0.37	0.44	0.41	0.50	0.16	1.26	.	1.11
Slovenia	28.32	38.06	30.54	41.46	51.36	41.98	45.01	23.32	40.22	102.08	159.33	70.88
Spain	42.46	53.92	48.16	63.42	75.44	71.03	83.19	49.21	95.40	153.79	90.89	51.14
Switzerland	15.99	19.31	22.79	23.83	29.71	50.41	50.60	53.71	65.61	68.37	70.56	23.81
Syria	1.59	12.39	1.08	5.42	11.74	3.93	12.62	19.54	34.97	64.26	45.10	16.16
Tunisia	0.12	–	–	–	–	4.53	7.51	2.54	18.33	61.98	5.08	1.24
Ukraine	22.56	25.16	49.61	60.91	67.72	52.63	76.19	45.78	55.06	76.76	110.06	64.22
United ArabEmirates	16.81	13.57	15.25	16.53	22.76	18.72	24.03	22.28	18.85	40.42	32.86	20.27
United Kingdom	3.47	4.18	8.36	10.48	12.58	11.02	16.91	15.80	27.95	39.28	33.53	20.15
USA	15.06	14.66	27.80	20.86	38.04	40.49	26.33	47.06	88.72	96.47	104.94	41.68
Others	35.58	50.69	96.72	104.67	163.87	231.62	252.88	277.89	445.12	538.99	699.64	438.04
Total	1051.45	1158.45	1224.67	1510.38	2007.60	2044.71	2238.42	2070.68	3366.42	4662.81	4532.84	2362.02

*FY - Financial year (April to March). Includes re-exports from 2004–2005 onwards (Provisional from 01.04.2013 to 30.09.2013).

Table 3.7C: Export of specialty and value added coffees: quantity (crop years 2003–2004 to 2012–2013)

(In MT)

Grade	2003–04	2004–05	2005–06	2006–07	2007–08	2008–09	2009–10	2010–11	2011–12	2012–13
Specialty Coffees										
Mysore Nuggets EB	1159.5	718.9	1256.5	1057.0	1147.7	700.7	915.4	914.2	1534.1	1890.4
Monsooned Malabar AA	2008.5	2339.7	2688.7	2575.1	3614.0	4091.8	3463.4	3496.8	2626.6	3537.1
Monsooned Malabar PB	–	–	–	–	–	–	–	–	–	–
Monsooned Malabar C	–	–	–	–	–	–	–	–	–	–
Monsooned Malabar BBB	–	–	–	–	–	–	–	–	–	–
Monsooned Arabica AA	–	–	–	–	–	–	–	–	–	–
Monsooned Robusta AA	1019.3	1120.0	1210.4	1581.4	1085.0	1267.7	1440.7	985.1	1209.9	1090.6
Monsooned Ar. Tr	–	8.7	69.0	30.0	12.8	54.5	89.0	207.0	156.0	211.5
Monsooned Rob. Tr	–	–	60.0	15.0	–	–	12.0	–	11.9	34.9
Monsooned Basanally	182.0	168.6	257.0	309.9	620.5	285.9	215.0	557.3	273.7	402.0
Monsooned Arb. BBB	–	–	–	–	–	–	–	–	–	–
Monsooned Rob. C	–	–	–	–	–	–	–	–	–	–
Monsooned Rob Bulk	–	–	–	–	–	–	–	–	–	–
Monsooned Rob Blacks	–	–	–	–	–	–	–	–	–	–
Robusta Kapi Royale	4338.2	3621.5	4286.1	3962.2	4218.4	3538.7	6432.5	9223.7	6714.2	6422.5
Others	–	–	–	–	–	–	–	–		
Subtotal	**8707.5**	**7977.4**	**9827.7**	**9530.6**	**10698.4**	**9939.3**	**12556.0**	**15396.1**	**12526.4**	**13589.0**
Value-added coffees										
Instant	45961.2	56079.4	51045.8	63515.2	62546.8	49323.1	73616.1	83062.2	87284.6	93912.7
Ground	137.4	26.9	93.6	303.2	191.9	230.5	150.6	176.8	175.0	167.7
Roasted	51.0	10.4	60.9	77.9	83.2	85.8	113.8	72.0	32.5	22.7
Subtotal	**46149.6**	**56116.7**	**51200.3**	**63896.3**	**62821.9**	**49639.4**	**73880.5**	**83311.0**	**87492.1**	**94103.1**
Grand total	**54857.1**	**64094.1**	**61028.0**	**73426.9**	**73520.3**	**59578.7**	**86436.5**	**98707.1**	**100018.5**	**107692.1**

Table 3.7D: Export of specialty and value added coffees: value (crop years 2003–2004 to 2012–2013)

(In Rs lakhs)

Grade	2003–04	2004–05	2005–06	2006–07	2007–08	2008–09	2009–10	2010–11	2011–12	2012–13*
Specialty coffees										
Mysore Nuggets EB	850.40	838.70	1393.40	1298.30	1509.50	1037.10	1655.00	2243.60	3797.80	3582.70
Monsooned Malabar AA	1438.10	1908.70	3092.50	3114.50	4298.40	6131.30	4927.00	6458.90	6875.10	8363.90
Monsooned Malabar PB	–	–	–	–	–	–	–			
Monsooned Malabar C	–	–	–	–	–	–	–			
Monsooned Mal BBB	–	–	–	–	–	–	–			
Monsooned Arabica AA	–	–	–	–	–	–	–			
Monsooned Robusta AA	464.10	574.30	863.80	1265.10	996.40	1476.90	1285.10	1036.60	1708.90	1792.40
Monsooned Ar. Tr	–	6.30	55.70	27.00	22.00	50.30	89.90	244.50	242.40	307.60
Monsooned Rob. Tr	–	–	30.80	9.90	–	–	11.00	17.30	45.2	
Monsooned Basanally	94.90	112.10	271.60	314.10	618.90	370.30	245.30	841.90	682.70	825.60
Monsooned Arb. BBB	–	–	–	–	–	–	–			
Monsooned Rob. C	–	–	–	–	–	–	–			
Monsooned Rob. Bulk	–	–	–	–	–	–	–			
Monsooned Rob. Blacks	–	–	–	–	–	–	–			
Robusta Kapi Royale	2296.00	2567.20	3347.50	3457.20	4837.50	4438.10	6655.60	10621.60	9950.10	10685.30
Subtotal	**5143.50**	**6007.30**	**9055.30**	**9486.10**	**12282.70**	**13504.00**	**14857.90**	**21458.10**	**23274.30**	**25602.70**
Value-added coffees										
Instant	30076.80	41324.10	41778.60	59287.90	68137.10	62984.80	80280.30	105908.10	131307.00	150250.5
Ground	106.40	31.40	121.40	330.40	208.70	331.50	358.00	335.20	476.30	500.4
Roasted	22.40	15.90	143.90	210.20	210.80	249.70	343.90	173.90	119.10	68.1
Sub-total	**30205.60**	**41371.40**	**42043.90**	**59828.50**	**68556.60**	**63566.00**	**80982.20**	**106417.20**	**131902.40**	**150819.00**
Grand total	**35349.10**	**47378.70**	**51099.20**	**69314.60**	**80839.30**	**77070.00**	**95840.10**	**127875.30**	**155176.70**	**176421.70**

Ar. Tr. = Arabica Triage. Rob. Tr. = Robusta Triage. GBE = Green Bean Equivalent.
*From 01.10.2012 to 30.09.2013. Includes re-exports from 2004-05 onward.

Table 3.8: Re-exports of coffee and types by countries – FY 2008/09

(Value in Rs lakh)

Destination	2008/09		2009/10		2010/11*		2011/12*		2012/13	
	Instant	Total	Instant	Total	Instant	Total	Instant	Total	Instant	Total
Ukraine	3575	3575	2769	2769	2118	2118	3071	3071	6285	6285
Russian Federation	2634	2634	24763	24763	17694	17694	30621	30621	28528	28528
Finland	2392	2392	3403	3403	1544	1544	2026	2026	3601	3601
Germany	1788	1788	665	665			3137	3137	2349	2349
Malaysia	1338	1338	1394	1394	883	883	1788	1788	3001	3001
Singapore	1264	1264	1234	1234	2593	2593	2547	2547	1738	1738
France	1031	1031	655	655	591	591	861	861	2128	2128
Latvia	781	781	760	760	606	606	1215	1215	1753	1753
Turkey	718	718	1160	1160	1506	1506	1572	1572	8952	8952
Egypt			823	823	940	940	2476	2476	1442	1442
USA	672	672	2202	2202	3148	3148	3438	3438	5700	5700
Switzerland	521	521	1171	1171	1352	1352				
Italy	479	479	706	706	817	817	479	479		
United Kingdom	420	420	459	459	499	499	733	733		
Poland	245	245					1746	1746	1559	1559
Taiwan	223	223	758	758	479	479	894	894	714	714
Japan	112	112	541	541	229	229	450	450	1661	1661
Korea, Republic of	76	76			259	259				
Myanmar					256	256				
Senegal							504	504	635	635
Netherlands	57	57								
Burkina Faso									602	602
Others	430	430	2721	2721	1505	1505	3130	3130	7043	7043
Total	**18755**	**18755**	**48548**	**48548**	**40128**	**40128**	**61601**	**61601**	**82511**	**82511**

WORLD COFFEE PRODUCTION

Among the plantation crops, coffee continues to occupy an important place in the country's economy. Indian coffee has created a niche for itself in the international market, particularly Robusta coffee, which is popular for its blending qualities. Indian Arabica coffee is also well received in the international market. India is Asia's third largest grower of coffee. World coffee production increased from 45 million tons in 1961 to 7.8 million tons in 2007. Corresponding area figures were 9.7 million and 10.4 million hectares (Table 3.9). Brazil topped the list from among the major top 20 producing countries at 2.7 million tons in 2011 (Table 3.9A). It was followed by Vietnam and Indonesia India came at the 7th position.

Detailed country wise information is as in Table 3.9B. Data regarding production of coffee in the exporting countries is available for members and non-member

Table 3.8A: Re-exports of coffee and types by countries – FY 2009/10

(Quantity in metric tons)

Destination	2009/10		2010/11*		2011/12*		2012/13	
	Instant	Total	Instant	Total	Instant	Total	Instant	Total
Russian Federation	21820	21820	16007	16007	20398	20398	18638	18638
Turkey	1059	1059	1464	1464	1118	1118	5610	5610
USA	1948	1948	2868	2868	2486	2486	3576	3576
Ukraine	2167	2167	1652	1652	1802	1802	3460	3460
Malaysia	1412	1412	915	915	1643	1643	2371	2371
Finland	3070	3070	1694	1694	1640	1640	2335	2335
Germany	444	444			2068	2068	1543	1543
Singapore	1201	1201	2615	2615	2486	2486	1469	1469
Switzerland	793	793	1227	1227	273	273		
Italy	735	735	759	759	308	308		
Belarus					538	538	1273	1273
France	565	565	511	511	533	533	1133	1133
Poland					1484	1484	1051	1051
Egypt			1004	1004	1776	1776	1046	1046
Japan	346	346			303	303	1044	1044
Latvia	603	603	455	455	851	851	1011	1011
Mali							722	722
Taiwan	729	729	467	467	698	698	507	507
Indonesia							483	483
Uzbekistan							377	377
Syria							345	345
Others	2183	2183	1130	1130	2140	2140	4050	4050
Total	42550	42550	36248	36248	42912	42912	52044	52044

countries. Breakdown of total production for exporting numbers producing both Arabica and Robusta coffee (Table 3.3.9C) shows that Brazil tops for both the varieties. Production of coffee both by the number and non-member countries (Table 3.9D) that while the production of non-number countries increased from 8.0 million bags in 2008 to 8.3 million bags, those of member countries increased from 128.6 million bags to 145.2 million bags during the same period. From the total production, Arabica coffee production increased from 78.6 million bags in 2004–2005 to 85.15 million bags in 2008–2009 and 88.7 million bags in 2012–2013. Brazil alone showed 46% increase followed by Columbia (12.13%) (Table 3.10) with regard to Robusta, Vietnam with over 37% share was at the top. It was followed by Brazil 24% and Indonesia around 12% (Table 3.11).

Table 3.9: Area and production of coffee in India and world

Area (ha.) production in tons

Year	India		World			
	Area	*Produ.*	*Area*		*Produ.*	
2007	343,000	288,000	10,366,922	A	7,792,960	A
2006	329,000	274,000	10,171,605	A	7,861,006	A
2005	329,000	276,000	10,484,643	A	7,276,333	A
2004	328,000	271,000	10,328,037	A	7,582,293	A
2003	323,000	275,000	10,224,395	A	7,179,592	A
2002	323,000	301,000	10,167,002	A	7,876,893	A
2001	321,000	301,000	10,704,085	A	7,407,986	A
2000	305,000	292,000	10,767,066	A	7,562,713	A
1999	280,000	265,000	10,295,938	A	6,789,637	A
1998	280,000	228,000	10,059,903	A	6,647,409	A
1997	242,000	205,000	9,848,839	A	6,000,920	A
1996	275,000	223,000	9,880,837	A	6,214,211	A
1995	275,000	180,000	9,806,328	A	5,537,023	A
1994	275,000	208,000	10,036,958	A	5,766,808	A
1993	265,000	162,000	10,181,358	A	5,555,144	A
1992	248,600	180,000	10,479,844	A	6,087,285	A
1991	270,800	170,000	10,928,457	A	6,099,605	A
1990	246,800	118,100	11,355,966	A	6,070,955	A
1989	243,100	214,700	11,263,151	A	5,908,050	A
1988	242,200	122,700	11,164,380	A	5,645,497	A
1987	243,500	192,100	10,853,050	A	6,385,160	A
1986	214,600	122,400	10,580,189	A	5,237,226	A
1985	209,400	195,100	10,350,547	A	5,824,530	A
1984	207,100	105,029	10,163,330	A	5,220,504	A
1983	201,000	130,000	10,142,872	A	5,582,080	A
1982	194,000	152,100	9,802,634	A	4,932,497	A
1981	190,000	118,600	10,385,160	A	6,080,258	A
1980	185,000	149,835	10,064,219	A	4,836,928	A
1979	180,000	110,488	9,773,493	A	4,971,186	A
1978	170,000	125,000	9,403,182	A	4,725,186	A
1977	160,000	102,300	8,987,687	A	4,399,391	A
1976	150,000	84,000	7,929,110	A	3,522,508	A
1975	145,000	92,506	8,998,436	A	4,603,209	A
1974	131,000	86,388	8,974,530	A	4,770,143	A

Table 3.9: Area and production of coffee in India and world (*Contd.*)

Area (ha.) production in tons

Year	India Area	India Produ.	World Area		World Produ.	
1973	130,000	91,072	8,876,898	A	4,185,724	A
1972	129,000	68,948	8,942,534	A	4,570,708	A
1971	128,000	110,231	9,071,139	A	4,663,275	A
1970	128,000	63,619	8,884,986	A	3,849,638	A
1969	128,000	73,430	8,993,300	A	4,272,399	A
1968	128,000	57,331	9,078,861	A	3,936,446	A
1967	126,000	78,500	9,406,925	A	4,332,681	A
1966	125,000	63,900	9,521,306	A	4,052,231	A
1965	122,000	60,900	9,777,738	A	4,981,569	A
1964	120,000	69,300	9,813,353	A	3,769,389	A
1963	118,000	56,200	10,339,766	A	4,152,127	A
1962	115,000	46,000	10,344,580	A	4,583,896	A
1961	96,000	43,200	9,755,805	A	4,527,246	A

A, May include official, semi-official or estimated data.

The production of green coffee increased from 101.4 million bags (60 kg) in 1992 to 122.6 in 2004/05 and further to 139.7 million bags in 2010/11 while Brazil is not mentioned in the production data upto 2002 Indonesia with 7.3 million bags in 1992 is shown as the leader. This is reduced to 6.2 million bags by 2002, went up to 8.4 million in 2004–2005 and 9.6 million bags in 1910–1911. Available data shows that with 43.6 million bags in 2004–2005 and 55.3 million in 2010/11, Brazil has been the Copper throughout. Brazil the major home of coffee production topped with 37%, followed by Vietnam 14.7% and central African Republic as 7.8% (Table 3.11). Graphs at Table 3.11A give projections for stocks in producing countries.

Green Bean exports increased from 86.2 million bags in 2004–05 to 94.0 million bags in 2008–09 further to 101.4 million bags in 2011/12. The share of Brazil was around 28.29%, the share of Vietnam varied from 16.5 to 20% during this period. Colombia came next at 12% in 2004–2005 dealing to 10% by 2008–2009 (Table 3.11B). With regard to Green Bean imports, EU-27 shared nearly 50%, followed by USA at around 25% (Table 3.11C). As regards ending shocks, Brazil has been leading with around 30–33%, followed by EU-27 with a share of 26% in 2004–2005 (Table 3.11D). EU-27 took the lead by 2012–2013 sharing over 35% followed by Brazil – over 22%.

Ending stocks in 2013/14 are forecast to continue rising in producing countries, particularly Brazil and Vietnam while consuming countries remain relatively flat. Global stocks have been rising over the last several years as world production outpaces consumption.

Global production is now forecast at 150.5 million bags, down 2.8 million from the previous year as Vietnam's record output is more than offset by declines in Brazil, Indonesia, Mexico and Central America. A modest increase in world exports is expected on strong shipments from Vietnam and Colombia.

Table 3.9A: Top rank countries of coffee green, 2011

Rank	Country	Production (Int. $1000)	Flag	Production (MT)	Flag
1	Brazil	2901244	*	2700440	
2	Vietnam	1371426	*	1276505	
3	Indonesia	681144	*	634000	
4	Colombia	503380	*	468540	
5	Ethiopia	398124	*	370569	
6	Peru	356200	*	331547	
7	India	324456	*	302000	
8	Honduras	303357	*	282361	
9	Guatemala	260896	*	242839	
10	Mexico	254683	*	237056	
11	Uganda	205601	*	191371	
12	Nicaragua	111372	*	103664	
13	Côte d'Ivoire	110659	*	103000	F
14	Costa Rica	107525	*	100083	
15	Philippines	95108	*	88526	
16	Papua New Guinea	91180	*	84870	
17	El Salvador	88199	*	82095	
18	Cameroon	75205	*	70000	F
19	Venezuela (Bolivarian Republic of)	74279	*	69138	Im
20	United Republic of Tanzania	65079	*	60575	

* : Unofficial figure
[ ]: Official data
F : FAO estimate
Im: FAO data based on imputation methodology

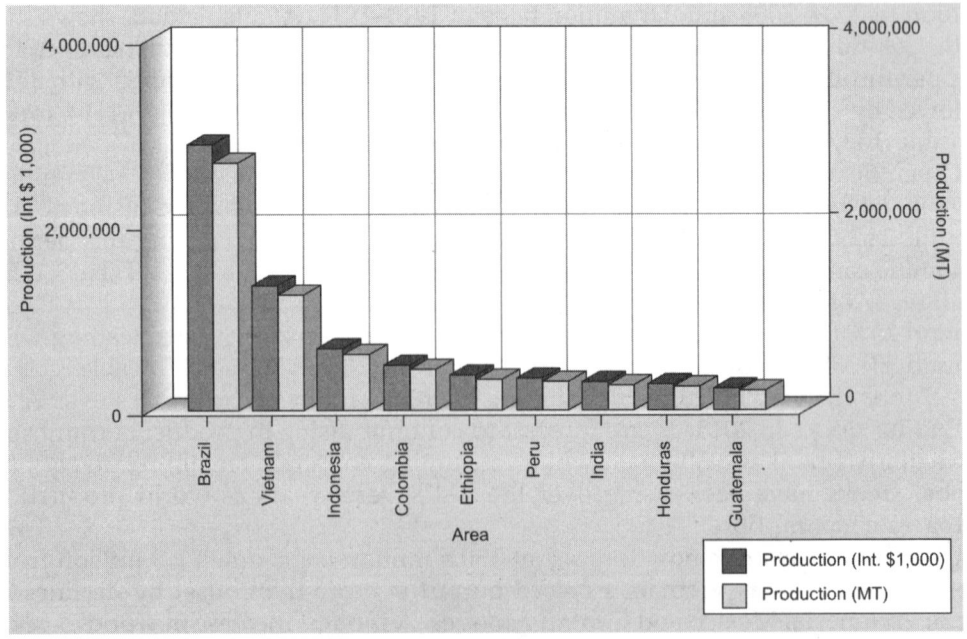

Top production–coffee, green, 2011

Table 3.9B: World production of coffee

(Tons)

Countries	1994–1996	1999–2001	2003–2005	2006	2007	2008	2009
Angola	2,760	3,620	1,960	2,100	2,160	2,160	
Belize		155	171	95	45	90	90
Benin	200	183	60	60	60	60	
Bolivia	20,518	26,238	24,741	25,272	25,422	25,422	
Brazil	1,202,207	1,784,994	2,197,651	2,573,368	2,249,010	2,796,927	2,432,904
Burundi	31,228	21,155	21,300	31,000	15,000	15,000	
Cambodia	213	300	307	310	310	310	
Cameroon	83,955	84,900	50,085	62,300	48,240	35,242	48,123
Central African Republic	13,833	12,153	4,380	1,500	2,400	3,300	3,600
China	3,156	12,504	22,241	23,000	26,000	26,500	27,000
Colombia	738,360	613,340	678,540	622,453	757,080	688,680	887,661
Comoros	93	97	100	100	100	100	
Congo	1,586	1,551	2,067	2,000	2,200	2,200	
Congo, Democratic Rep. of the	82,345	43,365	32,020	31,960	31,930	31,900	24,000
Costa Rica	150,730	153,184	127,976	101,038	124,055	107,341	91,627
Côte d'Ivoire	169,443	329,486	174,703	187,000	170,849	80,000	150,000
Cuba	16,940	18,080	13,680	13,500	13,500	6,240	7,980
Dominica	353	370	380	380	405	405	
Dominican Republic	41,198	38,544	37,551	41,352	41,232	41,232	
Ecuador	175,233	145,253	90,722	31,461	38,687	32,097	33,624
El Salvador	142,969	129,023	84,069	78,482	96,355	89,801	76,591
Equatorial Guinea	4,833	4,500	4,333	4,500	4,500	4,500	
Ethiopia	222,320	225,143	183,127	241,482	325,800	273,400	260,239
Gabon	212	128	120	120	125	125	125
Ghana	4,110	2,433	1,080	1,500	1,650	1,650	
Guatemala	221,707	293,760	247,585	220,500	240,332	248,614	
Guinea	26,917	19,043	20,820	23,226	26,115	18,000	
Guyana	295	103	150	150	160	160	
Haiti	29,000	28,667	31,333	21,120	47,000	35,000	
Honduras	135,804	185,421	183,671	199,399	201,987	190,137	205,800
India	203,667	286,000	274,000	274,000	288,000	262,000	
Indonesia	443,248	549,498	650,440	682,158	676,475	682,938	700,000
Jamaica	2,540	2,480	2,700	2,700	3,300	3,300	
Kenya	91,092	73,500	49,691	48,300	53,368	42,000	57,000
Lao People's Democratic Republic	9,210	22,275	25,317	25,250	33,200	38,985	46,035
Liberia	3,000	3,067	3,493	4,260	3,180	3,000	

(Contd.)

Table 3.9B: World production of coffee

(Tons)

Countries	1994–1996	1999–2001	2003–2005	2006	2007	2008	2009
Madagascar	68,667	62,537	64,530	61,635	67,000	67,000	
Malawi	5,099	3,880	1,785	2,091	1,403	1,122	
Malaysia	12,500	37,767	39,733	40,000	30,550	28,690	
Mexico	341,060	314,428	305,879	279,635	268,565	265,817	
Mozambique	883	733	600	600	600	600	
Myanmar	1,508	1,888	3,070	3,300	4,300	4,300	
Nepal	27	69	219	300	460	500	268
New Caledonia	47	38	34	25	21	21	
Nicaragua	48,346	80,265	78,572	70,455	100,000	72,727	
Nigeria	3,530	3,810	4,670	5,340	5,400	5,400	
Panama	10,923	12,451	12,506	12,844	13,790	13,324	
Papua New Guinea	63,939	76,587	68,420	46,900	75,400	75,400	
Paraguay	4,345	3,688	3,113	3,040	3,100	3,100	3,200
Peru	98,186	185,009	207,735	273,178	225,992	273,780	255,016
Philippines	138,474	107,984	105,033	104,093	97,877	97,428	96,433
Rwanda	12,837	17,755	17,473	21,000	14,683	20,724	28,000
Saint Vincent and the Grenadines	158	170	170	175	180	180	
Samoa	13	8	8	8	8	8	
Sao Tome and Principe	20	33	27	30	30	30	
Sierra Leone	25,943	15,117	17,667	18,000	18,000	18,000	
Sri Lanka	11,432	10,193	8,007	6,460	6,050	5,450	5,410
Tanzania, United Republic of	42,871	50,857	49,367	34,300	54,800	43,100	
Thailand	81,637	73,639	58,439	46,873	55,660	50,442	56,315
Timor-Leste	9,996	13,045	12,000	14,000	12,000	12,000	
Togo	15,027	16,367	7,333	8,900	9,300	9,500	
Tonga	19	15	15	18	18	18	
Trinidad and Tobago	733	434	348	350	350	350	
Uganda	222,587	197,589	159,684	133,310	175,346	211,726	195,871
United States of America	1,947	3,737	3,340	3,311	3,400	3,950	3,630
Vanuatu	33	32	15	15	15	15	
Venezuela	68,839	83,390	66,751	74,332	70,311	72,000	
Vietnam	239,367	732,100	846,167	985,300	1,251,000	1,067,400	1,176,000
Yemen	9,358	11,484	11,066	17,292	18,330	18,788	18,924
Zambia	1,465	4,880	5,187	3,900	4,500	4,500	
Zimbabwe	9,593	8,873	6,707	4,500	4,600	4,600	
World	**5,839,347**	**7,253,445**	**7,417,486**	**7,861,006**	**8,151,477**	**8,249,012**	**8,261,487**

Table 3.9C: International global production, consumption, exports and imports

(Total production of exporting members crop years 2007–2012)

Countries		2007	2008	2009	2010	2011	2012
TOTAL		1,16,612	1,28,523	1,22,599	1,33,470	1,34,401	1,44,061
Angola	(R)	36	38	13	35	29	50
Bolivia	(A)	133	135	142	130	147	150
Brazil	(A/R)	36,070	45,992	39,470	48,095	43,484	50,826
Burundi	(A)	133	412	112	353	204	483
Cameroon	(R/A)	795	750	750	608	555	850
Central African Republic	(R)	43	60	93	95	86	100
Colombia	(A)	12,516	8,664	8,098	8,523	7,653	8,000
Costa Rica	(A)	1,771	1,287	1,304	1,392	1,462	1,616
Côte d'Ivoire	(R)	2,317	2,397	1,795	982	1,906	2,000
Cuba	(A)	7	12	22	26	38	100
Ecuador	(A/R)	1,110	691	813	854	1,075	1,000
El Salvador	(A)	1,505	1,450	1,075	1,850	1,163	1,420
Ethiopia	(A)	5,967	4,949	6,931	7,500	6,008	6,500
Gabon	(R)	0	1	1	1	0	1
Ghana	(R)	31	27	33	112	122	85
Guatemala	(A/R)	4,100	3,785	3,835	3,950	3,840	3,500
Honduras	(A)	3,640	3,351	3,403	4,280	5,705	5,400
India	(R/A)	4,319	3,950	4,794	5,033	5,233	5,258
Indonesia	(R/A)	4,474	9,612	11,380	9,129	8,620	10,950
Kenya	(A)	652	541	630	658	680	850
Liberia	(R)	7	12	13	9	7	10
Malawi	(A)	19	21	17	17	27	20
Mexico	(A)	4,150	4,651	4,109	3,994	4,546	5,160
Nicaragua	(A)	1,905	1,445	1,871	1,669	1,774	1,530
Panama	(A)	176	149	138	114	104	100
Papua New Guinea	(A/R)	968	1,028	1,038	870	1,415	1,200

(Contd.)

Table 3.9C: International global production, consumption, exports and imports

(Total production of exporting members crop years 2007–2012)

Countries		2007	2008	2009	2010	2011	2012
Philippines	(R/A)	446	587	730	189	180	455
Rwanda	(A)	224	369	259	323	246	400
Sierra Leone	(R)	40	86	91	33	45	50
Tanzania	(A/R)	810	1,186	675	846	534	918
Thailand	(R)	650	675	795	829	823	850
Timor-Leste	(A)	36	48	47	60	44	75
Togo	(R)	125	138	204	161	142	150
Uganda	(R/A)	3,449	3,290	2,845	3,203	2,817	3,000
Vietnam	(R/A)	16,405	18,438	17,825	19,467	24,058	22,000
Yemen	(A)	198	220	135	160	158	200
Zambia	(A)	61	35	28	13	14	10
Zimbabwe	(A)	31	24	21	10	9	10
Non-member countries		7,295	8,019	7,066	7,898	9,447	8,783
Congo, Dem. Rep. of	(R/A)	416	422	346	305	350	450
Dominican Republic	(A)	465	645	352	378	682	550
Guinea	(R)	323	505	499	386	369	415
Haiti	(A)	359	359	351	350	349	325
Lao, People's Dem. Rep. of	(R)	393	406	434	541	468	550
Madagascar	(R)	614	728	457	529	603	575
Peru	(A)	3,063	3,872	3,286	4,069	5,581	4,750
Venezuela	(A)	1,520	932	1,214	1,202	901	1,000
Others	(R/A)	141	151	127	137	145	168

(A) – Arabica
(A/R) – Arabica/Robusta
Sources: ICO (Statistics on coffee 8/ICA 2007 – January 2013) India; Coffee Board, Bangalore.

Table 3.9D: Breakdown of total production for exporting members producing both arabica and robusta coffee 2007–2012

(000 bags)

Countries		2007	2008	2009	2010	2011	2012
Brazil	(A/R) Apr-Mar	36,070	45,992	39,470	48,095	43,485	50,826
	(A)	25,096	35,414	28,866	36,824	32,189	38,344
	(R)	10,974	10,578	10,604	11,271	11,296	12,482
Cameroon	(R/A) Oct-Sep	795	750	750	608	555	850
	(A)	87	82	82	67	83	128
	(R)	708	667	667	541	472	723
Congo, Dem. Rep. of	(R/A) Oct-Sep	416	422	346	305	350	450
	(A)	67	68	55	49	102	90
	(R)	349	354	291	256	249	360
Ecuador	(A/R) Apr-Mar	1,110	691	813	854	1,075	1,000
	(A)	677	352	415	436	548	620
	(R)	433	338	399	418	527	380
India	(A/R) Oct-Sep	4,319	3,950	4,794	5,033	5,233	5,258
	(A)	1,512	1,185	1,582	1,610	1,675	1,683
	(R)	2,807	2,765	3,212	3,422	3,559	3,576
Indonesia	(R/A) Apr-Mar	4,474	9,612	11,380	9,129	8,620	10,950
	(A)	850	1,826	2,162	1,917	1,810	2,300
	(R)	3,624	7,786	9,218	7,212	6,809	8,651
Papua New Guinea	(A/R) Apr-Mar	968	1,028	1,038	870	1,415	1,200
	(A)	958	1,017	1,028	861	1,400	1,188
	(R)	10	10	10	9	14	12
Tanzania	(A/R) Jul-Jun	810	1,186	675	846	534	918
	(A)	518	759	432	541	305	597
	(R)	292	427	243	305	230	321
Uganda	(R/A) Oct-Sep	3,449	3,290	2,845	3,203	2,817	3,000
	(A)	690	658	569	641	563	600
	(R)	2,760	2,632	2,276	2,563	2,253	2,400

A. Arabica, R. Robusta.
A/R, Both types: predominantly Arabica; R/A, Both types: predominantly Robusta.
Sources: ICO (Statistics on coffee 8/ICA 2007 – January 2013) India; Coffee Board, Bangalore.

Table 3.9E: Arabica coffee production

Thousand 60-kilogram bags*

	2004/05	2005/06	2006/07	2007/08	2008/09	2009/10	2010/11	2011/12	2012/13	2013/14
Arabica production						140	125	140	125	145
Bolivia	165	135	152	140	135	33,000	41,800	34,700	41,100	38,500
Brazil	34,300	26,000	36,000	27,650	40,500	300	235	210	225	200
Burundi	437	285	387	167	250	90	90	90	75	75
Cameroon	90	93	90	90	90	8,100	8,525	7,655	9,000	9,000
Colombia	11,532	11,953	12,164	12,515	8,664	105	100	90	80	70
Congo (Kinshasa)	58	54	200	212	100	1,475	1,575	1,775	1,675	1,425
Costa Rica	1,907	1,751	1,782	1,867	1,580	120	120	125	125	100
Cuba	150	125	100	70	127	500	500	500	475	450
Dominican Republic	481	310	390	465	545	375	400	400	405	400
Ecuador	398	439	450	419	360	1,300	1,860	1,200	1,125	800
El Salvador	1,329	1,387	1,300	1,515	1,550	6,000	6,125	6,320	6,325	6,350
Ethiopia	4,575	4,000	4,650	4,200	5,500	4,000	3,950	4,400	4,200	3,875
Guatemala	3,802	3,590	4,040	3,970	3,970	275	300	300	300	300
Haiti	365	356	362	350	360	3,550	3,975	5,600	4,600	5,000
Honduras	2,575	3,204	3,500	3,802	3,225	1,575	1,570	1,690	1,670	1,700
India	1,963	1,594	1,662	1,583	1,325	1,500	1,375	1,300	1,700	1,650
Indonesia	950	1,050	1,050	1,000	1,300	28	23	20	15	20
Jamaica	21	34	41	20	31	700	680	850	900	900
Kenya	754	867	867	699	900	25	25	25	25	25
Madagascar	25	37	35	30	30	25	25	25	25	25
Malawi	21	24	17	20	25	3,950	3,800	4,100	4,100	3,600
Mexico	3,800	3,800	4,000	4,250	4,300	1,925	1,740	1,880	1,850	1,500
Nicaragua	1,130	1,718	1,300	1,700	1,650	100	87	80	90	80
Panama	90	173	170	170	100	1,050	825	1,350	800	1,000
Papua New Guinea	948	1,270	810	970	1,000	25	25	25	25	25
Paraguay	26	45	20	28	25	3,300	4,100	5,200	4,300	4,100
Peru	3,550	2,420	4,550	3,950	4,000	20	35	30	30	25
Philippines	35	35	35	35	35	240	317	245	250	275
Rwanda	450	300	254	250	340	10				
Sri Lanka	10	10	9	10	10	400	600	365	575	650
Tanzania	480	500	515	505	650	818	644	875	650	700
Uganda	493	475	400	400	650	107	108	100	98	100
United States	146	168	154	153	133	725	625	700	730	800
Venezuela	800	820	862	1,000	1,000	450	650	800	850	800
Vietnam	383	335	500	400	480	150	145	150	150	150
Yemen	171	189	200	200	150	27	7	10	5	5
Zambia	110	103	56	60	39	21	10	8	8	5
Zimbabwe	120	66	45	30	22	76,501	87,106	83,343	88,691	84,835
Total	**78,643**	**69,716**	**83,120**	**74,896**	**85,152**					

* Coffee marketing year begins October in some countries and April or July (e.g. Brazil) in others.

Coffee Projected

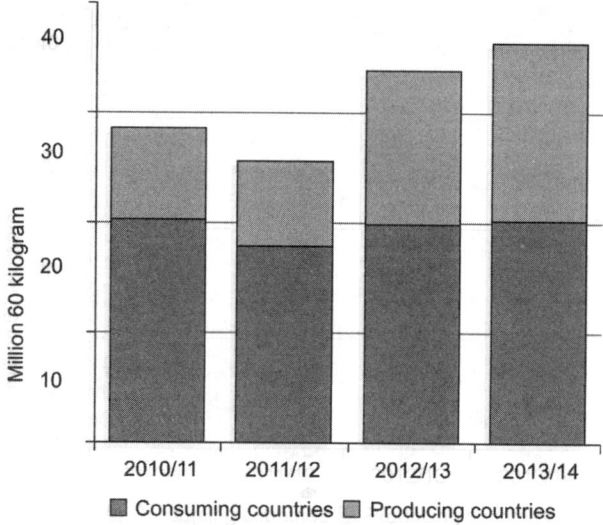

Stocks in producing countries to continue rising

2013/14 Forecast Overview

Brazil's production is forecast at 53.1 million bags, down 3.0 million from the previous year due primarily to Arabica trees entering the off-year of the biennial production cycle. Though the year-over-year difference in Arabica output is expected to narrow, last year was affected by frost and dry conditions in Minas Gerais, its main growing region. However, Arabica's off-year forecast continues its growth trend.

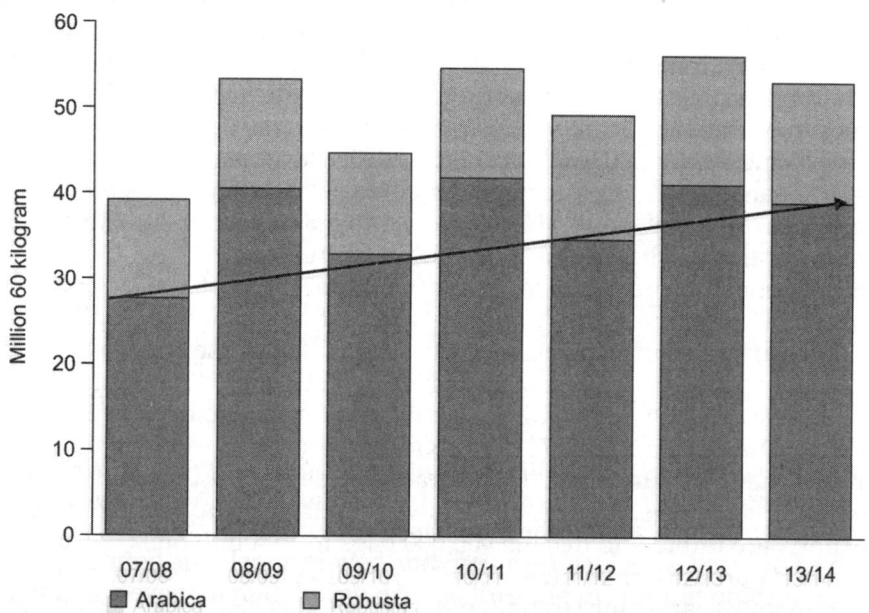

Brazil's off-year Arabica production continues growth trend

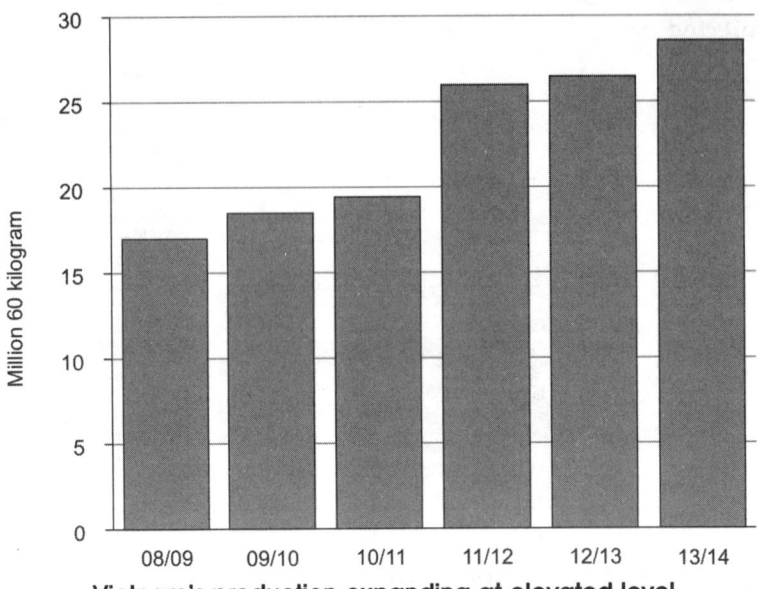

Vietnam's production expanding at elevated level

Following 3 years of expansion, the Robusta harvest is forecast to decline 1.1 million bags to 13.9 million as irregular rainfall combined with above average temperatures lower yields in Espirito Santo, where the vast majority is grown. Bean exports are forecast nearly flat at 27.5 million bags while ending stocks are expected to rise a second consecutive year.

Vietnam's production is forecast at a record 28.5 million bags, up 2.0 million from the previous year due to higher yields attributed to favorable weather as well as increased area harvested. Initial drought concerns in the coffee region's Central Highlands were much discussed in January and February, but were quieted by the normal arrival of the rainy season in late March. Favorable weather continued through May and led to good flowering and cherry development. Harvested area continues to expand and is likely above 625,000 hectares despite the government's goal of reducing area to 500,000 hectares by 2020, a level that was surpassed several years ago. Bean exports are forecast to increase 900,000 bags to 24.5 million while ending stocks are expected to almost double to 3.8 million bags. Consumption is forecast to continue rising as the coffee culture spreads.

Central America and Mexico account for one-fifth of the world's Arabica production. The region's production is forecast to decline 1.4 million bags to 16.9 million due to lower yields from coffee rust. The disease attacks the underside of the leaf, causing it to yellow and drop prematurely, reducing the plant's photosynthetic capacity and yield. El Salvador is forecast to decline 20%, followed by Mexico (–16%), Costa Rica (–15%), Nicaragua (–12%), Guatemala (–8%), and Panama unchanged. However, Honduras is expected to rebound 9% with the maturation of new trees. As a result of lower exportable supplies from the region, bean exports are forecast to decline 900,000 bags to 14.4 million.

Colombia's production is forecast at 10.0 million bags, up marginally from the revised previous year on the strength of recent months' deliveries, several of which approached or exceeded historical amounts. This turn-around for a second

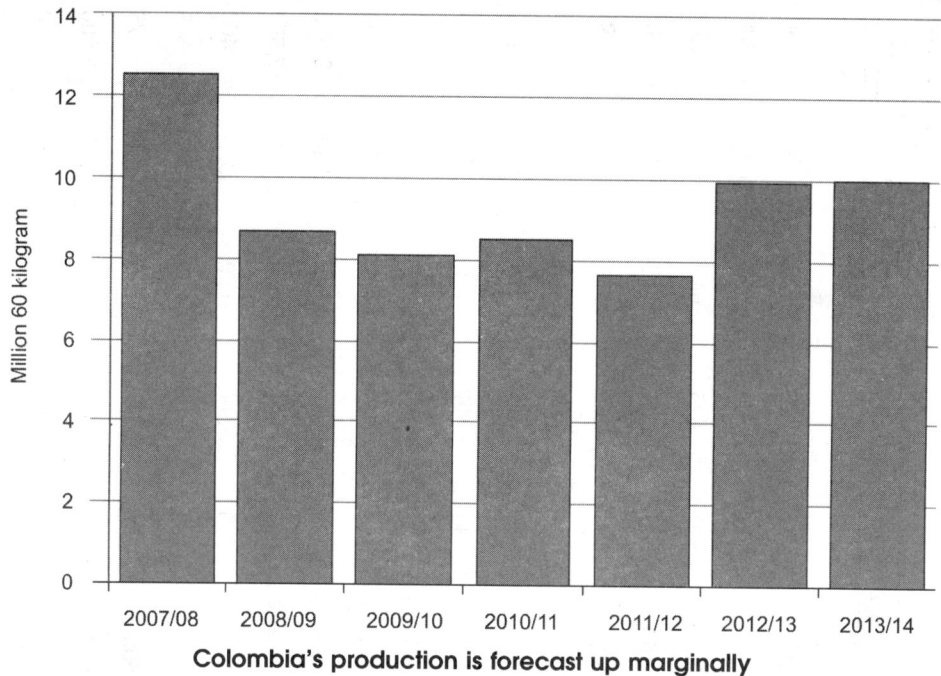

Colombia's production is forecast up marginally

consecutive year is in sharp contrast to significantly reduced output the previous four seasons caused by the spread of coffee cherry borer and rust. Bean exports are forecast to raise 900,000 bags to 9.0 million while imports are forecast to remain high at 700,000 bags.

Indonesia's production is forecast to drop 1.0 million bags to 9.5 million as dry weather at the beginning of the season reduced flowering, while excessive rain during cherry development further cut yields. Bean exports are forecast to decline 900,000 bags to 6.0 million.

India's production is forecast to slip 200,000 bags to 5.1 million on lower Robusta output in Karnataka, the largest coffee producing state. Heavy rains during the monsoon season caused some cherries to drop, lowering yield. Although bean exports are forecast to dip 75,000 bags to 3.7 million, this marks the fourth year of strong exports and declining stocks.

The **European Union** accounts for nearly half of world bean imports and is forecast to increase 600,000 bags to 45.5 million, with top suppliers including Brazil (28%), Vietnam (25%) and Honduras (7%). Ending stocks are expected to rise incrementally.

The **United States** imports the second-largest amount of coffee beans and is forecast to increase slightly to 23.5 million bags, with top suppliers including Brazil (25%), Vietnam (18%) and Colombia (13%). Ending stocks are forecast to rise marginally.

World production is revised up from the June 2012 estimate by 2.6 million bags to 153.3 million.

- Vietnam is up 1.6 million bags to 26.5 million on higher-than-anticipated yield.
- Colombia is raised 900,000 bags to 9.9 million on unexpected strong deliveries in the second half of the season, the highest percentage of the yearly total in nearly 40 years. Weak deliveries in the first half were similar in volume to previous seasons plagued by coffee cherry borer and rust.

Table 3.10: World robusta coffee production*

(*Thousand 60-kilogram bags***)

	2004/05	2005/06	2006/07	2007/08	2008/09	2009/10	2010/11	2011/12	2012/13	2013/14
Robusta production										
Angola	15	25	35	35	30	30	25	25	30	30
Brazil	9,300	10,100	10,700	11,450	12,800	11,800	12,700	14,500	15,000	15,200
Cameroon	700	757	735	705	560	500	625	645	550	625
Central African Republic	45	46	78	65	10	30	27	10	10	10
Congo (Kinshasa)	302	282	180	188	200	200	165	165	150	150
Cote d'Ivoire	2,301	1,962	2,847	1,600	1,853	2,350	1,600	1,600	1,800	2,000
Ecuador	335	345	355	283	275	260	250	200	185	175
Ghana	17	21	28	30	19	30	57	70	25	50
Guatemala	15	15	10	10	10	10	10	10	10	10
Guinea	316	525	475	400	400	445	325	425	375	400
India	2,709	3,023	3,138	3,082	3,050	3,250	3,465	3,540	3,580	3,500
Indonesia	7,500	8,400	7,000	6,500	8,700	9,000	7,950	7,000	8,800	7,550
Laos	385	417	400	400	350	390	500	450	375	400
Liberia	68	71	53	50	7	2	4	5	5	5
Madagascar	497	562	552	550	500	450	525	525	500	475
Malaysia	1,000	450	450	450	975	1,000	1,100	1,450	1,400	1,500
Mexico	100	200	200	250	250	200	200	200	200	200
Nigeria	45	69	50	40	30	30	30	40	30	35

Table 3.10: World robusta coffee production* *(Contd.)*

(Thousand 60-kilogram bags**)

	2004/05	2005/06	2006/07	2007/08	2008/09	2009/10	2010/11	2011/12	2012/13	2013/14
Papua New Guinea	50	63	32	43	35	35	40	50	50	50
Philippines	640	650	645	630	325	225	425	425	425	425
Sierra Leone	15	60	30	40	87	90	45	90	70	80
Sri Lanka	22	24	23	25	25	25	25	20	25	20
Tanzania	285	300	305	305	500	200	450	200	525	550
Thailand	884	1,000	750	600	800	900	850	850	850	850
Togo	166	140	134	135	185	436	615	560	250	400
Uganda	2,100	1,684	2,100	2,100	2,610	2,052	2,568	2,200	2,700	2,800
Vietnam	14,117	16,000	19,000	17,933	16,500	18,050	18,765	25,200	24,100	24,000
Total	**43,948**	**47,210**	**50,320**	**47,917**	**51,087**	**51,990**	**53,341**	**60,455**	**62,020**	**61,490**

* Coffee marketing year for producer countries begins either in October (Colombia), April (Indonesia) or July (Brazil), as examples.
** Coffee marketing year for non-producer countries begins in October.

Table 3.11: Coffee (green): production

(Unit: 1000 MT)

Country	1992	1999	2000	2001	2002	Annual growth rate 1992–2002
Indonesia	436.9	521.4	505.7	526.9	376.8	0.7%
Philippines	127.6	117.4	126.3	132.1	132.1F	–0.5%
Vietnam	119.2	553.2	802.5	840.6	688.7	22.9%
India	180	265	292	301	317	6.7%
Papua New Guinea	50.46	83.04	83	62.5	62.5	2.3%
Subtotal	1 024.5	1 648.9	1 955.2	2 024.2	1 704.6	7.1%
Asia & Pacific	1 024.5	1 648.9	1 955.2	2 024.2	1 704.6	7.1%
Rest of World	5 059.7	5 098.4	5 453.8	5 269.2	5 660.2	1.9%
World	6 084.2	6 747.4	7 409.0	7 293.4	7 364.8	3%

World ending stocks are raised 3.5 million bags to 33.8 million.

- Vietnam is revised up 1.1 million bags to 2.0 million on larger available supplies.
- European Union is raised 500,000 bags to 11.2 million on lower-than anticipated consumption.
- Brazil is 340,000 bags higher to 7.1 million bags, offsetting lower exports.
- Colombia is raised 320,000 bags to 750,000 due to increased supplies.

A dynamic model was used to make coffee projections. It covers the major exporting and importing countries of green coffee. Supply, demand and stock functions were estimated for each of the major exporting and importing countries. The model performs dynamic simulation forward in time and generates forecasts on the basis of assumptions for the future behavior of GDP, consumer price indices and exchange rates. For each year in the future, the International Coffee Organization's composite price is solved in order to achieve equilibrium between supply and demand for green coffee. This model was developed to provide forecasts for green coffee production, consumption and trade, assuming that coffee is treated as a homogeneous commodity with no distinction between Arabica and Robusta varieties.

The world's largest coffee producing region is likely to continue to be Latin America and the Caribbean although the projected annual growth rate for the region is expected to decrease from 1.7% in the previous decade to 0.4% annually during the projection period. Coffee production in Brazil in 2010 is expected to decrease to 1.3 million tons (22 million bags), compared to 2.1 million tons (35 million bags) in 1998–2000. In Brazil, improved prices from the mid-1990s stimulated planting and replanting after a period of decline when growers responded to lower prices by reducing the use of agricultural inputs and uprooting plants in marginal areas. In Colombia, based on the age profile of the coffee areas, output is projected to grow at an annual rate of 0.7% to 2010 to reach 747,000 tons (13 million bags), compared to 699,000 tons (12 million bags) in 1998–2000. Some plantings took place during the 1990s in response to the surge in demand for Colombian Milds, which fetch premium prices over other Arabicas.

Table 3.11A: Green coffee bean production*

*(Thousand 60-kilogram bags**)*

	2004/05	2005/06	2006/07	2007/08	2008/09	2009/10	Jun 2010/11
Production							
Angola	15	25	35	35	35	35	35
Bolivia	165	135	152	140	135	150	140
Brazil	43,600	36,100	46,700	39,100	53,300	44,800	55,300
Burundi	437	285	287	209	388	300	300
Cameroon	790	850	835	695	650	590	590
Central African Republic	45	21	45	50	10	10	10
Colombia	11,532	11,953	12,164	12,515	8,664	8,200	9,000
Congo (Kinshasa)	360	236	280	315	300	325	300
Costa Rica	1,907	1,751	1,782	1,867	1,580	1,456	1,380
Cote d'Ivoire	2,301	2,062	2,447	2,198	1,853	2,253	2,200
Cuba	150	125	100	70	127	120	120
Dominican Republic	481	310	390	465	545	500	500
Ecuador	733	784	805	702	637	635	650
El Salvador	1,329	1,387	1,400	1,650	1,550	1,400	1,475
Ethiopia	4,575	4,000	4,036	3,906	3,650	4,100	4,200
Ghana		17	29	27	19	23	21
Guatemala	3,817	3,715	4,050	4,110	3,980	4,160	4,010
Guinea	316	525	400	250	400	425	450
Haiti	365	331	337	335	360	300	350
Honduras	2,575	3,204	3,460	3,642	3,450	3,650	3,800
India	4,672	4,617	4,665	4,660	4,375	4,825	4,600
Indonesia	8,450	9,450	7,500	7,300	9,300	9,150	9,600
Jamaica		34	30	35	31	31	30
Kenya	756	869	869	700	884	850	850
Laos	385	417	400	350	350	350	350
Liberia	68	71	53	40	30	10	10
Madagascar	522	592	582	555	530	480	550
Malawi	21	24	17	25	25	25	25
Malaysia	1,000	700	500	930	952	1,000	1,000
Mexico	3,900	4,200	4,400	4,250	4,650	4,400	4,600
Nicaragua	1,130	1,718	1,300	1,850	1,650	1,950	1,800
Nigeria	45	59	51	42	51	40	40
Panama	90	173	170	170	120	120	120
Papua New Guinea	998	1,265	810	970	1,035	1,035	1,050

(Contd.)

Table 3.11A: Green coffee bean production*

*Thousand 60-kilogram bags***

	2004/05	2005/06	2006/07	2007/08	2008/09	2009/10	Jun 2010/11
Paraguay	26	45	20	28	25	25	25
Peru	3,550	2,420	4,400	2,800	4,000	3,300	4,000
Philippines	700	710	705	690	580	685	650
Rwanda	450	340	400	230	340	240	350
Sierra Leone	15	60	31	42	87	67	80
Sri Lanka	32	34	32	35	35	35	35
Tanzania	765	800	820	830	1,040	900	1,000
Thailand	884	1,000	750	900	800	900	900
Togo	166	140	180	255	200	250	250
Uganda	2,593	1,560	2,300	2,500	3,200	3,000	3,200
United States	146	168	154	151	133	106	110
Venezuela	800	820	862	900	900	725	690
Vietnam	14,500	16,335	19,500	18,000	18,000	17,500	18,725
Yemen	171	189	200	150	150	150	150
Zambia	110	103	56	60	35	35	35
Zimbabwe	120	66	45	31	25	30	30
Total	**122,616**	**116,810**	**131,548**	**121,762**	**135,168**	**125,656**	**139,696**

* Coffee marketing year for producer countries begins either in October (Colombia), April (Indonesia) or July (Brazil), as examples.
** Coffee marketing year for non-producer countries begins in October.

Table 3.11B: Green coffee bean exports*

*Thousand 60-kilogram bags***

	2008/09	2009/10	2010/11	2011/12	2012/13	2013/14
Bean exports						
Argentina	0	0	0	0	0	0
Bolivia	73	74	66	87	60	75
Brazil	28,396	26,580	31,810	26,556	27,465	27,500
Burundi	250	290	235	205	230	195
Cameroon	480	690	650	670	550	625
Central African Republic	6	25	22	7	5	5
Colombia	8,160	6,445	7,400	6,675	7,700	8,000
Congo (Kinshasa)	117	102	75	69	50	50
Costa Rica	1,385	1,200	1,255	1,455	1,450	1,200
Cote d'Ivoire	1,180	1,755	725	1,290	1,400	1,500
Cuba	6	7	5	11	10	10

Table 3.11B: Green coffee bean exports* *(Contd.)*

*Thousand 60-kilogram bags***

	2008/09	2009/10	2010/11	2011/12	2012/13	2013/14
Dominican Republic	42	36	48	47	40	40
Ecuador	179	450	425	575	575	575
El Salvador	1,506	1,236	1,770	1,130	1,000	750
Ethiopia	3,000	3,250	3,235	3,140	3,280	3,300
Ghana	18	30	57	70	25	50
Guatemala	3,783	3,860	3,650	3,875	3,800	3,450
Guinea	375	410	300	380	350	370
Haiti	17	10	7	9	10	10
Honduras	3,050	3,200	3,900	5,290	4,400	4,800
India	2,125	3,040	4,160	3,730	3,750	3,750
Indonesia	6,625	7,425	7,415	4,950	6,900	5,600
Jamaica	26	23	18	17	10	15
Kenya	980	740	650	800	850	850
Laos	250	290	400	350	275	300
Liberia	7	2	4	5	5	5
Madagascar	115	40	105	105	85	100
Malawi	25	24	24	24	24	24
Mexico	2,125	1,790	1,735	2,525	2,700	2,400
Nicaragua	1,425	1,650	1,525	1,675	1,675	1,350
Nigeria	1	3	2	10	5	5
Panama	45	53	37	30	40	35
Papua New Guinea	1,070	1,040	850	1,350	800	1,000
Paraguay	5	5	5	5	5	5
Peru	3,830	3,150	3,880	5,140	4,100	3,950
Rwanda	340	240	317	245	250	275
Sierra Leone	70	70	25	69	50	60
Tanzania	1,200	800	1,000	520	725	950
Thailand	4	4	15	15	20	25
Togo	188	436	615	560	250	400
Uganda	3,050	2,670	3,150	3,000	3,200	3,400
Venezuela	200	120	100	100	80	80
Vietnam	15,430	18,425	18,215	23,890	23,200	23,000
Yemen	35	30	20	20	20	20
Zambia	39	27	7	10	5	5
Zimbabwe	18	17	6	3	3	3
Total	**91,255**	**91,772**	**99,920**	**100,697**	**101,436**	**100,122**

* Coffee marketing year for producer countries begins either in October (Colombia), April (Indonesia) or July (Brazil), as examples.

** Coffee marketing year for non-producer countries begins in October.

Table 3.11C: Green coffee bean imports*

*(Thousand 60 kg bags**)*

	2004/2005	2005/2006	2006/2007	2007/2008	2008/2009	2009/2010	2010/2011	2011/2012	2012/2013	2013/2014
Bean imports										
Algeria	1,900	2,100	1,825	1,500	2,045	2,060	1,770	2,230	2,300	2,200
Argentina	500	490	510	490	480	500	510	500	525	500
Australia	800	850	900	920	950	1,040	1,115	1,140	1,175	1,200
Canada	2,140	1,960	1,950	1,940	1,940	2,010	2,305	2,225	2,400	2,300
China					320	425	680	625	900	1,000
Colombia					650	570	760	1,050	650	500
Costa Rica					15	130	175	65	40	50
Croatia					300	300	300	275	250	250
Ecuador					310	650	820	1,150	1,350	1,400
El Salvador					3	0	10	0	0	0
EU-27	40,950	41,775	44,325	43,550	43,350	44,200	44,270	43,635	45,000	44,300
Guatemala					60	60	0	0	0	0
India	688	366	334	330	560	725	820	880	820	800
Indonesia					90	425	190	930	300	200
Iran					25	125	25	40	40	40
Japan	6,600	6,400	6,200	6,150	6,375	6,160	6,900	5,965	7,000	6,700
Jordan					320	250	200	240	300	275
Korea, South	1,400	1,425	1,400	1,550	1,680	1,705	1,930	1,725	1,650	1,600
Malaysia	470	525	560	570	650	960	1,030	1,125	1,400	1,500

Table 3.11C: Green coffee bean imports* *(Contd.)*

*(Thousand 60 kg bags**)*

	2004/2005	2005/2006	2006/2007	2007/2008	2008/2009	2009/2010	2010/2011	2011/2012	2012/2013	2013/2014
Mexico	650	560	650	590	4	90	245	275	350	375
Morocco	480	700	960	970	600	580	540	700	725	700
New Zealand	670	575	590	590	150	160	150	170	180	190
Norway	1,550	1,275	1,490	1,710	610	580	620	570	525	550
Philippines	20,480	20,830	22,110	21,775	405	420	375	510	575	600
Russia					1,240	1,430	1,540	1,720	2,000	2,200
Serbia					590	525	520	570	575	575
South Africa					330	400	400	350	325	300
Switzerland					1,800	1,950	2,180	2,175	2,275	2,300
Thailand					130	205	620	410	500	500
Turkey					260	275	315	350	350	375
United States					21,660	20,240	22,460	23,700	22,400	22,200
Ukraine					80	100	100	115	150	125
Venezuela					0	310	620	570	600	630
Vietnam					70	#	#	#	#	300
Total	**81,394**	**82,160**	**86,807**	**85,855**	**88,052**	**89,610**	**94,670**	**96,105**	**97,930**	**96,735**

* Coffee marketing year for producer countries begins either in October (Colombia), April (Indonesia) or July (Brazil), as examples.
** Coffee marketing ear for non-producer countries begins in October. For each non-producing country, the balance between imports and exports was used in order to remove double-counting from these trade figures.

Table 3.11D: Green coffee bean-ending stocks

(Thousand 60 kilogram bags)

	2008/09	2009/10	2010/11	2011/12	2012/13	2013/14
Ending stocks						
Angola	20	11	5	2	1	0
Bolivia	44	35	19	4	4	4
Brazil	6,576	2,836	2,906	2,238	6,723	8,233
Burundi	18	23	15	15	5	5
Cameroon	219	44	34	24	24	24
Central African Republic	137	112	87	60	35	10
Colombia	209	284	99	249	434	159
Congo (Kinshasa)	31	34	24	10	10	10
Costa Rica	25	125	200	240	125	25
Cote d'Ivoire	88	93	408	118	110	100
EU-27	16,325	10,850	12,900	10,400	10,700	10,500
Ecuador	7	65	143	134	164	154
El Salvador	32	48	13	18	58	58
Ethiopia	120	70	100	230	220	170
Ghana	5	4	3	2	1	0
Guatemala	222	227	237	197	137	132
Guinea	12	7	2	12	7	7
Haiti	44	25	25	25	15	15
Honduras	50	218	30	90	70	50
India	2,568	2,633	1,742	1,432	1,157	737
Indonesia	1,208	1,603	83	88	98	128
Japan	2,050	1,950	2,550	2,140	2,600	2,500
Kenya	140	50	30	30	30	30
Madagascar	37	22	12	7	7	7
Mexico	109	124	89	102	27	12
Nicaragua	8	37	22	32	17	7
Norway	125	125	125	125	125	125
Papua New Guinea	21	36	21	31	36	36
Paraguay	39	24	10	5	5	5
Peru	84	74	124	14	44	24
Philippines	124	469	90	165	95	145
Switzerland	200	200	200	200	200	200
Tanzania	280	40	50	45	365	555
Thailand	42	92	10	0	0	75
Togo	0	0	0	0	0	0
Uganda	641	701	613	538	488	388
United States	5,333	4,250	4,580	5,100	5,200	5,200
Venezuela	349	390	232	103	54	100
Vietnam	2,307	1,012	800	1,070	845	595
Total	39,849	28,943	28,633	25,295	30,236	30,525

In Central America, output in Mexico in 2010 is expected to reach 273,000 tons (5 million bags), more or less the same as the base period. In Guatemala, the projected annual growth rate of 1.7% would take production to 348,000 tons (6 million bags) by 2010. A growth rate of 3.9% for El Salvador is likely to bring their output to 165,000 tons (3 million bags) by 2010, while Costa Rica should experience an increase of 4.2% that brings output to 194,000 tons (3 million bags).

In Africa, coffee production is expected to increase by 1.5% annually from the base period to 2010, mostly reflecting increases in yields rather than an expansion in area. Output is anticipated to increase from 961,000 tons (16 million bags) in 1998–2000 to 1.1 million tons (19 million bags) by the year 2010. Production in Ethiopia, the largest Arabica coffee producing country in Africa, is expected to expand by 1.6% annually to reach 207 000 tons (3 million bags) by 2010. Coffee output in Côte d'Ivoire is expected to increase by 3.8% per annum, which would likely bring its output to 217 000 tons (3.6 million bags) by 2010. The output in Uganda is projected to increase at a rate of 0.7% annually from 1998–2000 to 2010. Output may rise to 222,000 tons (4 million bags) by 2010 from 207,000 tons (3 million bags) in 1998–2000, through replanting and higher yields. Kenya, the African producer of Colombian Milds, is projected to expand output by 1.1% annually during the projection period to arrive at 88,000 tons (1.5 million bags).

Production in Asia is projected to grow by 2.1% annually to reach 1.7 million tons (29 million bags) by 2010. Much of the expansion is expected to occur in Indonesia, the largest producing country in the region. Its coffee production expanded rapidly during the 1970s, slowed in the 1990s and is projected to expand at a growth rate of 1.7% annually to 2010 when output is likely to reach 654,000 tons (11 million bags). Also, in India output is projected to rise at 3.1% annually to reach 409,000 tons (7 million bags) by 2010. An increase of 2.0% per annum is expected in Vietnam, where output could reach 561,000 tons (9 million bags) by 2010. An annual increase of 0.7% is expected for Thailand, where output is projected to reach 59,000 tons (1 million bags) by 2010.

In Oceania, Papua New Guinea is the only significant producing country. Its production has been relatively stable during the 1980s and its output in 2010 is estimated at 150,000 tons (3 million bags).

Consumption

World consumption of coffee is projected to increase by 0.4% annually from 6.7 million tons (111 million bags) in 1998–2000 to 6.9 million tons (117 million bags) in 2010.

Coffee consumption in developing countries is projected to grow from 1.7 million tons (29 million bags) in 1998–2000 to 1.9 million tons (32 million bags) in 2010, at an annual rate of 1.3%, while their share in the world market is expected to increase from 26% in the base period to 28% in 2010. The projected higher growth rate for developing countries compared to developed countries is due mainly to higher income and population growth in developing countries, with increased coffee consumption continuing to be concentrated in the major coffee producing countries.

Developed countries including countries in transition are likely to continue to account for the larger though slightly declining, share of world coffee consumption. In the base period their share of consumption was 74%, nearly 5 million tons (83 million bags), compared with 72% projected for 2010. Coffee consumption in developed countries is projected to grow by 0.1% annually to 5.0 million tons (83 million bags) by 2010. In Europe, demand for coffee is projected to increase by 0.4% per year to 3.1 million tons (51 million bags) by 2010. The European Community (EC) is projected to account for 2.2 million tons (36 million bags), or 68% of total consumption in Europe. Demand is expected to rise slightly in the EC, but growth in consumption in the rest of Europe, excluding the former Soviet Union/CIS, is expected to show a slight decline. Growth in the former Soviet Union/CIS is expected to be more or less the same as in the base period. In North America, demand is projected to decrease by 1.0% per year, mainly reflecting income and population growth in the region.

Trade

In 2010, global coffee net-exports is projected to reach 5.5 million tons (92 million bags). Latin America and the Caribbean, with an export of 2.9 million tons (48 million bags), is expected to continue to be the leading exporting region although there will be a decline in the net-exports of 0.5% annually. By contrast, in Africa there will be a net export increase at a rate of 1.6% annually, reaching 1.0 million tons (17 million bags) and accounting for a 18% share of global exports. In Asia, export availabilities are expected to grow to 1.5 million tons (24 million bags) in 2010, accounting for 27% of world coffee exports. Export availabilities from Oceania are estimated to increase by 7.3%, reaching 150,000 tons (2.5 million bags), about 3.0% of global export availabilities.

World coffee imports are expected to increase by 0.2% annually during the projection period to reach 5.5 million tons (92 million bags) by 2010. This compares with average imports of 5.4 million tons (90 million bags) in 1998–2000. Imports by developing countries are projected to reach 421,000 tons (7 million bags) in 2010, accounting for less than 8% of the world's total and similar to their share in 1998–2000. Reflecting the slower growth of consumption, import requirements of the developed countries are projected to grow at an annual rate of 0.1%, reaching 5.1 million tons (85 million bags) by 2010 and accounting for 92% of the global total. Import demand by North America is projected to decline moderately to 1.54 million tons (26 million bags) by 2010. Imports into Europe are projected to decrease marginally to 2.96 million tons (49 million bags) by 2010. Imports to Japan are projected to grow at 1.6% annually reaching 460,000 tons (7.7 million bags). Growth in import demand by the former Soviet Union/CIS, where consumption in soluble form has grown but no processing firm has been established in the area, is expected to remain low at less than 1% per annum during the projection period.

World Exports Coffee

Regarding global export volumes and earnings from coffee, the value of total exports in 2011 is forecast at US$ 23.5 billion from a total volume of 102.4 million bags, against US$ 16.7 billion for a volume of 96.8 million bags in 2010, according to ICO data.

International trade in Coffee has been steadily improving, Exporting increased from 79.6 million bags in 1991–1992 to 97.6 million bags in 2006–2007, further to 110.2 million bags in 2012–2013. The share of India in the world exports was 2.54% in 1991–1992 and varied from 3% to 4% in the subsequent years. During 2012–2013, India shared a total of 4.7% in the world exports.

Opening stocks of various types of coffee declined from 55.7 million bags in 1990 to 20.6 million bags in 2003 (Table 3.11D). Actual Projected consumption is in (Table 3.11E and F). There has been a regular decline, but having touched 29.7 million bags in 1997, it has been moving around 20–21 million bags (Table 3.12). Total coffee exported in the world increased from 101 million bags in 2008–2009 to 115.6 million bags in 2012/13 (Table 3.13). From October 12 to September 13, it was a bit lower at 110.7 million bags. Brazil as usual has been the leader in world exports with a share of over 27%. It was followed by Vietnam – over 20%. India with its share of just 4.5% is not a major player in coffee exports (Table 3.13A). Soluble coffee, around 13–14 million bags is also entering the export market (Table 3.13B). Here, again Brazil leader with a share of over 25%. Interesting by Malaysia and Indonesia takes the 2nd position with 14–15% share. India is also in the game with a small share of 10–11% (Table 3.13B).

IMPORTS

EU27 is the leading in Coffee imports (Table 3.14) accounting for over 40%. This is followed by United States with just half (20%) share. India, not to be left out imports less than 1% of the total coffee imported by different countries. Soluble coffee is also a major importer – over 110 million bags and Russia along with Philippine are the leader here in this case (Table 3.14A).

World picture of coffee production, supply and distribution shows that while total supply increased from 100.7million bags in 1976/77 to 286.5 million bags in 2013–2014, exportable production increased from 42.9 to 105.9 million bags during this period (Table 3.15) country wise details covering the period 2007/08 to 2010/13 are as in Tables 3.15A to D.

Consolidated data regarding world coffee production domestic consumption, ending stocks, beam exports and imports is given (Table 3.16) of the total world production of 150.7 million bags in 2012/13, 104.7 million bags were consumed domestically with ending stocks of 30.2 million bags. Bean exports were 101.4 million and imports as 98 million bags.

With regard to coffee consumption, it increased rapidly from 124.6 million bags to 140.7 million bags in 2012/13. EU27 with over 31% as its share the United just half of EU27 is the major consumer, followed by U.S.A. and Brazil. With regard to per capita consumption, however, Luxemburg with 18 kg is the top consumer. For behind are Denmark and Canada with 7 kg consumption levels of European Union, USA and Brazil, however, consume only 5, 4 and 3.5 kg per capita. India is more or less at the bottom with just 0.1 kg (Tables 3.16A and B).

Unit value of imports of green coffee (Table 3.17) increased from 108.45 US cents per pound in 2007 to 178.3 by 2012. But retail price during the same period increased from 428.5 cents per pound to 795.5 cents (Table 3.17A).

Issues and Uncertainties

Global green coffee demand and supply is likely to continue to grow although at a rate slower than in the previous decade. It is expected that several major changes would take place in the world coffee market to 2010. First, most production growth would come from Asia and Africa, instead of Latin America where most coffee had been produced. Second, the growth of consumption would be faster in developing

Table 3.11E: Coffee: actual and projected consumption

	Actual		Projected	Growth rates	
	1988–1990 Average	1998–2000 Average*	2010	1988–1990 to 1998–2000	1998–2000 to 2010
	000 tons			Percent per year	
WORLD	**5,709**	**6,681**	**6,947**	**1.6**	**0.4**
DEVELOPING	**1,627**	**1,710**	**1,951**	**0.5**	**1.3**
AFRICA	212	156	169	3	0.8
Cameroon	5	6	18	2.3	11.2
Côte d'Ivoire	3	3	2	0	−2.4
Ethiopia	71	99	87	3.3	−1.3
Kenya	5	3	4	4.8	3.7
Uganda	4	30	17	21.8	−5.3
Others	123	15	40	19	10.3
ASIA	**239**	**334**	**416**	**3.4**	**2.2**
India	52	56	96	0.8	5.5
Indonesia	73	122	111	5.3	−0.9
Philippines	39	49	60	2.2	2
Thailand	10	28	42	10.8	4
Viet Nam	9	15	26	5.9	5.4
Others	56	63	82	1.2	2.7
LATIN AMER. & CARIB.	**933**	**1,219**	**1,365**	**2.7**	**1.1**
Brazil	540	858	1 025	4.7	1.8
Colombia	83	96	92	1.5	−0.5
Costa Rica	23	14	11	4.9	−2.5
El Salvador	11	12	18	1	4.3
Guatemala	18	18	17	0.1	−0.8
Mexico	93	67	53	3.2	−2.4
Others	166	154	150	0.7	−0.3
OCEANIA				**12.9**	**0**
Papua New Guinea				12.9	0
DEVELOPED	**4,083**	**4,972**	**4,997**	**2**	**0.1**
NORTH AMERICA	**1,203**	**1,504**	**1,362**	**2.3**	**−1**
Canada	45	206	208	16.4	0.1
United States	1,157	1,299	1,154	1.2	−1.2
EUROPE	**2,541**	**2,974**	**3,087**	**1.6**	**0.4**
EC	**2,000**	**2,059**	**2,177**	**0.3**	**0.6**
France	367	394	424	0.7	0.7
Germany	758	838	878	1	0.5
Other Europe	**541**	**915**	**910**	**5.4**	**−0.1**
Former USSR/CIS	**1**			**−6.5**	**0**
OTHER DEVELOPED	**338**	**493**	**547**	**3.8**	**1.1**
Australia	15	56	57	14.1	0.2
Israel	5	31	31	18.8	0.2
Japan	309	373	426	1.9	1.3
New Zealand	3	11	11	15.6	0
South Africa	6	21	21	14	0

* Data for 1999 and 2000 partly estimated.

Table 3.11F: Coffee: actual and projected international trade

	Exports					Imports				
	Actual		Projected	Growth rates		Actual		Projected	Growth rates	
	1988–1990 Average	1998–2000 Average*	2010	1988–1990 to 1998–2000	1998–2000 to 2010	1988–1990 Average	1998–2000 Average*	2010	1988–1990 to 1998–2000	1998–2000 to 2010
	000 tons			Percent per year		000 tons			Percent per year	
WORLD	**4,455**	**5,207**	**5,510**	**1.6**	**0.6**	**4,688**	**5,419**	**5,510**	**1.5**	**0.2**
DEVELOPING	**4,455**	**5,207**	**5,510**	**1.6**	**0.6**	**314**	**381**	**421**	**2**	**1**
AFRICA	**927**	**849**	**996**	**−0.9**	**1.6**	**109**	**170**	**188**	**4.5**	**1**
Cameroon	114	69	106	−4.9	4.4					
Côte d'Ivoire	209	247	222	1.7	−1.1					
Ethiopia	73	104	119	3.6	1.4					
Kenya	107	70	79	−4.2	1.2					
Uganda	151	185	245	2.1	2.8					
Others	273	174	225	−4.4	2.6					
ASIA	**604**	**1,248**	**1,471**	**7.5**	**1.7**	**167**	**172**	**195**	**0.3**	**1.3**
India	109	233	325	7.9	3.4					
Indonesia	369	318	557	−1.5	5.8					
Thailand	47	51	40	0.8	−2.4					
Viet Nam	59	641	540	26.9	−1.7					
Others	20	5	9	−12.9	6.1					
LATIN AMER. & CARIB.	**2,861**	**3,036**	**2,893**	**0.6**	**−0.5**	**38**	**39**	**38**	**0.3**	**−0.3**
Brazil	1,064	1,217	481	1.4	−8.9					
Colombia	724	575	648	−2.3	1.2					
Costa Rica	139	124	186	−1.1	4.1					
El Salvador	126	120	148	−0.5	2.1					

(Contd.)

Table 3.11F: Coffee: actual and projected international trade

	Exports					Imports				
	Actual		Projected	Growth rates		Actual		Projected	Growth rates	
	1988–1990 Average	1998–2000 Average*	2010	1988–1990 to 1998–2000	1998–2000 to 2010	1988–1990 Average	1998–2000 Average*	2010	1988–1990 to 1998–2000	1998–2000 to 2010
	000 tons			Percent per year		000 tons			Percent per year	
Guatemala	183	278	339	4.3	2					
Mexico	233	259	241	1.1	-0.7					
Others	392	463	850	1.7	6.3					
OCEANIA	**63**	**74**	**150**	**1.6**	**7.3**					
Papua New Guinea	63	74	150	1.6	7.3					
DEVELOPED						**4,374**	**5,038**	**5,089**	**1.4**	**0.1**
NORTH AMERICA						**1,303**	**1,554**	**1,543**	**1.8**	**-0.1**
Canada						129	201	243	4.5	1.9
United States						1,174	1,353	1,300	1.4	-0.4
EUROPE						**2,666**	**2,973**	**2,957**	**1.1**	**-0.1**
EC						**2,043**	**2,059**	**2,035**	**0.1**	**-0.1**
France						369	398	399	0.8	0
Germany						778	852	860	0.9	0.1
Other Europe						623	914	922	3.9	0.1
OTHER DEVELOPED						**405**	**511**	**589**	**2.4**	**1.4**
Australia						44	57	65	2.6	1.3
Israel						19	27	30	3.6	1.1
Japan						319	394	460	2.1	1.6
New Zealand						7	11	13	4.6	1.7
South Africa						16	22	21	3.2	-0.5

* Data for 1999 and 2000 partly estimated.

Table 3.12: Opening stocks of coffee in exporting countries

(In million bags)

Crop year beginning	Columbian milds	Other milds	Brazilian	Robustas naturals	Total
1990	7.14	5.37	28.89	14.27	55.66
1991	7.67	4.94	28.41	11.95	52.97
1992	8.99	4.95	26.58	14.05	54.57
1993	6.70	3.19	23.65	8.98	42.52
1994	3.66	3.20	25.67	7.81	40.35
1995	6.21	4.21	21.90	7.37	39.69
1996	6.53	3.02	19.14	4.83	33.52
1997	4.41	2.17	17.91	5.29	29.78
1998	4.14	2.42	13.88	5.37	25.80
1999	3.30	2.04	13.00	5.07	23.40
2000	2.59	2.47	11.17	5.41	21.63
2001	1.96	2.61	10.79	5.74	21.09
2002	2.05	3.17	8.54	5.74	19.50
2003	1.90	2.86	9.57	6.31	20.64

Source: International Coffee Organization.

Table 3.13: Total coffee exports

(Thousand 60 kilogram bags)

	2008/09	2009/10	2010/11	2011/12	2012/13	Jun 2013/14
Angola	4	8	5	8	9	10
Bolivia	73	74	66	87	60	75
Brazil	31,475	29,780	35,010	29,843	31,000	31,040
Burundi	250	290	235	205	230	195
Cameroon	480	690	650	670	550	625
Central African Republic	6	25	22	7	5	5
Colombia	8,935	7,435	8,385	7,310	8,325	8,625
Congo (Kinshasa)	117	102	75	69	50	50
Costa Rica	1,385	1,200	1,255	1,455	1,450	1,200
Cote d'Ivoire	1,555	2,045	985	1,590	1,700	1,800
Cuba	6	7	5	11	10	10
Dominican Republic	42	36	48	47	40	40
Ecuador	861	1,140	1,250	1,521	1,675	1,750
El Salvador	1,510	1,240	1,772	1,130	1,000	750
Ethiopia	3,000	3,250	3,235	3,140	3,280	3,300
EU-27	225	170	490	405	450	400

(Contd.)

Table 3.13: Total coffee exports

(Thousand 60 kilogram bags)

	2008/09	2009/10	2010/11	2011/12	2012/13	Jun 2013/14
Ghana	18	30	57	70	25	50
Guatemala	3,815	3,890	3,725	4,050	3,870	3,500
Guinea	375	410	300	380	350	370
Haiti	17	10	7	9	10	10
Honduras	3,050	3,200	3,900	5,290	4,400	4,800
India	2,950	4,265	5,515	5,210	5,255	5,230
Indonesia	7,700	8,750	9,720	7,450	8,900	7,400
Jamaica	26	23	18	17	10	15
Kenya	980	740	650	800	850	850
Laos	250	290	400	350	275	300
Liberia	7	2	4	5	5	5
Madagascar	115	40	105	105	85	100
Malawi	25	24	24	24	24	24
Malaysia	1,100	1,460	1,675	1,950	2,200	2,350
Mexico	2,735	2,480	2,460	3,325	3,600	3,190
Nicaragua	1,585	1,806	1,665	1,780	1,775	1,450
Nigeria	1	3	2	10	5	5
Panama	45	53	37	30	40	35
Papua New Guinea	1,070	1,040	850	1,350	800	1,000
Paraguay	5	5	5	5	5	5
Peru	3,830	3,150	3,880	5,140	4,100	3,950
Rwanda	340	240	317	245	250	275
Sierra Leone	70	70	25	69	50	60
Tanzania	1,205	805	1,005	525	730	960
Thailand	644	684	1,207	750	820	775
Togo	188	436	615	560	250	400
Uganda	3,050	2,670	3,150	3,000	3,200	3,400
Venezuela	235	125	100	100	80	80
Vietnam	15,565	18,670	18,640	24,435	23,800	23,600
Yemen	35	30	20	20	20	20
Zambia	39	27	7	10	5	5
Zimbabwe	18	17	6	3	3	3
Total	**101,012**	**102,937**	**113,579**	**114,565**	**115,626**	**114,092**

A conversion factor of 2.6 was used to convert soluble coffee to the green bean equivalent.

Coffee marketing year for producer countries begins either in October (Colombia), April (Indonesia) or July (Brazil), as examples.

Coffee marketing year for non-producer countries begins in October.

For each non-producing country, the balance between imports and exports was used in order to remove double-counting from these trade figures.

Table 3.13A: Production and exports: India vs World[*]

(In '000 bags of 60 kilo each)

Year	Production		India's Share (%)	Exports		India's Share (%)
	World	India[@]		World	India[@]	
1991–92	101552	3000	2.95	79625	2024	2.54
1992–93	88913	2823	3.18	76780	1817	2.37
1993–94	90366	3533	3.91	73911	2907	3.93
1994–95	95154	3002	3.15	65718	2070	3.15
1995–96	85250	3717	4.36	74014	3572	4.83
1996–97	101865	3417	3.35	81745	2476	3.03
1997–98	95872	3805	3.97	77806	3685	4.74
1998–99	106163	4417	4.16	82554	3442	4.17
1999–00	115117	4867	4.23	92282	4214	4.57
2000–01	116619	5020	4.30	89248	4229	4.74
2001–02	108451	5010	4.62	90564	3730	4.12
2002–03	123723	4588	3.71	90007	3567	3.96
2003–04	103982	4508	4.34	87527	3826	4.37
2004–05	116062	4592	3.96	89546	2790	3.12
2005–06	111463	4567	4.10	88222	3581	4.06
2006–07	129138	4800	3.72	97620	3065	3.14
2007–08	119396	4367	3.66	96078	3389	3.53
2008–09**	128181	4372	3.41	97584	3286	3.37
2009–10**	123713	4827	3.90			

* Production and exports of ICO members.
** Provisional, subject to revision.
@ Board's Estimates
Source: ICO and Coffee Board.

countries than in developed countries, in contrast to the trend over the previous decade. Part of the growth in consumption in developing countries would come from the increase within the producing countries, and partially because of this, international trade would grow slower. This scenario, however, is subject to sudden and substantial changes in the world coffee economy.

Recent price crises have had an important implication for the world coffee economy. The price crisis, which has adversely and seriously affected incomes of all coffee producers, hit some producers more severely than others due to differences in various economic factors such as production cost and exchange rates. These variations may change the relative competitiveness among the exporters, and could therefore alter the pattern of the world coffee trade. In addition, various international initiatives are expected to take place as the exporters underline the importance of promoting higher quality coffee with the aim of improving prices through boosting consumption. All these factors may affect the demand and supply conditions in the world coffee markets to 2010 although the price would continue to be the primary determinant.

Table 3.13B: Soluble coffee exports

(Thousand 60 kilograms bags)

	2008/09	2009/10	2010/11	2011/12	2012/13	Jun 2013/14
Brazil	2,991	3,120	3,140	3,236	3,500	3,500
Colombia	725	925	935	610	600	600
Cote d'Ivoire	375	290	260	300	300	300
Ecuador	680	680	825	946	1,100	1,175
EU-27	225	170	490	405	450	400
India	825	1,225	1,350	1,475	1,500	1,475
Indonesia	1,075	1,325	2,305	2,500	2,000	1,800
Malaysia	1,100	1,460	1,675	1,950	2,200	2,350
Mexico	610	690	725	750	850	740
Nicaragua	160	156	140	105	100	100
Thailand	640	680	1,192	735	800	750
Vietnam	110	195	340	450	500	500
Total	9,553	10,951	13,457	13,642	13,975	13,750

A conversion factor of 2.6 was used to convert soluble coffee to the green bean equivalent.

Coffee marketing year for producer countries begins either in October (Colombia), April (Indonesia) or July (Brazil), as examples.

Coffee marketing year for non-producer countries begins in October.

For each non-producing country, the balance between imports and exports was used in order to remove double-counting from these trade figures.

New Thailand Coffee

In the lush hills of northern Thailand, a herd of 20 elephants is excreting some of the world's most expensive coffee. Trumpeted as earthy in flavor and smooth on the palate, the exotic new brew is made from beans eaten by Thai elephants and plucked a day later from their dung.

A gut reaction inside the elephant creates what its founder calls the coffee's unique taste. Stomach turning or oddly alluring, this is not just one of the world's most unusual specialty coffee but at $1,100 per kg ($500 per pound), it is also among the world's priciest. For now, only the wealthy or well-travelled have access to this brew, known as the Black Ivory Coffee. It was launched last month at a few luxury hotels in remote corners of the world first in Northern Thailand, then the Maldives and now Abu Dhabi with the price tag of about $50 a serving.

In the misty mountains where Thailand meets Laos and Myanmar, the coffee's creator cites biology and scientific research to answer the basic question: Why elephants? "When an elephant eats coffee, its stomach acid breaks down the protein found in coffee, which is a key factor in bitterness", said Blake Dinkin, who has spent $300,000 developing the coffee. "You end up with a cup that's very smooth without the bitterness of regular coffee".

The result is similar in civet coffee, or kopi luwak, another exorbitantly expensive variety extracted from the excrement of the weasel-like civet. But, the elephants' massive stomach provides a bonus. "Think of the elephant as the animal kingdom's equivalent of a slow cooker. It takes between 15 hours and 30 hours to digest the beans, which stew together with bananas, sugarcane and other ingredients in the elephant's vegetarian diet to infuse unique earthy and fruity flavors", said the 42-year-old Canadian, who has a background in civet coffee.

As for the coffee's inflated price, Dinkin half-joked that elephants are highly inefficient workers. It takes 33 kilograms (72 pounds) of raw coffee cherries to produce 1 kilogram of (2 pounds) Black Ivory coffee. The majority of beans get chewed up, broken or lost in tall grass after being excreted. Inevitably, the elephant coffee has become the butt of jokes. Dinkin shared his favorites—crapaccino. Good to the last dropping. Elephant poop coffee.

LOW GLOBAL PRICES LIKELY TO LIFT COFFEE EXPORTERS' HOPES OF REVIVING EXPORT

The Indian coffee industry is expecting that new supplies and the downswing in global prices owing to widespread rains in Brazil, the largest producer, to lift exports which have been going through a slack phase.

According to Coffee Board figures, exports have shown a 5% drop from January to September this year to 235,796 tons. A combination of tepid demand and higher prices has pulled down the shipments. Robusta cherry, which constitutes a major chunk of exports, has dropped by 19% during the period.

Indian robusta is traditionally priced higher in the global market thanks to its better quality. "Our exports suffered as the difference in prices of our robusta and that of Vietnam widened. Now, it has narrowed down to $250–300 per ton", said MP Devaiah, general manager of Allanasons, a major exporter.

Vietnam the largest producer of robusta coffee during the previous year has been able to sell at a cheaper rate in the international market. Global coffee prices have cooled after showers in Brazil. Arabica futures on ICE New York are around $1.90 per pound. The rains may lead to another revision of the Brazilian crop estimate, which determines coffee prices worldwide.

According to the September report of International Coffee Organization, the previous revision by Brazilian crop agency Conab put the production estimate at 45.14 million bags (each bag of 60 kg) for 2014–2015.

Indian coffee prices have declined slightly. Raw coffee prices of arabica parchment have dropped 5% to below Rs 11,000 per 50 kg. Robusta cherry is down by 6% to Rs 3,500 per 50 kg.

"We expect global prices to slide another 10%. Though there is a carryover stock of around 20,000 tons in India, overseas demand is for new crop slated to arrive by December. By that time, we hope the demand from Western Europe also improves", said Ramesh Rajah, President of Coffee Exporters Association of India.

Growers are awaiting a poor arabica crop and a better robusta crop in the next season. "The situation hasn't changed. We estimate the arabica crop to be 30% less to be in the range of 60,000–65,000 tons because of white stem borer attack. The robusta crop will be definitely better than the past year", said D Govindappa Jayaram, chairman of Karnataka Planters' Association.

The Coffee Board's post-blossom projections for 2014–2015 are 105,00 tons of arabica and 2.39 lakh tons of robusta. Growers' estimate of robusta crop is 2.20 lakh tons.

Table 3.14: Total coffee import

(Thousand 60 kilogram bags)

	2008–09	2009–10	2010–11	2011–12	2012–13	2013/14
Algeria	2,070	2,080	1,815	2,260	2,330	2,225
Argentina	680	740	800	740	800	750
Australia	1,225	1,330	1,390	1,450	1,500	1,525
Canada	2,865	3,170	3,375	3,390	3,550	3,450
China	435	610	930	1,025	1,600	1,800
Colombia	660	590	795	1,105	710	550
Costa Rica	15	130	175	65	40	50
Croatia	380	380	380	360	350	350
Cuba	240	220	225	225	225	200
Ecuador	389	732	883	1,150	1,350	1,400
El Salvador	157	136	147	185	175	190
EU-27	43,350	44,200	44,270	43,635	45,000	44,300
Guatemala	223	225	200	200	200	210
Honduras	18	18	23	15	15	15
India	560	725	820	890	830	810
Indonesia	290	570	565	1,535	825	700
Iran	185	335	330	300	205	190
Japan	7,005	6,680	7,460	6,555	7,800	7,450
Jordan	420	360	330	380	450	415
Kazakhstan	290	290	210	240	180	0
South Korea	1,680	1,705	1,930	1,725	1,650	1,600
Malaysia	650	960	1,030	1,125	1,400	1,500
Mexico	114	245	415	1,100	1,325	1,475
Morocco	600	580	540	700	725	700
New Zealand	290	310	300	310	340	365
Norway	700	670	710	655	615	640
Philippines	1,325	2,320	2,000	3,280	2,075	2,700
Russia	3,190	3,805	4,190	3,700	4,350	4,400
Serbia	660	595	620	755	800	800
South Africa	390	470	550	540	525	500
Switzerland	1,800	1,950	2,180	2,175	2,275	2,300
Thailand	400	545	1,050	990	1,150	1,200
Turkey	260	275	315	350	350	375
Ukraine	1,670	1,510	1,370	1,115	1,000	1,000
United States	22,250	20,870	23,110	23,825	22,800	22,700
Venezuela	5	316	622	576	606	636
Vietnam	95	75	350	370	450	450
Total	97,536	100,722	106,405	108,996	110,571	109,921

Source: USDA, Coffee.

Table 3.14A: Soluble coffee import

(Thousand 60 kilogram bags)

	2008–2009	2009–2010	2010–2011	2011–2012	2012–2013	2013–2014
Algeria	25	20	45	30	30	25
Argentina	200	240	290	240	275	250
Australia	275	290	275	310	325	325
Canada	925	1,160	1,070	1,165	1,150	1,150
China	115	185	250	400	700	800
Croatia	80	80	80	85	100	100
Ecuador	77	79	60	0	0	0
El Salvador	140	125	125	170	160	175
Guatemala	160	165	200	200	200	210
Honduras	10	10	15	15	15	15
Indonesia	200	145	375	470	375	350
Iran	160	210	305	260	165	150
Japan	630	520	560	590	800	750
Kazakhstan	290	290	210	240	180	0
Mexico	95	135	150	625	750	850
New Zealand	140	150	150	140	160	175
Norway	90	90	90	85	90	90
Philippines	920	1,900	1,625	2,770	1,500	2,100
Russia	1,950	2,375	2,650	1,980	2,350	2,200
Serbia	70	70	100	185	225	225
South Africa	60	70	150	190	200	200
Thailand	270	340	430	580	650	700
Ukraine	1,590	1,410	1,270	1,000	850	875
United States	590	630	650	125	400	500
Venezuela	5	316	622	576	606	
Vietnam	95	75	350	350	606	150
Total	**97,536**	**100,722**	**106,405**	**108,996**	**110,571**	**12,430**

A conversion factor of 2.6 was used to convert soluble coffee to the green bean equivalent.

Coffee marketing year for producer countries begins either in October (Colombia), April (Indonesia) or July (Brazil), as examples. Coffee marketing year for non-producer countries begins in October.

For each non-producing country, the balance between imports and exports was used in order to remove double-counting from these trade figures.

Table 3.15: Coffee world production, supply and distribution

	Beginning stocks	Arabica production	Robusta production	Production	Imports	Total supply	Exports	Domestic consumption	Ending stocks	Total distribution	Exportable production
Coffee, Green											
1976-77	38,984	42,977	17,807	61,162	534	100,680	56,561	18,452	25,667	100,680	42,922
1977-78	25,667	54,430	15,920	70,724	627	97,018	48,755	18,828	29,435	97,018	52,233
1978-79	29,435	59,847	18,770	79,018	678	109,131	64,612	19,462	25,057	109,131	60,035
1979-80	25,057	62,302	19,207	81,906	653	107,616	62,130	19,963	25,523	107,616	62,283
1980-81	25,523	63,154	22,584	86,174	S675	112,372	60,955	20,438	30,979	112,372	66,007
1981-82	30,979	75,132	22,396	98,023	755	129,757	65,359	20,556	43,842	129,757	77,771
1982-83	43,842	59,258	22,196	81,904	733	126,479	66,059	20,221	40,199	126,479	61,916
1983-84	40,199	70,459	17,905	88,801	606	129,606	68,191	20,577	40,838	129,606	68,490
1984-85	40,838	65,302	24,591	90,362	456	131,656	72,322	21,968	37,366	131,656	68,591
1985-86	37,366	71,299	23,998	95,750	397	133,513	70,478	21,220	41,815	133,513	74,777
1986-87	41,815	52,812	26,121	79,394	262	121,471	66,982	21,202	33,287	121,471	58,416
1987-88	33,287	78,985	23,810	103,170	296	136,753	67,504	21,075	48,174	136,753	82,310
1988-89	48,174	64,934	28,901	94,165	415	142,754	71,371	21,190	50,193	142,754	73,168
1989-90	50,193	69,118	27,542	96,958	258	147,409	83,402	20,995	43,012	147,409	76,157
1990-91	43,012	72,143	27,768	100,181	331	143,524	76,163	22,265	45,096	143,524	78,131
1991-92	45,096	73,980	29,809	104,064	291	149,451	80,887	22,266	46,298	149,451	81,950
1992-93	46,298	65,234	27,455	92,959	713	139,970	77,869	21,579	40,522	139,970	71,722
1993-94	40,522	65,052	27,146	92,406	585	133,513	76,284	22,928	34,301	133,513	69,764
1994-95	34,301	68,809	28,033	97,042	1,070	132,413	68,672	22,526	41,215	132,413	74,978

Table 3.15: Coffee world production, supply and distribution (*Contd.*)

	Beginning stocks	Arabica production	Robusta production	Production	Imports	Total supply	Exports	Domestic consumption	Ending stocks	Total distribution	Exportable production
1995-96	41,215	61,394	27,372	88,946	1,079	131,240	74,103	24,049	33,088	131,240	65,393
1996-97	33,088	66,452	37,236	103,786	1,091	137,965	84,509	24,361	29,095	137,965	79,780
1997-98	29,095	64,712	32,940	97,687	1,220	128,002	77,939	25,180	24,883	128,002	72,986
1998-99	24,883	74,859	34,060	108,953	1,435	135,271	85,133	25,738	24,400	135,271	83,533
1999-00	24,400	73,281	40,853	114,164	1,303	139,867	93,464	25,588	20,815	139,867	88,735
2000-01	20,815	70,362	46,820	117,217	1,488	139,520	90,847	26,303	22,370	139,520	91,069
2001-02	22,370	68,298	43,297	111,625	7,024	141,019	88,292	27,490	25,237	141,019	84,385
2002-03	39,452	85,085	41,855	126,968	87,976	254,396	93,936	112,832	47,628	254,396	99,628
2003-04	47,628	66,674	44,197	110,896	87,734	246,258	90,171	116,307	39,780	246,258	81,111
2004-05	39,780	77,898	43,668	121,591	89,728	251,099	93,878	115,792	41,429	251,099	90,673
2005-06	41,429	70,563	47,011	117,599	91,388	250,416	93,747	123,633	33,036	250,416	86,020
2006-07	33,036	83,690	49,903	133,618	97,298	263,952	104,804	123,036	36,112	263,952	101,795
2007-08	36,112	74,368	49,580	123,948	97,568	257,628	98,209	127,714	31,705	257,628	90,992
2008-09	31,705	85,152	51,087	136,239	97,536	265,480	101,012	124,619	39,849	265,480	102,013
2009-10	39,849	76,501	51,990	128,491	100,722	269,062	102,937	137,182	28,943	269,062	93,070
2010-11	28,943	87,106	53,341	140,447	106,405	275,795	113,579	133,583	28,633	275,795	103,791
2011-12	28,633	83,343	60,455	143,798	108,996	281,427	114,565	141,567	25,295	281,427	104,695
2012-13	25,295	88,691	62,020	150,711	110,571	286,577	115,626	140,715	30,236	286,577	111,166
2013-14	30,236	84,835	61,490	146,325	109,921	286,482	114,092	141,865	30,525	286,482	105,915

Note: After 2003/04, the database includes import and consumption data for non-producing countries.

Table 3.15A: World coffee supply and distribution, 2007–2008

(Thousand 60-kilogram bags*)

Country mktg year	Beginning stocks	Total production	Bean imports	Domestic Use	Bean exports	Ending stocks	Exportable production
Caribbean							
Dominican Republic	120	465	0	455	80	50	10
Total Caribbean							
2007–2008	306	920	0	884	128	213	36
Central America							
Costa Rica	77	1,867	0	280	1,588	76	1,587
El Salvador	31	1,515	1	224	1,465	18	1,291
Guatemala	125	3,980	0	338	3,820	10	3,642
Honduras	88	3,802	0	239	3,395	235	3,563
Nicaragua	186	1,700	0	165	1,610	81	1,535
Panama	29	170	0	65	100	34	105
Total Central America							
2007–2008	536	13,034	1	1,311	11,978	454	11,723
North America							
Mexico	390	4,500	15	2,200	2,420	270	2,300
Total North America							
2007–2008	6,090	4,653	23,730	26,168	2,420	5,870	2,300
Oceania							
Papua New Guinea	562	1,013	0	2	970	603	1,011
Total Oceania							
2007–2008	562	1,013	920	922	970	603	1,011
South America							
Brazil	8,361	39,100	0	17,390	23,770	2,781	21,710
Colombia	1,302	12,515	0	1,250	10,656	1,411	11,265
Peru	24	3,950	0	118	3,840	16	3,832
Venezuela	483	1,000	0	834	200	414	166
Total South America							
2007–2008	10,442	57,435	700	20,320	38,722	4,872	37,607
Southeast Asia							
Vietnam	791	18,333	65	885	15,700	2,604	17,448
Total Southeast Asia							
2007–2008	990	27,973	1,739	5,484	21,492	3,004	22,859
Sub-Saharan Africa							
Cote d'Ivoire	931	1,600	0	299	1,525	432	1,301
Ethiopia	1,000	4,200	0	2,000	2,300	900	2,200
Kenya	635	700	0	19	660	659	681
Liberia	0	50	0	9	41	0	41
Madagascar	604	580	0	450	210	524	130
Uganda	271	2,500	0	60	2,300	411	2,440
Total Sub-Saharan Africa							
2007–2008	4,721	12,910	410	3,716	9,791	4,252	9,614
World							
World	42,838	122,838	85,855	119,094	88,148	37,729	88,271

* One bag-132.276 pound.

Table 3.15B: World coffee supply and distribution, 2008–2009

(Thousand 60-kilogram bags*)

Country mktg year	Beginning stocks	Total production	Bean imports	Domestic Use	Bean exports	Ending stocks	Exportable production
Total Caribbean							
2008–2009	213	1,030	0	880	155	208	150
Central America							
Guatemala	10	3,700	0	335	3,400	18	3,365
Honduras	235	3,600	0	249	3,200	367	3,351
Total Central America							
2008–2009	454	12,162	3	1,365	10,795	614	10,797
North America							
Mexico	270	4,450	15	2,200	2,400	136	2,250
South America							
Brazil	2,781	51,450	0	17,940	27,300	6,011	33,510
Colombia	1,411	10,500	0	1,250	10,100	461	9,250
Total South America							
2008–2009	4,872	67,618	820	20,943	41,609	7,029	47,215
South Asia							
India	1,985	4,375	200	1,620	2,460	1,773	2,755
Sri Lanka	16	35	0	35	2	14	0
Total South Asia							
2008–2009	2,001	4,410	200	1,655	2,462	1,787	2,755
Southeast Asia							
Indonesia	158	7,600	400	2,445	5,500	183	5,155
Vietnam	2,604	19,670	70	933	18,800	2,611	18,737
Sub-Saharan Africa							
Cote d'Ivoire	432	2,150	0	315	1,600	417	1,835
Ethiopia	900	4,500	0	2,100	2,400	900	2,400
Uganda	411	2,700	0	100	2,700	311	2,600
Total Sub-Saharan Africa							
2008–2009	4,252	14,448	370	3,888	10,788	4,137	10,930

* One bag-132.276 pounds.

Table 3.15C: World coffee supply and distribution, 2009–2010

(Thousand 60-kilogram bags*)

Country mktg year	Beginning stocks	Total production	Bean imports	Domestic Use	Bean exports	Ending stocks	Exportable production
Total Caribbean							
2009–2010	208	1,020	0	855	150	223	165
Central America							
Guatemala	18	3,800	0	335	3,500	16	3,465
Honduras	367	4,000	0	249	3,600	494	3,751
Total Central America							
2009–2010	614	12,920	2	1,371	11,550	751	11,549
Mexico	136	4,500	20	2,200	2,400	56	2,300
Total North America							
2009–2010	5,336	4,660	23,670	26,150	2,400	5,116	2,300
Brazil	6,011	43,500	0	18,470	25,000	2,941	25,030
Peru	172	3,900	0	120	3,800	152	3,780
Total South America							
2009–2010	7,029	61,300	800	21,419	39,665	4,026	40,396
South Asia							
India	1,773	4,900	200	1,620	2,900	1,443	3,280
Total South Asia							
2009–2010	1,787	4,935	200	1,655	2,900	1,457	3,280
Indonesia	183	7,600	350	2,350	5,600	153	5,250
Vietnam	2,611	18,350	75	995	18,000	2,039	17,355
Ethiopia	900	4,300	0	2,200	2,400	600	2,100
Total Sub-Saharan Africa							
2009–2010	4,137	13,488	360	3,957	10,133	3,648	9,891
World							
World	40,063	127,443	86,357	121,059	91,725	35,293	91,474

* One bag-132.276 pounds.

Table 3.15D: World coffee supply and distribution, 2012–2013

(*Thousand 60-kilogram bags*)

Country	Beginning stock	Arabka production	Robusta production	Total production	Total import	Total supply	Total export	Domestic use	Ending stocks	Total distribution	Exportable production
Caribbean											
Cuba	0	125	0	125	225	350	10	340	0	350	0
Dominican Republic	0	475	0	475	0	475	40	435	0	475	40
Haiti	25	300	0	300	0	325	10	300	15	325	0
Jamaica	0	15	0	15	0	15	10	5	0	15	10
Trinidad and Tobago	0	0	0	0	0	0	0	0	0	0	0
Total Caribbean	25	915	0	915	225	1,165	70	1,080	15	1,165	50
Central America											
Costa Rica	240	1,675	0	1,675	40	1,955	1,450	380	125	1,955	1,295
El Salvador	18	1,125	0	1,125	175	1,318	1,000	260	58	1,318	865
Guatemala	197	4,200	10	4,210	200	4,607	3,870	600	137	4,607	3,610
Honduras	90	4,600	0	4,600	15	4,705	4,400	235	70	4,705	4,365
Nicaragua	32	1,850	0	1,850	0	1,882	1,775	90	17	1,882	1,760
Panama	0	90	0	90	0	90	40	50	0	90	40
Total Central America	577	13,540	10	13,550	430	14,557	12,535	1,615	407	14,557	11,935
East Asia											
China	0	0	0	0	1,600	1,600	0	1,600	0	1,600	0
Japan	2,140	0	0	0	7,800	9,940	0	7,340	2,600	9,940	0
Korea, South	0	0	0	0	1,650	1,650	0	1,650	0	1,650	0
Total East Asia	2,140	0	0	0	11,050	13,190	0	10,590	2,600	13,190	0
European Union											
EU-27	10,400	0	0	0	45,000	55,400	450	44,250	10,700	55,400	0
Total European Union	10,400	0	0	0	45,000	55,400	450	44,250	10,700	55,400	0

(*Contd.*)

Table 3.15D: World coffee supply and distribution, 2012–2013

(Thousand 60-kilogram bags)

Country	Beginning stock	Arabka production	Robusta production	Total production	Total import	Total supply	Total export	Domestic use	Ending stocks	Total distribution	Exportable production
Former Soviet Union - 12											
Kazakhstan	0	0	0	0	180	180	0	180	0	180	0
Russia	0	0	0	0	4,350	4,350	0	4,350	0	4,350	0
Ukraine	0	0	0	0	1,000	1,000	0	1,000	0	1,000	0
Total Former Soviet Union - 12	0	0	0	0	5,530	5,530	0	5,530	0	5,530	0
Middle East											
Iran	0	0	0	0	205	205	0	205	0	205	0
Jordan	0	0	0	0	450	450	0	450	0	450	0
Turkey	0	0	0	0	350	350	0	350	0	350	0
Yemen	0	150	0	150	0	150	20	130	0	150	20
Total Middle East	0	150	0	150	1,005	1,155	20	1,135	0	1,155	20
North Africa											
Algeria	0	0	0	0	2,330	2,330	0	2,330	0	2,330	0
Morocco	0	0	0	0	725	725	0	725	0	725	0
Total North Africa	25	0	0	0	3,055	3,055	0	3,055	0	3,055	0
North America											
Canada	0	0	0	0	3,550	3,550	0	3,550	0	3,550	0
Mexico	102	4,100	200	4,300	1,325	5,727	3,600	2,100	27	5,727	2,200
United States	5,100	98	0	98	22,800	27,998	0	22,798	5,200	27,998	0
Total North America	5,202	4,198	200	4,398	27,675	37,275	3,600	28,448	5,227	37,275	2,200
Oceania											
Australia	0	0	0	0	1,500	1,500	0	1,500	0	1,500	0
New Caledonia	0	0	0	0	0	0	0	0	0	0	0

Table 3.15D: World coffee supply and distribution, 2012–2013 *(Contd.)*

(Thousand 60-kilogram bags)

Country	Beginning stock	Arabka production	Robusta production	Total production	Total import	Total supply	Total export	Domestic use	Ending stocks	Total distribution	Exportable production
New Zealand	0	0	0	0	340	340	0	340	0	340	0
Papua New Guinea	31	800	50	850	0	881	800	45	36	881	805
Total Oceania	31	800	50	850	1,840	2,721	800	1,885	36	2,721	805
Croatia	0	0	0	0	350	350	0	350	0	350	0
Norway	125	0	0	0	615	740	0	615	25	740	0
Serbia	0	0	0	0	800	800	0	800	0	800	0
Switzerland	200	0	0	0	2,275	2,475	0	2,275	00	2,475	0
Total Other Europe	325	0	0	0	4,040	4,365	0	4,040	25	4,365	0
South America											
Argentina	0	0	0	0	800	800	0	800	0	800	0
Bolivia	4	125	0	125	0	129	60	65	4	129	60
Brazil	2,238	41,100	15,000	56,100	0	58,338	31,000	20,615	6,723	58,338	35,485
Colombia	249	9,000	0	9,000	710	9,959	8,325	1,200	434	9,959	7,800
Ecuador	134	405	185	590	1,350	2,074	1,675	235	164	2,074	355
Guyana	0	0	0	0	0	0	0	0	0	0	0
Paraguay	5	25	0	25	0	30	5	20	5	30	5
Peru	14	4,300	0	4,300	0	4,314	4,100	170	44	4,314	4,130
Venezuela	103	730	0	730	606	1,439	80	1,305	54	1,439	0
Total South America	2,747	55,685	15,185	70,870	3,466	77,083	45,245	24,410	7,428	77,083	47,835
South Asia											
India	1,432	1,670	3,580	5,250	830	7,512	5,255	1,100	1,157	7,512	4,150
Sri Lanka	0	10	25	35	0	35	0	35	0	35	0
Total South Asia	1,432	1,680	3,605	5,285	830	7,547	5,255	1,135	1,157	7,547	4,150

(Contd.)

Table 3.15D: World coffee supply and distribution, 2012–2013

(Thousand 60-kilogram bags)

Country	Beginning stock	Arabka production	Robusta production	Total production	Total import	Total supply	Total export	Domestic use	Ending stocks	Total distribution	Exportable production
Southeast Asia											
Indonesia	88	1,700	8,800	10,500	825	11,413	8,900	2,415	98	11,413	8,085
Laos	0	0	375	375	0	375	275	100	0	375	275
Malaysia	0	0	1,400	1,400	1,400	2,800	2,200	600	0	2,800	800
Philippines	165	30	425	455	2,075	2,695	0	2,600	95	2,695	0
Thailand	0	0	850	850	1,150	2,000	820	1,180	0	2,000	0
Vietnam	1,070	850	24,100	24,950	450	26,470	23,800	1,825	845	26,470	23,125
Total Southeast Asia	1,323	2,580	35,950	38,530	5,900	45,753	35,995	8,720	1,038	45,753	32,285
Sub-Saharan Africa											
Angola	2	0	30	30	0	32	9	22	1	32	8
Benin	0	0	0	0	0	0	0	0	0	0	0
Burundi	15	225	0	225	0	240	230	5	5	240	220
Cameroon	24	75	550	625	0	649	550	75	24	649	550
Central African Republic	60	0	10	10	0	70	5	30	35	70	0
Congo (Brazzaville)	0	0	0	0	0	0	0	0	0	0	0
Congo (Kinshasa)	10	80	150	230	0	240	50	180	10	240	50
Cote d'Ivoire	118	0	1,800	1,800	0	1,918	1,700	108	110	1,918	1,692
Equatorial Guinea	0	0	0	0	0	0	0	0	0	0	0
Ethiopia	230	6,325	0	6,325	0	6,555	3,280	3,055	220	6,555	3,270
Gabon	0	0	0	0	0	0	0	0	0	0	0
Ghana	2	0	25	25	0	27	25	1	1	27	24
Guinea	12	0	375	375	0	387	350	30	7	387	345
Kenya	30	900	0	900	0	930	850	50	30	930	850

Table 3.15D: World coffee supply and distribution, 2012–2013 *(Contd.)*

(Thousand 60-kilogram bags)

Country	Beginning stock	Arabka production	Robusta production	Total production	Total import	Total supply	Total export	Domestic use	Ending stocks distribution	Total distribution	Exportable production
Liberia	0	0	5	5	0	5	5	0	0	5	5
Madagascar	7	25	500	525	0	532	85	440	7	532	85
Malawi	0	25	0	25	0	25	24	1	0	25	24
Nigeria	0	0	30	30	0	30	5	25	0	30	5
Rwanda	0	250	0	250	0	250	250	0	0	250	250
Sierra Leone	0	0	70	70	0	70	50	20	0	70	50
South Africa	0	0	0	0	525	525	0	525	0	525	0
Tanzania	45	575	525	1,100	0	1,145	730	50	365	1,145	1,050
Togo	0	0	250	250	0	250	250	0	0	250	250
Uganda	538	650	2,700	3,350	0	3,888	3,200	200	488	3,888	3,150
Zambia	0	5	0	5	0	5	5	0	0	5	5
Zimbabwe	0	8	0	8	0	8	3	5	0	8	3
Total Sub-Saharan Africa	1,093	9,143	7,020	16,163	525	17,781	11,656	4,822	1,303	17,781	11,886
World											
World	25,295	88,691	62,020	150,711	110,571	286,577	115,626	140,715	30,236	286,577	111,166

Source: USDA Report.

Table 3.16: Coffee production, consumption, ending stock (export and import)

(Thousand 60-kilogram bags)

	2008–2009	2009–2010	2010–2011	2011–2012	2012–2013	2013–2014
Production						
Brazil	53,300	44,800	54,500	49,200	56,100	53,700
Vietnam	16,980	18,500	19,415	26,000	24,950	24,800
Indonesia	10,000	10,500	9,325	8,300	10,500	9,200
Colombia	8,664	8,100	8,525	7,655	9,000	9,000
Ethiopia	5,500	6,000	6,125	6,320	6,325	6,350
India	4,375	4,825	5,035	5,230	5,250	5,200
Honduras	3,225	3,550	3,975	5,600	4,600	5,000
Mexico	4,550	4,150	4,000	4,300	4,300	3,800
Peru	4,000	3,300	4,100	5,200	4,300	4,100
Guatemala	3,980	4,010	3,960	4,410	4,210	3,885
Other	21,665	20,756	21,487	21,583	21,176	21,290
11	136,239	128,491	140,447	143,798	150,711	146,325
Domestic Consumption						
EU-27	39,575	49,505	41,730	45,730	44,250	44,100
United States	22,650	22,060	22,888	23,405	22,798	22,800
Brazil	18,030	18,760	19,420	20,025	20,615	21,150
Japan	6,915	6,780	6,860	6,965	7,340	7,550
Russia	3,190	3,805	4,190	3,700	4,350	4,400
Canada	2,865	3,170	3,375	3,390	3,550	3,450
Ethiopia	2,500	2,800	2,860	3,050	3,055	3,100
Other	28,894	30,302	32,260	35,302	34,757	35,315
Total	124,619	137,182	133,583	141,567	140,715	141,865
Ending Stocks						
EU-27	16,325	10,850	12,900	10,400	10,700	10,500
Brazil	6,576	2,836	2,906	2,238	6,723	8,233
United States	5,333	4,250	4,580	5,100	5,200	5,200
Japan	2,050	1,950	2,550	2,140	2,600	2,500
India	2,568	2,633	1,742	1,432	1,157	737
Other	6,997	6,424	3,955	3,985	3,856	3,355
Total	39,849	28,943	28,633	25,295	30,236	30,525

Table 3.16: Coffee production, consumption, ending stock (export and import) *(Contd.)*

(Thousand 60-kilogram bags)

	2008–2009	2009–2010	2010–2011	2011–2012	2012–2013	2013–2014
Bean Exports						
Brazil	28,396	26,580	31,810	26,556	27,465	27,500
Vietnam	15,430	18,425	18,215	23,890	23,200	23,000
Colombia	8,160	6,445	7,400	6,675	7,700	8,000
Indonesia	6,625	7,425	7,415	4,950	6,900	5,600
Honduras	3,050	3,200	3,900	5,290	4,400	4,800
Peru	3,830	3,150	3,880	5,140	4,100	3,950
Guatemala	3,783	3,860	3,650	3,875	3,800	3,450
India	2,125	3,040	4,160	3,730	3,750	3,750
Ethiopia	3,000	3,250	3,235	3,140	3,280	3,300
Uganda	3,050	2,670	3,150	3,000	3,200	3,400
Other	13,806	13,727	13,105	14,451	13,641	13,372
Total	91,255	91,772	99,920	100,697	101,436	100,122
Bean Imports						
EU-27	43,350	44,200	44,270	43,635	45,000	44,300
United States	21,660	20,240	22,460	23,700	22,400	22,200
Japan	6,375	6,160	6,900	5,965	7,000	6,700
Canada	1,940	2,010	2,305	2,225	2,400	2,300
Algeria	2,045	2,060	1,770	2,230	2,300	2,200
Switzerland	1,800	1,950	2,180	2,175	2,275	2,300
Russia	1,240	1,430	1,540	1,720	2,000	2,200
Korea, South	1,680	1,705	1,930	1,725	1,650	1,600
Malaysia	650	960	1,030	1,125	1,400	1,500
Ecuador	310	650	820	1,150	1,350	1,400
Other	7,002	8,245	9,465	10,455	10,155	10,035
Total	**88,052**	**89,610**	**94,670**	**96,105**	**97,930**	**96,735**

Coffee marketing year for producer countries begins either in October (Colombia), April (Indonesia) or July (Brazil), as examples.
Coffee marketing year for non-producer countries begins in October.
Bean export and bean import data exclude soluble trade.

Table 3.16A: Domestic consumption of exporting members crop years
2006–2007 to 2011–2012

Countries	2007	2008	2009	2010	2011	2012
World Total	36,874	38,527	40,325	41,871	42,713	43,306
Total	33,383	34,930	36,727	38,269	39,111	39,707
Angola	30	30	30	30	30	30
Bolivia	60	60	60	60	60	60
Brazil	17,125	17,660	18,890	19,130	19,720	20,000
Burundi	1	1	1	2	2	2
Cameroon	69	69	69	69	69	69
Central African Republic	3	5	8	8	8	8
Colombia	1,281	1,291	1,270	1,308	1,413	1,413
Costa Rica	274	245	229	282	270	242
Côte d'Ivoire	317	317	317	317	317	317
Cuba	224	220	220	220	220	220
Ecuador	150	150	150	150	150	150
El Salvador	230	232	232	273	266	275
Ethiopia	2,894	3,048	3,210	3,383	3,383	3,383
Gabon	0	0	0	0	0	0
Ghana	2	2	2	2	2	2
Guatemala	300	335	320	340	340	340
Honduras	245	268	307	345	345	345
India	1,500	1,573	1,700	1,800	1,917	1,917
Indonesia	3,333	3,333	3,333	3,333	3,333	3,667
Kenya	50	50	50	50	50	50
Liberia	5	5	5	5	5	5
Malawi	1	1	1	1	1	1
Mexico	2,200	2,200	2,200	2,354	2,354	2,354

Table 3.16A: Domestic consumption of exporting members crop years 2006–2007 to 2011–2012 *(Contd)*

Countries	2007	2008	2009	2010	2011	2012
Nicaragua	192	194	197	199	200	200
Panama	67	67	67	67	67	67
Papua New Guinea	2	2	2	4	2	2
Philippines	1,060	1,720	1,820	2,125	2,175	2,175
Rwanda	1	1	1	1	1	1
Sierra Leone	5	5	5	5	5	5
Tanzania	47	47	47	47	47	47
Thailand	500	500	500	500	500	500
Timor-Leste	0	0	0	0	0	0
Togo	2	2	2	2	2	2
Uganda	140	140	140	140	140	140
Vietnam	938	1,021	1,208	1,583	1,583	1,583
Yemen	130	130	130	130	130	130
Zambia	1	1	0	0	0	0
Zimbabwe	4	4	4	4	4	4
Non-member countries	3,490	3,597	3,598	3,602	3,602	3,599
Congo, Dem. Rep. of	200	200	200	200	200	200
Dominican Republic	378	378	378	378	378	378
Guinea	50	50	50	50	50	50
Haiti	340	340	340	340	340	340
Lao, People's Dem. Rep. of	140	150	150	150	150	150
Madagascar	467	467	467	467	467	467
Peru	220	250	250	250	250	250
Venezuela	1,582	1,649	1,650	1,650	1,650	1,650
Others	113	113	113	117	117	114

Source: ICO (Statistics on coffee 8/ICA 2007 –January 2013).

Table 3.16B: Coffee consumption per capita

Countries	Unit	2002	2003	2004	2005	2006	2007
Albania	kg	1.3	1.4	1.2	1.1	1.8	2
Algeria	kg	3.5	3.3	4	3.5	3.3	2.5
Argentina	kg	0.8	1	1	1	1	1.1
Armenia	kg	3.4	2.8	2.3	2.3	1.6	1.7
Australia	kg	3.2	3.2	3.5	4.4	4.4	4.4
Austria	kg	6.6	6.3	7.6	5.2	5.1	8.6
Azerbaijan	kg			0.1	0.1	0.2	0.2
Belarus	kg	0.1	0.3	0.6	1.2	1.5	1.9
Belgium	kg	5.5	5.6	8.5	7.2	9.3	6.9
Bosnia and Herzegovina	kg	0.5	3.1	6.2	5.8	6.6	6.7
Brazil	kg	3.1	3.3	3.5	3.8	3.2	3.4
Bulgaria	kg	2.7	3.1	3.3	4	4.3	4.2
Canada	kg	4.4	4.1	5.4	5.5	6.3	7.2
Chile	kg	0.3	0.6	0.6	0.6	0.7	0.8
China	kg						
Colombia	kg	1.4	2	1.8	1.6	2	1.2
Croatia	kg	4.7	5	5.3	5.5	5.8	5.8
Czech Republic	kg	3.9	3.4	3	3	3	3.7
Denmark	kg	8.9	8.1	9.2	8.9	8.5	7.6
Egypt	kg	0.1	0.1	0.1	0.1	0.1	0.1
Estonia	kg	5.3	5.7	5.8	5.1	5.1	6.2
European Union	kg	4.8	4.8	5.1	4.7	4.8	4.9
Finland	kg	11	11.3	11.8	12	11.8	12
France	kg	5.6	5.3	4.9	4.9	5.4	5.6
Georgia	kg	0.4	0.6	1.1	1.4	1.6	2.2
Germany	kg	6.5	6.4	7.2	5.3	5.6	5.9
Ghana	kg						0.1
Greece	kg	4.6	5.3	4.9	4.7	4.8	5.5
Hungary	kg	3.4	3.5	3.5	3.2	3.2	3.2
Iceland	kg	8.8	8.8	8.9	9.6	8.6	8.9
India	kg	0.1		0.1	0.1		0.1
Indonesia	kg	1.5	1.4	1.3	0.7	1	1.5
Iran	kg					0.1	0.2
Ireland	kg	2	2.4	3.1	3.1	2.8	3.9
Israel	kg	3.6	4.4	4.3	4.8	4.2	4.4
Italy	kg	5.3	5.6	5.5	5.7	5.7	5.8
Japan	kg	3.6	3.4	3.7	3.8	3.9	3.6
Kazakhstan	kg	0.3	0.5	0.5	0.7	1	1.2
Kenya	kg	0.2	0.2	0.2	0.2	0.1	0.1
Kyrgyzstan	kg	0.1	0.2	0.2	0.3	0.4	0.3
Latvia	kg	4	4.4	4.3	4.3	4.9	5.1

Table 3.16B: Coffee consumption per capita

Countries	Unit	2002	2003	2004	2005	2006	2007
Lithuania	kg	3.9	3.4	4.3	4.5	4.8	5.4
Luxembourg	kg	15.4	13.5	16.9	17.5	18.1	18.2
Macedonia	kg	3.2	3.7	4	4.1	4.1	4.2
Malaysia	kg					0.5	0.3
Malta	kg	3.7	4.8	3.6	3.4	6.1	3.9
Mexico	kg	1.5	1.6	1.7	1.5	1	0.8
Moldova	kg	0.2	0.4	0.5	0.6	0.8	0.9
Mongolia	kg	0.3	0.2	0.3	0.4	0.4	1.7
Montenegro	kg					13.8	14.6
Morocco	kg	1	0.8	0.8	0.7	0.8	0.9
Netherlands	kg	8.8	10	9.9	6.4	8.2	8.6
New Zealand	kg	3.1	3.3	3.6	3.6	4	4.2
Nigeria	kg	0.1	0.1		0.1		0.1
Norway	kg	9.3	9.1	9.4	9.9	9.5	10.1
Pakistan	kg						
Peru	kg	1.7	1.9	1.4	1.8	1.3	1.9
Philippines	kg	1.7	1.4	1.4	1.7	1.5	1.5
Poland	kg	2.7	3	3	3.2	2.6	1.7
Portugal	kg	4	4	4.2	4	4.1	4.1
Romania	kg	2.1	2.2	2.3	2.4	2.4	2.4
Russia	kg	2	2.2	2.1	2.2	1.9	1.8
Serbia	kg					3.9	4.1
Singapore	kg						
Slovakia	kg	3.4	3.6	3.6	3.8	4	5.2
Slovenia	kg	6.5	5.9	6.4	6.1	6.1	6.9
South Africa	kg	0.4	0.4	0.6	0.7	0.9	0.8
South Korea	kg	1.7	1.7	1.8	1.8	1.7	1.5
Spain	kg	3.6	3.2	4	4.1	3.5	3.8
Sweden	kg	9.7	9.7	10.5	10	10.2	10
Switzerland	kg	6	6.7	5.1	8.4	6.5	7
Tajikistan	kg				0.1	0.1	0.2
Thailand	kg	0.4	0.4	0.3	0.3	0.2	0.4
Turkey	kg	0.4	0.4	0.6	0.8	1	1
Turkmenistan	kg						
Ukraine	kg	0.9	0.9	1	1.8	2.1	2.3
United Kingdom	kg	2.4	2.4	2.7	2.6	2.9	2.6
USA	kg	3.7	4	4	4.2	4.3	4.2
Uzbekistan	kg						
Venezuela	kg	2.9	2	2.5	2.4	2.8	2.5
Vietnam	kg	0.2	0.2	0.1	0.1	0.1	0.1
World	kg	1.2	1.1	1.2	1.2	1.2	1.2

Table 3.17: Unit value of imports (CIF) of green coffee by importing members from all sources in current terms 2007–2012

(US Cents per lb)

Importing member	2007	2008	2009	2010	2011	2012
Total	**108.45**	**135.33**	**119.56**	**126.23**	**220.76**	**178.25**
European Union	*101.78*	*130.18*	*112.67*	*116.45*	*206.33*	*163.07*
Austria	100.35	143.51	114.46	107.67	194.08	158.70
Belgium	110.76	134.46	120.35	119.74	224.65	178.29
Bulgaria	72.43	111.22	107.25	100.04	168.28	169.05
Cyprus	108.52	155.45	94.85	101.36	256.52	165.47
Czech Republic	95.38	129.77	107.49	104.16	228.42	166.31
Denmark	110.15	144.17	120.07	133.78	242.35	170.81
Estonia	99.33	106.96	120.73	63.96	617.67	147.88
Finland	119.03	140.15	130.62	166.41	294.91	210.65
France	98.57	129.58	111.88	119.79	214.36	164.34
Germany	100.77	127.80	112.30	118.52	213.21	162.49
Greece	102.23	191.72	103.48	111.36	190.94	150.63
Hungary	90.55	129.18	105.63	89.12	421.97	398.17
Ireland	167.95	253.25	422.72	228.63	237.29	238.37
Italy	98.44	127.21	107.23	106.26	185.20	151.36
Latvia	117.63	173.08	118.02	128.84	215.69	185.58
Lithuania	180.21	198.75	211.59	182.25	318.07	248.19
Luxembourg	179.75	221.45	169.42	174.05	331.01	281.29
Malta	280.14	—	1,292.22	139.96	338.40	201.83
Netherlands	111.78	138.50	125.40	138.53	240.21	180.59
Poland	86.07	124.76	95.19	87.31	166.01	133.27
Portugal	96.95	116.86	108.92	101.87	157.16	136.11
Romania	94.31	125.30	100.66	121.69	176.73	133.85
Slovakia	107.28	137.69	114.89	125.78	258.76	151.99
Slovenia	105.23	135.89	112.46	105.36	177.63	170.22
Spain	91.38	120.49	98.23	94.78	178.68	137.89
Sweden	116.94	138.34	123.51	154.89	283.52	221.62
United Kingdom	110.93	137.05	129.82	128.56	182.53	180.67
Other Importing Countries						
Japan	115.22	145.62	124.32	143.15	232.95	192.05
Norway	114.69	155.50	124.71	154.92	283.46	214.97
Switzerland	120.37	150.93	139.22	167.85	281.04	235.42
Tunisia	86.28	119.78	83.80	79.13	139.24	132.71
Turkey	103.44	124.07	91.09	108.44	176.63	163.58
USA	120.87	142.29	131.06	141.57	242.57	202.06

Source: ICO (Statistics on coffee 8/ICA 2007–2013).

Table 3.17A: Retail prices of roasted coffee in importing members countries in current terms 2007–2012

(US Cents per lb)

	2007	2008	2009	2010	2011	2012
European community						
Austria	428.46	499.45	706.94	613.51	848.45	795.49
Belgium	484.45	584.80	530.83	462.34	693.12	593.77
Bulgaria	333.00	429.21	386.80	331.24	437.08	337.83
Cyprus	562.96	652.53	588.06	512.18	603.71	525.59
Czech Republic	421.78	637.14	518.31	458.99	701.62	676.96
Denmark	471.10	580.52	537.13	489.42	735.04	671.65
Finland	318.91	395.05	347.11	323.37	587.39	464.79
France	333.52	403.51	378.90	332.22	428.14	381.83
Germany	467.41	544.59	476.80	430.78	527.34	459.10
Hungary	448.03	600.45	491.94	438.81	648.17	579.02
Italy	686.51	831.70	771.77	673.86	885.65	830.71
Latvia	471.08	644.40	607.26	535.08	915.35	761.79
Lithuania	451.89	575.80	511.26	470.42	815.96	695.00
Luxembourg	654.86	809.84	732.37	655.59	864.12	770.48
Malta*	1,185.21	1,395.36	1,303.26	1,196.01	1,501.11	1,375.05
Netherlands	435.76	533.31	472.99	420.82		
Poland	330.31	490.94	335.27	324.82	436.73	402.45
Portugal	498.45	610.20	537.19	456.80	559.97	553.42
Slovakia	375.87	557.23	508.59	448.50	606.97	664.80
Slovenia	447.93	548.83	484.43	398.67	500.58	436.38
Spain	374.90	451.48	419.59	358.80	454.25	434.11
Sweden	345.13	411.95	353.07	357.13	587.92	498.60
United Kingdom*	1,783.40	1,719.25	1,669.27	1,439.46	1,900.82	1,892.05
Other importing countries						
Japan	750.21	906.30	573.36	618.62	771.85	777.71
Norway	397.97	555.61	410.36	426.22	619.27	550.56
USA	340.70			369.7	523.40	558.20

* Soluble coffee.
A blank denotes that there were no imports of green coffee in the month.
Source: ICO (Statistics on coffee 8/ICA 2007–2013).

Annexures

Annexure 1: Statewise value of output - coffee

State/UTs	At current prices							At 2004-05 prices						
	2004-05	2005-06	2006-07	2007-08	2008-09	2009-10	2010-11	2004-05	2005-06	2006-07	2007-08	2008-09	2009-10	2010-11
Andhra Pradesh	1541	410	910	792	1254	978	2012	1541	372	776	582	878	566	768
Arunachal Pradesh	0	0	0	0	2	2	2	0	0	0	0	4	4	4
Assam	9368	11304	25	24525	49020	49574	59150	9368	7413	16	13761	21715	25553	22978
Karnataka	156342	178007	188346	215700	237266	365644	409025	156342	156814	162187	150812	144738	161931	166745
Kerala	20307	22304	22062	24194	28897	22993	22993	20307	22504	22242	21373	21391	22158	24551
Orissa	167	167	167	167	175	83	217	167	167	167	167	175	83	217
Tamil Nadu	12594	12904	16260	18156	18800	31299	26563	12594	12955	12405	12439	11187	13317	11459
Total	**200318**	**225096**	**227770**	**283534**	**335414**	**470690**	**519963**	**200318**	**200226**	**197793**	**199134**	**200089**	**223612**	**226721**

Annexure 2: Benefits of drinking coffee

If you thought your favorite cup of coffee was unhealthy, think again. Coffee's origin can be traced back to the 12th century in Ethiopia, where it is believed to have been first harvested. "Traders brought coffee to the Middle East from where it began to spread outward in the 15th century, penetrating every corner of Europe over the next 200 years". Brazil is one of the largest coffee producing countries in the world.

The last few years, urban India has acquired a new coffee culture. International chains are opening coffee shops and doing brisk business, even in smaller towns. While, South Indian filtered coffee has been a tradition, India in general is waking up to coffee. Coffee beans are cured either by air-drying or fermentation. The dried hulled beans are then roasted and ground. The green coffee beans have little flavor and aroma until they are roasted. Beans expand to one and a half times of their original size and become porous and are classified according to the color of roasting into light, medium and dark, Italian or French, which are very dark.

Most coffee beans are harvested directly from coffee trees while a special variety called Kopi Luwak also known as civet coffee beans are passed through the digestive tract of a cat-like animal called civet. The enzymes in the civet's digestive system breakdown some proteins that give the beans bitterness and its unique mellowness. Interestingly, this is the world's most expensive coffee, which typically sells for $200–600 / lb. These treasured coffee beans come from Indonesia and other Southeast Asian countries, and their supply is limited.

While there are several coffees, most of the world's coffee comes from two species: (1) coffea Arabica and (2) coffea Robusta. Both these kinds of coffee bushes bear the fruit called cherry. Most cherries have two coffee beans in them, but a small percentage of cherries of the Arabica have only one coffee bean and this is the rare pea-berry bean. This pea-berry has much more flavor than its sister bean on the same Arabica plant, which is called the plantation bean. Arabica provides more taste and flavor while Robusta more body and caffeine.

Other forms of coffee include: decaffeinated, instant, iced and flavored coffee. Many health-conscious people have turned to decaffeinated coffee, but there have been questions regarding safety of the decaffeinating process itself. Several decaffeination processes are available including water, steam, carbon dioxide, ethyl acetate and methyl chloride or coffee oils. However, now most decaffeinated coffee is made from methods which use water and steam with no chemical solvents and are therefore safe. Instant coffee powders contain dry, powdered water-soluble solids produced by drying very strong brewed coffee. The flavor of instant coffee is similar to that of freshly brewed coffee but the aroma is somewhat lacking in comparison with the freshly brewed beverage. These coffees should be kept packed in airtight containers because they tend to absorb moisture. Coffee contains more than 400 chemicals including trace amounts of vitamins, minerals and antioxidants. Caffeine is the main stimulant. A regular cup of coffee contains approximately 100 mg of caffeine. The caffeine content varies enormously depending on how strong the coffee is made. Caffeine increases epinephrine (adrenaline) release which stimulates the central nervous system, increases states of alertness and increases heart-beat.

Despite its growing popularity, most people believe coffee to be somewhat toxic addiction taken only as an indulgence or to overcome sleep and boost alertness. Several, health concerns have been attributed to coffee drinking including its addictive nature, ill-effects on digestion, bone health, cardiovascular health, disturbed sleep, high blood pressure, infertility and increased incidence in pancreatic or bladder cancer.

Annexure 3

Now Whistle at these Kettles

If you peek into the nearly two-millennia-old history of tea, you realise that what is served today at the cafes is a much-modified version. The British introduced it in India, and it soon became our very own beverage consumed for medicinal purposes or to feel rejuvenated. Usually, it is served as a welcome drink. Soon, coffee too became as popular and its interesting varieties lured the young and the old alike.

However, it's only after the commercial viability of coffee and tea was discovered that experiments with these began. A chain reaction of the increasing popularity of the beverages is the entry of popular western cafes like American global chain Starbucks, Coffee Bean and Tea Leaf, Italian Barista Lavazza, Britain's Café Coffee Day and Costa Coffee, and many more in India.

Over the past one decade or so, the outlets of these brands have ushered in a unique tradition. Coffee shops where the air breathes of coffee beans have become a popular hangout for the young. Unlike the fancier white-tablecloth restaurants, the casual ambience of cafes gave birth to coffee culture.

Brew-it-yourself Beverages

There is an emerging new world of tea connoisseurs and it is for them that chai-bars, tearooms and tea lounges are dotting big cities where they sample teas made from herbs, fruits, seeds and roots steeped in hot water. While the four basic teas are green, black, white and oolong, the exotic ones are blooming, chamomile tea, hibiscus, jasmine, orange pekoe, rooibos, pu-erh...

Cafes and tea bars also introduced a variety of coffee and tea-making machines in all shapes and sizes, which promise to steam up the beverage as per your liking. These machines can also be brought home. It won't be an exaggeration to say that these machines have elevated the mundane chore of coffee and tea making into an art.

From machines that automatically make tea and keep it warm for the whole day to the all-in-one grind-and-brew coffee makers that first grind the beans and then brew the coffee, these machines are home gadgets that come with press-button technology and timers.

Touch and get Going

All you have to do with these automatic devices is to put the ingredients in place before going to sleep, press the timer and you'll have a steaming cup of tea or coffee awaiting you when you wake up next morning. Many hi-tech tea-making machines come with a menu that tells you the ideal temperature and for how long any specific blend of tea leaves need to be infused to make a cup of tea of your choice.

Though the tea makers that brew loose or bagged tea are advanced versions of electric kettles, it is the coffee machines that have transformed into technological gizmos. These offer in-built timers that allow the units to be preset to brew coffee at the break of dawn. Some special machines even have in-built grinders for that unique bean-to-coffee cup experience. Shut-off timers automatically turn-off coffee-makers. In-built water filters are appreciated by people concerned about the quality of tap water.

A Popular Choice

Such is the rising demand of these coffee-makers that even Starbucks has launched its exclusive collection of automatic brewing machines to give coffee lovers its latte experience at home. The Verismo is a one-cup brewing machine that will allow Starbucks fans to brew coffee, latte and espresso at home, using single-serve coffee pods. Costing around Rs 12,000, it is a small price to pay to get the authentic taste of brand's coffee.

Most coffee and tea-makers are priced between Rs 5,000 and Rs 15,000. However, those who want a quality experience can go in for high-end models like De Longhi Magnifica (Rs 45,000) or the Krups Espresseria (Rs 31,000). And, for those who have enough to splurge and a passion for coffee to boast of, there is the GS3 coffee-maker by Italian company La Marzocco that costs an eye-watering Rs 4.14 lakh.

Tea-makers on the other hand are relatively evenly priced. Though a regular one can be bought between Rs 5,000 and Rs 15,000, there are no machines that are extravagantly priced. Almost all electric kettles have shut-off times, variable settings with preset temperatures. These are cheaper than automatic tea-makers, but perform the job equally well with a little manual help.

However, some purists feel that instead of parting with big money for a high-powered machine and grinder, not to mention the time spent figuring out how to make all sorts of adjustments, preparing quality coffee and tea should be best left to the professional chai-bars and coffee lounges.

Annexure 4: Bean counting

According to the Indian Coffee Board, the first planting of coffee in India happened in 1600 CE when saint Baba Budan planted seven seeds of mocha in the courtyard of his hermitage in Karnataka. Commercial plantation started during the 18th century. Traditionally, it is grown in the Western Ghats spread over Karnataka, Kerala and Tamil Nadu. Coffee is grown predominantly as an export commodity in India as about 65–70% of the total coffee produced in the country is exported. In 2013–14, the total production was over 3 lakh metric tones, of which about 70% was produced in Karnataka alone.

New Series of National Accounts A Review

The new series of national accounts with a revised base year of 2011– 12, released by the Central Statistics Office (CSO) on 30th January, is the product of substantial revisions in the methodology of compilation of data, its classifi cations including the presentation of data for the first time for institutional categories, and choice of new and more sources. The base year of the national accounts is revised from time to time, but this time the CSO has also revised the methodology of calculating these statistics inline with requirements of the System of National Accounts (SNA), an internationally accepted standard. This has meant that there have been substantial changes in the overall growth rates of the Indian economy for the past 3 years. According to the previous, 2004–05, series of national accounts, real growth of gross value added (GVA) at factor cost was 4.7%, and 5.0% for gross domestic product (GDP) at market prices for the year 2013–14. While these growth rates according to the 2011–12 series in the same year went up to 6.6% and 6.9%, respectively. The numbers for 2012–13 in the new series, however, improved only marginally from the old one. GVA at factor cost went from 4.5% to 4.9%, and GDP at market prices went from 4.7% to 5.1% for 2012–13. Why has this been so? Did the economy really surge ahead in 2013–14. These and other questions pertaining to sector-wise growth rates, which have also changed, need to be raised and scrutinised. In this note, we present key aspects of the new data series and issues that need to be addressed in the new methodology. This note presents a brief history of the conceptual understanding of national accounts that has developed in the SNA. What's New? The definitions used to calculate GVA have changed with the introduction of GVA at basic prices in accordance with SNA requirements. For the first time, data is classified using institutional categories, which distinguish between components within the institution (head offices, ancillaries, etc), as opposed to enterprises as units that was used previously. New data sources are now employed, which are recent, and hitherto not used to estimate national accounts in India. A noteworthy new source is MCA21, which has data from the e-governance initiative of the Ministry of Corporate Affairs (MCA). This data covers the private corporate sector in mining, manufacturing, and services comprehensively. MCA21 comprises annual accounts of companies, statutorily filed online with the MCA. This data allows for sector-wise savings and investment estimates that promise to be better than the previous method of relying on Reserve Bank of India (RBI) sample data.

Key macroeconomic aggregates present a synoptic view of the important macroeconomic aggregates from the new series of the National Accounts Statistics (NAS). Simultaneously, it makes a comparison of similar data available from the

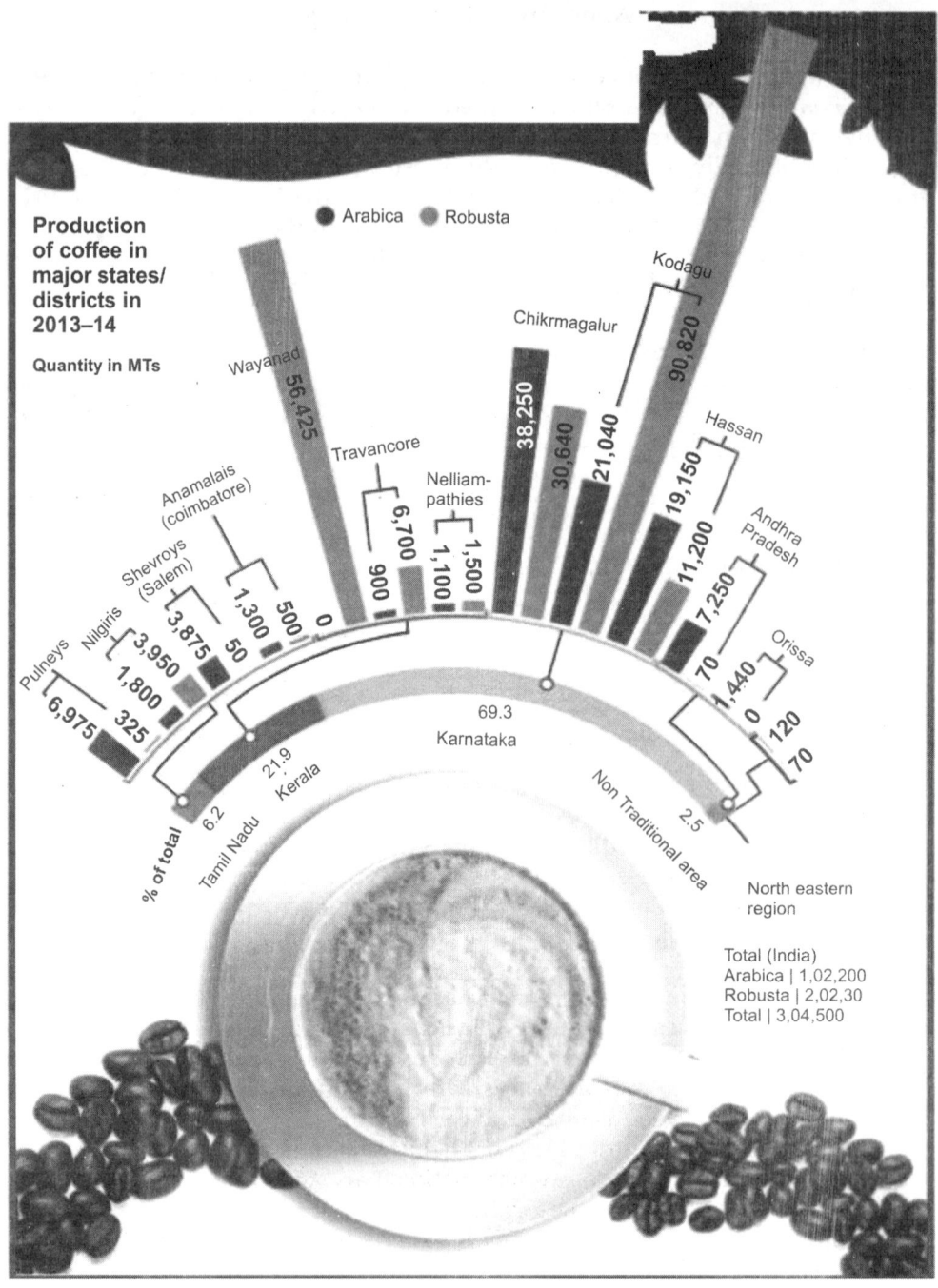

Production of coffee in major states/districts in 2013–14

Quantity in MTs

Arabica　Robusta

Wayanad 56,425

Travancore 6,700 · 900 · 0

Anamalais (coimbatore) 1,300 · 500

Shevroys (Salem) 3,875 · 50

Pulneys 6,975 · 325

Nilgiris 3,950 · 1,800

Nelliampathies 1,500 · 1,100

Chikrmagalur 38,250

30,640 · 21,040

Kodagu 90,820

Hassan 19,150 · 11,200

Andhra Pradesh 7,250 · 70

Orissa 1,440 · 0 · 120 · 70

% of total

6.2 Tamil Nadu · 21.9 Kerala · 69.3 Karnataka · Non Traditional area 2.5

North eastern region

Total (India)
Arabica | 1,02,200
Robusta | 2,02,30
Total | 3,04,500

Source: Coffee Board, govt. of India

2004–05 series. These aggregates are nominal numbers, not all of which have real counterparts. Some of the important ones having constant price numbers are presented. A few key elements of these macroeconomic aggregates are worth noting. Though we have placed in the front row the traditional measure of GVA at factor cost, the government has preferred to be relegated it to a statement at the end of the press release. We perceive this as an important economic variable from which the subsequent aggregates flow and therefore, it is necessary to note it at the outset. The other important aggregates which follow are GVA at basic prices and GDP (i.e. equivalent to the conventional GDP at market prices) with their component items of indirect taxes and subsidies.

What changed? The sizeable improvement in growth as per the new 2011–12 series for 2013–14 and the marginal improvement for 2012–13 is the first issue we deal with. The change in growth of GVA from 2012–13 to 2013–14 according to the new series is mainly in four sectors: agriculture (from 1.2% to 3.7%), mining (–0.2% to 5.4%), construction (–4.3% to 2.5%) and trade, repair, hotels and restaurants (10.3–13.3%). While if one compares figures for 2013–14 between the two data series, distinct changes are seen in three sectors. Mining was –1.4% in the old series, it increased to 5.4% according to the new series, manufacturing increased from –0.7% to 5.3%, and trade, repair, hotels and restaurants increased from 1.0% to 13.3%. For some of these sectors, fresh data from the private corporate sector have been used at least partially if not wholly. For the manufacturing sector, the MCA21 database has been used to supplement the information available in the Annual Survey of Industries (ASI) which was used in the older series.

Similarly, the "enterprises approach" adopted for mining and manufacturing using MCA21 data to account for head offices, ancillary activities, etc. were previously not covered under the earlier used "establishment approach". To what extent the use of fresh data and classifications has contributed to the changes in sector-wise growth and overall growth is, however, still difficult to discern. The other change is to do with the estimates of savings and investments, which show an increased share for the private corporate sector, while a decrease in share of household savings. This is discussed later in this note. What Do other Indicators Say? Other macroeconomic indicators do not seem to corroborate findings of the new series of national accounts. For instance, the infrastructure index for mining has registered a decline of (–)0.6% during 2013–14, whereas real GVA growth in the new series says the sector grew by 5.4% that year. Likewise, the index of industrial production (IIP) was almost stagnant during the same year with a –0.1% growth preceded by a growth of just 1.1% in 2012–13, but GVA growth in 2013–14 was 6.3% and in 2012–13 was 5.3%. These numbers, and the lack of any corroborative evidence so far, do raise misgivings about the new NAS data (saving and investment). The most noteworthy aspect of the NAS data generated by the new series concerns the sector-wise profile of domestic saving and investment. This has come about, as explained earlier, due to the use of MCA21 data instead of the RBI sample statistics for the private corporate sector. Other components of estimation have remained the same. For gross capital formation (GCF), aggregate estimation by the commodity-flow method continues to be used. From this aggregate, fresh estimates of corporate sector GCF combined with public sector investment are deducted to arrive at the residual figure for household sector investment in physical assets. This is combined with fresh saving estimates of the private corporate sector and the public sector and financial savings of the household sector to derive aggregate domestic savings. As a result of these changes, the relative shares of sectors in domestic saving and GCF have undergone some significant changes. First, because of MCA21 data, the savings and GCF of the private corporate sector have expanded rather sizeably. In absolute terms, revised savings of the private corporate sector have risen from the old series to the new by 28.5% for 2011–12 and by 47.4% for 2012–13. In terms of relative shares, the sectors share was around 23% in 2011–12 and 2012-13, and this increased to 29% in 2011–12, 31% in 2012–13, and further to 35% in 2013–14. It is in the estimation of GCF that a more significant increase has occurred for the private corporate sector. In absolute terms, GCF of the sector has increased from the old series to the new by 28.5% for 2011–12 and by 45.4% for 2012–13. The relative share of the private corporate sector has shot up from 28.5% in the old series of GCF to 40% in the revised series for 2012–13. Correspondingly, because of the residual method, there has occurred a sharp reduction in the relative share of the household sector from 46% in the old series to 38% in the revised series for the same year; this share has further slipped to 34% in 2013–14 while the corporate sector share has remained at around 40%.

Institutional Classification

The institutional categories used have been set out as per the recommendations of the SNA. There are data given separately for financial and non-financial corporations and again, separately for these corporations in the public and private sectors. Similar data are given for the household sector. An attempt has been made to present a summary picture of the distribution of GVA by the three traditional categories of public sector, private corporate sector, and household sector using the new series. It is possible to make a comparison of the relative shares in GVA with their relative shares in domestic savings and GCF. The key results described here tell us about the broad structures of saving and investment in the economy: (i) The household sector is the one which has a much higher share in savings (59% to 67%) than its share in GVA (around 45% in each year). The private corporate sector has almost similar shares in GVA and saving. The public sector has the least share in saving, which is lower than its relative share in GVA. (ii) In GCF, the private corporate sector and the public sector have much higher shares in GCF than their relative shares in GVA. The household sector, though, accounts for the largest share in savings, has a share in total GCF lower than that of private corporate sector. (iii) These results confirm the widely held view regarding the surplus and deficit sectors in investment and investible resources in the economy.

References CSO (2012)

National Accounts Statistics: Sources and Methods, Central Statistics Office. MOSPI (2009): Report of the High Level Committee on Estimation of Saving and Investment, Ministry of Statistics and Programme Implementation, Government of India. RBI (2008): State Finances: A Study of Budgets of 2008–09, Reserve Bank of India, December. SNA (1968): A System of National Accounts, Studies in Methods, Series F, No 2 Rev 3, United Nations. (1993): System of National Accounts 1993, United Nations. (2008): System of National Accounts 2008, United Nations. New Series of National Accounts—A Background Note on the Genesis. The government's press note on the release of National Accounts Statistics (NAS) revising the base year from 2004–05 to 2011–12, states that apart from a shift in the reference year for measuring real growth, conceptual changes have been incorporated as recommended by the international guidelines on the subject, which have resulted in comprehensive revisions in the methodology of compilation, in adoption of revised classification systems including the presentation for the first time of data for the institutional categories, and in the inclusion of new and more recent data sources. This reference to international guidelines has an interesting background. The compilation practices of India's NAS have always broadly followed the United Nations System of National Accounts (SNA). The UN-SNA underwent periodic changes in 1968, 1993 and 2008. The presentation of accounts in India's NAS in recent years has generally conformed to the standards set in SNA 1968, but the compilation practices in regard to sector-wise data were changed to cover some of the recommendations of SNA 1993 to the extent that data is available (CSO 2012: 6). The comprehensive revisions in the methodology of compilation and classification systems referred to in the government press note have involved some radical departures that were proposed by SNA 1993 and the latest SNA 2008 in defining gross domestic product (GDP), which has now been adopted by the Government of India. This radical departure indicated above, takes three forms: (i) The concept of gross value added (GVA) at factor cost is not a concept to be explicitly used in the SNA; it is a measure of income and not output with observable sector of prices; (ii) GDP at market prices is the GDP in SNA, as transactions are valued at the actual price agreed upon by the transactors—at market prices and (iii) The SNA introduces an intermediary concept called GVA at basic prices covering value added at factor cost plus indirect taxes on production net of production subsidies. Though these recommendations were made in SNA 1993, these were not been implemented in . India for over two decades, until now. GVA at basic prices, the concept of GVA at basic prices was introduced by the SNA 1993 and carried forward in an identical fashion in SNA 2008. In the entire SNA system, the basic output aggregate is GDP measured at purchasers' prices. These purchasers' values include indirect taxes net of subsidies. It is in the classification of indirect taxes (net of subsidies) that distinguishes the SNA 1993 and SNA 2008 from the SNA 1968. The two former SNAs classify indirect taxes (net of subsidies) into two categories: (i) indirect taxes on production (net of subsidies on production) and (ii) indirect taxes on products (net of subsidies on products). The SNA 1968 made no such distinction, and covered all indirect taxes under one bracket, whether levied on units of commodities such as excise duties, sales taxes, and customs duties are, or on production activities involving the employment of land, labour and the use of fixed assets or on general business activities attracting business licence fees, transaction (e.g. stamp) duties, and real estate taxes. GVA at basic prices includes the contribution of factors of production (land, labour, capital, and entrepreneurship) in the production process and the amount appropriated by the government in the form of taxes on production (net of subsidies on production). These taxes on production are said to be taxes levied on some aspect of a business or the other. In the Indian NAS, some examples of taxes on production specified are: land revenue, stamps and registration fees, and profession taxes. Subsidies on production are: subsidies to the railways, input subsidies to farmers, subsidies to village and small industries, administrative subsidies to corporations or cooperatives, etc. Thus, the basic price receivable by the producer from the purchaser for a good or service covers both factor cost and the taxes on production (net of subsidies on production), which are incurred before the product is ready for sale; it is thereafter that indirect taxes on products are levied (except valued added tax, VAT). GDP at Market Prices According to the 1993 and

2008 SNAs, GDP at market prices is the true measure of GDP covering all indirect taxes net of all subsidies. They recognise that such GDP is equivalent to the sum of GVA at factor cost plus all taxes on products (net of product subsidies) plus all taxes on production (net of production subsidies). Extending the above logic, SNA 2008 makes a distinction between GDP and value added in these terms: value added is of analytical interest because when the value of taxes on products (less subsidies on products) is added, the sum of value added for all resident units gives the value of gross domestic product (GDP). At the same time, the same SNA (2008:104) concedes that "the underlying rationale behind the concept of gross domestic product (GDP) for the economy as a whole is that it should measure the total gross value added from all institutional units resident in the economy". Thus, the distinction made in the SNA between GDP and value added appears to be just hair-splitting. A close study of SNA 2008 suggests that the above assertion on GDP at market prices is not an unequivocal statement. In explaining the concept, SNA 2008 makes a clear distinction between a situation with VAT and that without VAT. It argues thus: "The traditional concept of 'market' price becomes somewhat blurred under a system of VAT or similar deductible taxes because there may be two different prices for a single transaction: one from the seller's point of view and another from the purchaser's, depending upon whether or not the tax is deductible" (SNA 2008: 103). It then recommends that in the SNA the term "market prices" should be avoided. In micro accounts, GVA is equivalent to output valued at producers' prices less intermediate consumption valued at purchasers' prices. Thus, in the presence of VAT, the producers' price would exclude invoiced VAT, and hence "it would be inappropriate to describe this measure as being at market prices" (SNA 2008:104). On the other hand, in the absence of VAT, total value of intermediate inputs consumed is the same whether they are valued at producers' or purchasers' prices, in which case the measure of GVA is the same as the one that uses producers' prices, to value both inputs and outputs. The SNA (2008: 104) asserts thus: "It is an economically meaningful measure that is equivalent to the traditional measure of gross value added at market prices". It must be recognized that netting of VAT on intermediate inputs is at the micro or individual transaction level. At the aggregate level for the system as a whole, VAT on inputs is not entirely foregone by the government. It is just that the double taxation of inputs is avoided by the net ting process; it is once collected at some initial stage. Studies have shown that in all countries including India (RBI 2008), introduction of VAT has resulted in better tax buoyancy. Therefore, whether there is VAT or not, the collection of indirect taxes adds to the producers' prices and hence the traditional measure of GDP at market prices becomes a meaningful measure. GDP at Factor Cost by bringing the concept of GVA at basic prices to the forefront, the government's new methodology has relegated to the background yet another traditional concept, namely, GDP at factor cost. It has great economic meaning. Admittedly, it is a measure of income and not output (SNA 1968: 154). It is a measure of GVA derived from gross value of output less the value of intermediate costs, devoid of "other taxes on production". The SNA 1993 and SNA 2008 have argued that "the conceptual difficulty with gross value added at factor cost is that there is no observable vector of prices such that gross value added at factor cost is obtained directly by multiplying the price vector by the vector of quantities of inputs and outputs that defines the production process" (SNA 1993: 154 and SNA 2008:104). But, both SNA 1993 and SNA 2008 recognise that GVA at factor cost can be derived from GVA at basic prices by subtracting other taxes on production, less subsidies on production. When there is a clear-cut method of deriving GDP at factor cost, there is no justifi able reason to exclude the concept from the SNA, as has been argued in identical terms in both SNAs. Apart from the fact that it is a value added concept, and useful for economic analysis, and to ascertain the distribution of incomes amongst the factors of production, there are a few other strong reasons why GDP at factor cost should be held out as one of the primary measures in the SNA. First, as a value added concept, GDP can be derived in three different ways as recognised by all the SNAs: (i) by production method; (ii) by expenditure method and (iii) by income method. The aggregates derived by the three methods become very relevant for the SNA. Second, SNAs conclude that GVA at factor cost can be derived by a circuitous method of deducting from GVA at basic prices, the indirect taxes on production (net of their subsidies). But, many systems of national accounts, like India's, derive rather directly, the gross primary incomes first as summation of compensation for employees (CE), operating surplus and mixed income (OS/MI), and then add production taxes less production subsidies to estimate GVA at basic prices. Finally, the entire SNA literature accepts GDP as a value added concept and no economic logic would allow indirect taxes to be part of value addition.

MCA 21 has been a long-standing issue concerning, particularly, the estimates of corporate saving and investment. Initially, when the government statistical system had not developed, the Reserve Bank of India (RBI) with its vast resources, took the initiative of producing a vast array of national level statistics. One of its coveted initiatives was the generation of basic data on the private corporate sector based on a system of sample studies. Though the government has achieved considerable advancement in producing firm national accounts statistics over the years, it has continued to depend on the RBI for corporate sector data. With the explosive growth of private sector companies, RBI's sample studies have become unrepresentative of the corporate sector as a whole. As brought out by the High-Level Committee on Estimation of Saving and Investment (MOSPI 2009: Chaired by C Rangarajan), there have been serious drawbacks in the results of the RBI sample studies based on paid-up capital as the blowing up factor, particularly in regard to corporate savings and investment. The committee had strongly urged the government to firm up the data flowing from the Ministry of Corporate Affairs' online data reporting for companies under their e-governance initiative (MCA21). It is now reported that the government has succeeded in achieving this goal. It appears that there has been an all-round improvement in data on corporate sector savings and investment. As shown in the main article, there was about a 40% improvement in corporate sector savings in the revised series as compared with the data from the existing series for 2012–13. Likewise, corporate investment has shown a 45% rise for the same year. Correspondingly, based on the conventional residual method, the household savings in the form of physical assets has shown an absolute decline of about 16.0%. It must be clarified here that the above unqualified approval of data improvement relates to only saving and investment and not necessarily of the new data on value added.

4

Rubber

NATURAL RUBBER

Plantings of para rubber, the tree *Hevea brasiliensis*, are usually called plantations. Natural rubber, also called India rubber or *caoutchouc*, as initially produced, consists of suitable polymers of the organic compound isoprene, with minor impurities of other organic compounds plus water. Forms of polyisoprene that are useful as natural rubbers are classified as elastomers. Currently, rubber is harvested mainly in the form of the latex from certain trees. The latex is a sticky, milky colloid drawn off by making incisions into the bark and collecting the fluid in vessels in a process called "tapping". The latex then is refined into rubber ready for commercial processing.

Natural rubber is a solid product obtained through coagulating the latex produced by certain plants, particularly the Brazilian rubber-tree (*Hevea brasiliensis*). This raw material is usually tapped from the rubber tree, which is native to Amazonia. Although there are a large number of species that exude secretions similar to latex when the bark is cut, only a few produces sufficient quantities of a quality adequate for exploitation on economic bases.

Rubber is found in the fluid of some specific plants but it can also be produced synthetically. Synthetic rubber is produced through the process of polymerization of various monomers. Naturally, rubber is produced by the process of tapping of the plant called *Hevea brasiliensis*. The rubber tree is a native of the Amazon River basin in South America. The ideal rubber growing regions should be 8° North of equator, 10° South of equator, high temperature, altitude not beyond 400 m and high humidity. These plants generally have 32 years of economic life but they may live up to 100 years or even more than that. The plantation would start its yield from 6th year onward. The natural rubber produced is processed to convert into a storable and marketable form.

Rubber was known to the indigenous peoples of the Americas long before the arrival of European explorers. In 1525, Padre d'Anghieria reported that he had seen Mexican tribes people playing with elastic balls. The first scientific study of rubber was undertaken by Charles de' la Condamine, when he encountered it during his trip to Peru in 1735. A French engineer that Condamine met in Guiana, Fresnau studied rubber on its home ground, reaching the conclusion that this was nothing more than a "type of condensed resinous oil".

The first use for rubber was an eraser. It was Magellan, a descendent of the famous Portuguese navigator, who suggested this use. In England, Priestley popularized it to the extent that it became known as India Rubber. The word for rubber in Portuguese-borracha-originated from one of the first applications for this product, when it was used to make jars replacing the leather borrachas that the Portuguese used to ship wine.

Returning to the works of Condamine, Macquer suggested that rubber could be used to produce flexible tubes. Since then, countless craftsmen have become involved with rubber; Goldsmith Bernard, herbalist Winch, Grossart, Landolles and others. In the 1820, British industrialist Nadier produced rubber threads and attempted to use them in clothing accessories. This was the time when America was seized by rubber fever, and the waterproof footwear used by the indigenous peoples became a success. Waterproof fabrics and snow-boots were produced in New England.

The Para rubber tree is indigenous to South America. Charles Marie de' La Condamine is credited with introducing samples of rubber to the Academie Royale Des Sciences of France in 1736. In 1751, he presented a paper by Francois Fresneau to the Académie (eventually published in 1755) which described many of the properties of rubber. This has been referred to as the first scientific paper on rubber. In England, Joseph Priestley, in 1770, observed that a piece of the material was extremely good for rubbing off pencil marks on paper, hence the name "rubber". Later, it slowly made its way around England.

In 1832, the Rosburg factory was setup. Unfortunately, cold weather affected goods made from nonvulcanized natural rubber, leaving them brittle and with a tendency to gum together if left in the sun, all discouraging consumers. After a long period attempting to develop a process to upgrade rubber qualities (such as including nitric acid) that almost ruined him, in 1840 Goodyear discovered vulcanization, quite by accident.

An interesting fact: in 1815, a humble sawyer-Hancock-became one of the leading manufacturers in the UK. He had invented a rubber mattress and through an association with MacIntosh he produced the famous waterproof coat known as the "macintosh". Furthermore, he discovered how to cut, roll and press rubber on an industrial scale. He also noted the importance of heat during the pressing process, and built a machine for this purpose.

Natural rubber has been used for trival purposes for many centuries. Its "discovery" is generally attributed to Christopher Columbus, who observed the inhabitants of Haiti using rubber to make playballs; it was probably also used by them in various religious rites. Europeans later discovered that rubber could be extracted from many different kinds of trees and shrubs mostly native to the tropics. Toward the end of the 18th century European scientists started to look at the properties of this curious material. The British scientist Joseph Priestley, observing its ability to rub out pencil marks, gave rubber its English name. Its name in French, caoutchouc, is more apt, however, coming from the Indian-American word cachuchu, "the wood that weeps". By the start of the 19th century, rubber was an expensive curiosity with no serious uses. Thomas Hancock devised methods for mechanically working rubber so it could be shaped, and he built England's first rubber factory in 1820. In 1823, Charles, MacIntosh devised a practical method of water proofing fabric with rubber.

MacIntosh discovered the use of benzene as a solvent, while Hancock discovered that prior chipping and heating were required in order to ensure that the rubber dissolved completely. Hancock also discovered how to manufacture elastic balls.

Finally, in 1842, Hancock came into possession of vulcanized rubber produced by Goodyear, seeking and finding the secret of vulcanization that brought him a vast fortune.

ANCIENT MESOAMERICANS RUBBER INDUSTRY

The Mesoamericans were robust users of rubber, according to historical and archeological records. With it they made sandals, rubber bands and also balls, which they used to play a ceremonial game in stone-walled courts. Each of these items need different qualities in the rubber of which they are made. A ball requires elasticity for bounciness, a rubber band requires strength, and a sandal requires wear and resistance. A new study reports that the Mesoamericans, which include the Aztec and the Maya, knew how to make different kinds of rubber, mixing latex from rubber trees with juice squeezed from morning glory vines in different proportions. "It is a pretty safe bet that they were engineering materials to suit their needs", It wasn't just a haphazard concoction".

Tarkanian and his co-author, Dorothy Hosler, also an MIT researcher, experimented with samples of latex and morning glory vine juice from Mexico and achieved three kinds of rubber with different mixtures. Bounciness is maximized when 50% of the mixture is juice while longevity and wear are maximized when 25% of the mixture is juice. And strength, required for a rubber band, is maximized when no juice is added. The earliest records indicate that mesoamericans were using rubber by 1600 BC. Thousands of years later, in 1839; Charles Goodyear discovered vulcanization, the chemical process used to produce rubber today.

In 1845, RW Thomson invented the pneumatic tire, the inner tube and even the textured tread. In 1850 rubber toys were being made, as well as solid and hollow balls for golf and tennis. The invention of the velocípede by Michaux in 1869 led to the invention of solid rubber, followed by hollow rubber and finally the reinvention of the tire, because Thomson's invention had been forgotten. The physical properties of rubber were studied by Payen, as well as Graham, Wiesner and Gérard.

South America remained the main source of the limited amounts of latex rubber used during much of the 19th century. In 1876, Henry Wickham gathered thousands of Para rubber tree seeds from Brazil, and these were germinated in Kew Gardens, England. The seedlings were then sent to India, Ceylon (Sri Lanka), Indonesia, Singapore, and British Malaya. Malaya (now Malaysia) was later to become the biggest producer of rubber. In the early 1900s, the Congo Free State in Africa was also a significant source of natural rubber latex, mostly gathered by forced labor. Liberia and Nigeria also started production of rubber.

In India, commercial cultivation of natural rubber was introduced by the British planters, although the experimental efforts to grow rubber on a commercial scale in India were initiated as early as 1873 at the Botanical Gardens, Calcutta. The first commercial *Hevea* plantations in India were established at Thattekadu in Kerala in 1902.

Finally, Bouchardt discovered how to polymerize isoprene between 1879 and 1882, obtaining products with properties similar to rubber. The first bicycle tire dates back to 1830, and in 1895 Michelin had the daring idea of adapting the tire to the automobile. Since then, rubber has held an outstanding position on the global market.

As rubber is an important raw material that plays a leading role in modern civilization, chemists soon became curious to learn more about its composition in order to synthesize it. In the XIX century, work focused on this objective, soon discovering that rubber is an isoprene polymer.

The Russians and the Germans broke fresh ground in their efforts to synthesize rubber. But, the resulting products were unable to compete with natural rubber. It was only during World War I that Germany pressured by circumstances had to develop the industrialized version of this synthetic product. This was the springboard for the massive development of the synthetic rubber industry all over the world, producing elastomers.

The history of natural rubber in Brazil is a tale that is just as exciting as the Gold Rush in the USA. For almost 50 years during the second half of the 19th century through to the second decade of the 20th century-natural rubber underpinned one of the most important development booms in Brazil. At that time, the industrial revolution was expanding rapidly as the world lived through a time of prosperity and discoveries that was reflected in all sectors. Automobiles, trams, telephones, electric light and other innovations changed the landscapes and customs of towns and cities. New markets opened up. This was the Belle Époque period, whose splendor has been portrayed in literature and film for subsequent generations.

Thanks to its multiple applications, particularly in the expanding automobile industry, rubber produced from latex tapped from rubber-trees became a product in demand worldwide. And there was no lack of rubber-trees in the Brazilian Amazon. This brought a boom to Northern Brazil which at that time was one of the poorest and least-inhabited parts of the country. Eager to work the rubber-groves of Amazonia, leading foreign banks and companies setup shop in the towns of Belém and Manaus.

The capital of Amazonas State becomes the economic heart of Brazil. It was equipped with water and electricity supplies, in addition to telephones and large buildings such as the Amazonas Theater, still today a symbol of the wealth brought in by Brazil's rubber boom. Thousands of immigrants flowed in, mainly fleeing the drought that assailed Northeast Brazil during the 1870s, invading the forest to tap the latex and turn it into rubber.

The output of Amazonia reached 42,000 tons a year, with Brazil dominating the global natural rubber market. This euphoria lasted through to 1910, when the situation began to change: rubber exports began to appear on the market from British Colonies, and Brazil was unable to withstand this fierce competition.

In 1876, the British smuggled out rubber-tree seeds from Amazonia to the Botanical Gardens in London. Through grafting, they developed more resistant varieties that were later sent to the Colonies in Asia where massive rubber plantations were established, particularly in Malaysia, Ceylon and Singapore.

The difference between latex production techniques in Brazil and Asia was a significant factor in the development of this business, due to these plantations. While the rubber trees of Asia were set only four meters apart, it was sometimes necessary to walk miles between one tree and the next in Amazonia, limiting the amount of latex collected and increasing its price. Obviously, the well-organized plantations of the Far East resulted in a significant increase in productivity, making them more competitive.

In Brazil, the Government was unwilling to change these methods. It believed that tapping these rubber trees would ensure the presence of Brazilians in the Amazon region, guaranteeing national sovereignty over this largely unpopulated area. It opted for geopolitics represented by human settlements instead of geo-economics that could have produced higher gains.

This relative immobility cost Brazil dear; its exports shrank as they were unable to withstand the competition of Asian rubber, tapped at far lower prices. Consequently, production began to drop, bringing the decades of boom to an end for much of Northern Brazil. The companies that had set up shop in Manaus and Belém left in search of other more productive regions. The immigrants went home, and leading names in the world of the arts no longer performed at the Amazonas Theater. This golden age of opulence slipped into history.

In the late 1920s, Brazil was still attempting to catch up this lost ground with the help of an unexpected partner: US industrialist Henry Ford, who had developed a new scheme—the production line that was to change the face of industry for ever, and at that time accounted for 50% of the world's vehicle output. In order to loosen the grip of the British Colonies in Southeast Asia on the rubber market—the precious raw material for making tires—Ford planted no less than 70 million rubber tree seedlings in an area covering one million hectares in Para State.

This ambitious project was soon christened Fordlândia by the local residents. It was designed to produce 300,000 tons of natural rubber a year, accounting for one half of global consumption. But, the Ford Project succumbed to the hostile environment of the Amazon rainforest and was abandoned, posting huge losses.

Within this context, Asia dominated global supplies of natural rubber with over 90% of the output. However, significant changes redistributed the production among the main competitors. Accounting for one-third of global output in 1985, Malaysia fell back due to alterations in its production profile, which began to stress non-agricultural investments. Its position as the world largest natural rubber producer went to Thailand. Based on advantages in terms of available land and labor, Indonesia has maintained a significant share in global output since the 1980s.

Other countries have been successfully deploying their low-cost labor-forces and easily-available lands to expand in this sector, particularly India and China. By 2001, natural rubber consumption accounted for some 40% of the total amount of rubber consumed worldwide.

In the 1970s and 1980s, the natural rubber industry still forged ahead. Further new materials and new uses appeared. We saw the advent of epoxidized natural rubber—a rubber derived from natural rubber but with high damping characteristics, oil resistance and gas permeability equal to halobutyl rubbers. Thermoplastic natural rubber is a blend of natural rubber with polyprohylene to give a recyclable rubber. New liquid natural rubbers have been developed for a variety of uses.

NATURAL RUBBER DEVELOPMENTS

There were a whole series of developments in natural rubber science and technology in the 1940s, 50s, and 60s which led to a range of new materials derived from it and new uses. For example, rubber in roads' is not new. The first rubberized bitumen was laid in the Rue Ferrier, Geneva, in 1947 by Ashaltiques Geneva, and subsequently in Acre Lane in London in 1950. By 1955, 112.65 km (70 miles) had been laid in the

UK. It was reported to give non-slip properties, one-third improvement in life and was much more resistant to low temperatures.

In 1952, the first liquid rubber Rubbone was produced by the mechanical working of softened rubber with chemical plasticizers (6–8 hours in a two blade mixer at 120–140°C). This was used for textile machinery components, printers' rollers and prototype manufacturing. Then there was Positex in 1952—a latex which was processed to give the rubber particles, a positive charge for the wool industry and methyl methacrylate grafted (MG) rubber in 1954 for making very hard rubber (96 IRHD), or adhesives if only 30% is grafted. New uses saw the first rubber-metal laminated bridge bearings in 1957 on the Pelham Bridge in Lincoln, and oil-extended natural rubber to improve the grip of unstudied winter tires in 1967.

VARIETIES

The major commercial source of natural rubber latex is the para rubber tree (*Hevea brasiliensis*), a member of the spurge family, Euphorbiaceae. This species is widely used because it grows well under cultivation and a properly managed tree responds to wounding by producing more latex for several years.

Many other plants produce forms of latex rich in isoprene polymers, though not all produce usable forms of polymer as easily as the Pará rubber tree does; some of them require more elaborate processing to produce anything like usable rubber, and most are more difficult to tap. Some produce other desirable materials, for example gutta-percha (*Palaquium gutta*) and chicle from Manikara species. Others that have been commercially exploited, or at least have shown promise as sources of rubber, include the rubber fig (*Ficus elastica*), Panama rubber tree (*Gasticalla astilla* elastic), various spurges (*Euphorbia spp.*), lettuce (*Lactuca* species), the related *Scorzonera tau-saghyz*, various *Taraxacum species*, including common dandelion (*Taraxacum officinale*) and Russian dandelion (*Taraxacum kok-saghyz*), and guayule (*Parthenium argentatum*). The term **gum rubber** is sometimes applied to the tree-obtained version of natural rubber in order to distinguish it from the synthetic version. Many high-yielding clones have been developed for commercial planting. These clones yield more than 2,000 kg of dry rubber per hectare per year, when grown under ideal conditions.

As there is a well organized network of private nurseries in the traditional area, availability of quality planting material has not been a problem in the case of rubber. However, the Board has been maintaining a limited number of nurseries in order to ensure reliable supply of recommended types of planting material. Nurseries have also been established by the Rubber Board in all the District Development Centers. Apart from this, two regional nurseries are functioning, one each in Hillara in Assam and Mendipathar in Meghalaya.

The Government of India set up the National Seed Corporation, a public sector undertaking in the year 1963 to organize the development of a sound seed industry in India. In the initial stages, the primary responsibility of the corporation was to serve as a foundation seed production, storage and supply organization of the released hybrids of maize. Later, hybrids of other crops, viz. sorghum, bajra were added in the list and seed multiplication of high yielding strains of wheat and paddy was taken up besides seeds of selected vegetable varieties, fiber and fodder crops. As the seed industry grew and since the progressive seed growers and seed producers in the private sector were associated with the National Seeds Corporation (NSC) in the seed multiplication program, the task of certification was maintained by NSC. Keeping in view the increased requirement of seeds, need was felt to establish a large number of seed producing and supplying organizations in the public as well as private sector.

In order to regulate the growing seed industry, Government of India enacted the Seeds Act in the year 1966. The Seed Rules framed under the Seeds Act were notified in 1968. With experiences gained in the application of various provision of the Seeds Act and Rules made thereunder and the suggestions received by the Government from concerned quarters, several amendments have been carried out in the Seeds Act and Rules from time to time. Government of India declared seeds as an essential commodity under the Essential Commodities Act, 10 of 1955 and Seed (Control) Order was issued in December, 1983.

The Essential Commodities Act, 1955 (10 of 1955) was amended by an Order of the Government dated 24th February, 1983, thereby, declaring that the seeds used for sowing or planting (including seedlings and tubers, bulbs, rhizomes, roots, cuttings and all types of grafts and other vegetatively propagated material, of food crops or cattle fodder) to be essential commodities for the purposes of the Act, namely: (1) seeds of food crops and seeds of fruits and vegetables; (2) seeds of cattle fodder and (3) jute seeds.

The Seeds (Control) Order, 1983 prohibits to carry on business of selling, exporting or importing seeds at any place except under and in accordance with the terms and conditions of the license granted to any person under this order. Certification agency shall ensure that the seed conforms to the standards laid down in the manual known as "Indian Minimum Seed Certification Standards" published by Central Seed Committee and amended from time to time. DAC has, however, formulated a proposal for revising the Seed Act. The proposal aims at setting up a National Seeds Board to advise the Government. on matters connected with seeds sector, to facilitate supply of quality seed to farmers and regulate sale, import and export of seeds.

At present, there is no legislation to regulate production and sale of vegetatively propagated planting material of most horticulture crops by nurseries. A mechanism to ensure the quality of planting material needs to be developed through registration and quality control. This could be achieved by establishing an Apex Body for the purpose.

Five high yielding clones of rubber have been introduced under Category III of planting material recommendation. India has achieved highest productivity of 1576 kg/hectare during the IX plan period. Protocols have been evolved for somatic embryogenesis and field level evaluation of plants generated by this technique has been in progress. Genetic transformation of *Hevea* has been attempted using genes conferring tolerance to drought and tapping panel dryness (TPD). Recommendations have been issued for intercropping of banana and pineapple with rubber in the Northeast. The norms for Diagnosis and Recommendation Integrated System (DRIS) have been evolved. The infrastructure for offering discriminatory fertilizer recommendation has been augmented with the establishment/strengthening of 10 regional soil testing laboratories. Low frequency tapping systems have been studied and ad-hoc recommendations issued for on-farm evaluation. Latex diagnosis parameters have been identified to assess the status of exploitation of rubber trees. Experiments on cropping systems based on rubber have been laid out and based on the results obtained; ad-hoc recommendations have been issued. Based on research findings, the outbreak of *Corynespora* leaf disease in the southern parts of Karnataka and Northern part of Kerala has been controlled effectively. Biogas generation using rubber latex serum has been perfected and the technique has been widely accepted. A semi-automatic cleaning machine for upgradation of low quality sheet rubber has been developed. Integrated drying systems incorporating solar, biogas and smoke drying have been developed. Pilot plant-scale production of styrene grafted natural rubber (SGNR) using gamma radiation has been made and the material has been found acceptable by the footwear manufacturing industry as a substitute for the synthetic rubber.

TYPES OF RUBBER

Rubbers include natural rubbers (NRs) and synthetic rubbers (SRs). Natural rubber is a naturally occurring substance obtained from the exudations of certain tropical plants. Synthetic rubber is artificially derived from petrochemical products. Among the most important synthetics are styrene butadiene, polybutadiene and isoprene (commonly classified as "general-purpose" synthetic rubbers), as well as ethylenepropylene rubbers (often referred to as "specialty rubbers").

Synthetic Rubber

- Styrene butadiene (SBR) latex and solid
- Polybutadiene (BR)
- Isobutene-isoprene (IIR)
- Halo-isobutene-isoprene (CIIR/BIIR)
- Chlorobutadiene (CR) latex and solid
- Acrylonitrile-butadiene (NBR) latex and solid
- Isoprene (IR)
- Ethylene-propylene nonconjugated diene (EPDM).

Natural Rubber

- Liquid forms
- Latex concentrates
- Specialty types (liquid).

Dry/Solid Rubber

- Conventional rubber (sheet rubber, crepe rubber)
- Technically specified rubber (mainly block rubber)
- Specialty types (solid).

Processing

The latex will coagulate in the cups if kept for long. The latex has to be collected before coagulation. The collected latex, "field latex", is transferred into coagulation tanks for the preparation of dry rubber or transferred into airtight containers with sieving for ammoniation. Ammoniation is necessary to preserve the latex in colloidal state for long.

Latex is generally processed into either latex concentrate for manufacture of dipped goods or it can be coagulated under controlled, clean conditions using formic acid. The coagulated latex can then be processed into the higher-grade, technically specified block rubbers such as SVR 3L or SVR CV or used to produce Ribbed Smoke Sheet grades.

Naturally, coagulated rubber (cup lump) is used in the manufacture of TSR10 and TSR20 grade rubbers. The processing of the rubber for these grades is a size reduction and cleaning process to remove contamination and prepare the material for the final stage of drying.

Synthetic Rubber

In 1826, Michael Faraday—although he was not aware of the class of molecule known as polymers—discovered that natural rubber is composed of units of a chemical compound, isoprene. Later 19th century, French and German chemists showed how isoprene could be converted into rubber. No practical means of producing synthetic rubber, however, was devised until Germany, deprived of access to Asian rubber during .World War I, undertook limited production of synthetic rubber. Interest in synthetic rubber, however, evaporated after the war, and subsequent economic depression discouraged further effort. In 1941–1942, the United States, similarly faced with the loss of Asian rubber, undertook a program—second in scale only to the nuclear-bomb project—to develop a supply of this vital strategic material. By 1945, plants were producing 1 million tons of synthetic rubber a year. During the 1950s and 60s, many other countries started production, and synthetic rubber has now become a universally available commodity.

The importance of the rubber industry ever since it first appeared and the decisive role that it has played in the development of modern civilization prompted much interest in discovering its chemical composition in order to synthesize this product. Through these research projects, the tire industry saw the possibility of breaking away from the grip of the world natural rubber plantations. The drop in natural rubber production in Brazil coincided with World War I (1914–1918), triggering the need for lower-cost products with steadier supplies in order to manufacture tires. The pressures imposed by the conquest of the plantations of Asia by the Japanese prompted the development of a rubber that was able to meet the extraordinarily high demands of the troops at that time, although its structure differed somewhat from its natural counterpart.

This was how GR-S, Buna S, Hycar OS and SBR appeared which are styrene and butadiene copolymers. The launch-pad for the massive development of the synthetic rubber industry, this product could be vulcanized easily, and became the flagship of the world rubber industry, although its properties did not correspond to all the qualities of natural rubber. But, its costs and main characteristics made it into an unbeatable competitor. Although synthetic rubber had been known since 1875, its production had been expensive and almost negligible.

During World War II, a crucial historical episode altered the scenario for this market. On December 7, 1941, the USA entered the War. Three months after the attack on Pearl Harbor, the Japanese invaded Malaysia and the Dutch East Indies, desperate to take over natural rubber production from the allies. This gave the Axis control over 95% of world rubber supplies, plunging the USA into a crisis. Each Sherman tank contained twenty tons of steel and half a ton of rubber. Each warship contained 20,000 rubber parts. Rubber was used to coat every centimeter of wire used in every factory, home, office and military facilities throughout the USA. There was no synthetic alternative. Looking at all the possible sources, at normal consumption levels, the nation had stocks for around year. And these reserves also had to supply the largest and most critical industry in the history of the world during a time of rapid expansion: the arms segment. The response of Washington was rapid and dramatic. Four days after Pearl Harbor, the use of rubber in any product that was not essential to the war drive was banned. The speed limit on US highways fell to 35 miles an hour, in order to reduce wear and tear on tires countrywide. Rubber chips were sold a penny or more per pound weight at over 400,000 depots all over the country. Even President Franklin Roosevelt's pet dog Fala saw his rubber toys melted. This was the largest recycling campaign ever recorded in history, ensuring the success of the Allies through to 1942.

Under these circumstances, an order was sent to all chemists and engineers to develop a synthetic rubber industry. In 1941, the total output of synthetic rubber barely topped 8,000 tons, consisting largely of products not suitable for tires. The nation's survival depended on its capacity to manufacture over 800,000 tons of products that had barely begun to be developed. There were few detailed instructions on how the factories should organize themselves to produce this vast amount. No facility had been built, nor was there any way of producing enough raw materials to produce rubber. The US industrial sector had never been called upon to shoulder such a massive task, achieving so much so quickly. The engineers were given just 2 years to reach this target. If the synthetic rubber program failed, the capacity of the USA to fight the war would be blunted. This US drive was to help spread synthetic rubber throughout the world's market, even in Brazil as it strove to consolidate its industrial park during the post-War years.

A wide variety of synthetic rubbers have been developed since this product was first discovered. As massive investments were required to develop these different varieties, the production technology was heavily concentrated in long-established global enterprises such as DuPont, Bayer, Shell, Basf, Goodyear, Firestone, Michelin, EniChem, Dow, and Exxon. The use of rubber is widespread, as the characteristics and properties of these elastomers make them useful in almost all economic sectors: automobiles, footwear, civil construction, plastics, hospital materials and others that are of crucial importance in the daily life of society. As they are most widely used to produce tires, the SBR and BR varieties are the most widely consumed type of synthetic rubber.

Although synthetic rubber may be obtained in many different ways, most of it is produced through the system shown at the next page:

Main Synthetic Rubber Production System

A wide variety of synthetic rubbers have been developed since this product was first discovered. As massive investments were required to develop these different varieties, the production technology was heavily concentrated in long-established global enterprises such as DuPont, Bayer, Shell, Basf, Goodyear, Firestone, Michelin, EniChem, Dow, and Exxon.

The use of rubber is widespread, as the characteristics and properties of these elastomers make them useful in almost all economic sectors: automobiles, footwear,

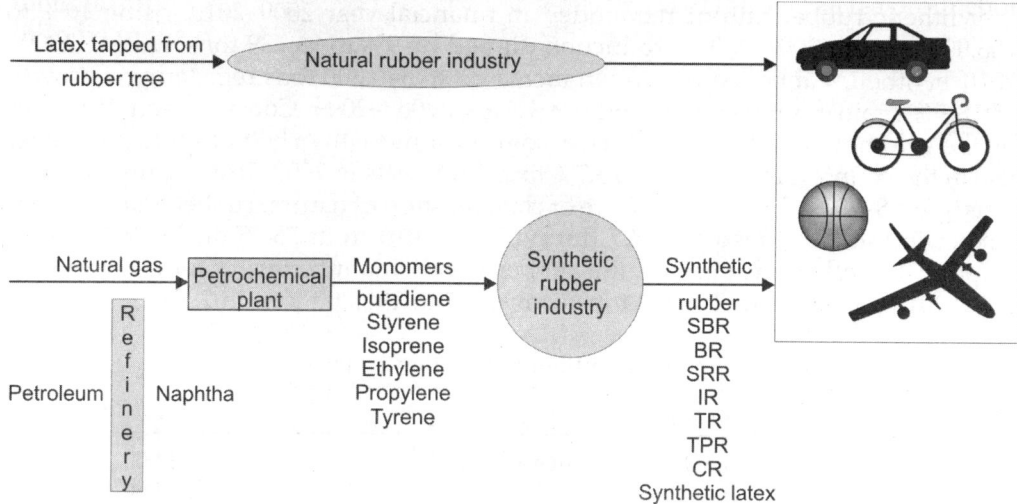

civil construction, plastics, hospital materials and others that are of crucial importance in the daily life of society. As they are most widely used to produce tires, the SBR and BR varieties are the most widely consumed type of synthetic rubber.

Main types and applications for synthetic rubbers

Name	Type of rubber	Asphalt modifications	Footwear	Adhesives	Technical goods
eSBR	Styrene-butadiene in emulsion	–	X	X	X
sSBR	Styrene-butadiene in solution	X	X	X	X
BR	Polybutadiene	–	X	–	X
NBR	Nitryl	–	X	–	X
EPDM	Ethylene-propylene	X	–	–	X
IIR	Butyl	–	–	X	X
CR	Polychloroprene	X	X	X	X
TR	Plastics	X	X	X	–
Latex	Various types of latex	X	X	–	X

Name	Type of rubber	Tires	Treads	Plastic modifications
eSBR	Styrene-butadiene in emulsion	X	X	–
sSBR	Styrene-butadiene in solution	X	X	–
BR	Polybutadiene	X	X	X
NBR	Nitryl	–	–	X
EPDM	Ethylene-propylene	X	–	X
IIR	Butyl	X	–	–
CR	Polychloroprene	–	–	–
TR	Plastics	–	–	X
Latex	Various types of latex	–	X	–

Synthetic rubber output rebounded in financial year 2009–2010, rising 10% to 106,000 tons. In 2008–2009, production dipped by 9% to 96,739 tons. During 2009–2010, synthetic rubber consumption increased to 340,000 tons registering a growth of 18.7% against a negative growth of 1.4% in 2008–2009. Consumption of rubber by the automotive tire sector, which accounts for more than half of synthetic rubber use in the country, increased by 28.7% to 238,000 tons in 2009–2010, against 185,000 tons in 2008–2009. The relative share of consumption of natural rubber and synthetic rubber in India changed to 73:27 during 2009–2010 from 75:25 during 2008–2009. Import of synthetic rubber by the rubber goods manufacturing industry during 2009–2010 increased to 250,000 tons compared to 190,000 tons in 2008–2009.

Synthetic rubber production in India

Sl. No.	Product	Manufacturer	Capacity
1	SBR	Synthetics & Chemicals Ltd.	41,000
		Apar Ltd.	5,000
2	BR	Reliance Industries Ltd.	73,000
3	NBR	Apar Ltd.	8,000
4	EPDM	Herdillia Unimers Ltd.	10,000
5	VP Latex	Apcotex	1,000 (D.WT)
		ENPRO	1,000 (D.WT)

MOTIVATION

Natural rubber is an elastic hydrocarbon polymer called polyisoprene and is found in the sap (latex) of certain trees. Synthetic rubber is made from polymers that are engineered synthetically by a process called polymerization, which is a chemical reaction produced when two or more molecules combine to form larger molecules with repeated structural units.

AREA AND PRODUCTION

Available data regarding area under rubber is divided into planted and replanted (Table 4.1) holdings and estates (Table 4.1A). Distribution of area as between holdings and estates is shown in Table 4.1B. Classification of holdings by size is Tables 4.1C and D. Total capable area during 1970–1971 was 141 thousand hectares. It has been regularly increasing: 563 thousand hectares in 2000–2001 to 735 thousand hectares in 2011–2012. Area in India on which rubber is produced can be divided into two zones: (1) traditional and (2) nontraditional. Traditional zone comprises South-West coastal regions of India, i.e. Kanyakumari in Tamil Nadu and some districts of Kerala. Nontraditional zone constitutes coastal regions of Karnataka, Goa, Andhra Pradesh, Orissa, some areas of Maharashtra, Northeastern States (mainly Tripura) and Andaman and Nicobar Islands.

Production of rubber separately for holdings and estates is available (Table 4.2). Grade-wise distribution of rubber production is as in Table 4.2A. All India area, production is shown in Table 4.2B.

Table 4.1: New planted and replanted area with rubber

(Hectares)

Year	New planted	Replanted	Total	Year	New planted	Replanted	Total
1956-57	12030	737	12767	1983-84	18805	5641	24446
1957-58	14278	1394	15672	1984-85	22365	5217	27582
1958-59	12605	1874	14479	1985-86	21222	5759	26981
1959-60	9963	1641	11604	1986-87	19856	5563	25419
1960-61	12104	1385	13489	1987-88	19535	6517	26052
1961-62	14485	2446	16931	1988-89	19471	6998	26469
1962-63	13222	2499	15721	1989-90	20175	6854	27029
1963-64	6551	2309	8860	1990-91	15143	7154	22297
1964-65	5800	2692	8492	1991-92	13851	7100	20951
1965-66	4749	4163	8912	1992-93	11000	7200	18200
1966-67	5886	4039	9925	1993-94	9200	6000	15200
1967-68	6614	2905	9519	1994-95	7500	7000	14500
1968-69	6079	1905	7984	1995-96	7800	7500	15300
1969-70	6709	1920	8629	1996-97	10400	7000	17400
1970-71	6655	2089	8744	1997-98	13300	7500	20800
1971-72	3044	1473	4517	1998-99	8800	6000	14800
1972-73	3775	1704	5479	1999-00	6000	6000	12000
1973-74	3975	1576	5551	2000-01	4600	5000	9600
1974-75	4310	2200	6510	2001-02	6380	5930	12310
1975-76	4561	3099	7660	2002-03	5390	7890	13280
1976-77	4882	3172	8054	2003-04	6980	7350	14330
1977-78	4770	3645	8415	2004-05	12500	7130	19630
1978-79	8450	4050	12500	2005-06	16750	7520	24270
1979-80	12300	4065	16365	2006-07	21500	8380	29880
1980-81	19308	5476	24784	2007-08	22750	8500	31250
1981-82	18100	4188	22288	2008-09	30200	10000	40200
1982-83	19884	4963	24847	2009-10	25500	11000	36500

Table 4.1A: Production of holdings estates

Year	Holdings	Estates	Total
1950-1951	3387	12443	15830
1955-1956	6450	17280	23730
1960-1961	6528	19169	25697
1965-1966	20424	30106	50530
1966-1967	24165	30653	54818
1967-1968	30215	34253	64468

(Contd.)

Table 4.1A: Production of holdings estates

Year	Holdings	Estates	Total
1968-1969	36312	34742	71054
1969-1970	43785	38168	81953
1970-1971	51538	40633	92171
1971-1972	57630	43580	101210
1972-1973	66247	46117	112364
1973-1974	75331	49822	125153
1974-1975	79260	50883	130143
1975-1976	84616	53134	137750
1976-1977	93848	55784	149632
1977-1978	94135	52852	146987
1978-1979	88767	46530	135297
1979-1980	103210	45260	148470
1980-1981	107700	45400	153100
1981-1982	109160	43710	152870
1982-1983	117789	48061	165850
1983-1984	125912	49368	175280
1984-1985	136335	50115	186450
1985-1986	149673	50792	200465
1986-1987	168195	51325	219520
1987-1988	181710	53487	235197
1988-1989	204000	55172	259172
1989-1990	239400	57900	297300
1990-1991	268500	61115	329615
1991-1992	302700	64045	366745
1992-1993	327500	65990	393490
1993-1994	367950	67210	435160
1994-1995	405900	65915	471815
1995-1996	436500	70410	506910
1996-1997	475000	74425	549425
1997-1998	507000	76830	583830
1998-1999	527000	78045	605045
1999-2000	544600	77665	622265
2000-2001	553770	76635	630405
2001-2002			631400
2002-2003			699435
2003-2004			711650
2004-2005			749665
2005-2006			802625
2006-2007			852895
2007-2008			825345
2008-2009			864500

Table 4.1B: District/state/union territory-wise area of rubber under holdings and estates

(Hectares)

District/States/Union Territory	2003–2004			2004–2005			2005–2006		
	Holdings	Estates	Total	Holdings	Estates	Total	Holdings	Estates	Total
Thiruvananthapuram	27793	715	28508	28001	715	28716	28197	723	28920
Kollam	27726	9091	36817	27877	9097	36974	28007	7268	35275
Pathanamthitta	41899	6036	47935	41958	6040	47998	42001	7550	49551
Alappuzha	3854	0	3854	3897	0	3897	3934	0	3934
Kottayam	107972	4097	112069	108062	4039	112101	107575	4060	111635
Idukki	34347	4123	38470	34434	4165	38599	34671	4173	38844
Ernakulam	54184	2856	57040	54301	2769	57070	54483	2806	57289
Thrissur	9297	4176	13473	9535	4141	13676	9848	4210	14058
Palakkad	28653	1038	29691	29642	947	30589	31050	902	31952
Malappuram	27315	2590	29905	28466	2557	31023	30065	2523	32588
Kozhikode	14307	3374	17681	14595	3367	17962	14992	3245	18237
Wynad	6655	0	6655	7135	0	7135	7777	0	7777
Kannur	33468	1204	34672	34913	1204	36117	37159	1207	38366
Kasargod	22266	567	22833	23227	526	23753	24856	518	25374
Kerala	**439735**	**39867**	**479602**	**446043**	**39567**	**485610**	**454615**	**39185**	**493800**
Tamil Nadu	12302	6331	18633	12367	6275	18642	12495	6320	18815

(Contd.)

Table 4.1B: District/state/union territory-wise area of rubber under holdings and estates

(Hectares)

District/States/ Union Territory	2003–2004			2004–2005			2005–2006		
	Holdings	Estates	Total	Holdings	Estates	Total	Holdings	Estates	Total
Tripura	21665	9105	30770	22860	9205	32065	24884	9305	34189
Assam	12161	1680	13841	12380	1677	14057	13152	1696	14848
Meghalaya	3525	1233	4758	3757	1077	4834	4202	858	5060
Nagaland	1934	157	2091	2028	156	2184	2117	157	2274
Manipur	1296	477	1773	1309	477	1786	1352	477	1829
Mizoram	624	85	709	415	83	498	426	81	507
Arunachal Pradesh	342	37	379	379	37	416	388	37	425
Karnataka	14593	5867	20460	15177	6012	21189	17100	6053	23153
A & N Islands	127	835	962	127	716	843	44	718	762
Goa	343	412	755	349	412	761	316	388	704
Maharashtra	124	58	182	94	58	152	91	58	149
Orissa	392	88	480	368	88	456	377	88	465
West Bengal	365	96	461	380	93	473	392	131	523
Andhra Pradesh	124	0	124	124	0	124	107	0	107
Grand total	509652	66328	575980	518157	65933	584090	532058	65552	597610
Percentage share	88.48	11.52	100.00	88.71	11.29	100.00	89.03	10.97	100.00

Table 4.1B: District/state/union territory-wise area of rubber under holdings and estates *(Contd.)*

(Hectares)

District/States/ Union Territory	2006–2007			2007–2008			2008–2009		
	Holdings	Estates	Total	Holdings	Estates	Total	Holdings	Estates	Total
Thiruvananthapuram	28537	723	29260	28914	726	29640	29309	700	30009
Kollam	28324	7246	35570	28678	7082	35760	28960	6705	35665
Pathanamthitta	42160	7491	49651	42318	7542	49860	42473	7341	49814
Alappuzha	4080	0	4080	4210	0	4210	4254	0	4254
Kottayam	107794	4056	111850	108040	3995	112035	108306	4270	112576
Idukki	34900	4110	39010	35227	4108	39335	35514	3867	39381
Ernakulam	54794	2796	57590	55127	2803	57930	55419	2890	58309
Thrissur	10282	4228	14510	10667	4123	14790	10927	3767	14694
Palakkad	32286	878	33164	33415	870	34285	34146	694	34840
Malappuram	31783	2372	34155	33326	2574	35900	34361	2570	36931
Kozhikode	15702	3238	18940	16302	3298	19600	16752	3187	19939
Wynad	8340	0	8340	8890	0	8890	9315	0	9315
Kannur	38768	1107	39875	40516	1064	41580	41648	722	42370
Kasargod	26285	460	26745	27770	460	28230	28856	522	29378
Kerala	**464035**	**38705**	**502740**	**473400**	**38645**	**512045**	**480240**	**37235**	**517475**
Tamil Nadu	12643	6590	19233	13080	6330	19410	13344	6011	19355
Tripura	28166	9680	37846	31200	9965	41165	38595	11475	50070
Assam	14160	1730	15890	16500	1725	18225	21942	1763	23705

(Contd.)

Table 4.1B: District/state/union territory-wise area of rubber under holdings and estates

(Hectares)

District/States/Union Territory	2006–2007			2007–2008			2008–2009		
	Holdings	Estates	Total	Holdings	Estates	Total	Holdings	Estates	Total
Meghalaya	4721	610	5331	5664	1166	6830	6574	1166	7740
Nagaland	2329	157	2486	2540	157	2697	3318	197	3515
Manipur	1382	477	1859	1437	477	1914	1903	477	2380
Mizoram	445	80	525	468	83	551	652	83	735
Arunachal Pradesh	409	37	446	421	37	458	683	37	720
Karnataka	19955	6080	26035	22780	6050	28830	26065	6350	32415
A & N Islands	44	685	729	44	685	729	44	836	880
Goa	384	388	772	320	666	986	344	666	1010
Maharashtra	113	58	171	315	58	373	592	58	650
Orissa	412	88	500	440	88	528	467	103	570
West Bengal	406	120	526	435	113	548	435	145	580
Andhra Pradesh	111	0	111	111	0	111	180	0	180
Grand total	**549715**	**65485**	**615200**	**569155**	**66245**	**635400**	**595378**	**66602**	**661980**
Percentage share	**89.36**	**10.64**	**100.00**	**89.57**	**10.43**	**100.00**	**89.94**	**10.06**	**100.00**

Table 4.1C: Classification of estates according to size

(Area in the hectares)

Year	Upto ha. units	Upto ha. area	Above 40 ha. and upto 200 ha. units	Above 40 ha. and upto 200 ha. area	Above 200 ha. and upto 400 ha. units	Above 200 ha. and upto 400 ha. area	Above 400 ha. and upto 600 ha. units	Above 400 ha. and upto 600 ha. area	Above 600 ha. and upto 800 ha. units	Above 600 ha. and upto 800 ha. area	Above and 800 ha. units	Above and 800 ha. area	Total area	Total unit
1955-56	209	6781	179	15047	33	9578	15	7513	4	2762	6	5898	446	47579
1960-61	271	7590	216	17812	29	8082	18	8768	5	3437	8	7841	547	53530
1965-66	325	9556	248	20476	30	8551	19	9400	4	2696	10	13024	636	63703
1970-71	309	8771	273	21318	29	8219	20	9966	6	4036	12	15088	649	67398
1975-76	289	8235	242	19332	27	7366	17	8100	9	6138	14	18018	598	67189
1980-81	258	7289	228	18659	25	7481	15	8208	10	6885	17	20201	553	68723
1985-86	137	4320	171	14408	24	7305	18	9046	14	9294	20	28249	384	72622
1990-91	120	3407	130	11348	22	6262	22	11051	17	11415	21	34135	332	77618
1991-92	123	3478	130	11533	22	6217	21	10622	17	11423	21	34618	334	77891
1992-93	126	3543	132	11555	22	6285	21	10649	17	11504	21	34679	339	78215
1993-94	129	3628	132	11406	22	6280	21	10679	17	11406	21	34928	342	78327
1994-95	130	3659	132	11377	22	6266	21	10638	17	11230	21	34858	343	78028
1995-96	114	3286	134	12291	25	7589	19	9835	15	10116	19	31459	326	74576
1996-97	112	3214	134	12262	25	7610	20	10303	13	8682	19	31738	323	73809
1997-98	111	3165	136	11732	23	6821	22	11396	11	7328	19	29212	322	69654
1998-99	111	3171	136	11743	23	7059	21	10775	11	7313	19	29279	321	69340
1999-00	111	3188	137	11680	23	7159	20	10301	11	7284	19	28695	321	68307
2000-01	108	3118	135	11591	24	7487	21	10720	9	5887	19	28509	316	67312

Table 4.1D: Classification of holdings and estates according to size at the end of each year

(Area in hectares)

| | Holdings | | | | | | | |
| | 2 hectares and below | | Above 2 hectares and upto and including 4 hectares | | Above 4 hectares and upto and including 20 hectares | | Total | |
Year	Units	Area	Units	Area	Units	Area	Units	Area
1990-91	763022	332401	13100	33149	4465	31915	780587	397465
1991-92	797429	342010	13556	35569	4562	33044	815547	410623
1992-93	824298	351571	13627	36450	4575	33138	842500	421159
1993-94	845402	359451	13714	37205	4584	33437	863700	430093
1994-95	862728	365654	13994	37849	4678	34016	881400	437519
1995-96	892094	375957	14474	39079	4721	34463	911289	449499
1996-97	912112	384008	14724	40145	4801	35284	931637	459437
1997-98	935456	394412	17210	44104	5058	36364	957724	474880
1998-99	948553	402336	17317	44515	5108	36850	970978	483701
1999-00	963613	407601	17627	45031	5249	37645	986489	490277
2000-01	968656	412574	17647	45088	5257	37696	991560	495358
2001-02	980511	414146	18141	45803	5530	39012	1004182	498961
2002-03	991042	428753	11377	34281	4810	39860	1007229	502894
2003-04	1000254	435198	11400	34350	4890	40104	1016544	509652
2004-05	1012557	443077	11500	34640	4945	40440	1029002	518157
2005-06	1032728	455483	11665	35280	4995	41295	1049388	532058
2006-07	1055885	471590	11925	36280	5050	41845	1072860	549715
2007-08	1079950	488300	12200	37530	5160	43325	1097310	569155
2008-09	1114540	511218	12580	38790	5310	45370	1132430	595378

Statewise area production and yield (Tables 4.3A to D) shows that total production of rubber in 1950–1951 was just 15.8 thousand tons. It increased to 27 thousand tons in 1961, 92.2 thousand tons in 1970–1971, 549.4 thousand tons in 1996–1997 and 861.95 thousand tons in 2010–2011. Along with area, productivity levels have also been going up from 654 kg/hectares in 1970–71, it touched 1,503 kg. hectares in 1996–1997 and 1867 in 2008–2009. One reason for increasing yield level is the new varieties introduced (Tables 4.3B to C). Statewise distribution of rubber is shown in Table 4.3E.

Kerala is the major producer accounting for over 90% of total production. Other smaller States are (Karnataka, Tamil Nadu and Northeastern States). District-wise distribution of rubber production in Kerala shows that the top district is Pathanamthitta, followed by Kollam and Kannur (Table 4.3F). Distribution of area and production in the Northeastern region is as in Tables 4.3G to I. Northeastern States together have a share of 4.6% while Karnataka and Tamil Nadu account for 2.57% and 2.97%, respectively. Rubber is also grown on a limited scale in a few

Table 4.2: Production of holdings estates

Year	Holdings	Estates	Total	Year	Holdings	Estates	Total
1950-51	3387	12443	15830	1986-87	168195	51325	219520
1955-56	6450	17280	23730	1987-88	181710	53487	235197
1960-61	6528	19169	25697	1988-89	204000	55172	259172
1965-66	20424	30106	50530	1989-90	239400	57900	297300
1966-67	24165	30653	54818	1990-91	268500	61115	329615
1967-68	30215	34253	64468	1991-92	302700	64045	366745
1968-69	36312	34742	71054	1992-93	327500	65990	393490
1969-70	43785	38168	81953	1993-94	367950	67210	435160
1970-71	51538	40633	92171	1994-95	405900	65915	471815
1971-72	57630	43580	101210	1995-96	436500	70410	506910
1972-73	66247	46117	112364	1996-97	475000	74425	549425
1973-74	75331	49822	125153	1997-98	507000	76830	583830
1974-75	79260	50883	130143	1998-99	527000	78045	605045
1975-76	84616	53134	137750	1999-00	544600	77665	622265
1976-77	93848	55784	149632	2000-01	553770	76635	630405
1977-78	94135	52852	146987	2001-02	555320	76080	631400
1978-79	88767	46530	135297	2002-03	580080	69355	649435
1979-80	103210	45260	148470	2003-04	647095	64555	711650
1980-81	107700	45400	153100	2004-05	685595	64070	749665
1981-82	109160	43710	152870	2005-06	739530	63095	802625
1982-83	117789	48061	165850	2006-07	789805	63090	852895
1983-84	125912	49368	175280	2007-08p	764675	60670	825345
1984-85	136335	50115	186450	2008-09p	804950	59550	864500
1985-86	149673	50792	200465	2009-10p	773250	58150	831400

other Eastern and Western states in India. It is primarily the selected rubber yielding varieties which are responsible for increasing yield levels. Tapped area, production and average yield are given in Table 4.3I.

Rubber cultivation has been successfully introduced in the nontraditional areas like Karnataka, Andaman and Nicobar islands, Goa and Maharashtra and in the Northeastern States viz. Assam, Meghalaya and Tripura. It has been recently introduced in certain other States including Orissa. However, in spite of all this expansion, Kerala enjoys a near monopoly position with 92% of the total production in the country followed by Tamil Nadu and Karnataka with 3.4% and 2.4% of the total production, respectively.

The new areas coming under cultivation have surged more than three times. The estimates made by the Rubber Board. People in the Northern parts of Kerala have taken up rubber cultivation in a big way. Planters also take up cultivation of inter-crops like banana, pineapple, ginger, turmeric, vegetables, herbs and tuber crops.

Table 4.2A: Grade-wise production of natural and synthetic rubber

(Tons)

Natural rubber

Grade	1987-88	1988-89	1989-90	1990-91	1991-92	1992-93	1993-94	1994-95	1995-96	1996-97	1997-98	1998-99	1999-00	2000-01	2001-02
RSS	162815	177625	207180	236530	263220	281335	315535	342775	373455	396160	436560	436275	454180	455175	
Latex Concentrates (drc)	27688	32478	36910	39440	43425	46245	48810	52655	59695	61550	55400	64565	60640	65975	
Solid Block Rubber	11246	15354	17160	16980	25870	27107	31240	40390	41110	51960	49910	59715	60095	60225	
Pale Latex Crepes	2112	2440	2409	2725	2900	2608	2985	2790	2310	1565	1315	1980	1845	1975	
Others	31336	31275	33641	33940	31330	36195	36590	33205	30340	38190	40645	42510	45505	47055	
Total	235197	259172	297300	329615	366745	393490	435160	471815	506910	549425	583830	605045	622265	630405	

(Tons)

Synthetic rubber

Grade	1987-88	1988-89	1989-90	1990-91	1991-92	1992-93	1993-94	1994-95	1995-96	1996-97	1997-98	1998-99	1999-00	2000-01	2001-02
SBR 1502	8098	12075	9988	11962	8962	8099	4620	9289	11608	9897	6243	3035	239		
SBR 1712	6753	8325	8228	8745	8458	5406	1646	5425	7645	6265	5031	1183			
SBR 1958	13395	17131	18835	19808	21027	21355	22667	21773	17704	20529	17770	15139	12322	12482	15197
Latex(drc)*	1008	1141	1326	1501	1902	1908	2153	3044	3389	4064	3038	1984	1411	1422	1642
Nitrile	708	67				3108	2592	2614	2837	4300	3619	4445	5280	5151	6275
Polybutadiene	14488	15650	15105	15277	17365	17377	14728	19320	21442	15547	32789	36760	35750	40670	41994
EPDM						2	1170	2194	3598	3597	3136	4619	4811	4304	3835
Others	18			12		637	57	22	—	364	367	425	480	1431	710
Total	44468	54389	53482	57293	57726	57892	49633	63681	68223	64563	71993	67590	60293	65460	69653

Table 4.2B: Area and production of natural rubber

Year	Production (thousand metric tons)	Tappable area (thousand hectare)	Production index
1985–1986	200.5	223	100.0
1986–1987	219.5	237	109.1
1987–1988	235.2	249	117.4
1988–1989	259.2	266	129.3
1989–1990	297.3	289	148.3
1990–1991	329.6	306	164.4
1991–1992	366.7	325	183.2
1992–1993	393.5	341	197.0
1993–1994	435.2	358	217.5
1994–1995	472.0	515	236.0
1995–1996	507.0	530	253.3
1996–1997	549.4	540	275.0
1997–1998	655.8	545	328.0
1998–1999	591.8	629	296.0
1999–2000	682.6	647	332.2
2000–2001	631.0	563	275.6
2001–2002	638.0	567	254.3
2002–2003	707.0	570	352.6
2003–2004	778.2	576	389.2
2004–2005	772.0	584	385.0
2005–2006	853.0	598	425.4
2006–2007	811.0	615	404.5
2007–2008	881.0	662	439.4
2008–2009	865.0	680	431.2
2009–2010	831.4	695	414.7
2010–2011	862.0	700	429.9
2011–2012	903.7	735	450.7
2012–2013	798.2	760	398.1

Table 4.3A: Area, production and average yield statewise rubber

Area: in hectares;   Production: in tons;   Yield: per hectare in kg.

Year	Karnataka				Kerala				Tamil Nadu				Other States				All India			
	Area	T. Area	Prod.	Yield	Area	T. Area	Produ.	Yield	Area	T. Area	Produ.	Yield	Area	T. Area	Produ.	Yield	Area	T. Area	Produ.	Yield
1970–71	–	–	–	–	–	–	867.7	–	–	–	–	–	–	–	–	–	203.0	141.0	92.2	654
1971–72	–	–	–	–	–	–	–	–	–	–	–	–	–	–	–	–	209.0	149.0	101.2	679
1972–73	–	–	–	–	–	–	–	–	–	–	–	–	–	–	–	–	213.0	155.0	112.4	725
1973–74	–	–	–	–	–	–	–	–	–	–	–	–	–	–	–	–	218.0	166.0	125.2	754
1974–75	–	–	–	–	–	–	–	–	–	–	–	–	–	–	–	–	221.0	171.0	130.1	761
1975–76	–	–	–	–	–	–	128.8	–	–	–	–	–	–	–	–	–	224.0	178.0	137.8	774
1976–77	–	–	–	–	–	–	–	–	–	–	–	–	–	–	–	–	231.0	186.0	149.6	804
1977–78	7.9	3.9	2.0	513	221.8	177.9	135.9	764	12.2	9.0	9.0	1000	3.3	0.2	0.1	500	245.2	191.0	147.0	770
1978–79	8.1	3.9	2.1	538	224.8	177.0	123.7	699	12.3	9.0	9.4	1044	4.0	0.4	0.2	500	249.2	190.3	135.4	712
1979–80	8.2	4.0	2.5	625	229.4	178.8	136.6	764	13.0	9.2	9.1	989	5.9	0.5	0.2	400	256.5	192.5	148.4	771
1980–81	8.5	4.0	2.1	525	238.3	179.9	140.3	780	15.5	9.7	10.4	1072	6.9	0.6	0.2	333	269.2	194.2	153.1	788
1981–82	8.9	4.3	2.6	605	248.0	181.2	139.5	770	15.7	9.9	10.5	1061	8.3	0.8	0.3	375	280.9	196.2	152.9	779
1982–83	9.5	4.4	3.1	705	256.2	184.3	152.7	829	15.8	10.0	9.7	970	9.5	1.0	0.4	400	291.0	199.7	165.9	831
1983–84	10.1	5.2	2.8	538	294.3	187.7	162.2	864	16.3	10.6	9.7	915	11.0	1.0	0.6	600	331.7	204.5	175.3	857
1984–85	10.8	5.4	3.1	574	312.0	193.3	172.1	890	16.5	10.7	10.6	991	12.5	1.1	0.7	636	351.8	210.5	186.5	886
1985–86	11.2	5.6	4.1	732	326.7	205.8	184.6	897	16.7	10.6	11.0	1038	14.7	1.3	0.8	615	369.3	223.3	200.5	898
1986–87	11.7	5.9	4.8	814	337.7	218.8	202.1	924	16.8	11.0	11.8	1073	17.8	1.4	0.8	571	384.0	237.1	219.5	926
1987–88	12.0	6.1	5.2	852	350.9	230.0	216.6	942	17.0	11.5	12.5	1087	20.7	1.5	0.9	600	400.6	249.1	235.2	944
1988–89	12.8	6.2	6.2	1000	366.7	246.7	238.4	966	17.0	11.6	13.4	1155	27.2	1.6	1.2	750	423.7	266.1	259.2	974
1989–90	13.2	6.5	6.5	1000	376.8	268.7	275.4	1025	17.1	11.8	14.1	1195	33.6	2.1	1.4	667	440.7	289.1	279.3	966

Table 4.3A: Area, production and average yield statewise rubber (Contd.)

Area: in hectares; Production: in tons; Yield: per hectare in kg.

Year	Karnataka				Kerala				Tamil Nadu				Other States				All India			
	Area	T. Area	Prod.	Yield	Area	T. Area	Produ.	Yield	Area	T. Area	Produ.	Yield	Area	T. Area	Produ.	Yield	Area	T. Area	Produ.	Yield
1990–91	14.0	6.9	6.7	971	407.8	285.0	307.5	1079	17.2	11.9	13.6	1143	36.1	2.6	1.8	692	475.1	306.4	329.6	1076
1991–92	14.4	7.4	7.2	973	419.2	301.3	343.1	1139	17.2	12.2	14.0	1148	37.7	3.6	2.4	667	488.5	324.5	366.7	1130
1992–93	14.6	7.9	7.9	1000	428.9	316.8	368.6	1164	17.3	12.3	14.3	1163	38.6	4.0	2.7	675	499.4	341.0	393.5	1154
1993–94	14.9	8.4	8.6	1024	437.1	313.4	408.3	1303	17.3	12.3	14.7	1195	39.1	4.5	3.5	778	508.4	338.6	435.2	1285
1994–95	15.0	9.2	9.7	1054	443.3	319.0	442.8	1388	17.4	12.6	15.1	1198	39.9	5.6	4.2	750	515.5	346.3	471.8	1362
1995–96	16.3	9.5	10.3	1084	449.0	328.8	474.6	1443	17.9	12.4	17.3	1395	40.8	5.7	4.7	825	524.1	356.4	506.9	1422
1996–97	17.3	9.8	11.2	1143	455.6	335.4	512.8	1529	18.2	12.7	18.5	1457	42.1	7.7	7.0	909	533.2	365.6	549.4	1503
1997–98	–	–	–	–	–	–	541.9	–	–	–	–	–	–	–	–	–	–	–	–	–
1998–99	–	–	–	–	–	–	559.1	–	–	–	–	–	–	–	–	–	–	–	–	–
1999–00	–	–	–	–	–	–	572.8	–	–	–	–	–	–	–	–	–	–	–	–	–
2000–01	–	–	–	–	–	–	579.9	–	–	–	–	–	–	–	–	–	–	–	–	–
2001–02	–	–	–	–	–	–	581.0	–	–	–	–	–	–	–	–	–	–	–	–	–
2002–03	–	–	–	–	–	–	596.7	–	–	–	–	–	–	–	–	–	–	–	–	–
2003–04	–	–	–	–	–	–	–	–	–	–	–	–	–	–	–	–	–	–	–	–
2004–05	–	–	–	–	–	–	–	–	–	–	–	–	–	–	–	–	–	–	–	–
2005–06	–	11.8	14.9	1270	–	396.4	739.2	1865	–	14.5	23.6	1624	–	24.4	24.9	1022	–	447.0	802.6	1796
2006–07	–	12.4	16.1	1300	–	399.6	783.3	1960	–	14.7	24.0	1640	–	27.3	29.5	1079	–	454.0	852.9	1879
2007–08	–	12.8	16.6	1298	–	401.4	753.1	1876	–	14.7	23.8	1617	–	29.9	31.9	1064	–	458.8	825.4	1799

Source: Area and Production of Principal Crops in India (Various Issues), Directorate of Economics and Statistics, Department of Agriculture and Co-operation, Ministry of Agriculture.

Table 4.3B: Statewise area and production of natural rubber in India during 2010–2011

Traditional region	Total area (hectares)	Production (tons)
Kerala	534228	770580
Tamil Nadu	19767	25160
Subtotal	*553995*	*795740*
Non-traditional Region		
A. Northeastern Region		
Tripura	59285	25875
Assam	32659	8050
Meghalaya	10584	5135
Other NE	11157	2140
Subtotal	*113685*	*41200*
B. Others		
Karnataka	38110	23705
A & N Islands	879	312
Goa	1081	361
Maharashtra	1173	72
Others	2637	560
Subtotal	*43880*	*25010*
Grand total	**711560**	**861950**

Recently, climate change is affecting rubber farming. As warm nights are increasing steadily, rubber productivity is adversely affected. For instance, the productivity of rubber trees in India declined to 1796 kg/hectare in 2009 from 1903 kg/hectare in 2008. Climate change is an important cause for this fall in productivity. Unlike the world production of rubber, which has been unstable during the last 10 years, Indian production is consistently growing at 6%.

Small Holders

India is the third largest producer of natural rubber next only to Thailand and Indonesia accounting for 9.2% of the global output. The country has the distinction of having the highest of having the highest average yield per hectare. The country is also the fourth largest consumer next to USA, China and Japan. The increase in production of rubber during the period 1990–1991 to 2008–2009 has been phenomenal. During the last 60 years the area, production and productivity have increased by 6.2, 54.7 and 6.6 times, respectively. Table 4.3B has been described the growth in natural rubber production in India.

Table 4.3C: Selected rubber-yielding species

Scientific name	Common name	Distributional range
Castilla elastica sesse	Panama rubber tree	America (Mexico, Central America, Western South America), widely naturalized in tropics
Ficus vogelII (Miq.) Miq.	West African rubber tree	Africa (Macaronesia, Northeast tropical Africa, East tropical Africa, West-Central tropical Africa, West tropical Africa, South tropical Africa, South Africa and Western Indian Ocean)
Funtumia africana Africa (Benth.) Stapf	Lagos silk rubber tree	Africa (East tropical Africa, West-Central tropical West tropical Africa and South tropical Africa)
Hevea brasiliensis (Willd.ex Adr. Juss.)	Rubber tree Muell. Arg.	Southern America (Brazil, Bolivia, Colombia, Peru); also cultivated and naturalized elsewhere
Holarrhena floribunda (G. Don) Durand and Schinz	False rubber tree	Africa (West-Central tropical Africa, West tropical Africa)
Funtumia elastic	–	Africa (Northeast tropical Africa, East tropical Africa, West-Central tropical Africa, West tropical Africa); also cultivated elsewhere
Ficus elastica	Indian rubber plant	Asia-tropical (India, China, Malaysia); widely cultivated elsewhere
Parthenium argentatum	Guayule	Northern America (South-Central US, Mexico)
Taraxacum koksahgyz	Russian dandelion	Asia-temperate former Soviet Union and China

Growth in natural rubber production in India

Year	Tapped area (000 hectare)	Product (tons)	Productivity (kg/hectare)	Annual growth in production (%)
1950–1951	75	15,830	284	
1990–1991	306	329,615	1,076	10.9
1998–1999	387.1	605,045	1,563	3.6
2008–2009	463.1	864.5	1,867	–

A salient feature of the rubber industry is its dominance by small holders. Currently, 86% of the area and production in the country is contributed by small holdings. The average size of holding is less than half hectare. However, in spite of the predominance of small holdings, the national average productivity is 1,563 kg/ hectare. Though natural rubber is processed into different marketable forms in India,

Table 4.3D: Statewise area under rubber at the end of each year

(Hectares)

State	2000–01	2001–02	2002–03	2003–04	2004–05	2005–06	2006–07	2007–08	2008–09
Kerala	474365	475039	476047	479602	485610	493800	502740	512045	517475
Tamil Nadu	18710	18704	18631	18633	18642	18815	19233	19410	19355
Traditional total	493075	493743	494678	498235	504252	512615	521973	531455	536830
Tripura	26495	27947	28853	30770	32065	34189	37846	41165	50070
Assam	12117	12806	13208	13841	14057	14848	15890	18225	23705
Meghalaya	4029	4354	4586	4758	4834	5060	5331	6830	7740
Nagaland	1791	2024	2087	2091	2184	2274	2486	2697	3515
Manipur	1588	1698	1708	1773	1786	1829	1859	1914	2380
Mizoram	585	619	696	709	498	507	525	551	735
Arunachal Pradesh	280	323	372	379	416	425	446	458	720
Northeast total	46885	49771	51510	54321	55840	59132	64383	71840	88865
Karnataka	19735	20017	20294	20460	21189	23153	26035	28830	32415
A&N	931	960	960	962	843	762	729	729	880
Goa	872	843	870	755	761	704	772	986	1010
Maharashtra	189	165	200	182	152	149	171	373	650
Orissa	493	517	552	480	456	465	500	528	570
West Bengal	388	430	494	461	473	523	526	548	580
Andhra Pradesh	102	109	109	124	124	107	111	111	180
Others total	22710	23041	23479	23424	23998	25863	28844	32105	36285
Non-traditional Total	69595	72812	74989	77745	79838	84995	93227	103945	125150
Grand total	562670	566555	569667	575980	584090	597610	615200	635400	661980
Annual growth rate	0.73	0.69	0.55	1.11	1.41	2.31	2.94	3.28	4.18

Table 4.3E: Statewise area and production of rubber

(Area in hectare/production in tons)

State	2000–2001		2001–2002		2002–2003		2005–2006		2006–2007	
	Area	Prod.	Area	Prod.	Area	Prod.	Area	Prod.	Area	Prod.
Arunachal Pradesh	280	16	323	42	372	24	425	59	446	114
Assam	12117	2456	12806	1755	13208	1991	14848	3372	15890	4939
Manipur	1588	198	1698	198	1708	229	1829	119	1859	139
Meghalaya	4029	1717	4354	2378	4586	2648	5060	3340	5331	3967
Nagaland	585	64	619	63	2087	438	2274	548	2486	660
Tripura	1791	285	2024	393	28853	12234	34189	16322	37846	18705
Mizoram	–	–	–	–	–	–	507	77	525	88

Source: Rubber Board, Guwahati.

Table 4.3F: District wise production of natural rubber-Kerala

(Tons)

District	1970-71	1975-76	1980-81	1985-86	1990-91	1993-94	1994-95	1995-96	1996-97	1997-98	1998-99	1999-00	2000-01	2001-02	2002-03	2003-04
Alappuzha	1713	2409	2771	2722	2140	2804	2973	3135	3386	3706	3868	3954	4003	4114	4356	5093
Ernakulam	11907	12292	13929	19419	37586	53395	58206	62159	66604	69967	71593	72663	73557	73219	73752	79647
Idukki	—	10187	11140	15611	26638	34286	36540	38356	40712	43380	44005	44853	45405	45260	45294.63	49496
Kannur	5251	10238	12298	9841	16808	22196	24506	26876	30559	33646	36164	37992	38459	38800	40658	50381
Kasargod	—	—	—	7424	13149	16264	17709	18971	20372	21669	22898	23732	24024	24125	25794.68	29758
Kollam	16141	24185	25561	19807	26951	34315	36773	38821	41160	43130	44405	45727	46289	46854	48386.38	50035
Kottayam	26907	34021	36132	50134	82852	105198	113225	120946	129871	135125	137820	139550	141266	140543	143244.1	152682
Kozhikode	7656	10076	10730	8602	12769	16743	18124	19490	20640	21559	21833	22593	22871	22884	23490	25544
Malappuram	6451	9132	10571	11419	14855	20269	22330	24430	27405	29907	31740	32606	33007	32904	33883	39959
Palakkad	1466	3816	4516	7150	12531	18389	20414	22571	25275	28076	30150	31235	31619	31759	34334	40916
Pathanamthitta	—	—	—	16245	34264	45616	49924	52974	56894	59131	60711	61664	62423	62502	62833.17	67985
Thiruvananth apuram	3581	5223	5933	8475	15513	23457	25437	27298	29046	30717	31309	32913	33318	34205.65	36026	
Thrissur	5700	7190	6739	6079	9108	12639	13790	15513	17615	18361	18775	19431	19670	19762	19932.05	21383
Wynad	—	—	—	1635	2357	2740	2879	3015	3217	3561	3828	3907	3955	4038	4753	6230
Total	86773	128769	140320	184563	307521	408311	442830	474555	512756	541935	559099	572820	579866	580970	596737	619109

Table 4.3G: The statewise target of new planting and replanting

(Area in hectare)

States	2002–03	2003–04	2004–05	2005–06	2006–07	Total
Tripura	700	700	700	700	700	3500
Assam	400	400	400	400	400	2000
Meghalaya	75	75	75	75	75	375
Nagaland	50	50	50	50	50	250
Manipur	50	50	50	50	50	250
Arunachal Pradesh	50	50	50	50	50	250
Mizoram	35	35	35	35	35	175
Total new planting						

Source: Rubber Board, Guwahati.

Table 4.3H: Statewise share of area and production of rubber in North-eastern states

(In %)

States	2005–2006		2006–2007	
	Share of area (%)	Share of production (%)	Share of area (%)	Share of production (%)
Tripura	5.72	2.03	6.15	2.19
Assam	2.48	0.42	2.58	0.58
Meghalaya	0.85	0.42	0.87	0.47
Nagaland	0.38	0.07	0.40	0.08
Manipur	0.31	0.01	0.30	0.02
Mizoram	0.08	0.01	0.09	0.01
Arunachal Pradesh	0.07	0.01	0.07	0.01
Total	**9.89**	**2.97**	**10.47**	**3.35**

Source: Rubber Board, Guwahati.

about 72% are made as ribbed smoked sheets. Concentrated latex (11%) and technically specified rubber (10%) are the other two major forms of natural raw rubber in the country.

GM rubber

Kerala has challenged the Genetic Engineering Appraisal Committee's (GEAC) decision to allow open field trials of genetically modified (GM) rubber in the State. GEAC, the country's apex body that approves release of GM crops, had given a go-ahead to the Rubber Research Institute of India (RRII) to carry out the trials in Chetchackal, Thombikandom in Kottayam. The Supreme Court had directed GEAC to seek permission from the state government, the local government and farmers before permitting any GM trials". But, the directions were ignored by GEAC while giving approval in a meeting held on November 15.

Table 4.3I: Tapped area, production and average yield per hectare in different states

(Area in hectares, production in ones and yield per hectare in kilograms)

Year	Kerala			Tamil Nadu			Karnataka			Others			Total		
	Tapped area	Production	Yield	Tapped area	Production	Yield	Tapped area	Production	Yield	Tapped area	Production	Yield	Tapped area	Production	Yield
1993-94	313416	408311	1304	12215	14720	1205	8410	8626	1026	4509	3503	777	338550	435160	1285
1994-95	318965	442830	1389	12550	15065	1200	9175	9700	1057	5580	4220	756	346270	471815	1362
1995-96	328812	474555	1443	12420	17335	1396	9530	10275	1078	5682	4745	835	356444	506910	1422
1996-97	335400	512756	1529	12730	18505	1454	9760	11160	1143	7690	7004	911	365580	549425	1503
1997-98	342420	541935	1583	13000	19175	1475	10365	12150	1172	11185	10570	945	376970	583830	1549
1998-99	349683	559099	1599	13215	20263	1533	10685	12549	1174	13517	13134	972	387100	605045	1563
1999-00	355342	572820	1612	13377	21134	1580	10980	13115	1194	15101	15196	1006	394800	622265	1576
2000-01	359780	579866	1612	13651	21611	1583	11043	13368	1211	15427	15560	1009	399901	630405	1576
2001-02	360006	580350	1612	13677	21631	1582	11110	13465	1212	15920	15954	1002	400713	631400	1576
2002-03	363791	594917	1635	14065	22253	1582	11278	13659	1211	18819	18606	989	407953	649435	1592
2003-04	381970	655135	1715	14170	22520	1589	11488	14070	1225	20307	19925	981	427935	711650	1663
2004-05	391397	690768	1765	14325	22690	1584	11560	14440	1249	22438	21767	970	439720	749665	1705
2005-06	396385	739225	1865	14505	23555	1624	11755	14940	1271	24370	24905	1022	447015	802625	1796
2006-07	399635	783275	1960	14650	24020	1640	12414	16125	1299	27321	29475	1079	454020	852895	1879
2007-08	401420	753135	1876	14730	23820	1617	12850	16450	1280	29830	31940	1071	458830	825345	1799
2008-09	401706	782685	1948	15113	24355	1612	13635	19175	1406	32676	38285	1172	463130	864500	1867

In his letter dated December 2, the agriculture minister asked Union Environment Minister Jairam Ramesh to revoke the approval and not allow any field trials without prior permission of the state. "We have already stated to the Central Government that Kerala wishes to remain a state free of GM crops. This is not only to protect its agriculture, but also its agro-biodiversity and the highly pristine and valuable biodiversity", the minister writes.

According to RRII, GM rubber plant has certain genes about which even scientists are apprehensive. Some of these genes are the MnSOD gene construct, which has CaMV 35 S promoter (from virus) and NPT II Kanamycin resistance and GUS reporter genes from E Coli.

"Rubber seeds are used in the production of cattle feed. Rubber tree based honey is also consumed on a large scale in Kerala. Therefore more clarity and scrutiny is needed before proceeding with the project", Andhra Pradesh had reported cattle deaths after grazing on Bt Cotton farms.

"We are not against biotechnology or research in genetics, but we will not permit open field trials of GM crops until all biosafety concerns in this respect are addressed both at social and scientific levels. In case of endosulfan, Kerala has already paid a social price and does not want any other catastrophe to happen".

The 11th schedule gives the government the right to decide what to grow. Besides, Kerala is amongst the few states which has setup biodiversity management committees under the Biological Diversity Act, 2001. These committees facilitate local level decision making on use of biological resources in their area and can play a crucial role on defending the State government's stand.

Rubber Takes Root in New Regions

Supply shortage and record prices have prodded planters to expand rubber acreage this year. Farmers in regions where rubber trees are not normally grown have taken up rubber farming in a big way, thanks to the unrelenting rally in prices. A half of the new land brought under rubber this year is in States such as Karnataka, Maharashtra, Orissa and the Northeastern States, Rubber Board officials said. The rest of the expansion is seen in the rubber belt of Kerala and Tamil Nadu. "It is difficult to find land in Kerala", said Satish Abraham, president, Latex Manufacturers Association. He said rubber was now being cultivated as an inter crop in many new regions of the state. Rubber was replacing many other crops. Experts said rubber replanting was progressing at a slower pace. "Replanting will slow down when prices are high", said a Rubber Board official adding that even scrap rubber was getting nearly Rs 200 per kg.

Rubber Board estimates show the area under rubber has been expanding by around 6,000 hectares since the beginning of this decade. However, this increased to 22,700 hectares by 2007–2008 and to 30,200 hectare in the subsequent year. The provisional figure for 2009–2010 put the new plantation at 25,500 hectares. The extended rainy season this year has forced growers to cut back production.

Small Farmers

Since majority of the old senile unproductive plantation of coffee, rubber, coconut, arecanut, spices are with small farmers, group approach will greatly help. Some of the developmental schemes where financial assistance to individual farmers are available can be scientifically modified to suit group farming.

The small holder sector in the case of rubber is reasonably well organized through the formation of the Rubber Producers' Societies (RPS). The initiative taken by the Rubber Board for introducing group processing in RPS is a welcome step, which is absent in other crops such as coconut, coffee, arecanut and spices. Formation of such societies encouraged by the respective Boards will lead to organized marketing of the crops and in establishing storage facilities at reasonable costs. Right from raising quality-planting materials, organizing input supply like fertilizers, pesticides, water management, etc. can be jointly organized and utilized, even by arranging credit facilities.

The need for supporting the formation of voluntary organizations as mentioned earlier was felt necessary and the RPS have been promoted in this backdrop. These RPSs are envisaged to undertake group processing and marketing, distribution of inputs and also to function as an extension arm of the Rubber Board. There are about 2,100 societies at the moment and regular. Extension service is being dispensed through a good number of these societies. The Board also has adopted participatory extension management. The uses of farmer resource persons have also been tried extensively during the last couple of years, the results of which are quite encouraging. As a result of these efforts, the productivity of natural rubber increased from 284 kg/hectare to 1,576 kg/hectare during the last 5 decades, which is a remarkable achievement considering the nature of the sector, which is dominated by small holdings.

Recent Initiatives

The Rubber Board plans to bring more land under rubber cultivation and increase productivity. According to government estimates, India would become the second largest consumer of rubber after China in the next decade. The Rubber Board is planning to invest Rs 2,445 million in Northeastern States during the 11th plan period. The government of India had approved the plan submitted by the Board. The intention is to expand the area of rubber plantations in states such as Assam, Tripura, Meghalaya, Nagaland, Manipur, Mizoram and Arunachal Pradesh. India produced 864,500 tons of rubber during 2008–2009, of which 37,240 tons were from Northeastern States. The Rubber Board has identified that around 450,000 hectares of land in these states is ideal for rubber cultivation. But, only 72,000 hectares has been planted so far.

Recently, the Rubber Board has appointed a consultant to develop a rubber tapping machine. The basic design has already been completed. Rubber tapping requires skill. It has to be executed without damaging the cambium—the soft tissue between the tree trunk and the bark. There is severe shortage of tappers. With the help of a machine, even an unskilled person can do tapping. In Kerala alone, there are about 250,000 rubber tappers.

At present, the rubber tapping style is debated. Till now, rubber tapping has followed a common style the inclined downward tapping. Now, a new method called inclined upward tapping is advocated. It promises considerably higher output from each tree. Experiments have shown that the new method produces 45% more rubber. However, the Rubber Board is not convinced of the advantages of the new method.

Role in the Indian Economy

India is the third largest producer, fourth largest consumer of natural rubber and fifth largest consumer of natural and synthetic rubber together in the world, is considered to be one of the key players in the global rubber based industries for natural rubber, synthetic rubber, rayon/nylon tire cord, steel cord, 6carbon black and rubber chemicals, etc is being met from indigenous sources. Rapid progress has also been made in the production of natural rubber. Rubber is a core sector in the Indian national economy. There are around 6,000 units comprising 30 large-scale, 300 medium-scale and around 5,600 small-sector industries/tiny-sector units manufacturing around 35,000 rubber products. The sector employs around 40 million people including around 22,000 technically qualified support personnel. The industry accounts for a turnover of Rs 200 billion contributing Rs 40 billion to the national exchequer through taxes, duties and other levies. These units manufacture more than 35,000 rubber products, employing 400,000 people, which include 22,000 technically qualified support personnel, contributing Rs 40 billion to the national exchequer through taxes, duties and other levies.

The wide range of rubber products manufactured by the Indian rubber industry comprises all types of heavy duty earth moving tires. Auto tires, tubes, automobile parts, footwear, belting, hoses, cycle tires and tubes, cables and wires, camelback, battery boxes, latex products, pharmaceutical goods, besides molded and extruded goods for mass consumption. The products manufactured also cover hi-tech industrial items. The important areas which the industry caters to include all the three wings of defense, civil, aviation, aeronautics, railways, agriculture, transport as also textile engineering industries, pharmaceuticals, mines, steel plants, ports, family planning programs, hospitals, sports, practically to every conceivable field.

The rubber industry in India is basically divided in two sectors tire and non-tire sector produces all types of auto tires, conventional as well as radial tires and exports to advance countries like USA. The non-tire sector comprises the medium scale, small scale and tiny units. It produces high technology and sophisticated industrial products. The small scale sector accounts for over 50% of production of rubber goods in the non-tire category. Going by share of rubber consumption, automotive tire sector is the single largest sector accounting for about 50% consumption of all kinds of rubbers, followed by bicycles tires and tubes 15% footwear 12%, belts and hoses 6%, camelback and latex products 7%. All other remaining rubber products put together account for 10%.

The plantation sector with an estimated production of over 631 hundred thousand tons of natural rubber and a projected production of more than 1 million tons in near future, contributes to the rapid growth of the Indian rubber industry. Kerala, with a total area of 3.84 lakh hectares under rubber cultivation and an annual production of 3.70 lakh tons, produces over 90% of India's natural rubber. Of the total area, 92% is represented by small holdings with an average area of around 0.5 hectares. There are about 10 lakh growers and 3.5 lakh workers engaged in the rubber sector of which more than 90% belong to Kerala. A sound network of intermediate rubber units engaged in rubber compounding, crumb rubber manufacture, etc exist in the State.

Quality Planting Material Generation

The Rubber Board is maintaining one Central Nursery and eight regional rubber nurseries in different parts of the country including the nontraditional region other than NE states. These nurseries scientifically produce good quality budded plants and are the sources of genuine bud wood material required by private nurseries to produce budded plants. Even though the Board is in a position to meet only around 10% of the total planting material requirement in the country, it is very much necessary to maintain the nurseries already established by the Board in order to ensure quality control and check unscrupulous trading practices by the private nursery owners. Periodic incorporation of organic manure in bulk quantities for enrichment of soil fertility, augmentation of irrigation facilities, repairs to civil construction, etc. are the major items of work envisaged in the nurseries during the next 5 years.

Apiculture-extra income generation activity from rubber plantations-rubber plantations are good sources of honey and bee keeping in rubber estates will add to the financial viability of the plantations. In fact, this potential of rubber plantations is only sparingly utilized now. This activity will help the growers increase their net farm income in addition to providing extra employment opportunities. Financial support to 3,000 growers Rs 3,000/- per grower will be provided for establishing bee-keeping units in rubber plantations. The financial provision made is Rs 4.50 crore.

As many as one million planters are involved in NR plantations in the country. India has the advantage of the highest number of technical personnel for the rubber industry in the world. Also, cost of labor in India is significantly lower than in USA. Railways, defense, space research, mining ports, agriculture, transport, textile, steel plants and many other industrial sectors in India are highly developed and generate a huge demand for rubber products. A billion strong populations ensure a huge demand for consumer rubber products. This has further helped in the radical and rapid growth of the Indian rubber industry. A sustained boom in the vehicle industry and overall industrialization further enhance the growth prospects.

The government has decided to setup a Rubber Development Fund for promotion of natural rubber, widely grown in Kerala, Tamil Nadu and Karnataka. A bill to this effect was passed by Parliament on December 18, 2009. The Bill was earlier passed by the Lok Sabha on November 24, 2009.

With the passing of the Rubber Amendment Bill 2009, the government would be introducing a system for collection of rubber that would be determined on the basis of self assessment. The government also made it clear that small growers would be given more representation in the Rubber Board. Also, natural rubber has been excluded from the scope of Indo-ASEAN free trade agreement.

In the next 5 years, about 130,000 hectares of land needs to be replanted. The 11th plan (2007–2012) outlay for Rubber Board was Rs 5,800 million, up from Rs 4,150 million in the 10th plan. The government is concentrating on the plantation sector as it is labor intensive.

Future Prospects

The future for natural rubber looks bright. Even increasing volumes are being produced. At 5.92 million tons per annum, natural rubber has 39% of the world rubber consumption of 15.14 million tons per annum. The earthquake bearing market will take off when people realize that such system saves not only lives but also the contents of the buildings. Powder-free surgical gloves are on the way and this, achieved by polymer coatings both on the inside and out, will eliminate the protein allergy problem. All predictions of future cars see them continuing to use rubber tires. The space shuttles land on all natural rubber tires because of the superb performance of this 500-year-old polymer. With space travel around the corner, natural rubber has a guaranteed future.

World rubber consumption is forecast to rise 4.1% per year through 2013 to 26.9 million metric tons, according to a report from industry research firm Fredonia Group. Majority of rubber demand is accounted for by the motor vehicle sector, particularly for usage in tires. The largest national rubber market, China, will consume over one-third of all new rubber demand in the world through 2013, and account for 30% of the global rubber market in 2013.

Demand for non-tire rubber products is expected to benefit from rising industrialization levels in developing countries. Tire rubber demand will continue to benefit from strong growth in Asia. Concerns related to the environment and high gasoline prices will boost the popularity of more fuel-efficient smaller cars resulting in a decline in rubber usage per tire through 2013. Demand for synthetic rubber will register slightly slower growth than demand for natural rubber through 2013, but the former will remain more important.

Measures Needed

Though rubber productivity is satisfactory, efforts are being made to improve it through the Rubber Plantation Development Scheme in the 11th five-year plan (2007–2012). The scheme provides subsidy on planting, supplies critical inputs with price concession, and assists soil and water conservation and generation and distribution of quality planting materials. The export of rubber is promoted through export promotion schemes, which include participation in international trade fairs, assistance to exporters to participate in trade fairs and organizing buyer-seller meets.

However, there is one serious anomaly. There is 70% input duty on latex while 20% or Rs 20 per kg on rubber. Latex is a wet form of rubber with about 60% rubber and 40% water. Nearly 900 units (most of them small-scale) use latex for making foam mattresses, surgical and other gloves, balloons and hot water bottles. The high-import duty of 70% on latex makes their operations uncompetitive. The import duty on latex needs to be in tune with the duty on rubber.

The industry recently sought a hefty increase in the subsidy on rubber output to Rs 100,000 per hectare in the 12th five-year plan (2012–2017). It urged the government a one-time subsidy of Rs 100,000 per hectare to small farmers for a period of 3 years for planting rubber trees. The government at present provides a subsidy of Rs 19,500 per hectare on rubber cultivation in the traditional areas (Kerala and Kanyakumari) and Rs 30,000 in nontraditional areas. A hefty subsidy is expected to help increase production in newer areas like the Northeastern States.

Because of rising prices of rubber, both in domestic and international markets, more growers in India are turning to rubber cultivation. The industry has requested the Rubber Board to increase the acreage of rubber plantation substantially, especially in the North-East. Similarly, nontraditional areas where rubber cultivation could be increased should be identified.

Steps Needed for Growth

Efforts would be needed to achieve global competitiveness with respect to quality and cost and market development for the domestically produced rubber. It would also be necessary to promote natural rubber as a green commodity *vis-à-vis* its synthetic counterparts.

Agroclimatic zoning, enhanced productivity, better disease/stress management, sustainable farming systems, higher ancillary income, environmentally sound processing methods and improved product quality would be needed for achieving competitiveness and sustainability.

It would be necessary to generate additional income from rubber plantations through tapping ancillary products such as rubber wood, honey, rubber seed and also by resorting to intercropping with annual and perennial crops. Productivity increase through replanting and rejuvenation with better varieties has more scope than horizontal area expansion.

In the field of processing and marketing, thrust will have to be given for quality improvement, reduction in cost of processing, value addition and for promoting environmentally sound processing methods while providing market information on rubber and rubber wood. Strengthening of research and development and also providing testing support to the manufacturing industry and providing market information on rubber products will be necessary.

Promotion of rubber wood as an ecofriendly timber and improving processing and marketing of the same are important for improving the economic viability of rubber plantations.

As market development for rubber is considered very important in the present context, it will be necessary to encourage manufacturing of export-oriented products having locational advantages. Price stabilization fund which could be used to protect growers at the time of crisis to ensure fair price needs to be established.

Increased community participation would be necessary for creation of infrastructure and strengthening of existing processing and marketing channels in order to cater to the needs of export sector.

Sanitary and phytosanitary measures play an important role as nontariff barriers in the world trade organization (WTO) regime. With the liberalized import and export of commodities, the risk of entry of new pests and disease is higher and hence steps to be taken to avoid such risks.

Present Position

The happy days seem to have petered out. In the last 3 years, situation has changed for the worse with frequent fluctuation in rubber prices. Today, around 95% of the 11 lakh growers who fit into the small category are tightening their belts following rapid plunge in the price levels since last September.

Rubber prices	Rs 240
August 2011	Rs 150
Brief period in 2013.	
Prices started tumbling September, 2013.	
Rs 142 kg February, 2014.	

The rubber prices touched a high of 240 in August 2011. Volatility increased in the subsequent years. But, the growers had no reason to complain when the prices were hovering in the range of 170–180 per kg. The prices had fallen to 150 per kg for a brief period in early 2013. But after September, 2013; things began to take a turn for the worse. The prices touched a low of 142 in February, far below the breakeven level. The growers can't easily shift to other crops. The reason: there are no dependable crops that will provide a steady income. Though pepper prices are up, its production has come down in Kerala. Recent decision for procurement by State agencies may bring temporary relief.

In addition, the industries suffer from:

1. Unattractive financial assistance to meet our incentives for the growers to undertake scientific planting
2. Low price of rubber
3. Inadequate infrastructure for primary processing
4. Stiff competition from natural and synthetic rubber some of the major constraints are discussed in detail below.

Consumption of Rubber

India is one of the major consumers of rubber. All the three types of rubber: (1) natural, (2) synthetic and (3) reclaimed are growing fast. Table 4.4A gives details of production and consumption of all the three types subcategory wise. Growth rates of production and consumption of rubber (Table 4.4B) show a very fluctuating trend. Details about the consumption of all the categories of these three types at the all India level are provided in the Table 4.4C during 1985–1986 and 2012–2013 shows an increase of 3.5 times for natural, 5.3 times synthetic and 2.5 times reclaimed. Statewise consumption of all kinds of rubber shows that the share of natural rubber is 70% (Table 4.4D). Type-wise consumption of natural and synthetic rubber is shown in Tables 4.4E and F.

Consumption of natural as well as synthetic rubber statewise is shown in Tables 4.5A and B. Kerala is the top consumer of natural rubber followed by Maharashtra, Punjab and Gujarat. With regard to the consumption of synthetic rubber also, Kerala leads the country and is followed by Maharashtra, Gujarat and Madhya Pradesh.

Major consumers of rubber in India are the tire and tube industry (Tables 4.5C to E) and the production of other rubber goods like contraceptive, carbon black, foot wear and cycle tires as well as tubes (Table 4.5F). There are about 6,000 units comprising 30 large scale, 300 medium-scale and around 5,600 small scale and tiny sector units in India. These units manufacture more than 35,000 rubber products, employing about 4 lakhs people, which also includes 2,200 technically qualified support personnel, contributing Rs 40 billion to the National exchequer through taxes, duties and other levies. The production in the near future is projected to be more than 1 million tons. The prospects of growth are further enhanced by a boom in the vehicle industry, improved living standard of the people and rapid overall industrialization. Currently, the per capita consumption of rubber in India is only 800 gm compared to 12–14 kg in Japan, USA and Europe.

IMPORTS, EXPORTS AND STOCKS

The accelerated growth in demand for natural rubber in India made the country a net importer of natural rubber in 1947. The situation remained unchanged until 1970. But, during the first 3 years of 1970s, owing to the industrial recession and slackness in demand, import of natural rubber was banned from April 1973. Apart from this measure, limited quantities of natural rubber were exported during 1973–1974, 1974–1975, 1976–1977 and 1977–1978. To overcome occasional glut in the

Table 4.4A: Annual production and consumption of rubber in India

(*Metric tons*)

Categories production	2000-01	2001-02	2002-03	2003-04	2004-05	2005-06	2006-07	2007-09	2008-09
Natural rubber (NR)									
Ribbed smoked sheet (RSS)	455172	453465	450220	-490070	532155	566445	612735	583875	617125
Solid block rubber	60225	65650	74940	87665	84275	92540	98500	100705	110275
Latex concentrates (DRC)	65975	62990	74325	81860	78795	90950	86780	88305	88070
Pale latex crepes	1975	1645	1750	1765	2070	2555	2055	NA	NA
Others	47055	47650	48200	50290	52370	50135	52825	52460	49030
Total	630405	631400	699435	711650	749665	802625	852895	825345	864500
Synthetic rubber (SR)									
Styrene butadiene (SBR)	13342	16182	16512	18673	18893	14470	12285	16879	12523
Poly-butadiene (BR)	40670	41994	50977	55652	63762	67286	71730	74045	71758
Others	11448	11477	12912	14041	11554	15882	15498	15362	12458
Total	65460	69653	80401	88366	94209	97638R	99513	106286	96739
Total NR & SR	695865	701053	729836	800016	843874	900263	952408	931631	961239
Consumption									
Natural rubber (NR)									
Ribbed smoked Sheet (RSS)	463280	446150	492980	501625	519855	561655	561580	577635	597440
Solid block Rubber	61680	82850	87305	98205	117130	115840	132755	155670	146060
Latex concentrates (DRC)	70870	72595	77540	78660	71880	74670	76190	77715	80520
Pale latex crepes	2250	2360	2615	2515	2210	2435	2170	NA	NA
Others	33395	34255	34985	38595	44330	46510	47610	50435	47700
Total	631475	638210	695425	719600	755405	801110	820305	861455	871720

(*Contd.*)

Table 4.4A: Annual production and consumption of rubber in India

(Metric tons)

Categories production	2000-01	2001-02	2002-03	2003-04	2004-05	2005-06	2006-07	2007-09	2008-09
Out of which auto tyre manufacturers	305718	304425	353032	378185	406226	442921	462081	495577	508121
Synthetic rubber (SR)									
Styrene butadiene (SBR)	54935	55945	65110	71030	75610	80885	98170	110965	111745
Poly-butadiene (BR)	49810	49995	55170	61120	64620	69080	79900	88205	82740
Others	65925	68590	74570	78040	84420	87530	92760	97985	98465
Total	170670	174530	194850	210190	224650	237495	270830	297155	292950
Out of which auto tyre manufacturers	98362	95277	107483	119367	131267	141580	170809	191507	185094
Total NR & SR	802145	812740	890275	929790	980055	1038605	1091135	1158610	1164670
Out of which auto tyre manufacturers	404080	399702	460515	497552	537493	584501	632890	687084	693215
Reclaimed rubber (RR)									
Production	62120	63550	67385	70990	73060	76645	78495	83075	86390
Consumption	62260	63875	67320	70460	72905	76535	78435	83165	86030
Out of which auto tyre manufacturers	13256	12925	16138	18244	19908	21978	23714	27589	29191

NA, not available.
Source: Various issues of Rubber Statistical News, Robber Board, India.

Table 4.4B: Growth rate of production and consumption

Year	Production	Consumption	Supply gap	Production growth rate (%)	Consumption growth rate (%)
1995-96	506,910	525,465	18,555	7.40	8.20
1996-97	549,425	561,765	12,340	8.40	6.90
1997-98	583,830	571,820	12,010	6.30	1.80
1998-99	605,045	591,545	13,500	3.60	3.40
1999-00	622,265	628,110	5,845	2.80	6.20
2000-01	630,405	631,475	1,070	1.30	0.50
2001-02	631,400	638,210	6,810	0.20	1.10
2002-03	649,435	695,425	45,990	2.90	9.00
2003-04	711,650	719,600	7,950	9.60	3.50
2004-05	749,665	755,405	5,740	5.30	5.00
2005-06	802,625	801,110	1,515	7.10	6.10
2006-07	852,895	820,305	32,590	6.30	2.40
2007-08	825,345	861,455	36,110	3.2	5.00
2008-09	864,500	871,720	7,220	4.70	1.20
2009-10	831,400	930,565	99,165	3.8	6.80
2010-11	861,950	947,715	85,765	3.70	1.80
2011-12	903,700	964,415	60,715	4.80	1.80

market and also in accordance with the new economic policy of Government of India, all restriction on export of natural rubber was removed since 1991. But, the indigenous production was insufficient to meet internal consumption and natural rubber continued to be deficit in the country. Though export was freely allowed, only nominal quantities were actually exported. However, India has been exporting significant quantities of rubber in the form of value-added products. The export earnings from rubber products during 199–200 were Rs 5,730 million.

Total production of all the three types of rubber: natural, synthetic and reclaimed is not sufficient to meet the growing demand of the industry. The consumption of NR rose 5.6% in the first half of the financial year 2012–2013 while production increased only 1.1%. This would exert pressure on supplies and prices of the commodity in the local market. Of course, rise in the production of automotive tires is the primary reason for the increase in consumption, which is placed at 1,006,000 tons with an annual deficit of 76,000 tons. In 2011–2012, production and consumption stood at 903,700 tons and 964,415 tons, respectively (Table 4.6).

At the end of May 2013, Rubber Board indicated a stock of 235,000 tons in the country, but the tire industry doubted the estimate. According to the industry, the growers have rubber with them, but they are awaiting a higher price to release it. When rains stop, more rubber will be off-loaded, as the growers know that prices will fall once tapping begins. Tire consumption in the replacement sector is good while the original equipment manufacturing (OEM) segment continues to experience a slack demand.

Table 4.4C: Consumption of natural synthetic and reclaimed rubber in India

(Thousand million tons)

Year	Natural	Synthetic	Reclaimed
1985-86	237.4	70.0	38.2
1986-87	257.3	71.8	38.6
1987-88	287.5	76.4	41.1
1988-89	313.8	84.1	42.4
1989-90	341.8	93.5	43.9
1990-91	364.3	104.7	52.5
1991-92	380.1	105.6	54.0
1992-93	413.8	106.6	62.0
1993-94	448.8	109.5	63.1
1994-95	485.8	122.7	65.6
1995-96	525.5	134.1	65.8
1996-97	561.8	142.8	66.6
1997-98	571.8	160.9	70.1
1998-99	591.5	156.3	63.1
1999-00	622.3	167.2	64.0
2000-01	627.8	169.4	63.8
2001-02	638.0	191.7	66.4
2002-03	716.0	204.0	70.0
2003-04	719.7	210.2	69.6
2004-05	745.3	222.8	72.2
2005-06	801.1	237.5	76.5
2006-07	820.3	270.8	78.4
2007-08	853.0	297.2	80.0
2008-09	871.7	293.0	86.4
2009-10	930.6	347.7	93.5
2010-11	947.7	411.8	100.3
2011-12	964.4	423.4	102.4
2012-13 (up to Jan)	818.3	371.1	95.9

Table 4.4D: Statewise consumption of all kinds of rubber

(Tons)

State/Union territory	2005-06				2006-07			
	Natural	Synthetic	Reclaimed	Total	Natural	Synthetic	Reclaimed	Total
Andhra Pradesh	37209	15274	5419	57902	33792	17163	6440	57395
Delhi	15778	1949	1156	18883	16643	1896	1164	19703
Goa & Daman	35192	5751	1010	41953	34606	7267	1078	42951
Gujarat	48336	12869	1986	63191	60193	16762	2337	79292
Haryana	48572	8875	1420	58867	48297	10297	1645	60239
Jharkhand	1197	284	160	1641	1203	286	155	1644
Karnataka	55404	16400	6499	78303	57202	19523	7143	83868
Kerala	135792	48666	8995	193453	126809	50572	8440	185821
Madhya Pradesh	30685	18914	3485	53084	33901	20055	3071	57027
Maharashtra	106096	38698	12288	157082	106654	39998	12689	159341
Orissa	31300	5969	249	37518	33981	8369	262	42612
Pondicherry	2714	1956	115	4785	1884	1859	105	3848
Punjab	82813	10165	17723	110701	78794	12760	15588	107142
Rajasthan	54013	11540	1624	67177	55294	15263	1952	72509
Tamil Nadu	49485	21868	6450	77803	64731	30060	8717	103508
Uttar Pradesh	32485	7578	4461	44524	30588	7769	4036	42393
West Bengal	31087	10558	3435	45080	31955	10737	3542	46234
Others	2952	181	60	3193	3778	194	71	4043
Total	801110	237495	76535	1115140	820305	270830	78435	1169570

Table 4.4E: Typewise consumption of natural rubber

Type	1999-00	2000-01	2001-02	2002-03	2003-04	2004-05	2005-06	2006-07	2007-08	2008-09	2009-10
RSS grades	462120	463280	446150	492980	501625	519855	561655	561580	577635	597440	621435
Solid block rubber	64385	61680	82850	87305	98205	117130	115840	132755	155670	146060	190545
Latex concentrate (DRC)	66775	70870	72595	77540	78660	71880	74670	76190	77715	80520	82515
Others	34830	35645	36615	37600	41110	46540	48945	49780	50435	47700	36070
Total	**628110**	**631475**	**638210**	**695425**	**719600**	**755405**	**801110**	**820305**	**861455**	**871720**	**930565**

Table 4.4F: Typewise consumption of synthetic rubber

Type	1998-99	1999-00	2000-01	2001-02	2002-03	2003-04	2004-05	2005-06	2006-07	2007-08	2008-09	2009-10
Styrene butadiene rubber@	51245	53790	54935	55945	65110	71030	75610	80885	98170	110965	111745	138905
Polybutadiene	44040	49245	49810	49995	55170	61120	64620	69080	79900	88205	82740	104465
Butyl	35910	37925	39940	40385	44850	47400	51900	53090	55825	59260	58960	66080
Polychloroprene	4680	5115	5310	5655	5450	5775	6220	6510	6640	6850	6775	6890
Nitrile	6455	6605	5875	6405	7055	7280	7935	8115	9195	9135	9430	8260
Latex (DRC)	5050	5025	5030	5180	5605	5970	6190	6460	6550	6420	6900	7135
EPDM	5965	6190	5920	6430	6730	7040	7195	7515	7830	8450	8305	8020
Others*	3050	3325	3850	4535	4880	4575	4980	5840	6720	7870	8095	7955
Total	**156395**	**167220**	**170670**	**174530**	**194850**	**210190**	**224650**	**237495**	**270830**	**297155**	**292950**	**347710**
Annual growth rate	2.81	6.92	2.06	2.26	11.64	7.87	6.88	5.72	14.04	9.72	1.42	18.69

@ Includes SBR Latex, VP Latex and Nitrite Latex.

* Includes SBR Latex, VP Latex and Nitrite Latex.

Table 4.5A: Consumption of natural rubber by states

(Thousand metric tons)

Grade	1980–1981	1985–1986	1990–1991	1991–1992	1992–1993	1993–1994	1994–1995	1995–1996	1996–1997	1997–1998	1999–2000	2000–2001	2002–2003	2003–2004	2004–2005	2005–2006	2006–2007	2007–2008	2008–2009	2009–2010
Andhra Pradesh	2.7	4.5	8.9	14.0	15.0	15.0	18.3	20.0	21.9	22.7	19.7	19.9	21.1	24.2	36.5	37.2	33.8	36.2	50.9	52.9
Delhi	8.5	10.2	15.6	16.3	17.2	18.8	18.7	19.6	18.6	17.5	18.9	18.4	17.7	17.2	16.6	15.8	16.6	16.3	16.1	13.1
Goa and Daman	2.6	4.2	6.2	7.9	10.5	9.4	8.9	12.7	18.8	23.1	23.5[a]	23.6[a]	18.3[a]	31.7[a]	36.6[a]	35.2[b]	34.6	34.7	32	28.5
Gujarat	3.2	5.0	6.9	8.4	15.6	20.3	21.8	23.4	25.1	30.8	32.4	35.1	39.7	37.5	46.8	48.3	60.2	66.7	65.7	68.2
Haryana	15.7	18.8	22.7	24.6	27.2	31.1	29	29.9	30.9	34.4	37.0	38.6	46.4	47	47.7	48.6	48.3	49.7	50	50.5
Karnataka	8.6	11.7	17.0	18.5	19.6	21.1	22.3	23.7	25.3	26.0	29.7	31.2	45.8	46.3	49.2	55.4	57.2	55.8	56.3	64.2
Kerala	20.8	28.3	55.4	51.2	52.5	54.1	64.7	67.3	69.9	68.5	86.8	88.2	126.1	124.6	125.0	135.8	126.8	142.2	139.3	147.1
Madhya Pradesh	NA	0.9	4.1	5.3	9.6	12.7	14.7	17.0	19.7	21.8	26.7	27.7	31.9	31.1	31.3	30.7[c]	33.9[c]	32.4[c]	29.6[c]	33.0[c]
Maharashtra	30.3	37.3	47.2	49.3	49.2	52.0	58.6	62.4	60.8	54.8	68.7	68.3	84.7	90.4	97.1	106.1	106.7	111.7	109.6	116.4
Punjab	14.1	27.2	46.2	51.6	53.8	55.4	58.0	61.3	62.7	78.2	79.2	82.8	85.5	84.2	81.6	82.8[d]	78.8[d]	83.6[d]	81.8[d]	75.9[d]
Rajasthan	7.3	12.2	17.9	18.0	22.4	23.4	25.0	27.2	29.5	30.9	37.5	35.9	41.1	42.1	47.1	54.0	55.3	59.4	53.0	49.6
Tamil Nadu	18.8	19.1	21.2	20.4	22.0	25.3	25.9	29.2	34.8	37.1	32.0	32.6	32.8	34.7	37.6	49.5	64.7	60.6	64.4	68.4
Uttar Pradesh	24.5	29.4	46.8	47.4	45.0	52.9	62.1	65.8	64.5	63.2	61.7	55.7	32.9	33.5	33.2	32.5	30.6[e]	31.2[e]	51.2[e]	83.9[e]
West Bengal	30.1	27.5	42.3	38.3	38.5	40.6	41.2	42.2	40.3	38.9	43.0	43.3	39.0	37.1	34.8	31.1	32	33.7	30.1	30.7[b]

[a] Excluding Daman
[b] Including Dadra and Nagar Haveli
[c] Including Chattisgarh
[d] Including Chandigarh.

Table 4.5B: Consumption of synthetic rubber by states

State	1984-85	1989-90	1990-91	1991-92	1992-93	1993-94	1994-95	1995-96	1996-97	1997-98	1999-00	2000-01	2002-03	2003-04	2004-05	2005-06	2006-07	2007-08	2008-09	2009-10 (P)
Andhra Pradesh	574	2,202	2,594	3,865	5,124	5,673	6,121	7,138	8,325	9,709	11,238	9,330	7,937	8,515	11,489	15,274	17,163	17,323	19,632	21,925
Delhi	1,621	2,764	3,747	3,696	3,696	3,172	2,581	2,579	2,578	2,576	2,371	2,176	2,083	2,012	2,036	1,949	1,896	1,822	1,890	1,360
Goa & Daman	1,409	1,624	1,501	1,235	1,375	2,008	2,311	2,545	2,802	3,086	5,312[a]	8,556[a]	14,004[a]	7,694[a]	7,860[a]	5,751[a]	7267	8760	8323	10280
Gujarat	774	1,254	1,402	1,339	2,851	3,457	3,690	4,485	5,450	6,625	5,302	6,213	7,868	8,994	10,935	12,869	16,762	18,875	18,866	26,380
Haryana	6,589	6,866	7,106	6,593	6,554	6,591	7,481	8,028	8,614	9,244	8,761	7,596	6,631	8,230	8,919	8,875	10,297	9,975	9,185	9,835
Karnataka	4,130	5,867	6,602	6,459	6,689	6,755	7,200	7,641	8,109	8,608	8,539	9,312	14,382	15,344	16,242	16,400	19,523	22,640	19,960	25,690
Kerala	6,197	13,352	15,232	14,893	15,646	16,441	18,984	21,564	24,495	27,825	31,068	32,978	36,438	46,921	49,746	48,666	50,572	53,998	48,504	61,135
Madhya Pradesh	*	480	1,040	1,246	1,954	2,500	2,504	3,082	3,794	4,670	9,609	11,404	13,370	15,577	16,826	18,914[b]	20,055[b]	23,815	23,123	26,210
Maharashtra	13,868	20,181	21,370	20,904	20,932	21,928	22,947	23,102	23,258	23,415	26,783	25,989	33,654	37,655	40,528	38,698	39,998	41,897	42,033	46,755
Punjab	3,467	2,885	3,735	5,025	4,859	5,494	5,515	6,543	7,762	9,209	8,463	8,001	8,935	8,573	9,228	10,165[c]	12,760[c]	11,696	13,200	13780
Rajasthan	3,676	7,052	6,932	6,265	6,385	6,173	6,526	7,128	7,785	8,503	9,395	8,423	9,003	9,318	9,990	11,540	15,263	18669	18450	20,320
Tamil Nadu	6,496	8,022	11,254	9,294	7,786	8,088	10,602	11,606	12,706	13,910	10,737	12,945	14,026	14,372	14,999	21,868	30,060	34,205	34,723	38,970
Utter Pradesh	7,141	10,732	11,396	11,934	10,218	10,716	12,550	13,649	14,845	16,145	13,977	11,539	7,637	7,754	7,231	7,578[d]	7,769[d]	8,137	11,360	19510
West Bengal	8,351	9,428	9,635	10,030	9,942	9,481	8,627	9,322	10,073	10,885	9,706	10,217	11,519	11,184	10,511	10,558	10,737	12427	12254	10,550
Others	1,107	841	1,189	2,872	4,813	5,413	5,011	5,673	2,214	6,505	5,959	5,991	7,563	11,047	8,110	181	194	226	217	110
Total	**65,400**	**93,550**	**104,735**	**105,650**	**108,690**	**113,943**	**122,650**	**134,085**	**142,810**	**160,915**	**167,220**	**170,670**	**194,850**	**210,190**	**224,650**	**237,495**	**270,830**	**297,155**	**292,950**	**347,710**

* Included in others upto 1984-85

[a] Excluding Daman, Dadra and Nagarhaveli

[b] Including Chattisgarh

[c] Including Chandigarh

[d] Including Uttaranchal

P = Provisional

Table 4.5C: Production of tubes

Year	2001-02	2002-03	2003-04	2005-06	2006-07	2007-08	2008-09	2009-10
Truck & Bus	7291	7852	8851	10522	11257	12016	11,911	14,142
Tractor	925	824	906	1232	1425	1443	1,333	1,970
Car	4277	4728	5331	6990	8509	11490	10,773	9,922
Jeep	972	1036	1056	1066	1132	1416	1,411	1,430
LCV	1835	2133	2633	3775	4156	4147	4,213	4,912
Motor Cycles	11372	13978	15415	22263	28067	30817	31,527	37,095
Scooter	5122	5750	5624	7044	7461*	9128*	8242*	11610*
Moped	151	176	270	227	—	—	—	—
A.D.V	216	231	187	165	213	181	184	235
OTR	13	15	19	38	48	60	60	68
Industrial	61	65	50	99	108	112	79	64
Total	**32235**	**36788**	**40342**	**53421**	**62376**	**70810**	**61,491**	**69,838**

Table 4.5D: Production of automobile types and tubes

	Car tyres (thousand nos)	2-Wheelers tyres (thousands nos)	Giant tyres (thousand nos)	Tractor tyre/ADV tyres (thousands nos)	OTR tyre aero tyre (thousand nos)	Giant tubes (thousand nos)
1980-81	1,063.2	2,016.0	3,700.8	1,225.2	26	3,264
1985-86	1,480.8	4,648.8	4,785.6	1,279.2	29	3,792
1990-91	2,462.4	6,942.0	6,087.6	1,707.6	47	4,944
1991-92	2,198.4	6,067.2	6,052.8	1,761.6	44	4,512
1992-93	2,185.2	5,926.8	6,720.0	1,792.8	48	4,584
1993-94	2,649.6	7,293.6	7,053.6	1,825.2	52	5,148
1994-95	3,042.0	8,380.8	7,855.2	1,879.2	47	7,276
1995-96	3,546.8	7,849.1	8,786.6	1,786.9	43	8,787
1996-97	3,598.5	7,799.1	8,835.0	1,932.8	30	8,835
1997-98	3,873.9	7,799.8	9,208.1	2,049.1	37	9,208
1998-99	4,156.0	10,151.9	10,490.0	2,476.5	37	8,002
1999-00	4,657.0	12,208.0	11,881.0	2,534.0	36	8,641
2000-01	6,813.0	20,700.0	12291.0	2,796.0	38	8,573
2001-02	7,481.0	20,957.0	9,980.0	2,455.0	46	8,216
2002-03	8,544.0	25,714.0	12,817.0	2,453.0	51	8,817
2003-04	11,397.0	26,130.5	13,457.0	2,712.4	74	9,758
2004-05	13,324.0	28,243	12,530.1	2,144.6	89	10,492
2005-06	14,878.0	30,572	13,513.1	2,445.2	105	11,754
2006-07	15,554.1	35,272.0	14,486	2,833.5	133	12,682
2007-08	16,437.0	39,521	15,257	2,593.8	141	13,459
2008-09	16,570.0	41,030	14,912	2,817.3	136	13,245
2009-10	20,047.0	49,222	17,348	3,652.2	161	16,112
2010-11	20,043.2	63,258	18,496	4,037.9	91	16,996
2011-12	27,141.0	67,051.0	18,996	4,312.9	98.0	17,549
2012-13	23883*.0	44,234	14,812	3,520.0	225	13,500

ADR, Animal Drawn Vehicle.   * Apr-Sep
OTR , off the Road

Table 4.5E: Production of tyres

(*Lakh nos*)

Category	1982	1985	1986	1987	1988	1989	1990	1991	1992-93	1993-94	1994-95	1995-96	1996-97	1997-98	1998-99	1999-00	2000-01	2001-02	2002-03	2003-04	2004-05	2005-06	2006-07	2007-08	2008-09	2009-10	2010-11	2011-12	2012-13
Truck & bus	34.91	36.07	38.55	39.4	48.74	50.87	51.54	53.79	62.69	65.91	73.09	76.20	80.15	79.79	78.35	87.94	86.12	84.74	98.63	108.21	110.91	119.41	136.47	131.37	128.39	148.11	135.00	160.85	127.09
Light commercial vehicle	7.94	9.86	9.51	9.94	12.95	14.03	15.14	12.44	15.02	17.48	18.81	11.66	17.98	18.30	18.26	18.68	21.08	23.52	28.44	32.61	39.45	45.29	53.43	53.20	52.98	57.30	28.40	66.88	44.95
Passenger car	9.77	15.36	14.61	15.57	19.51	22.57	24.77	21.93	23.04	28.44	32.19	32.60	38.13	41.80	41.56	46.57	68.13	74.81	85.44	113.97	133.24	148.78	155.54	164.37	165.70	200.47	262.01	271.41	238.83*
Tractor & trailor	6.85	8.94	7.84	7.89	11.22	12.19	13.27	13.98	16.25	19.97	20.2	22.37	19.89	19.77	21.90	22.58	22.85	22.55	24.20	24.17	28.15	31.13	42.18	39.34	39.15	49.23	54.23	56.67	36.06ª
ADV	4.65	4.11	2.52	2.07	4.66	3.93	4.55	5.89	5.5	5.67	5.84	5.18	4.77	4.10	4.76	4.36	5.11	4.88	4.56	2.94	1.97	3.24	4.01	4.90	2.81	2.94	3.11	2.93	7.42
OTR	0.12	0.15	0.13	0.12	0.2	0.28	0.29	0.45	0.39	0.37	0.39	0.36	0.30	0.36	0.37	1.72	0.38	0.46	0.51	0.74	0.89	1.05	1.15	1.41	1.36	1.61	1.91	1.96	2.25
Others: scooter, motorcycle, moped, industrial	23.93	34.24	36.66	35.73	60.17	63.63	69.42	68.84	76.51	86.84	109.29	120.90	125.00	146.47	155.07	158.65	115.34	126.24	161.48	264.25	286.20	311.40	404.11	402.58	415.99	497.59	638.74	677.32	442.38
Total	88.38	108.86	109.96	110.87	157.53	167.61	179.13	177.40	199.51	222.82	259.99	278.94	297.65	310.59	334.12	357.17	424.41	435.14	515.85	546.90	600.82	660.31	735.44	811.03	821.07	971.36	1191.97	1253.97	922.05

ADV, Animal Drawn Vehicle; OTR, Off the Road.

Lakh = 0.1 million

*Excluding Jeep tyre in 2013

a w.e.f 2012-13 Industrial & A.D.V Tyre Production merged on other Tyres new category.

Table 4.5F: Production of rubber goods other than automobile tyres and tubes *

Product	1980	85-86	90-91	91-92	92-93	93-94	94-95	95-96	96-97	97-98	98-99	99-00	2000-01	2001-02	2002-03	2003-04	2004-05	2005-06	2006-07	2007-08	2008-09	2009-10	2010-11	2011-12
Contraceptives	362	696	1,004	965	1,019	933	1159	1,089	1,165	1,233	1,348	1,348	2,611	2,370	2134	2342	2071	2882	3615	3334	2690	2802	3332	2722
Rubber/canvas footwear	43	37	30	27	28	30	32	28	28	28	28	28	20	17	15	13	12	25	28	31	32	35	29	31
Bicycle tyres	27	36	24	22	19	13	11	10	10	12	10	12	23	40	45	42	40	96	93	95	87	79	103	95
Bicycle tubes	12	27	18	18	18	19	17	18	18	23	16	16	14	40	45	42	40	111	108	118	107	92	106	94
Conveyor belting	7	6	16	16	12	11	10	11	14	14	13	11	17	14	19	17	18	26	24	23	24	27	34	30
Reclaimed rubber	24	25	52	54	62	63	64	66	67	70	64	63	63	66	63	70	72	77	79	82	59	94	104	100
Rubber hoses	5	5	5	5	4	4	3	5	6	6	6	3	2	2	2	3	4	5	6	7	6	5	6	6
Carbon black	66	93	119	128	165	164	178	234	255	218	259	282	283	257	220	247	376	395	423	427	382	424	620	556

* For Automobile tyres and tubes, See Table 113.05.

Table 4.6: Production and consumption of natural rubber

(Tons)

Year	Production	Total consumption	Consumptionby auto tire manufacturers
2007–2008	825,345	861,455	495,577
2008–2009	864,500	871,720	508,121
2009–2010	831,400	930,565	576,210
2010–2011	861,950	947,715	597,623
2011–2012	903,700	964,415	NA
2012–2013*	930,700	NA	NA

* Estimates

Although crude oil prices have fallen in the last quarter of calendar year 2012, consumption of synthetic rubber (SR) has not risen. SR is a downstream product of crude oil. In 2011–2012, while the NR consumption showed 1.8% growth at 964,415 tons, the SR use recorded a growth of 2.8% at 423,350 tons. In tire segment, the ratio of NR to SR is 70:30. The average price of SR declined from Rs 245 per kg in April 2012 to Rs 175 per kg in November of that year. During this period, NR price crashed from Rs 211 to Rs 179.

> The Rubber Board has announced a cash award of Rs 500,000 to those who develop a mechanized rubber tapping device. The Board will take-up research required for its further development and commercialization, in collaboration with the investor. The selected designers will have to present their models and demonstrate them before an expert committee constituted by the Board. Based on demonstration and field trial, a suitable model will be selected for further joint development and commercial application. The Board is showing interest in the on-going efforts to bring about technological innovations in the field of rubber tapping and to address the problems of shortage of skilled tappers.

In order to meet, the gaps between production and consumption (Table 4.6A), the country has to import rubber. Rubber imports by India hit an all-time high in the financial year 2011–2012 at 205,050 tons as against 188,337 tons in 2010–2011: a growth rate of 9%. The 2009–2010 figures were 176,756 tons. Typewise data for import and export of natural rubber shows that total imports have gone up 20.2 thousand tons in1999–2000 to estimated 176.8 thousand tons in 2009–2010 (Tables 4.6B and C).

This is attributed to poor local production and the lower price tag in the global markets. Imports are likely to go up as the SMR 20 grade rubber, which is almost equivalent to the local RSS 4 grade, is much cheaper in the Bangkok and Kuala Lumpur markets.

The falling rupee is making NR imports costlier, but the tire units have no option but to continue shipments, mainly because of tight supplies in the domestic market. Another reason is the wide gap between global and Indian prices. The global price of block rubber SMR 20, which is imported for use in tires, is at around Rs 132.84

Table 4.6A: Imports of natural rubber

(Tons)

Year	Imports
2001–2002	49,769
2002–2003	26,217
2003–2004	44,199
2004–2005	72,835
2005–2006	45,285
2006–2007	89,799
2007–2008	86,394
2008–2009	77,762
2009–2010	176,756
2010–2011	188,387
2011–2012	205,050
2012–2013*	250,000

*Estimates

per kg. This is cheaper because the price of domestic RSS 4 has been rising because of a shortage in the market. On 10th June, 2013, RSS 4 price stood at Rs 173 per kg.

The Industry's Views

The industry is urging the government to lower import duty on raw material such as butyl rubber and hi-tech synthetic rubbers. It also wants the duty on finished products to be kept high. The All India Rubber Industries Association (AIRIA) has asked for reduction in customs duty on NR from the current 20% or Rs 20 a kg to 7.5% or Rs 10 a kg, whichever is lower.

At the current international price of Rs 160 a kg for NR, the import duty of Rs 20 works out to around 12.5%, which is much higher than the import duty on finished rubber products at 10% leading to an inverted duty structure.

The AIRIA has sought permission for duty-free import of 100,000 tons to bridge the demand-supply gap. It has also asked for allowing NR import under the ASEAN free trade agreement (FTA) on reduced customs duty, in line with the concessional tariff on finished products. This is a precondition for providing a level-playing field for local rubber based units. Despite all that imports of natural rubber have increased from 49.7 thousand tons in 2001–2002 to an estimated 250 thousand tons in 2012–2013.

Tables 4.6D to G present summarized the position regarding production imports, exports consumption and stocks of natural, synthetic and reclaimed rubber. Monthly Stocks of synthetic rubber for the period 1998 to 2009–2010 are shown in Table 4.7. They vary from month to month. Stocks of natural rubber with growers and dealers show that they had been increasing from year to year (Table 4.7A). India has been exporting natural rubber to various parts of the world (Table 4.8). Total exports. There is no trend in the quantity exported from year to year. Malaysia is the major importer of Indian natural rubber followed by USA.

Table 4.6B: Typewise import of natural rubber

(Tons)

Type	1999–00	2000–01	2001–02	2002–03	2003–04	2004–05	2005–06	2006–07	2007–08	2008–09	2009–10
RSS grades	11143	3088	27403	11755	11758	20919	6992	33111	26349	27220	73392
Solid block rubber	6012	2647	19516	12751	30539	50720	37433	55075	58595	49130	98574
Latex concentrates (DRC)	2849	3075	2515	1243	1757	979	783	1401	855	1412	4439
Pale latex crepe	209	160	297	378	100	152	77	76	129	–	51
Others	–	–	38	90	45	65	–	136	466	–	300
Total	**20213**	**8970**	**49769**	**26217**	**44199**	**72835**	**45285**	**89799**	**86394**	**77762**	**176756**

Table 4.6C: Typewise export of natural rubber

(Tons)

Type	1999–00	2000–01	2001–02	2002–03	2003–04	2004–05	2005–06	2006–07	2007–08	2008–09	2009–10
RSS grades	5282	12605	6199	43688	38951	24028	35187	31786	28675	14209	2827
Solid block rubber	657	684	714	4637	19807	11558	13396	8454	8240	9283	7999
Latex concentrates (DRC)	49	65	82	6927	17125	10496	24153	16056	22639	20836	13106
Others	–	–	–	59	22	68	1094	249	799	2598	1158
Total	**5988**	**13354**	**6995**	**55311**	**75905**	**46150**	**73830**	**56545**	**60353**	**46926**	**25090**

Table 4.6D: Production, import, export and consumption of natural and synthetic rubber

(Tons)

Year	Production			Import			Export	Consumption		
	Natural	Synthetic	Total	Natural	Synthetic	Total	Natural	Natural	Synthetic	Total
1995–96	506910	68223	575133	51635	71735	123370	1130	525465	134085	659550
1996–97	549425	64563	613988	19770	91050	110820	1598	561765	142810	704575
1997–98	583830	71993	655823	32070	86389	118459	1415	571820	160915	732735
1998–99	605045	67590	672635	29534	97548	127082	1840	591545	156395	747940
1999–00	622265	60293	682558	20213	104842	125055	5989	628110	167220	795330
2000–01	630405	65460	695865	8970	106923	115893	13356	631475	170670	802145
2001–02	631400	69653	701053	49769	111572	161341	6995	638210	174530	812740
2002–03	649435	80401	729836	26217	129902	156119	55311	695425	194850	890275
2003–04	711650	89240	800890	44199	104733	148932	75905	719600	210190	929790
2004–05	749665	93854	843519	72835	113095	185930	46150	755405	224650	980055
2005–06	802625	97638	900263	45285	132118	177403	73830	801110	237495	1038605
2006–07	852895	99513	952408	89799	171998	261797	56545	820305	270830	1091135
2007–08	825345	106286	931631	86394	195705	282099	60353	861455	297155	1158610
2008–09	864500	96739	961239	77762	190630	268392	46926	871720	292950	1164670
2009–10	831400	106743	938143	176756	250210	426966	25090	930565	347710	1278275

Table 4.6E: Production, import, export, consumption and stock of natural rubber

(Tons)

Year	Production	Annual growth rate	Import	Total supply	Export	Consumption	Annual growth rate	Total demand	Excess (+)/ Deficiency (−) compared with demand	Stock at the end of the period*
1996–97	549425	8.39	19770	569195	1598	561765	6.91	563363	+ 5832	107310
1997–98	583830	6.26	32070	615900	1415	571820	1.79	573235	+ 42665	147300
1998–99	605045	3.63	29534	634579	1840	591545	3.45	593385	+ 41194	187965
1999–00	622265	2.85	20213	642478	5989	628110	6.18	634099	+ 8379	192570
2000–01	630405	1.31	8970	639375	13356	631475	0.54	644831	− 5456	183900
2001–02	631400	0.16	49769	681169	6995	638210	1.07	645205	+35964	193070
2002–03	649435	2.86	26217	675652	55311	695425	8.96	750736	−75084	117995
2003–04	711650	9.58	44199	755849	75905	719600	3.48	795505	−39656	85190
2004–05	749665	5.34	72835	822500	46150	755405	4.98	801555	+20945	110385
2005–06	802625	7.06	45285	847910	73830	801110	6.05	874940	−27030	93020
2006–07	852895	6.26	89799	942694	56545	820305	2.40	876850	+65844	165290
2007–08	825345	−3.23	86394	911739	60353	861455	5.02	921808	−10069	164280
2008–09	864500	4.74	77762	942262	46926	871720	1.19	918646	+23616	196230
2009–10	831400	−3.83	176756	1008156	25090	930565	6.75	955655	+52501	253975

* Including year end adjustment.

Table 4.6F: Production, import, consumption and stock of synthetic rubber

(Tons)

Year	Production	Import	Total	Consumption	Excess(+)/ deficiency (–) compared with demand	Stock at the end of the period
1991–92	57726	39210	96936	105650	– 8714	11470
1992–93	57892	47362	105254	108690	– 3436	12390
1993–94	49633	64338	113971	113395	+ 576	14665
1994–95	63681	73860	137541	122710	+ 14831	20285
1995–96	68223	71735	139958	134085	+ 5873	18760
1996–97	64563	91050	155613	142810	+ 12803	31560
1997–98	71993	86389	158382	160915	– 2533	29030
1998–99	67590	97548	165138	156395	+ 8743	42410
1999–00	60293	104842	165135	167220	– 2085	43505
2000–01	65460	106923	172383	170670	+ 1713	45220
2001–02	69653	111572	181225	174530	+ 6695	51930
2002–03	80401	129902	210303	194850	+ 15453	67385
2003–04	89240	104733	193973	210190	– 16217	51170
2004–05	93854	113095	206949	224650	– 17701	33470
2005–06	97638	132118	229756	237495	– 7739	25730
2006–07	99513	171998	271511	270830	+ 681	26410
2007–08	106286	195705	301991	297155	+4836	31250
2008–09	96739	190630	287369	292950	–5581	25670
2009–10	106743	250210	356953	347710	+9243	34910

Future of Rubber in India

Futures trading in Rubber flagged off on 15 March 2003 for the very first time in India via National Multi-Commodity Exchange (NMCE) of India Ltd. Ahmedabad, and the product soon became a role model as a truly efficient and liquid market. If futures are meant for the price discovery and price risk management for real hedgers, rubber futures should be considered as a great success. NMCE has provided an unbiased credible online platform to all the participants giving equal opportunities of the fair and transparent trade. Rubber futures have been used by the rubber industry whose offices are largely located in the south. It includes the traders, exporters, user industry, manufacturers, etc.

NMCE has CWC warehouses at Kottayam, Aluva, Ernakulam, Kakkanad, Kakkanchery, Kozhikode, Trichur, Palakkadu, etc in South were Rubber is stored. NMCE has facilitated a delivery of 101,625 tons of rubber up to July 2012 since its inception. After a detailed cost study by the Costing Branch of Finance Ministry, in 1998 GoI announced Rs 35 a kg, to a large extent, as the benchmark price.

But, rubber historical prices show that 1998–1999 to May 2002 price of RSS 4 remained lower than Rs 3,500 per quintal. Since rubber futures trading started in

Table 4.6G: Production, consumption and export of reclaimed rubber

(Tons)

Year	Production*	Consumption	Export
1990–91	53629	52500	985
1991–92	54185	54015	573
1992–93	61490	62470	379
1993–94	62780	63110	810
1994–95	64425	64655	1928
1995–96	65780	65775	2078
1996–97	66670	66585	3306
1997–98	69840	70085	2271
1998–99	63980	63095	1252
1999–00	64080	63450	2184
2000–01	62120	62260	3349
2001–02	63550	63875	5766
2002–03	67385	67320	7625
2003–04	70990	70460	9462
2004–05	73060	72905	12313
2005–06	76645	76535	18270
2006–07	78495	78435	19100
2007–08	89250	83165	29675
2008–09	91350	86030	32710
2009–10	100767	92250	36477

*Indigenous purchase by manufacturers.

India, it has never gone below this scale, and also absurd volatility in its prices has now become unusual. This gives a very relevant example of market participation by the actual rubber growers who are now benefited by the futures trading mechanism and have consistently managed to gain a price that is approximately 94% higher than the cost price of rubber. The rubber growers of Kerala have heaved a sigh of relief, by getting consistently good prices due to the efficient price discovery and price dissemination contributed by futures trading on the NMCE.

RUBBER BOARD

The Rubber Board is a statutory body constituted by the GoI, under the Rubber Act 1947, for the overall development of the rubber industry in the country.

Genesis of the Rubber Board

Commercial cultivation of natural rubber was introduced in India by the British, although the experimental efforts to grow rubber on a commercial scale in India were initiated as early as 1873 at the Botanical Gardens, Calcutta. The first commercial *Hevea* plantations in India were established at Thattekadu in 1902. The

Table 4.7: Stock of synthetic rubber at the end of each month

(Tons)

Month	1998-99	1999-00	2000-01	2001-02	2002-03	2003-04	2004-05	2005-06	2006-07	2007-08	2008-09	2009-10
April	29420	41020	44500	45180	51395	66840	50120	30770	24620	25770	33030	24590
May	31980	39350	44180	43440	52900	64870	47560	27720	24615	26980	37550	26700
June	31630	39980	46875	42070	54445	60780	44775	25940	25180	27155	42970	29130
July	33895	40920	47900	44435	57125	58890	43905	22840	23480	26345	44070	30195
August	36390	40530	47210	46255	60995	55930	43290	22860	22000	27570	43650	32600
September	34675	40820	47530	46245	63320	55510	42570	23590	24950	27550	40240	33170
October	34240	37805	47010	46710	67410	53820	41490	23960	26440	27195	38480	34820
November	36640	37920	46180	47775	68665	51580	40330	24780	27670	25780	35420	36165
December	37960	40495	45655	48225	68520	52210	39340	23980	27010	26435	37725	37415
January	38150	39690	47040	49010	68995	52470	38110	24360	25460	28190	35020	36555
February	40440	39785	46240	49840	65625	52570	34230	24665	25700	28220	27630	35490
March	42410	43505	45220	51930	67385	51170	33470	25730	26410	31250	25670	34910

Table 4.7A: Stock of natural rubber with growers, dealers and manufacturers at the end of each month

(*Tons*)

Month	2007-08			2008-09			2009-10		
	G & D	M	T	G & D	M	T	G & D	M	T
April	91425	69175	160600	84680	68710	153390	142350	41115	183465
May	81315	64540	145855	82990	66360	149350	139175	44465	183640
June	61295	62415	123710	80800	55315	136115	137925	49145	187070
July	43040	48195	91235	70875	44660	115535	138805	49290	188095
August	40790	41820	82610	78060	36270	114330	142692	52958	195650
September	40405	41005	81410	93420	34055	127475	155982	53258	209240
October	63815	40445	104260	110015	39495	149510	172505	55760	228265
November	98580	49770	148350	130005	44555	174560	191275	53595	244870
December	128740	62115	190855	168730	38960	207690	214075	55665	269740
January	149415	75925	225340	199360	40220	239580	228312	63218	291530
February	118695	79365	198060	174295	42485	216780	209615	64965	274580
March	88485	75795	164280	157845	38385	196230	185244	68731	253975

Note: G - Growers, D - Dealers & Processors, M - Manufacturers, T - Total. Stock with manufacturers includes stock in transit as well as imported rubber.

Table 4.8: Country-wise export of natural rubber

(Quantity in tons and value in '000 Rs)

Country	2004-05		2005-06		2006-07		2007-08		2008-09		2009-10	
	Quantity	Value	Quantity	Value	Quantity	Value	Quantity	Value	Quantity	Value	Quantity	Value
China	16485	828886	26521	1691729	16592	1654157	20222	1807846	5518	608156	1747	182549
Sri Lanka	10246	515956	7556	496359	4760	418513	2789	227446	1982	226020	1182	140372
Malaysia	4388	224289	6363	481289	10412	1097676	12092	1117024	13510	1588812	6925	715632
Germany	2779	103511	5680	258628	2658	179704	2480	157526	1296	96202	1276	116776
Belgium	212	7844	2501	194920	2324	148944	2873	182442	2046	150472	876	72091
Turkey	1858	85344	2355	127893	1751	103398	1178	85213	902	89687	502	38790
UK	331	12338	2098	121510	1238	79527	1177	71048	749	59248	183	13774
USA	–	–	1954	97795	1567	125413	4888	307633	8289	579655	3076	306340
Spain	2153	82615	1634	91101	1204	95540	1052	65774	1106	81263	384	35045
Korea	301	16336	1360	83006	608	66451	776	77131	1101	114652	75	4635
Nepal	1585	83481	1201	91819	656	67489	685	60570	983	104909	309	25211
Others	5812	292800	14607	846863	12775	1100565	10141	783426	9444	802969	8555	854797
Total	**46150**	**2253400**	**73830**	**4582912**	**56545**	**5137377**	**60353**	**4943079**	**46926**	**4502045**	**25090**	**2506012**

Others include Indonesia, UAE, Egypt, Netherlands, Singapore, Iran, Ukraine, Italy, Poland, Brazil, Bulgaria, Vietnam, etc.

importance of rubber production in India from strategic and security reasons had been realized by the government during the Second World War period. The rubber growers in India were encouraged to produce the maximum rubber required for the use during war. After the war, there were growing demands from the growers for setting up a permanent organization to look after the interests of the industry. Thereupon the government setup an ad-hoc committee in 1945 to study the situation and to make appropriate recommendation. On the recommendation of this ad-hoc committee, the government passed the Rubber (Production and Marketing) Act, 1947, on 18th April 1947, and the "Indian Rubber Board" was constituted forthwith. The Rubber Production and Marketing (Amendment) Act, 1954 amended the name of the Board as "The Rubber Board".

Legislative Enactments on Rubber

As noted above, a consideration of the post war natural rubber scenario prompted the Government of India to pass the Rubber (Production and Marketing) Act, 1947 to provide for the overall promotion and development of the sector under its guidance and control. As envisaged in the Act, the Indian Rubber Board was set up as the statutory organization responsible for assisting the government in implementation of the various provisions of the Act. The Act which came into force on April 18, 1947 has since undergone many amendments.

The Rubber production and Marketing (Amendment) Act of 1954 which took effect on August 1, 1954 made some important changes in the constitution of the Board now renamed as The Rubber Board. It clearly defined the role of the Board in the development of the industry and in formulating and implementing necessary research and development programs. This was followed by notification of the Rubber Rules, 1955 laying down guidelines for the Board to follow in carrying out the purposes of the Act. The Rules have been subjected to need based amendments from time to time. The Rubber (Amendment) Act of 1960 made certain alterations in the rate and procedure of collection of rubber. The Rubber (Amendment) Act of 1982 provided for the Central Government to appoint a part time or whole time Chairman for the Board and, if necessary, an Executive Director for exercising such powers and performing such duties as may be prescribed or delegated to him by the Chairman. The 1994 Amendment refixed the maximum rate that can be levied on rubber.

The Rubber Act, 1947

An Act to provide for the development under the control of the union of the rubber industry whereas it is expedient to provide for the development under the control of the union of the rubber industry is hereby enacted as follows:

Short title and extent:

1. This Act may be called The Rubber Act, 1947.
2. It extends to the whole of India except the State of Jammu and Kashmir.

The Rubber Rules, 1955: (Ministry of Commerce and Industry) (Notification) (Rubber Control) New Delhi, the 1st August 1955.

S.R.O 1662: In exercise of the powers conferred by Section 25 of the Rubber Act, 1947 (XXIV of 1947), and in supersession of the Rubber (Production and Marketing) Rules, 1947, the Central Government hereby makes the following rules (Published in the Gazette of India (Extraordinary) Part II, Section 3, Page 1613, dated 1st August, 1955).

Functions of the Rubber Board

The functions of the Board as defined under the Act are:

1. To promote by such measures as it thinks fit the development of the rubber industry.
2. Without prejudice to the generality of the foregoing provision the measures referred to therein may provide for:
   a. Undertaking, assisting or encouraging scientific, technological or economic research.
   b. Training students in improved methods of planting, cultivation, manuring and spraying.
   c. The supply of technical advice to rubber growers
   d. Improving the marketing of rubber.
   e. The collection of statistics from owners of estates, dealers and manufacturers.
   f. Securing better working conditions and the provision and improvement of amenities and incentives to workers.
   g. Carrying out any other duties which may be vested with the board as per rules made under this act.
3. It shall also be the duty of the Board:
   a. To advise the Central Government on all matters relating to the development of the rubber industry, including the import and export of rubber.
   b. To advise the Central Government with regard to participation in any international conference or scheme relating to rubber.
   c. To submit to the Central Government and such other authorities as may be prescribed, half yearly reports on its activities and the working of this Act
   d. To prepare and furnish such other reports relating to the rubber industry as may be required by the Central Government from time to time.

Constitution

The Rubber Board functions under the Ministry of Commerce and Industry of the Government of India. The Board has a Chairman appointed by the Central Government. He is the principal executive officer responsible for the proper functioning of the Board and implementation of its decisions and discharge of its duties under the Rubber Act.

There are 25 other members of the Board consisting of:

1. Two members to represent the State of Tamil Nadu. One of them shall be a person representing rubber producing interest.
2. Eight members to represent the State of Kerala. Six of them shall be representing the rubber producing interest, three of such being persons representing the small growers.
3. Ten members to be nominated by the Central Government, two of whom shall represent the manufacturers and four labors.
4. Three members of parliament two of whom shall be elected by the House of the People and one by the Council of States.
5. The Rubber Production Commissioner of the Rubber Board (ex-officio).
6. The Executive Director (ex-officio).

One of the members is elected as Vice-Chairman on an annual basis. The Board meets periodically for transacting business. The committees are formed to scrutinize various matters and make recommendation to the Board. Besides the Executive Committee and the Research and Development Committee (statutory committees) the Board has five other committees, viz.

1. Planting Committee
2. Statistics and Import/Export Committee
3. Market Development Committee
4. Labor Welfare Committee
5. Staff Affairs Committee.

Organizational Setup and Control

The Chairman who is the administrative head of the Board exercises control over all the departments. The activities of the Board are classified under nine departments: Administration, Finance and Accounts (F and A), Rubber Production (RP), Research (RRII), Processing and Product Development (P and PD), Statistics and Planning (S and P), Training, Licensing and Excise Duty (L and ED) and Market Promotion.

Publicity and Public Relations (P and PR) Division, Vigilance Division and Internal Audit Division although grouped under Administration and Finance and Accounts Department, for general purposes, function directly under the Chairman.

The Board has its headquarters complex located at Kottayam in Kerala State. The Chairman's Office together with the central offices of Administration, Finance & Accounts, Rubber Production, Statistics and Planning and Licensing and Excise Duty departments function in own building in the municipal town of Kottayam. The Rubber Research Institute of India (RRII) the Research Department of the Board, is situated 7 km eastwards in the suburban village of Puthuppally. The Institute is also housed in Board's own building which is set amidst a 28 hectare Rubber Experiment Station. The Training Department of the Board is also housed on an adjacent plot of land in a picturesque building.

Departments and Divisions

- Rubber Production Department
- Rubber Research Institute of India
- Processing and Product Development Department
- Training Department
- Administration Department
- Finance and Accounts Department
- Licensing and Excise Duty Department
- Statistics and Planning Department
- Market Promotion Department.

WORLD SITUATION

World area under rubber during 1961 was 3.9 million hectares producing 2.1 million tons of rubber. Corresponding figures for 2007 are 8.6 million hectares and 10.2 million tons (Table 4.9). Of the top 20 producers, Thailand produced 3.3 million tons in 2011, being followed by Thailand (3.3 million), Indonesia (3.1 million) and Malaysia (10.0 million), India occupies the fifth position with 8.9 million tons

(Table 4.9A). Detailed data series for all the countries producing rubber is shown in Table 4.9B. This includes countries like Dominican Republic which produced just 13 tons and Bangladesh me thousand tons. With saturation in rubber consumption in western countries and the shift in consumption of rubber to the Asia-Pacific region, the focal point for development in this decade will be India. The industry is expected to grow at over 8% per annum. There exists tremendous scope for expansion and development in coming years, provided basic raw materials, particularly natural and synthetic rubber, are made available in adequate quantity at reasonable prices.

In fact, India and China are the only two countries in the world with the capacity to consume the entire indigenous production of natural rubber, and thereby obviate the compulsion and over-dependence on exports of surplus quantity of natural rubber. Distribution of area into small holdings and Estates for some of the selected countries is shown in Tables 4.9C and D.

Table 4.9: Area and production of natural rubber in India and world

Area (hectares); Production (tons)

	India			World		
Year	Area		Production	Area		Production
2007	450,000	F	819,000	8,567,576 A		10,287,941 A
2006	450,000		852,895	8,522,039 A		10,185,619 A
2005	447,000		802,625	8,808,077 A		9,381,093 A
2004	440,000		749,665	8,130,629 A		9,153,461 A
2003	428,000		711,650	8,056,128 A		8,187,288 A
2002	408,000		649,435	7,847,340 A		7,590,006 A
2001	401,000		631,000	7,765,881 A		7,330,965 A
2000	400,000		630,000	7,563,460 A		7,040,376 A
1999	395,000		622,000	7,522,515 A		6,736,299 A
1998	387,000		605,000	7,460,540 A		6,644,476 A
1997	377,000		550,000	7,348,371 A		6,642,776 A
1996	366,000		507,000	7,237,095 A		6,535,677 A
1995	356,000		472,000	7,211,919 A		6,326,517 A
1994	339,000		394,000	6,974,977 A		6,048,608 A
1993	331,000		367,000	6,975,105 A		5,793,058 A
1992	323,000		366,700	6,850,704 A		5,632,954 A
1991	306,400		329,600	6,747,889 A		5,403,982 A
1990	289,100		297,300	6,655,790 A		5,225,425 A
1989	266,100		259,200	6,601,438 A		5,143,902 A

Table 4.9: Area and production of natural rubber in India and world *(Contd.)*

Area (hectares); Production (tons)

Year	India Area		India Production	World Area		World Production	
1988	249,100		235,200	6,430,494	A	5,119,374	A
1987	237,100		219,500	6,340,552	A	4,824,479	A
1986	223,300		200,500	6,130,847	A	4,616,828	A
1985	210,500		186,500	6,049,333	A	4,247,161	A
1984	204,500		175,300	5,663,605	A	4,100,807	A
1983	199,700		165,900	5,588,449	A	4,035,568	A
1982	196,200		152,900	5,553,618	A	3,763,673	A
1981	194,200		153,100	5,412,471	A	3,754,740	A
1980	192,500		148,400	5,411,787	A	3,748,108	A
1979	190,300		135,400	5,623,976	A	3,800,000	A
1978	191,000		147,000	5,433,481	A	3,674,133	A
1977	186,000		149,600	5,364,701	A	3,606,015	A
1976	178,000		137,800	5,393,247	A	3,576,326	A
1975	171,000		130,100	5,187,221	A	3,269,255	A
1974	166,000		125,200	5,289,063	A	3,361,652	A
1973	155,000		112,400	5,305,485	A	3,404,407	A
1972	149,000		101,200	4,995,756	A	3,058,785	A
1971	141,000		92,200	4,921,659	A	3,036,401	A
1970	138,000	F	89,905	4,621,270	A	2,986,300	A
1969	120,000	F	79,951	4,654,764	A	2,919,332	A
1968	110,000	F	68,844	4,336,252	A	2,671,760	A
1967	102,000	F	62,502	4,280,446	A	2,473,498	A
1966	88,000	F	53,195	4,297,109	A	2,471,089	A
1965	82,000	F	49,387	4,396,958	A	2,383,817	A
1964	74,000	F	44,248	4,205,949	A	2,292,485	A
1963	60,000	F	37,200	4,175,782	A	2,223,002	A
1962	52,000	F	31,357	4,065,498	A	2,159,128	A
1961	45,000	F	26,992	3,879,860	A	2,120,070	A

A, May include official, semi-official or estimated data.
F, FAO estimate.

Table 4.9A: Top rank countries of natural rubber, 2011

Rank	Country	Production (Int. $1,000)	Flag	Production (MT)	Flag
1	Thailand	3,830,585	*	3,348,897	
2	Indonesia	3,532,620	*	3,088,400	
3	Malaysia	1,140,029	*	996,673	Im
4	India	1,019,550	*	891,344	Im
5	Viet Nam	903,212	*	789,635	
6	China, mainland	858,850	*	750,852	
7	Côte d'Ivoire	273,052	*	238,717	
8	Brazil	188,158	*	164,498	
9	Sri Lanka	180,952	*	158,198	
10	Myanmar	171,148	*	149627	
11	Nigeria	164,140	*	143,500	F
12	Philippines	160,708	*	140,500	*
13	Guatemala	118,312	*	103,435	Im
14	Liberia	72,061	*	63,000	F
15	Cameroon	63,482	*	55,500	F
16	Cambodia	49,723	*	43,471	Im
17	Mexico	43,743	*	38,243	
18	Ghana	23,088	*	20,185	
19	Ecuador	22,493	*	19,665	Im
20	Bolivia (Plurinational State of)	20,004	*	17,489	Im

*:   Unofficial figure
[ ]:   Official data
F: FAO estimate
Im: FAO data based on imputation methodology.

Top production—natural rubber, 2011

Table 4.9B: World rubber statistics area under rubber in main producing countries

(In thousand hectares)

Country	End of	Holdings	Estates	Total
Indonesia	2009	NA	NA	3435
Thailand	2009	NA	NA	2756
Malaysia	2009	1177	60	1237
China	2008	NA	NA	932
India	2009	620	67	687
Vietnam	2009	325	349	674
Myanmar	2006	NA	NA	295
Nigeria	2009	112	61	173
Brazil	2009	NA	NA	159
Cote d'Ivoire	2009	112	50	162
Sri Lanka	2009	NA	NA	124
Liberia	1999	49	60	109
Philippines	2008	NA	NA	123
Cameroon	2005	4	36	40
D.R. of Congo	1999	10	25	35

NA: Not available.
Note: Estate area refers to holdings of 40 hectares and over except for India where it refers to holdings of over 20 hectares.
Source: Rubber Statistical Bulletin of the International Rubber Study Group.

Table 4.9C: Production of rubber

(Tons)

Countries	1994–1996	1999–2001	2003–2005	2006	2007	2008	2009
Bangladesh	2,733	3,667	5,233	5,300	5,300	5,300	
Brazil	47,790	81,967	98,770	105,434	113,297	120,905	
Cambodia	37,476	42,076	26,291	21,389	17,923	31,676	
Cameroon	53,194	56,427	47,297	46,000	52,000	52,000	52,000
China	400,159	483,000	551,134	538,000	588,380	547,861	565,000
Côte d'Ivoire	75,169	123,394	143,789	130,000	188,532	188,532	
Guatemala	29,180	42,514	52,274	50,500	70,000	70,000	
India	457,667	627,667	754,647	831,000	819,000	819,000	
Indonesia	1,523,556	1,571,083	2,043,020	2,350,000	2,755,172	2,921,872	
Malaysia	1,090,633	859,633	1,093,433	1,283,600	1,199,600	1,072,400	857,019
Mexico	46,305	22,167	26,332	24,221	27,709	27,709	
Myanmar	23,167	28,400	42,700	43,000	45,000	45,000	
Nigeria	120,000	107,333	142,000	142,500	143,000	143,000	
Philippines	60,800	75,933	238,310	351,556	404,072	411,044	390,962
Sri Lanka	108,169	90,153	97,020	109,140	117,550	129,240	136,000
Thailand	2,056,648	2,379,180	2,948,629	3,071,218	3,022,324	3,166,910	3,090,280
Vietnam	131,990	284,033	421,367	546,100	605,800	659,600	
World	6,327,380	7,035,880	8,907,224	9,816,211	10,353,292	10,569,082	10,280,888

Table 4.9D: Area under rubber in main producing countries

(In thousand hectares)

Territory	Holding			
	End of	S	Estates	Total
Thailand	2000	1,895	85	1,980
Malaysia	2000	1,245	186	1,431
Sri Lanka	2000	101	57	158
Indonesia	2000	2,823	549	3,372
China	1998	NA	NA	NA
India	2000	496	67	563
Brazil	1998	100	80	180
Nigeria	1999	90	60	150
Liberia	1999	49	60	109
Vietnam	1997	35	240	275
D.R. of Congo	1999	10	25	35
Philippines	1999	–	92	92
Myanmar	1995	59	46	105
Cote d' Ivoire	1998	26	70	96
Cameroon	1997	2	40	42

NA: Not available.

Global Trends

Natural rubber production is confined to developing countries, particularly Asia. The world natural rubber output increased from 6.8 million tons in 1998 to 9.8 million tons in 2007. There was a slight decline recently, production being 9.6 million tons in 2009 (Table 4.10). In terms of country wise share in the world production, Thailand accounted for 30.3% followed by Indonesia at 28.4%, Malaysia at 10.8%, India at 8.8% and Vietnam at 6.6% at the end of 2008.

Thus, Thailand, Indonesia and Malaysia account for around 70% of world rubber production and have formed the International Rubber Consortium (IRC). These three countries produced 7 million tons of rubber in 2007, of which they exported 5.55 million tons. Thailand, world's largest producer plans to raise rubber production from the estimated 3.16 million tons in 2009 to 3.3 million tons in 2010. China is the largest consumer, accounting for 3.6% of the total global consumption, followed by USA at 10.9%, India at 9.1%, Japan at 8.9% and Malaysia at 4.8%. Rubber plantations give yield only after 6 years of being planted and are productive for about 25 years. As expected, natural rubber producing regions—Asia-Pacific and Africa—hold the trade surplus, while all other regions hold the trade deficit. For synthetic rubber, traditionally North America and Europe provide the major trade surplus while Asia-Pacific is the major deficit region. However, increasingly Asia-Pacific has started to turn the situation around.

As for the production of synthetic rubber, the top position was held by USA until 2007, China has now overtaken as the top producer. Japan comes next. India is more or less at the bottom with around 90 thousand tons (Tables 4.10A and B).

Table 4.10: Production of natural rubber in main producing countries

(In thousand tons)

Country	1998	1999	2000	2001	2002	2003	2004	2005	2006	2007	2008	2009
Thailand	2,076	2,155	2,346	2,320	2,615	2,876	2,984	2,937	3,137	3,056	3,090	3,164
Indonesia	1,714	1,599	1,501	1,607	1,630	1,792	2,066	2,271	2,637	2,755	2,751	2,440
Malaysia	886	769	928	882	890	986	1169	1126	1,284	1,200	1,072	856
India	591	620	629	632	641	708	743	772	853	811	881	820
Vietnam	218	262	291	313	331	364	419	482	555	606	660	724
China	450	460	445	478	527	565	573	510	533	590	560	637
Sri Lanka	96	97	88	86	91	92	95	104	109	118	129	137
Brazil	70	87	88	88	89	94	101	107	108	116	123	104
Philippines	68	65	67	71	76	84	80	79	75	93	95	87
Liberia	75	100	105	107	109	107	115	111	101	106	81	77
Cambodia	39	46	42	42	43	32	34	30	32	33	37	45
Nigeria	65	58	55	45	42	38	45	40	41	42	49	45
Others*	472	552	179	581	253	282	322	335	326	275	508	481
World	6,820	6,870	6,764	7,252	7,337	8,020	8,746	8,904	9,791	9,801	10,036	9,617

Italics: estimated, *: countries not reported separately.
Source: "Rubber Statistical Bulletin" of the International Rubber Study Group.

Future Trend

In India, the demand-supply gap for natural rubber (NR) is widening. It may go up to 150,000 tons in 2013–2014. The country is forced to depend on imports. NR is the major raw material for Indian rubber industries, accounting for 35–45% of raw material cost. The global rubber shortage may widen to one million tons by 2020 as demand from tire makers will boost consumption to about 15.4 million tons.

Asia is now the focus of growth in the rubber industry. The entire world's natural rubber is grown in this region (Thailand, Indonesia, India, Malaysia, Sri Lanka, etc.) While European Union and the US have almost become a saturated market for the rubber industry, all the action is shifting to Asia. The largest investments in new synthetic rubber plants are coming up here. Production of all auto majors is also shifting to Asia. In terms of consumption, Asia's share in the world auto market is also growing.

Highest growth and availability of technically trained manpower for the rubber industry is in this region. Low demand growth for end products, high labor costs, very strict environmental norms and nonavailability of natural rubber in the backyard are propelling the world's major input suppliers for the rubber industry to look toward Asia.

With saturation in rubber consumption in western countries and the shift in consumption of rubber to the Asia-Pacific region, the focal point for development in this decade will be India. The industry is expected to grow at over 8% per annum. There exists tremendous scope for expansion and development in coming years, provided basic raw materials, particularly natural and synthetic rubber, are made available in adequate quantity at reasonable prices.

Table 4.10A: Production of synthetic rubber in main producing countries

(In thousand tons)

Country	1998	1999	2000	2001	2002	2003	2004	2005	2006	2007	2008	2009
USA	2,600	2,354	2,397	2,062	2,164	2,270	2,325	2,366	2,606	2,697	2,314	1,962
China	589	754	836	1,052	1,133	1,272	1,478	1,632	1,845	2,215	2,325	2,856
Japan	1,520	1,577	1,592	1,466	1,522	1,577	1,616	1,627	1,607	1,655	1,651	1,303
Russian Federation	621	737	837	919	919	1,070	1,116	1,146	1,219	1,210	1,173	971
Rep. of Korea	547	655	678	663	685	710	720	770	848	1,010	970	1,149
Germany	619	720	849	828	869	888	905	855	865	803	791	655
France	606	592	669	672	681	718	776	655	664	655	566	465
Taiwan	472	495	465	480	523	529	545	575	600	600	552	520
Brazil	310	363	373	342	384	407	429	416	418	425	392	385
U.K.	252	283	286	333	337	327	351	344	305	318	302	248
Italy	290	279	285	274	250	244	235	233	235	235	220	200
Mexico	173	171	187	173	182	180	188	182	186	204	198	164
Netherlands	184	185	200	188	176	176	180	186	192	194	177	166
Poland	94	97	102	83	82	85	104	104	120	123	114	112
India	66	66	60	69	78	86	95	96	101	104	99	104
Canada	191	195	186	146	136	74	84	64	79	93	96	74
Belgium	95	100	104	104	104	104	108	106	107	107	94	104
Others*	651	717	713	629	652	624	706	743	656	740	709	649
World	9,880	10,340	10,819	10,483	10,877	11,341	11,961	12,100	12,653	13,388	12,743	12,087

Italics: estimated, *: countries not reported separately.
Source: "Rubber Statistical Bulletin" of the International Rubber Study Group.

Table 4.10B: Country-wise production of natural rubber

(Tons)

Country	2009	2010*	Change (%)
Thailand	3,164,000	3,240,000	2.4
Indonesia	2,440,000	2,592,000	6.2
Malaysia	857,000	1,000,000	16.7
India	820,000	895,000	9.1
Vietnam	724,000	770,000	6.4
China	646,000	680,000	5.3
Sri Lanka	137,000	142,000	3.7
Cambodia	34,000	49,000	43.9
Total	**8,822,000**	**9,369,000**	**6.2**

* Estimated.

In fact, India and China are the only two countries in the world with the capacity to consume the entire indigenous production of natural rubber, and thereby obviate the compulsion and over-dependence on exports of surplus quantity of natural rubber. Automotive sectors of China and India will continue to support demand. Strong vehicle output will definitely lead to strong tire sales, especially for replacement as 75% of tires are sold to the replacement markets. Global tire demand is expanding at a faster pace than production, led by growth in China, as vehicle sales are increasing.

World Consumption

China being the fastest growing economy of the world is also the world's largest natural rubber consuming country. At 3,460 thousand tons it consumes 36.8 of the rubber world over. USA is the second largest consumer of rubber at 1,041 thousand tons, followed by India and Japan (Table 4.11). Other major consuming countries include Malaysia, Korea and Indonesia.

With regard the consumption of synthetic rubber, it is again China which is the leader followed by USA, for behind, consumption of India is less than 3% (Table 4.11A). Country-wise imports of natural rubber (Table 4.12) show that China leads in the world followed by USA and Japan. As regards exports (Tables 4.12A and B), Thailand is the leader, followed by Indonesia and Malaysia.

Table 4.11: Consumption of natural rubber in main consuming countries

(In thousand tons)

Country	1998	1999	2000	2001	2002	2003	2004	2005	2006	2007	2008	2009
China	839	852	1,080	1,330	1,395	1,538	2,000	2,266	2,743	2,812	2,940	3,460
USA	1,157	1,116	1,195	974	1,111	1,079	1,144	1,159	1,003	1,018	1,041	687
India	580	619	638	631	680	717	745	789	815	851	881	905
Japan	707	734	752	729	749	784	815	857	874	887	878	636
Malaysia	334	344	364	401	408	421	403	387	383	450	469	470
Indonesia	97	116	139	142	145	156	196	221	355	391	414	422
Thailand	186	227	243	253	278	299	319	335	321	374	398	399
Rep. of Korea	283	333	332	332	326	333	352	370	364	377	358	330
Brazil	185	184	227	216	233	256	285	302	294	345	357	254
Germany	247	226	250	246	247	258	242	259	269	282	247	171
France	223	240	270	282	226	218	230	230	220	220	200	109
Spain	157	153	163	176	181	188	192	186	189	195	178	124
Canada	148	140	148	131	155	146	146	156	145	138	138	103
Italy	146	134	139	137	134	138	151	154	148	144	134	90
Taiwan	97	105	92	90	107	115	120	114	100	115	97	90
UK	139	127	123	98	76	91	86	82	68	91	77	43
Russian Fed.	6	15	36	36	19	32	29	34	41	42	39	25
Others*	1,029	975	1,122	1,129	1,084	1,183	1,263	1,299	1,345	1,412	1,327	1,072
World	6,560	6,640	7,313	7,333	7,554	7,952	8,718	9,200	9,677	10,144	10,173	9,390

* Countries not reported separately.
Source: "Rubber Statistical Bulletin" of the International Rubber Study Group.

Table 4.11A: Consumption of synthetic rubber in main consuming countries

(In thousand tons)

Country	1998	1999	2000	2001	2002	2003	2004	2005	2006	2007	2008	2009
China	1,000	1,285	1,455	1,575	1,941	2,193	2,467	2,597	3,064	3,587	3,479	4,266
USA	2,354	2,218	2190	1,840	1,895	1,926	1,907	2,002	2,001	1,929	1,734	1,448
Japan	1,116	1,133	1,138	1,085	1,096	1,111	1,146	1,156	1,171	1,162	1,138	832
Brazil	300	309	357	334	344	352	431	405	425	477	481	445
Germany	582	565	632	613	612	615	625	635	635	599	586	450
Russian Federation	358	436	539	575	551	619	597	568	572	597	533	374
Rep. of Korea	277	394	382	373	365	352	349	344	364	347	329	278
France	451	434	482	465	469	493	420	355	311	316	316	237
India	155	164	171	172	192	203	223	233	264	290	294	321
Spain	229	242	269	262	295	294	303	254	262	258	259	182
Italy	275	287	291	275	261	251	255	242	252	255	238	170
Taiwan	272	263	262	232	282	290	294	280	303	282	212	175
Canada	238	239	233	228	228	225	232	226	216	200	164	158
Mexico	165	169	160	142	132	140	146	145	154	162	149	132
UK	177	189	188	167	210	204	214	222	201	169	149	133
Others*	1,921	1,873	2,015	1,915	2,004	2,080	2,231	2,236	2,496	2,634	2,542	2,153
World	9,870	10,200	10,764	10,253	10,877	11,348	11,840	11,900	12,691	13,264	12,603	11,754

* Countries not reported separately.
Source: "Rubber Statistical Bulletin" of the International Rubber Study Group.

Picture regarding world production, consumption and stocks of both natural and synthetic rubber (Table 4.13) show that synthetic rubber has been keeping higher stock, although consumption of synthetic rubber has always been higher than that of natural.

Forecasts made by the experts for the coming few years regarding rubber consumption are presented in Tables 4.14; 4.14A and B.

Rubber Takes Root in New Regions on Record Prices

Supply shortage and record prices have prodded planters to expand rubber acreage. Farmers in regions where rubber trees are not normally grown have taken up rubber farming in a big way, thanks to the unrelenting rally in prices.

A half of the new land brought under rubber this year is in states such as Karnataka, Maharashtra, Orissa and the North-Eastern states, Rubber Board officials said. The rest of the expansion is seen in the rubber belt of Kerala and Tamil Nadu. "It is difficult to find land in Kerala", said Satish Abraham, president, Latex Manufacturers Association. He said rubber was now being cultivated as an inter crop in many new regions of the state.

Rubber Board former vice chairman Siby Monippally said rubber was replacing many other crops. Experts said rubber replanting was progressing at a slower pace. "Replanting will slow down when prices are high", said a Rubber Board official adding that even scrap rubber was getting nearly Rs 200 per kg.

Table 4.12: Country-wise import of natural rubber

(In thousand tons)

Country	1998	1999	2000	2001	2002	2003	2004	2005	2006	2007	2008	2009
China	411	402	820	943	915	1,150	1,206	1,445	1,885	1,889	1,948	2,463
USA	1,177	1,116	1,192	972	1,126	1,120	1,156	1,170	1,012	1,029	1,052	705
Japan	678	755	802	713	772	792	801	849	886	850	849	596
Rep. of Korea	282	332	331	330	326	342	352	371	365	378	359	332
Germany	247	226	250	245	266	283	270	282	296	330	282	230
Brazil	115	98	139	128	144	162	184	195	179	221	235	152
France	223	240	270	282	254	236	244	246	236	243	223	137
Spain	159	161	171	184	186	191	194	193	195	203	185	130
Canada	148	141	150	132	155	148	152	160	150	144	143	106
Italy	148	131	136	135	146	149	159	159	162	160	145	95
Turkey	84	69	86	79	95	109	120	130	133	145	138	106
Taiwan	97	105	92	90	106	115	120	115	102	116	99	90
UK	139	127	123	98	94	99	100	96	80	103	90	53
India	29	20	11	35	26	46	63	62	50	113	81	160
Mexico	82	82	90	67	67	74	76	79	75	72	70	59
Argentina	42	22	27	23	26	34	36	41	41	39	34	34
Others*	656	620	752	823	671	723	898	933	988	1017	995	862
World	4,717	4,647	5,442	5,279	5,375	5,773	6,131	6,526	6,835	7,052	6,928	6,310

* Countries not reported separately.
Source: "Rubber Statistical Bulletin" of the International Rubber Study Group.

Table 4.12A: Country-wise export of natural rubber

(In thousand tons)

Country	1998	1999	2000	2001	2002	2003	2004	2005	2006	2007	2008	2009
Thailand	1,839	1,886	2,166	2,042	2,354	2,574	2,637	2,632	2,772	2,704	2,675	2,726
Indonesia	1,641	1,495	1,380	1,497	1,502	1,661	1,875	2,025	2,287	2,407	2,296	1,991
Malaysia	425	436	430	345	887	947	1,106	1,128	1,131	1,018	917	704
Vietnam	191	218	254	270	455	432	513	554	704	716	659	731
Liberia	75	100	105	107	109	107	115	111	101	106	81	77
India	2	3	13	4	44	63	72	60	71	30	77	16
Cambodia	33	39	39	38	40	36	32	28	25	25	15	36
Sri Lanka	41	43	33	32	36	35	40	32	46	50	46	54
Nigeria	47	38	36	30	24	22	29	25	24	25	26	32

Source: "Rubber Statistical Bulletin" of the International Rubber Study Group.

Table 4.12B: Country-wise export of natural rubber

	2011–0012		2010–2011	
	Quantity in tons	Share in tons (%)	Quantity	Share (%)
Sri Lanka	6.623	24.4	2,619	8.8
Malaysia	4,273	15.7	6,555	22
China	2,890	10.6	8,463	28.3
Germany	2,732	10.1	1,375	4.6
Brazil	2,598	9.6	1,406	4.7
Italy	2,366	8.7	1,035	3.5
Belgium	1,613	5.9	950	3.2
Spain	982	3.6	644	2.1
Nepal	432	1.6	409	1.4
Indonesia	415	1.5	313	1
Pakistan	359	1.3	1,641	5.5
Egypt	311	1.2	395	1.3
Turkey	265	1	348	1.2
USA	254	0.9	1,075	3.6
Netherland	214	0.8	83	0.3
UAE	187	0.7	105	0.3
Russia	127	0.5	85	0.3
Singapore	114	0.4	95	0.3
Bahrain	96	0.4	16	0.1

Table 4.13: Production, consumption and stock of natural and synthetic rubber (in thousand tons)

Year	Natural rubber				Synthetic rubber			
	Production	Consumption	Excess (+) or deficiency (−) compared with consumption	Stock at the end of the year	Production	Consumption	Excess (+) or deficiency (−) compared with consumption	Stock at the end of the year
1996	6,440	6,110	+330	2,130	9,740	9,570	+170	2,340
1997	6,470	6,460	+10	2,250	10,080	10,000	+80	2,400
1998	6,820	6,560	+260	2,560	9,880	9,870	+10	2,450
1999	6,870	6,640	+230	2,760	10,340	10,200	+140	2,700
2000	6,764	7,313	−549	2,247	10,819	10,764	+55	2,700
2001	7,252	7,333	−81	1,972	10,483	10,253	+230	2,900
2002	7,337	7,554	−217	1,976	10,877	10,877	0	2,731
2003	8,020	7,952	+68	2,020	11,341	11,348	−7	2,748
2004	8,746	8,718	+28	2,048	11,961	11,840	+121	2,869
2005	8,904	9,200	−296	1,752	12,100	11,900	+200	3,069
2006	9,791	9,677	+114	1,866	12,653	12,691	−38	3,031
2007	9,801	10,144	−343	1,523	13,388	13,264	+124	3,154
2008	10,036	10,173	−137	1,386	12,743	12,603	+140	3,294
2009p	9617	9390	+227	1613	12087	11754	+333	3627

Source: "Rubber Statistical Bulletin" of the International Rubber Study Group.

Table 4.14: Forecasts of rubber consumption

('000 tons)

	2007	2008	%	2009	%	2010	%	2011	%
Natural rubber									
North America	1,157	1,179	2.0	742	−37.1	780	5.1	877	12.4
Latin America	565	562	−0.5	410	−27.0	414	1.0	435	5.0
European Union (EU)	1,377	1,188	−13.8	760	−36.0	766	0.9	793	3.5
Non-Europe	273	254	−7.1	161	−36.5	143	−11.4	138	−3.6
Africa	118	112	−4.8	99	−11.7	105	6.6	104	−0.9
Asia-Pacific	6,726	6,807	1.2	6,981	2.6	7,142	2.3	7,296	2.2
World	10,230	10,088	−1.4	9,140	−9.4	9,337	2.2	9,630	3.1
Synthetic rubber									
North America	2,129	1,898	−10.9	1,497	−21.1	1,387	−7.4	1,566	12.9
Latin America	864	890	3.0	667	−25.0	682	2.2	730	7.0

(Contd.)

Table 4.14: Forecasts of rubber consumption

('000 tons)

	2007	2008	%	2009	%	2010	%	2011	%
European Union	2,514	2,372	−5.6	1,810	−23.7	1,905	5.2	1,932	1.4
Non-EU Europe	1,014	912	−10.1	746	−18.1	801	7.4	805	0.5
Africa	105	106	0.2	94	−10.8	100	6.4	97	−3.0
Asia/Pacific	6,527	6,274	−3.9	6,184	−1.4	6,441	4.2	6,579	2.1
World	13,284	12,586	−5.3	11,118	−11.7	11,439	2.9	11,836	3.5
Total rubber									
North America	3,286	3,077	−6.4	2,239	−27.2	2,167	−3.2	2,443	12.7
Latin America	1,429	1,452	1.6	1,077	−25.8	1,096	1.8	1,165	6.2
European Union	3,891	3,560	−8.5	2,569	−27.8	2,671	4.0	2,725	2.0
Non-EU Europe	1,287	1,165	−9.4	908	−22.1	944	4.0	943	−0.1
Africa	223	217	−2.4	193	−11.2	205	6.5	201	−1.9
Asia-Pacific	13,253	13,082	−1.3	13,165	0.6	13,583	3.2	13,875	2.2
World	23,514	22,674	−3.6	20,258	−10.7	20,777	2.6	21,466	3.3

Notes:
1. The regions are defined as follows: North America (Canada and US), Latin America (Brazil, Mexico and other Latin America), European Union (Austria, Belgium/Luxembourg, Czech Republic, Finland, France, Germany, Italy, Netherlands, Poland, Portugal, Slovakia, Slovenia, Spain, Sweden, UK and other European Union), Non-EU (Russian Federation, Turkey, Ukraine and other Europe), Africa (South Africa and other Africa), Asia-Pacific (Australia, China, India, Indonesia, Japan, Republic of Korea, Malaysia, Taiwan, Thailand and other Asia)
2. Total may not add up due to rounding and balancing adjustments.

Table 4.14A: Forecasts of natural rubber consumption

('000 tons)

	2007	2008	%	2009	%	2010	%	2011	%
Thailand	3,056	3,090	1.1	3,000	−2.9	3,290	9.7	3,274	−0.5
Indonesia	2,755	2,751	−0.2	2,777	0.9	2,841	2.3	3,036	6.4
Malaysia	1,200	1,072	−10.6	859	−19.9	892	3.9	891	−0.1
Other Asia	2,375	2,488	4.8	2,326	−6.5	2,584	11.1	2,844	9.1
Africa	445	443	−0.4	438	−1.2	466	6.6	478	2.5
Latin America	228	241	5.6	233	−3.1	247	5.8	255	3.1
World	9,687	9,877	2.0	9,433	−4.5	10,108	7.2	10,556	4.2

Notes:
1. The regions are defined as follows: Other Asia (Bangladesh, Combodia, China, India, Myanmar, Papua New Guinea, Philippines, Sri Lanka and Vietnam), Africa (Cameroon, Cote d'Ivotre, Ghana, Liberia, Nigeria, D.R. of Congo and other Africa), Latin America (Brazil, Guatemala, Mexico and other Latin America).
2. Total may not add up due to rounding and balancing adjustments.

Table 4.14B: Forecasts of synthetic rubber consumption

('000 tons)

	2007	2008	%	2009	%	2010	%	2011	%
North America	2790	2410	−13.6	1903	−21.0	1979	4.0	2103	6.3
Latin America	684	691	1.0	582	−15.8	730	25.5	736	0.8
European Union	2684	2502	−6.8	2065	−17.5	2097	1.6	2068	−1.4
Non-EU Europe	1288	1207	−6.3	944	−21.8	981	3.9	1001	2.1
South Africa	71	78	9.9	66	−15.8	71	8.5	72	0.8
Asia/Pacific	5916	5926	0.2	6077	2.6	6530	7.5	6810	4.3
World	13,434	12,813	−4.6	11,637	−9.2	12,389	6.5	12,790	3.2

Notes:
1. The regions are defined as follows: North America (Canada, US), Latin America (Argentina, Brazil, Mexico), European Union (Austria, Belgium, Czech Republic, Finland, France, Germany, Italy, Netherlands, Poland, Spain, Sweden and UK), Non-EU (Bulgaria, Romania, Russian Federation, Turkey, Federal Republic of Yugoslavia and other Europe), Asia-Pacific (Australia, China, India, Indonesia, Iran, Japan, Republic of Korea, Malaysia, Taiwan and Thailand).
2. Total may not add up due to rounding and balancing adjustments.

More people are taking to rubber planting across the globe as shortages and a rising demand are pushing prices to record levels. International prices stood at Rs 292.98 per kg in 2011. Local prices which stood at around Rs 139 per kg in January 2010 rose to Rs 240.50 per kg on February 19, 2011. The shortage is estimated at around 85,000 tons last year and 1 lakh tons this year.

Rubber Board estimates show the area under rubber has been expanding by around 6,000 hectares since the beginning of this decade. However, this increased to 22,700 hectare by 2007–2008 and to 30,200 hectare in the subsequent year. The provisional figure for 2009–2010 put the new plantation at 25,500 hectares. The extended rainy season this year has forced growers to cut back production.

RUBBER AND RUBBER PRODUCTS

Tariffs and Protection in the Asean—India Agreement

Attempting to provide a conceptual basis for disaggregate-level analysis of the implications of the ASEAN-India Free Trade Agreement on rubber and rubber products, this article critically assesses the key provisions of the accord. The analysis reveals that the categorization of tariff lines under six different groups is the most crucial component governing tariff policy and the implementation period. India's negative balance of trade in rubber and rubber products with ASEAN and the high annual average growth rate of imports of finished rubber products underline the need for close monitoring of the trends in external trade with the trading bloc at the disaggregate level.

The signing of the Association of Southeast Asian Nations (ASEAN)- India Free Trade Agreement (AIFTA) in 2009 was important in India's engagements in Regional Trade Agreements (RTAs) for three reasons. First, the AIFTA covers the largest number of countries compared to the 17 other RTAs so far signed by India. Second,

India's total merchandize trade with the ASEAN is significant *vis-à-vis* other RTAs. Third, no other RTA has generated such sharp polemical exchanges cutting across regions and sectors on the potential threat of cheaper imports into the country. However, the perceived vulnerability of various sectors in India has not been based on an objective understanding of the provisions related to tariff policy, tariff reduction commitments, and the implementation period. Moreover, implications of the interlinkages between the tariff policy and the implementation period committed to by India and the ASEAN have not been critically assessed. In effect, there has been an absence of comprehensive sector-specific analyzes from a policy perspective. Against this background, this article attempts to explore the tariff policy, tariffs, and tariff reduction commitments on rubber and rubber products in Chapter 40 of the Harmonized System. The study assumes importance as the share of rubber and rubber products sector in India's total merchandise trade with the ASEAN is significant in relation to the share of the sector in the country's total merchandise trade with the world. More importantly, the ASEAN accounted for 12.92% of the country's total value of exports and 26.69% of imports of rubber and rubber products with notable sector-wise differences (GoI, 2012). Hence, a critical assessment of the key provisions of the AIFTA on rubber and rubber products is attempted to provide a conceptual basis for disaggregate-level analyzes and monitoring outcomes from a policy perspective.

Objectives

The following are the three specific objectives here: (1) to understand the tariff policy, tariffs and tariff reduction commitments on rubber and rubber products under the AIFTA; (2) to examine the tariff preferences and differential levels of protection provided to three broad groups under rubber and products and (3) to highlight the policy implications for India.

Methodology

Our database consists of the ASEAN-India Trade in Goods Agreement, schedules of the tariff commitments under the AIFTA, and external trade data on rubber and rubber products provided by the department of commerce, Ministry of Commerce and Industry. The analysis focuses on the technical contents of the AIFTA pertaining to the inclusion of tariff lines (products) under the six listed categories: (1) normal track-1 (NT-1), (2) normal track-2 (NT-2), (3) sensitive track (ST), (4) special products (SP), (5) highly sensitive list (HSL), and (6) exclusion list (EL)—as well as the implementation period and tariff reduction commitments. Among the six categories, SP is excluded from the analysis as it is not applicable to rubber and rubber products. Singapore is excluded from the country-wise analysis as its tariffs on all originating goods are zero from the date of entry of the agreement. The analysis of the tariff policies is based on the destination-wise classification of tariff lines into three groups—tariff elimination, tariff reduction, and exclusion list—as India has three separate implementation periods with reciprocal and nonreciprocal provisions pertaining to NT-1, NT-2 and ST with the ASEAN-5 (Brunei Darussalam, Indonesia, Malaysia, Thailand and Singapore), the CLMV (Cambodia, Lao PDR, Myanmar and Vietnam), and the Philippines.

Rubber and rubber products contained in the mandatory 85 tariff lines at the six-digit levels are grouped into raw materials (tariff lines included under HS 4001-03), intermediate products (tariff lines included under HS 4004-08), and finished rubber products (tariff lines included under HS 4009-17) to focus on the conceptual basis of the tariff policies. Differential levels of protection are analyzed by linking the categorization of the three product groups with the average final tariffs at the end of the implementation period.

Categorization of Product Groups

The most crucial component in tariff policy under the AIFTA is perhaps the categorization of tariff lines under six different groups. The categorization prefixes both the tariff policy and the implementation period under the Trade in Goods Agreement. Table 4.15 summarizes the details. From the angle of tariff policy, the tariff lines under NT-1 and NT-2 represent tariff elimination, while ST, SP and highly sensitive list (HSL) are concerned with tariff reduction. The tariff lines under EL are excluded from tariff reduction. As the tariff policy progresses from NT-1 to HSL, the longevity of the implementation period increases with country and group-specific differences. A salient feature of the AIFTA has been the nonreciprocal nature of the implementation period of India's tariff concessions to the CLMV. The four-country group is required to fulfill its commitments only at a later stage for products covered under NT-1, NT-2 and ST. The preferential treatment given to the CLMV has policy implications for India arising from the differential tariff rates in the ASEAN during the implementation period.

Functionally, the two key factors governing the trade-off between India and the ASEAN are the categorization of tariff lines under each product group and the final tariff rates. India's tariff commitments are given at the eight-digit level of the HS (12,169 products) and almost 75% of them are covered in NT-1 and NT-2 while the share of products in the EL is around 10% (George, 2010). Table 4.15A shows the sector-wise tariff lines of India and the ASEAN member countries on rubber and rubber products. Table 4.15A indicates that India has the lowest number of tariff lines on raw materials, finished products, and all rubber and rubber products. Malaysia has the highest number of tariff lines in all sectors other than finished products. Though the number of tariff lines beyond the mandatory six-digit level is an indication of the trade-related importance of a product, the disaggregate level classification has potential for trade facilitation and revenue generation. However, from a policy angle, category-wise classification of the tariff lines assumes more importance under the AIFTA. Table 4.15B provides the category-wise shares of tariff lines of the ASEAN and India.

Table 4.15B reveals that more than 52% of India's tariff lines on rubber and rubber products are categorized for tariff elimination (NT-1 and NT-2), 40.23% for tariff reduction (ST), and 6.89% are excluded from tariff reduction. This is in contrast to the varied strategies pursued by the ASEAN member countries. At first look, India is one among the six countries having a liberal tariff policy, with less number of tariff lines in the EL than Brunei (48.79%), Vietnam (39.61%) and Myanmar (21.26%). However, Indonesia and Lao PDR with no tariff lines under the EL deserve attention.

The analysis on category-wise shares of the countries provides only a broad outline on the tariff policy pursued on rubber and rubber products under the AIFTA. At the disaggregate level, it is imperative to understand the sector-wise shares in categorization to assess country specific tariff policies and preferences across the three broad product groups.

Table 4.15: Categorization of tariff lines, tariff policy and implementation period under AIFTA

Category	Tariff policy	ASEAN-5 and India	CLMV and India	Philippines and India
			Implementation period	
Normal track-1	Tariff elimination	January 2010 to December 2013	January 2010 to December 2013 for India and January 2010 to December 2018 for CLMV	January 2010 to December 2018
Normal track-2	Tariff elimination	January 2010 to December 2016	January 2010 to December 2016 for India and January 2010 to December 2021 for CLMV	January 2010 to December 2019
Sensitive track*	Tariff reduction	January 2010 to December 2016	January 2010 to December 2016 for India and January 2010 to December 2021 for CLMV	January 2010 to December 2019
Special products	Tariff reduction	Applicable to India only for palm oil, coffee, black tea and pepper; January 2010 to December 2019	Applicable to India only for palm oil, coffee, black tea and pepper; January 2010 to December 2019	Applicable to India only for palm oil, coffee, black tea and pepper; January 2010 to December 2019
Highly sensitive list	Tariff reduction	January 2010 to December 2019 for Indonesia, Malaysia and Thailand	January 2010 to December 2024 for Vietnam and Cambodia	Applicable to the Philippines only. January 2010 to December 2022
Exclusion list	Excluded from any tariff reduction		Only annual tariff review	

* Applicable to tariff lines with most favored nation (MFN) tariff rates above 5%.
Source: GoI (2010).

Table 4.15A: Sector-wise tariff lines on rubber and rubber products (Nos)

Country	Raw materials	Intermediate products	Finished products	Total
India	32	26	116	174
Malaysia	120	41	122	283
Vietnam	46	12	149	207
Thailand	48	12	119	179
Indonesia	48	12	119	179
Myanmar	46	12	149	207
Philippines	48	12	125	185
Cambodia	48	12	119	179
Brunei Darussalam	46	12	149	207
Lao PDR	48	12	119	179

Source: GoI (2010).

Table 4.15B: Category-wise shares of tariff lines on rubber and rubber products (%)

Country	NT-1	NT-2	ST	HSL	EL	Total
India	44.83	8.05	40.23	0.00	6.89	100.00
Malaysia	36.40	9.88	41.70	6.01	6.01	100.00
Vietnam	60.39	0.00	0.00	0.00	39.61	100.00
Thailand	66.48	15.64	13.97	0.00	3.91	100.00
Indonesia	34.64	0.00	65.36	0.00	0.00	100.00
Myanmar	57.00	0.00	21.74	0.00	21.26	100.00
Philippines	41.08	21.63	22.70	1.08	13.51	100.00
Cambodia	69.27	0.00	28.49	0.00	2.24	100.00
Brunei Darussalam	51.21	0.00	0.00	0.00	48.79	100.00
Lao PDR	94.97	3.35	1.68	0.00	0.00	100.00

Source: GoI (2010).

Table 4.15C shows the sector-wise shares of different categories. Table 4.15C is illustrative of a sector specific tariff policy and differential levels of protection accorded to the tariff lines. In the raw materials sector, all the countries have included a majority of tariff lines in NT-1, with the exception of the Philippines. Four ASEAN member countries have committed all tariff lines in the raw materials sector to NT-1. However, the Philippines (52.1%) and India (28.1%) are the two countries that have adopted a highly protective tariff policy for all forms of natural rubber (NR). In the case of intermediate products, India has adopted a cautious strategy of placing a substantial share of tariff lines in ST (77.0%) and EL (11.5%). The strategies of ASEAN members vary; from inclusion of all tariff lines in NT-1 (Vietnam, Cambodia and Brunei) to Myanmar committing 41.7% of the tariff lines to the EL. India's tariff policy in value-added finished products is unique in that no tariff line on rubber and rubber products is included in the EL. Instead, the largest number of tariff lines are included in NT-1 (47.4%), followed by ST (41.4%).

Table 4.15C: Sector-wise shares of the tariff lines under different categories (%)

Country	Raw materials (HS 4001 - 4003)						Intermediate products (HS 4004-08)						Finished products (HS4009-17)					
	NT-1	NT-2	ST	HSL	EL	Total	NT-1	NT-2	ST	HSL	EL	Total	NT-1	NT-2	ST	HSL	EL	Total
India	65.6	28.1	0.0	6.3	0.0	100.0	7.7	3.8	77.0	0.0	11.5	100.0	47.4	11.2	41.4	0.0	0.0	100.0
Malaysia	72.5	0.0	14.2	12.5	0.8	100.0	2.4	0.0	85.4	12.2	0.0	100.0	12.4	9.0	55.7	9.0	13.9	100.0
Vietnam	100.0	0.0	0.0	0.0	0.0	100.0	100.0	0.0	0.0	0.0	0.0	100.0	45.0	0.0	0.0	0.0	55.0	100.0
Thailand	97.9	0.0	0.0	2.1	0.0	100.0	75.0	0.0	16.7	0.0	8.3	100.0	52.9	23.6	18.5	0.0	5.0	100.0
Indonesia	77.1	0.0	22.9	0.0	0.0	100.0	41.7	0.0	58.3	0.0	0.0	100.0	16.8	0.0	83.2	0.0	0.0	100.0
Myanmar	100.0	0.0	0.0	0.0	0.0	100.0	50.0	0.0	8.3	0.0	41.7	100.0	44.3	0.0	29.5	0.0	26.2	100.0
Philippines	47.9	0.0	0.0	0.0	52.1	100.0	41.7	41.6	16.7	0.0	0.0	100.0	38.4	28.0	32.0	1.6	0.0	100.0
Cambodia	75.0	0.0	25.0	0.0	0.0	100.0	100.0	0.0	0.0	0.0	0.0	100.0	63.8	0.0	32.8	0.0	3.4	100.0
Brunei Darussalm	100.0	0.0	0.0	0.0	0.0	100.0	100.0	0.0	0.0	0.0	0.0	100.0	32.2	0.0	0.0	0.0	67.8	100.0
Lao PDR	100.0	0.0	0.0	0.0	0.0	100.0	83.3	0.0	16.7	0.0	0.0	100.0	94.2	5.0	0.8	0.0	0.0	100.0

Source: GoI (2010).

Conversely, Brunei (67.8%), Vietnam (55.0%), Myanmar (26.2%), and Malaysia (13.9%) accord higher protection to value-added products. A closer understanding of the priorities of tariff policy and differential levels of protection pursued by individual countries require a comparative analysis of the destination-wise shares of tariff lines and average final tariffs at the end of the implementation period across sectors. Table 4.15C summarizes the country and sector-specific priorities.

Table 4.15D summarizes the priorities and strategies pursued on rubber and rubber products by the signatories of the AIFTA. In the raw material sector, although the Philippines have the largest share of tariff lines under the EL, India's average final tariff rate is the highest (31.11%). More precisely, tariff lines on all important forms of NR are protected by India with a high rate of tariffs. Conversely, the average final tariff rates of ASEAN members on tariff lines in the raw material sector varied from 2.39–5%. Vietnam, Myanmar, Brunei and Lao PDR have included all the tariff lines in the tariff elimination category. In the intermediate products sector, India has adopted a more liberal and cautious approach of committing the highest share of tariff lines (77.0%) in the tariff reduction category, followed by the EL (11.5%) with 10% and 5% average final tariffs, respectively. The ASEAN countries that follow a relatively more protective policy in this sector are Malaysia, Indonesia, Thailand, Myanmar, the Philippines and Lao PDR, with average final tariff rates ranging from 4.46–20.0%. However, Vietnam, Cambodia and Brunei have included all the tariff lines in the tariff elimination category. India has pursued the most liberal tariff policy in the case of value-added finished products by including 58.6% of the tariff lines in the tariff elimination category and the remaining tariff lines (41.4%) in the tariff reduction category with a 5.0% average final tariff rate. Along with Indonesia, the Philippines and Lao PDR, it has excluded all tariff lines in the finished products group from the EL. In sharp contrast, all the other ASEAN countries barring Lao PDR follow a more protected tariff policy with average final tariff rates ranging from 3.78% (Myanmar) to 23.18% (Vietnam). At the disaggregate level, the share of tariff lines included in the EL by Brunei (67.8%), Vietnam (55%), Myanmar (26.2%) and Malaysia (13.9%) deserve attention. In sum, India's tariff policy on rubber and rubber products under the AIFTA focuses on providing more protection to the raw materials sector while the ASEAN countries have a protected tariff policy on value-added finished products.

RUBBER DREAM STORY UNRAVELS IN GOD'S OWN COUNTRY

The predicament of Thomas Baby sums up what Kerala's rubber cultivators are going through today. Like most of his fellow farmers, Baby has only rubber on his small 2.5 acre patch, where he used to earlier grow ginger, banana, tapioca and other short-duration crops.

Baby shifted to rubber as he saw it to be a source of regular and reliable income. The crop has been the lifeline for the people of Pala in Kottayam district, which, along with Idukki and Pathanamthitta, forms Kerala's traditional rubber belt. But now, Baby is struggling to keep afloat a family that includes an unemployed wife, two school-going children and an aged mother.

"I tap once in every 3 days, and each time it costs me Rs 400 for 200 trees at Rs 2 per tree. After paying the tapper's wages, I am left with a daily income of just Rs 150 at the current rubber price of Rs 116 per kg (for top RSS-4 sheet grade)", Baby says.

Table 4.15D: Destination-wise shares of tariff lines and average final tariffs (%)

Country	Raw material			Intermediate products			Finished products		
	Tariff elimination	Tariff reduction	Exclusion list	Tariff elimination	Tariff reduction	Exclusion list	Tariff elimination	Tariff reduction	Exclusion list
India	65.6 (0.0)	6.3 (5.0)	28.1 (31.11)	11.5 (0)	77.0 (5.0)	11.5 (10.0)	58.6 (0)	41.4 (5.0)	0
Malaysia	86.7 (0.0)	13.3 (4.31)	0	2.4 (0)	97.6 (6.93)	0	21.4 (0)	64.7(7.63)	13.9 (22.65)
Vietnam	100.0 (0.0)	0	0	100 (0)	0	0	45 (0)	0	55 (23.18)
Thailand	97.9 (0.0)	2.1 (5.0)	0	75 (0)	16.7 (5.0)	8.3 (20.0)	76.5 (0)	18.5 (5.0)	5 (10.0)
Indonesia	77.1 (0.0)	22.9 (2.39)	0	41.7 (0)	58.3 (4.46)	0	16.8 (0)	83.2 (4.66)	0
Myanmar	100.0 (0.0)	0	0	50 (0)	8.3 (1.0)	41.7 (5.0)	44.3 (0)	29.5 (3.78)	26.2 (5.07)
Philippines	47.9 (0.0)	0 (3.0)	52.1 (0)	83.3 (5.0)	16.7	0(0)	66.4 (4.82)	33.6	0
Cambodia Darussalam	75.0 (0.0)	25.0 (5.0)	0	100 (0)	0	0	63.8 (0)	32.8 (5.0)	3.4 (13.0)
Brunei	100.0 (0.0)	0	0	100 (0)	0	0	32.2 (0)	0	0
Lao PDR	100.0 (0.0)	0	0 (0)	83.3 (5.0)	16.7	0	99.2 (0)	0.8 (5.0)	0

Figures in parentheses are the average final tariffs at the end of the implementation period.
Source: GoI (2010).

"It is suicidal to be a rubber farmer today. At the same time, we don't have the resources to shift to any other crop. But Baby and other rubber farmers in Kerala, which accounts for 80% of the country's production, saw much better days only 3 years ago when RSS-4 prices scaled Rs 240–250 levels.

During the boom, this cash crop spread from the three central Kerala districts to even non-traditional growing areas elsewhere in the state. From their lows of below Rs 20 per kg in the late 1990s, rubber prices rose gradually to embark on a bull run that took them to their Rs 250 peaks in 2011. It has been a slippery slope since— more so in the last 1 year. The impact of this can be gauged if one considers Kerala's annual rubber production of roughly 800,000 tons. A fall of Rs 100/kg translates into an income loss of Rs 8,000 crore for farmers, with obvious cascading effects on consumption and spending across the state.

Almost 80% of farmers have now stopped deploying workers for tapping, whose wages too had spiraled along with rubber prices in the boom, but which haven't adjusted downward along with plunging rubber realizations. They remain in the Rs 2–3 per tree range, depending upon the availability of workers. "Only farmers who tap the trees themselves can today engage in production, as it will at least save wages. But if prices go down further, even that wouldn't be possible. They will then have to leave their trees idle and scout for other jobs", says Thankachan, a 300-tree grower in Thodupuzha.

It is not growers alone who are affected. At Kanjirappally, a major plantation center, many rubber traders have shut shop as farmers have ceased tapping. P M Abdul Azeez, who trades in scrap rubber, says he used to get 200 kg of material every day. "These days, I have to wait for 2 weeks to get the same quantity". During the boom, growers constructed new houses, bought swanky cars, and enrolled children for professional courses at private institutions. As plantation real estate values soared and rubber prices crossed Rs 200, banks, too, rushed to give educational loans to children of cultivators.

Low rubber realizations have now left their imprint on banks, not just in terms of local deposits and credit offtake; in many cases, even repayment of educational loans availed during the boom isn't happening, confirmed an official at a leading private sector bank's Kanjirappally branch. There has been impact elsewhere too. Ligo Francis, manager of a Maruti showroom at Kanjirappally, said that compared to last year, car sales in the area have nearly halved. The high prices enjoyed in the last few years attracted many new farmers into rubber cultivation. This was partly enabled by the price crisis in coconut during the previous decade. Hence, many farmers uprooted coconut trees and planted rubber. In non-traditional areas such as Kozhikode, Kannur, Kasargod and Wayanad, where coconut, areca, cashew or spices were grown, rubber plantations sprung up. According to Rubber Board statistics, the country's overall area under the crop rose by nearly a third, from 5.84 lakh hectares to 7.76 lakh hectares, between 2004–2005 and 2013–2014. Much of this was in Kerala. Rubber also became a source of valuable real estate.

Even in remote North Kerala villages, an acre of rubber plantation began commanding a price of Rs 40 lakh. "NRIs, especially Muslims, came in search of rubber land mainly as a real estate investment. But these have turned into idle investments, as there is no tapping, and nobody to buy the land even if one wants to sell", said Muhammed Ali, a real estate broker at Puthuppaddy in Kozhikode. "If prices had stayed at Rs 200, more land in Kerala would have been turned into rubber plantations. The fall in prices has changed that trend", says Joy Vadakkel, a nursery owner at Pala. The crash in the rubber market has also hit the subsidiary business of rearing rubber saplings. The rate of saplings that was Rs 140 a year back, has fallen to Rs 40 this season. Kerala has around a thousand rubber nurseries that together prepared 1 crore saplings annually. "This year, we could sell only half of them. The unsold saplings had to be destroyed", said Josekutty Antony, secretary of the All Kerala Rubber Nurseries Association.

Many rubber farmers blame the free import policy of the Congress government for their crisis. "Why should we blame the BJP? We are suffering for the wrong policy of the previous government", said farmer C J Jose of Melukavu near Pala. In the last 6 years, rubber imports have quadrupled to 325,000 tons even as domestic output has hovered around 900,000 tons.

The Kerala government, for now, has decided to give growers an additional Rs 5 over the Rubber Board's indicative market price. This support, through procurement by agencies such as Kerala State Co-operative Rubber Marketing Federation (Rubber Mark) and Marketfed, will continue until the market price reaches a target level of Rs 176 per kg.

Conclusion

The observations from the analysis highlight four important points: (1) the crucial role of categorization of tariff lines in prefixing the tariff policy; (2) the reciprocal and non-reciprocal blocs of countries in ASEAN related to the implementation period; (3) the varied tariff policies and rates followed by ASEAN member countries, contrary to the popular perceptions and (4) the contrasting sector-specific tariff preferences between India and the ASEAN. Apparently, the underlying factors behind the varied strategies are dependent on a host of factors in the trade-centric agenda of the agreement. India's strategy of pursuing an inverted tariff structure on rubber and rubber products under the AIFTA may have been guided by the composition of the total value of exports to and imports from ASEAN. The country's large rubber products manufacturing base absorbs its entire domestic production of NR. However, the AIFTA has the potential of giving rise to major structural adjustments in the prevailing equations among the NR production, processing, rubber products manufacturing, and external trade sectors in the country.

This assumes importance for two reasons: (1) India's negative balance of trade in rubber and rubber products with the ASEAN (more than $535 million in 2010–2011) and (2) a higher annual average growth rate of imports of finished rubber products into India (27.35%) from the ASEAN than exports (17.88%) from India to the group in the last decade. Therefore, a close monitoring of the trends in external trade of rubber and rubber products with the ASEAN at the disaggregate level assumes importance, given the context of market integration.

Annexure

Annexure 1: Statewise value of output-rubber

State/UTs	At current prices							At 2004-05 prices						
	2004-05	2005-06	2006-07	2007-08	2008-09	2009-10	2010-11	2004-05	2005-06	2006-07	2007-08	2008-09	2009-10	2010-11
Andhra Pradesh	0	0	5	10	10	10	10	0	0	5	8	8	8	8
Arunachal Pradesh	21	23	45	47	17	17	31	21	14	28	29	8	8	8
Assam	1301	2200	2593	4133	11305	11305	16336	1301	1325	1469	2288	4736	4736	4919
Goa	352	292	297	391	391	402	299	292	177	180	189	189	195	299
Karnataka	8045	9982	3811	14945	24146	24491	45047	8045	8301	8983	9164	11699	11866	13206
Kerala	360305	464683	701740	671683	776394	806318	1367753	360305	385599	407094	392869	408708	388886	401979
Maharashtra	17	20	21	22	0	0	0	17	20	21	22	0	0	0
Manipur	75	31	53	174	20	465	20	75	45	53	139	8	175	8
Meghalaya	1273	1336	2605	2871	3938	3184	5025	1273	1273	1512	1601	2196	1733	1957
Mizoram	23	27	23	42	0	0	0	23	29	23	42	0	0	0
Nagaland	163	209	252	293	778	778	778	163	133	160	186	186	186	186
Orissa	11	23	24	31	31	30	30	11	22	23	30	30	29	29
Tamil Nadu	9587	15810	22108	21640	24628	28394	47812	9587	9628	9799	9717	9936	10074	10264
Tripura	5760	6910	10080	15224	14713	15627	17076	5760	6419	8710	9926	9593	9819	11134
West Bengal	33	45	65	103	103	118	123	33	45	47	52	52	53	53
A & N Islands	167	130	126	116	229	229	340	167	131	116	107	148	148	99
Total	**387080**	**501781**	**743841**	**731632**	**856703**	**891356**	**1500784**	**387080**	**413278**	**438220**	**426361**	**447497**	**427911**	**444045**

5

Cocoa

Common name: Cocoa
Botanical name: *Theobroma cacao*
AKA: Chocolate

A BRIEF HISTORY

"This *name chocolate is an Indian name*, and is compounded from Atte, as some say or as others, Atle, which in the Mexican language signifieth "water" and from the sound which the water (wherein is put the chocolate) makes, as Choco, Choco, Choco, when it is stirred in a cup by an instrument called a Molinet, or Milinillo, until it bubble and rise into a froath" – Thomas Gage.

Unlike Columbus, Cortez readily estimated the great value of the cocoa bean. In fact, he and his crew were fascinated by native cocoa drinking customs. Chronicler Bernial Diaz de Castillo observed that royalty drank cocoa from vessels of gold, and that ground cocoa was kept by the wealthy in gold containers. This spoke volumes about the high value the Mexicans placed on this bean. The Aztec made a drink of finely ground cocoa beans, mixed in water and beaten to a froth with a wooden molinet. People of high rank drank cocoa in large quantities. The great emperor Monetzuma reputedly consumed as many as fifty goblets of the drink daily. The Aztecs spiced their cocoa with native vanilla and chile peppers, and some added honey to the mix. The Spaniards took up cocoa drinking as well, finding in cocoa a refreshing, satisfying and inspiring beverage.

Thousands of years ago, dense equatorial rainforest covered much more of the South American continent than today. Verdant forest and running rivers made up the landscape of the territory known as Amazonia, and forest covered much of the corridor of land we now call Central America. In this vibrantly alive landscape, wild cacao flourished. The exact origin of cacao remains shrouded in mystery and hard to pin down, due to the vastness of this wild and bio-diverse landscape. Wild species of cacao, with their fruit pods clustered on forest trees, provided food for birds and animals. The pods were either collected when they fell to the ground, or were gathered from trees, opened by claws or beaks, and the white, fruity insides eaten for their sweet and nourishing mucilage. The large "beans" inside the pods were eaten too, and many were later excreted by the creatures who ate them, sprouting in new soil and making new trees. In this way, the cacao trees were further disseminated as fertilized seeds made their way into new soil and the populations of cacao grew and spread.

According to the best estimates of archeologists, either the ancient Olmec, or the Maya, whose civilization flourished from the Yucatan Peninsula to the Pacific coast of Guatemala, are believed to have cultivated the cacao tree for the very first time around 1000 BC. This occurred during what is referred to as the Preclassic Period of Mesoamerican history, which spanned from approximately 2000 BC to 250 AD. The oldest evidence of cocoa consumption is residue in a ceramic pot recovered from a Mayan site at Rio Azul in the Northeastern part of Guatemala. According to anthropologists, this confirms the use of cacao by the Olmec.

THE COCOA TREE

Cocoa beans come from Amazon and Orinoco rainforest tree Theobroma cacao (name was given by Swedish botanist Carl von Linné). This tree needs shade so usually grows under rainforest trees near rivers. About 3 or 4 thousand years ago cocoa tree was cultivated and spread out to Central America. The tree grows upto 15 m height (if cultivated only about 8 m to easier harvesting). Theobroma cacao can live up to 100 years. Cacao leaves are bright green, about 15 cm long and 8 cm wide. Stabile temperature between 21°C and 32°C is needed and a lot of rain during year. Cocoa tree growns worldwide in tropical forest within 20 latitude of the equator. Most important producers of cocoa are: Brazil, Dominican Republic, Ecuador, Colombia, Cameroon, Cote D'Ivoire, Ghana, Nigeria, Indonesia and Malaysia.

SEAFARING EXPLORES AND COCOA

The intrepid seafaring legend *Christopher Columbus and his crew were actually the first non-natives to encounter cacao.* In 1502, Columbus was aboard the Santa Maria, moored off the island of Guanaja on the coast of Honduras, when he was visited by an Aztec chief in splendid raiments, bearing gifts. Among the cloth, copper objects and wooden weapons presented to Columbus were cocoa beans which neither he nor his crew recognized. The Aztec chief offered to exchange some of the cocoa beans for goods aboard the ship, and this perplexed Columbus and crew. To demonstrate the value of cocoa, the chief had some cocoa beverage prepared by his servants. The Aztec called the drink cacahuatl which literally means "bitter water". Columbus found the beverage bitter, spicy, and not altogether pleasant, and was not especially impressed. Although the Aztecs appeared to place high value on cocoa beans, Columbus and crew did not. The Genoan sailor subsequently described cocoa beans as "almonds, which are called cacao and serve as coins in New Spain". Columbus reputedly brought some beans back to the Spanish royal court along with numerous other treasures. But, neither Columbus nor any of his crew members appreciated the significance of cocoa, or grasped its high place in Mesoamerican society. As a result, cocoa received only fleeting attention in the Spanish court. The real discovery of the value of cacao was left to a subsequent and infinitely more shrewd explorer.

The Aztecs regarded cocoa as a sacred plant, and they valued cocoa beans as currency. Girolamo Benzoni, in his "History of the New World noted—they call the fruit cacahuate and use it for money. The tree on which it grows is not very tall, and only thrives in hot, shady places, as even minimal exposure to the sun kills it". In a subsequent entry, the author remarked "sometimes when passing through a village, I would come across an Indian who would offer me a drink of chocolate. I would refuse it; the Indian would be most astonished by my refusal, then laugh, and go on his way. In the long run, finding myself often in places where there was not a drop of wine, I learned to do as the others, so that I would not be drinking only water all the time. Its taste is not all bitter. It nourishes and refreshes the body, and is not intoxicating".

In 1544, a delegation of Mayan nobles visited the court of Spain's Prince Philip. Among the many treasures they bore were cocoa beans. In 1585, the first eagerly awaited commercial shipment of cacao beans arrived in Seville, borne on the shoulders of Spanish sailors returning from Veracruz. With a mighty and triumphant shout, cocoa crossed the great Atlantic Ocean and planted its flag in Spain. Its campaign to capture the palates of Europeans had begun in earnest. The Spaniards took up cocoa drinking with enthusiasm, and set a new course for the consumption of this beverage by adding boiling water to the bean paste and making a hot drink. Flavored variously with ginger, cinnamon, pepper and nutmeg, the hot cocoa beverage captured the palates and the imaginations of the Spanish.

Cocoa soon made its way from Mexico to Spain not just in the form of dried cocoa beans, but also in pressed tablets or slabs. Today, this is still a typical method of cocoa preparation. Cocoa beans are fermented for about 4 days, they are dried in the sun, and then they are roasted so the thin shell that surrounds them can be easily removed. The inside cocoa "nibs" are ground finely for a long time until they form a pliable mass. The finely ground beans are typically mixed with vanilla, cinnamon and vanilla. This preparation is rolled into balls, or pressed into tablets or slabs, and can be stored for later use. Today, you can find such preparations made fresh throughout South America, and you can also buy them in markets.

Chocolate of fine and good quality is prepared by crushing the roasted and hulled beans between rollers, then mixing them with sugar, vanilla, or occasionally with other spices, and allowing this mixture to cool. The chocolate beverage is prepared in various ways: it is simply boiled with water, with some sugar added to it. But, it is also consumed with the unavoidable milk, with a lot of sugar, or with eggs. Since chocolate is actually a thin paste or soup, and its infusion is not prepared from cacao seeds or leaves as in the case of tea or coffee, it is more appropriate for chocolate than for the two other beverages to be taken with toast, cookies, and all kinds of other things.

While several European companies were raising stars in the chocolate field, two United States (US)-based chocolate companies would become titans in the world of cacao. Hershey's Chocolate was founded in 1895 by Milton Hershey, and their eventual arch-rival Mars Co was founded by Frank Mars in 1922. Both companies would become huge, and both would generate not only mountains of chocolate products, but staggering wealth as well. Not surprisingly, the rivalry between Hershey's and Mars boils on to this day. At almost double the retail sales of Hershey's, Mars is the big gorilla in the world of cocoa. Both companies are leaders in cocoa research. Each has delved deeply into the compounds in cocoa, their biological activity, and their health benefits. It is Mars, although, that has done the most thorough job of patenting findings related to cocoa. Their patents on methods of cocoa processing and the sale of cocoa products for health benefits are vast, broad and restrictive, and it is only a matter of time before there is a major legal showdown between Mars and entities who believe that their patent goes too far.

Cocoa tree became cultural plant in central America probably about 1500 BC when Olmecs established first plantations. Later central American civilizations of Toltecs and Mayas continued in planting cocoa. About 1000 AD cocoa beans were already used as a currency. Mayas used the cocoa beans to prepare very nourishing drink which they called Xocolatl. Columbus was first European who saw cocoa in today's Nicaragua in 1502. But, he did not care about cocoa because he searched way to India.

Hernando Cortez discovered real importance of cocoa in central American Society and also thanks to nourishing cocoa drink conquered Aztec empire in 1521. Cortez brought back to Europe the first cocoa in 1528. It took more than 100 years to spread cocoa to other European countries. Chocolate became popular drink in European higher society during 17th and 18th century. The first machine-made chocolate was produced in Barcelona about year 1780. Thanks to industrial revolution and its inventions and massive expansion of sugar production chocolate became not only drink but also confectionery in 19th century.

IMPORTANCE OF COCOA

Cocoa was an important commodity in Pre-Columbian Mesoamerica. Spanish chroniclers of the conquest of Mexico by Hernán Cortés relate that when Moctezuma II, emperor of the Aztecs, dined he took no other beverage than chocolate, served in a golden goblet and eaten with a golden spoon. Flavored with vanilla and spices, his chocolate was whipped into a froth that dissolved in the mouth. It is reported that Montezuma II may have consumed no fewer than 50 portions each day, and 200 more by the nobles of his court. Chocolate was introduced to Europe by the Spaniards and became a popular beverage by the mid-1600s. They also introduced the cacao tree into the West Indies and the Philippines. The cacao plant was first given its botanical name by Swedish natural scientist Carl Linnaeus in his original classification of the plant kingdom, who called it *Theobroma* ("food of the gods") *cacao*.

During the 18th century, Dutch merchants controlled virtually the entire trade in cocoa beans. Amsterdam developed into the most important cocoa port in the world and thereby stimulated a local cocoa industry. Dutch initiatives established the basis of modern cocoa processing and included the invention of the cocoa press to remove the fat from cocoa mass and development of the Dutch Process of alkalization (CJ van Houten). These advances became the basis of Dutch supremacy in cocoa processing that remains true today.

Originating from the Americas, the cocoa bean enriches life throughout the world today. Its real value was probably first discovered by the Aztecs in Central America and was used as means for payment as well as the ingredient for a powerful "drink of gods". It may have originated in the foothills of the Andes in the Amazon and Orinoco basins of South America where today, examples of wild cacao still can be found. However, it may have had a larger range in the past, evidence for which may be obscured because of its cultivation in these areas long before, as well as after, the Spanish arrived. It may have been introduced into Central America by the ancient Maya, and cultivated in Mexico by the Olmecs, then by the Toltecs and later by the Aztecs. It wasn't until the beginning of the 16th century that cocoa was brought into Europe during the initial visit of Columbus to the "new world". Although the Spanish tried to keep this developing cocoa and chocolate industry to themselves, this new "taste" quickly found its way to the rich and wealthy of other countries.

According to legend, cocao cultivation was initiated by the Mayan demigod king Hun-Apu, or Hunahpu. Hunahpu was one of the two Mayan Twins, brother to Xbalanque. The two play heavily in early Mayan mythology. In constant strife with other gods of the period, they were eventually burned to death and their remains thrown into a river, where they transformed themselves into catfish and lived on happily for a long time. The significance of this is that cacao is considered divine in origin, and this establishes its importance in the world of the Maya. The Maya so highly valued cacao, they used cocoa beans as currency, and to pay taxes. Like many events which occurred a long time ago, the specifics of cacao's rise to popularity remain largely veiled by the mists of time. But we do know this much, that from the very onset of its use, cacao was assigned high status.

In the Mayan and Aztec cultures, cocoa and its preparation featured prominently. *The typical preparation of cocoa involved harvesting the beans from their pods, fermenting the beans, roasting them, and grinding them into a paste. The paste was mixed with water, to which was often added corn, chile peppers, and other spices.* Vigorously mixed with a grooved beating utensil known as a molinet, cocoa was transformed into a frothy beverage. Since sugar was not yet a known food item, cocoa was consumed unsweetened. Drunk on occasion by most people, cocoa was a more regular beverage of the more privileged including priests, rulers, soldiers and other members of high social rank. Cocoa was typically prepared in, and drunk from, a gourd.

Cocoa bean (also *cacao bean*, often simply *cocoa* and *cacao*) is the dried and fully fermented fatty seed of *Theobroma cacao*, from which cocoa solids and cocoa butter are extracted. Cocoa beans are the seeds of the fruit or "pod" of the cocoa tree. The cocoa tree grows in the warmest regions on earth within 20° North and South of the equator. They can be classified in groups according to its geographic origin as well as characteristics, value and application; (West) Africa, Central and South America, Asia/Oceania. Approximately 60% of world production originates from Africa, mainly produced within a network of small farms and cooperatives.

VARIETIES

There are three main varieties of cacao: (1) Forastero, (2) Criollo and (2) Trinitario. The first comprises 95% of the world production of cocoa, and is the most widely used. Overall, the highest quality cocoa beans come from the Criollo variety, which is considered a delicacy. Criollo plantations have lower yields than those of Forastero, and also tend to be less resistant to several diseases that attack the cocoa plant; hence very few countries still produce it. One of the largest producers of Criollo beans is Venezuela (Chuao and Porcelana). Hacienda San José, located in Paria/Venezuela, cultivates Criollo beans. The total area of this Hacienda is 320 hectares, of which 185 hectares are devoted to cacao with a density of 1.000 plants per hectare. Trinitario is a hybrid between Criollo and Forastero varieties. It is considered to be of much higher quality than the latter is, but has higher yields and is more resistant to disease than the former.

Name of variety	Recommended state
VTLCC-1	Karnataka, Kerala and Tamil Nadu
VTLCH-1	Karnataka, Kerala, Tamil Nadu, Andhra Pradesh, Maharashtra, Goa, Meghalaya
VTLCH-2	Karnataka, Kerala, Tamil Nadu, Andhra Pradesh, Maharashtra, Meghalaya, Goa Puducherry, Andaman & Nicobar Islands, Assam, West Bengal and Orissa
VTLCH-3	Karnataka, Kerala, Tamil Nadu, Andhra Pradesh, Maharashtra, Goa, Meghalaya, Puducherry, Andaman & Nicobar Islands, Assam and West Bengal.
VTLCH-4	Karnataka, Kerala, Tamil Nadu, Andhra Pradesh, Maharashtra, Meghalaya, Puducherry, Andaman & Nicobar Islands, Assam, West Bengal and Goa
CCRP-1	Kerala, Karnataka, Tamil Nadu and Andhra Pradesh
CCRP-2	Kerala, Karnataka, Tamil Nadu and Andhra Pradesh
CCRP-3	Kerala and Karnataka
CCRP-4	Kerala, Karnataka, Tamil Nadu and Andhra Pradesh
CCRP-5	Kerala
CCRP-6	Kerala
CCRP-7	Kerala, Karnataka, Tamil Nadu and Andhra Pradesh
CCRP-8	Kerala, Karnataka, Tamil Nadu and Andhra Pradesh
CCRP-9	Kerala, Karnataka, Tamil Nadu and Andhra Pradesh
CCRP-10	Kerala, Karnataka, Tamil Nadu and Andhra Pradesh

HEALTH BENEFITS OF COCOA CONSUMPTION

Chocolate and cocoa contain a high level of flavonoids, specifically epicatechin, which may have beneficial cardiovascular effects on health. The ingestion of flavonol-rich cocoa is associated with acute elevation of circulating nitric oxide, enhanced flow-mediated vasodilation, and augmented microcirculation.

Prolonged intake of flavonol-rich cocoa has been linked to cardiovascular health benefits, although it should be noted that this refers to raw cocoa and to a lesser extent, dark chocolate, since flavonoids degrade during cooking and alkalizing processes. Milk chocolate's addition of whole milk reduces the overall cocoa content per ounce while increasing saturated fat levels, possibly negating some of cocoa's heart-healthy potential benefits. Nevertheless, studies have still found short-term benefits in low-density lipoprotein (LDL) cholesterol levels from dark chocolate consumption.

Hollenberg and colleagues of Harvard Medical School studied the effects of cocoa and flavanols on Panama's Kuna Indian population, who are heavy consumers of cocoa. The researchers found that the Kuna Indians living on the islands had significantly lower rates of heart disease and cancer compared to those on the mainland who do not drink cocoa as on the islands. It is believed that the improved blood flow after consumption of flavonol-rich cocoa may help to achieve health benefits in hearts and other organs. In particular, the benefits may extend to the brain and have important implications for learning and memory.

Foods rich in cocoa appear to reduce blood pressure but drinking green and black tea may not, according to an analysis of previously published research in the April 9, 2007 issue of Archives of Internal Medicine, one of the *Journals* of the American Medical Association (JAMA)/Archives journals.

In June of 2009, Mars Botanicals, a division of Mars Inc., the candymaker and food company, launched Cirku, a cocoa extract high in flavanols. A 15-year study of elderly men published in the *Archives of Internal Medicine* in 2006 found a 50% reduction in *cardiovascular* mortality and a 47% reduction in *all-cause* mortality for the men regularly consuming the most cocoa, compared to those consuming the least cocoa from all sources.

NONHUMAN ANIMAL CONSUMPTION

Chocolate is a food product with appeal not only to the human population, but to many different animals as well. However, chocolate and cocoa contain a high level of xanthines, specifically theobromine and to a much lesser extent caffeine that is detrimental to the health of many animals, including dogs and cats. While these compounds have desirable effects in humans, they cannot be efficiently metabolized in many animals and can lead to cardiac and nervous system problems, and if consumed in high quantities, even lead to death. However, since the beginning of the 21st century, some cocoa derivatives with a low concentration of xanthines have been designed by specialized industry to be suitable for pet consumption, enabling the pet food industry to offer animal-safe chocolate and cocoa flavored products. It results in products with a high concentration of fiber and proteins, while maintaining low concentrations of sugar and other carbohydrates, thus enabling it to be used to create healthy functional cocoa pet products.

CHILD LABOR

- According to an International Labor Organization report, in 2002, more than 109,000 children were working on cocoa farms in Côte d'Ivoire (Ivory Coast), some of them in "the worst forms of child labor". The International Labor Organization later reported that 200,000 children were working in the cocoa industry in Ivory Coast in 2005.
- The first allegations that child slavery is used in cocoa production appeared in 1998. The International Labor Organization report in 2005 failed to fully characterize this problem, but estimated that up to 6% of the 200,000 children involved in cocoa production could be victims of human trafficking or slavery.

The Cocoa Protocol is an effort to end these practices. It has, however, been criticized by some groups including the International Labor Rights Forum as an industry initiative which falls short.

Today cocoa is consumed widely throughout Europe and the Americas, and to a lesser extent in other parts of the world. Large commercial cacao plantations operate in the Ivory Coast, Brazil, Ghana, Malaysia, Mexico, Indonesia, Nigeria, Cameroon, Ecuador, Columbia, the Dominican Republic, Mexico, and Papua New Guinea.

Annual cocoa bean yield is at about three-and-a-half million tons per year, as of 2010. The US, Germany, France, United Kingdom (UK), and Russia are the largest consuming areas for cocoa, in that order. Small cocoa plantations can be found in just about every other tropical location large or small. Cocoa, the food of the gods and the electuary of lovers has captivated humanity with its exotic flavor and sensuous mouth feel. Well done, bravo! Cocoa is the heroic delight, the preferred food of children and poets alike. The world would be a poorer place if not for heavenly cocoa!

POSITION IN INDIA

Production

According to Food and Agriculture Organization (FAO), the production of cocoa in India increased from 300 tons in 1977 to 10.2 thousand tons in 2007 from a corresponding area of 300 and 30.3 thousand hectares. Statewise production (Table 5.1) shows that all India production as 10.2 thousand tons in 2006–2007. India has also been exporting cocoa (Table 5.2) shown in annexure at the end of chapter. This increased to 14.4 thousand tons in 2011 according to FAO (Table 5.3 and 5.3A) occupying 18th position in the world.

The two sources of production data vary as usual—the range in both the cases being more or less the same. Kerala predominates, with more than 50% share. Karnataka, Tamil Nadu and Andhra Pradesh are responsible for the rest of production.

Cadbury India is the largest buyer in Indian market with a purchase of around 10,000 tons beans and an equal quantity through imports to meet its requirement. The consumption is projected to grow by 20%. The four Southern states led by Kerala, monopolize the cocoa cultivation in the country. But, the production has been languishing around 9,000–10,000 tons for some years without much increase in the area.

Encouraged by the high prices, 12,269 hectares were added during 2009–2010 of which 7,317 hectares came under cocoa cultivation in Tamil Nadu alone, the highest among all cocoa producing states. Although the state entered the cocoa scene in a big way only a few years ago and has made rapid progress. The cultivation has picked up well in Dindigul, Namakkal, Coimbatore and Kanyakumari where it is grown as intercrop in vast irrigated coconut farms. Andhra Pradesh added 2,908 hectares and Karnataka 1,708 hectares while the accretion was minimum at 336 hectares in Kerala—all of which are expected to yield beans in a few years. Andhra Pradesh has 16,969 hectares for cocoa, the largest in the country. But when it comes to production, Kerala leads with 6,344 tons out of a total of 12,954 tons of cocoa beans produced in 2009–2010, followed by Karnataka with 3,006 tons. The production was 11,820 tons in 2008–2009. "The addition of more land for cocoa cultivation is good for the crop. Around 10–15 lakh saplings are planned a year, which could lead to increase in production".

Even with this small production base, India is in a position to have substantial increase in the cocoa manufactures particularly chocolates, etc. from Rs 22.8 million in 1992–1993 to 422.6 million in 2007–2008.

It is an important commercial crop grown the world over, in India. It is being cultivated in Kerala, Karnataka and Tamil Nadu. The current area under cocoa is

Table 5.1: Statewise area, production and productivity of cocoa

Area = in hectares; Production = in tons; Productivity = kg/hectare

Years		Andra Pradesh	Kerala	Karnataka	Tamil Nadu	Total
199394	Area	835	8200	2800	48	11883
	Production	30	5270	1400	42	6742
199495	Area	979	6900	2800	48	10727
	Production	30	4300	1400	42	5772
199596	Area	1031	7900	2800	49	11780
	Production	539	4455	1400	43	6282
1996 97	Area	1208	8364	2773	49	12394
	Production	720	3537	1397	43	5697
199798	Area	670	8525	2800	43	12038
	Production	123	3794	1300	37	5281
199899	Area	670	8909	2780	43	12402
	Production	150	3686	1325	37	5198
	Productivity	224	414	477	860	494
199900	Area	2744	8949	4400	92	16185
	Production	771	4000	1550	40	6361
	Productivity	280	446	352	434	378
200001	Area	2740	8500	4400	100	15740
	Production	800	4000	1700	40	6540
	Productivity	293	470	402	434	400
200102	Area	2700	8680	4400	350	16130
	Production	800	4100	1700	180	6780
	Productivity	460	472	402	500	500
200203	Area	6393	9295	6000	205	21893
	Production	633	5109	2500	155	8397
	Productivity	370	550	416	750	560
200304	Area	8537	10220	6000	400	25157
	Production	690	5870	2500	170	9230
	Productivity	370	630	420	500	500
200405	Area	10170	10220	6000	1421	27811
	Production	650	5900	2500	200	9250
	Productivity	170	700	750	300	515
200506	Area	11830	10220	6000	1421	29471
	Production	715	6490	2750	220	10175
	Productivity	187	770	825	330	530
200607	Area	11900	10220	6800	1421	30341
	Production	1520	5800	2650	220	10180
	Productivity	550	675	600	300	530
200708	Area	12734	10530	7200	1421	31885
	Production	1580	6000	2760	220	10560
	Productivity	560	680	600	300	535
200809	Area	14061	10708	7250	2030	34049
	Production	2600	6100	2890	230	11820
	Productivity	565	685	600	350	550

Table 5.3: Area and production of cocoa beans in India and world

Area (hectares); Production (tons)

| Year | India | | World | |
	Area	Production	Area	Production
2007	30,341	10,180	8,306,724 A	4,161,631 A
2006	29,471	10,175	8,564,431 A	4,287,359 A
2005	27,811	9,250	8,775,876 A	4,047,154 A
2004	25,157	9,230	8,535,413 A	4,010,594 A
2003	21,893	8,397	7,728,280 A	3,576,369 A
2002	16,130	6,780	7,024,190 A	3,285,126 A
2001	15,740	6,540	7,169,366 A	3,116,111 A
2000	16,185	6,361	7,602,980 A	3,379,696 A
1999	12,402	5,198	6,549,540 A	2,975,516 A
1998	12,038	5,281	6,653,276 A	3,309,913 A
1997	12,394	5,697	6,497,606 A	3,015,559 A
1996	11,780	6,282	6,469,469 A	3,244,996 A
1995	10,727	5,772	6,562,754 A	2,991,189 A
1994	11,883	6,742	5,759,369 A	2,672,355 A
1993	20,000	6,000	5,752,452 A	2,673,398 A
1992	20,000	6,000	5,729,876 A	2,677,316 A
1991	20,000	6,000	5,684,345 A	2,532,616 A
1990	20,000	6,000	5,709,925 A	2,532,083 A
1989	20,000	6,000	5,514,974 A	2,641,015 A
1988	20,000	6,000	5,655,180 A	2,563,339 A
1987	20,000	7,000	5,275,079 A	2,055,935 A
1986	20,000	6,000	5,247,633 A	2,118,410 A
1985	20,000	6,000	5,046,026 A	2,014,015 A
1984	20,000	6,000	4,768,166 A	1,810,611 A

Table 5.3: Area and production of cocoa beans in India and world *(Contd.)*

Area (hectares); Production (tons)

Year	India Area		India Production	World Area		World Production	
1983	20,000		6,000	4,658,944	A	1,604,673	A
1982	20,000		6,000	4,678,395	A	1,611,358	A
1981	20,000		6,000	4,848,332	A	1,735,292	A
1980	20,000		6,000	4,740,389	A	1,670,684	A
1979	1,000	F	800	4,632,803	A	1,659,914	A
1978	630	F	500	4,581,600	A	1,495,418	A
1977	380	F	300	4,436,820	A	1,452,549	A
1976	0	NR	0	4,309,667	A	1,366,556	A
1975	0	NR	0	4,360,731	A	1,561,669	A
1974	0	NR	0	4,398,854	A	1,556,484	A
1973	0	NR	0	4,316,724	A	1,402,108	A
1972	0	NR	0	4,299,404	A	1,510,770	A
1971	0	NR	0	4,423,360	A	1,638,900	A
1970	0	NR	0	4,358,554	A	1,543,448	A
1969	0	NR	0	4,260,157	A	1,418,917	A
1968	0	NR	0	4,079,359	A	1,246,628	A
1967	0	NR	0	4,217,406	A	1,390,556	A
1966	0	NR	0	4,076,790	A	1,344,411	A
1965	0	NR	0	4,589,429	A	1,228,709	A
1964	0	NR	0	4,541,277	A	1,544,612	A
1963	0	NR	0	4,516,075	A	1,280,516	A
1962	0	NR	0	4,468,792	A	1,213,107	A
1961	0	NR	0	4,403,484	A	1,186,364	A

* - Unofficial figure; F - FAO Estimate; NR - Not reported by country;
A, May include official, semi-official or estimated data.

Table 5.3A: Top rank countries of cocoa beans, 2011

Rank	Country	Production (Int. $1,000)	Flag	Production (MT)	Flag
1	Côte d'Ivoire	1,619,460	*	1,559,441	
2	Indonesia	739,611	*	712,200	
3	Ghana	726,962	*	700,020	
4	Nigeria	415,395	*	400,000	F
5	Cameroon	282,468	*	272,000	F
6	Brazil	258,089	*	248,524	
7	Ecuador	232,790	*	224,163	
8	Togo	103,848	*	100,000	F
9	Peru	58,674	*	56,500	
10	Dominican Republic	56,368	*	54,279	
11	Colombia	45,943	*	44,241	
12	Papua New Guinea	43,616	*	42,000	F
13	Mexico	22,211	*	21,388	
14	Venezuela (Bolivarian Republic of)	18,692	*	18,000	*
15	Malaysia	16,589	*	15,975	Im
16	Uganda	16,328	*	15,723	Im
17	Guinea	15,577	*	15,000	F
18	India	14,954	*	14,400	
19	Sierra Leone	12,461	*	12,000	*
20	Guatemala	11,347	*	10,927	

*:   Unofficial figure
[ ]:   Official data
F: FAO estimate
Im: FAO data based on imputation methodology.

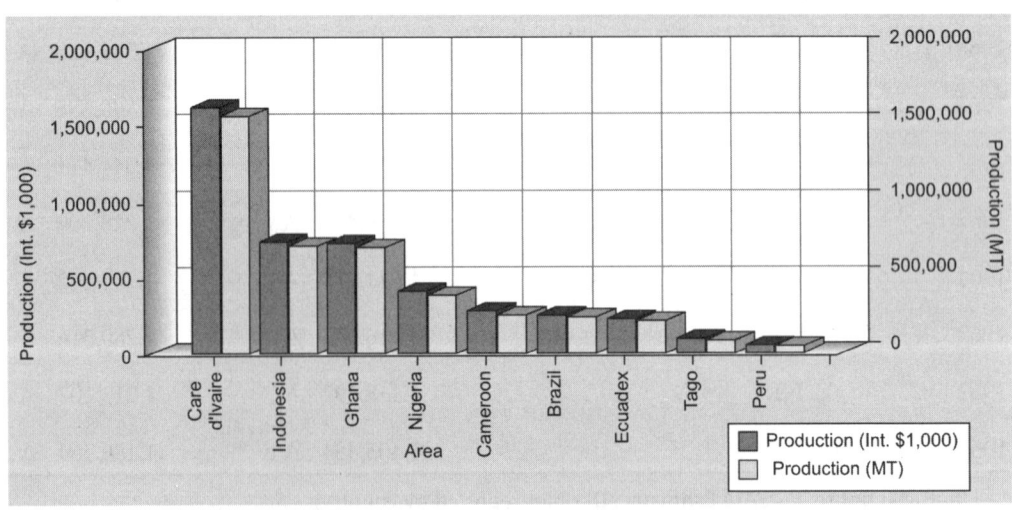

Top production—cocoa beans, 2011

very small. There is a lot of potential for area expansion as a mixed crop. Kerala accounts for about 76% of the area and 78% of the total production in the country. The remaining area and production is contributed by Karnataka. It is being grown in some pockets in Tamil Nadu and Andhra Pradesh also.

Major Cocoa Growing Belts in India

Andaman and Nicobar Islands	All parts of Andaman and Nicobar Islands
Andhra Pradesh	East Godavari, West Godavari, Visakhapatanam, Vizianagaram, Krishna, Khammam
Assam	Barpeta, Baksa, Bongaigaon, Cachar, Chirang, Darrang, Dhemaji, Dhubri, Dibrugarh, Goalpara, Golaghat, Hailakandi, Jorhat, Karbi Anglong, Kamrup, Karimgang, Kokrajhar, Lakhimpur, Marigaon, N.C. Hills, Nagaon, Nalbari, Sibsagar, Sonitpur, Tinsukia, Udaiguri
Goa	North and South Goa
Karnataka	Uttara and Dakshina Kannada, Shimoga, Mysore, Davanagere, Kodagu, Mandya, Chickmagalore, Hassan, Tumkur.
Kerala	Idukki, Kottayam, Malappuram, Trissur, Kozhikode, Kasaragod
Maharashtra	Raigad, Ratnagiri, Sindhudurg, Thane
Meghalaya	East Khasi Hills, Jaintia Hills, West Garo Hills, East Garo Hills
Orissa	Balasore, Bhadrak, Cuttak, Dhenkanal, Ganjam, Jagatsinghpur, Jajapur (Jajpur), Puri
Puducherry	Karaikal, Mahe, Puducherry, Yanam
Tamil Nadu	Coimbatore, Erode, Thanjavur, Truchirapally, Salem, Theni, Madurai
West Bengal	Jalpaiguri, Cooch Behar, 24 Parganas (North and South), Howrah, Nadia, Darjeeling.

Post-harvesting Management

The harvested pods are broken for extraction of beans by hitting them or a hard surface. The beans are then extracted excluding the placenta. The pods may be kept to a week before breaking and extracting beans for fermentations. The fermented beans have a moisture content of about 55%. The beans are to be skin dried within 24 hours after fermentation to avoid mound growth. During drying biochemical oxidation of excess acetic acid from the bans takes place.

Dry cocoa beans can be store be stored for a long stored for a long period under suitable conditions. The storage life is decided by the relative humidity and temperature prevailing in the store house. It is found that at 85% relative humidity, the moisture contents exceed 8%. The practice followed at present is to shift the beans to other regions of the country where the conditions are suitable.

Good Fortunes for Organic Cocoa Farming in India

Demand for organic cocoa is rising in the world, particularly in the US and Europe. To cash in on the trend, major chocolate companies are jumping on to the organic bandwagon. While South America and Africa are the main sourcing countries, a Swiss company has launched a chocolate based on organic cocoa from India recently. "Eating habits are changing in the US and Europe. People aware of the environment and ecological issues prefer organic products even in chocolates", said Antony Panakal of Switzerland-based Chocolate Stella, which recently launched Indian brand of chocolate made of organic cocoa grown in Kerala. The company has introduced single origin organic chocolates in several developing countries.

According to Antony, nearly 15–20% of world cocoa production is of the organic variety. This could increase to 30% considering the rising demand. Chocolate Stella sources most of its organic cocoa from South America. In India, the company has tied up with Indian Organic Farmers Producer Company (IOFPCL).

Indian organic cocoa production is largely confined to Kerala. "It is done mostly in Idukki and Kottayam districts. Although we have not done an exact calculation, it is estimated that about 10–20% of the total cocoa production of over 12,000 tons in the country is organic". The Southern states are the major cocoa producers in the country.

There are several enquiries from European companies for organic cocoa. "The problem is our production of organic cocoa is not big. But, the premium price is an incentive for the farmers to increase their cultivation.

Export

The primary product is chocolate confectionary which increased from 147 tons in 1992–1993. Having touched 1,552.13 tons in 2003–2004, it again fell down to 1,137 tons in 2007–2008. We can find that the main exporters are also the main producers of cocoa beans. Although countries like Brazil and Malaysia are main producers, they are not necessarily large exporters due to the size of their processing industry, which absorbs local production. In Latin America for example, the Dominican Republic exports more cocoa beans than Brazil.

WORLD

World production of cocoa increased from 1,186.4 thousand tons in 1961 to 4,161.6 thousand tons in 2007. Corresponding area figures are 4,403.5 and 8,306.7 thousand hectares (Table 5.3). Thereafter production declined for a few years and again touched 4,197 thousand tons in 2010–2011 according to USA. Côte d'Ivoire has been the top producer with 1,600–1,800 thousand tons in some years accounting for 40% of the world production (Table 5.3A).

PROCESSING

Cocoa processing consists in the production of two intermediate products: (1) cocoa butter and (2) cocoa powder. This operation is known as converting or grinding. Cocoa butter and powder are recombined, in varying proportions, to make chocolate which also incorporates other inputs, most importantly milk and sugar. Cocoa powder is also used without the butter in confectionary products. Butter and powder are produced in fixed proportions, given the fat content of the beans, and powder is normally seen as a by-product.

The harvested pods are opened—typically with a machete—the pulp and cocoa seeds are removed and the rind is discarded. The pulp and seeds are then piled in heaps, placed in bins, or laid out on grates for several days. During this time, the seeds and pulp undergo "sweating", where the thick pulp liquefies as it ferments. The fermented pulp trickles away, leaving cocoa seeds behind to be collected. Sweating is important for the quality of the beans, which originally have a strong bitter taste. If sweating is interrupted, the resulting cocoa may be ruined if underdone the cocoa seed maintains a flavor similar to raw potatoes and becomes susceptible to mildew. Some cocoa producing countries distill alcoholic spirits using the liquefied pulp.

Demand: Grindings

Once cocoa beans have been harvested, fermented, dried, and transported, cocoa processing is the next key step in preparation for commercial consumption. From supply of beans to demand by processors, it is important to analyze the import market for indications of cocoa trade balance. In general, grindings from cocoa beans serve as the key focus for market analysts for an overall view of anticipated demand relative to supply.

While processors of cocoa beans are located throughout the world, the highest percentage is based in Europe, followed by Asia and Oceania, Americas and then Africa (Table 5.3B and Fig. 5.1).

In terms of cocoa beans, market analysts provide ongoing tracking of grindings to compare and analyze against production estimates. Providing a breakdown of grindings per region for a 3 year time frame, International Cocoa Organization (ICCO) shows a relatively constant market share for the Americas (~22%) and Africa (~17%) while Europe (~39%) has slightly declined and Asia and Oceania (~22%) have increased. Origin grindings have slightly increased to 41% out of total grindings over the time frame.

The supply chain illustrates a simple version of the cocoa supply chain (Fig. 5.2). Producers sell their cocoa beans, via a cooperative and/or a local buyer or "traitant", to exporters. Some or all the major exporters are either multinational converters or local companies controlled by the converters. A small amount of generally low quality cocoa may be processed and sold locally. Both sets of domestic marketing agents sell to exporters, who are associated with importers and processor in Europe and North America, or who trade on the London or New York commodity exchanges. A few exporters operate out of one or two ports in each country. Processors grind cocoa into butter, powder and liquor, which they sell to chocolate manufacturers and other food processors, who ultimately sell their products to consumers. Both processors and chocolate manufacturers are concentrated Transnational Corporations (TNCs). The intent in this section is to describe the chain more in depth up to the level where the actors of the West and Central Africa (WCA) producing countries get.

The cocoa pods take about 5 months from flowering to ripeness and are exposed to a number of pests and diseases (capsids, swollen shoot virus and phytophthora). Ripe fruits are harvested by farmers with long-handled knives or machetes when the fruit has achieved a deep yellow color (for most varieties). The harvested pods are collected together, broken open, usually with a wooden baton and the wet beans

Table 5.3B: Grindings of cocoa beans

('000 tons)

	2009–2010	2010–2011	2011–2012
Europe	1,492	1,595	1,554
Germany	361	439	421
Netherlands	500	525	490
Others	631	631	643
Share of total	41.2%	41.7%	39.1%
America	801	839	865
Brazil	223	236	243
United States	380	390	400
Others	198	213	222
Share of total	22.1%	22.0%	21.8%
Asia and Oceania	689	770	897
Indonesia	120	170	270
Malaysia	298	305	312
Others	271	295	315
Share of total	19.0%	20.1%	22.6%
Africa	642	618	657
Côte d'Ivoire	390	340	380
Ghana	200	220	222
Others	52	58	55
Share of total	17.7%	16.2%	16.5%
World total	3,624	3,822	3,973
Origin total	3,624	3,822	3,973
Origin grindings	1,423	1,472	1,621

Note: Total differs from sum of constituents due to rounding.
Source: LMC of February, 2012.

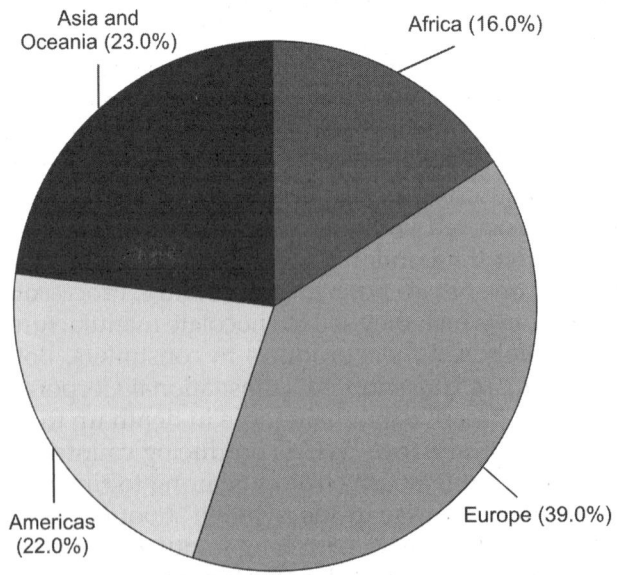

Fig. 5.1: World grindings of cocoa beans

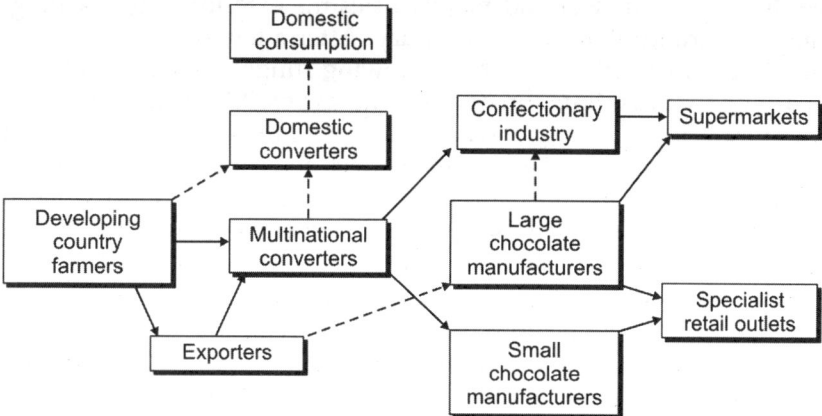

Fig. 5.2: The basic cocoa supply chain

Source: Gilbert (2006).

covered with sweet mucilage are removed by hand. Ripe fruits are sometimes left in the field for up to 10 days, a practice called pod storage which is supposed to enhance the flavor but is usually done to allow enough labor to be assembled to break the pods all on the same day, often a Saturday morning. The pod husk is discarded and the wet cocoa beans with their sweet mucilage are then fermented for a number of days; without this vital process, the chocolate flavor will not be fully developed on subsequent roasting in the factory.

The fermented beans are dried by spreading them out over a large surface and constantly raking them. In large plantations, this is done on huge trays under the sun or by using artificial heat. Small plantations may dry their harvest on little trays or on cowhides. Finally, the beans are trodden and shuffled about (often using bare human feet) and sometimes, during this process, red clay mixed with water is sprinkled over the beans to obtain a finer color, polish, and protection against molds during shipment to factories in the US, the Netherlands, UK, and other countries. Drying in the sun is preferable to drying by artificial means, as no extraneous flavors such as smoke or oil are introduced which might otherwise taint the flavor.

For successful flavor development, a fermentation pile (from 90 kg to 250 kg of wet beans) are built up on plantain leaves and then covered with more leaves; these piles should be constructed away from full sunlight and ideally should be turned after about 3 days to ensure even conditions throughout the pile. Plastic sheets are sometimes used. On larger holdings, this fermentation can conveniently be carried out in wooden boxes usually 1.2 m by 1.2 m and beans are to a depth of 0.9 m and again would be turned at the third day; this would be about 1 ton of wet beans. On completion of fermentation, the cocoa is carried to the villages for drying on raised bamboo mats (in Ghana for example) or on concrete (Côte d'Ivoire). This can take from 7 days to 10 days or even longer in cloudy/rainy conditions. Drying on concrete can lead to the beans drying quickly and can potentially introduce various sorts of externally imposed contamination. On raised bamboo mats the drying beans can be conveniently sorted and debris moved and their use enables the beans to be rolled up in the mat in the event of rain during drying. Rushing the drying process stops some of the chemical reactions started during fermentation and prevents escape of the remaining acids in the beans resulting in acidic flavors in the cocoa. Very fast drying can leave the cotyledons wet and merely dries the exterior of the bean, giving the misleading appearance that the cocoa is dry. After a few days in this situation, the moisture will migrate out to the shell, allowing fungal development and growth. Artificial drying should mimic sun drying as far as possible, using low temperatures/ ambient air for the initial drying and higher temperatures only for the final stage. Sun drying allows the sun and wind to take their effect, and combined with stirring ensures thorough drying; a process that also allows the removal of defective beans. When cocoa beans crackle in the hand if rubbed together, then they have achieved the desired level of about 7.5% moisture and after cooling for 24 hours are ready for sale.

The purchase of cocoa from farmers and its movement to port is in the hands of private operators. In Côte d'Ivoire, for instance, itinerant buyers (traitants) with small pick-up trucks regularly come to the villages to buy cocoa for cash after a rapid quality and moisture check followed by crude weighing. The scales are rarely checked by the relevant authorities. The cocoa is delivered that same day to the collection center in the nearest large town then moved to the exporters store in the port areas of Abidjan or San Pedro.

The only state intervention is in Ghana where the government controlled Quality Control Division (QCD) undertakes grading and sealing of cocoa into export sacks. Stating buying premises are required under the cocoa marketing legislation. The cocoa can be brought into the metal roofed shed by the farmer where it is weighed on certified scales. Quality and moisture content are thoroughly checked often in the presence of the farmer by the manager of the buying shed who usually provides a check to the farmer and keep a detailed payment record. The marketing system in Ghana and the resulting high quality has been founded on the principal that cocoa bags are officially graded and sealed by QCD as close to the farm as possible in the village buying sheds. Cocoa may remain in villages for some weeks both before and after sealing by QCD. Once an adequate quantity of sealed cocoa and transport is available, then the buyer will move to the "hand over point" where the cocoa is sold to the government owned Cocoa Marketing Company (CMC) at a fixed price. The cocoa is purchased by CMC from the Licensed Buying Companies (LBCs) and placed into large piles in airy warehouses close to the port from which vessels can are loaded after fumigation. Competition among LBCs exists but varies in degree across villages (Teal et al., 2006).

In the Northern Hemisphere cocoa stocks can be stored for several years, as storage conditions tend to be good in cold climates. Storing cocoa at its point of origin in warmer climates can be difficult, but the degree of difficulty varies across countries. In Ghana properly prepared cocoa is reportedly very resilient and can be stored for some time despite the humidity and heat (Varangis and Schreiber, 2001). In general, cocoa needs to be moved from its point of origin as soon as possible because of the effects of heat and moisture. Cocoa that is delivered to a port wet can rapidly develop mold and problems with free-fatty acids and ochratoxin (fungal toxin). Much cocoa is dried at port in order to prevent mold from forming. This process is delicate: exporters want parcels to arrive at their final destination with no less than 5.5% moisture and no more than 7.5–8.0%. The fabric and the ventilation in many of the cocoa stores are poorer than desirable. In the case of Ghana, cocoa may remain in these stores for some weeks. Cocoa may also remain on lorries in the port area for some days waiting to be unloaded. On unloading at the exporters' store, the cocoa would be checked again for quality, re-dried if necessary (in artificial driers), sieved and bagged into export sacks. The bagging stage would be omitted if cocoa is being shipped as bulk in containers or as megabulk (direct in the hold of the vessel). Cocoa may be ready for export within 7 days of arrival at the exporters' store. For container shipments (either as bags or bulk in containers), the speed of loading of the container vessel requires that containers are stuffed well ahead of the estimated time of arrival of the vessel.

Along with farmers in neighboring Côte d'Ivoire, Ghana's 600,000–800,000 cocoa growers are known to receive the lowest share of the export price in the world, roughly half (Varangis and Schreiber, 2001). At 30%, the export tax is the highest by far among all the major cocoa-producing countries. Marketing costs are also relatively high at 15%, and the costs of the Cocobod and its subsidiaries account for around 5%. Producer prices in Nigeria are determined by market conditions in both the internal and international cocoa markets. As a result of liberalization, cocoa farmers in Nigeria receive well above 80% of the *free on board* (FOB) export price. The poor state of the WCA infrastructure hampers production and limits the marketing network.

Cocoa beans undergo many different stages of processing before they can be mixed with other ingredients to produce chocolate Cocoa butter and liquor are used to make chocolate while cocoa powder is used in beverages and other confectionery. Good quality chocolate will contain a relatively high percentage of cocoa (up to 70%); however, most of the popular bars in the UK and North America contain only 20% (Oxfam, 2002).

Since there has been little processing of cocoa historically in Africa, exports have closely matched production. In 2000, only 8% of beans were processed within Africa, and the remainder exported. Both tax incentives offered by African governments and the advantages under backward integration have encouraged the multinational processors to build or buy plants in WCA. In the past, local processing firms have used lower quality beans, while exporting the higher quality ones. Storage of cocoa has also been in Europe and North American because the logistics and the temperate and semiarid climates are better suited to storage. Processors of beans into liquor or who manufacture chocolate is flavor conscious, and hence will pay more for well-fermented cocoa (Bloomfield and Lass, 1992).The usual buyers of beans of irregular or unpleasant flavor are those companies who press beans to extract butter or cake. They buy the majority of cocoa from Cote d'Ivoire, Nigeria, Malaysia and Indonesia.

Cocoa processing at origin has traditionally been an area of controversy (Bloomfield and Lass, 1992). The rationale for promoting local processing has been to generate employment, promote industrialization, and add value to raw materials and to process sub-quality beans that would otherwise not be exportable or would pull down the average price of bean exports. Local processing lacked competitiveness compared with processing in consumer countries. Processing at origin suffers from a number of drawbacks including sourcing of beans from only one origin, transport costs to end-users, shipment of cocoa liquor and butter in solid form as contrasted with shipment by processors in consumer countries in liquid and heated form, tariff escalation, and competition from industrialized-country processors who ship on a just-in-time basis, as contrasted with producers countries who have less control over the delivery date. Many origin processing companies have not met quality and hygiene standards demanded by end-users. Given these many marketing constraints, producer country.

Processors have had to compete primarily on a cost basis. This has been possible either through subsidized inputs or through the use of low quality beans and low cost of production.

The beans should be dry for shipment (usually by sea) to the US and Europe. Traditionally exported in jute bags, over the last decade the beans are increasingly shipped in "Mega-Bulk" bulk parcels of several thousand tons at a time on ships, or in smaller lots of around 25 tons in 20' containers. Shipping in bulk significantly reduces handling costs; however shipment in bags, either in a ship's hold or in containers, is still commonly found. The Netherlands is the leading cocoa processing country, followed by the US.

To make 1 kg (2.2 pounds) of chocolate, about 300–600 beans are processed, depending on the desired cocoa content. In a factory, the beans are roasted. Next they are cracked and then de-shelled by a "winnower". The resulting pieces of beans are called nibs, and are ground, using various methods, into a thick creamy paste, known as chocolate liquor or cocoa paste. This "liquor" is then further processed into chocolate by mixing in (more) cocoa butter and sugar (and sometimes vanilla and lecithin as an emulsifier), then refined, conched and tempered. Alternatively, it can be separated into cocoa powder and cocoa butter using a hydraulic press or the Broma process. This process produces around 50% cocoa butter and 50% cocoa powder. Standard cocoa powder has a fat content of approximately 10–12%. Cocoa butter is used in chocolate bar manufacture, other confectionery, soaps and cosmetics.

Adding an alkali produces Dutch process cocoa powder, which is less acidic, darker and more mellower in flavor than what is generally available in most of the world. Regular (non-alkalized) cocoa is acidic, so when cocoa is treated with an alkaline ingredient, generally potassium carbonate, the pH increases. This process can be done at various stages during manufacturing including during nib treatment, liquor treatment or press cake treatment. Another process that helps to develop the flavor is roasting. Roasting can be done on the whole bean before shelling or on the nib after shelling. The time and temperature of the roast affect the result: a "low roast" produces a more acid, aromatic flavor, while a high roast gives a more intense, bitter flavor lacking complex flavor notes.

Originally, cocoa was mainly cultivated in the tropical rainforests in South America. Once established in Ghana, cocoa production expanded rapidly in Africa and by the mid 1920s, WCA has become the main producer. Cocoa grows naturally in tropical rain forests. This habitat provides heavy shade and rainfall, uniform temperature and constant relative humidity and is typically only found within 10° of the equator. There are basically three types of cocoa grown: (1) Criollo, (2) Forestaro and (3) Trinitario (a cross between Criollo and Forestaro). Each type has its own characteristics of growth vigor, fermentation requirements, disease susceptibility and fat content. Forestaro is the most commonly grown comprising some 93% of world production.

WCA produces about 70% of world cocoa. About 90–95% of all cocoa is produced by smallholders with farm sizes of 2–5 hectares. Cocoa and coffee are both dependent on natural resources and unskilled or semiskilled low cost labor rather than technology as the dominant portion of their total costs. The most prominent issue receiving attention in the media now is the concern that child labor, under unsafe conditions and possibly as slaves, is used on the plantations. Eliminating such practices remains a challenge.

With such relatively simple and widely available production technology, countries which have traditionally been heavily dependent on cocoa production are vulnerable to the entry of new competitors. Proper farm management and maintenance (sanitation, weeding and removing parasites) and technologies such as high-yielding varieties (HYV) are important in maintaining and enhancing productivity.

Given the perennial nature of the crops, the two basic moments of choice for the farmer include the choice of planting given the already available stock of trees and the choice of maintenance and harvesting intensity. Once planted, the cocoa trees can have a productive life of more than 30 years, with yields per tree that rise gradually and eventually fall as the tree grows older. In WCA, the main crop harvest for cocoa starts in the September–October period and can extend into the January–March period. The clearing is done manually which together with the no-tillage method used when planting, causes minimum or no disturbance to the soils. Mechanical fermentation and drying facilities in some cases have enabled economies of scale and a reduction in costs.

Cocoa serves as an important crop around the world: a cash crop for growing countries and a key import for processing and consuming countries. Cocoa travels along a global supply chain crossing countries and continents. The complex production process involves numerous parties including, farmers, buyers, shipping organizations, processors, chocolatiers and distributors. Cultivation of cocoa at the farm level is a delicate process as crops are susceptible to various conditions including weather patterns, diseases, and insects. Unlike larger, industrialized agribusinesses, the vast majority of cocoa still comes from small, family-run farms, who often confront outdated farming practices and limited organizational leverage. A steady demand from worldwide consumers draws numerous global efforts and funds committed to support and improve cocoa farm sustainability.

Cocoa trades on two world exchanges: (1) London [London International Financial Futures Exchange (LIFFE-Pound)] and (2) New York [Intercontinental Exchange (ICE-USD)]. In 2011, trading volume of cocoa futures on the ICE was 4.95 million metric tons, outpacing production by 750,000 tons. Conversely, ICE traded 3.8 million tons in 2010, 390,000 tons less than total production. Comparatively, ICE traded 5.2 million metric tons of coffee futures in 2011 and 5.5 million metric tons in 2010.

They are the basis of chocolate. A cocoa pod (fruit) has a rough leathery rind about 3 cm thick (this varies with the origin and variety of pod). It is filled with sweet, mucilaginous pulp (called "baba de cacao" in South America) enclosing 30–50 large seeds that are fairly soft and pale pink or lavender in color. The word "cocoa" is derivative of "cacao". "Cocoa" can often also refer to the drink commonly known as hot chocolate; to cocoa powder, the dry powder made by grinding cocoa seeds and removing the cocoa butter from the dark, bitter cocoa solids; or to a mixture of cocoa powder and cocoa butter.

WORLD PRODUCTION

Cocoa is grown principally in West Africa, Central and South America and Asia. In order of annual production size, the eight largest cocoa producing countries at present are Côte d'Ivoire, Ghana, Indonesia, Nigeria, Cameroon, Brazil, Ecuador and Malaysia. These countries represent 90% of world production (Fig. 5.3).

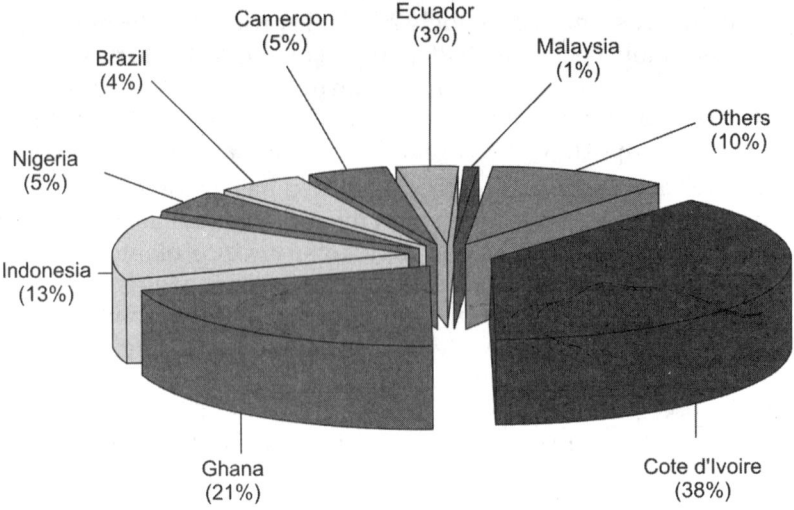

Fig. 5.3: Share of countries in total cocoa beans production (2005/2006 crop year forecasts)

Source: United Nations Conference on Trade and Development (UNCTAD) based on the data from International Cocoa Organization, quarterly bulletin of cocoa statistics.

In the early 1970s, production was concentrated on Ghana, Nigeria, Côte d'Ivoire and Brazil, but it has now expanded to areas such as the Pacific region where countries like Indonesia have shown spectacular growth rates in production. By 2005–2006, world production increased by 131.7% (2.8% annual).

Numerous cocoa market experts and analysts provide reports based on historical, current, and projected levels. Cocoa bean production is closely monitored as trade balances, pricing, and futures contracts depend largely on supply side factors.

As depicted below, total production has increased in absolute terms from 2000. 3.66 million metric tons in 2007–2008 and 3.98 million metric tons in 2011–2012 (Table 5.4). Change in production has not been linear, however, and has fluctuated in various patterns among the different regions. Africa has been and is projected to remain the principal cocoa producer with 73% market share last year.

Dry weather patterns across West Africa early in the 2011/2012 season caused forecasts of production shortfalls. However, increased rains through March 2012 have changed these projections. Production for the 2011/2012 season is expected to approximately match demand.

Consumption

Although cocoa is largely produced in developing countries, it is mostly consumed in industrialized countries. For cocoa, the buyers in the consuming countries are the processors and the chocolate manufacturers. A few multinational companies dominate both processing and chocolate manufacturing. The following graph represents the main consumers of cocoa, based on the apparent domestic cocoa consumption, which is calculated as grindings plus net imports of cocoa products and of chocolate products in beans equivalent. There no data available regarding total consumption Cocoa country-wise. Per capita consumption of cocoa beans is

Table 5.4: Production of cocoa region wise

'000 tons

	2007–08 Total	2008–09 Total	2009–10 Total	2010–11 Total	2011–12 Total	07/08–11/12 % Change
Total production ('000 tons)	3,667	3,507	3,569	4,197	3,987	8.73%
% Change	**7.2%**	**–4.4%**	**1.8%**	**17.6%**	**–5.0%**	
Total Africa	2,603	2,451	2,428	3,076	2,801	7.61%
% Change	**9.5%**	**–5.8%**	**–0.9%**	**26.7%**	**–8.9%**	
Cameroon	188	210	205	230	220	17.02%
Cote d'Ivoire	1,431	1,234	1,184	1,668	1,400	–2.17%
Ghana	730	730	740	860	870	19.18%
Nigeria	200	210	230	240	230	15.00%
Other Africa	55	67	69	78	81	47.27%
Total Asia and Oceania	614	596	642	563	623	1.47%
% Change	**–3.3%**	**–2.9%**	**7.7%**	**–12.3%**	**10.7%**	
Indonesia	500	490	530	450	500	0.00%
Malaysia	32	25	20	18	18	–43.75%
Other Asia	82	81	92	95	105	28.05%
Total Americas	450	459	499	558	563	25.11%
% Change	**10.7%**	**2.1%**	**8.5%**	**12.0%**	**0.8%**	
Brazil	170	155	159	197	185	8.82%
Ecuador	115	130	150	160	170	47.83%
Other Latin America	165	174	189	201	208	26.06%

Source: ICCO; USDA; Reuters; LMC Report, February, 2012.

the highest (8.1 kg/annum) is in Estonia, followed by Luxembourg (5.2 kg), France (4.2 kg) and UK (4.6 kg).

Production Trends and Yields

Figs 5.4A and B; Tables 5.5 and 5.6, show the trend in West and Central Africa (WCA) cocoa production in terms of area harvested in hectares and production quantity in metric tons. Production had a steady upward trend that got steeper in the early 1990s. There was a decline right after the 2000 international price shocks and then there was a gradual increase as prices regained their upward trend. Since 2004, the area harvested has declined with the production quantity has remained the same. On average, cocoa yield has gradually increased throughout the 1980–2007 period; the yield has specifically accelerated upward since 2002 (Tables 5.6 and 5.6A).

A brief discuss as about the production pattern in each of the major WCA cocoa producing countries in order of production quantity is given at the next page. The Central African Republic is omitted here for its production level in cocoa is negligible.

Côte d'Ivoire

Côte d'Ivoire is the world's largest producer of cocoa, accounting for around 40% of global supply with a recorded production of 1.3 million tons in 2007. The country's economic growth tends to reflect fluctuations in revenue from this all-important crop [*Economist Intelligence Unit* (EIU), 2008]. Together, cocoa and coffee account for 60% of the area under cultivation in Côte d'Ivoire. The cocoa and coffee region in the south-west is linked to the second major port, San-Pédro (Abidjan being the first). Cash crops are grown in the coastal region and the south of the country is also the site of most manufacturing activity. Côte d'Ivoire has been going through adverse conditions such as the depletion of the labor force in the cocoa-producing zone, the persistence of roadblocks and corruption on the transport routes, the failure to sustain agricultural extension services, and the instabilities of domestic farm gate prices. Another factor contributing to the decline of the sector is the deterioration in the quality of cocoa beans; the Ivorian cocoa is attracting a lower price on the world markets as a result of the lower use of pesticides and of problems with drying the

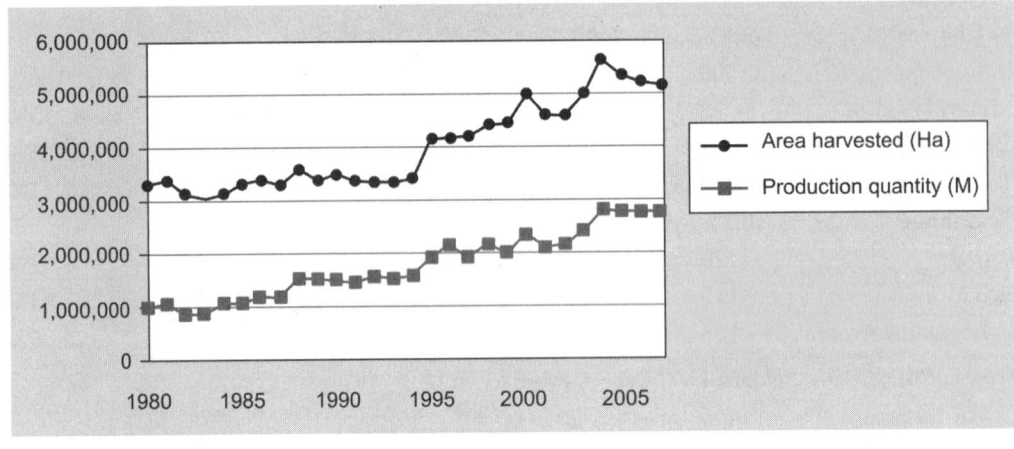

A

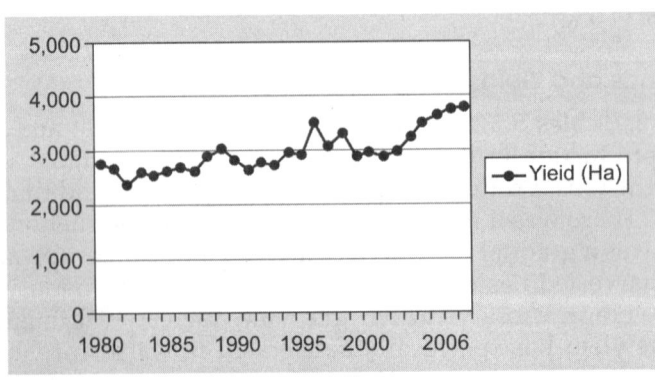

B

Figs 5.4A and B: (A) WCA cocoa production trend (1980–2007), (B) WCA average cocoa yield trend (1980–2007)

Table 5.5: WCA cocoa production (2000–2007)

Country	Element	2000	2001	2002	2003	2004	2005	2006	2007
Cameroon	Area harvested (hectares)	370,000	370,000	370,000	375,000	375,000	400,000	370,000	378,000
	Production quantity (million tons)	122,600	122,100	125,000	154,965	166,754	178,500	164,553	179,239
CAR	Area harvested (hectares)	1,000	1,000	1,000	1,000	1,000	1,000	1,000	1,000
	Production quantity (million tons)	50	50	50	50	50	50	50	50
DRC	Area harvested (hectares)	21,724	20,752	19,16	19,033	18,900	18,767	18,633	19,000
	Production quantity (million tons)	6,582	6,235	75,750	5,710	5,670	5,630	5,590	5,700
Côte d'Ivoire	Area harvested (hectares)	2,000,000	1,777,550	1,880,000	2,000,000	2,050,000	1,800,000	1,700,000	1,700,000
	Production quantity (million tons)	1,401,101	1,212,428	1,264,708	1,351,546	1,407,213	1,286,330	1,254,500	1,300,000
Ghana	Area harvested (hectares)	1,500,000	1,350,000	1,195,000	1,500,000	2,000,000	1,850,000	1,835,000	1,725,000
	Production quantity (million tons)	436,600	389,591	340,562	497,000	737,000	740,000	734,000	690,000
Liberia	Area harvested (hectares)	24,000	10,000	10,000	15,000	15,000	17,000	17,000	17,000
	Production quantity (million tons)	3,100	1,000	1,500	2,500	2,500	3,000	3,000	3,000
Nigeria	Area harvested (hectares)	966,000	966,000	1,030,000	1,002,000	1,062,000	1,062,000	1,104,000	1,110,000
	Production quantity (million tons)	338,000	340,000	362,000	385,000	412,000	441,000	485,000	500,000
STP	Area harvested (hectares)	24,000	24,000	24,000	28,000	21,000	26,000	22,000	22,000
	Production quantity (million tons)	3,418	3,200	3,200	3,700	2,800	3,500	3,000	3,500
Sierra Leone	Area harvested (hectares)	30,000	30,000	30,000	33,000	33,000	33,000	38,000	33,000
	Production quantity (million tons)	11,000	11,000	11,000	12,000	12,000	12,000	13,940	12,000
Togo	Area harvested (hectares)	21,400	21,400	18,000	19,000	35,000	90,000	104,000	104,000
	Production quantity (million tons)	6,600	6,500	6,000	7,900	21,700	59,000	73,000	70,000

Source: FAOSTAT (2008).

Table 5.5B: Cocoa international trade

('000 tons)

	Exports				Imports			
	Actual		Growth rates		Actual		Growth rates	
	1988–1990 Average	1998–2000 Average	1988–1990 to 1998–2000	1998–2000 to 2010	1988–1990	1998–2000	1988–1990	1998–2000
World	**1,765**	**2,220**	**2.3**	**2.8**	**1,723**	**2,337**	**3.1**	**2.2**
Developing	**1,765**	**2,220**	**2.3**	**2.8**	**176**	**334**	**6.6**	**0.0**
Africa	1,225	1,731	3.5	2.8	2	4	7.1	0.0
Côte d'Ivoire	694	1,115	4.8	3.0				
Ghana	251	340	3.1	3.0				
Nigeria	143	148	0.3	2.9				
Cameroon	96	95	-0.2	0.2				
Latin America and Caribbean	236	97	-8.5	2.7	7	70	25.7	-7.7
Brazil	112	3	-30.4	20.3		61		-12.5
Colombia	6		-23.8			1		4.5
Ecuador	57	48	-1.8	-1.0		2		
Mexico	1	2	7.9			4		5.9
Other Latin America	61	46	-2.8	3.1	7	1	-15.6	13.0
Near East					5	31	21.0	-0.5
Far East	304	391	2.5	2.8	162	230	3.5	1.4
Indonesia	92	328	13.5	4.3		14		0.0
Malaysia	164	18	-19.7	4.0	1	87		0.0
Developed					**1,547**	**2,002**	**2.6**	**2.5**
North America					335	487	3.8	0.3
Canada					23	52	8.3	4.1
United States					312	435	3.4	-0.2

Table 5.5B: Cocoa international trade *(Contd.)*

('000 tons)

	Exports				Imports			
	Actual		Growth rates		Actual		Growth rates	
	1988–1990 Average	1998–2000 Average	1988–1990 to 1998–2000	1998–2000 to 2010	1988–1990	1998–2000	1988–1990	1998–2000
Europe					1,030	1,323	2.5	3.5
EC					921	1,233	3.0	3.7
Austria					14	20	3.8	2.6
Belgium/Luxemburg					46	26	-5.5	10.3
Denmark					3	11	16.2	4.8
Finland							-9.8	56.6
France					63	145	8.7	2.4
Germany					275	226	-2.0	0.5
Greece					5	3	-4.9	2.5
Ireland					11	8	-2.7	-3.0
Italy					51	73	3.7	1.4
Netherlands					258	444	5.6	7.0
Portugal							-9.9	21.6
Spain					42	54	2.4	-0.6
Sweden					2		-42.7	
United Kingdom					151	177	1.6	1.3
Other Europe					109	90	-1.9	-0.1
Poland					24	30	2.2	2.4
Switzerland					21	22	0.5	0.8
Former USSR					130	138	0.6	-1.1
Oceania								
Other Developed					52	55	0.6	1.7
Japan					46	48	0.3	1.4

Table 5.6: World production of cocoa beans

(Tons)

Countries	1994–1996	1999–2001	2004	2005	2006
Bolivia	3,825	4,273	4,268	4,358	4,474
Brazil	294,686	195,818	196,005	208,620	212,270
Cameroon	122,242	120,233	166,754	178,500	164,553
Colombia	52,304	46,574	36,356	37,099	37,000
Côte d'Ivoire (Ivory Coast)	1,054,654	1,258,851	1,407,213	1,286,330	1,254,500
Dominican Republic	65,037	35,955	47,985	31,361	32,000
Ecuador	86,830	90,197	123,623	106,143	87,561
Equatorial Guinea	3,927	4,800	3,000	3,000	3,000
Ghana	364,992	420,130	737,000	740,000	734,000
India	6,265	6,033	8,510	10,440	10,175
Indonesia	290,300	405,627	641,700	642,900	580,000
Malaysia	142,906	70,536	33,400	27,964	31,937
Mexico	44,017	38,613	43,975	36,366	38,151
Nigeria	283,000	301,000	412,000	441,000	485,000
Papua New Guinea	32,092	40,400	38,900	47,800	51,100
Philippines	7,905	6,942	5,648	5,679	5,415
Sao Tome and Principe	3,975	3,605	2,800	3,500	3,000
Sierra Leone	10,579	10,973	12,000	12,000	13,940
Spain	3,617	3,610	1,970	1,880	1,560
Togo	8,567	6,700	21,700	59,000	73,000
Venezuela	16,921	15,293	17,515	16,946	17,151
World	2,969,491	3,155,841	4,043,784	3,992,226	3,938,740

Source: FAO.

crop and storing it. Ageing plantations, it is estimated that 50% of total plantations in Côte d'Ivoire are more than 30 years old, are also contributing to the trend.

Ghana

Cocoa is the main cash crop in Ghana with a production of 690,000 million tons in 2007 a drop from 734,000 million tons in 2006. Ghana has about 600,000–800,000 cocoa growers. Cocoa grows in all the regions south of Northern region: Eastern, Volta, Western, Central, Ashanti and Brong Ahafo. In Ashanti and the Central regions, cocoa production is highest and infrastructure is relatively more enhanced (Hatting et al., 1998). The volatility of the commodity market, resulting in low and unstable farm-gate prices create a vicious circle of lower investments, lower productivity, lack of competitiveness and deteriorating incomes.

Table 5.6A: Cocoa bean consumption per capita

Countries	Unit	2002	2003	2004	2005	2006	2007
Albania	kg	0.5	0.4	0.4	0.5	0.5	0.5
Algeria	kg	0.4	0.4	0.5	0.5	0.5	0.6
Argentina	kg	0.4	0.5	0.5	0.6	0.7	0.8
Armenia	kg	0.8	1	1.2	1.2	1.4	1.9
Australia	kg	1.8	1.6	1.7	1.9	2.3	2.8
Austria	kg	2.3	2.7	3	1.8	2.5	1
Azerbaijan	kg	0.5	0.6	0.9	1	1.1	1.1
Belarus	kg	0.6	0.9	0.6	0.8	1.4	1.5
Belgium	kg	0.1	0.1	0.1	0.1	0.2	0.2
Bosnia and Herzegovina	kg	1.4	1.2	2.1	2.1	2.3	2.5
Brazil	kg	0.7	0.5	0.5	0.6	0.6	0.8
Bulgaria	kg	1.6	1.7	1.4	1.6	2.4	1.5
Canada	kg	1.2	1.3	1.8	0.5	1.6	0.9
Chile	kg	0.9	0.9	0.9	1	1.1	1.1
China	kg				0.1	0.1	0.1
Colombia	kg	0.9	0.9	0.8	0.8	0.9	1.1
Croatia	kg	1.7	1.7	1.2	1.3	0.2	1.1
Czech Republic	kg	3.1	2.9	3.1	2.8	5.2	3
Denmark	kg	3.4	3.2	4.4	6.4	4	4.6
Egypt	kg	0.1	0.1	0.2	0.2	0.1	0.1
Estonia	kg	4.4	5.1	8.3	7	7.1	8.1
European Union	kg	2	2.1	2	2.3	2.5	2.6
Finland	kg	1.2	1.4	1.4	1.6	1.7	2.1
France	kg	3.8	4	4.1	4.2	3.9	4.2
Georgia	kg	0.4	0.7	1.2	1.4	1.6	1.8
Germany	kg	2.4	2.3	1.6	2	2	2.6
Ghana	kg	0.2	0.2	0.2	0.3	0.3	0.3
Greece	kg	1.9	2	2.3	2.4	2.6	2.7
Hungary	kg	2.2	2.2	2.6	2.3	3.2	2.8
Iceland	kg	4.3	4.3	4.5	4.5	4.5	5
India	kg						
Indonesia	kg	1.1	1.5	1.3	1.7	0.8	1.2
Iran	kg	0.2	0.2	0.3	0.3	0.2	0.4
Ireland	kg	1.7	1.7	1.7	1.7	1.7	1.7
Israel	kg	2.6	3	3.2	2.9	2.7	3.3
Italy	kg	1.4	1.6	1.4	1.6	1.5	1.7
Japan	kg	1.1	1.3	1.3	1.3	1.4	1.6
Kazakhstan	kg	1.2	1.3	1.7	1.4	1.8	2.1
Kenya	kg	0.1			0.1	0.1	0.1
Kyrgyzstan	kg	0.4	0.5	0.7	0.7	0.8	1.3
Latvia	kg	1.9	2	2.5	2.4	2.9	2.7

(Contd.)

Table 5.6A: Cocoa bean consumption per capita

Countries	Unit	2002	2003	2004	2005	2006	2007
Lithuania	kg	0.6	0.5	0.5	0.7	0.4	0.7
Luxembourg	kg	5.3	5.3	5.2	5.2	5.1	5.2
Macedonia	kg	2.2	1.8	1.9	1.9	2.1	2.4
Malaysia	kg	1	2.1	1.2	2.7	2.5	1.2
Malta	kg	3	3.4	3.5	2.8	3.1	2.8
Mexico	kg	0.9	0.9	0.8	0.9	0.4	0.4
Moldova	kg	0.5	0.6	0.9	0.9	1.2	1.2
Mongolia	kg	0.6	0.9	0.9	1.2	1.2	1.4
Montenegro	kg					2.6	3.1
Morocco	kg	0.3	0.3	0.3	0.3	0.4	0.4
Netherlands	kg						0.1
New Zealand	kg	0.1		0.1			
Nigeria	kg	0.1	0.1	0.1	0.1	0.1	0.1
Norway	kg	3	3.1	3.5	3.5	3.5	3.7
Pakistan	kg						
Peru	kg	0.8	0.8	0.8	0.7	0.7	1
Philippines	kg	0.8	0.4	0.5	0.6	0.5	0.6
Poland	kg	1.2	1.3	0.9	1.4	1.8	1.6
Portugal	kg	2	1.9	2	2.2	2.1	2.5
Romania	kg	0.8	0.8	0.9	1	1.2	1.4
Russia	kg	1.3	1.2	1.3	1.5	1.4	1.6
Serbia	kg					1	1.1
Singapore	kg						
Slovakia	kg	1.3	1.3	1.1	1.1	1.2	1.4
Slovenia	kg	4.2	4	2.3	3	3.6	3.7
South Africa	kg	0.2	0.3	0.3	0.3	0.3	0.4
South Korea	kg	0.4	0.4	0.4	0.4	0.6	0.7
Spain	kg	2.3	2.4	2.6	3	3.3	2.9
Sweden	kg	2.2	1.5	2.1	1.5	1.1	1.1
Switzerland	kg	0.8	1.3	1.2	1.2	1.5	1.9
Tajikistan	kg		0.2	0.3	0.6	0.5	0.7
Thailand	kg	0.2	0.1	0.3	0.3	0.4	0.3
Turkey	kg	0.4	0.6	0.6	0.5	0.3	0.3
Turkmenistan	kg	0.3	0.5	0.8	0.6	0.6	0.3
Ukraine	kg	0.1	0.1	0.3	0.4	0.5	1.3
United Kingdom	kg	1.9	2.2	2.4	2.8	3.8	4.6
USA	kg	2.4	2.8	2.9	3.3	3.2	2.6
Uzbekistan	kg	0.1	0.1				0.2
Venezuela	kg	0.6	0.5	0.6	0.7	0.8	0.8
Vietnam	kg			0.1	0.1	0.1	0.1
World	kg	0.5	0.6	0.6	0.6	0.6	0.6

Cameroon

In 2007, 179,000 tons of cocoa was produced in Cameroon. Cocoa production is spread across the Southwest, Center, South, Littoral, East, and West regions. In the South and Center Provinces of Cameroon, about 75% of rural households produce cocoa on small plots that are concentrated along roadsides (Leakey and Tchoundjeu, 2008). Many of the cocoa plots there are now relatively old coexist with indigenous timber and fruit trees. North of Yaoundé, where population pressure is higher, farmers have developed cocoa based mixed cropping systems. Staple food crops such as maize and cassava are integrated within the tree crops. The Cameroonian government plans to boost cocoa and coffee output by increasing the area under cultivation, introducing higher-yielding strains and providing more technical, financial and institutional support to farmers. In 2006 the state-run Cameroon Cocoa Development Authority (Sodecao) acquired 11,500 hectares of land from traditional rulers in the Center and East provinces for distribution to farmers to open new cocoa farms. Plans have also been developed to improve rural infrastructure and empower farmers to negotiate better prices with buyers. A cocoa and coffee development fund was created in March 2006 to fund these initiatives with proceeds from an export tax, the net effect of which need to be assessed.

Nigeria

Cocoa's contribution to Nigeria's total exports earnings during the past two decades dropped considerably due to the enormity of foreign exchange earning of crude petroleum. Even so, cocoa remains Nigeria's major agricultural export of which the country is the fifth largest exporter of in the world. Cocoa output ranges between 185,000 tons and 215,000 tons in recent years. Oyo is one of the five cocoa-producing States in the Southwest cocoa belt, which accounts for about 70% of Nigeria's annual demand for labor in the area of production and marketing in the cocoa belt area contributes to some rural migration (Folayan et al., 2007). cocoa production [*Wet annular burnable absorber* (WABA), 2007].

Sierra Leone

In Sierra Leone, since the civil war of 1991–2002, cocoa has been one of the most significant exports. The war lasted longest in the Eastern borderlands, where both cocoa and coffee are grown (EIU, 2007). About 85% of Sierra Leone's cocoa is grown in the Kenema and Kailahun districts in the East (Bah, 2007). In 2007, 12,000 million tons of cocoa was produce on 33,000 hectares compared to respectively, almost 14,000 million tons and 38,000 hectares a year before. Typically, crop production is characterized by low yields and productivity and occurs in a setting severely deprived of institutional facilities. The typical farmer exhibits a very poor knowledge of agronomy and is inhibited by the absence of institutional credit as well as organized markets for farm produce. There seems to not be any adequate framework for sector policy as no official comprehensive and coherent agricultural and food security policies have ever been adopted.

Togo

Cocoa is one of Togo's main cash crops at a total production of 70,000 million tons in 2007. Togo has considerable agricultural potential because of its varied climate, but the sector is dominated by subsistence farming and is poorly integrated with the rest of the economy. Productivity is low because of a lack of irrigation and fertilizers. Just as the case in the rest of the WCA region, development is hampered by a shortage of rural credit institutions and the poor rural infrastructure.

Democratic Republic of Congo

The Democratic Republic of Congo produced 5,700 million tons of cocoa in 2007. The country has a more dynamic coffee sector which is discussed in part III of the paper.

Sao Tomé and Principe

The agricultural exports for Sao Tomé and Principe are composed almost entirely of cocoa, which has been the dominant crop since the 1890s with an export value share of agricultural exports of 94% in 2005 [Food and Agriculture Organization of the United Nations (FAOSTAT), 2008]. As a result of falling prices, the division of former estates into numerous small landholdings, ageing trees and other local supply-side constraints, cocoa production has fallen from a peak of 4,500 tons in 1994 to an estimated 3,500 tons in 2007. The eastern slopes and coastal flatlands of the country are covered by cocoa plantations within a dense and well-watered jungle. The soils of this volcanic island are of basaltic origin and are thus relatively deep, permeable, and resistant to erosion, as well as highly suitable for cocoa (Eyzaguirre, 1986).

Liberia

Liberia is a tiny producer, with less than 5,000 tons of cocoa beans a year; the country is dwarfed by the 1.35 million tons harvested in neighboring top producer, Côte d'Ivoire. Throughout the 14 years civil war which ended in 2003, there was no replanting or maintenance, but the old trees were harvested, and sometimes not by the owner. The 2007 output was about 3,600 tons; put precise figures are hard to find for much of the cocoa is shipped out of neighboring Guinea. The International Institute of Tropical Agriculture's (IITA) Sustainable Tree Crop Program (STCP) with funding from the US Agency for International Development (USAID) and the World Cocoa Foundation plans to bring hybrid cocoa seeds from Cote d'Ivoire to cultivate and gradually replace old trees. The farmers are encouraged to plant at least a hectare of cocoa in existing growing areas, with each hectare accounting for around 1,000 trees. These are high yielding, disease resistant and early maturing varieties. Right now, farmers are getting a yield which is as low as 150 kg/hectares, but it is believed that if farmers follow the recommended cultural practices the yield can get as high as 800 kg/hectares; and harvesting can start as early as in 3 years. The quantities produced are not expected to have any impact on the international market price, but farmers are expected to be able to make a fairly good living from cocoa. Production is expected to provide income for some 30,000 families, or 150,000 of Liberia's 3.1 million inhabitants.

Production and export and other relevant statistics since 1980, for the purpose of this report, are displayed in the Statistical Annexure at the end of the chapter. Low farm gate prices can be a significant disincentive to good crop husbandry and to the adoption of improved technologies in WCA. For instance, Ghana's yields are only a little over half of those in Côte d'Ivoire. Productivity is low generally in WCA because of a lack of irrigation and fertilizers; development is hampered by a shortage of rural credit institutions and the poor rural infrastructure.

In 2007, WCA per country cocoa yields ranged between a low of 50 kg/hectares (CAR) and a high of 765 kg/hectares (Côte d'Ivoire). The average yield for the region was 380 kg/hectares compared to a world average of 541 kg/hectares. Côte d'Ivoire, the number one producer also has the highest yield in the WCA region. Ghana is the second producer with 17% of WCA output and has a yield of 400 kg/hectares. Togo produces only close to 2% of the WCA output but has the second highest yield of 673 kg/hectares.

Marketing and Value Chain

The Cocoa Value Chain

This section provides a description of the cocoa production processes along the value chain in order to provide an understanding of circumstances and the market environment faced by all the actors involved. The value chain analysis (VCA) studies the sequence of processes of a good or service until the production of the final product (Talbot, 2002; Laven, 2005; Gilbert, 2006). The VCA framework examines the nature of the commodity flows to and from each stage and the geographic distribution of the flows; and is complemented by more traditional industrial organization models in which questions of strategic behavior and market power can be more satisfactorily addressed. Commodity chains can also be viewed as a series of transactions, beginning with the transfer of the raw product to a first stage processor, and ending with the sale of the finished product to the final consumer. These transactions can take place on a free market; they may be completely removed for the market, as is the case for a vertically integrated TNC; or they may be structured by oligopolistic sellers and or oligopsonistic buyers using contracts that are indirectly affected by spot market supply and demand conditions. The amount of value added to the product at each stage, are determined by the rules governing the transactions, and by their relations to transactions at the other stages.

The cocoa supply chain is more complicated than that of coffee because the final product, chocolate, exhibits greater variety than roast and soluble coffee, and because chocolate incorporates other raw material inputs such as sugar and milk. Nevertheless, both crops need some kind of preliminary but rudimentary processing soon after they are harvested. Talbot (2002) mentions the implications of green coffee being much closer to its final consumption end, whereas there is another set of intermediate storable product in the cocoa chain. The existence of the intermediate storable products of cocoa butter and the powder opened the possibility for cocoa traders to integrate forward into cocoa processing without directly threatening the chocolate manufacturer's market. The movement of cocoa traders into processing was also facilitated by decisions of the chocolate manufacturers to focus on the marketing of chocolates and the design of new products, and to externalize the less profitable grinding operations.

World Trade

Total quantity of cocoa which enters the world market export/import is around 3,000 tons (Table 5.5). Of the world production, Africa, particularly Côte d'Ivoire is the main producer. As for imports, it is primarily the developed world, particularly Europe, which is more significant.

Cocoa beans can be stored for about 6 months and can therefore, be the form in which it is traded in the world market. The roasting and cracking of the beans to extract the nibs is a much more capital-intensive process. However, cocoa powder, cocoa butter, and chocolate are also storable, so there is an international trade of these intermediate products as well. The following figure graphs the export values of intermediate cocoa products other than the raw cocoa beans between 1980 and 2005. It shows that at home processing of cocoa butter, cocoa paste, cocoa husks and shells, and cocoa powder for export has seen some growth since 2000. However, this is so only in the four major producing countries (Côte d'Ivoire, Ghana, Cameroon and Nigeria).

It has been shown in a number of cases that when premium quality beans are used, the country concerned would most likely have received a higher return from exporting raw cocoa than cocoa products, once the costs of processing and the additional taxing are taken into account. Also, cocoa processing seems to not generate much employment as the method is more capital than labor intensive; the contribution to industrialization is trivial.

The first processing factory in Ghana was built in 1947 by Gill and Duffus, then the world leading cocoa trader (now part of Archer Daniels Midland Company of the US) (Talbot, 2002). After independence, the state nationalized the cocoa processing industry, so that by the mid-1980s, Ghana's three cocoa processing factories were all State owned. Despite some management issues and diseases in cocoa trees, thanks to significant investment in processing capacities made in the country, Ghana is expected to record a strong increase in grinding activities, up by 29,000–150,000 tons in the current season (ICCO, 2008). US Company, Cargill has begun construction of a US$70 million factory at Tema to add value to Ghana's raw cocoa beans. The plan is to process 65,000 metric tons of cocoa annually into liquor, butter and powder. It will be the fifth cocoa-processing factory in Ghana. However, local processing companies have raised concerns over the lack of light crop cocoa beans, which are sold at a discount over the main crop. Light crop beans are found throughout the year but feature mainly in Ghana's June–September mid crop, rather than the October–May main crop. Local processors fear when there might not be enough light crop beans to match processing capacity; less profitable plants may be forced to close down. In fact, a major local cocoa processing company, West Africa Mills Company (WAMCO), has reduced activity in one of its location in the beginning of 2008 (Fig. 5.6).

Côte d'Ivoire has the leading position of cocoa processing among the producing countries. A processor based in France, provides marketing and technical assistance as well as an outlet to local ones (Bloomfield and Lass, 1992). The company also produces small quantities of chocolate for the domestic market. Barry Callebaut, the Swiss-Belgian chocolate group, is working on boosting its cocoa processing capacity since 2007 by more than 50% in the country within 2 years. This was in response to growing demand for cocoa liquor. The company will double the amount of beans it buys from farmers in order to secure its supply of raw materials. The planned increase will create round 60 new jobs in Barry Callebaut's existing cocoa processing facilities in Côte d'Ivoire.

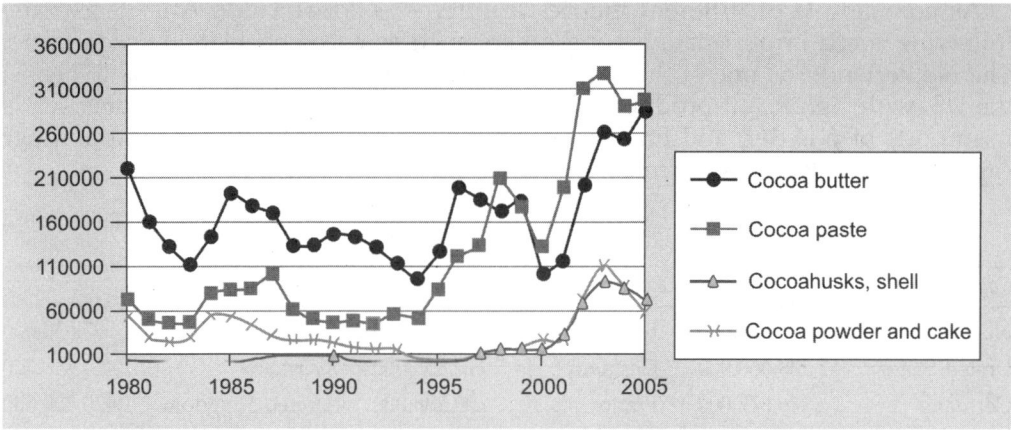

Fig. 5.6: WCA cocoa product export values (Int. $1,000) (1980–2005)

Source: Computed from FAOSTAT (2008).

In Nigeria, local processing companies, represented by the Cocoa Processors' Association of Nigeria (COPAN), have criticized the new customs tariffs imposed by the European Union (EU) countries to Nigerian exports of cocoa semi-finished products (ICCO, 2008). This was the result of the failure of trade talks related to the Economic Partnership Agreement (EPA) between the EU and Nigeria. Hence, instead of entering duty free, Nigerian cocoa semi-finished products have since been facing customs tariffs between 2.8% and 6.1%, depending on the product concerned. During the first 4 months of the current season, these exports have declined by 20% over the same period a year earlier.

Imports of cocoa beans and cocoa semi-finished products are usually subject to either an import tariff or an indirect tax such as Value Added Tax (VAT) also known as Goods and Services Taxes (GST), or both, as they enter the markets of cocoa consuming countries (ICCO, 2008). Major cocoa importing countries include the EU, US, Malaysia, Canada, the Russian Federation, Japan and Switzerland; together they import about 76% of world trade in cocoa beans and 50% of world trade in cocoa semi-finished products. The average (weighted) VAT rate was 6.7%, where weights are derived from imports of cocoa beans and cocoa semi-finished products. VAT is uniform for all forms of cocoa for each country.

Overall, it is estimated that imports of cocoa beans and cocoa semi-finished products face an average (weighted) import tariff of 1.2%, where trade values are used as weights. Tariff escalation is a taxation system in which tariffs vary according to the product, from no tariffs or low tariffs on raw materials to the highest tariffs on finished goods. Tariff escalation reduces the means of accumulating skills and capital and thus limits the scope for processing for exporting countries. This is so for exports of cocoa semi-finished products to Japan, Russia and Malaysia. The impacts of escalating tariffs on processing and destination choices of WCA countries require further analysis.

It is worthwhile to note the ranking of cocoa importing countries depends on the composition of the goods imported: trade is not only tracked by cocoa beans but also by semi-finished products of cocoa.

As an example of different metrics of interest, Global Trade Atlas tracks the following cocoa import data among others such as cocoa shells and cocoa paste. The Netherlands, as one of the main ports into Europe, leads in imports of beans; the US, with significant production of cocoa complementary food products, leads in imports of powder; and France, one of the biggest chocolate consumption per capita markets, leads in chocolate preparations.

2009 imports ($USD value)

Cocoa beans		Cocoa powder and cake		Chocolate preparations	
Netherlands	2,075,860,000	United States	337,074,000	France	1,597,530,000
United States	1,228,060,000	Germany	110,855,000	Germany	1,465,840,000
Germany	976,677,000	France	100,286,000	United Kingdom	1,420,300,000
Malaysia	768,199,000	Japan	75,873,000	United States	1,407,960,000
France	493,246,000	Russia	73,286,000	Netherlands	762,134,000
Belgium	462,689,000	Spain	70,486,000	Canada	683,774,000
United Kingdom	426,156,000	Netherlands	67,114,000	Spain	535,130,000
Spain	244,124,000	Italy	61,799,000	Belgium	531,020,000
Singapore	208,586,000	Australia	59,417,000	Italy	480,966,000
Italy	206,966,000	China	47,147,000	Japan	479,535,000

Source: FAOSTAT as of March, 2012.

West and Central Africa

WCA exports are dominated by just a few agricultural commodities. For some countries, the dependence on just a few commodities is tremendous, making them and the producers extremely vulnerable. Given the harshness of the world market at times of instabilities, the relatively heavy reliance on the export of cash crops creates economic insecurity at the national and local levels by affecting the trade balance of the state and the income level of smallholders.

In the WCA region, cocoa and coffee represent a large source of foreign exchange. In 2005, the value share of cocoa and coffee to total agricultural exports were about 52 and 3%, respectively; and the value share to total merchandise exports were 4.5 and 20% when accounting for Nigeria and almost 16 and 1% without Nigeria, for cocoa and coffee, respectively. In this report, 10 major WCA cocoa and coffee producing countries are the object of the analysis and they include Cameroon, the Central African Republic (CAR), Côte d'Ivoire, the Democratic Republic of Congo (DRC), Ghana, Liberia, Nigeria, Sao Tomé and Principe (STP), Sierra Leone and Togo. Figure 5.5.6 shows the trend in WCA cocoa and coffee world export value shares (%) between 1980 and 2005. WCA has maintained a high market share for cocoa of close to 70% for over two decades; 98% of this share belongs to four West African countries: Cote d'Ivoire, Ghana, Nigeria and Cameroon. On the other hand, coffee has seen a recent decline in market share down to 1.5% in 2005.

Cocoa Growing Countries

Cocoa powder and chocolate are made from the dried seeds that are found in pods on the cacao tree. In the 18th century the Swedish botanist, Carolus Linnaeus, renamed the cocoa tree giving it the Greek name the Obroma Cacao, now its official botanical name, which literally means "food of the Gods". Although a native of the Amazon basin and other tropical areas of South and Central America, where wild varieties still grow in the forests, the cocoa growing area has extended to the Caribbean and beyond. Different types of cocoa are selected for cultivation in the various growing areas.

1. Mexico
2. Costa Rica
3. Panama
4. Jamaica
5. Cuba
6. Balti
7. Dominican Republic
8. Grenada
9. Trinidad and Tobago
10. Venezuela
11. Colombia
12. Ecuador
13. Peru
14. Brazil

15. Sierra Leone
16. Ivory Coast
17. Ghess
18. Toga
19. Nigeria
20. Cameroon
21. Equatorial Guinea
22. Gabon
23. Ferando pessoa

24. Sio Tome
25. Congo
26. Sri Lanka
27. Malaysia
28. Sabals
29. Indonesia
30. Philippines
31. Papus New Guinea
32. Fiji islands
33. W. Samos

Most of the world's cocoa is grown in a narrow belt 10° either side of the equator because the trees grow well in humid tropical climates with regular rains and a short dry season. Even temperatures between 21°C and 23°C with a fairly constant rainfall of 1,000–2,500 mm per year, are needed without hot dry winds and drought.

Many countries now grow cocoa but the main producers are:

- West Africa: Ghana which grows some of the best quality cocoa in the world, Nigeria and Cote D'Ivoire.
- South America: Brazil and Ecuador.
- Asia: Malaysia and Indonesia where cocoa is a relatively new crop, are becoming increasingly important growing areas.

Cocoa was first planted in Ghana, now a major producer, in 1879 and as in the rest of West Africa, cocoa is grown almost entirely on smallholdings where the whole family works together. Cocoa farming is a small, unsophisticated business as the current planting patterns of cocoa trees make mechanization impractical. In Asia, public and private plantations have been developed as well as the small farms.

Types of Cocoa

There are three broad types of cocoa *Forastero* and *Crillo* plus *Trinitario* which is a hybrid of Forastero and Crillo. Within these types are several varieties. Forastero, which now forms the greater part of all cocoa grown, is hardy and vigorous producing beans with the strongest flavor. Amelonado is the Forastero variety most widely grown in West Africa and Brazil. It has a smooth yellow pod with 30 or more pale to deep purple beans.

Crillo with its mild or weak chocolate flavor is grown in Indonesia, Central and South America. Crillo trees are not as hardy and they produce softer pods which are red in color, containing 20–30 white, ivory or very pale purple beans.

Trinitario plants are not found in the wild as they are cultivated hybrids of the other two types. Trinitario cocoa trees are grown mainly in the Caribbean area but also in Cameroon and Papua New Guinea. The mostly hard pods are variable in color and they contain 30 or more beans of variable color but white beans are rare.

Cocoa trees resemble English apple trees, seldom reaching more than 7.5 meters (25 feet) high and they are carefully pruned so that pods can be more easily harvested. To flourish they need to be shaded from direct sun and wind particularly in the early stages of growth. Two methods are used to establish cocoa trees:

1. Young trees are interspersed with new permanent or temporary shade trees such as coconut, plantains and bananas, following the clear-felling of the forest. In Asia where large plantations have been developed, cocoa trees and coconut trees are planted together and both crops are harvested commercially.
2. Alternatively forest trees are thinned out and the cocoa trees are planted between established trees.

Cocoa trees begin to bear fruit when they are 3–4 years old. The pink and white flowers, then the pods grow straight out of the trunk and main branches which is most unusual. Like most tropical plants, flowers are present throughout the year but appear in abundance before the rain starts. Only a small proportion of all the flowers develop into fruit over a period of about 5 months.

Each tree will yield 20–30 pods per year and the peak time for harvesting is between September and December in West Africa.

Cocoa Pods: The pods are hard and melon shaped, between 15–20 cm long and each weighing about 450 g each. When the pods are ripe they change from green to yellow, red or orange. Each pod contains 20–40 seeds which when dried are the cocoa beans of commerce. It takes the whole year's crop from one tree to make 450 g of chocolate.

Harvesting Ripe Pods and Curing the Cocoa Beans

The harvesting of the pods is very labor intensive and on the West African small-holdings the whole family, together with friends and neighbors help out. Ripe pods are gathered every few weeks during the peak season. Workers cut the high pods from the trees with large knives attached to poles, taking care not to damage nearby flowers or buds. The women of the family collect the pods in large baskets which they carry on their heads to be piled up ready for splitting. The pods are split open by hand and the seeds or beans, which are covered with a sweet white pulp or mucilage, are removed ready to undergo the two part curing process-fermentation followed by drying. This prepares the beans for market and is the first stage in the development of the delicious chocolate flavor.

Methods of fermentation vary considerably from country to country but basically there are two methods: (1) HEAP and (2) BOX.

Traditionally, the HEAP method is used on the farms in West Africa. Wet cocoa beans, surrounded by the pulp, are piled on banana or plantain leaves which are spread out in a circle on the ground. More leaves are put on top to cover the heap and it is left for 5–6 days, turning to ensure even fermentation. Cocoa is also fermented in baskets lined and covered with leaves - a method used in Nigeria. During fermentation the pulp and astringency of the beans are removed as the sugar in the pulp turns to alcohol and vinegar-like liquids, which drain away and the true chocolate flavor starts to develop. When fermentation is complete the wet mass of beans is dried, traditionally by being spread in the sun on mats.

In the West Indies, Latin America and in Malaysia the Box method is used in the plantations while on small farms the traditional heap method is still used. Box fermentation involves the use of strong wooden boxes with drainage holes or gaps in the slats in the base to allow the passage of air and the removal of liquid products of fermentation. The process takes 6–8 days during which time the beans are mixed twice. The fermented beans are then dried by means of special drying equipment rather than out in the sun.

The cured beans are packed into sacks for transportation to Singapore where Cadbury process the cocoa beans. Stringent quality control procedures are carried out as samples are checked to ensure that standards are maintained before cocoa beans are bought from the farmer and again during transportation.

Cadbury's cocoa factory at Singapore operates 24 hours a day, 7 days a week, producing the basic ingredients from which all Cadbury chocolate products are made. 18,000 tons of cocoa beans are processed each year using the latest technological control systems to ensure that the end product is of the highest quality. On arrival at the factory, the cocoa beans are sorted and cleaned. They are then treated through a micronizer to break the shell and a winnower to remove the shell. The beans are broken down into small pieces called nibs and are subsequently roasted at a temperature of 135°C. The actual roasting time depends on whether the end use is for cocoa or chocolate.

During roasting, the cocoa nibs darken in color and acquire their characteristic chocolate flavor. This flavor however, had actually started to develop during fermentation back on the farm. Cocoa nibs are ground in stone mills until the friction and heat of the milling reduces them to a thick chocolate colored liquid, known as "mass", which contains 53–58% cocoa butter and solidifies on cooling. This is the basis of all chocolate and cocoa products. Cocoa powder is made by extracting about half the cocoa butter in heavy presses. The amount of cocoa butter removed is specified in the Australia New Zealand Food Authority (ANZFA) food laws. The solid blocks of compressed cocoa remaining after extraction is pulverized into a fine powder to produce a high-grade cocoa powder for use as a beverage or in cooking. The extracted cocoa butter is used in the recipes for the wide range of Cadbury's chocolate, the most famous brand being Cadbury's Dairy Milk, Australia's favorite molded chocolate bar.

Chocolate Making

Cadbury make a variety of chocolates for different purposes but the two main types are: (1) Cadbury's Dairy Milk (milk chocolate) and (2) Cadbury's Old Gold (dark chocolate). The special taste and texture of Cadbury's chocolate are based on long traditions of expertise in recipe and processing which are unique to Cadbury. Techniques are improving all the time and new technology enables the whole process to be finely tuned to the consumer's evolving tastes and preferences.

Production starts at the Singapore cocoa factory where the top quality cocoa beans are processed to produce the cocoa mass containing 53% cocoa butter plus extracted cocoa butter, the basis for all chocolate products. When dark chocolate is made, the "mass" goes straight to the Cadbury factory in Ringwood, Victoria or Claremont, Tasmania. At the milk processing factory in Burnie, fresh liquid full cream milk is collected and condensed for transport by road tanker to Claremont. Sugar is added to the condensed milk with some of the cocoa mass, making a rich creamy chocolate liquid which is then evaporated to make milk chocolate crumb. As these ingredients are cooked together the very special rich creamy taste of Cadbury's chocolate is produced. 22,000 tons of crumb a year are produced at Claremont to be made into chocolate at the Cadbury chocolate factories at Claremont and Ringwood.

On arrival at the chocolate factory the crumb is passed through a pin mill and mixed with additional cocoa liquor and cocoa butter as well as special chocolate flavorings. The amount of emulsifiers added depends on the consistency of the chocolate required; thick chocolate is needed for molded blocks while a thinner consistency is used for assortments and covered bars. Both milk and dark chocolate undergo the same final special production stages, such as refining and conching which produce the famous smoothness, gloss and snap of Cadbury's chocolate.

The most important component of chocolate, as far as texture is concerned, is the fat and the special processes known as conching and tempering which are very carefully controlled to produce chocolate with the fat in a specific physical structure. The fat must coat individual particles of cocoa, milk and sugar, combining them together to form the solid chocolate. Conching involves mixing and beating the semi-liquid mixture to develop the flavor, removing unwanted volatile flavors and reducing the viscosity and particle size.

Tempering is the final crucial stage. It is a complex process which in simple terms involves mixing and cooling the liquid chocolate under carefully controlled conditions to ensure that the fat in the chocolate crystallizes in its most stable form. Highly sophisticated machinery has been developed for this process and the control of it is one of the skills of the chocolatier.

Without the right tempering, the chocolate would be very soft and gritty as large crystals would form and the lovely gloss and snap of top quality chocolate would soon disappear. Tempered chocolate is used in a number of ways to produce Cadbury's famous brands. Cadbury's chocolate production is a highly sophisticated, computer controlled process, with much of the new specialist machinery being produced to Cadbury's own design and specification.

The Claremont factory alone produces 26,000 tons of molded chocolate blocks and assortments each year whilst the Ringwood facility produces 26,000 tons of chocolate bars, novelty and seasonal products each year. Blocks of solid chocolate, with or without added ingredients such as nuts and raisins are known in the industry as "molded" products. Tempered chocolate is poured into bar shaped moulds, shaken and cooled then the unmolded blocks continue to high speed wrapping plants. One of the most recently commissioned plants has the potential for producing 700 blocks per minute.

Cadbury's Dairy Milk, Australia's favorite molded chocolate block is available in a wide range of block sizes to suit all ages and all eating occasions. Dairy Milk is also the main ingredient of other Cadbury favorites such as Hazelnut and Fruit and Nut.

Molded blocks come in different sizes:

- Large blocks: 250 g and 400 g, with even larger blocks for special occasions, bought for sharing or as a gift.
- Smaller blocks: 150 g, 100 g and chunky bars to share or enjoy as a "big eat"
- Snack size: For the lunch box.
- Treat size: Small individual bars to enjoy as a small treat.

In bar products such as Crunchie, Cherry Ripe, or Time Out, the chocolate covers the center filling. This is achieved by the "enrobing" process where the centers pass on a continuous belt beneath a curtain of liquid chocolate.

Assortments such as the boxed selection Cadbury's Milk Tray or the twist wrapped Cadbury's Roses are made either by the same "enrobing" method or "shelling". Here, the liquid chocolate is deposited into a mould to form a shell into which the center is deposited and then this is sealed with the "back". Another process used is "panning" where pieces of biscuit, raisins or caramel are coated with chocolate in a revolving drum. Shell Easter eggs are made by the "shell molding" process while Cadbury has a special unique process for products like Yowie and Cadbury's famous Creme Eggs.

Australian food laws are quite specific about what can and cannot be called "chocolate". It is any product that is obtained from cocoa nibs, cocoa mass, cocoa, fat-reduced cocoa or any combination of two or more of these ingredients, with or without extracted cocoa butter and sucrose.

Chocolate must contain not less than 15% total dry cocoa solids, excluding cocoa butter. It is the cocoa solids that give the chocolate its rich flavor and the amounts included in the recipe vary with different brands, giving them their own characteristic taste.

Milk chocolate must contain a minimum of 14% milk solids or 27% as in Cadbury's Dairy Milk. There is another range of products popularly referred to as "compounded chocolates" many of which in fact should be called "chocolate flavored cake coverings" because they do not contain cocoa butter. Vegetable fats are used which not only alters their texture but also their melting properties.

Chocolate is a recipe product and different traditions and tastes have developed in different countries of the world. Dark chocolate is the most popular in Europe and their chocolate has a higher level of cocoa solids giving it a much stronger flavor. Milk chocolate is the preferred choice in Australia while the Americans favor dark chocolate with the smoky flavors of South American beans.

Another important difference between the recipe traditions of European and UK chocolates is the kind of milk used. European manufacturers use dried milk powder, often mixed with whey powder. However, UK style manufacturers and Cadbury Australia use fresh milk. Indeed, Cadbury Australia believes that the very best milk chocolate is made with fresh milk. It is the special flavors produced when fresh milk, cocoa mass and sugar are cooked together in the first stages of the chocolate crumb making process that give Cadbury's Diary Milk its very special taste.

COCOA PROJECTIONS

Introduction

The projections employed dynamic time series models to analyze the world cocoa economy. Essentially, autoregressive distributed lag models were used to capture the dynamic process of market adjustment in the world cocoa bean market. The forecasts are obtained from "s" step a-head ADL models, where "s" is the forecast horizon. International cocoa prices were included as exogenous factors. Their values over the forecast horizon were obtained from their autoregressive representations. Projections were based on the assumption of normal weather conditions, and a continuation of the past trends in yields, planted areas, population and income growth. Adjustments were made to reflect current policies and future market prospects. The forecasting models captured cycles and trends in the world cocoa beans market to a satisfactory level.

Production

World cocoa production is projected to grow at a rate of 2.2% a year, from 1998–2000 to 2010, compared with the 1.7% growth during the previous decade, and reach 3.7 million tons. During the same period, Africa's share in the global production is expected to decrease slightly from 69% to 68%, while the share of the Far East is projected to remain at 18% and that of Latin America and the Caribbean at 14%.

Africa is expected to remain the world's leading cocoa producing area over the next decade. Production in Côte d'Ivoire, the world's largest cocoa bean producer, should grow by 2.3% a year from 1.2 million tons of the base period to 1.6 million tons in 2010, and account for 44% of global cocoa production due mainly to the increased foreign direct investment followed by the market liberalization. Yields in Côte d'Ivoire are well below levels seen in Asia partly because of less use of agricultural inputs. However, the recent surge in world cocoa prices has made it easier for the growers to use more inputs. If this trend continues, volume of cocoa produced in Côte d'Ivoire could increase further. Output in Ghana, the second largest cocoa bean producer in Africa, would grow from 410,000 tons in 1998–2000 to 490,000 tons in 2010, and an annual average growth rate of 1.6%. The corresponding growth rate for the previous decade was 3.3%. The lower projected growth rate over the next decade would result from the outbreak of diseases (such as swollen shoot virus, black pod and mirids), increased competition at the world market and low export prices. Over the same period, Nigeria and Cameroon are projected to increase outputs by 1.4% and 0.3%, respectively.

Cocoa production in Latin America is projected to increase from 397,000 tons during the base period to 520,000 tons in 2010, and an annual growth rate of 2.5%. Outputs in Brazil, the largest cocoa bean producer in the region, and Colombia, the third largest, are expected to fall, but an increase in outputs in other cocoa producing countries in the region would more than offset the decline. Output in Brazil is projected to increase by 2.2% annually and reach 180,000 tons by 2010. The production and yields of cocoa beans in Brazil have decreased during the previous decade because of the detrimental production loss caused by witches' broom disease. The recently found (discovered?) use of new varieties would not bring the production back to the level achieved during the 1980s, because some producers have already switched to alternative crops, discouraged by the recent low world prices. During the same period, output in Ecuador, the second largest cocoa bean producer in Latin America, would increase by 0.8% annually and reach 94,000 tons. Ecuador has successfully used a new variety resistance to the witches' broom disease, which had also affected their cocoa production areas. However, growth is expected to be only slight because of the increasing costs of production and lower returns to growers. In Colombia, outputs are projected to fall by 3.1% per annum. On the other hand, outputs in Dominican Republic and Mexico are expected to grow by 1.8% and 0.5%, respectively.

In the Far East, production had grown rapidly over the past two decades, and this growth is likely to continue. Production in the Far East is projected to grow by 2.7% per year from 509,000 tons during the base period to 680,000 tons in 2010 reflecting the expected improvement in yields. The Far East is expected to replace Latin America and the Caribbean as the second largest cocoa producing region by 2010. Most of the production growth in Asia would come from Indonesia, the world's third largest cocoa bean producer after Côte d'Ivoire and Ghana. Production in Indonesia is projected to grow by 3.5% annually to 574,000 tons in 2010 and account for 16% of the global production by 2010, compared to 14% in 1998–2000. In Indonesia, the Government policies had encouraged expansion of production, and most of the increases during the last two decades were bulk cocoa coming from hybrid trees. While the expansion of production area in Indonesia has slowed since the late 1990s, yields in the country are still the highest among major cocoa producing countries. A close link between the world market prices and the producer prices in Indonesia also contributed to the country's high yields. Since the growers earn a high proportion of the market prices, they can invest in inputs, which in turn results in improvement in yields. Production in Malaysia, where expansions of urban areas and real estate development have reduced cocoa producing areas, is projected to fall by 1.7% annually and reach 43,000 by 2010. The downward trend has been observed since the early 1990s when the outbreak of disease coincided with the deterioration of country's macroeconomic conditions. In addition, farmers switched to production from cocoa to more lucrative crops, such as palm oil, in response to the fall in world cocoa prices during the 1990s. Therefore, outputs in Malaysia are unlikely to rebound to the level achieved a couple of decades ago.

Consumption

In 2010 world grindings of cocoa beans, a proxy for world cocoa consumption, would amount to 3.6 million tons, reflecting an average annual increase of 2.1% from 2.8 million tons during the base period. Consumption will continue to be concentrated in developed counties, which are expected to account for 64% of world cocoa consumption in 2010. Consumption in these countries is projected to increase at an annual rate of 2.2% from 1.8 million tons during the base period to 2.3 million tons in 2010.

Consumption in Europe is projected to grow by 1.7% per annum and reach 1.4 million tons. Europe is likely to continue to be the world's largest cocoa consuming area, accounting for 40% of global cocoa consumption in 2010. Chocolate and cocoa based products in the EU are currently governed by a 2000 directive which authorizes the replacement of cocoa butter by less expensive cocoa butter substitutes upto five of the total weight of the finished product. Under the Directive, chocolate products that contain vegetable fats other than cocoa butter may be marketed in the EU provided that their labeling is supplemented by a statement. Member countries have until August 2003 to implement national laws to enforce this directive. Consumption in North America, the world's second largest cocoa consuming area, is likely to grow by 3.6% per annum and reach 703,000 tons. In the former Soviet Union/Commonwealth of Independent States (CISs), consumption is expected to grow by 0.8% per annum from 65,000 tons to 71,000 tons, reflecting expected increase in income in these countries. In Japan, consumption is expected to increase from 48,000 tons during the base period to 56,000 tons in 2010 (Table 5.6A).

Consumption in developing countries as a group is expected to amount to 1.3 million tons by 2010, an annual growth rate of 1.8%. Africa, where capital formation for grindings has grown rapidly over the past decade, will remain the largest consuming region in this group, accounting for 35% of the consumption of developing countries. The share of consumption in Latin America and Caribbean, where the relative cost for grindings are higher compared to Africa, is expected to decrease from 32% to 28%. In the Far East, where per capita consumption is still small, the share in consumption is projected to increase from 31% during the same period to 34% by 2010.

Trade

By 2010, the world cocoa market is expected to be approximately in balance. Beans will continue to form the large majority of cocoa exports, despite some increase of processing capacity in producing countries, especially those in Africa. Global cocoa bean exports are projected to reach 3.0 million tons by 2010, an average annual growth rate of 2.8%. Total exports from Africa are expected to grow by 2.8% annually from 1.7 million tons during the base period to 2.3 million tons in 2010, with Côte d'Ivoire, Ghana and Nigeria achieving an annual average growth rate of about 3%. Exports from Côte d'Ivoire are projected to increase to 1.5 million tons by 2010, or 51% of the global cocoa exports, although this growth is subject to the development of its current political instability. Exports from Ghana would reach 469,000 tons or 16% of the world total. The share of African exports in the world market is expected to remain stable, about 78% of the global exports.

Exports from the Far East, which increased rapidly during the 1980s and continued to grow at a lower rate during the 1990s, are expected to grow further and reach 529,000 tons by 2010. The increase in the Far East during the 1980s resulted mainly from rapidly growing shipments from Malaysia that accounted for 54% of the exports from the region. However, exports fell dramatically during the 1990s when farmers switched production. The increase in exports during the current decade is likely to result mostly from the increase in yields, and the share of the Malaysian exports in the region should increase only slightly, from 4.6% during the base period to 5.3% in 2010. On the other hand, exports from Indonesia grew rapidly during the 1980s and 1990s and are projected to continue to grow at 4.3% per year over the next decade and account for 98% of cocoa bean exports from the Far East by 2010, compared to 30% during the 1980s and 84% during the 1990s.

In Latin America and the Caribbean, cocoa exports are projected to increase from 97,000 tons during the base period to 130,000 tons reflecting increased exports from Brazil where production is expected to recover from the loss caused by the witches' broom disease.

Global cocoa imports are expected to increase by 2.2% annually between 1998–2000 and 2010, compared with 3.1% during the previous decade. Imports in developed counties as a group are expected to grow at an annual rate of 2.5% to 2.6 million tons. Europe should continue to be the main consumer of cocoa, accounting for 65% of global cocoa imports in 2010. In North America, imports are projected to grow by 0.3% per year, to reach 505,000 tons by 2010. Shipments to the countries of the former Soviet Union/CISs are likely to decrease slightly by 1.1% per annum. In Japan, imports are expected to increase by 1.4% per year from 48,000 tons in 1998–2000 to 56,000 tons in 2010. Imports in developing countries as a group are projected to remain unchanged and would account for 11.3% of world cocoa imports, compared with the 14% during the previous decade (Table 5.6A).

Issues and Uncertainties

The projections show an approximate balance in the world cocoa economy by 2010. However, in any single year, the size of a surplus or deficit continues to depend on weather conditions, market prices and changes in the level of stocks. Analysis on market prospects to 2010 suggests that global cocoa trade will continue to expand. However, the rate of expansion would be slower compared to the previous decade constrained by lower consumption growth in most of the major markets. Prices of cocoa beans in 2000/2001 were at their lowest levels in three decades, mainly due to a fundamental oversupply. Although some recovery in cocoa prices has occurred since mid-2001 as a result of the combination of reduced world cocoa bean production and increased speculative buying, prices of cocoa are not likely to improve significantly in the medium term, with low consumption expansion and steady production growth.

In the period to 2010, cocoa exports from developing countries would continue to be mainly in the form of beans. This suggests that the benefits of cocoa processing in adding value will continue to be enjoyed mainly by the importing countries. Cocoa producing countries have been aware of the need for developing the local grindings of beans to add value to their exports. Some African countries have increased their local processing capacity by providing subsidy, but most producing countries have not yet been able to increase the value addition to their exports. A major obstacle hindering the local processing of beans has not been the processing capacity itself, but the high degree of vertical integration of the multinational firms in the cocoa and chocolate industry, most of which have traditionally been established in importing countries. What the producing countries need most are efficient and sophisticated marketing skills. Unless this issue is solved, the benefit of value addition will continue to be distributed mostly among traditional bean importing countries while income of farmers would stay low.

World Cocoa by 2020

Chocoholics may want to start hoarding their sweet treats! The world will run out of cocoa—the basic ingredient of chocolate—within the next 7 years due to pressures of rising global demand, experts have warned. Industry experts who met at the British Library in London last week have even predicted the exact date of the impending meltdown—October 2, 2020. "There will be a chocolate shortage and there is not a solution to the problem. Seven years is what we think we have left", chocolate taster and expert Angus Kennedy said. Confectionery giants noted that there are just not enough cocoa plantations across the globe to cater to the soaring chocolate demand, the "Daily Star" reported.

They warned that world would need the equivalent of another planet Earth to fill the gap needed to keep the chocolate industry going. "We need another Earth basically if we carry on at this rate. We are destroying the whole thing. The problem we have got is that much of the space that was used for cocoa plantations is no longer there", Kennedy said. Chocolate prices may increase over the next few years as cocoa becomes harder to get hold of. With the result, many big chocolate brands will fill small-sized bars with more nuts and fruit as they are cheaper to produce.

There is very little growth projected for cocoa consumption in Europe and America but in Asia it is set to go sky high, said Kennedy.

Expert Says 2014 May See Chocolate Drought

The world is facing a "chocolate drought". The warning is prompted by fears that the globe's sustainable cocoa supplies could be exhausted by 2014. If the crisis spirals out of control—as may be the case, with one man hanging on to power despite the rising popularity of his electoral opponent and de jure winner of last year's elections—there is every chance of shortages due to falling production in the battle zone. Political unrest has depleted the number of cocoa farmers there. Many fled the country or are smuggling the crop into Ghana, where it sells at a far higher price. Chocolate makers are now facing the highest cocoa prices for more than 30 years.

Chocolate producers were facing "one of the biggest challenges to hit the industry in recent history". Supplies of sustainable cocoa are set to run out, it's that simple. The Ivory Coast is a complete no-go area for cocoa traders as it is too dangerous, so training new farmers and trying to cut problems in the region is now impossible. So in effect, its sustainability is not sustainable.

It is not surprising the sale of conflict cocoa—some may call it blood beans—continues, for the bitter truth is that Ivory Coast produces 32% of the world's total supply and cutting it out of sourcing calculations is no trifling matter. So, a contraband cocoa channel has been in operation and beans are making their way under couverture of darkness to international markets via soft-centered neighbors. To avert a 2014 cocoa crisis and spur an early settlement of the Ivorian stalemate, an awareness campaign run by socially—conscious chocolatiers on the lines of those on fur and diamonds—could be the answer, with ethical cocoa as the ultimate aim.

Annexures

Table 5.2: Export of cocoa products

Quantity (Qty.) - Tons value – Rs lakhs

Description	1992–1993		1993–1994		1994–1995		1995–1996		1996–1997	
	Qty.	Value	Qty.	Value	Qty.	Value	Qty.	Value	Qty.	Value
Cocoa beans whole/broken raw/roasted	0	0	0	0	0	0	00	0	0	0
Cocoa powder of coating sugar/sweetening material	8	1.62	48	36.62	83	62	57	52	86	55
Other food products containing cocoa										
Chocolate confectionary	147	109.76	92	85.67	301	232	595	492	653	543
Cocoa shells husks skins and others										
Cocoa butter fat and oil	2	85	118	105.77	379	391	300	342	498	382
Other food products preparations										
Total		196.38		228.06		685		886		980

(Contd.)

Table 5.2: Export of cocoa products

Quantity (Qty.) - Tons value - Rs lakhs

Description	1997–1998		1999–2000		2000–2001		2001–2002		2002–2003	
	Qty.	Value	Qty.	Value	Qty.	Value	Qty.	Value	Qty.	Value
Cocoa beans whole / broken raw / roasted	0	0	78.50	5.42	181.90	11.25	21.20	7.21	12.20	10.97
Cocoa powder of coating sugar / sweetening material	171	126	250.50	278.85	284.50	305.11	221.60	237.74	30.00	25.57
Other food products containing cocoa			342.70	335.94	254.80	215.83	357.10	439.73	245.62	245.46
Chocolate confectionary	762	600	821.20	678.31	453.90	434.93	579.80	659.71	981.76	968.29
Cocoa shells husks skins and others			0	0	0.10	0.44	161.70	10.85	32.80	4.24
Cocoa butter fat and oil	96	118	0	0	187.50	390.29	8.50	5.19	1.30	1.02
Other food products preparations			0	0	9.32	9.38	11.00	16.87	Negligible	
Total	**844**		**1,298.52**		**1,367.24**		**1,377.30**		**1,255.55**	

Table 5.2: Export of cocoa products (*Contd.*)

Quantity (Qty.) - Tons value - Rs lakhs

Description	2003–2004		2004–2005		2005–2006		2006–2007		2007–2008	
	Qty.	*Value*	*Qty.*	*Value*	*Qty.*	*Value*	*Qty.*	*Value*	*Qty.*	*Value*
Cocoa beans whole/ broken raw/roasted	15.12	11.48	30.67	23.62	27.30	4.18	0.362	0.297	12.50	13.42
Cocoa powder of coating sugar/ sweetening material	15.93	7.15	44.37	29.94	27.16	36.18	22.795	45.247	8.57	10.11
Other food products containing cocoa	6.84	10.64	12.35	21.61	691.94	649.74	1497.154	1609.82	3562.42	2661.37
Chocolate confectionary	1552.13	1827.41	1266.26	1758.20	1610.64	1218.91	1060.566	1625.367	1137.08	1173.52
Cocoa shells husks skins and others	0	0	6.00	1.84	185.85	34.67	1.53	1.421	75.07	22.54
Cocoa butter fat and oil	66.07	91.14	686.94	1,033.80	374.20	483.70	483.38	729.653	182.05	343.65
Other food products preparations	0	0	0	0	27.35	52.85	0.1	0.12	1.00	1.24
Total		**1,947.82**		**2,869.01**		**2,480.23**		**4,011.925**		**4,225.85**

Annexure 1: Statewise value of output - at cocoa

| State/UTs | At current prices | | | | | | | At 2004-05 prices | | | | | | |
	2004-05	2005-06	2006-07	2007-08	2008-09	2009-10	2010-11	2004-05	2005-06	2006-07	2007-08	2008-09	2009-10	2010-11
Andhra Pradesh	1010	1322	1719	1719	5778	1428	4472	1010	260	308	312	879	217	680
Karnataka	1634	1700	1800	1042	2312	4698	1342	1634	335	322	189	352	852	243
Kerala	1013	995	1167	1950	2013	2149	3258	1013	652	706	1149	742	754	1055
Tamil Nadu	131	136	134	148	184	728	728	131	27	26	27	28	110	110
Total	**3787**	**4152**	**4820**	**4859**	**10287**	**9002**	**9800**	**3787**	**1274**	**1362**	**1676**	**2000**	**1932**	**2088**

Annexure 2: Agro min plans to make India global cocoa hub

India is preparing to become the global hub for cocoa production with the ministry of agriculture charting a blueprint to overcome the shortage of cocoa and increase exports of the commodity in next 5 years. Cocoa is primarily used as a raw material for chocolates and the increasing demand for dark chocolate is expected to push up global cocoa demand by 30% to 4.5 million metric tonnes (MT) by 2020.

The decision has been taken considering the volatility in international cocoa supply that is influenced by many factors from extreme weather, pests and disease to speculation and political instability leading to fluctuations in imports. According to the blueprint, which has been reviewed by HT, initial trials of special cocoa seeds have already shown huge acceptance with Indian farmers.

The draft acknowledge a commercial benefit with a ready and grow market in India for dark chocolate. India currently cultivates cocoa in 71.365 hectares with a total production of 15.133 MT. India has an average productivity of 450 kg/ha, which is lower than the global average of 504 kg/ha.

We will hold a meeting with stake holders soon including the chocolate industry and farmers, said a source in directorate of cashewnut and cocoa development board (DCCD). The Centre is expected to float a paper soon soliciting response from the stake holders.

The proposal includes introduction of cocoa in potential states such as Maharashtra, Goa and Odisha. It is already farmed in Andhra Pradesh, Kerala, Karnataka and Tamil Nadu. Going forward the government plans to initiate tripartite agreement between the state government, processing industries and farming community for guaranteed procurement with remunerative prices.

A meeting with major chocolate manufacturers and agriculture ministry is also expected to be held soon to promote contract farming of cocoa.

Bitter Sweet Opportunity

- The decision has been taken considering the volatility in international cocoa supply.
- Rising demand for dark chocolate expected to push up global cocoa demand to 4.5 million MT by 2020.
- According to the draft, initial trials of special cocoa seeds has shown huge acceptance with Indian farmers.

Index